Pirate Math

Developing Mathematical Reasoning with Games and Puzzles
Book 2

Michael Serra

Publisher
Executive Editor
Project Administrator
Production Manager
Angela Snead

Editor/Copyeditor
Designer
Technical Artist
Compositor
Emily Reed

Proofreader/Puzzle Tester
Jennifer North-Morris

Cover Designer
Lumina Designworks

Printed in the USA
Lightning Source

Playing It Smart
PO Box 27540
San Francisco, CA 94127
mserramath@gmail.com
www.michaelserra.net
ISBN 978-0-9834-0991-5

Contents

Acknowledgements

Polyominoes play a major role in *Pirate Math,* so a special thanks goes out to polyomino creator, Solomon Golumb. Some of the puzzles and games appearing in math puzzle books today can be traced back to Martin Gardner. *Pirate Math,* like many puzzle books, owes much to these two champions of recreational mathematics.

To the teachers Diane Garfield and Amber Lewis-Francis, thank you for letting me into your classroom to try these new games and puzzles with your students. Your efforts in preparing students to think and explain their reasoning made my visits a learning experience for all of us. I am especially indebted to the students for encouraging me with their wonderful enthusiasm and creativity.

I am grateful to Jennifer North-Morris for field-testing the exercises and puzzles in *Pirate Math.* Jennifer was not only helpful in identifying errors, but she was instrumental in finding additional solutions to puzzles.

A thank you to Emily Reed for turning my manuscript into something I am proud to share. Emily is the book's editor, copy editor, designer, and compositor. Thank you, Emily, for your excellent work.

Thanks also to Terry Lockman and Jill Zwicky of Lumina Designworks for their innovative cover design.

We greatly appreciate the support of May Ho, who encouraged us to follow our dream of publishing our own books.

Once again, I want to thank my wife, Angela Snead, who helped me turn my classroom activities into a format all teachers can use. To the project administrator, production manager, and publisher, thank you for your continued support and enthusiasm.

Introduction

Seaward ho! Hang the treasure! It's the glory of the sea that has turned my head.

—Robert Louis Stevenson, *Treasure Island*

Pirate Math takes you to sun-drenched tropical islands in search of buried treasures. With treasure map in hand, you will follow clues and solve puzzles, uncovering secret passages and hidden caves. Ah, what glorious adventures await you in your quest for pirate treasure!

Stories of the hunt for buried treasure have been depicted in film and literary fiction; yet they have their basis in history. Sharing these historical stories and modern day films with your students will set the stage for their classroom explorations.

The pirate most responsible for the legends of buried pirate treasure was 17th-century Captain William Kidd. Originally from Scotland, Kidd was raised in New York and became a wealthy merchant. British investors convinced him to become a pirate in order to plunder competing French commercial ships. Kidd sailed under the *Jolly Roger* (a flag flown to identify a ship's crew as pirates) in the Red Sea and Indian Ocean. With the law in pursuit, Kidd left chests containing 100 pounds of gold and silver and other valuable items from a plundered ship with an associate named Gardiner. As the story goes, Gardiner buried the treasure on his secret hideout, near Long Island, New York. Upon Kidd's return to England, he was arrested, tried, and executed. Although much of Kidd's treasure was recovered, the public's fascination with the case grew. Rumors spread of a fortune in gold that Kidd had secretly buried and was still to be found.

Another documented case of buried treasure involved Francis Drake, who attacked a Spanish mule train and then buried the gold and silver. After burying the booty, he left men to guard the spot while he returned to his ships. Six hours later he returned, retrieved the loot, and sailed for England.

Did pirates often bury their plunder? For much of human history, if you had some valuables you wanted to hide, burial was a good plan. As adventurous as it sounds there is little evidence of pirates burying treasure and creating a treasure map. (Drake did not create a map.) Pirates usually spent their ill-gotten gains as soon as possible on liquor, gambling, and women—rarely holding on to the loot long enough to bury it for retrieval later. But we don't want to let facts get in the way of a good story, or an exciting treasure hunt.

Treasure Maps in Literature and Film

Although there are no documented cases of an actual pirate treasure map, it is a favorite literary device. With its stereotypical tattered and wrinkled chart, and over-sized "X" to denote the treasure's location, the treasure map can be found in many novels. There were early tales of treasure with maps, most notably Edgar Allan Poe's *The Gold-Bug* (1843). Forty years later, Robert Louis Stevenson popularized the search for buried treasure with his novel

Treasure Island (1883). Arthur Conan Doyle published "The Adventure of the Musgrave Ritual" in *Strand Magazine*. In this short story, Sherlock Holmes deduces that the ritual is a guide to a treasure buried on the Musgrave estate.

The plot of the 1984 film *Romancing the Stone* centers on using a treasure map to find an enormous emerald. The clever twist involved a map that only made sense when it was folded in a particular way. In the 1994 comedy *City Slickers 2: The Legend of Curly's Gold* and the 2004 film *National Treasure*, treasure maps played prominent roles. In 2011, Steven Spielberg brought the animated 3-D movie *The Adventures of Tintin: Secret of the Unicorn* to the screen. The story has it all—treasure maps, a search for clues to sunken treasure, and battles with pirates.

Polyominoes + Pirates = *Pirate Math*

As a high school student I happened upon Martin Gardner's "Mathematical Games" column in *Scientific American*. On many occasions Mr. Gardner's column explored the world of polyominoes, a creation of mathematician Solomon Golumb. Gardner's column of mathematical recreations, and polyominoes in particular, have had an enormous influence on my classroom teaching and now in *Pirate Math*. In *Pirate Math* I have combined the fun and challenge of polyominoes with the excitement and adventure of pirate maps and treasure hunts.

One of the goals in *Pirate Math* is to teach graphing. There are games teaching graphing in the coordinate plane (Chapter 2), using polar coordinates (Chapter 3), on a spherical surface (Chapter 4), and in three dimensions (Chapter 5). *Pirate Math* also contains a collection of puzzles that help develop reasoning and problem solving, which is at the heart of all mathematics.

As with all of the books in the series "Developing Mathematical Reasoning with Games and Puzzles," our objective is to encourage beginner-level puzzle solvers. At a time when complex mysteries are neatly solved in one-hour TV shows, perseverance is a quality that is sadly under-utilized. Thomas Edison said, "Genius is one-percent inspiration and ninety-nine percent perspiration." The puzzles in *Pirate Math* are not the type that require the solver to "think outside of the box" or to have a "Eureka moment." Instead, they are designed to strengthen your problem solving skills, help you learn some mathematics, and have fun along the way. I sincerely hope you enjoy the experience!

> It's not that I am so smart, it's just that I stay with problems longer.
> *Albert Einstein*

Features of Pirate Math

In mathematics teaching, what matters is not whether a problem is plausibly real or artificial, but whether it is such that pupils are prepared to enter into the spirit of the mental world it conjures up.
—A. Gardiner

Common Core State Standards (CCSS)

The CCSS for Mathematics consist of Standards for Content and Mathematical Practices. By playing the games and solving the puzzles in *Pirate Math*, students will practice the skills described in the CCSS. The Standards for Mathematical Practices identify eight mathematical habits that mathematics educators should develop in their students. The Standards for Mathematical Practices are:

- Make sense of problems and persevere in solving them
- Reason abstractly and quantitatively
- Construct viable arguments and critique the reasoning of others
- Model with mathematics
- Use appropriate tools strategically
- Attend to precision
- Look for and make use of structure
- Look for and express regularity in repeated reasoning

Making sense of the puzzles, persevering in solving them, constructing viable arguments, and attending to precision are essential tools for the puzzle solver. Using appropriate tools strategically, making use of structure, and looking for regularity in repeated reasoning are useful skills taught while playing the Buried Treasure games.

Game Sheets

You will find game sheets for *Pirate Math* in Appendix 1. I suggest you begin with the simpler games and gradually move up to more challenging ones. After playing with some of these games, I encourage you to create some of your own buried treasure games and share them with us at *www.michaelserra.net.*

Hints and Answers

Many puzzles have hints to assist you in solving the puzzles. Look at the examples in the chapter first, then make a serious effort at solving the puzzles. Only if you need more direction, turn to the hints. Puzzles with hints are marked with an $\hbar$. You will find the hints in Appendix 4. Answers to investigations, exercises, and puzzles are found in Appendix 5.

Problem Solving and Puzzle Solving Tips

During my years of teaching, I have come up with a few rules to assist in the successful use of puzzles in the classroom. First, it is very important to establish a safe classroom environment. Students need to feel comfortable asking questions and exploring ideas without the fear of being criticized or marked down for a wrong answer. The same is true during puzzle solving. Second, allow plenty of time for students to experiment and ponder challenges—don't rush toward the answer. Third, nothing succeeds like success. Start with puzzles that everyone can accomplish to help boost confidence. Fourth, praise good effort rather than complimenting students for being smart. While some students enjoy challenging puzzles requiring additional insight or cleverness, these "trick problems" can turn off other students. Finally, focus on games and puzzles that stress sequential reasoning and good old-fashioned "stick-to-it-ness."

Stanford psychologist Carol Dweck conducted studies with early adolescents. In these experiments researchers gave the students some difficult IQ test questions. After the test, some youngsters were complimented for their effort and told, "You must have worked really hard." The others were praised for their ability, and told, "You must be smart at this." Students who were praised for their intelligence were more likely to turn down the chance to try a new exercise that they could learn from. According to Dweck, they didn't want to do anything that could expose their deficiencies and call into question their talent. However, of the students who were praised for their hard work, ninety percent of them were eager to try the new task.

Mueller, Claudia M. and Dweck, Carol S., "Praise for Intelligence Can Undermine Children's Motivation and Performance," Journal of Personality and Social Psychology (1998)

Puzzles and mathematical problem solving share similar strategies. Here are a number of those strategies and their corresponding sections in this book.

1. Solve simpler or analogous problems first (find all the pentominoes in Section 1.3).
2. Look for patterns (Pentomino puzzles 7–9 in Section 1.3).
3. Work backwards from the desired result to the given information (longitude and latitude activities in Section 4.1).
4. Make a table (solving and creating ciphers in Section 7.2).
5. Use manipulatives (the Soma Cube puzzle in Section 5.2).
6. Pay attention to detail (Buried Treasure in Section 2.2).
7. Plan ahead (Pirate Treasure with geometric constructions in Section 6.2).
8. Check your answer to see if it is reasonable and accurate (all puzzles and games).

And remember, the time it takes to solve a puzzle has no relationship to how intelligent you are. Many ordinary people became great thinkers because of concentrated and deliberate effort. Perseverance is incredibly important to mathematics and puzzle solving.

A Closer Look at Pirate Math

Chapter 1 introduces polyominoes. These shapes are the "treasures" you will be searching for in the different Buried Treasure games throughout *Pirate Math.* Strategic planning, recognizing patterns, understanding symmetry and transformations are all key to success in the games in Chapters 2–5. Visual thinking, careful logical reasoning, and perseverance are valuable tools for solving the puzzles in *Pirate Math.*

In Chapter 2, you will play Buried Treasure games in the Cartesian Coordinate Plane and then solve puzzles using what you have learned about the rectangular coordinate system. The chapter concludes with a hunt for pirate treasure buried on tropical islands with the help of coordinate geometry.

In Chapter 3, you will play Buried Treasure games in the Polar Coordinate Plane and then solve polar coordinate grid puzzles. In the last section you will use polar coordinates to follow clues to buried pirate treasure on exotic isles.

In Chapter 4, you will use longitude and latitude lines to help you locate positions on the earth and then play Buried Treasure games using these skills. The chapter finishes with you solving puzzles on spherical surfaces and locating an actual sunken ship off the Florida Keys.

Students playing Spherical Buried Treasure

In Chapter 5, your visual thinking skills will be put to the test as you learn to sketch 3-D polyominoes on isometric grids. You will then play Buried Treasure games with these 3-D polyominoes. The chapter concludes with 3-D puzzles.

Chapter 6 takes you to mysterious treasure islands for some geometry fun. In Section 6.1 you will learn or review some geometry. You will then use your geometry and reasoning skills to find pirate treasure buried on island hideaways in Section 6.2.

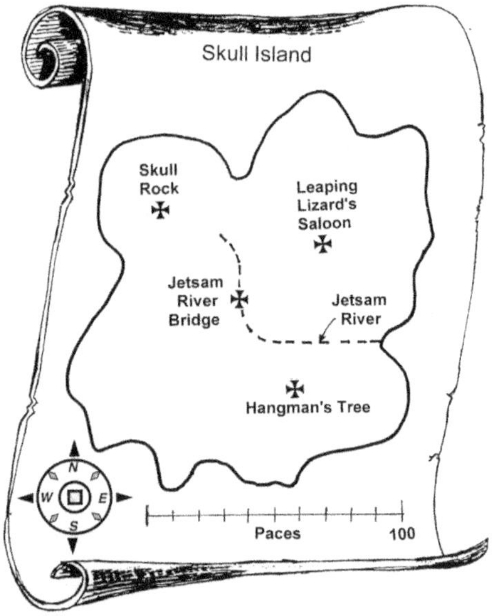

In Chapter 7 you visit tropical isles for some cipher adventures. In Section 7.1 you will learn about cryptography. You will learn how to create and decipher secret messages using a variety of cipher systems. In Section 7.6 you will use these skills to decipher messages and find treasure buried on pirate islands.

The Appendices contain the following sections: Appendix A1 is where you will find the Buried Treasure Game Sheets; Appendix A2 reviews linear equations; Appendix A3 shows you how to build spherical and 3-D Buried Treasure game equipment; Appendix A4 has the hints; and Appendix A5 has the answers.

Using Pirate Math

Pirate Math teaches reasoning and perseverence using puzzles and games. There are mathematical exercises and examples embedded in the chapters in order to prepare the student for the games and puzzles to follow. If the math review is extensive, linear equations for example, then the material is placed in an appendix (A2). If choosing chapters randomly instead of going through *Pirate Math* sequentially, I suggest the teacher, parent, or student browse through the book once to see where certain topics are reviewed or introduced before you begin your mathematical journey.

5th graders playing Buried Treasure

10th graders playing 3-D Buried Treasure

Classroom Setting

Pirate Math can be used as a supplement with school mathematics curriculum or as extra-curricular activities for students. The puzzles make excellent classroom openers, end-of-period thought provokers, or take-home activities for students to do during school breaks.

Each of these coordinate geometry games, played as part of your school mathematics curriculum, will create an exciting change of pace. They introduce new graphing concepts while providing the drill and practice necessary for mastery. I found students developed strategies and reasoning skills faster and deeper with these games than with traditional methods. When playing the more advanced versions of Buried Treasure (i.e. polar, spherical, 3-D), young students gain a great sense of accomplishment from topics usually reserved for advanced level mathematics.

The games and puzzles in *Pirate Math* are also wonderful cooperative problem solving activities for your classroom. I encourage teachers to post group solutions on classroom bulletin boards to showcase student work. Another great way to introduce a puzzle into your lesson is to use a document camera. You can project a puzzle worksheet onto a screen for the entire class to see and discuss. A student can write on the worksheet as the class solves the puzzle together. For a more dramatic effect, project the games and puzzles onto a white board and have students fill in the parts of the puzzle as they explain their reasoning to the rest of the class. The games and puzzles can also be dropped into PowerPoint™ or Keynote™ to create presentations for classroom use or to share on "Back to School Night."

Home School Setting

For the homeschool teacher, finding supplemental materials can be challenging. Textbook instruction in mathematics can be very dry if done in an isolated setting and drill-like manner. Integrating home mathematics instruction with games and puzzles creates a fun and playful environment for the students. The lessons in *Pirate Math* can be used as starting points for your students to explore mathematics in their own way and at their preferred pace.

Many parents are looking for opportunities to do mathematics with their children. I encourage the whole family to participate in these games and puzzles. Finding pirate treasure on mysterious islands provides a fun setting for students and parents to work on problem solving and mathematics together. Try it. I think you'll "dig it."

Chapter 1 Polyomino Warm-Up Puzzles

I do not think that there is any other quality so essential to success of any kind as the quality of perseverance.

—John D. Rockefeller

This chapter introduces you to some fun shapes called **polyominoes**. Polyominoes are the "buried treasure" you will be looking for in the games and puzzles throughout this book. We begin with some polyomino puzzles to get you warmed up for the activities in the following chapters.

Exercises and puzzles with hints are marked with an ℏ and can be found in Appendix 4. Investigation, exercise, and puzzle answers can be found in Appendix 5.

1.1 Polyominoes

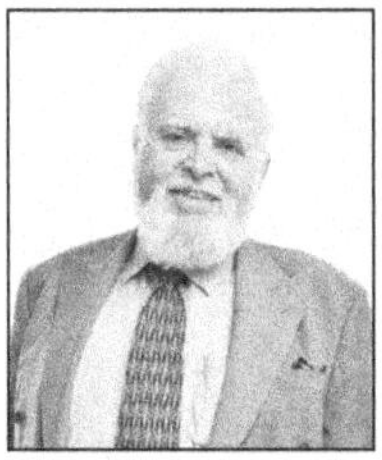

In 1953, mathematician Solomon Golumb "invented" and named polyominoes. He introduced them to the world of recreational mathematics at the Harvard Mathematics Club. A few years later, polyominoes appeared in Martin Gardner's "Mathematical Games" column in the May 1957 issue of *Scientific American*. Polyomino play is now a classic activity in recreational mathematics. The list of contributors to the study (or play) of polyominoes reads like a "Who's Who" of contemporary mathematics.[1]

What are Polyominoes? Polyominoes are shapes made by connecting congruent squares complete side to complete side. The name came from the domino. Dominoes are examples of two squares connected side to side.

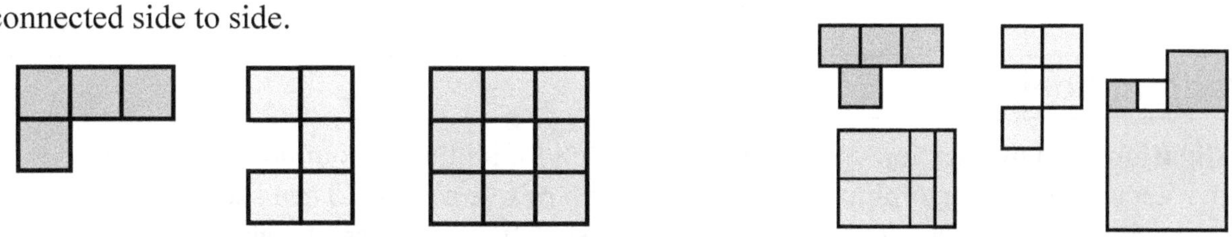

Tetromino **Pentomino** **Octomino** **Not Polyominoes**

Two polyominoes are considered different (distinct) if and only if they cannot be obtained from each other by rotating or flipping.

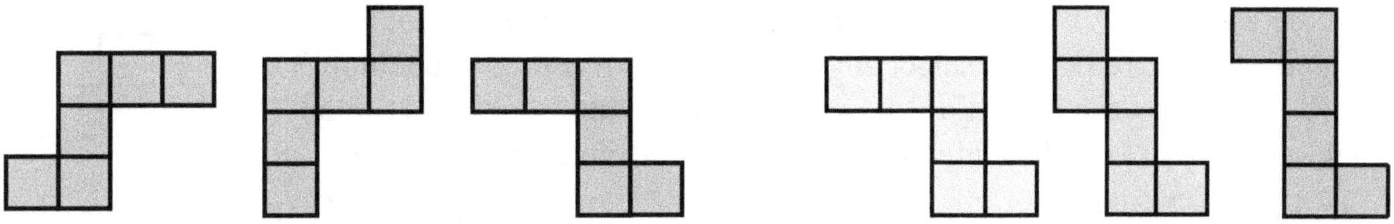

These are the same **These are different**

1.2 Monomino, Domino, Trominoes, and Tetrominoes

Polyominoes are named according to the number of squares they contain. The smallest, the *mono*mino, contains one square; the *do*mino contains two squares; the *tro*mino contains three squares; the *tetro*mino contains four squares, and so on. There is only one monomino, and only one domino, but there are two different trominoes (straight and bent). These smaller polyominoes are shown below.

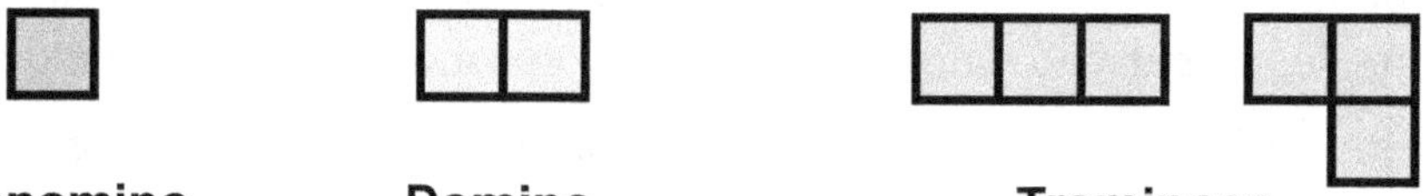

Monomino **Domino** **Trominoes**

1.2 Investigation 1: There are five different tetrominoes. Four of them are shown below. Sketch the remaining tetromino in the grid on the right. Check your answer in Appendix 5.

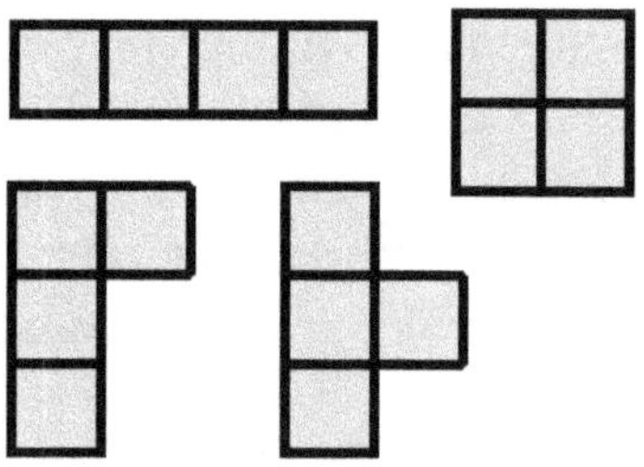

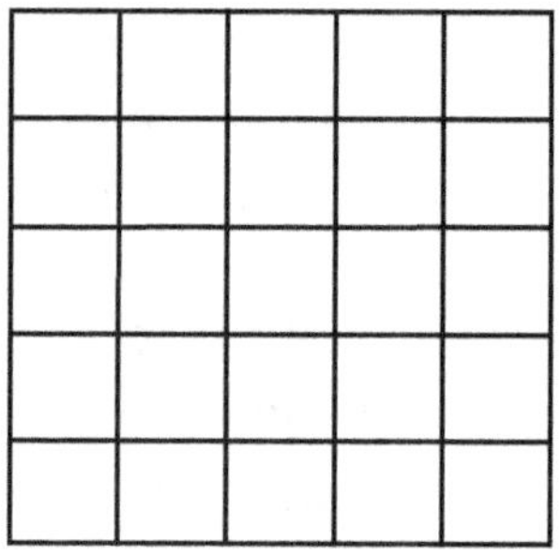

1.3 Pentominoes

1.3 Investigation 1: In this section you are going to search for all the pentominoes. Hint: Be organized. First sketch the pentomino with a longest chain of five squares. Then sketch all the pentominoes with a longest chain of four squares. Next, sketch all the possible pentominoes with a longest chain of three squares. This is where it can get tricky. Here is one possible approach. Take the five tetrominoes and find all the different ways an additional square can be added. Eliminate any duplicates.

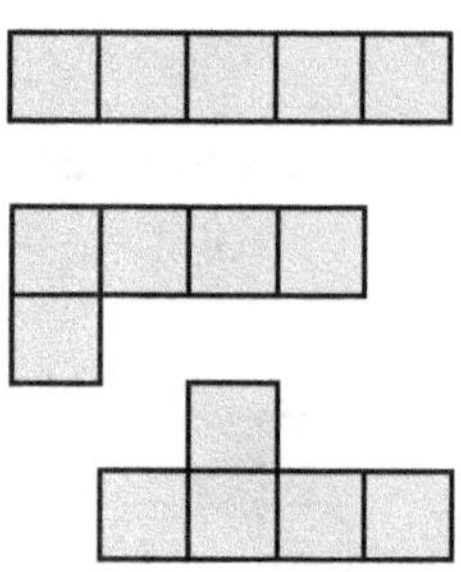

For example: Suppose we have found all the pentominoes with a longest chain of five squares and all the pentominoes with a longest chain of four squares (shown on the right). Next we look for all the pentominoes with a longest chain of three squares. To do this, select any tetromino with a longest chain of three squares. We select the tetromino shown below left. Next we record all the places that a fifth square can be added that result in a new pentomino with a longest chain of three squares.

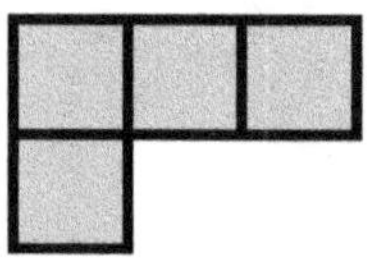

Tetromino

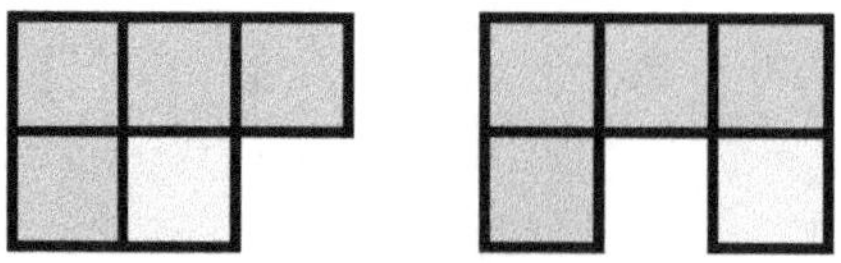

Two new pentominoes

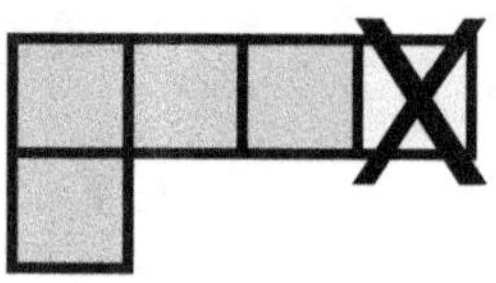

Not new

Next, do the same with the other tetromino having a longest chain of three squares. You might use tracing paper or patty paper to see whether two pentominoes are identical or different. Once you are convinced you have found all the pentominoes with a longest chain of three squares, search for all the pentominoes with a longest chain of two squares. When you have found all the pentominoes, sketch them below. Check your answer in Appendix 5.

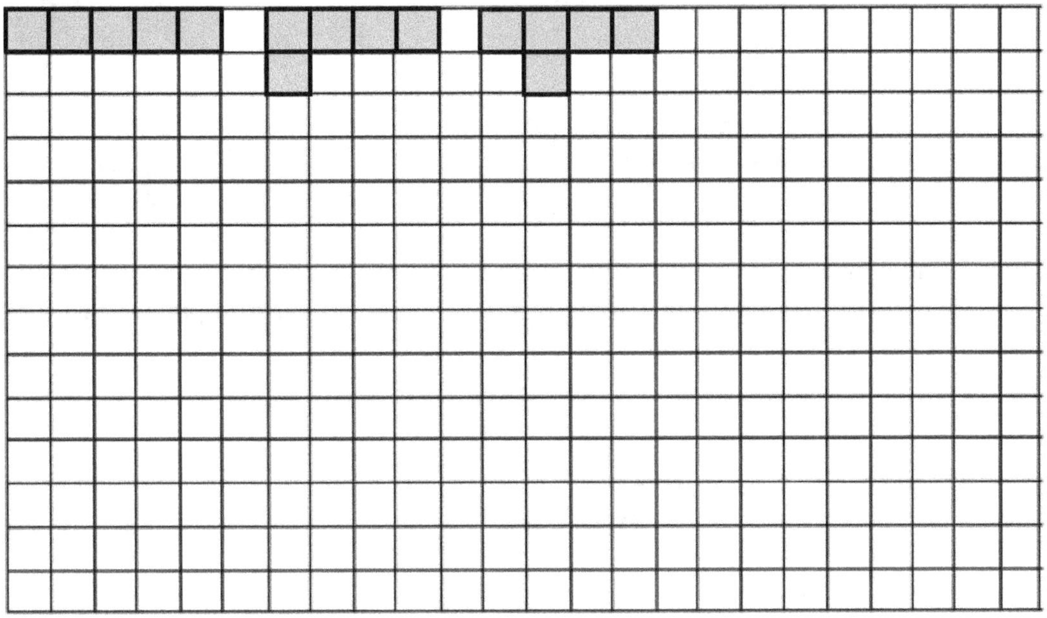

Pentomino Puzzle 1 *h*

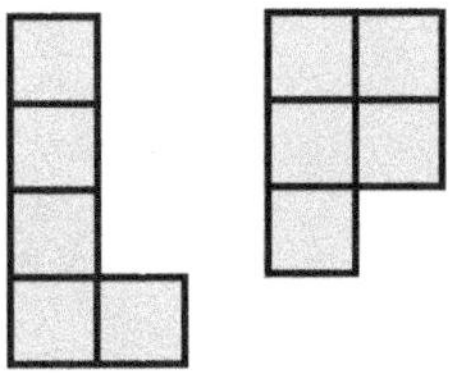

There are less than 15 pentominoes. They have been named with letters of the alphabet that correspond to their shape. For example, seven of the pentominoes can be seen as the last seven letters of the alphabet (*T*, *U*, *V*, *W*, *X*, *Y*, and *Z*). Others can be viewed as letters as well (for example: *F*, *L*, *I*, *P*, and *N*). Two examples (the letters *L* and *P*) are shown at right. Name each of the pentominoes you found above by placing a capital letter next to it.

Pentomino Puzzle 2 *h*

The type of symmetry a pentomino has determines the number of different orientations it can take. The *X*-pentomino has both a horizontal line of **reflectional symmetry** and a vertical line of reflectional symmetry thus it has only one orientation. The *U*-pentomino and *T*-pentomino have one line of reflectional symmetry and thus each has four orientations. The *Z*-pentomino has 180° **rotational symmetry** and thus has four orientations. See examples below. For more on reflectional and rotational symmetry see the hint for this puzzle.

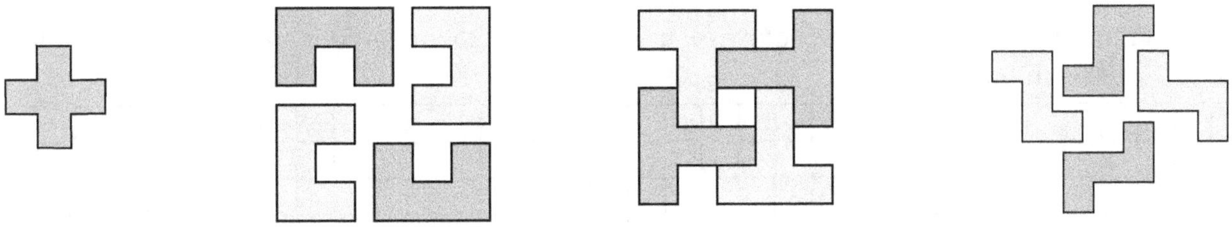

The *L*-pentomino has neither reflectional symmetry nor rotational symmetry. It has eight different orientations, as shown below left. When the eight orientations are combined they can create lovely designs with rotational symmetry like the one shown below right.

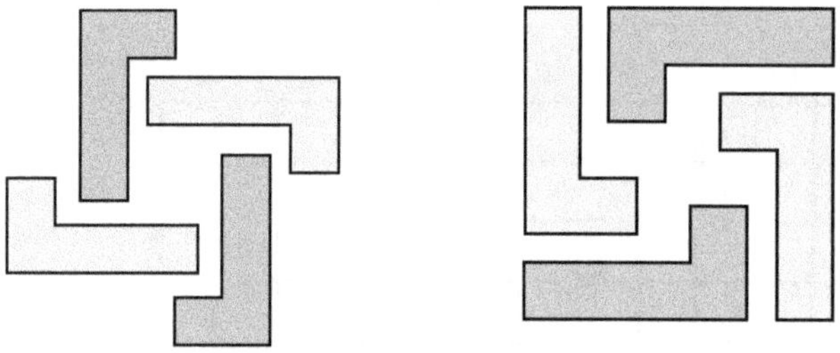

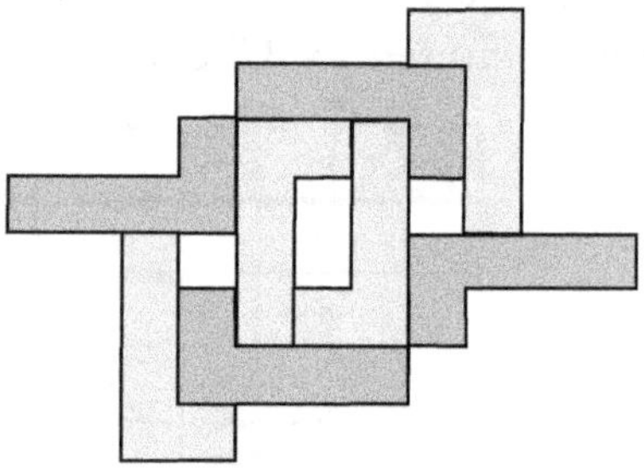

Sketch all the possible orientations of the remaining pentominoes with no symmetry in the four grids below. When you do this with some thought you can create beautiful patterns with rotational symmetry.

F

P

Y

N

Pentomino Puzzle 3 *h*

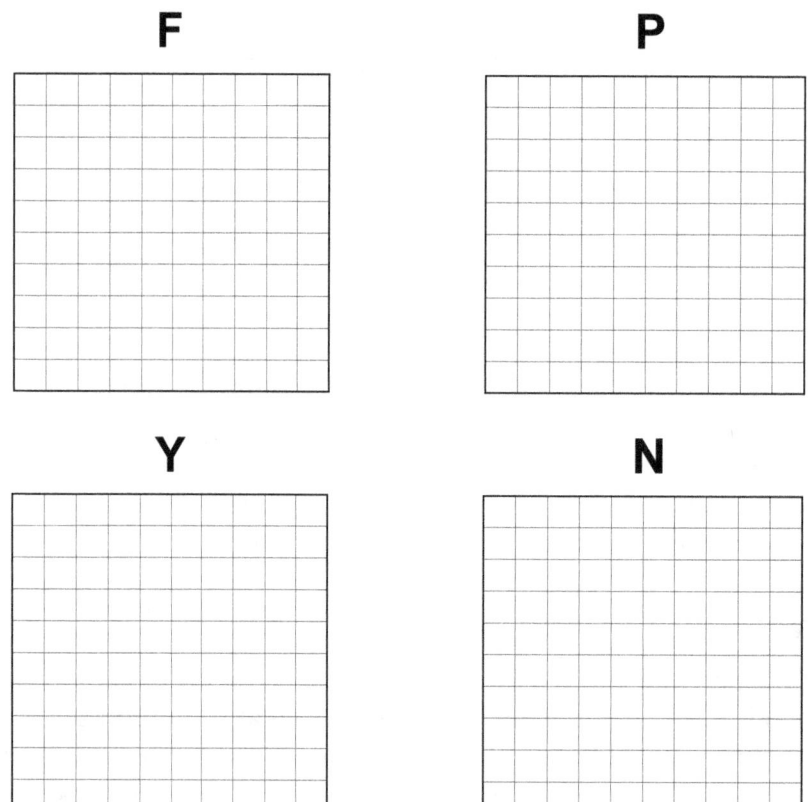

Which pentominoes can fold into a box without a lid? Circle them on your answers from Pentomino Puzzle 1 or sketch them below.

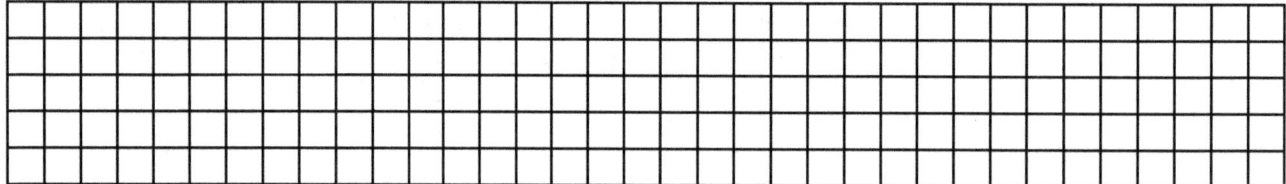

Pentomino Puzzle 4 *h*

Cover each 5×5 grid of squares with five pentominoes. You may use the same pentomino more than once. Do it a different way each time.

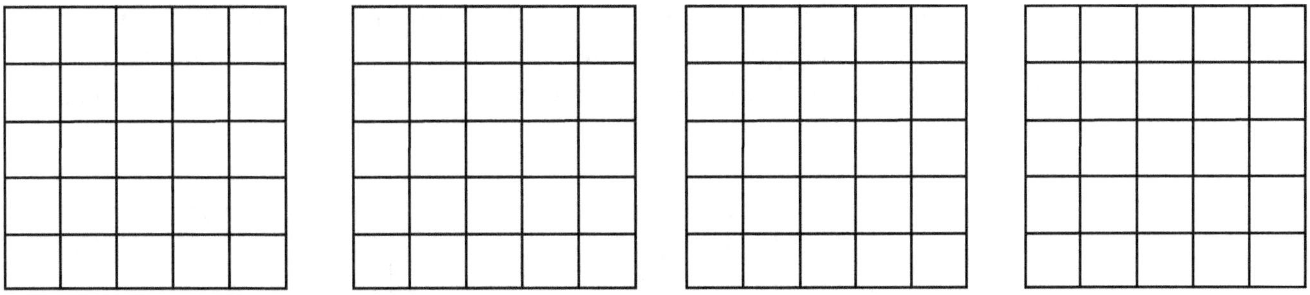

Pentomino Puzzle 5 *h*

The first 5×5 grid has been filled with five different pentominoes. Cover the remaining three 5×5 grids with five *different* pentominoes. Do it a different way each time.

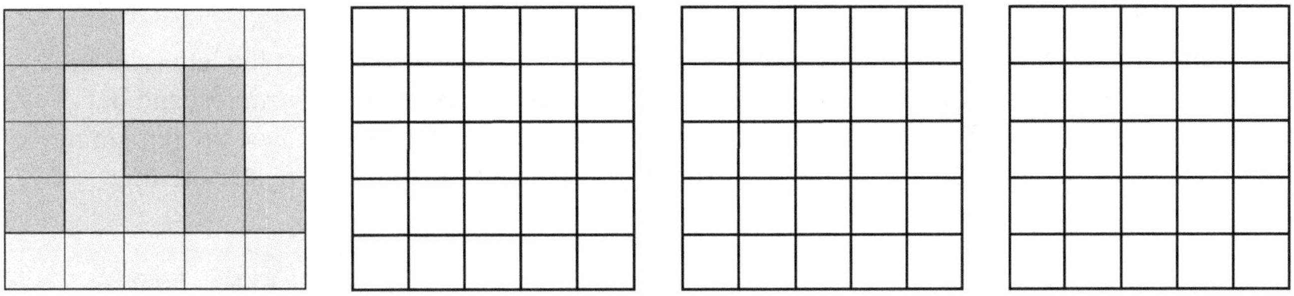

Pentomino Puzzle 6 *h*

A **sudoku** is a logic puzzle in a grid of squares called *cells*. Some cells contain given numerals. The object is to fill in all the empty cells. In the more common 9×9 sudoku (on the right) every row, column, and non-overlapping 3×3 box must contain the numerals 1 through 9. In the pentomino sudoku below, every row, column, and pentomino region must contain the numerals 1 through 5. Complete the pentomino sudoku by filling in all the empty cells.

4			3	
	2			1
		1		
	5			2

		7		1		9		
		2		6	5		7	4
8	9		4				1	
	8		5	9		2		
2		3			6	1		
	1				2		4	5
	4	1		2				7
9			8	5		3	2	
5					7		6	

Chapter 1.3

The 12 pentominoes can be arranged into a 6×10, 5×12, 4×15, and even a 3×20 rectangle.

Pentomino Puzzle 7

The pentominoes shown below right can be arranged into the 5×12 rectangle so the letters form five geometry terms: *central angle*, *straightedge*, *circumcenter*, *proportional*, and *Euler segment*. The *Y*-pentomino has already been correctly placed. Place the remaining pentominoes in the grid to spell out the five geometry terms.

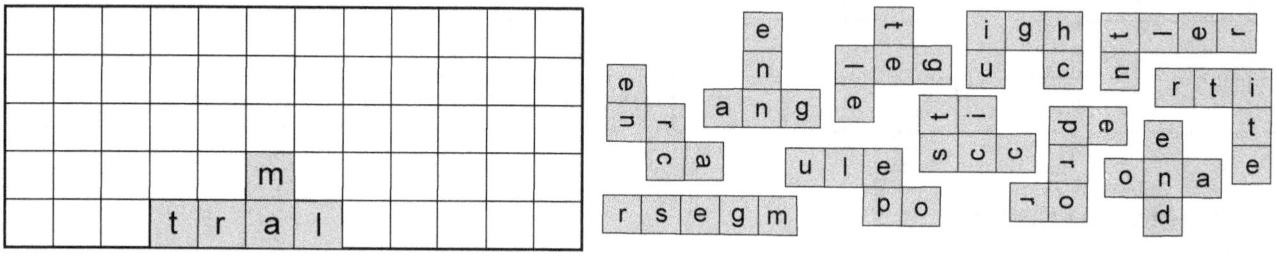

Pentomino Puzzle 8

The pentominoes shown below right can be arranged into the 6×10 rectangle so the letters form five geometry terms: *coordinate*, *hypotenuse*, *hemisphere*, *octahedron*, and *protractor*, and one mystery geometry term. The *T*-pentomino has already been correctly placed. Place the remaining pentominoes in the grid to spell out the five geometry terms and discover the mystery term.

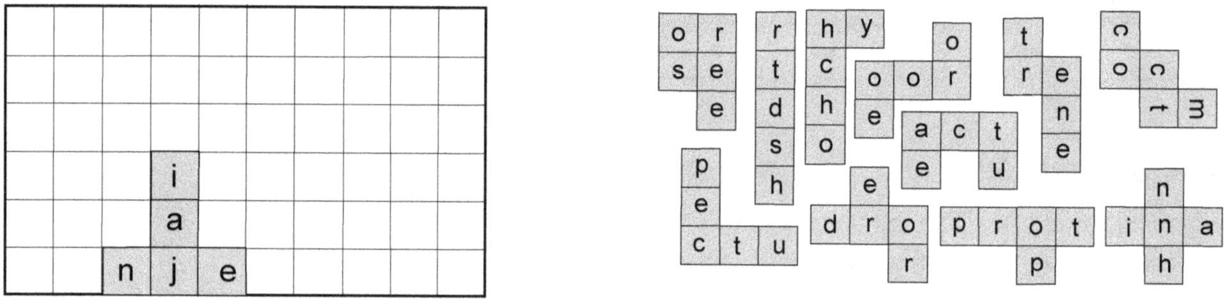

Pentomino Puzzle 9

The pentominoes shown below right can be arranged into the 6×10 rectangle so the letters form six geometry terms. One of the geometry terms is *postulates*. The *U*-pentomino has already been correctly placed. Place the remaining pentominoes in the grid to spell out the remaining five mystery terms.

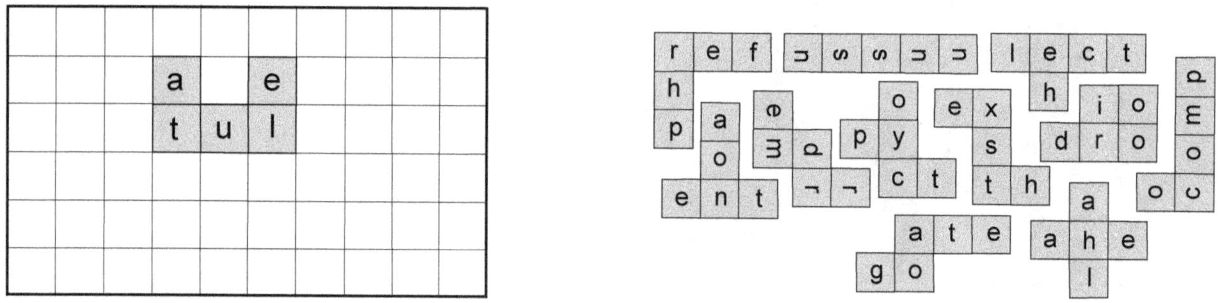

Pentomino Puzzle 10 *h*

In the puzzle on the right all 12 pentominoes have been arranged into a 6×10 rectangle, but some of them have been hidden. The 12 pentomino shapes are identified by the letters *T*, *U*, *V*, *W*, *X*, *Y*, *Z*, *F*, *L*, *I*, *P*, and *N*. These letters are given as clues. If the letter *F*, for example, is in a square, then the *F*-pentomino covers that square. Use logical reasoning to determine the location of all the pentominoes.

V	V	V	U	U	X				
Z	Z	V	U	X	X	X			
Y	Z	V	U	U	X			W	L
Y	Z	Z					F		
Y	Y								P
Y					I				

Pentomino Puzzle 11 *h*

There are 2,339 arrangements of the 6×10 pentomino rectangle, not counting rotations and reflections. One is shown below left. Purchase or create a complete set of pentominoes (you might cut them from graph paper). Find an arrangement of the 12 pentominoes into a 6×10 rectangle where the *I*-, *T*-, *Y*-, and *P*-pentominoes are at the four corners of the rectangle, the *V*-pentomino is in the position shown, and the *X*-, *N*-, and *Z*-pentominoes do not touch the rectangle's perimeter (below right).

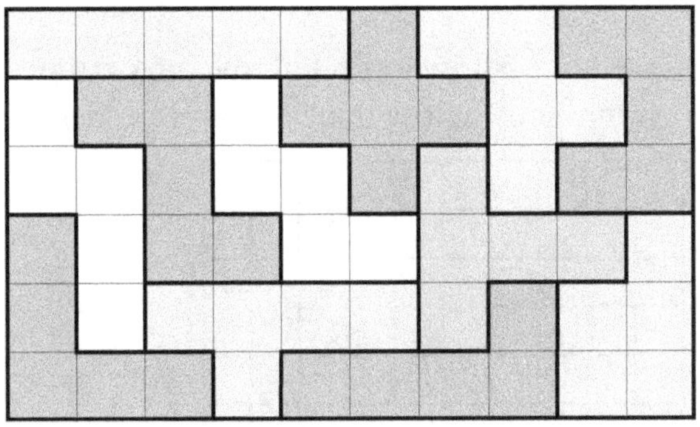

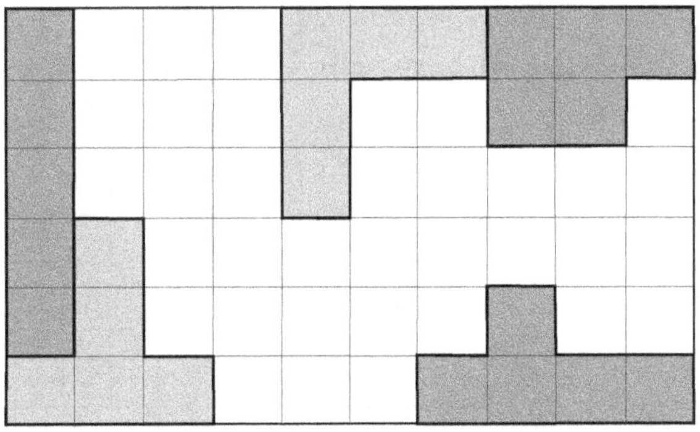

Pentomino Puzzle 12 *h*

Of the 2,339 arrangements of the 6×10 pentomino rectangle, only two of them have every piece touching the perimeter. Find one such arrangement of the 12 pentominoes where the *L*-, *U*-, *Z*-, and *I*-pentominoes are at the four corners of the rectangle, the *Y*-pentomino is in the position shown, and every pentomino touches the rectangle's perimeter.

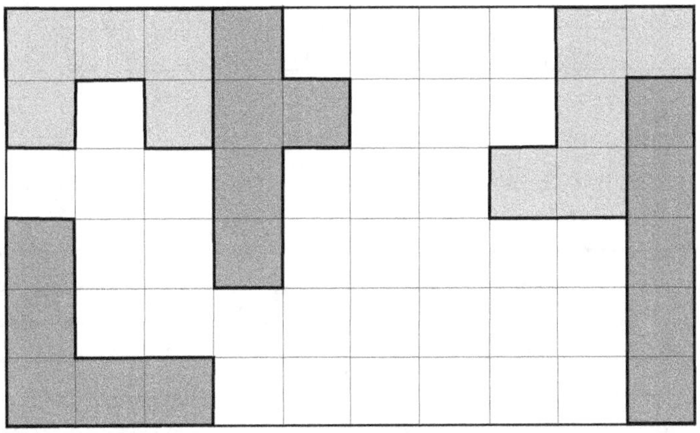

1.4 Hexominoes

You could start sketching hexominoes and hope to find them all. However, there are so many it would be difficult to know, by trial and error, if you had found all of them. Being organized in your search is very important. One possible approach would be to take the pentominoes and find all the different ways you can add an additional square. Be on the lookout for duplicates. There are more than 30 hexominoes but less than 40. To get you started, the hexominoes with a longest chain of 6 and 5 are shown below.

All the hexominoes with a longest chain of six squares: 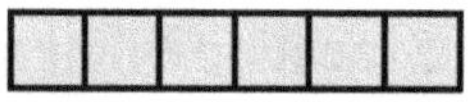

All the hexominoes with a longest chain of five squares:

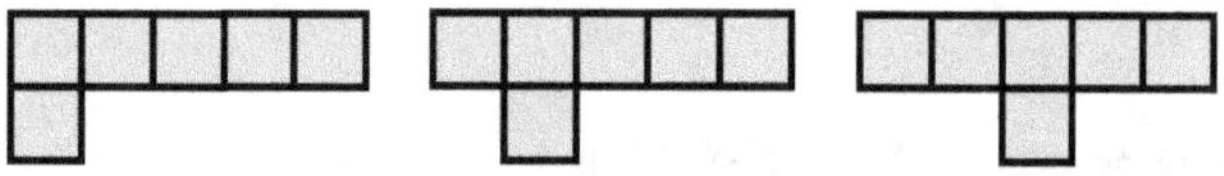

In the following investigations you are going to search in an organized way for all the possible hexominoes. First, you will search for all the hexominoes with a longest chain of four squares. Next, you will search for all the hexominoes with a longest chain of three squares. Finally, you will search for the hexomino with a longest chain of two squares.

To find all the hexominoes with a longest chain of four squares you will use the *L*- and *Y*-pentominoes. Why these? We use the *L*- and *Y*- pentominoes because they are the only pentominoes with a longest chain of four squares.

1.4 Investigation 1: Add one square to each of the *L*-pentominoes below to find all the hexominoes with a longest chain of four squares. (There are more *L*-pentominoes below than you will need.)

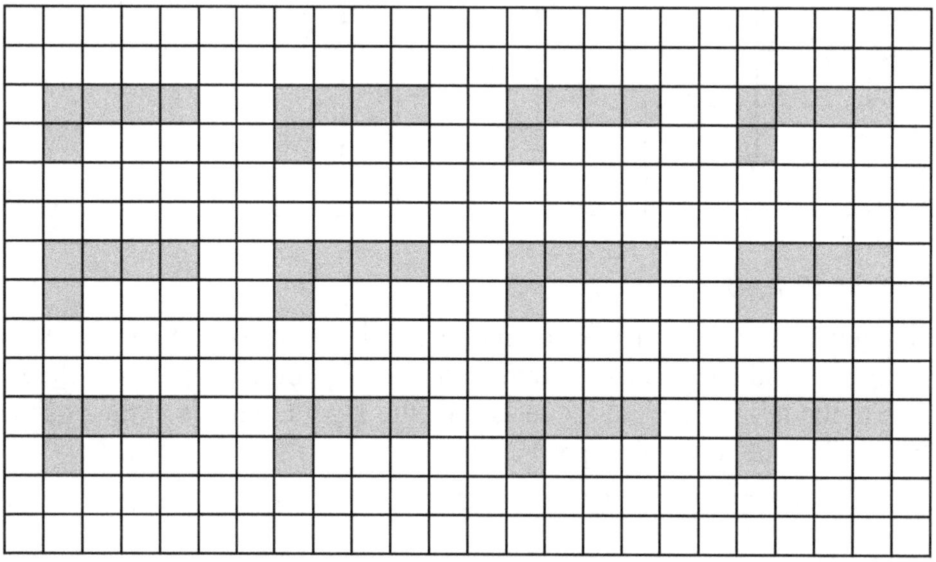

1.4 Investigation 2: Add one square to each of the *Y*-pentominoes below to find more hexominoes with a longest chain of four squares. Eliminate those that you already found in Investigation 1. (There are more *Y*-pentominoes below than you will need.)

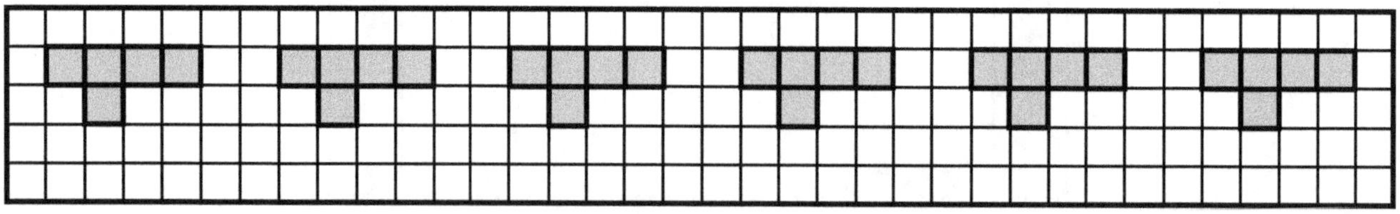

Since there are no more pentominoes with a longest chain of four squares, you should have found all the hexominoes with a longest chain of four squares. Sketch them in the grid below.

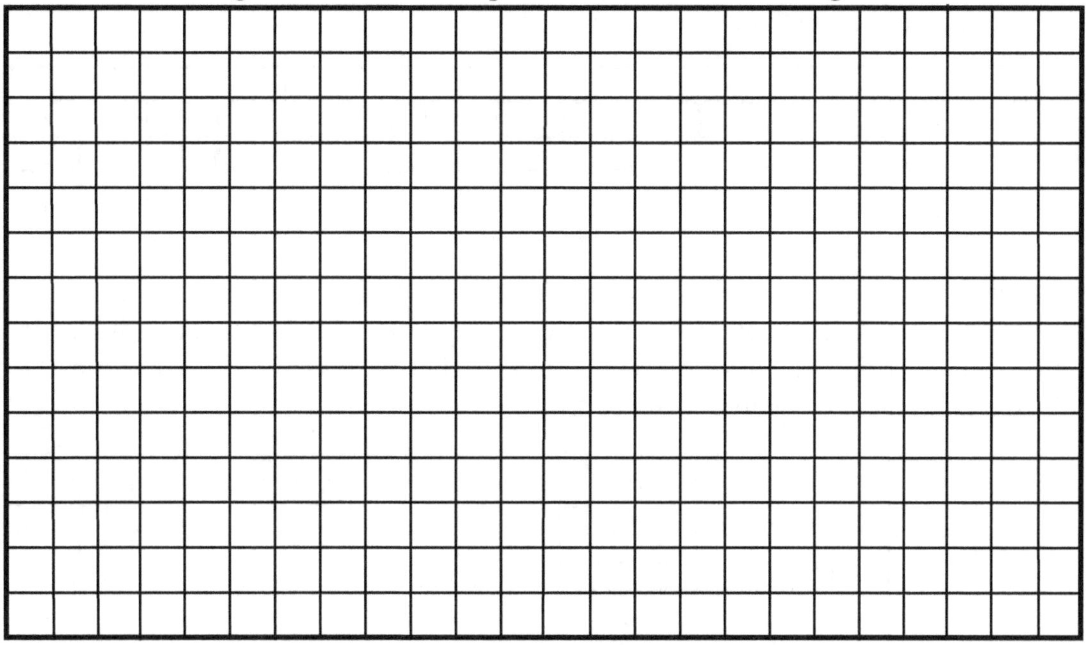

Next, find all the hexominoes with a longest chain of three squares. You will use the *V*-, *P*-, *U*-, *N*-, *T*-, *F*-, *Z*- and *X*-pentominoes.

1.4 Investigation 3: Add one square to each of the *V*-pentominoes below to find hexominoes with a longest chain of three squares. (There may be more *V*-pentominoes below than you need.)

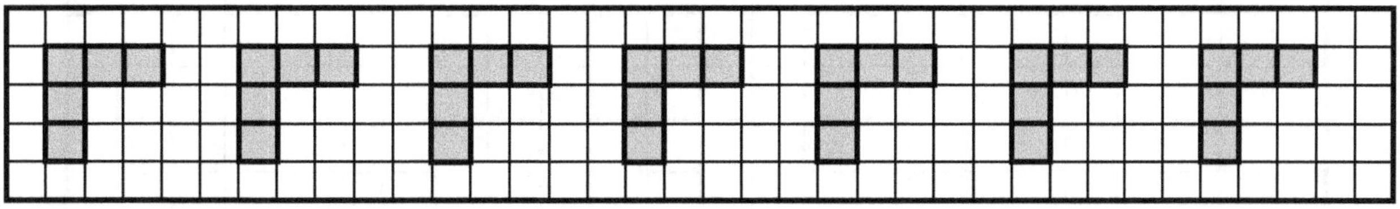

1.4 Investigation 4: Add one square to each of the *P*-pentominoes below to find more hexominoes with a longest chain of three squares. Eliminate any you found in earlier investigations. (There may be more *P*-pentominoes below than you need.)

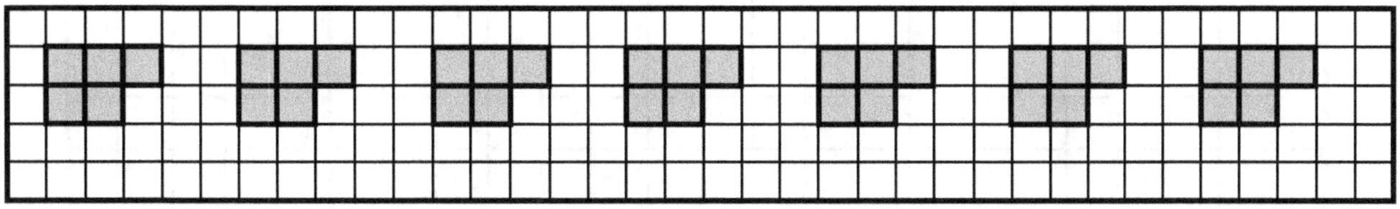

1.4 Investigation 5: Add one square to each of the *U*-pentominoes below to find more hexominoes with a longest chain of three squares. Eliminate any you found in earlier investigations. (There may be more *U*-pentominoes below than you need.)

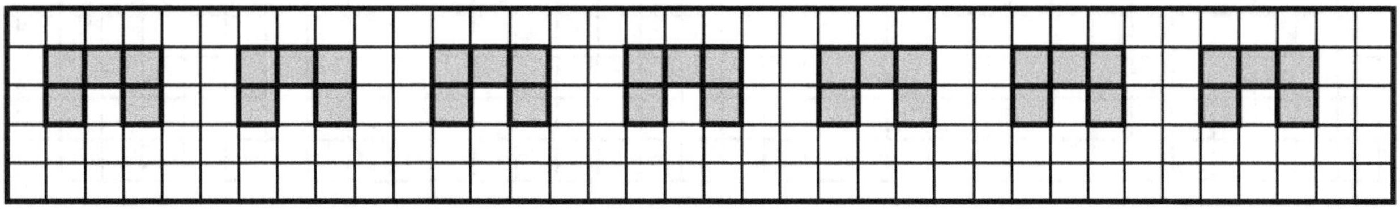

1.4 Investigation 6: Add one square to each of the *N*-pentominoes below to find more hexominoes with a longest chain of three squares. Eliminate any you found in earlier investigations. (There may be more *N*-pentominoes below than you need.)

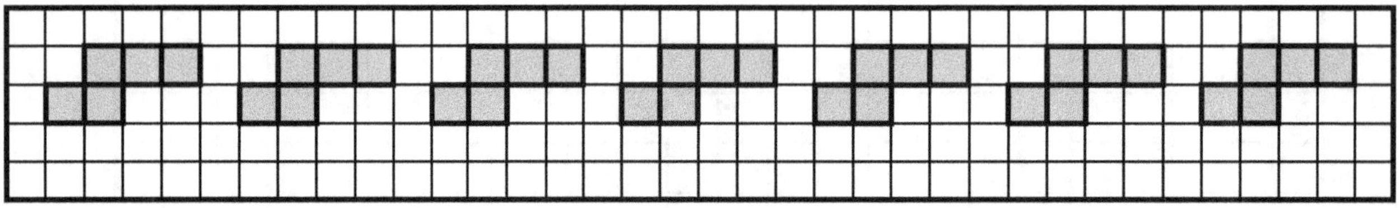

1.4 Investigation 7: There are not too many hexominoes left to find. Add one square to each of the *T*-, *F*-, *Z*-, and *X*-pentominoes below to see if there are any remaining hexominoes with a longest chain of three squares. Eliminate any you found in the earlier investigations. (There may be more *T*-, *F*-, *Z*-, and *X*-pentominoes below than you need.)

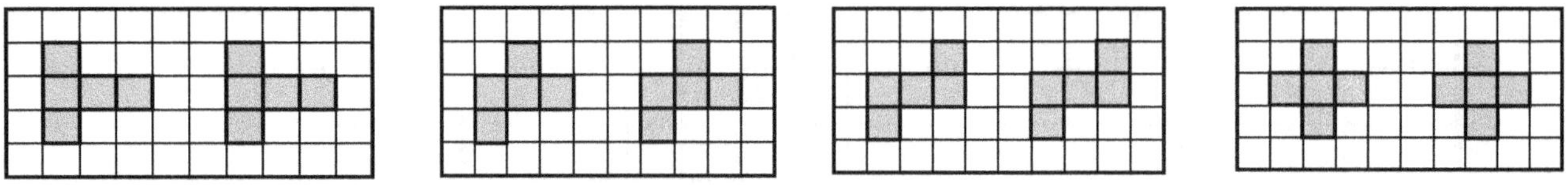

How many new hexominoes with a longest chain of three squares did you find in Investigation 7? Since there are no more pentominoes with a longest chain of three squares, you should have found all the hexominoes with a longest chain of three squares. Sketch them in the grid below.

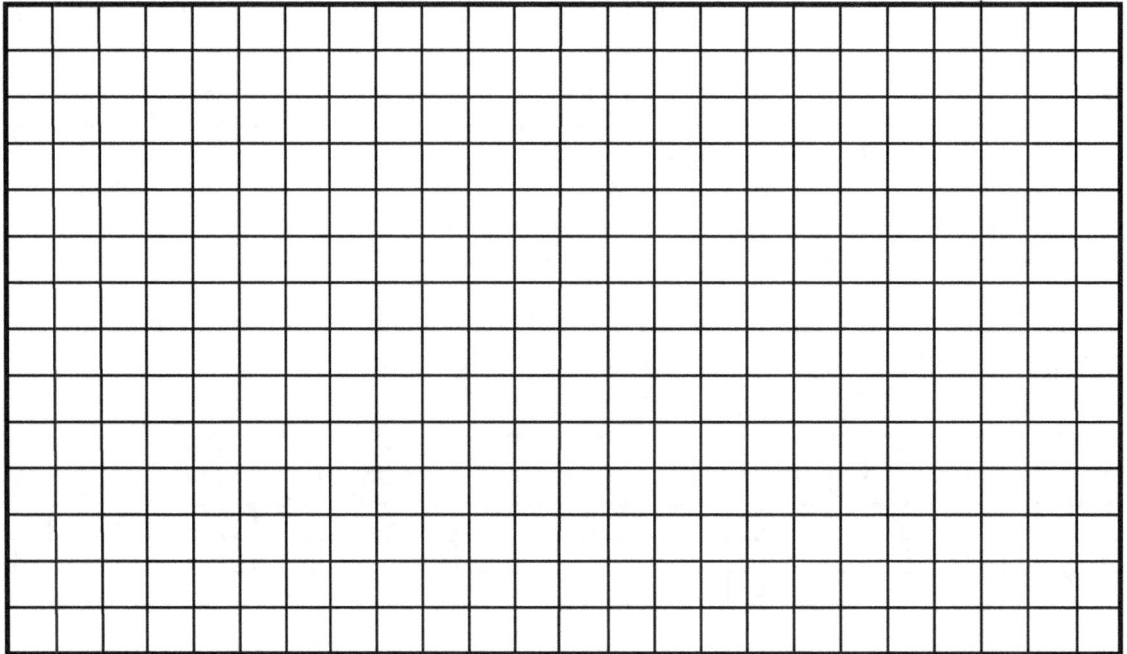

1.4 Investigation 8: Finally, find all the hexominoes with a longest chain of two squares.

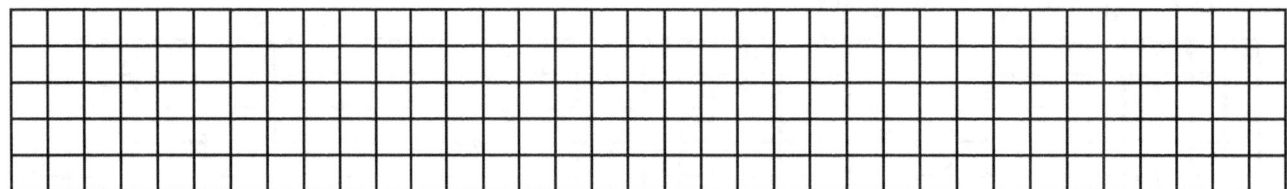

After completing Investigations 1–8, you should now have found all the hexominoes.

Hexomino Puzzle 1 ħ Sketch all the hexominoes in the grid below.

Hexomino Puzzle 2 ħ Which hexominoes can fold into a box with a lid? Circle them on your answers from Hexomino Puzzle 1.

Hexomino Puzzle 3 ħ The hexomino that forms a 1×6 rectangle and the hexomino that forms a 2×3 rectangle have both rotational and reflectional symmetry. Which hexominoes have only reflectional symmetry? (More than seven do.) Which have only rotational symmetry? (More than four do.) Sketch them in the grid below.

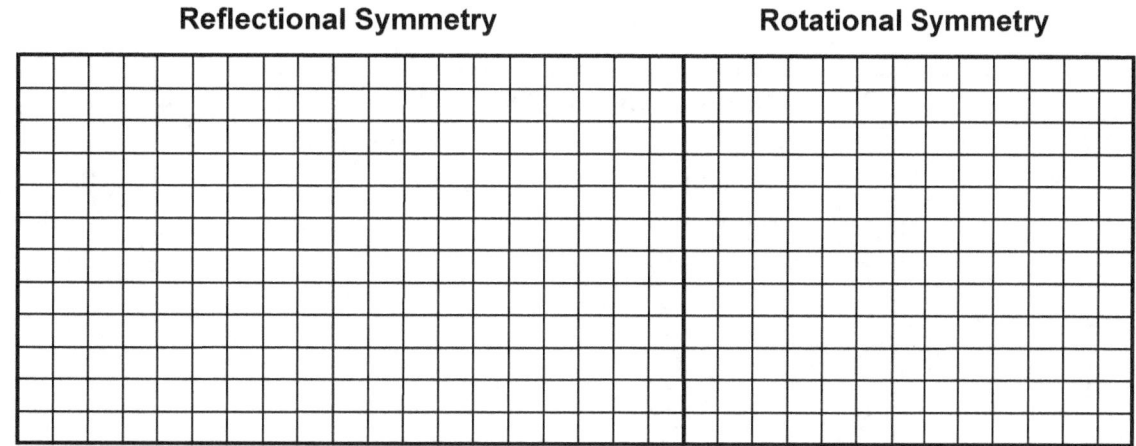

Reflectional Symmetry **Rotational Symmetry**

Hexomino Puzzle 4 *h*

All the hexominoes have the same area (six squares) but they do not all have the same perimeter. Some have a perimeter of 14, some have a perimeter of 12, and one has a perimeter of 10 (the 2×3 rectangle). Sketch the hexominoes with a perimeter of 12 in the grid below. Without counting the squares, can you identify which hexominoes have a perimeter of 12 and which have a perimeter of 14?

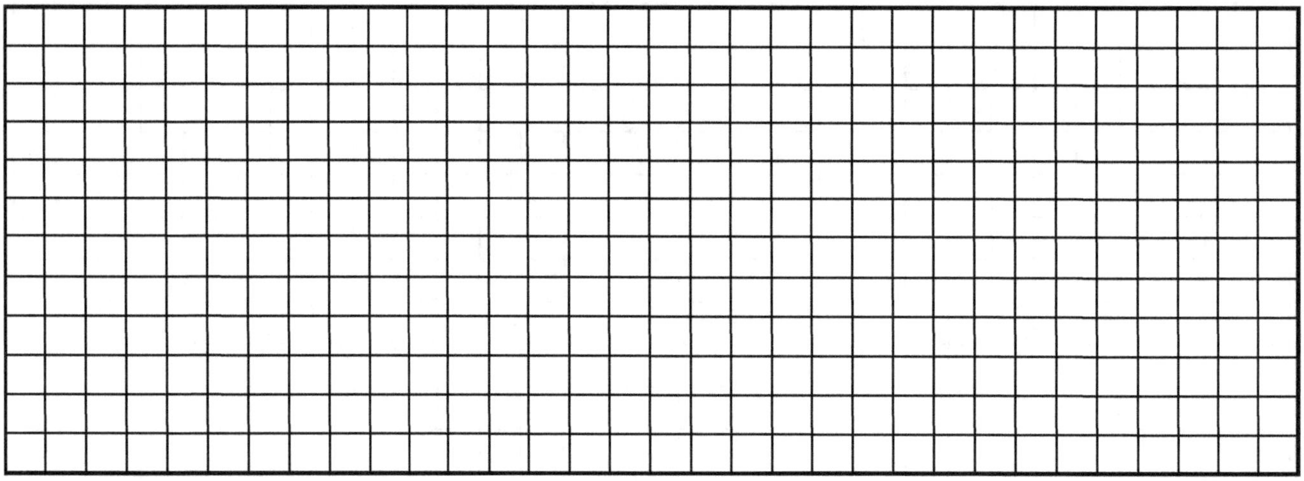

Hexomino Puzzle 5 *h*

The first 6×6 grid has been filled with six different hexominoes. Cover each of the remaining three 6×6 grids with six *different* hexominoes. Do it a different way each time.

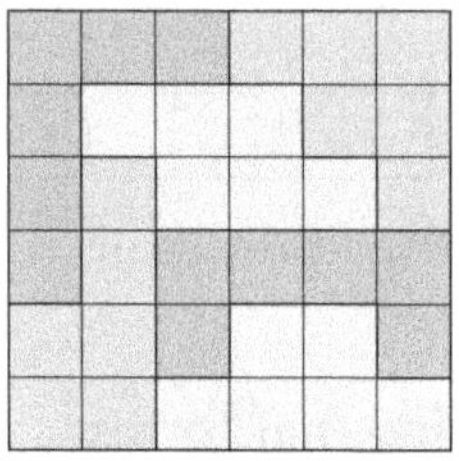

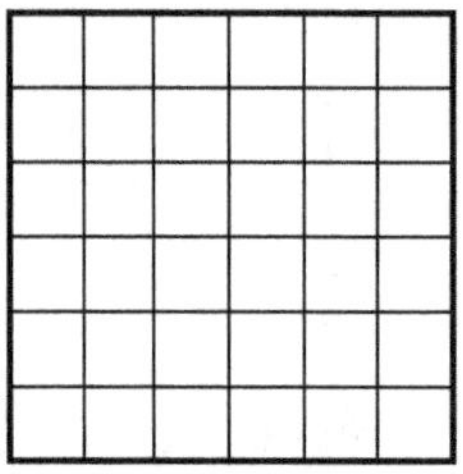

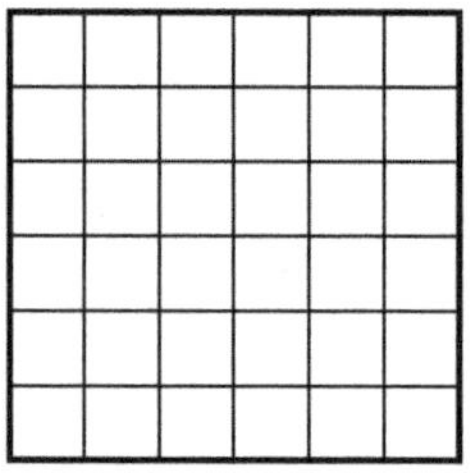

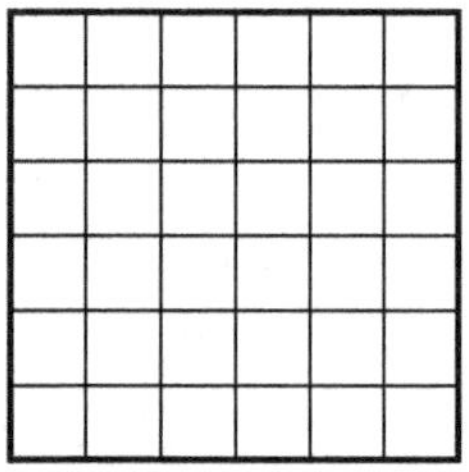

Hexomino Puzzle 6 *h*

In Section 1.3 you saw a pentomino sudoku like the one on the right. Every row, column, and pentomino region must contain the numerals 1 through 5.

	2		4		6
		5			
					3
6	1		5		
				4	
3		1			

The hexomino sudoku on the left has six different hexominoes filling the 6×6 grid. Every row, column, and hexomino region must contain the numerals 1 through 6. Complete the sudoku by filling in the empty cells.

4			3	
	2			1
		1		
	5			2

1.5 Combinatorial Geometry

The patterns made with polyominoes lend themselves to a variety of mathematical explorations. These explorations are examples of **combinatorial geometry**, a branch of geometry that deals with the ways in which geometrical shapes can be combined. The following puzzles feature some possible explorations.

Polyomino Puzzle 1 ℏ

It is possible to fill a 4×4 grid with four identical tetrominoes. This can be done with four of the five tetrominoes. The four possibilities are shown below left. Can you fill a 4×4 grid with a combination of exactly two different tetrominoes? One solution is shown below right. If rotations and reflections are not counted as different, how many different solutions can you find?

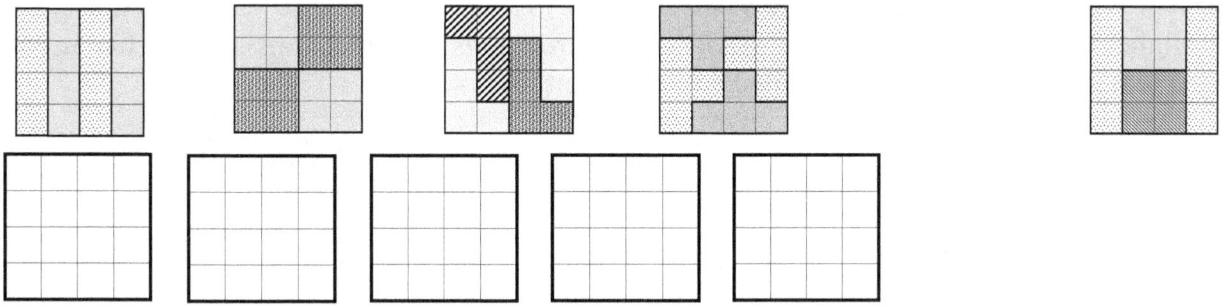

Polyomino Puzzle 2 ℏ

A polyomino is ***n*-rectifiable** if, and only if, *n* copies of the polyomino can be arranged to form a rectangle. The monomino, domino, both trominoes, and four of the five tetrominoes are rectifiable. The monomino, domino, the straight tromino, the straight tetromino, and the square tetromino are 1-rectifiable since they are already rectangles. See below.

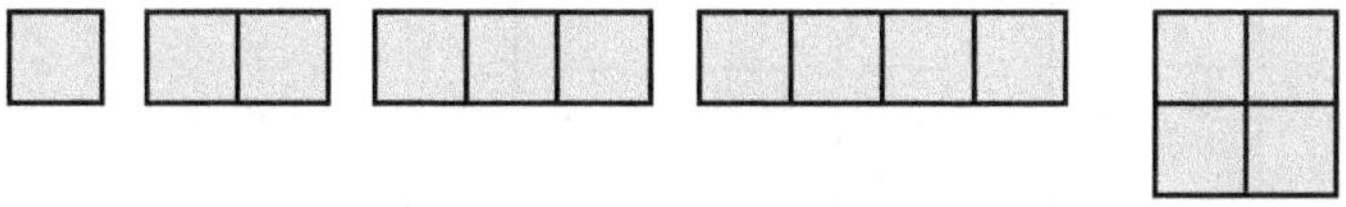

The bent tromino and the *L*-tetromino are 2-rectifiable since they form rectangles with two copies of the polyomino. See below left. The *T*-tetromino is 4-rectifiable, as you saw in the previous puzzle. One example of a 2-rectifiable hexomino is shown below right. Which of the pentominoes and remaining hexominoes are 2-rectifiable? Sketch them in the grid below.

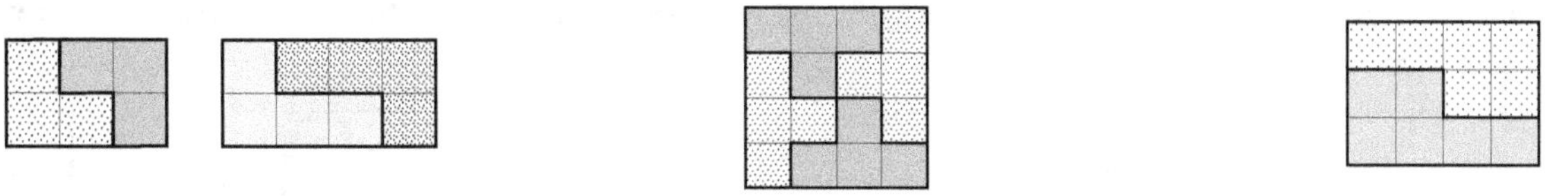

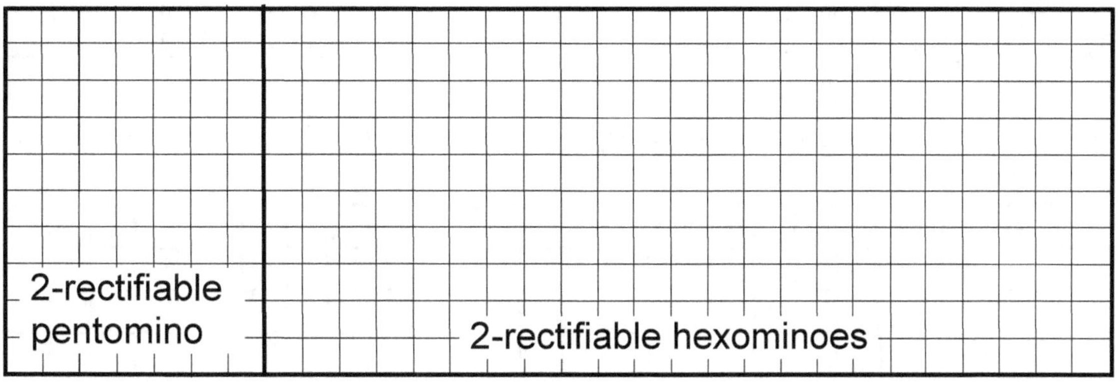

Polyomino Puzzle 3

Some of the pentominoes clearly can tile the plane without gaps or overlaps, as shown below. Are there any pentominoes that do not tile the plane?

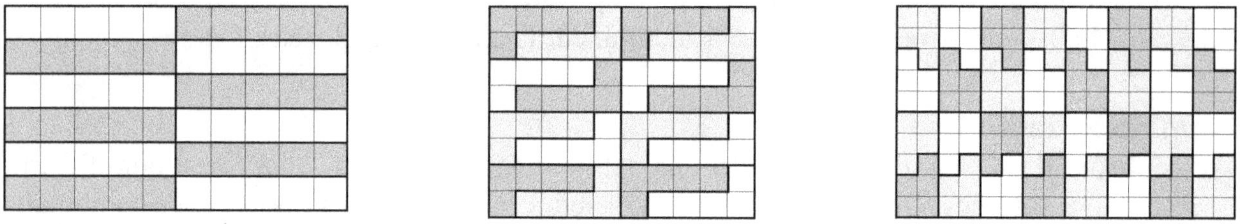

Polyomino Puzzle 4 ℏ

An $n \times n$ grid of squares is **deficient** if any one square is missing from the grid. The diagrams below show all the possible deficient 4×4 grids (not counting rotations and reflections). Notice that in each case the remaining 15 squares can be tiled with five bent trominoes.

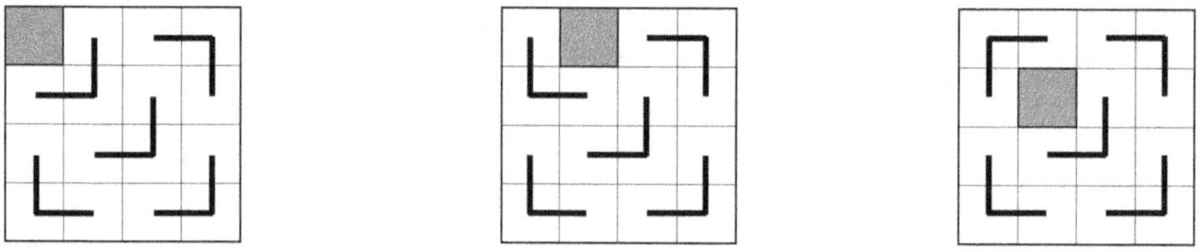

Can all 8×8 deficient boards also be tiled by bent trominoes? Find all 8×8 deficient boards and show whether or not you can tile each of them with 21 bent trominoes. Five deficient 8×8 boards are shown below.

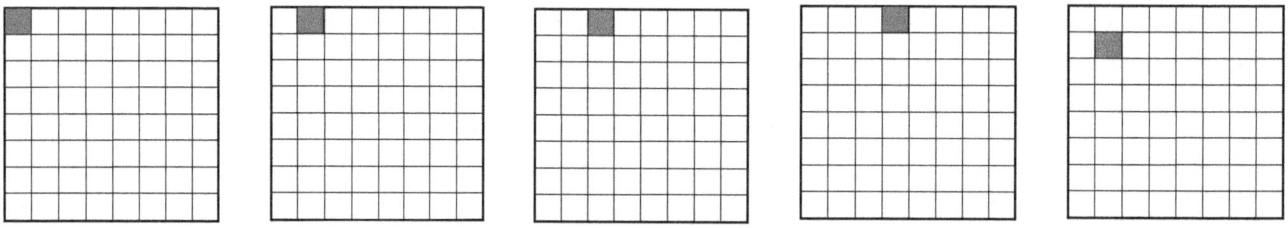

Polyomino Puzzle 5 ℏ

A 4×4 grid of squares can easily be covered with eight dominoes (below left). If you remove two adjacent corner squares of the 4×4 grid, it is still possible to cover the 14 squares with seven dominoes (below right).

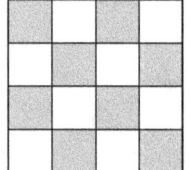

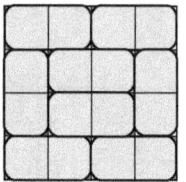

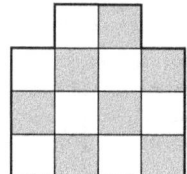

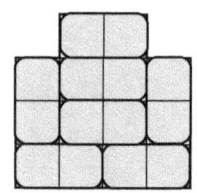

However, if you remove two opposite corner squares of the 4×4 grid, it appears to be impossible to cover the 14 squares with seven dominoes (below).

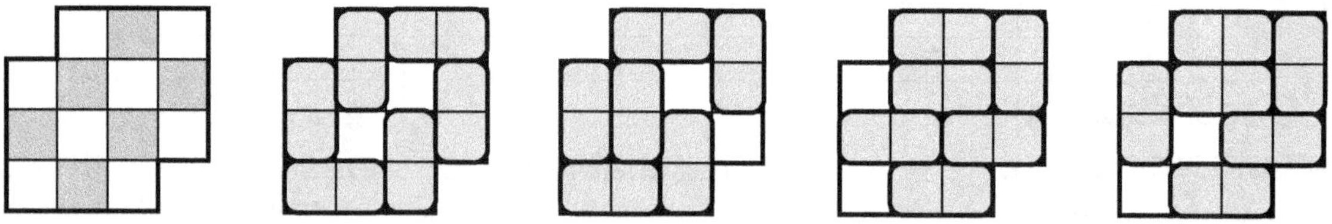

A chessboard has 64 squares. It is certainly possible to cover the entire chessboard with 32 dominoes. If you remove two opposite corners of the chessboard, can you still cover all 62 remaining squares with 31 dominoes? If not, can you explain why not?

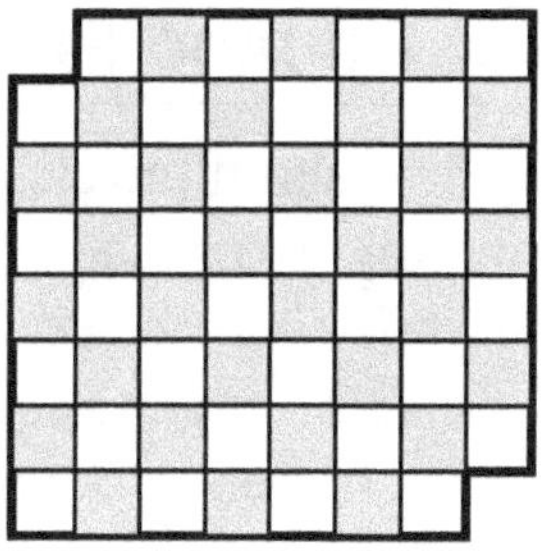

Polyomino Puzzle 6 *ℏ*

The complete set of the five tetrominoes can be arranged into a variety of shapes, including the staircase shown at right. There are a total of 20 squares in the complete set of tetrominoes. If they could be arranged into a rectangle it would have to be either a 4×5 or a 2×10 rectangle. But it turns out you cannot arrange all five into a rectangle (See examples below). Can you explain why not?

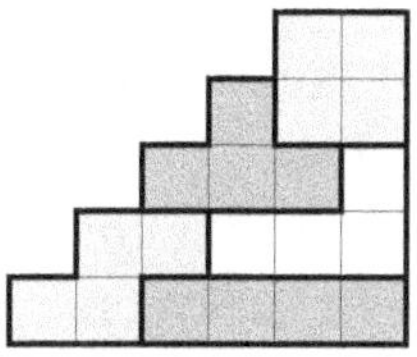

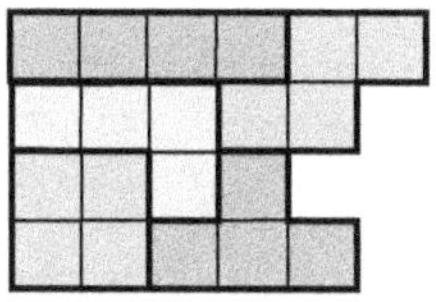

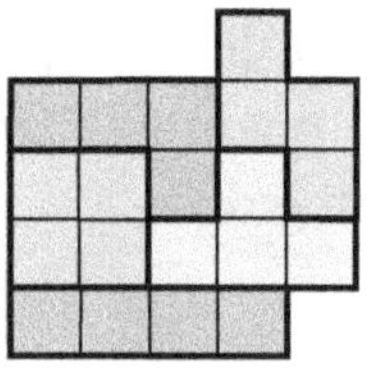

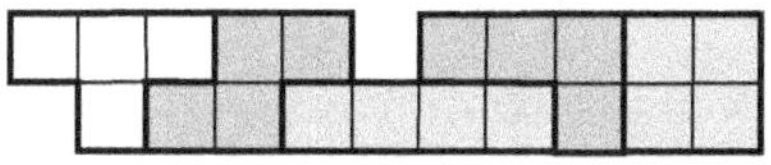

Polyomino Puzzle 7 *ℏ*

The total area covered by the 35 hexominoes is 6×35, or 210 squares. So it would seem a number of rectangles could be formed from all the hexominoes: 3×70, 5×42, 6×35, 7×30, 10×21, and 14×15. It turns out, however, that no rectangle can be formed using all 35 hexominoes. Explain why not.

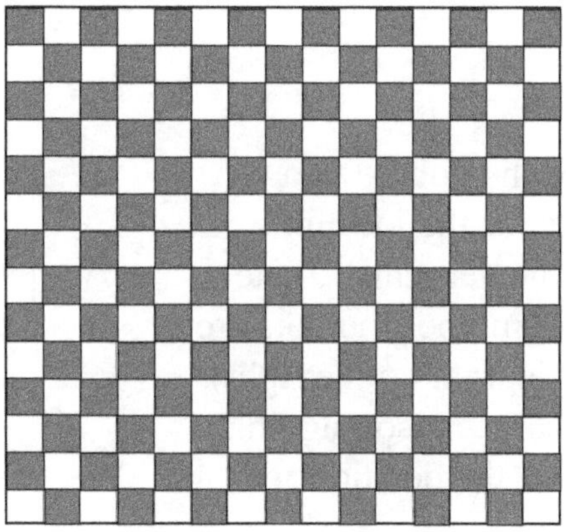

14×15 rectangle

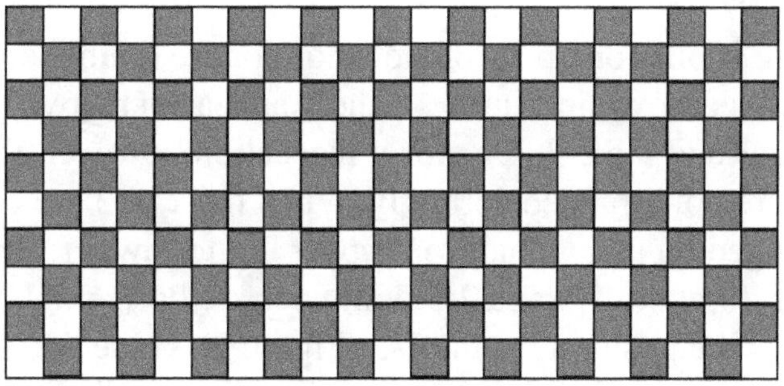

10×21 rectangle

Explorations in combinatorial geometry can be quite challenging because there are few rules or formulas to guide the investigations. Cleverness and ingenuity are two very useful mental tools for solving puzzles in combinatorial geometry. This next set of puzzles, Domino Puzzles, rely more on logical reasoning and perseverance. One important logical strategy used in domino puzzles is indirect proof.

1.6 Domino Puzzles

The next set of puzzles involve polyominoes with only two squares, dominoes. The game of Dominoes is believed to have originated in China in the 12th century. Today the game is played on every continent[2]. The most popular domino set is the "double-six." This set contains all the pairs of the numbers from zero (or blank) to six. The set contains 28 "bones" or tiles, shown in the diagram on the right. There are 56 squares in the 28 bones and therefore a complete set of double-six dominoes can be arranged into a 7×8 rectangle.

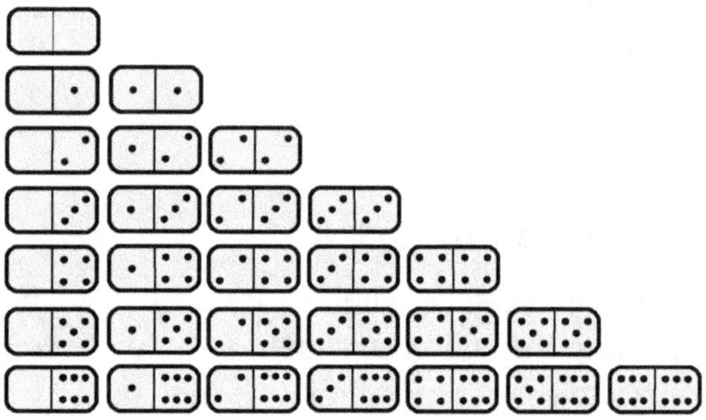

A number of dominoes have been arranged into a rectangle in each puzzle below. The outlines of the individual dominoes, however, have been removed. To solve the puzzle you will need to use sequential reasoning and clues from the arrangement of the dots.

Let's look at an example.

Example A

All ten dominoes with zeros, ones, twos, and threes {0-0, 0-1, 0-2, 0-3, 1-1, 1-2, 1-3, 2-2, 2-3, 3-3} have been arranged into a 4×5 rectangle. The outlines of the individual dominoes have been removed. Use your reasoning and visual thinking to sketch the outlines for the individual dominoes.

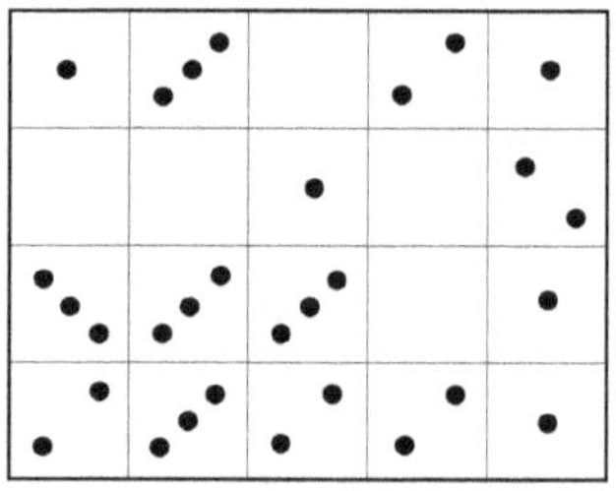

Solution

There is only one possible location for the double one (1-1) and the double two (2-2), as shown in Figure 1. There appear to be two possibilities for the locations of the 1-3 and the 2-3. On closer inspection however, the dots on the vertical 1-3 and 2-3 are not arranged correctly. When the 2 or 3 are on vertical dominoes the dots are arranged on a diagonal from upper left to lower right (See the diagram on the right). Therefore, the 1-3 and 2-3 dominoes are horizontal. Using the same reasoning, this forces the position for the 3-3 (Figure 2). Once the 3-3 is located, the positions of the remaining five dominoes are forced as well (Figure 3).

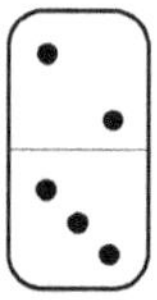

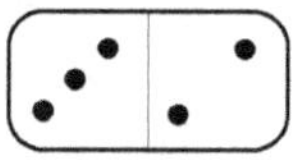

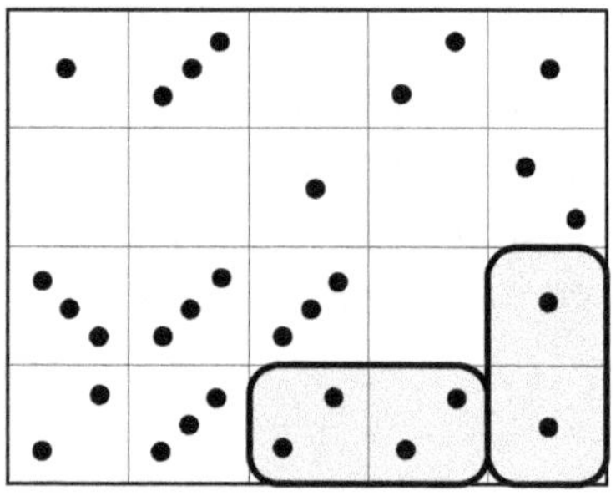

Figure 1

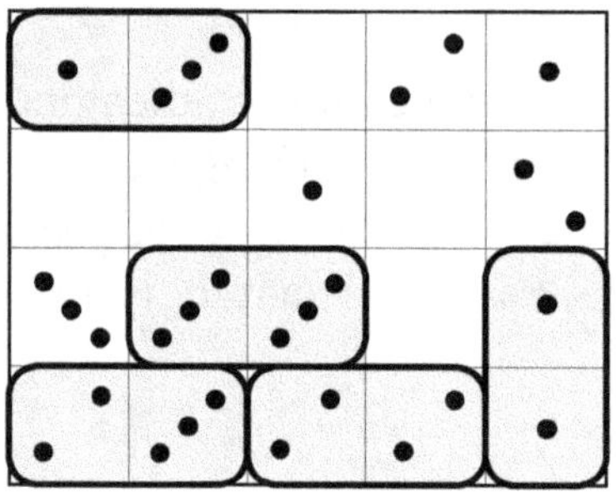

Figure 2

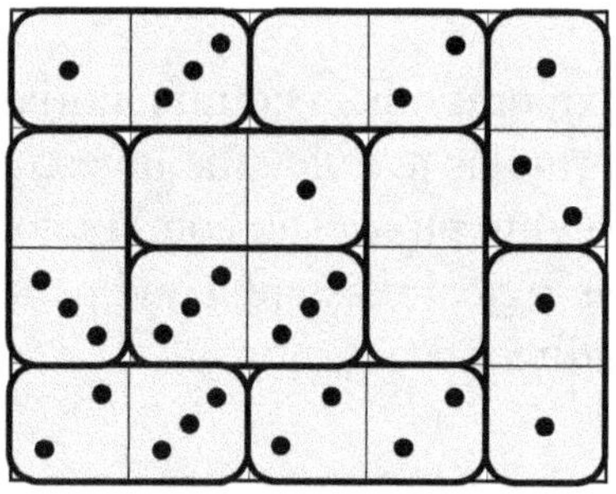

Figure 3

Domino Puzzle 1 uses the 15 dominoes with zeros, ones, twos, threes and fours. They have been arranged into a 5×6 rectangle. Domino Puzzle 2 uses the 21 dominoes with zeros, ones, twos, threes, fours, and fives. They have been arranged into a 6×7 rectangle. The outlines of the individual dominoes have been removed. Use your sequential reasoning and visual thinking skills to solve these domino puzzles. Use the small set of dominoes below each puzzle to help you keep track of the dominoes found. You might also use tracing paper or patty paper to help you visualize the positions of the dominoes.

Domino Puzzle 1

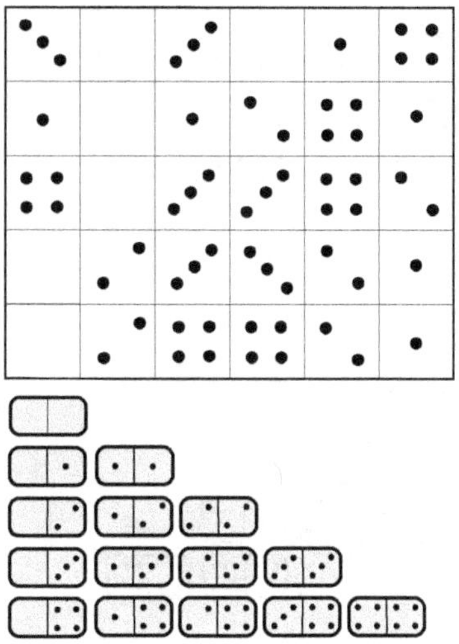

Domino Puzzle 2

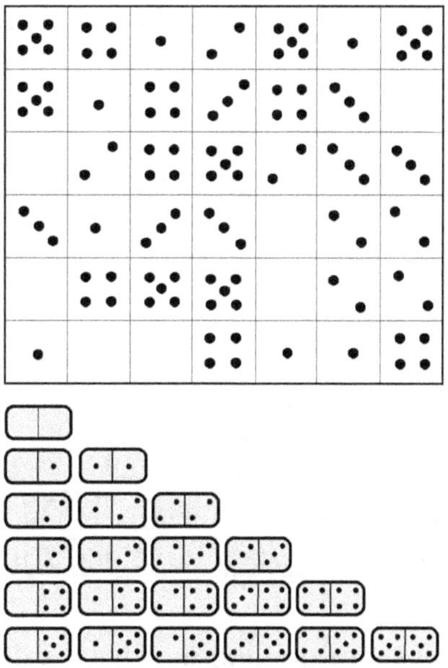

Domino Puzzles 3–6 use the entire double-six set. The 28 dominoes have been arranged into 7×8 rectangles. The outlines of the individual dominoes have been removed. Use your sequential reasoning and visual thinking skills to solve these domino puzzles.

Domino Puzzle 3

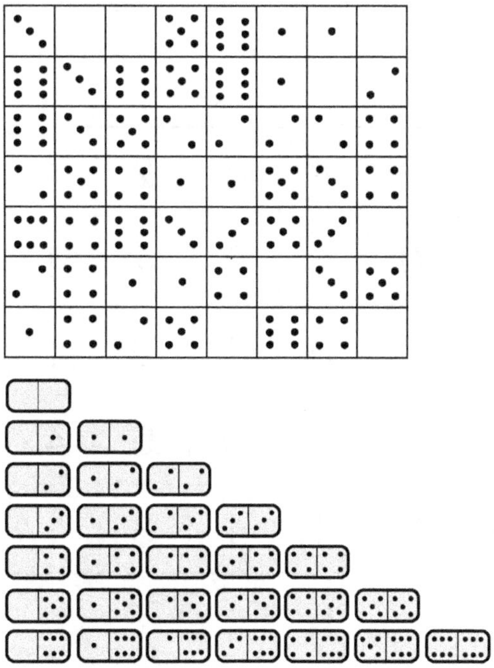

Domino Puzzle 4

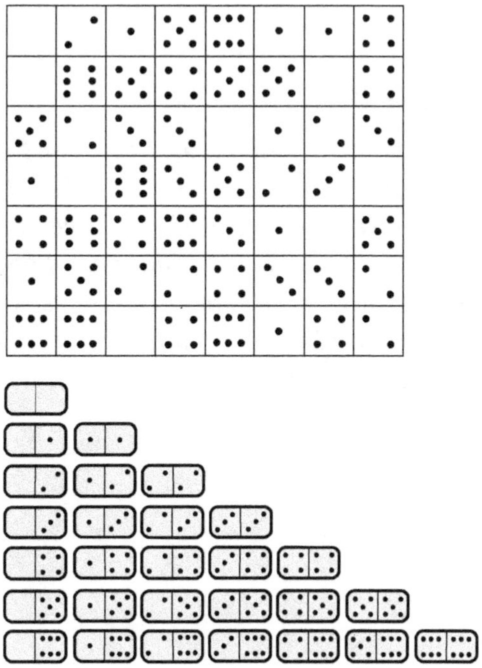

Domino Puzzle 5

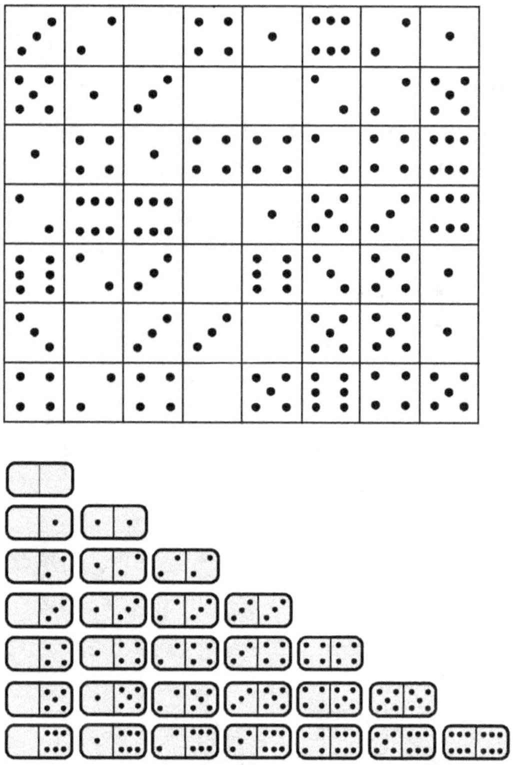

Domino Puzzle 6

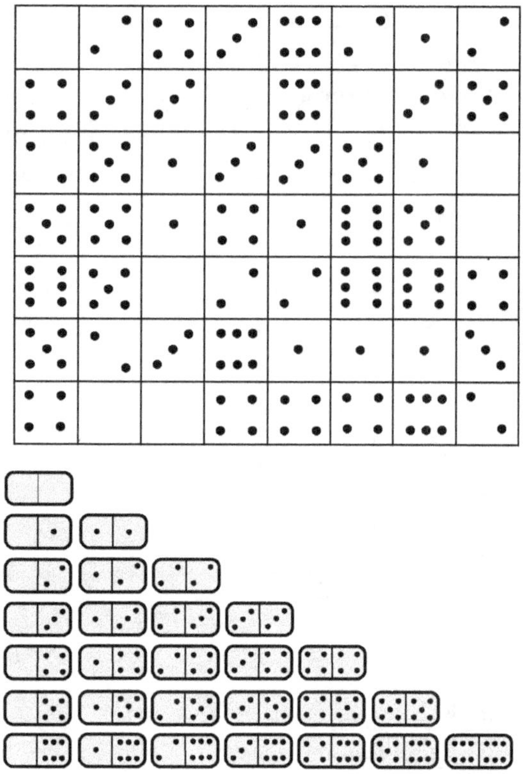

In this next set of domino puzzles the dots are replaced with their numerals. This may make the puzzle more difficult, since the 2, 3, and 6 no longer give you clues about their orientation. Let's look at an example.

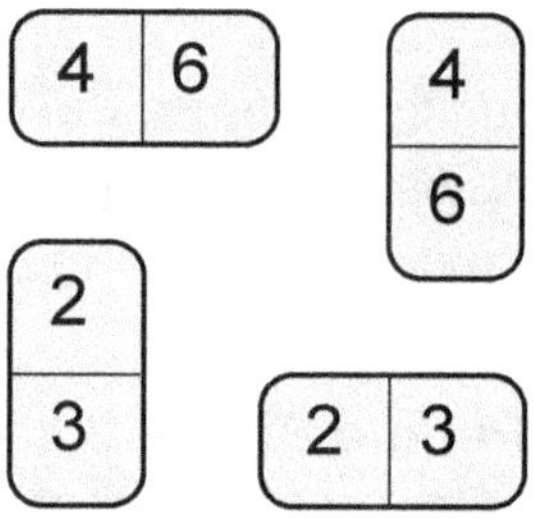

Example B

All 15 dominoes with zeros, ones, twos, threes, and fours {0-0, 0-1, 0-2, 0-3, 0-4, 1-1, 1-2, 1-3, 1-4, 2-2, 2,3, 2-4, 3-3, 3-4, 4-4} have been arranged into a 5×6 rectangle. The outlines of the individual dominoes have been removed. Use reasoning and visual thinking to sketch the outlines for the individual dominoes.

3	2	4	4	2	4
3	0	1	2	4	4
2	0	0	1	3	1
2	2	3	0	0	4
3	0	1	1	3	1

Solution

There is only one possible location for the 1-1, 3-3, 3-4, and the 0-4 (Figure 4). This forces the 1-3, the 1-4, and the 2-4 (Figure 5). This leaves only one location for the 4-4, which forces the 0-2 (Figure 6). Once the 0-2 is located then the other three possible 0-2 positions are eliminated (Figure 6). This forces the 2-2, then 0-3, then 2-3, then 0-0, then 1-2, and finally 0-1 (Figure 7).

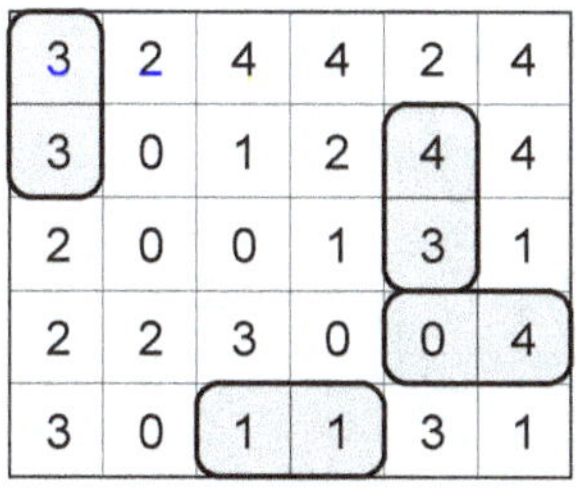

Figure 4

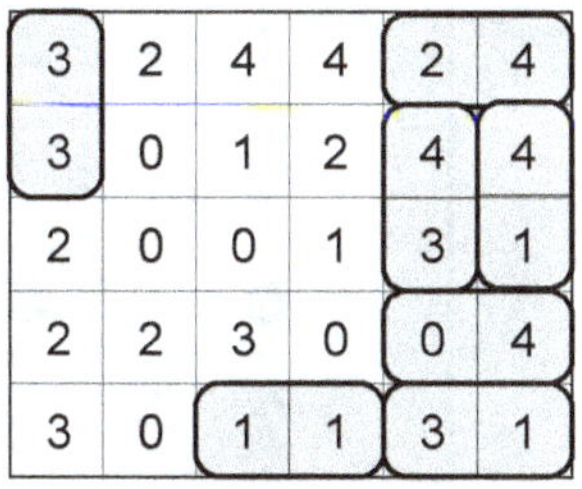

Figure 5

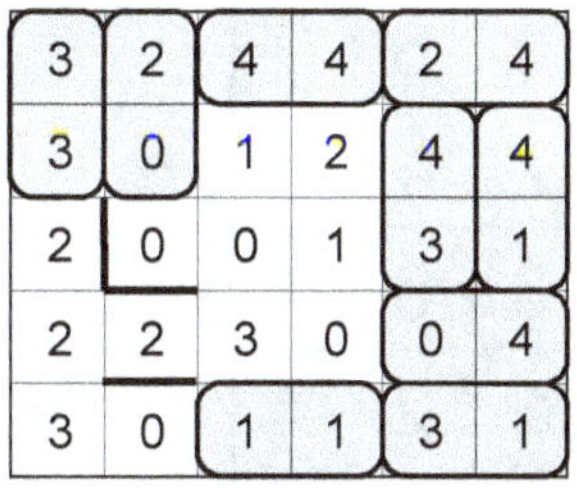

Figure 6

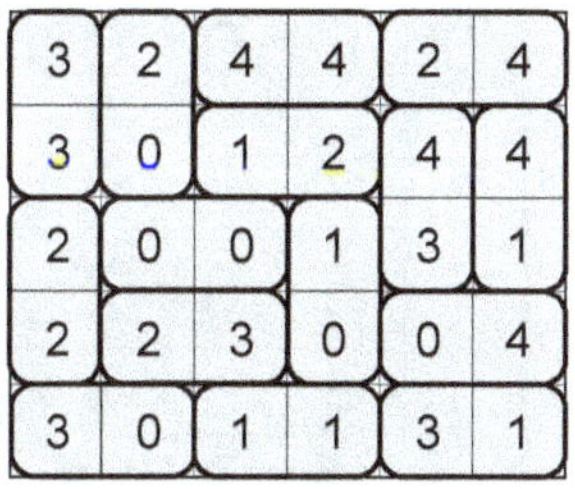

Figure 7

Domino Puzzles 7–10 use the entire double-six set. The 28 dominoes have been arranged into a 7×8 rectangle. The outlines of the individual dominoes have been removed. Use sequential reasoning and deductive logic to solve these domino puzzles.

Domino Puzzle 7

0	5	6	2	5	4	5	0
0	1	1	4	0	2	3	2
6	4	2	2	3	6	1	4
3	1	0	3	3	4	5	0
4	6	1	4	1	4	3	1
3	0	3	5	6	5	5	6
6	2	1	2	5	2	0	6

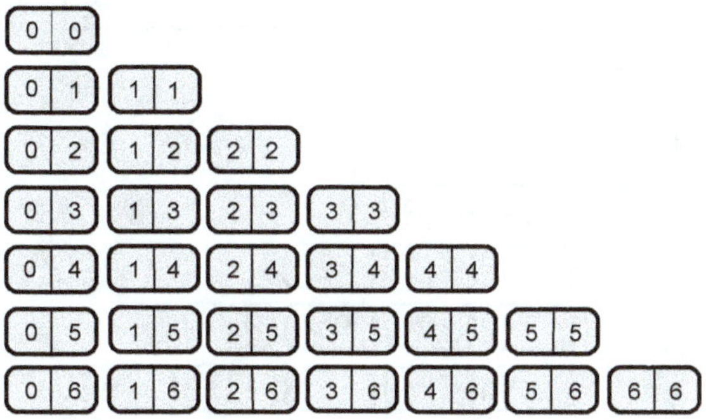

Domino Puzzle 8

5	0	4	1	3	6	4	3
5	2	6	5	2	5	3	1
0	3	6	1	6	0	6	2
4	1	4	4	3	1	2	4
5	3	2	3	3	0	2	6
1	2	6	0	4	6	1	0
0	5	4	5	2	5	1	0

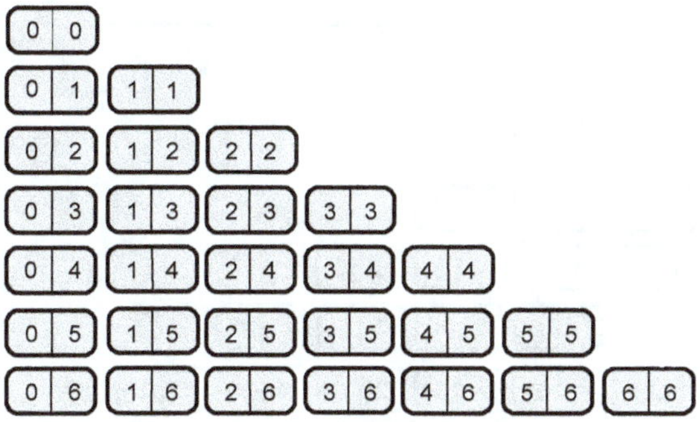

Domino Puzzle 9 ℏ

4	1	5	4	2	2	1	5
0	3	1	3	6	4	0	6
0	6	0	6	3	0	5	2
2	4	5	5	3	2	4	1
6	5	0	2	5	3	5	4
1	3	2	1	6	1	2	4
3	6	6	3	0	1	4	0

0|0
0|1 1|1
0|2 1|2 2|2
0|3 1|3 2|3 3|3
0|4 1|4 2|4 3|4 4|4
0|5 1|5 2|5 3|5 4|5 5|5
0|6 1|6 2|6 3|6 4|6 5|6 6|6

Domino Puzzle 10

0	4	1	0	2	4	3	1
0	1	3	6	0	3	5	4
6	2	6	4	2	6	1	4
5	3	1	1	2	0	2	6
1	5	4	5	3	0	2	4
1	3	2	5	4	3	3	2
5	0	6	6	0	5	6	5

0|0
0|1 1|1
0|2 1|2 2|2
0|3 1|3 2|3 3|3
0|4 1|4 2|4 3|4 4|4
0|5 1|5 2|5 3|5 4|5 5|5
0|6 1|6 2|6 3|6 4|6 5|6 6|6

Domino Puzzle 11 ℏ

2	4	6	6	3	5	6	0
2	3	1	0	6	5	4	2
1	1	3	0	4	1	4	2
0	2	5	4	0	6	3	3
3	1	2	1	4	6	1	6
6	5	5	5	0	3	2	2
4	5	0	0	4	3	1	5

0|0
0|1 1|1
0|2 1|2 2|2
0|3 1|3 2|3 3|3
0|4 1|4 2|4 3|4 4|4
0|5 1|5 2|5 3|5 4|5 5|5
0|6 1|6 2|6 3|6 4|6 5|6 6|6

Domino Puzzle 12

0	1	4	4	6	6	6	6
5	1	4	4	6	2	0	1
5	1	3	3	5	5	1	1
4	1	0	5	5	5	5	3
2	2	2	6	2	2	2	2
1	0	0	3	3	3	3	4
0	0	4	4	6	6	3	0

0|0
0|1 1|1
0|2 1|2 2|2
0|3 1|3 2|3 3|3
0|4 1|4 2|4 3|4 4|4
0|5 1|5 2|5 3|5 4|5 5|5
0|6 1|6 2|6 3|6 4|6 5|6 6|6

Chapter 2 Rectangular Buried Treasure

Creative thinking is a skill that can be practiced and nurtured.

—Edward de Bono

2.1 The Positive Coordinate System

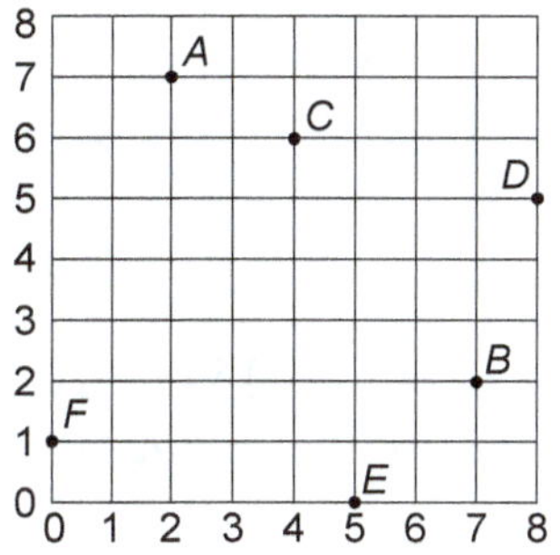

A coordinate system locates points on a rectangular grid. The point where the two axes cross is called the **origin** and has coordinates (0, 0). Points are located by using an **ordered pair** of numbers. They are called *ordered* pairs because order is important. The first number of the pair moves you horizontally while the second number moves you vertically. The ordered pair (2, 3) locates a point two units to the right of the origin and three units up from the origin. Notice that point *A* (2, 7) and point *B* (7, 2) are two different points.

Exercises in the Positive Coordinate System

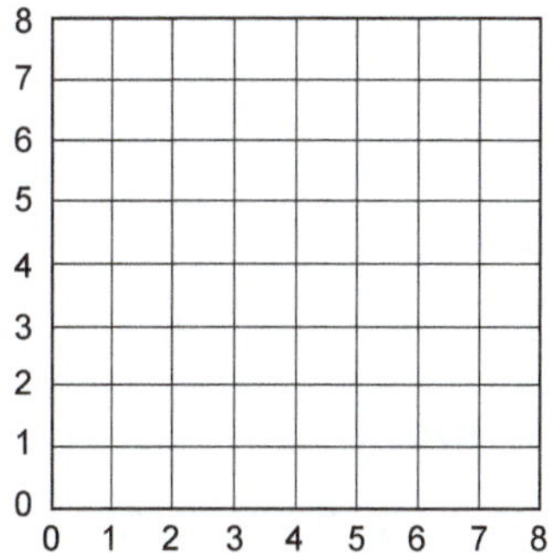

Find the coordinates of the points shown on the coordinate grid above.

1. Point *A* (,) 2. Point *B* (,) 3. Point *C* (,)

4. Point *D* (,) 5. Point *E* (,) 6. Point *F* (,)

Locate the following points on the coordinate grid shown at right.

7. Point *G* is (2, 4) 8. Point *H* is (7, 8)

9. Point *I* is (6, 1) 10. Point *J* is (1, 6)

11. Point *K* is (0, 4) 12. Point *L* is (2, 0)

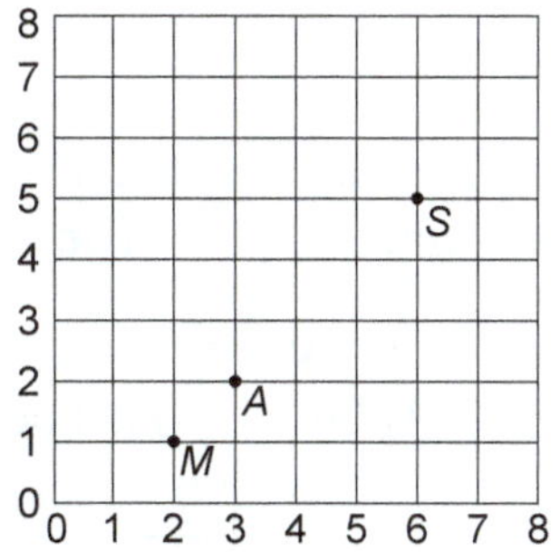

Points that lie on the same line are **collinear**. Points *M*, *A*, and *S* on the graph at right are collinear.

Example A

Collinear points M(2, 1), A(3, 2) and S(6, 5) are shown on the graph at right. Locate another point on the same line as the line containing the three given points. What are the coordinates of that point?

Solution

One approach is to use your ruler and carefully draw a line through the three given points. Notice that the line also passes through point (4, 3). Put a dot at the point (4, 3) and label it point *R*.

Another approach is to look for a pattern of movement from one point to another. Do you see a pattern in how you can move between the points on the graph? Complete the ordered pairs below to find other points that are collinear with points *M*, *A*, *S*, and *R*, then check your answer on the next page.

T(5 ,____) or *U*(7 ,____) or *V*(8 ,____) or *W*(1 ,____)

Chapter 2.1

You should have gotten: $T(5, 4)$ or $U(7, 6)$ or $V(8, 7)$ or $W(1, 0)$

For each exercise below, locate another point on the same line as the line containing the two given points.

13. Given points C and R, find another point that is collinear and label it point O.

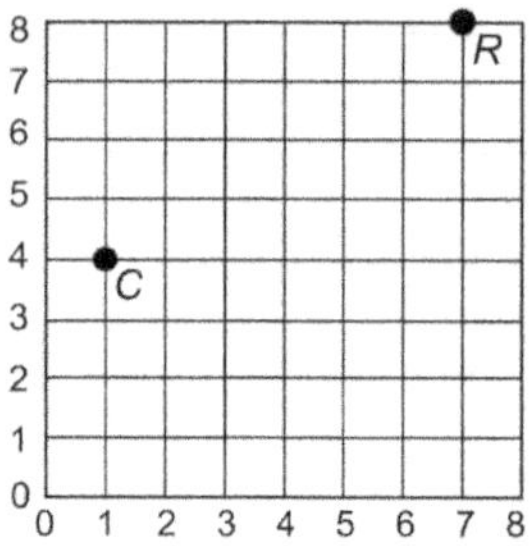

14. Given points N and A, find another point that is collinear and label it point T.

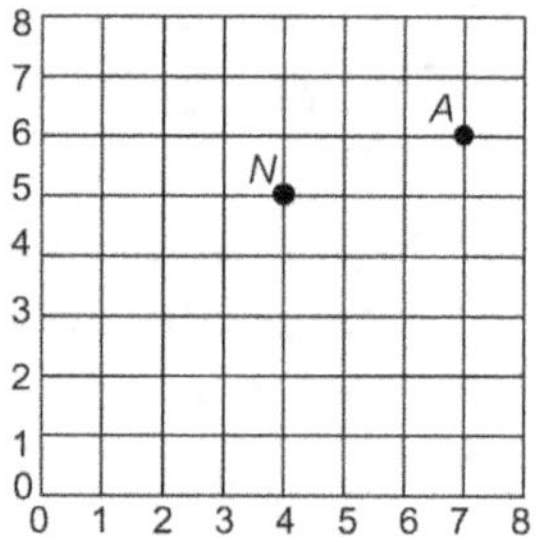

For Exercises 15 and 16 below, locate and label each pair of points on the graph provided. Then locate another point that is on the same line as the line containing the two given points.

15. Given $A(1, 6)$, $B(3, 2)$, find another point on the line and label it point N.

16. Given $C(0, 7)$, $D(8, 3)$, find another point on the line and label it point O.

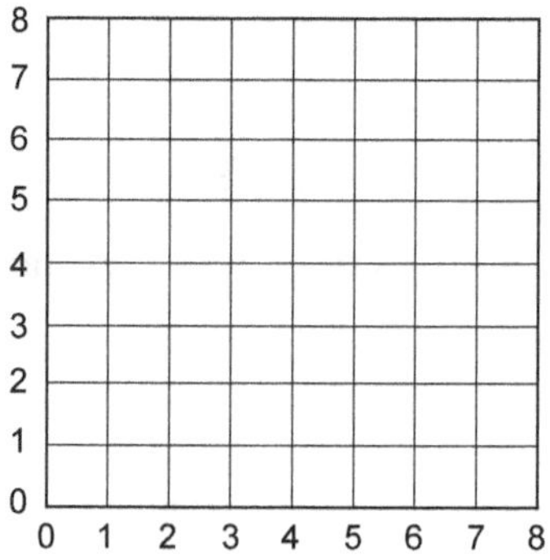

Example B

Find the coordinates of the corners of the tetromino on the right.

Solution

There are six corners on this tetromino. They are (2, 7), (1, 7), (1, 4), (3, 4), (3, 5), and the indented corner (2, 5).

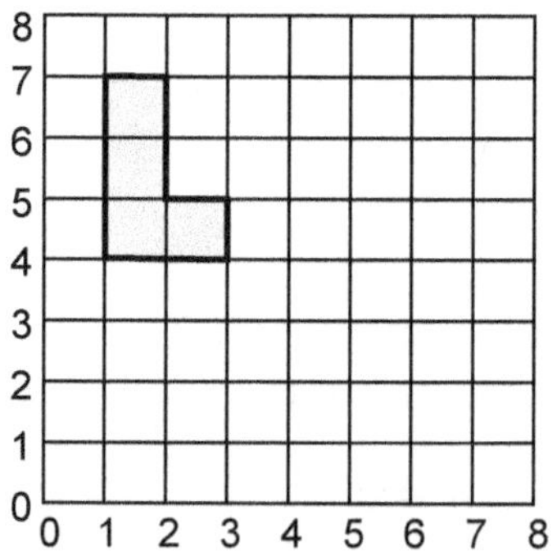

For Exercises 17 and 18, name the coordinates of the corners of the tetromino below left and the pentomino below right.

17. There are eight corners. One corner is (6, 4) but (7, 5) is not a corner.

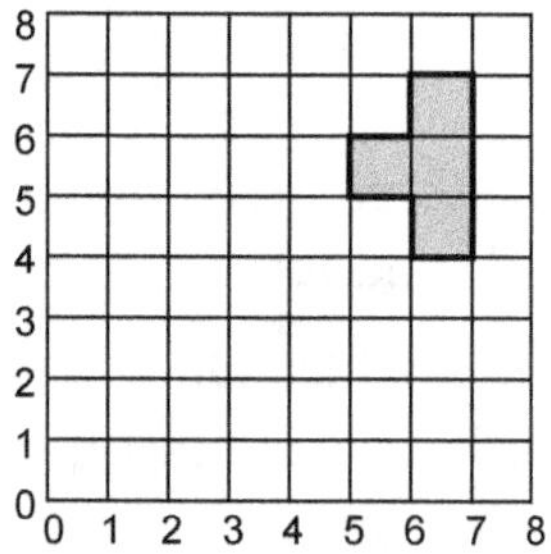

(5, 5), (5,__), (6, 4), (6,__),
(6,__), (6,__), (7,__), (7,__),

18. There are ten corners. One corner is (3, 1) but (5, 1) is not a corner.

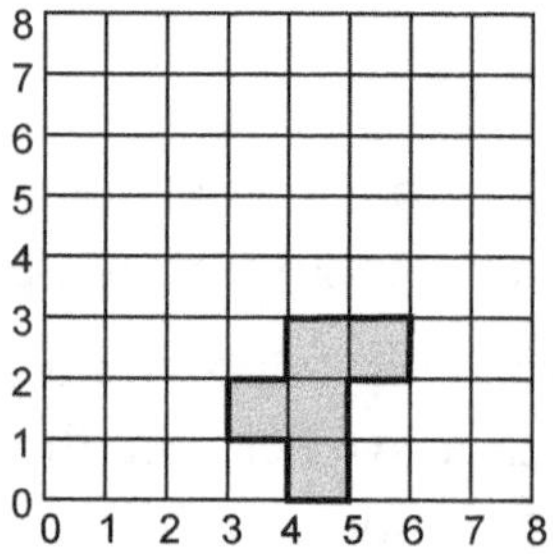

(3, 1), (3,__), (4,__), (__,__), (__,__),
(__,__), (__,__), (__,__), (__,__), (__,__),

For Exercises 19 and 20, shade a pentomino in the grid given the coordinates of only some of its corners. For each exercise there is only one solution.

19. Five of the six corners include:
(2, 3), (2, 5), (4, 4), (4, 5), (5, 3)

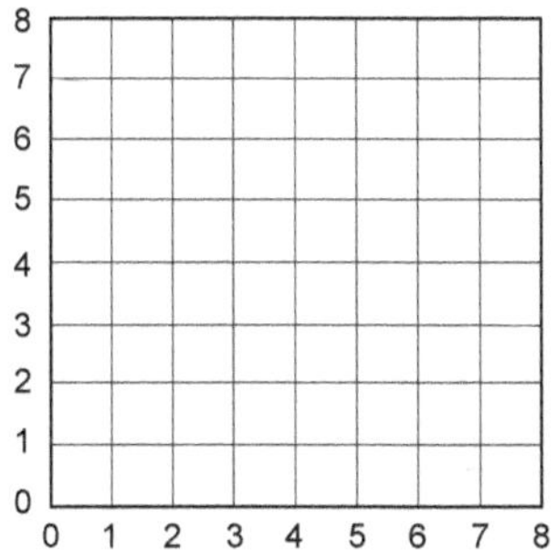

20. Five of the eight corners include:
(1, 3), (1, 5), (4, 3), (4, 5), (3, 3)

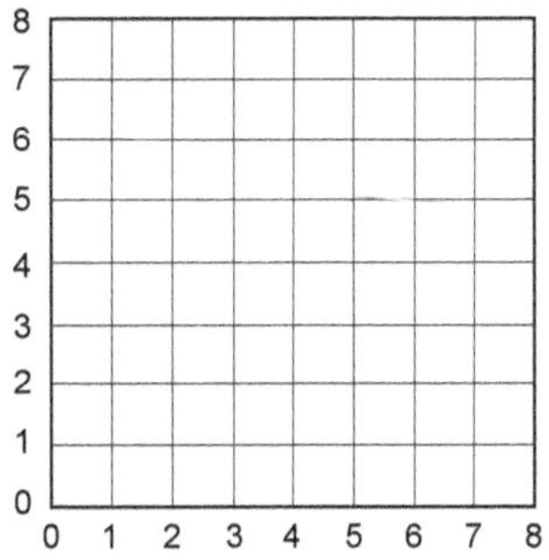

Example C

On the grid to the right each E represents a point on an edge of a pentomino and each C represents a point on a corner. An X means the pentomino does not pass through that point (a miss). From these clues, locate the pentomino.

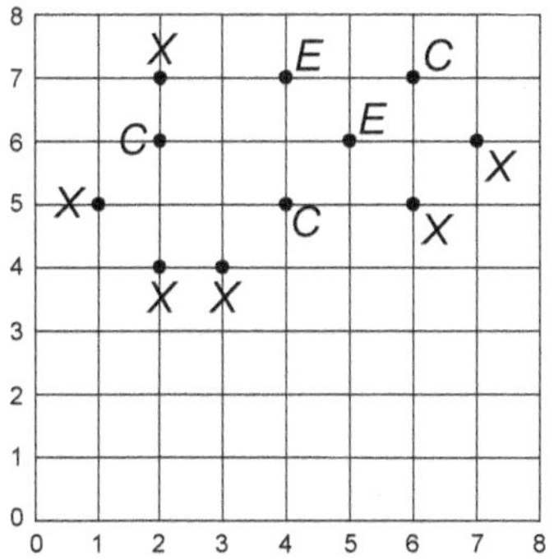

Solution

Since the points (1, 5), (2, 4), (2, 7), (3, 4), (6, 5), and (7, 6) are marked with an *X*, those points are not part of the pentomino. This means that the pentomino cannot be in any of the shaded squares. If the points marked with a *C* indicate corners, and points marked with *E* indicate edges, then the pentomino can be located using logical reasoning.

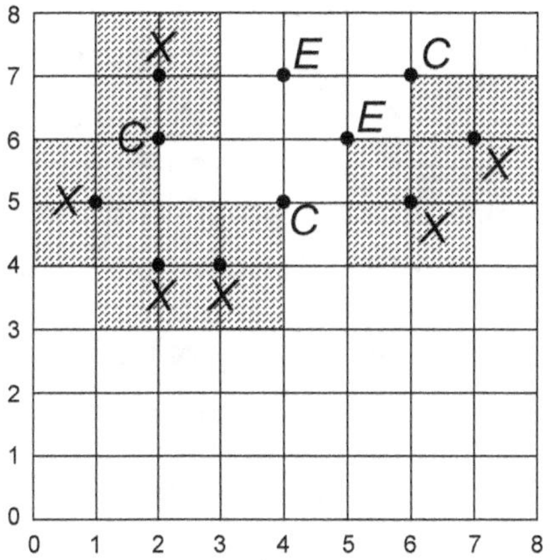

The corners: (2, 5), (2, 6), (3, 6), (3, 7), (6, 7), (6, 6), (4, 6), and (4, 5). The edge points include: (3, 5), (4, 7), (5, 7), and (5, 6). The pentomino is the *N*-pentomino.

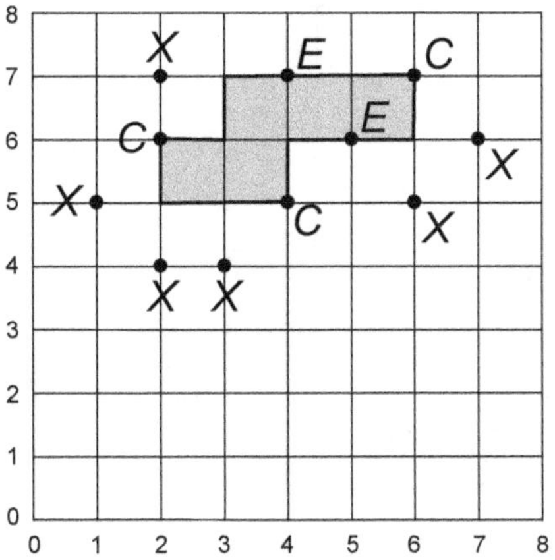

In Exercises 21–24, sketch a pentomino given the clues: *C* for corner point, *E* for edge point, *X* for a point that is not on the pentomino, and *I* for interior point. (The *P*-pentomino is the only pentomino with an interior point.)

21.

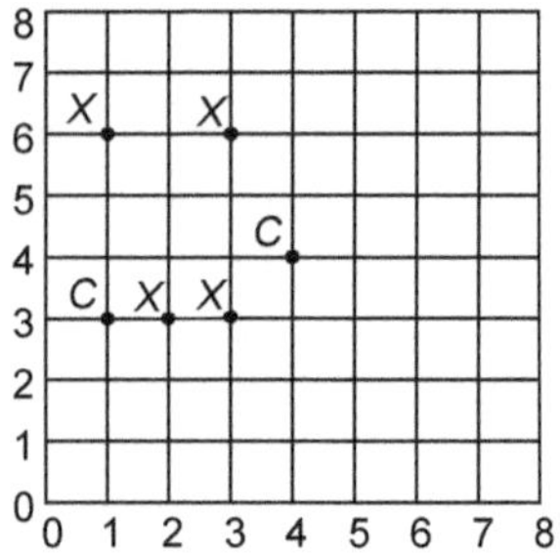

22. *h*

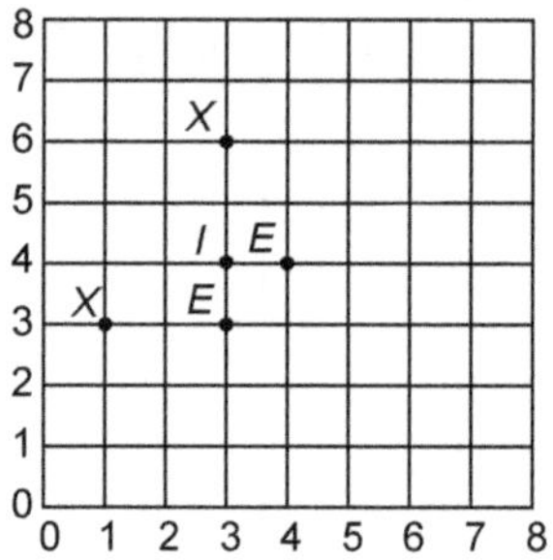

23.

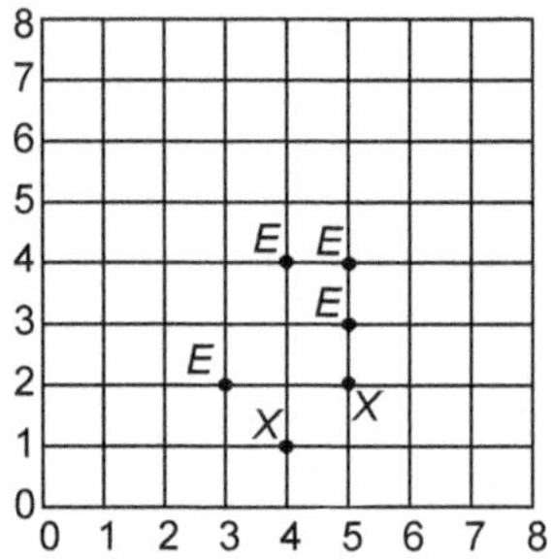

24. *h*

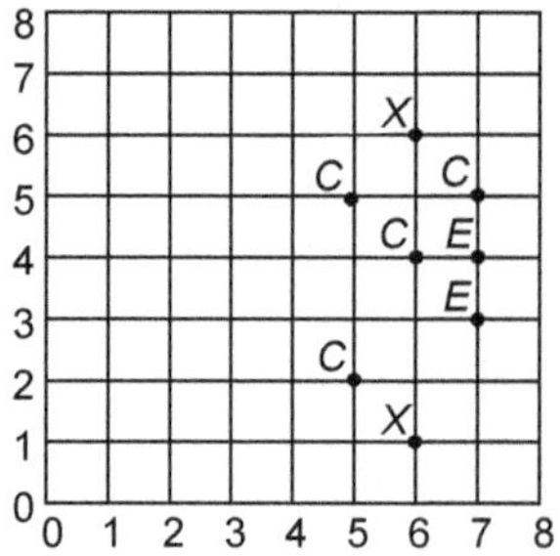

2.2 Introduction to Buried Treasure

Buried Treasure is a variation of a game called Battleship[3], played in math classes for at least a hundred years and later made available by the toy company Milton Bradley. In our game, two teams will be searching for buried treasure rather than sinking warships. Each team hides their buried treasure on their grid for the other team to find.

Before the game begins, each player or team hides his or her buried treasure on their game sheet in the grid labeled **Our Team's Buried Treasure**. For example, the *I*-pentomino in the grid below right has been hidden as buried treasure. Game sheets for playing Buried Treasure are located in Appendix 1. Each team needs two game sheets. One sheet has **Our Team's Digs** above the table and **Other's Team's Buried Treasure** below the grid. The other sheet has **Other Team's Digs** above the table and **Our Team's Buried Treasure** below the grid. I recommend that you print the two game sheets back to back.

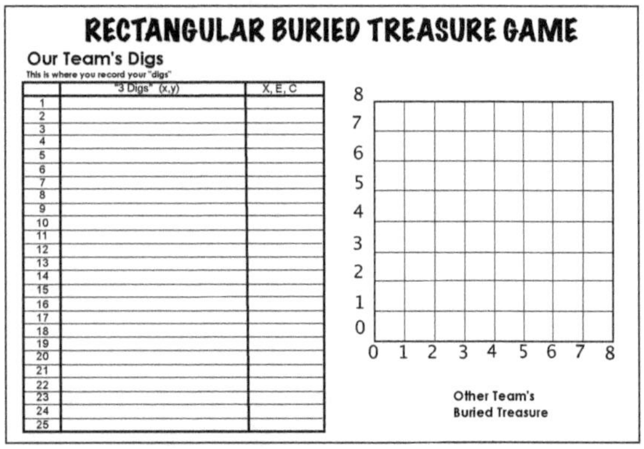

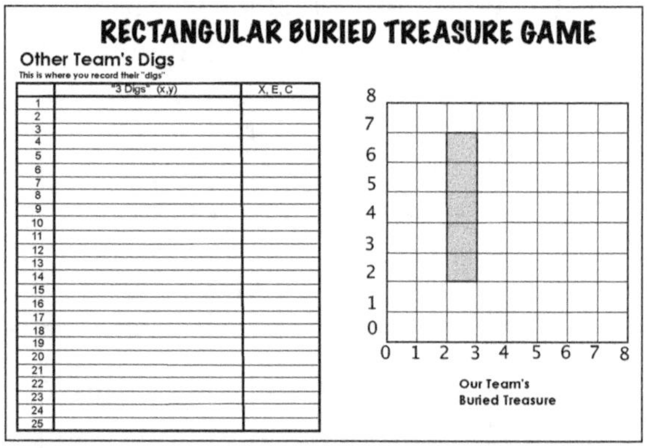

Do not let your opponent see where you have hidden your treasure. You might hide your game sheets in a book or magazine, place a screen between the teams, or cover your team's buried treasure beneath a post-it™ note.

You will search for your opponent's treasure in the grid labeled **Other Team's Buried Treasure**. Each team tries to locate the other team's hidden treasure by taking turns calling out a pair of numbers called **coordinates** indicating where they would like to "dig" for treasure.

Level 1A In this first Buried Treasure game both teams are trying to be the first to locate where the other team has buried their treasure. Both teams will be hiding the same shape, the *I*-pentomino, shown to the right. Determine which team plays first by flipping a coin or rolling a die.

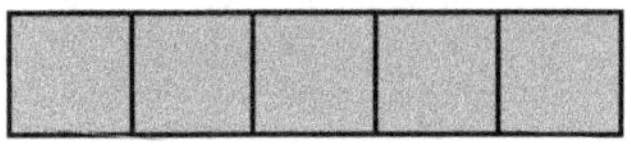

Rules for Level 1A:

1. The first team to dig for treasure calls out three sets of ordered pairs, or *digs*. Teammates record all ordered pairs on their team's dig table and on the grid labeled **Other Team's Buried Treasure** (See below).
2. The second team responds after each guess whether the ordered pair is a hit or a miss. If it is a hit, they tell the first team whether it is a corner or an edge of the *I*-pentomino.
3. Next, it is the second team's turn to dig for treasure. Continue taking turns with three digs at a time.
4. When one team has located at least two of the four corners of the pentomino with their digs then that team may guess the location of the treasure. Guessing the location of the treasure must happen when it is your turn but before you have taken your three digs. To guess, sketch on your grid where you think the *I*-pentomino is hidden and show it to the other team. If a team guesses correctly, they win and the game is over. If a team guesses incorrectly, they lose and the game is over. If the team that has located two corners is not ready to guess where the treasure is located, the game continues.

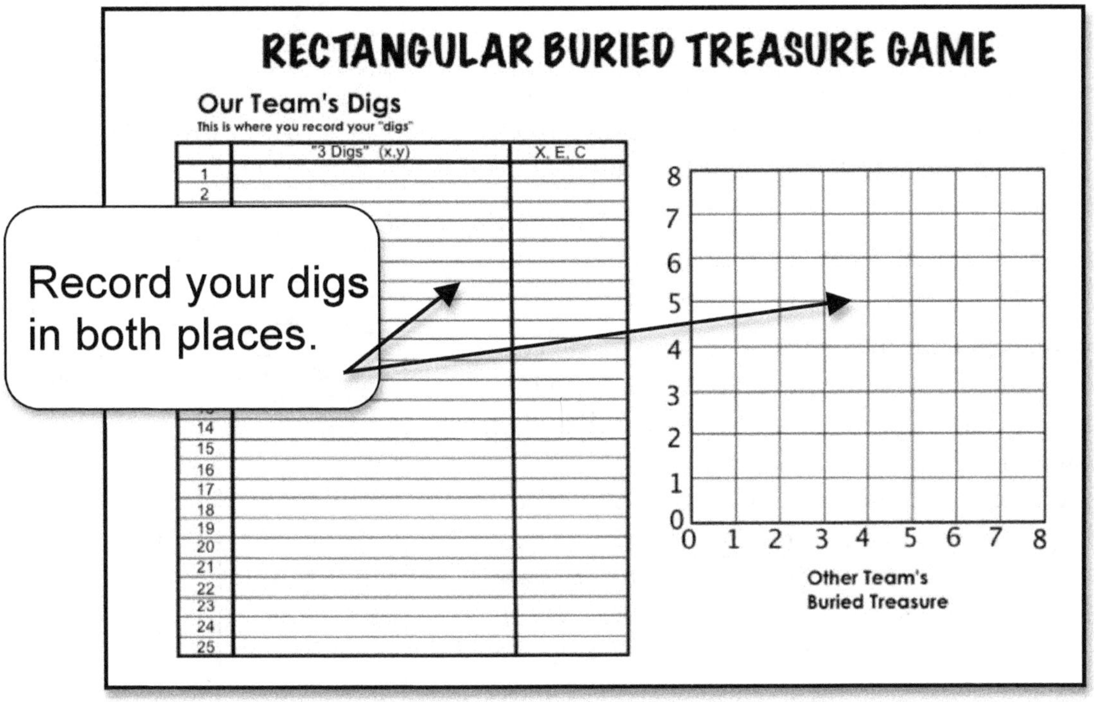

Basic Strategies:

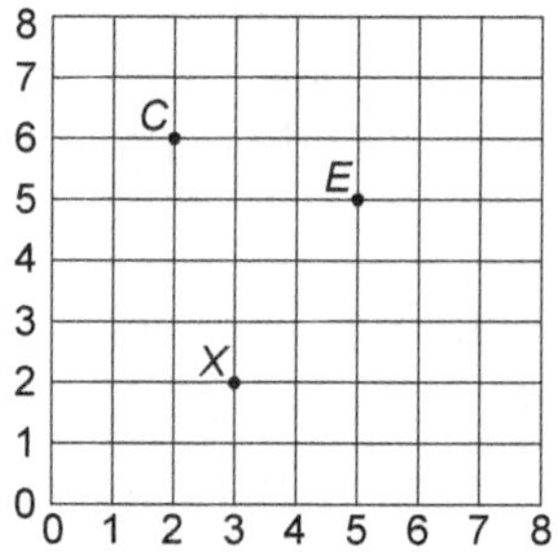

1. Create a symbol system so if one of your digs is a hit you can tell if it is on an edge or a corner. For example, you might use a *C* next to a point to indicate a corner hit and an *E* next to a point to indicate an edge hit. You might put an *X* through a point that is a miss and shade areas where the pentomino cannot be hidden.

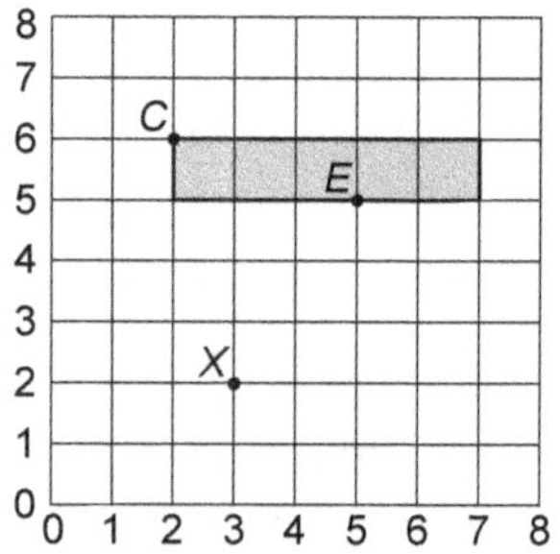

2. Use the corner (*C*), edge (*E*), and miss (*X*) clues to determine possible locations of the buried treasure pentomino. This will guide your next set of guesses. For example, the two guesses, *C* and *E*, shown leave only one possible location for the *I*-pentomino treasure. Do you understand why?

2.3 Variations on Buried Treasure

Level 1B In this variation, each team selects any one of the 12 pentominoes[4] and hides it on their game sheet labeled **Our Team's Buried Treasure**. Since teams do not know the pentomino shape chosen by the other team, the task will be more challenging than in Level 1A. Determine which team plays first by flipping a coin or rolling a die.

Rules for Level 1B:

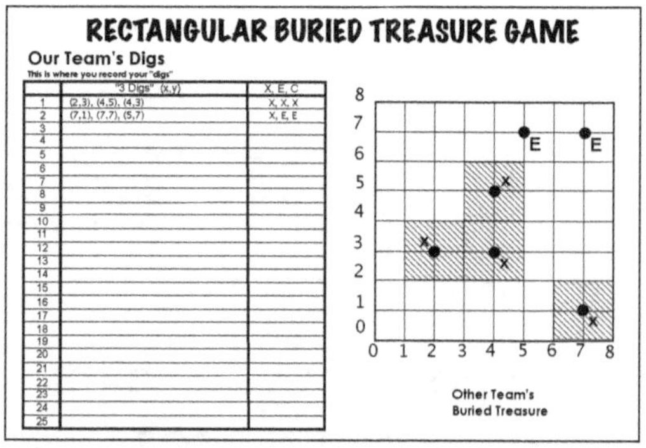

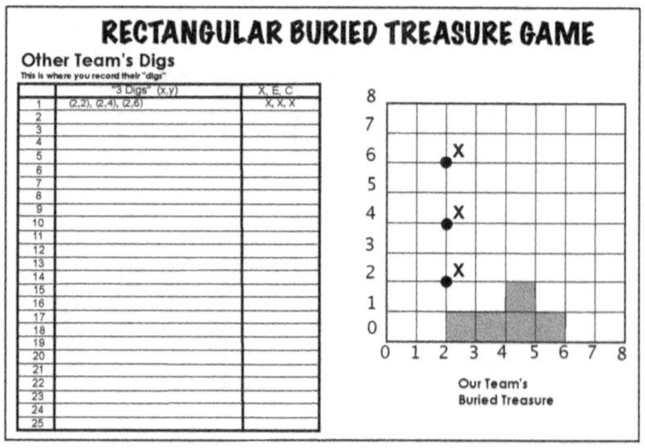

1. The first team calls out three sets of ordered pairs, or *digs*.
2. The second team responds after each guess whether it is a hit or miss. If it is a hit, they tell the other team whether it is a corner, edge, or interior point of the pentomino.
3. Then it is the second team's turn to take three digs. Continue taking turns with three digs at a time.
4. When one team has located at least three of the corners of the pentomino with their digs, then that team may take a guess as to the location of the remaining corners. Guessing the location of the treasure must happen when it is your turn but before you have taken your three digs. Shade in where you think the other team's pentomino shape is on the grid labeled **Other Team's Buried Treasure**. Show it to the other team. If correct, you win. If you guess incorrectly, you lose. If a team that has located three corners does not wish to guess, the game continues until one team is ready to take a guess on the treasure location.

More Strategies:

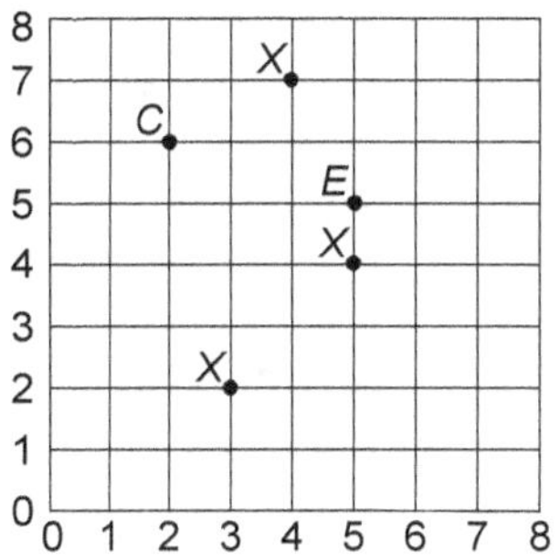

When you don't know which of the pentominoes are hidden, your search is trickier. On the grid to the right, the first guess was a miss at (3, 2); the second guess located a corner at (2, 6); and the third guess located an edge at (5, 5). The fourth guess was a strategic move at (5, 4) to see if the edge was vertical or horizontal. You now know the pentomino treasure is horizontal. With the (4, 7) guess you eliminate two more positions for another square connected to the four horizontal squares.

The five guesses above leave a small number of possible locations for the hidden pentomino. Four are shown below. What are three good digs for the next turn?

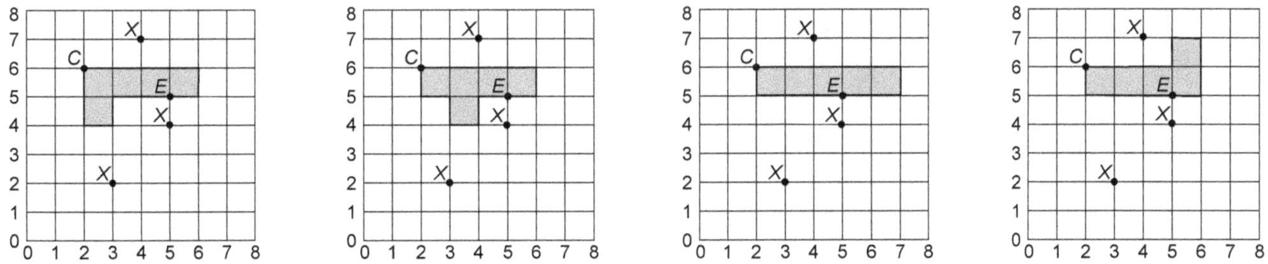

Notice that (3, 4) and (6, 6) are two important points to try next. Depending on the responses to those two digs the third dig might be either (4, 4) or (6, 5).

The playing field for Levels 1C through 1E is still an 8×8 grid.

Level 1C

- Each team hides two identical pentominoes.

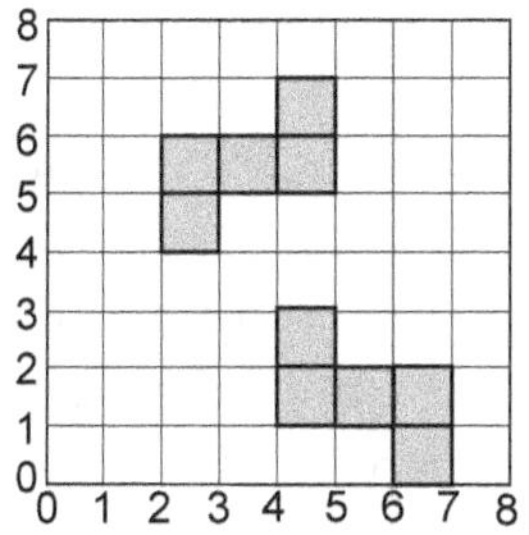

Level 1D

- Each team hides two different pentominoes.

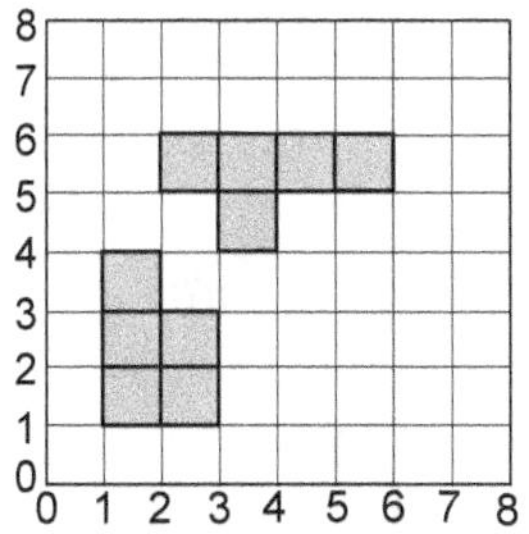

Level 1E

- Each team hides two different polyominoes (pentominoes or smaller).
- No information is given about hits or misses until after all three ordered pairs are given. For example, if the first dig was a miss, the second dig hit an edge, and the third hit a corner, the response would be: "miss, edge, corner."

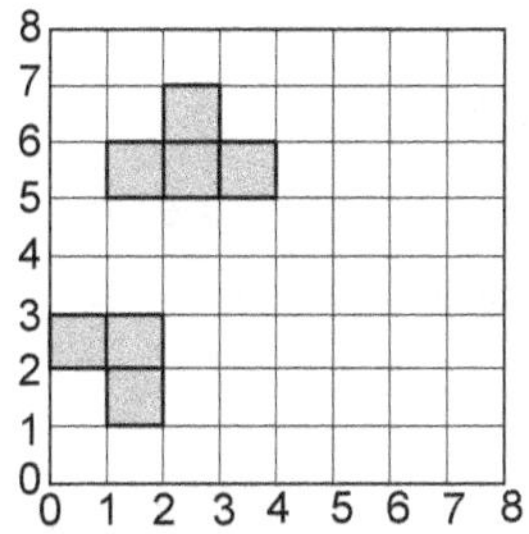

The playing field for Levels 1F through 1L is increased to a 15×15 grid. No information is given about hits or misses until after all three ordered pairs are given.

Level 1F

- The playing field is a 15×15 grid.
- No information is given until after all three ordered pairs are given.

Level 1G

- Teams take four digs at a time but they must lie on a straight line. To do this you must give a starting point, then a rule for moving to the next point. The rule for moving is a movement up or down followed by a movement to the right or left. Your dig requests can look like this:

  "Start at (0,10), then move down 1, then right 4.
  Do this two more times."

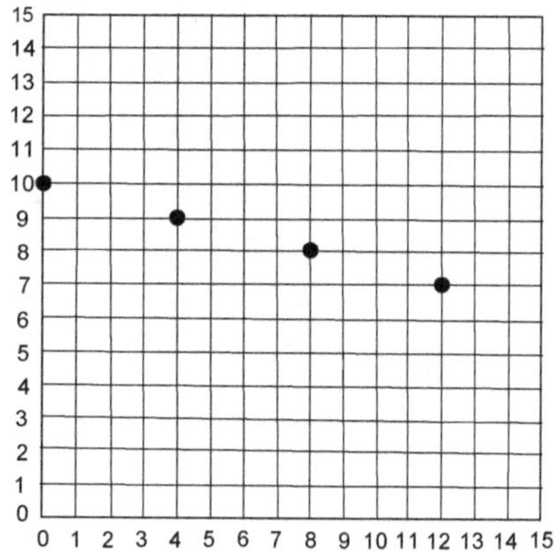

Level 1H

- Teams have a choice of how they take their digs. Teams can take up to six digs at a time but they must lie on a straight line (using the movement rule from level 1G). Alternately, teams can take three digs anywhere they wish.

Level 1I

- At the beginning of the game, players agree to hide four one-unit squares. These four squares (16 ordered pairs) are where enemy pirates are spying on your buried treasures. When someone digs one of the corners of one of the squares they get to ask the other team a question that can be answered with a "yes" or "no." Only one question per square.

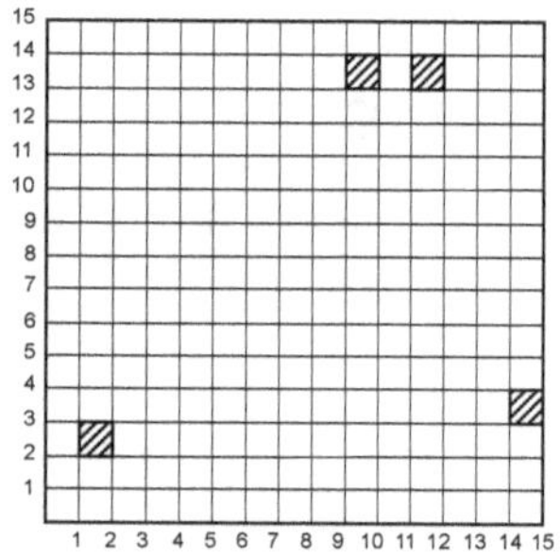

Level 1J

- Each team hides five different pentominoes with no two pentominoes touching. After hiding the pentominoes count the number of pentomino squares in each row and column and place the sums at the top of each column and to the right of each row (See example at right). Each team tells the other team the number of squares in each row and column. (As a check, these numbers should total 25 for all the rows and 25 for all the columns.)

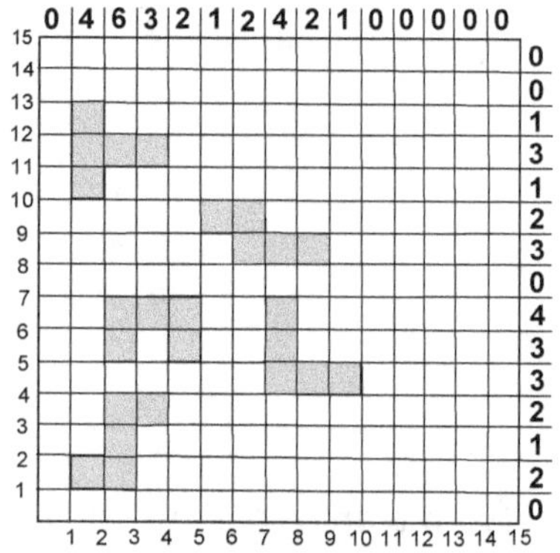

Level 1K

- Each time one of your digs locates a corner of a treasure you roll a die to determine how many free digs you get to take immediately.

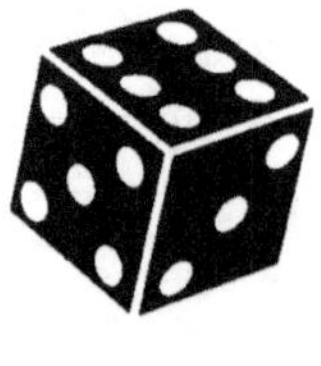

Level 1L

- Both teams agree to add a new special rule.

2.4 The Cartesian Coordinate System

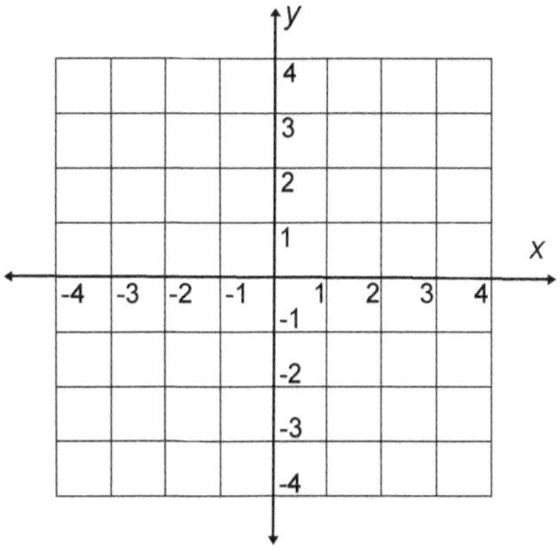

One of the big events in mathematics history was the joining of algebra and geometry by French mathematician and philosopher Rene Descartes (1596–1650).[5] By taking two number lines and placing them at an angle to each other, Descartes created a coordinate system that came to be known as the **Cartesian Coordinate Plane**. Using this coordinate system, mathematicians are able to visualize equations from algebra and algebraically describe the shapes of geometry. The modern rectangular coordinate plane places two number lines (called the *x*- and *y*- axes) at right angles to each other. The point where the two number lines cross (0, 0) is called the **origin**.

The ordered pair (2, 3) locates a point two units to the right of the origin and three units up from the origin. The ordered pair (-1, -2) locates a point one unit to the left of the origin and two units down from the origin.

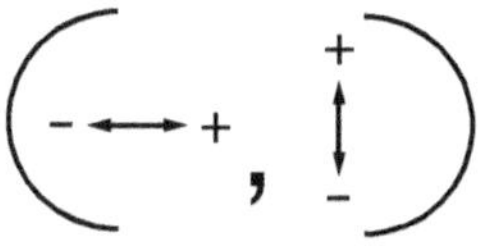

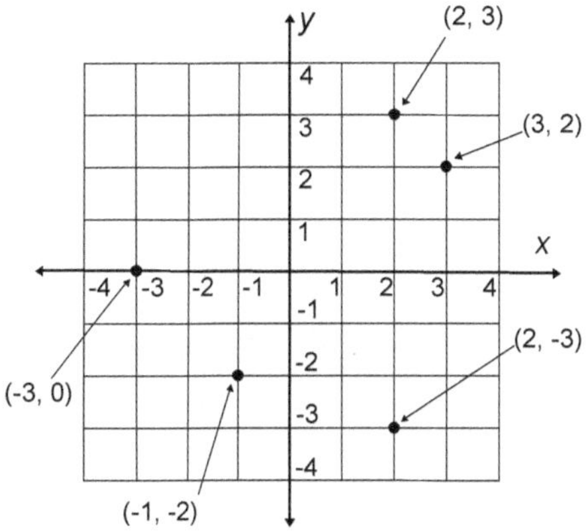

The symbols shown at left help you remember that the first number in the ordered pair moves right (+) or left (–) and the second number moves up (+) or down (–). To locate the point (2, -3) on the coordinate graph, you begin at the origin (0, 0) then move horizontally (right or left) according to the first number in the ordered pair. The first number in this ordered pair is 2, so you move horizontally two units to the right. Next you move vertically (up or down) according to the second number in the ordered pair. In this example, you move three units down since the number is a negative 3.

Exercises in the Cartesian Coordinate System

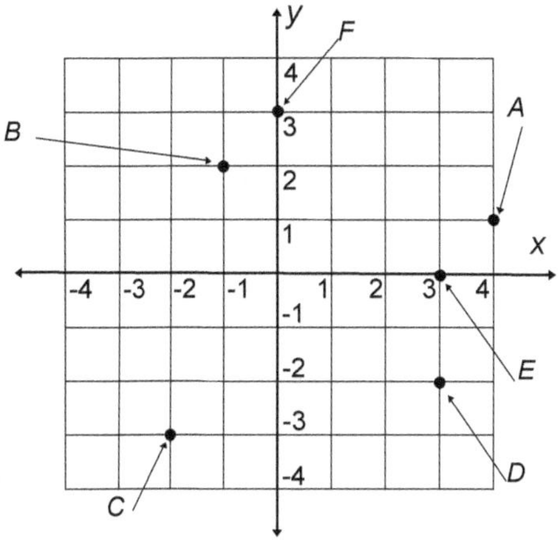

Find the coordinates of the points shown on the coordinate grid to the right.

1. Point *A* (,) 2. Point *B* (,)

3. Point *C* (,) 4. Point *D* (,)

5. Point *E* (,) 6. Point *F* (,)

Chapter 2.4

Locate the following points on the coordinate grid shown at right. Label each point with its letter.

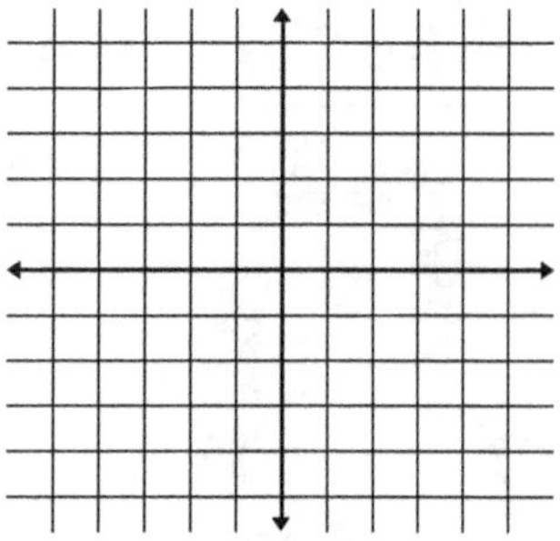

7. Point *F* is (2, 0)
8. Point *G* is (2, -1)
9. Point *H* is (-3, 2)
10. Point *I* is (-3, -4)
11. Point *J* is (0, -3)
12. Point *K* is (0, 0)

Find the coordinates of the four vertices in each special quadrilateral[6] in Exercises 13–15.

13. *ABCD* is a rectangle.

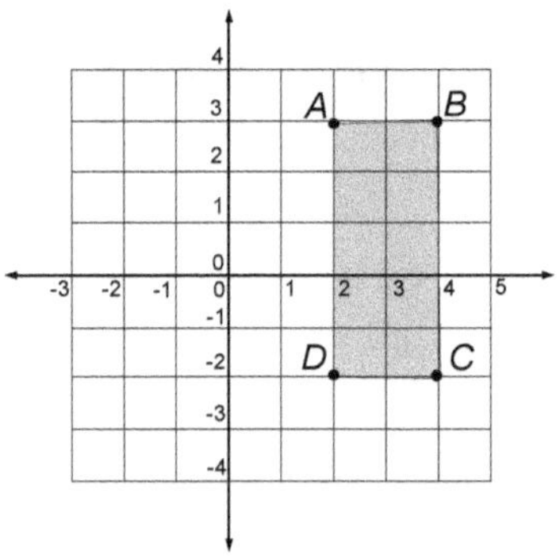

A(,), *B*(,),
C(,), *D*(,)

14. *EFGH* is a parallelogram.

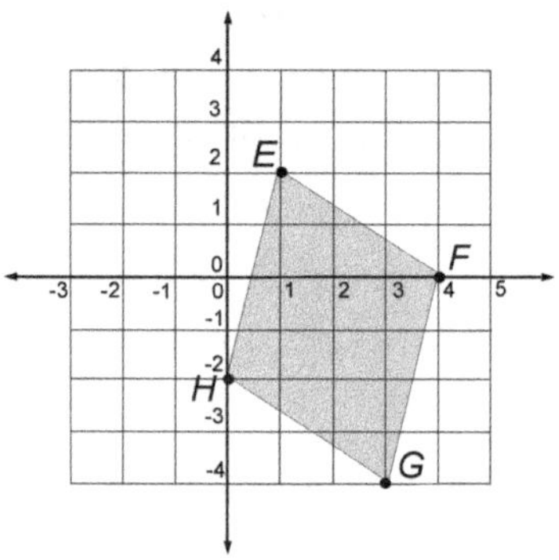

E(,), *F*(,),
G(,), *H*(,)

15. *MNOP* is a trapezoid.

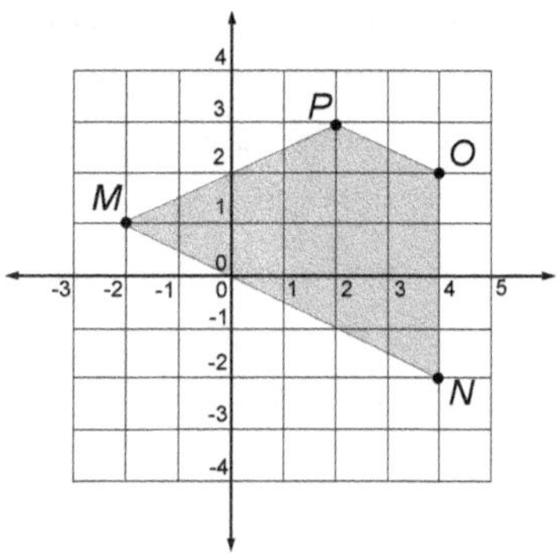

M(,), *N*(,),
O(,), *P*(,)

In Exercises 16–18, graph the four points and identify the types of special quadrilateral. Then find the coordinates of the point of intersection of the two diagonals.

16. *I*(5, 2), *J*(4, -1), *K*(1, 0), *L*(2, 3)

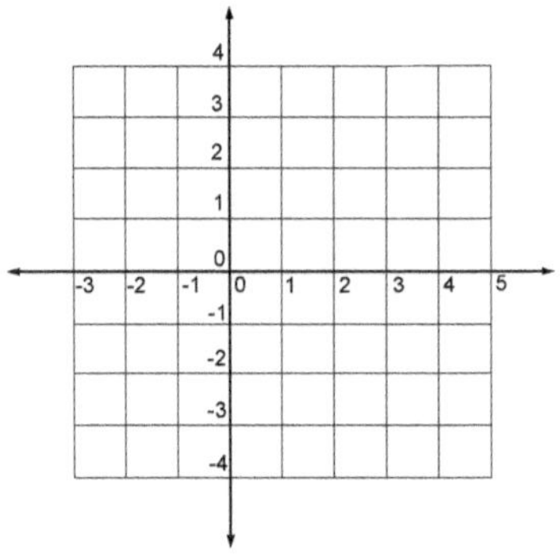

IJKL is a __________.

Diagonals intersect at (,).

17. *Q*(-3, -4), *R*(3, -2), *S*(5, 4), *T*(-1, 2)

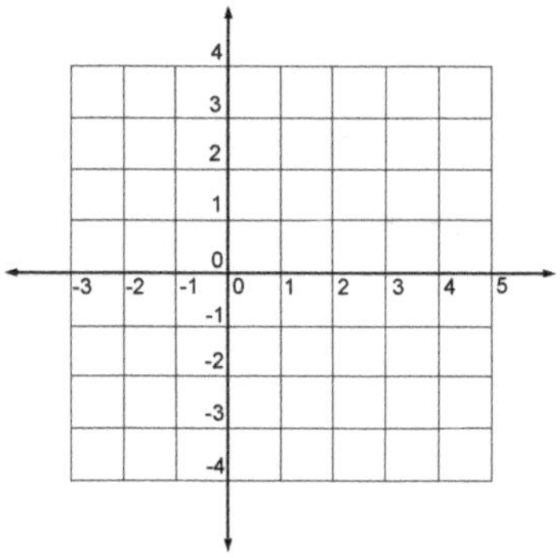

QRST is a __________.

Diagonals intersect at (,).

18. *U*(-1, -3), *V*(5, -1), *W*(4, 2), *X*(1, 3)

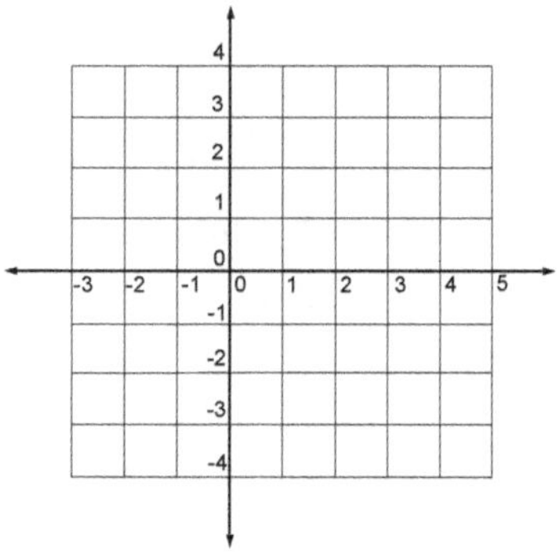

UVWX is a __________.

Diagonals intersect at (,).

Collinear Points and the Slope of a Line

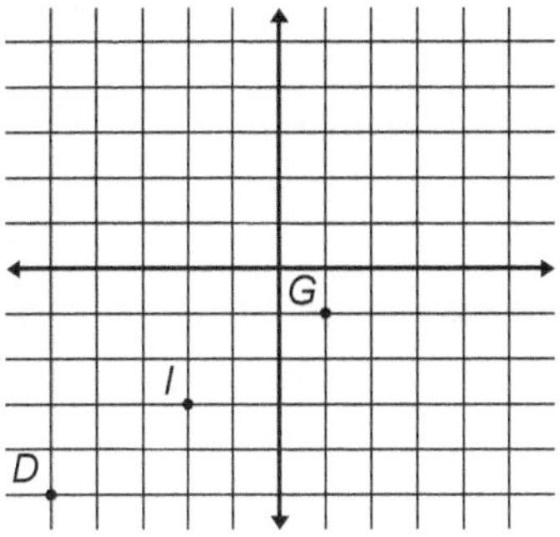

Points *D*, *I*, and *G* are collinear points. (They lie on the same line).

For each exercise below, locate and label each pair of points on the graph provided. Then, locate another point that is on the same line as the line containing the two given points. (The three points are collinear).

19. Given *R*(-5, -3), *T*(-1, 5), find another point on the line and label it point *A*.

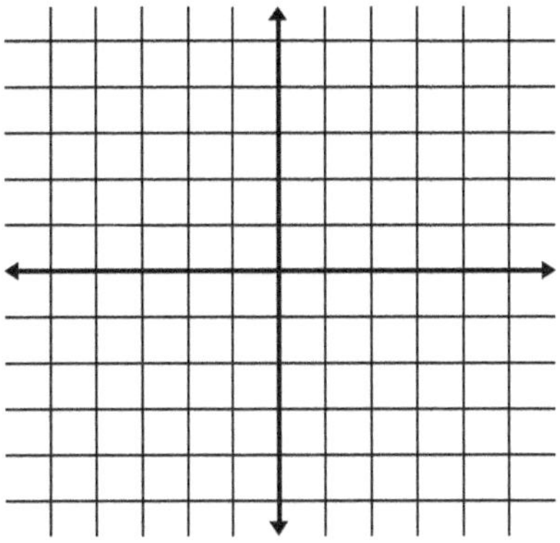

20. Given *Z*(4, -3), *N*(0, 3), find another point on the line and label it point *E*.

The most basic property of lines is their "straightness." The slope of a line is a measure of its steepness. Lines on the coordinate plane do not change direction; they have a constant slope.

Example D

Locate point A (-5, -5). From point A move 2 units up then 3 units to the right. Label the new location point B. From point B, do the same thing; move 2 units up then 3 units to the right. Label that new location point C. Continue in this way one more time, by moving 2 units up then 3 units to the right, and label this next point D. Draw a line through the four points.

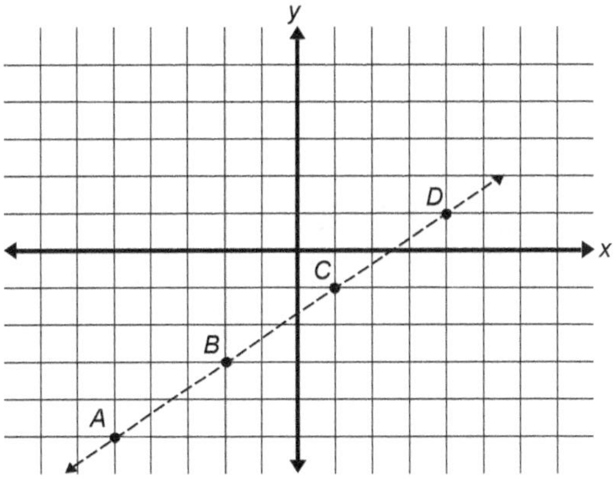

Solution

See the graph to the right.

In each exercise below, first locate the starting point on the coordinate grid and label it. Second, locate the next three points by moving according to the given rule. Finally, draw one line through all four points showing that they are collinear.

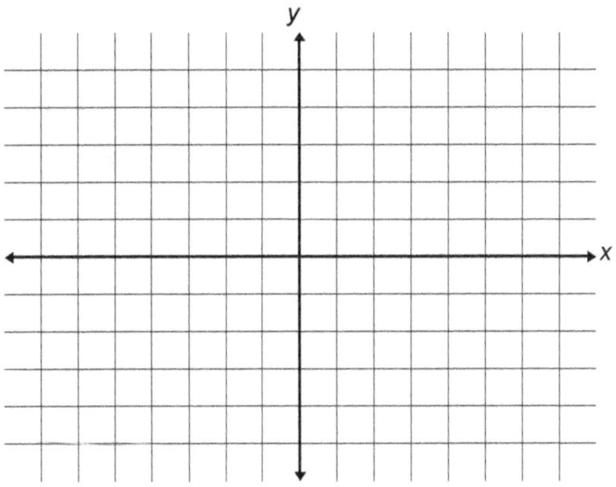

Starting Point	Movement Rule (slope)
21. *P*(-5, -3)	"up 1 then right 2"
22. *Q*(-4, 5)	"down 2 then right 3"
23. *R*(3, 4)	"down 1 then left 2"
24. *S*(-3, -5)	"up 3 then left 0"

Transformations on the Cartesian Coordinate Plane

By moving a geometric figure according to certain rules you can create an **image** of the original. This is called a **transformation.** If the image created is identical to the original, then the process is called a **rigid transformation**.

A **translation** (or *slide*) is the simplest rigid transformation. You can translate a figure on the coordinate plane by selecting a distance and a direction, called a **translation vector**, to locate the image.

Example E

Translate the pentomino using the translation vector < 3, -4 > then identify the coordinates of the indented corners.

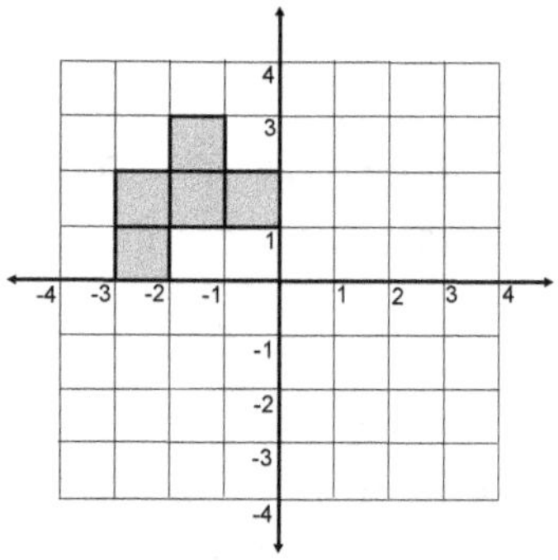

Solution

The translation vector <3, -4> tells you that every point of the original figure moves 3 units in the positive *x* direction then 4 units in the negative *y* direction. Thus the image of the original *F*-pentomino is shown to the right and down from the original figure. Notice that the coordinates of the indented corners before the translation are (-2, 1), (-2, 2), (-1, 2) and after the translation they are (1, -3), (1, -2), (2, -2).

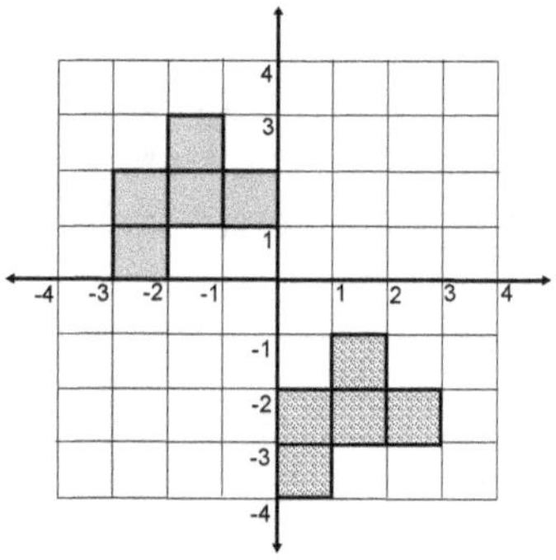

Coordinates before translation	Coordinates after translation
(-2, 1)	(1, -3)
(-2, 2)	(1, -2)
(-1, 2)	(2, -2)

A **reflection** (or *flip*) is also a rigid transformation. To reflect a figure on the coordinate plane you first select a line of reflection.

Example F

Reflect the F-pentomino across the vertical y-axis, then identify the coordinates of the indented corners before the reflection and after.

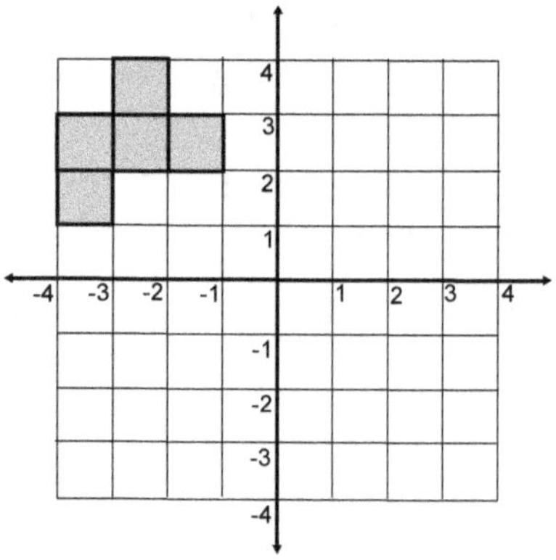

Solution

Picture the y-axis as a wire and the pentomino as a piece of cardboard taped to the wire. Visualize spinning the wire so that the pentomino flips over. Notice that however far a point is to one side of the wire, it reappears after the flip, the same distance on the other side. The coordinates of the indented corners before the reflection are (-3, 2), (-3, 3), (-2, 3). After the reflection they are (3, 2), (3, 3), (2, 3).

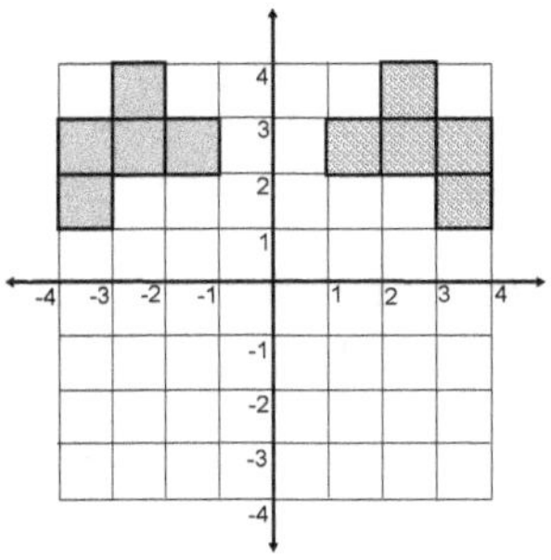

Coordinates before the reflection	Coordinates after the reflection
(-3, 2)	(3, 2)
(-3, 3)	(3, 3)
(-2, 3)	(2, 3)

A **rotation** (or *turn*) is also a rigid transformation. You can rotate a figure on the coordinate plane by selecting a center of rotation and an amount of turning (in degrees) to locate the image.

Example G

Rotate the N-pentomino 180° (a half-turn), clockwise about the origin (0, 0), then identify the coordinates of the indented corners before the rotation and after.

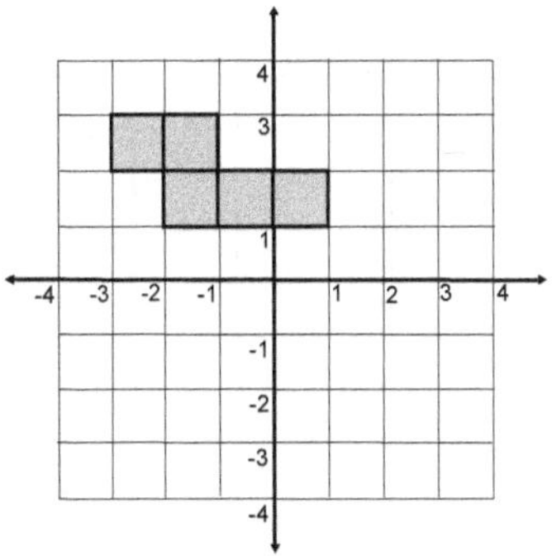

Solution

Picture the N-pentomino as a piece of cardboard connected to the origin by an invisible wire. Visualize rotating the wire 180° about the origin so that the pentomino rotates to its new position. The coordinates of the indented corners before the rotation are (-2, 2) and (-1, 2). After the rotation they are (2, -2) and (1, -2).

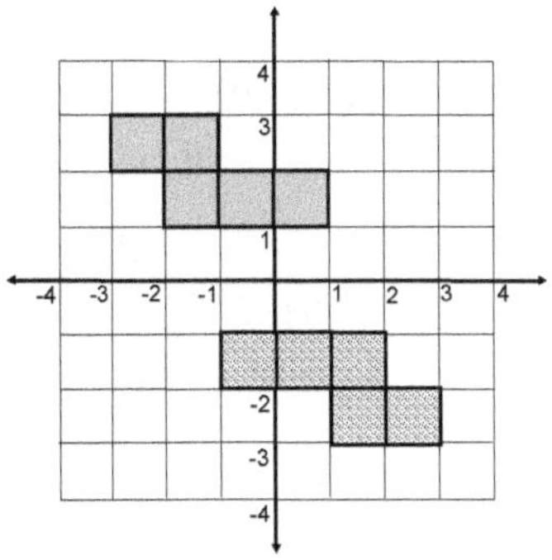

Coordinates before the rotation	Coordinates after the rotation
(-2, 2)	(2, -2)
(-1, 2)	(1, -2)

Exercises on the Cartesian Coordinate Plane

Find the coordinates of the missing fourth vertex and complete the special quadrilateral on each of the coordinate grids below.

25. Quadrilateral *ABCD* is a square.
Find point *D*. *D*(,).

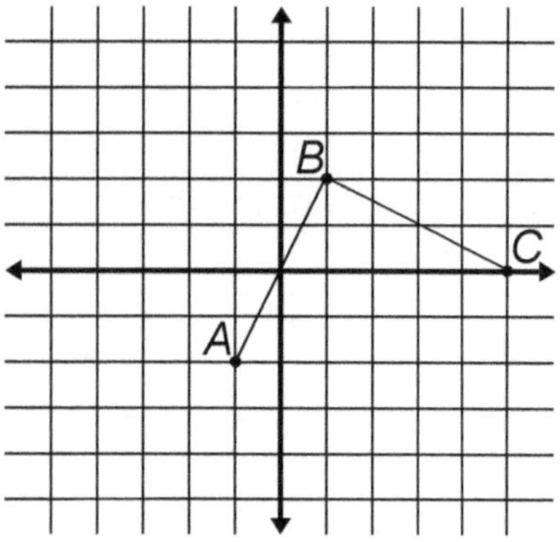

26. Quadrilateral *EFGH* is a rectangle.
Find point *F*. *F*(,).

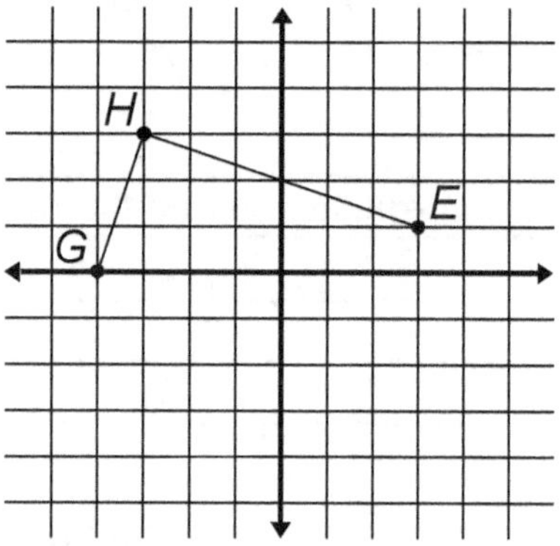

27. Quadrilateral *JKLM* is a rhombus.
Find point *K*. *K*(,).

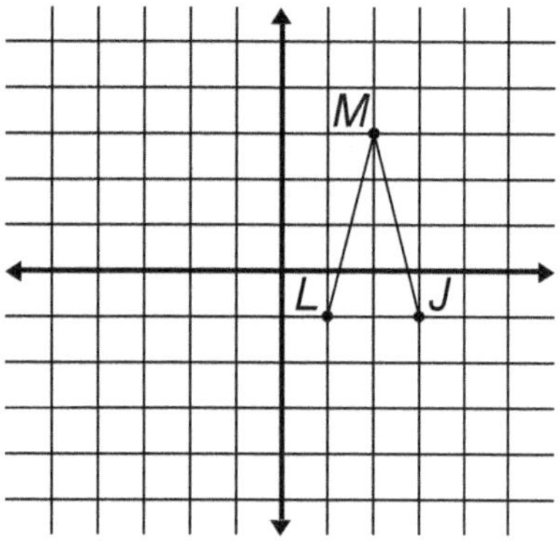

28. Quadrilateral *PQRS* is a kite. Find point *P*. *P*(,).

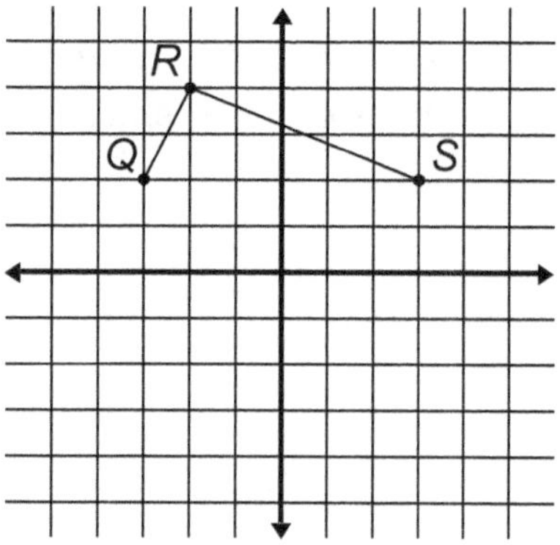

In Exercises 29–30 graph the three given points and find the remaining fourth point to create the special quadrilateral. Then find the coordinates of the point of intersection of the two diagonals.

29. *TUVW* is a parallelogram.
T(-3, -5), *U*(3, -3), *W*(-5, 3)
Find point *V*. *V*(,).

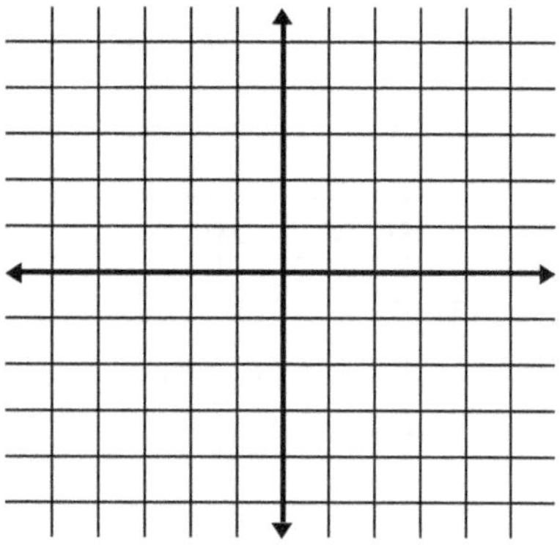

Diagonals intersect at (,).

30. *NOXY* is an isosceles trapezoid.
N(-1, -4), *O*(3, -4), *X*(5, 5)
Sides $\overline{NY}$ and $\overline{OX}$ are equal.
Find point *Y*. *Y*(,).

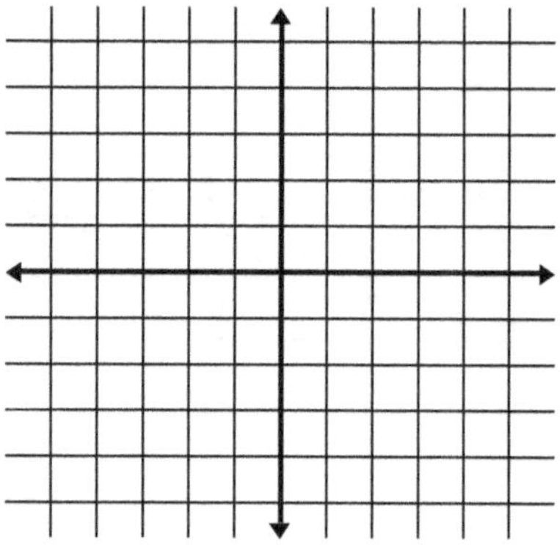

Diagonals intersect at (,).

To help you visualize translations, reflections, and rotations it is helpful to use tracing paper or patty paper.

Translation with patty paper

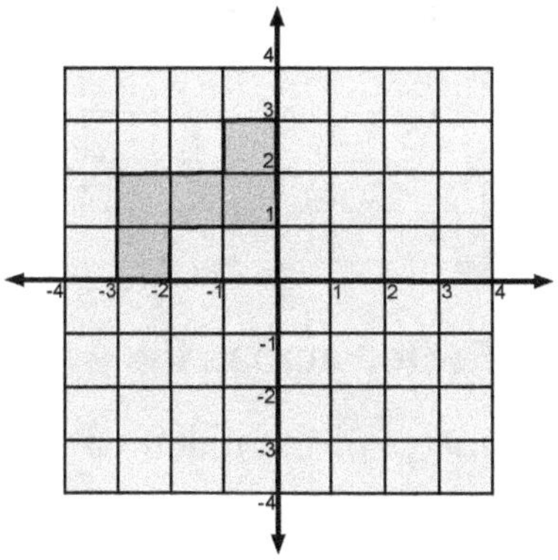

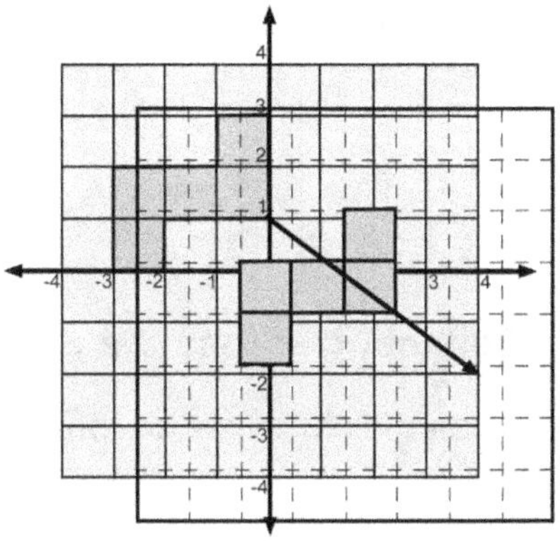

Translating <4, -3>

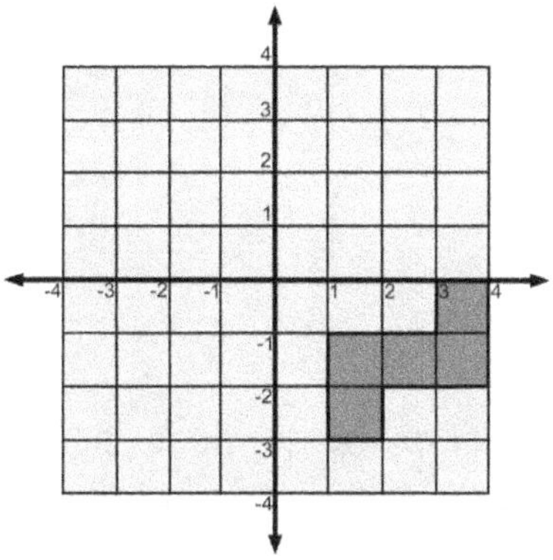

Translated <4, -3>

Translate the pentominoes by the translation vector indicated. Next, identify the coordinates of the indented corners before and after the translation.

31. Translate by the vector < -4, 3 >.

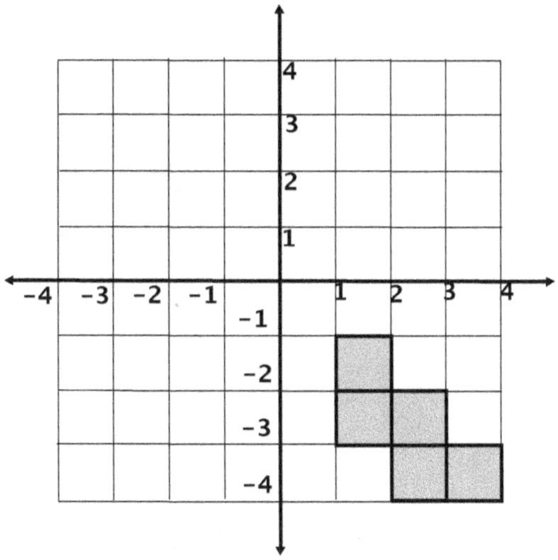

(*x*, *y*) before translation	**(*x*, *y*) after translation**
(2, -2)	(,)
(3, -3)	(,)
(2, -3)	(,)

32. Translate by the vector < 0, -5 >.

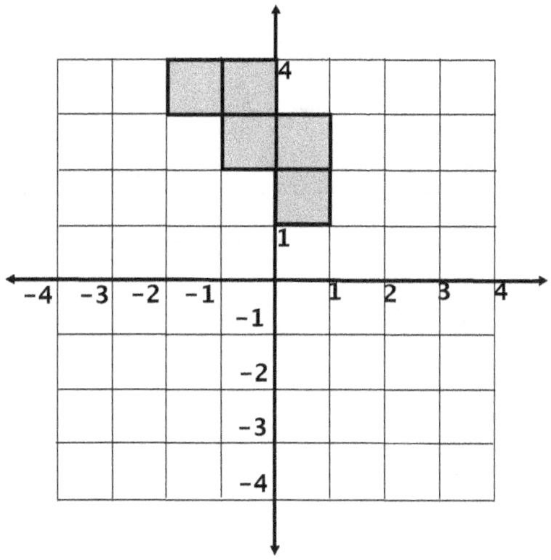

(*x*, *y*) before translation	**(*x*, *y*) after translation**
(-1, 3)	(,)
(0, 3)	(,)
(0, 2)	(,)

Reflection with patty paper

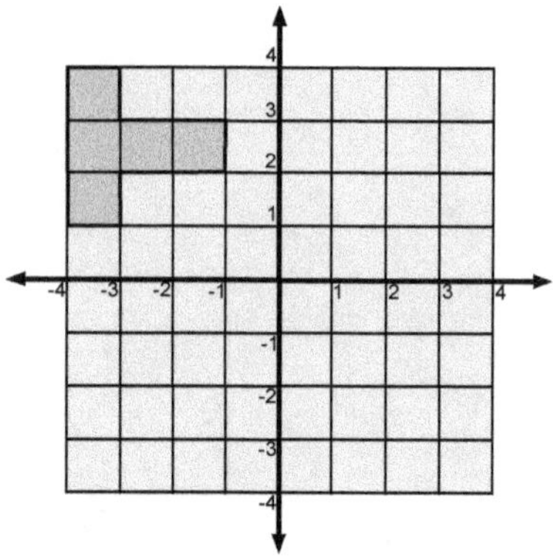

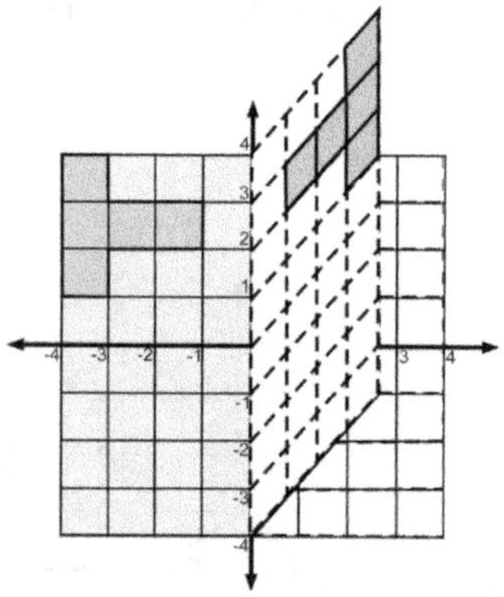

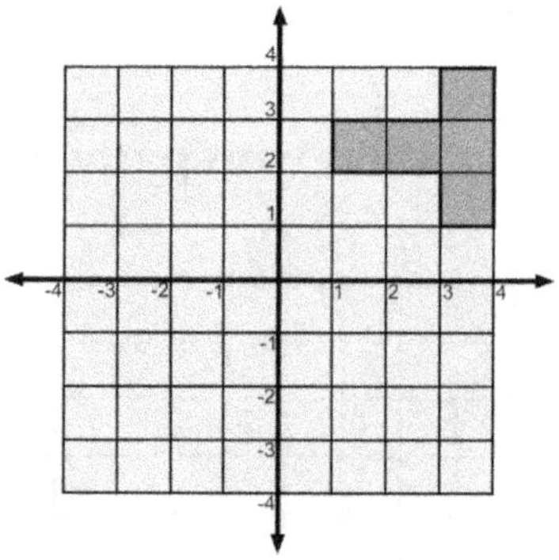

Reflecting across the *y*-axis **Reflected across the *y*-axis**

Reflect the pentominoes across the indicated axes. Next, identify the coordinates of the indented corners before and after the reflection.

33. Reflect across the y-axis. *h*

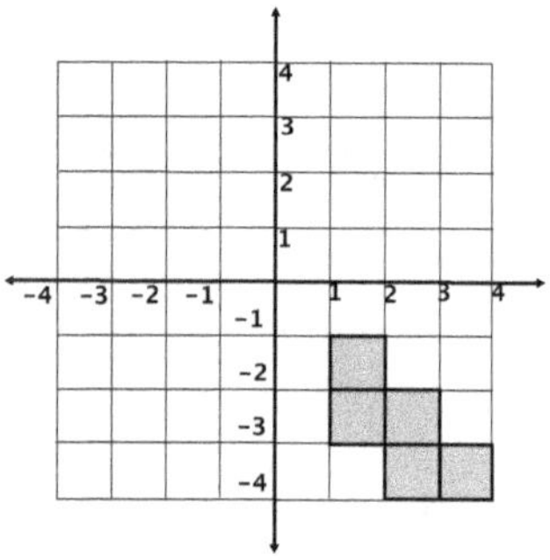

(*x*, *y*) before reflection	(*x*, *y*) after reflection
(2, -2)	(,)
(2, -3)	(,)
(3, -3)	(,)

34. Reflect across the y-axis.

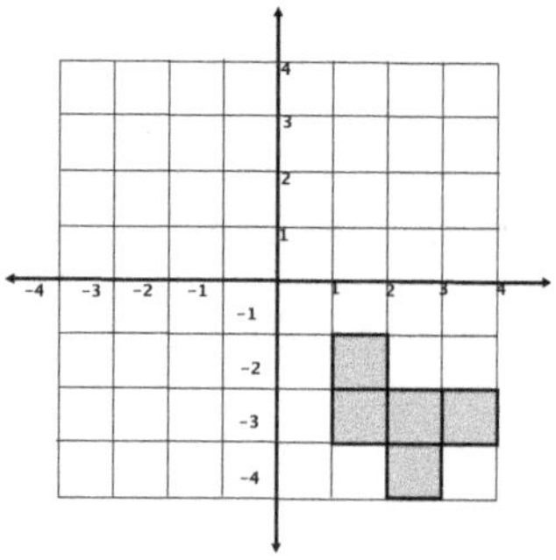

(*x*, *y*) before reflection	(*x*, *y*) after reflection
(2, -2)	(,)
(2, -3)	(,)
(3, -3)	(,)

35. Reflect across the x-axis. *h*

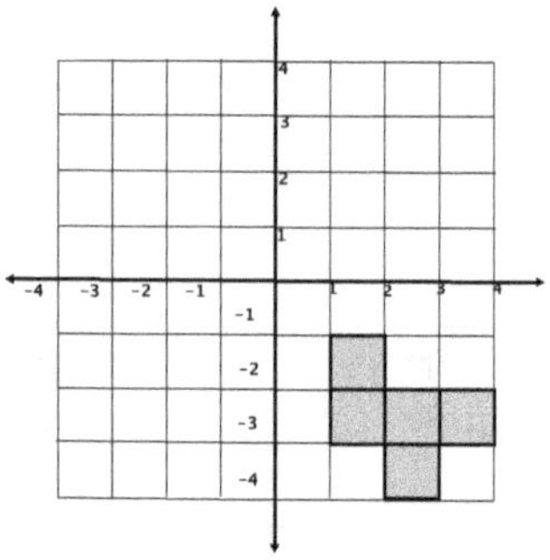

(*x*, *y*) before reflection	(*x*, *y*) after reflection
(2, -2)	(,)
(2, -3)	(,)
(3, -3)	(,)

36. Reflect across the x-axis.

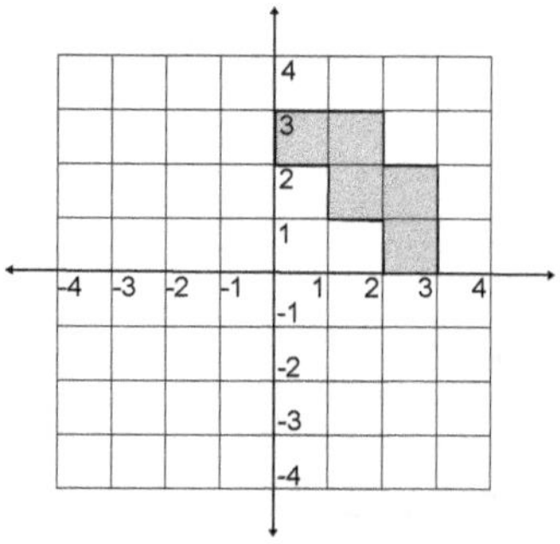

(*x*, *y*) before reflection	(*x*, *y*) after reflection
(1, 2)	(,)
(2, 1)	(,)
(2, 2)	(,)

Rotation with patty paper

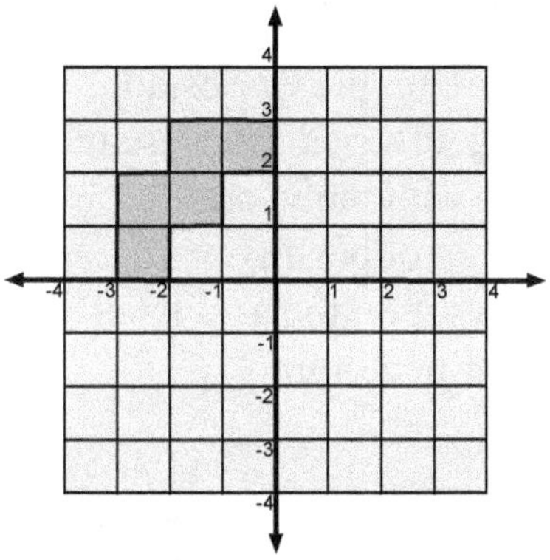

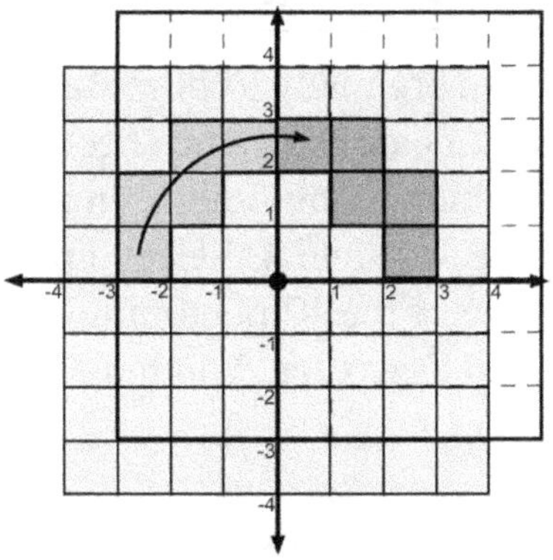

Rotating

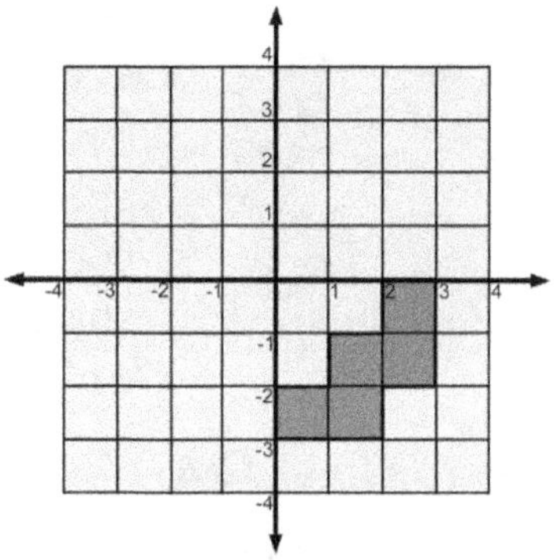

Rotated 180° about the origin

For each exercise below, rotate the pentomino the given amount of degrees about the origin. Next, identify the coordinates of the indented corners before and after the rotation.

37. Rotate clockwise 90° about the origin.

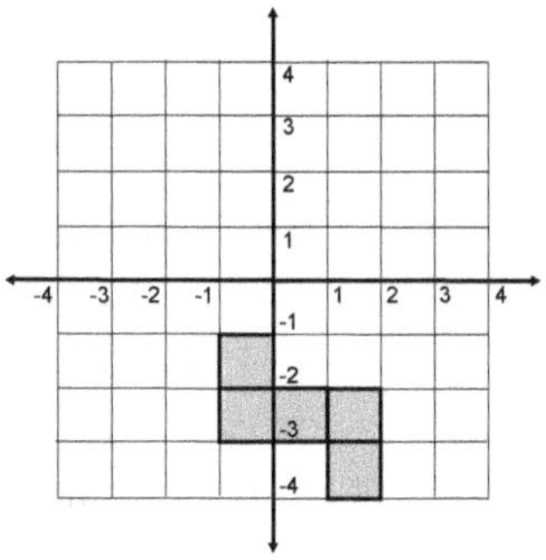

(*x*, *y*) before rotation	**(*x*, *y*) after rotation**
(0, -2)	(,)
(1, -3)	(,)

38. Rotate clockwise 180° about the origin.

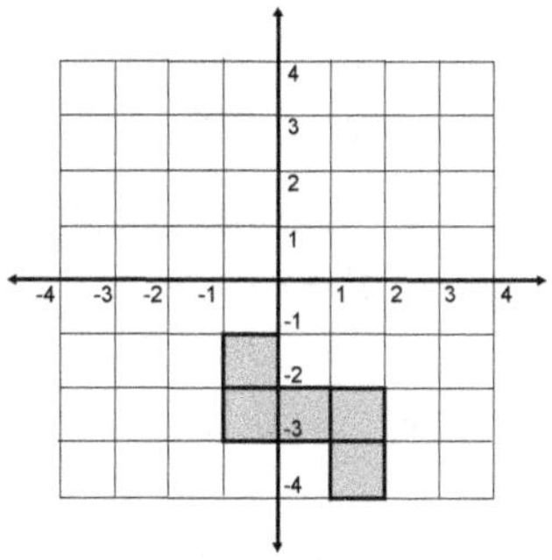

(*x*, *y*) before rotation	**(*x*, *y*) after rotation**
(0, -2)	(,)
(1, -3)	(,)

39. Rotate clockwise 180° about the origin.

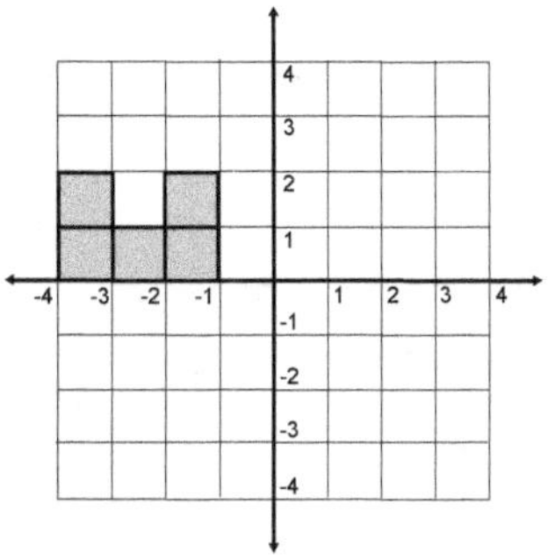

(*x*, *y*) before rotation	**(*x*, *y*) after rotation**
(-3, 1)	(,)
(-2, 1)	(,)

40. Rotate counter-clockwise 270° about the origin.

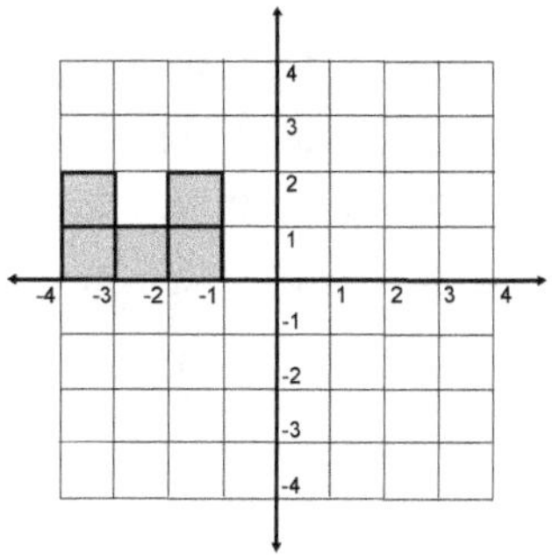

(*x*, *y*) before rotation	**(*x*, *y*) after rotation**
(-3, 1)	(,)
(-2, 1)	(,)

2.5 Buried Treasure with the Cartesian Coordinate System

Level 2A Now you are ready to play Buried Treasure on the Cartesian coordinate system. Locate the game sheet for Level 2A Buried Treasure in Appendix 1. This first playing field is on an 8×8 grid with the x- and y-coordinates between -4 and 4. Select a partner and an opposing team. Each team selects any one of the 12 pentominoes and draws it on the grid labeled **Our Team's Buried Treasure**. You have hidden your pentomino.

Rules for Level 2A:

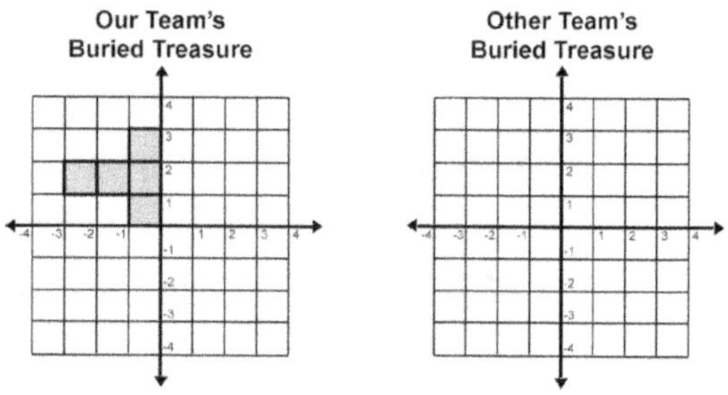

1. The first team to dig for treasure calls out three sets of ordered pairs, or *digs*.
2. The second team does not respond until after all three digs have been taken. If there are any hits, they tell the first team whether each hit is a corner or an edge of the pentomino.
3. Next, it is the second team's turn. They do the same. Continue taking turns.
4. When one team has located at least two corners of a pentomino with their digs then that team may guess the location of the pentomino treasure. Guessing must happen when it is your turn but before you have taken your three digs. To guess, sketch on your grid where you think the pentomino is hidden and show it to the other team. If a team guesses correctly, they win and the game is over. If a team guesses incorrectly, they lose and the game is over. If the team that has located two corners is not ready to guess where the treasure is located, the game continues.

Basic Strategies:

1. As suggested earlier, create a system on the grid to determine if the dig is a hit or a miss. For example, *X* for miss; *C* for corner; *E* for edge; *I* for interior point. If you get a hit that is an interior point, you are in luck; only one pentomino has an interior point.

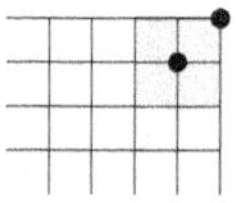

2. Don't waste digs by placing them in a corner. For example, corner dig (15, 15) shown at right covers only one square while dig (14, 14) covers the same corner square and three other squares.

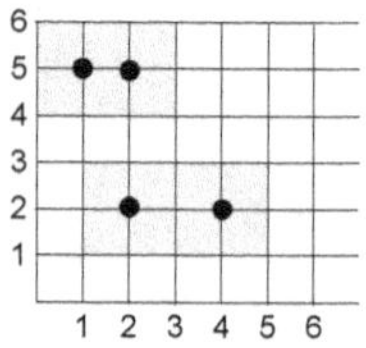

3. Don't waste digs by placing them next to each other. For example, the two digs (1, 5) and (2, 5) shown at right cover six squares, while the two digs (2, 2) and (4, 2) cover eight squares.
4. The other team does not tell you which individual dig is a hit or miss until after all three of your digs are complete. Therefore, do not spread your digs too far apart.

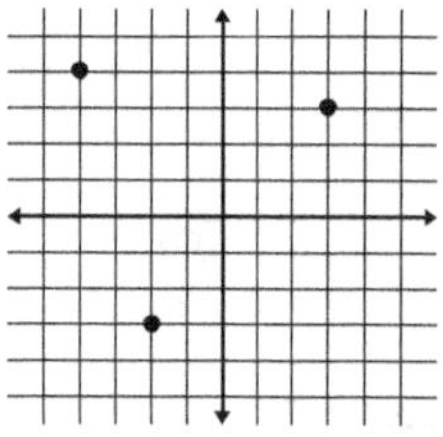

Not such a great idea

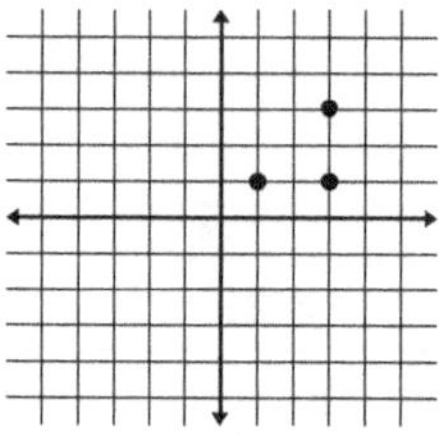

A better idea

2.6 Variations on Cartesian Buried Treasure

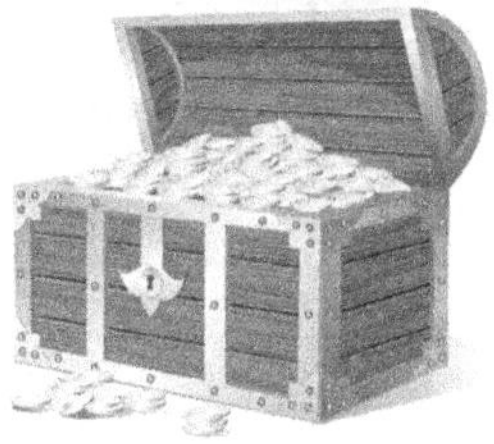

Level 2B The same playing field (an 8×8 grid) and rules as Level 2A except each team selects any one of the 12 pentominoes and hides two of them anywhere on the playing field.

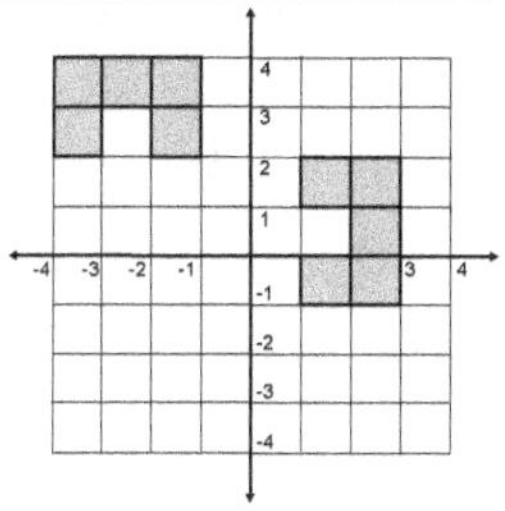

Level 2C

- Each team hides two different pentominoes.

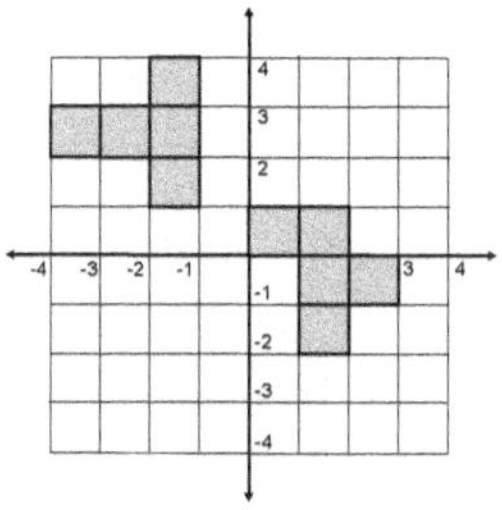

Level 2D

- Each team hides two different polyominoes (hexominoes or smaller).
- Each team takes four digs but no information is given about hits or misses until after all four ordered pairs are given.

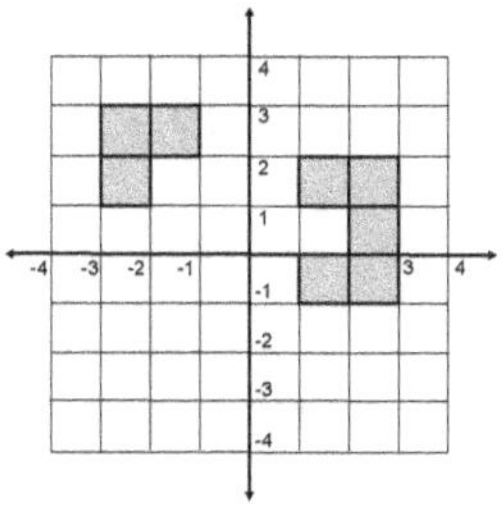

The playing field for Levels 2E through 2L is increased to a 20×20 coordinate grid where the horizontal (x-values) and vertical (y-values) range from -10 to 10.

Level 2E

- Each team hides two identical polyominoes (hexominoes or smaller).
- Each team takes four digs but no information is given about hits or misses until after all four ordered pairs are given.

Level 2F

- Each team hides two different polyominoes (hexominoes or smaller).
- Each team takes four digs but no information is given about hits or misses until after all four ordered pairs are given.

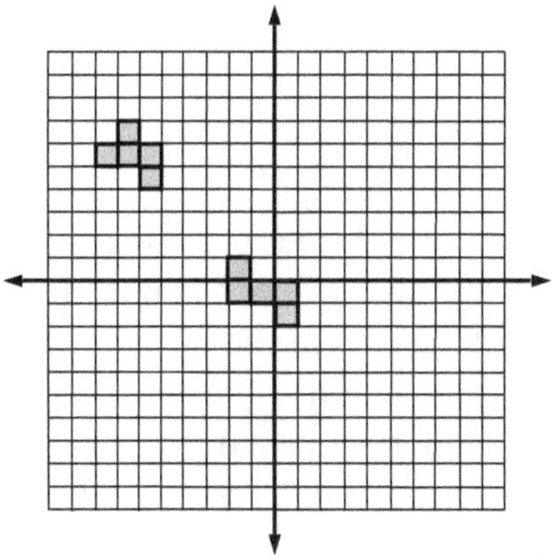

Level 2G

- Each team hides four pentominoes consisting of two pairs of identical pentominoes (such as two L-pentominoes and two U-pentominoes). The pairs must be arranged so one of the pair is a reflection of the other.

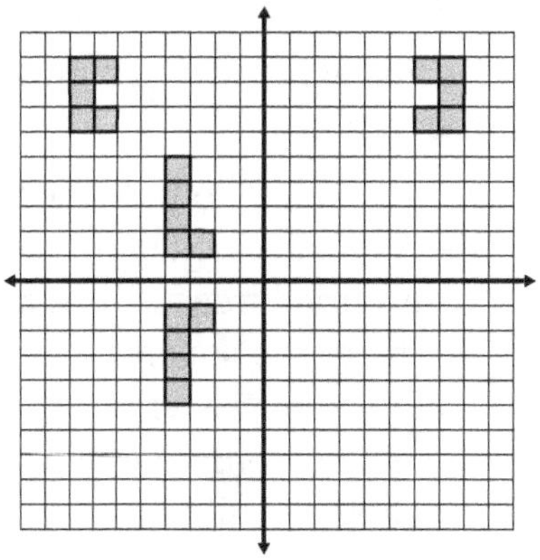

Level 2H

- Each team hides four pentominoes consisting of two pairs of identical pentominoes (such as two *T*-pentominoes and two *V*-pentominoes). The pairs must be arranged so one of the pair is a 180° rotation of the other.

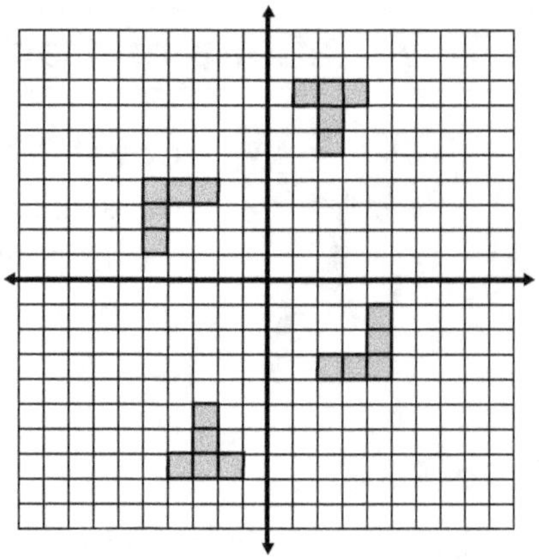

Level 2I

- Each team hides four pentominoes consisting of two pairs of identical pentominoes (such as two *L*-pentominoes and two *U*-pentominoes). The pairs must be arranged so one of the pair is a reflection of the other.
- Teams take six digs at a time but they must lie on a straight line. To do this you must give a starting point, then a rule for moving to the next point. The rule for moving is a movement up or down followed by a movement to the right or left. Your dig request can look like this:

  "Start at (9, -9), then move up 1 then left 2. Do this four more times."

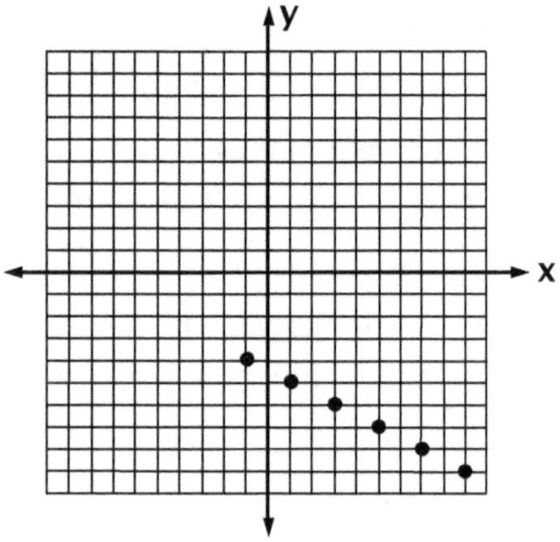

Level 2J

- Each team hides four pentominoes consisting of two pairs of identical pentominoes (such as two *L*-pentominoes and two *U*-pentominoes). The pairs must be arranged so one of the pair is a reflection of the other.
- Teams can either take eight digs at a time, but they must lie on a straight line; or, they can take four digs anywhere on the grid.

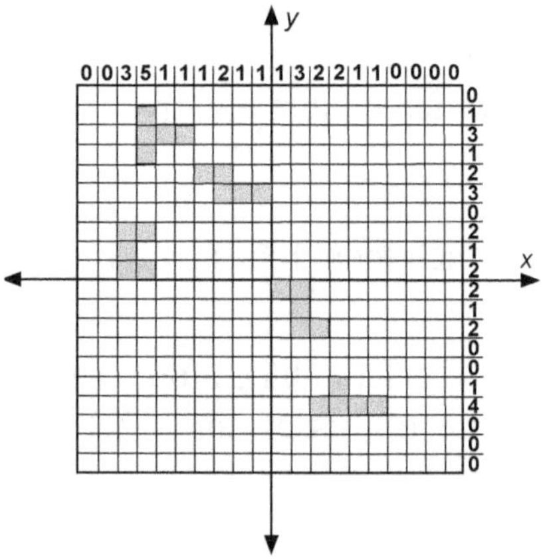

Level 2K

- Each team hides five different pentominoes with no two pentominoes touching. After hiding the pentominoes, count the number of pentomino squares in each row and column. Place the sums at the top of each column and to the right of each row (see example). Each team tells the other team the number of squares in each row and column. (As a check, these numbers should total 25 for all the rows and 25 for all the columns.)

Level 2L

- Teams agree on the number and types of polyominoes they are to hide.
- Players agree to hide four one-unit squares—one in each of the four quadrants. These squares are enemy pirates spying on your buried treasures. When someone digs one of the corners of one of the squares they get to ask the other team a question that can be answered with a "yes" or "no." For example: "Is there a pentomino in the first quadrant (positive *x*- and *y*-values)." Only one question is allowed per square.

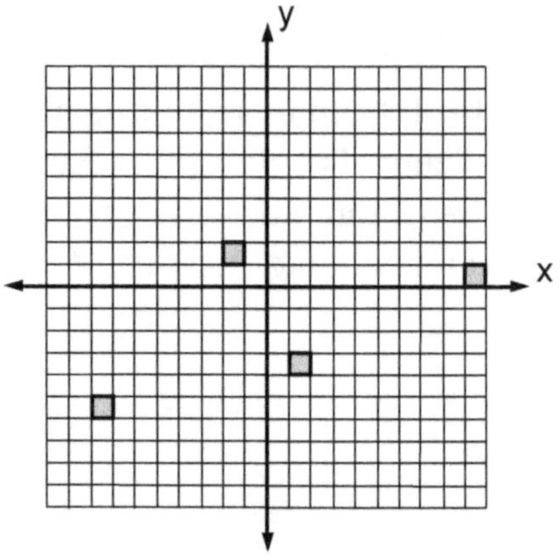

2.7 Buried Treasure with Equations

Level 3A At this level each team tries to locate the other team's two buried treasures (two different pentominoes) using linear equations. See Appendix 2 for more on graphing linear equations.

Rules for Level 3A:

1. A turn consists of either calling out the coordinates for three digs, or by calling out one linear equation. Think of the equation as a metal-detecting ray that sweeps the grid for buried treasure. The equation must be of the form $y = mx + b$ (where m is the slope of the line and b is where the line crosses the y axis).
2. If team A chooses to take three digs instead of a linear equation, they call out the coordinates of three digs. The second team does not respond until after all three digs have been taken. If there are any hits, they tell the first team whether each hit is a corner, edge, or an interior point of the pentomino.
3. If team A calls out a linear equation, they record the equation on their table of digs and then plot the points and the line on the grid labeled **Other Team's Buried Treasure**.
4. Team B records the equation on the **Other Team's Digs** table and then plots the line on the grid labeled **Our Team's Buried Treasure**. Team B then determines if the graph of the equation passes through one of their buried treasures.
5. One line (or metal-detecting ray) will locate a buried treasure if the line passes through any portion of the buried treasure. If the line passes through a buried treasure, the team spokesperson says, hit and identifies the type of buried treasure by saying, for example, "You hit my *U*-pentomino." If the line passes through more than one buried treasure, the spokesperson says two treasures are hit and names them. A response might be, "You hit my *T*-pentomino and *U*-pentomino."

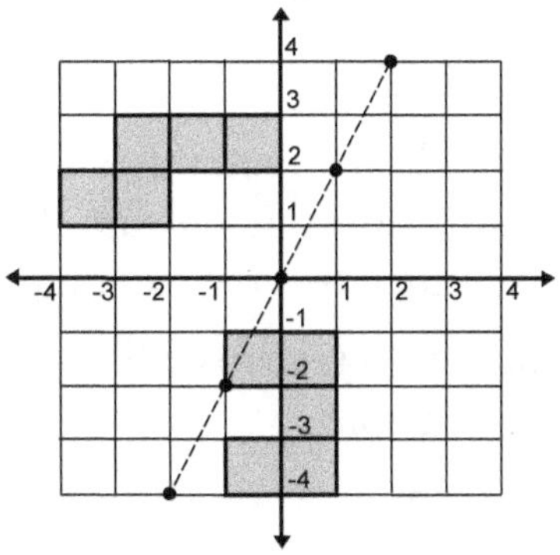

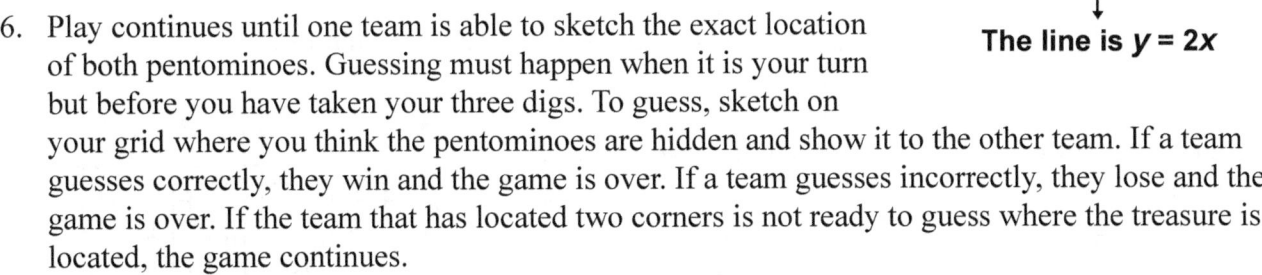

The line is $y = 2x$

6. Play continues until one team is able to sketch the exact location of both pentominoes. Guessing must happen when it is your turn but before you have taken your three digs. To guess, sketch on your grid where you think the pentominoes are hidden and show it to the other team. If a team guesses correctly, they win and the game is over. If a team guesses incorrectly, they lose and the game is over. If the team that has located two corners is not ready to guess where the treasure is located, the game continues.

Basic Strategies:

1. Just as in earlier games, create a symbol system to determine if the dig is a hit or a miss (for example, *X* for miss; *C* for corner; *E* for edge; *I* for interior point).
2. Don't waste digs by playing them too close together or too far apart.
3. If your team calls out a linear equation, pick "nice" equations so players on your team and players on the other team do not make mistakes graphing the lines. Nothing ruins a game like a mistake in graphing.

2.8 Variations on Buried Treasure with Equations

Level 3B At this level, you use two pentominoes and the playing field is increased to a 20×20 coordinate grid where the horizontal (*x*-values) and vertical (*y*-values) range from -10 to 10. A turn consists of either calling out the coordinates for three digs or by calling out one linear equation. The equation must be of the form $y = mx + b$. You still give a response, hit or miss, after each dig or equation. For example,

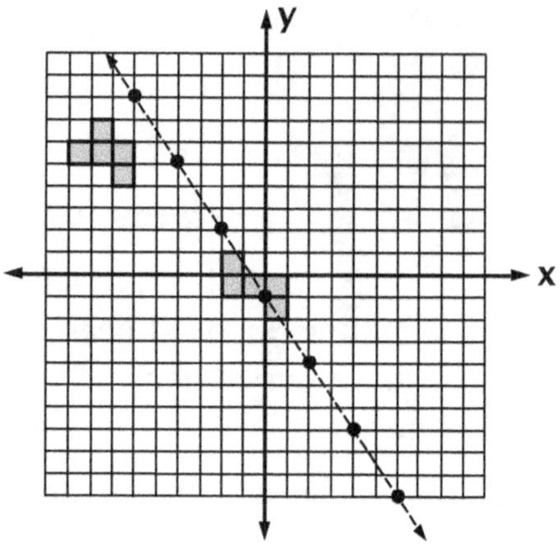

Team A: "*y* = -(3/2)*x* – 1"

Team B: "You hit my *Z*-pentomino!"

The playing fields for Levels 3C through 3G also use a 20×20 coordinate grid.

Level 3C

You hide three different pentominoes instead of two. You give a response, hit or miss, after each dig or equation.

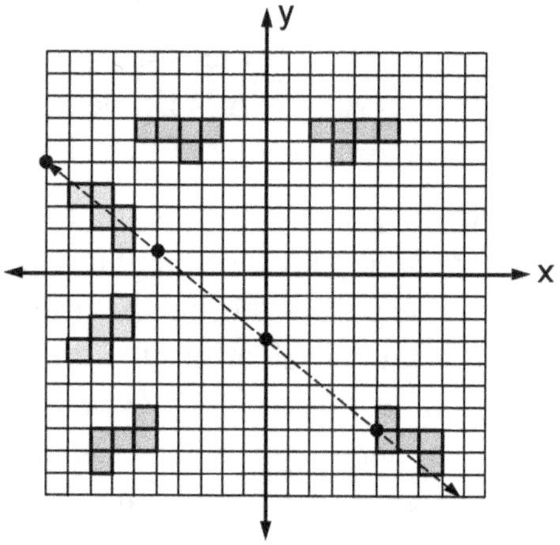

Level 3D

You hide six pentominoes (three different pairs of identical pentominoes). Each pair of pentominoes are reflections of each other. See the example to the right.

You give a response, hit or miss, after each dig or equation. For example,

Team A: "*y* = -(4/5)*x* – 3"

Team B: "You hit one of my *W*-pentominoes and one of my *Z*-pentominoes."

Level 3E

You hide three different pentominoes. At this level, players can either:

- Take four digs at a time and nothing is said about a hit or miss until the completion of the four digs or,
- Call out two parallel equations and a response is given about each equation after it is announced. For example,

  Team A: "*y* = -(3/2)*x* – 1"

  Team B: "You missed."

  Team A: "*y* = -(3/2)*x* – 9"

  Team B: "You hit my *T*-pentomino."

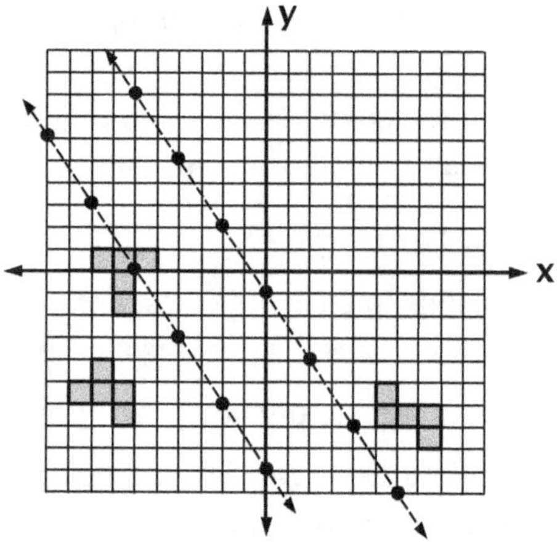

Level 3F

You hide three different pentominoes. At this level, players can either:

- Take four digs at a time and nothing is said about a hit or miss until the completion of the four digs; or,
- Call out two equations, but the lines must pass through the origin. No response is given about the two equations until after both equations are announced. For example,

Team A: "$y = (3/4)x$"

"$y = -(5/3)x$"

Team B: "You hit my *Z*-pentomino and my *W*-pentomino."

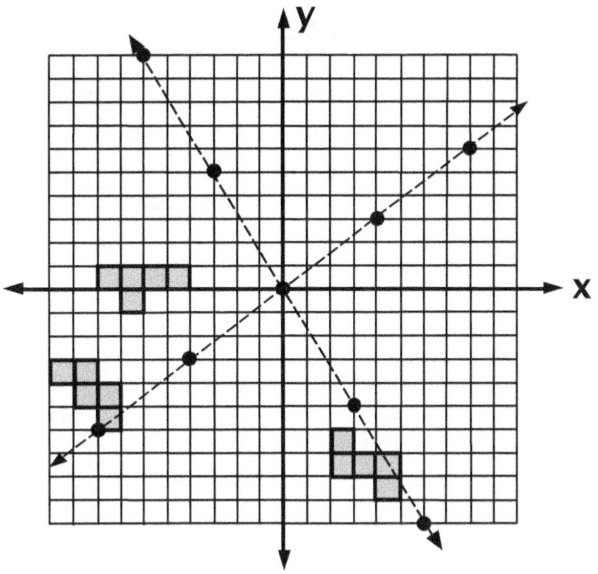

Level 3G

At this level, you hide six pentominoes (three different pairs of identical pentominoes). Each pentomino in the pair is a reflection (across the *x*- or *y*-axis) of the other. After hiding the pentominoes, count the number of pentomino squares in each row and column and place the sums at the top of each column and to the right of each row (see example). Each team tells the other team the number of squares in each row and column. (As a check, these numbers should total 30 for all the rows and 30 for all the columns.) Players can either:

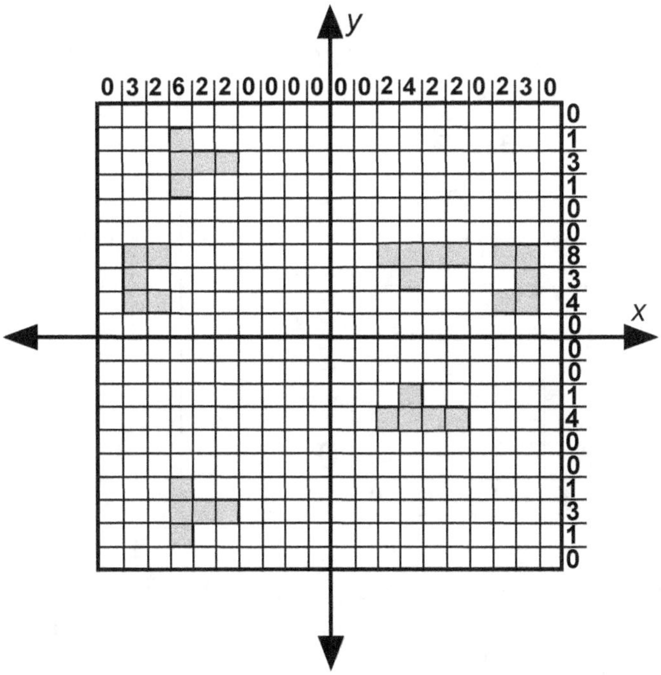

- Take four digs at a time and nothing is said about hit or miss until the completion of the four digs; or,
- Call out two equations, but the equations must pass through the *y*-axis. No response is given about the two equations until after both equations are announced.

2.9 Buried Treasure Puzzles

In this first set of tetromino buried treasure puzzles, the goal is to find the one tetromino hidden in a 4×4 grid of squares. The numbers along the right vertical edge and the bottom edge indicate the number of squares occupied by the hidden tetromino in that particular row or column. Occasionally, a portion of a tetromino is shown. Some puzzles may have more than one solution.

BTP 1

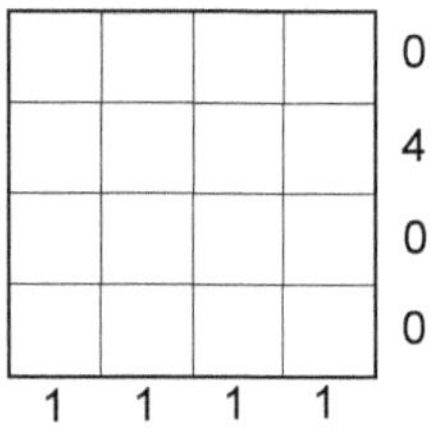

BTP 2

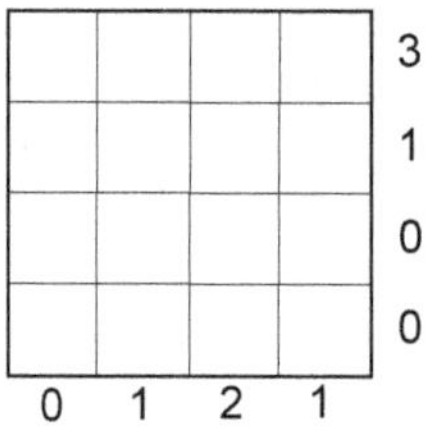

BTP 3

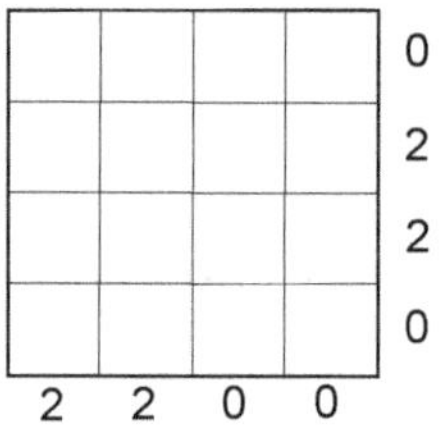

BTP 4

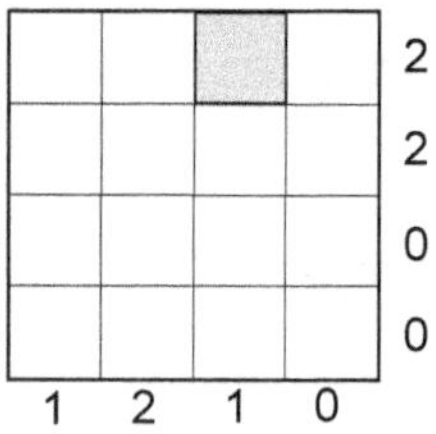

In this second set of tetromino buried treasure puzzles, the goal is to find the two different tetrominoes hidden in a 6×6 grid of squares. The two tetrominoes will not occupy adjacent squares, horizontally, vertically, or diagonally. Occasionally, a portion of a tetromino is shown.

BTP 5

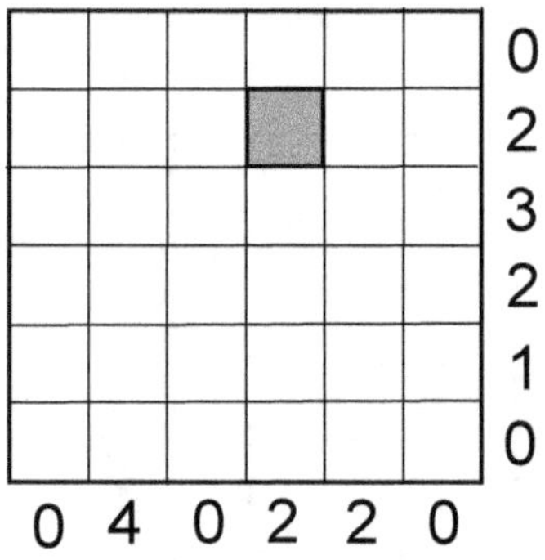

BTP 6

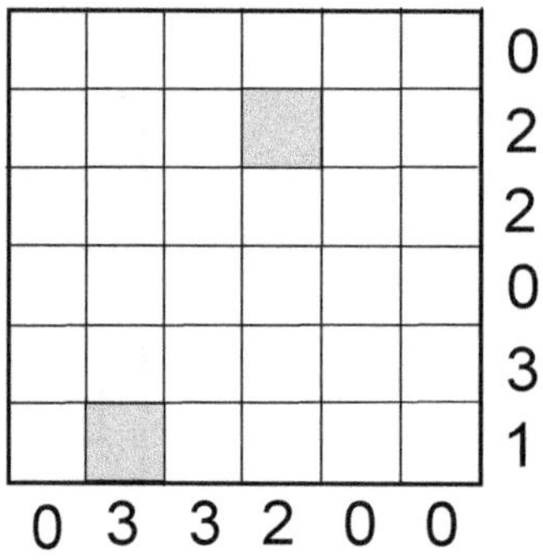

BTP 7 *h*

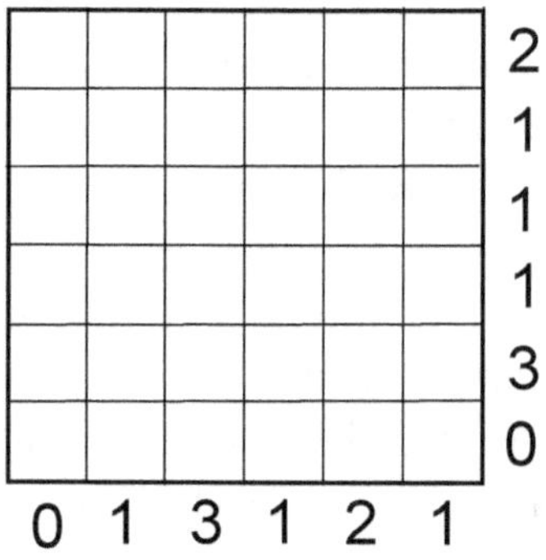

In this third set of tetromino buried treasure puzzles, the goal is to find the three different tetrominoes hidden in a 6×6 grid of squares. No two tetrominoes will occupy adjacent squares, horizontally, vertically, or diagonally. Occasionally, a portion of a tetromino is shown.

BTP 8

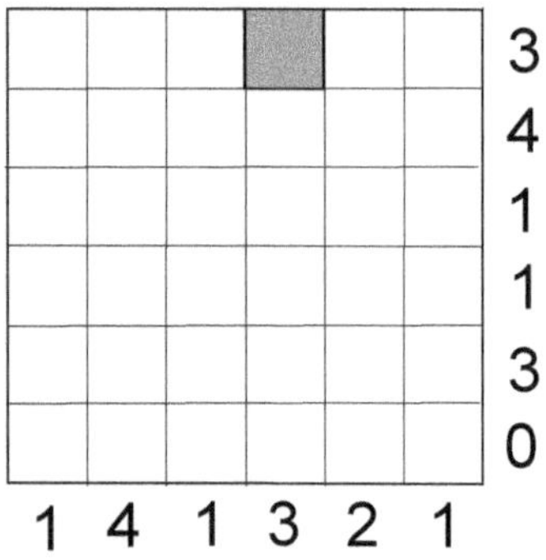

BTP 9

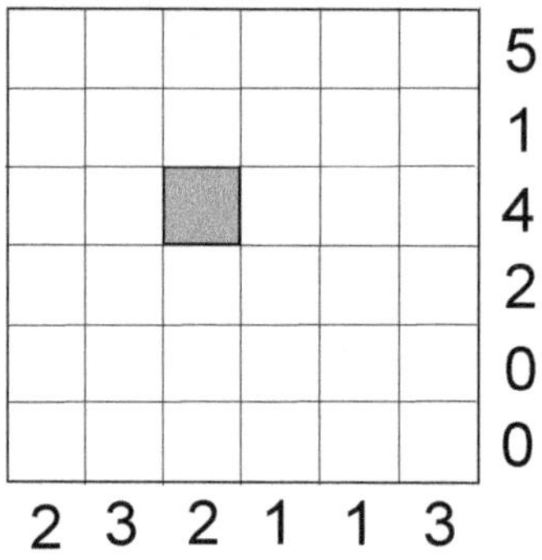

BTP 10 *h*

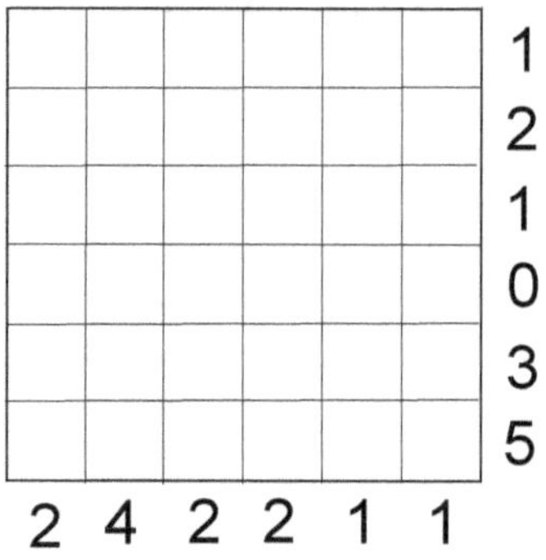

In this fourth set of tetromino buried treasure puzzles, the goal is to find two pairs of tetrominoes hidden in an 8×8 grid of squares. No two tetrominoes will occupy adjacent squares, horizontally, vertically, or diagonally. Each tetromino has a twin that is its reflection. The pairs may or may not share the same line of reflection. Occasionally, a portion of a tetromino is shown.

BTP 11 *h*

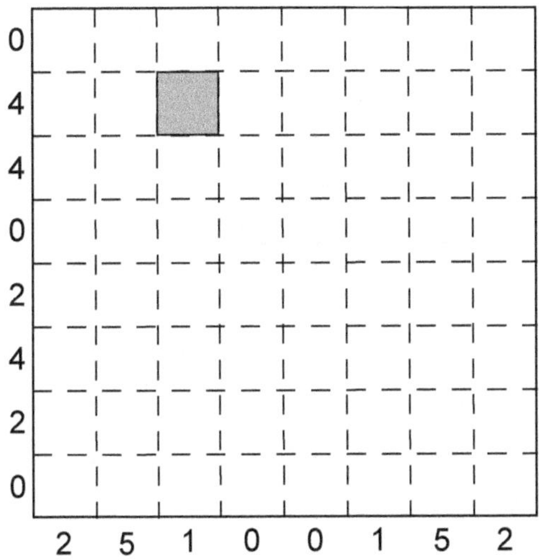

BTP 12

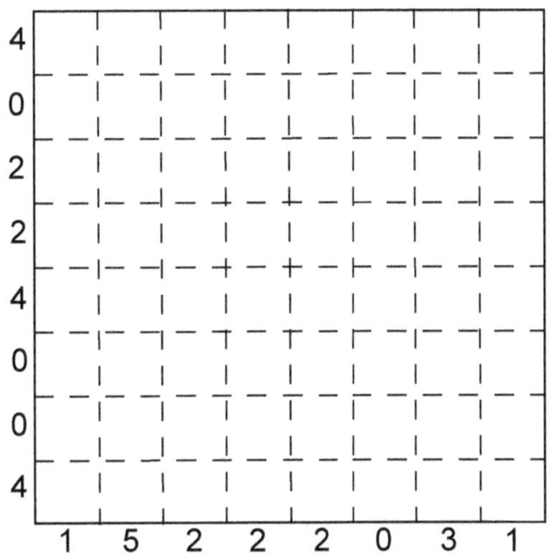

In this fifth set of tetromino buried treasure puzzles, the goal is to find two pairs of tetrominoes hidden in an 8×8 grid of squares. No two tetrominoes will occupy adjacent squares, horizontally, vertically, or diagonally. Each tetromino has a twin that is a rotation of it. The pairs may or may not share the same center of rotation. Occasionally, a portion of a tetromino is shown.

BTP 13 *h*

Both rotations are 90°

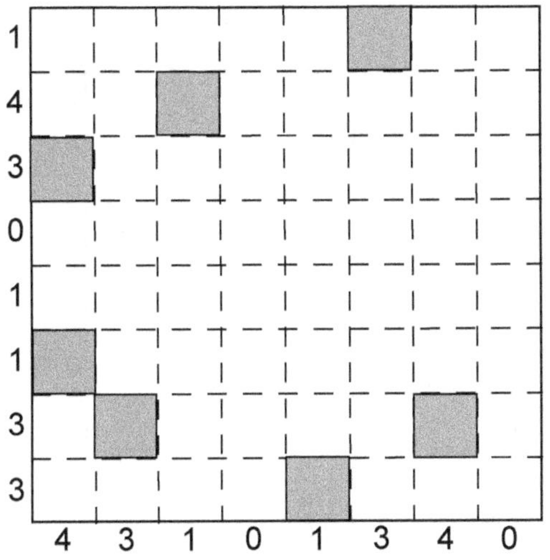

BTP 14

Both rotations are 180°

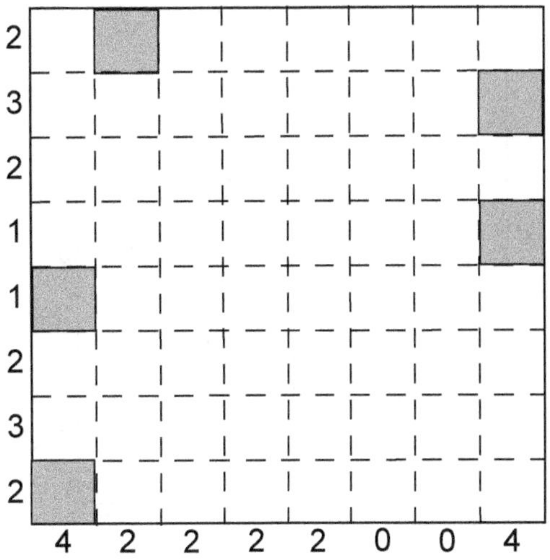

Chapter 2.9

For puzzles 15–18 the goal is to find all five tetrominoes in each 8×8 grid. Tetrominoes will not occupy adjacent squares, horizontally, vertically, or diagonally. The numbers along the right vertical edge and the bottom edge indicate the number of squares occupied by the hidden tetrominoes in that particular row or column. Occasionally, portions of tetrominoes are shown. The five tetrominoes are shown shaded below.

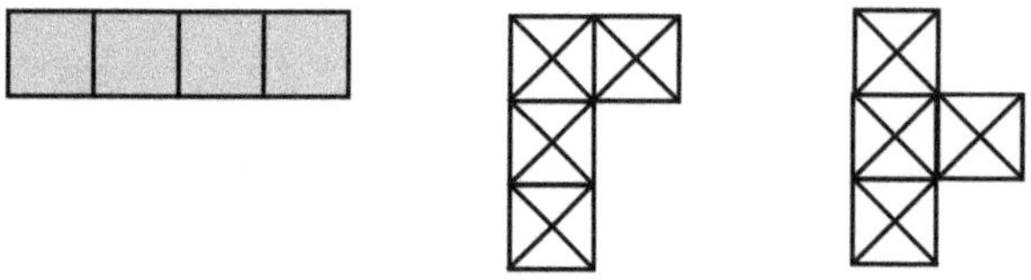

BTP 15

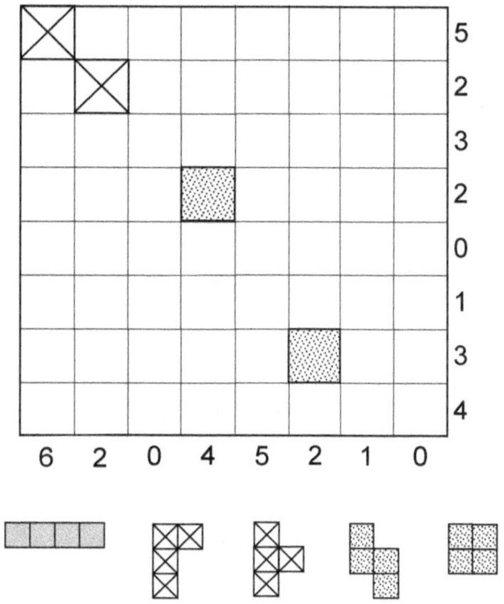

BTP 16

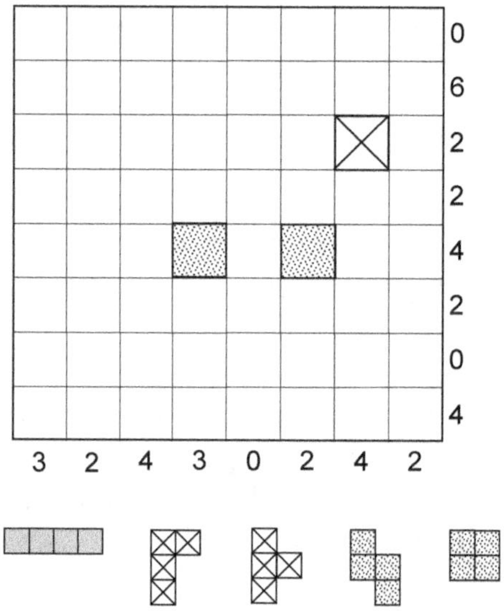

BTP 17

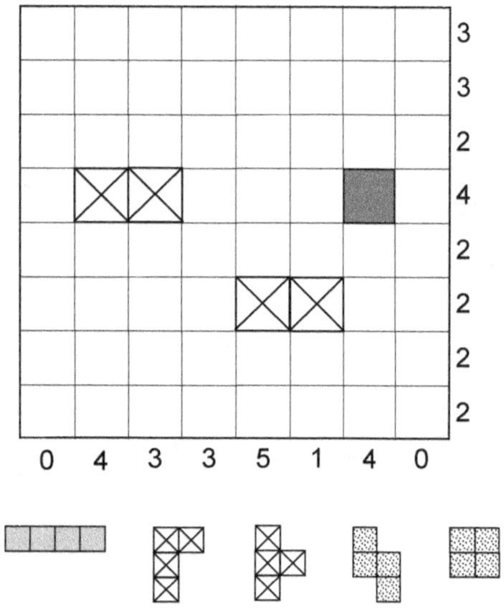

BTP 18

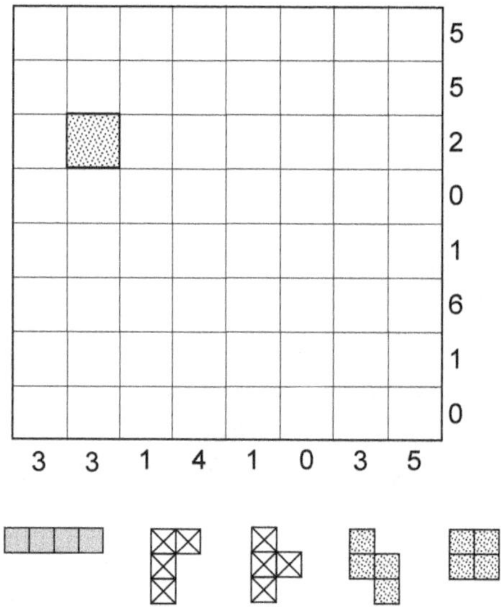

For Puzzles 19–22 sketch a pentomino buried treasure given the coordinates of only some of its corners. There are multiple solutions. Different solutions may include the same pentomino in a different position or a completely different pentomino. Find at least three solutions for each puzzle.

BTP 19

Five of the corners include: (2, 5), (3, 5), (4, 5), (5, 5), (4, 7)

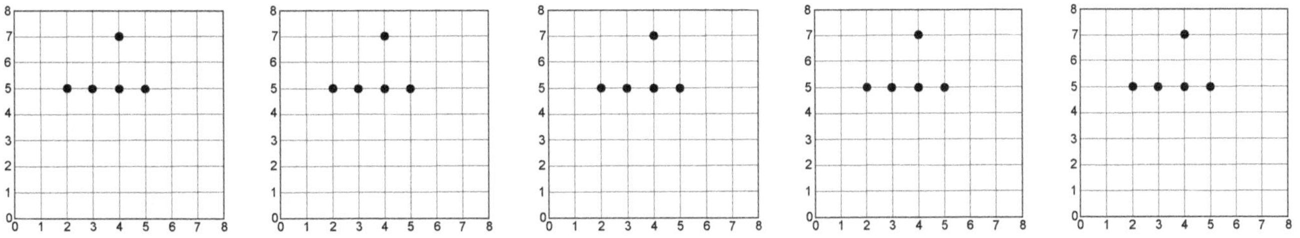

BTP 20

Five of the corners include: (2, 3), (2, 5), (3, 4), (4, 4), (4, 5)

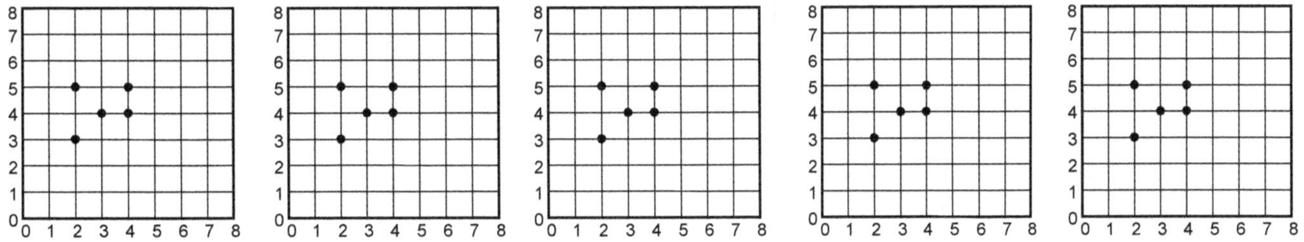

BTP 21

Five of the corners include: (2, 5), (3, 3), (3, 4), (4, 4), (4, 5)

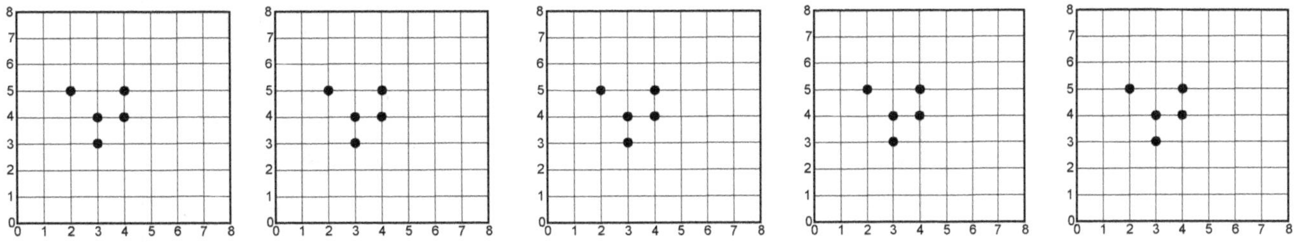

BTP 22

Five of the corners include: (3, 3), (4, 4), (5, 5), (5, 4), (3, 6)

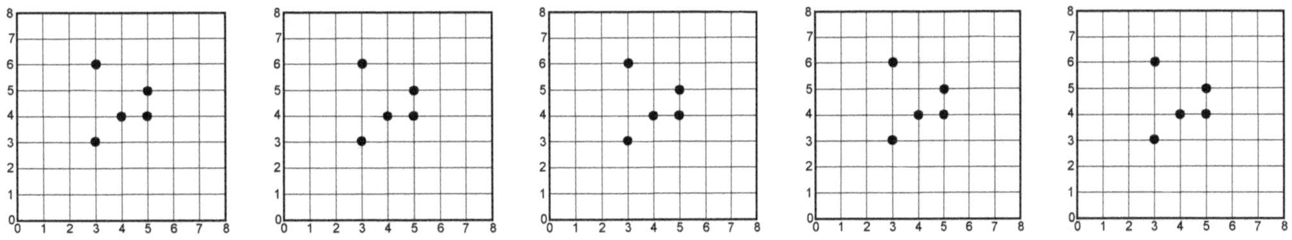

In Puzzles 23–28 one pentomino buried treasure has been hidden in the 8×8 grid. Some points in the grid have been identified as a corner, an edge, or an interior point of the pentomino. Other points not on the pentomino are identified as misses. Use the clues: corner (*C*), edge (*E*), miss (*X*), and interior (*I*) to determine the location of the hidden pentomino. See the example on the right.

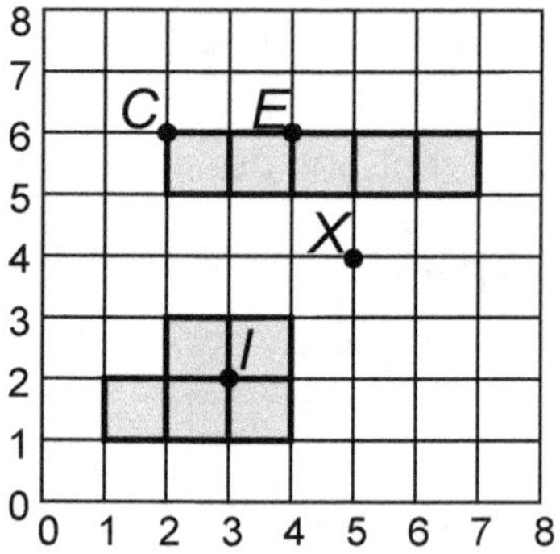

BTP 23

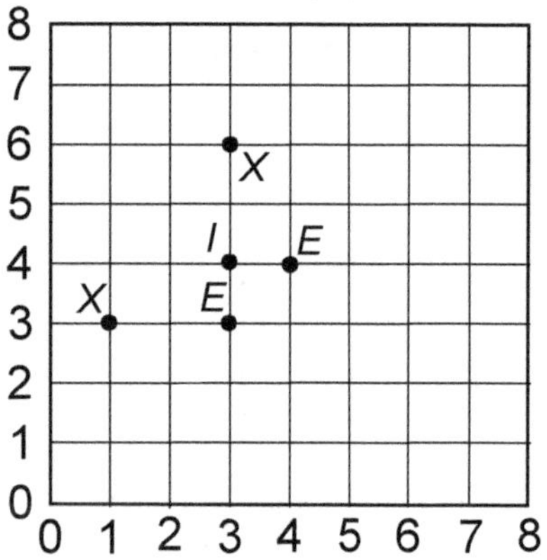

BTP 24

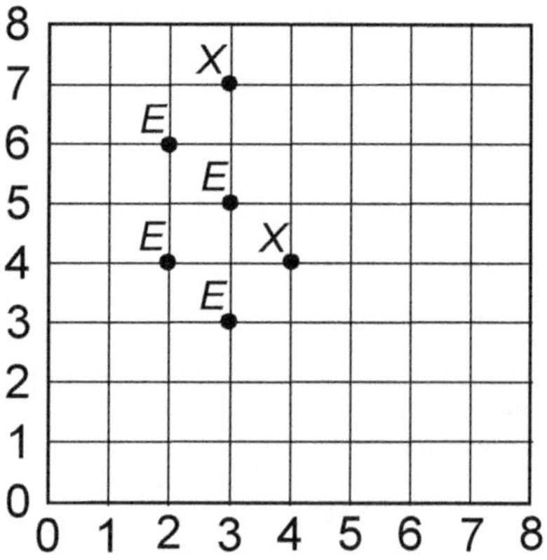

BTP 25

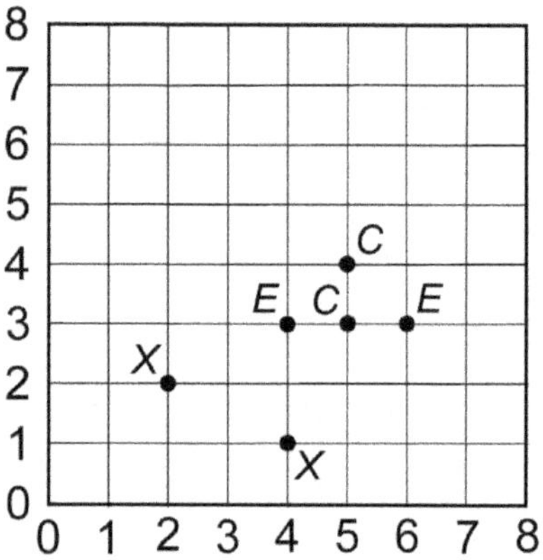

BTP 26

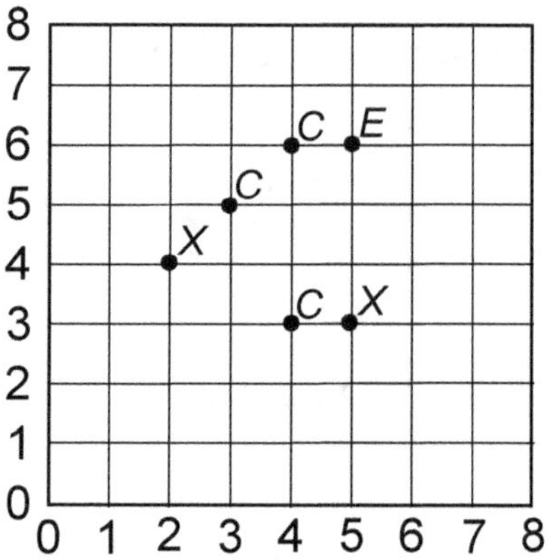

BTP 27

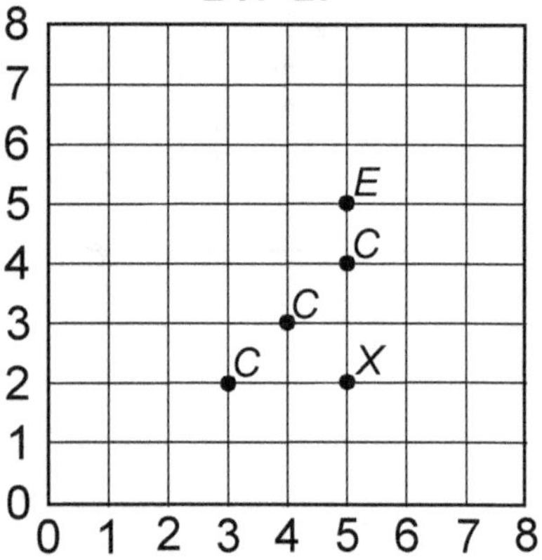

BTP 28

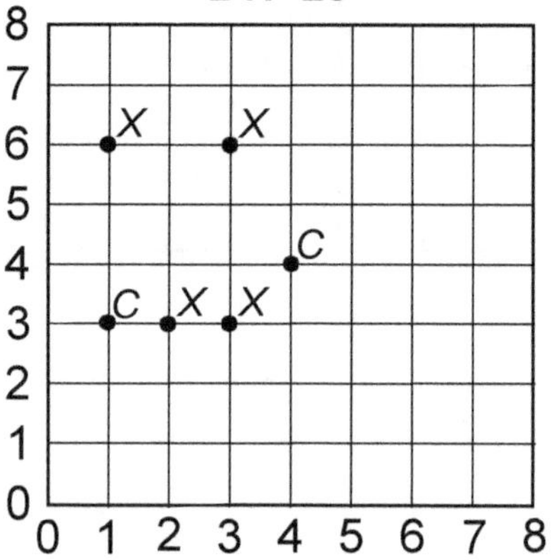

For puzzles 29 and 30 below, sketch a pentomino given the coordinates of some of its corners. Each puzzle has only one solution.

BTP 29 Four of the six corners include:
(2,3), (3,-1), (2,0), (3, 1)

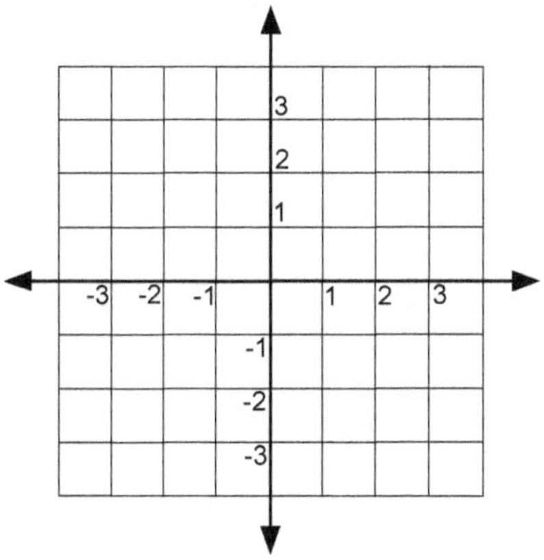

BTP 30 Five of the ten corners include:
(-1,-3), (-3,0), (-2,-2), (-4,-1), (-3,-3)

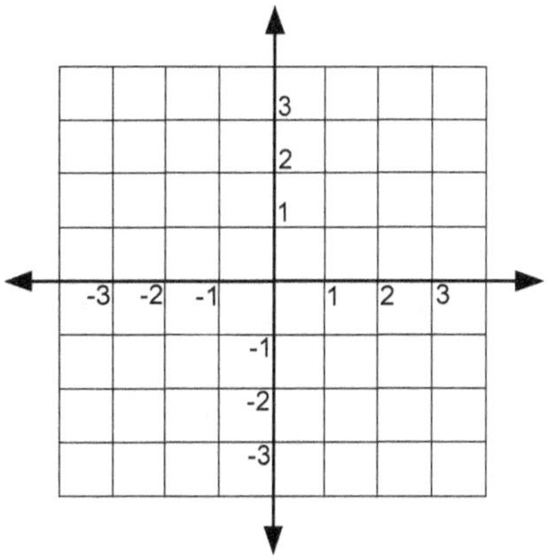

On the coordinate grids for puzzles 31 and 32 below, each *E* represents an edge of a pentomino, each *C* represents a corner, and an *X* means the pentomino does not pass through that point. Locate and sketch the pentomino.

BTP 31 *h*

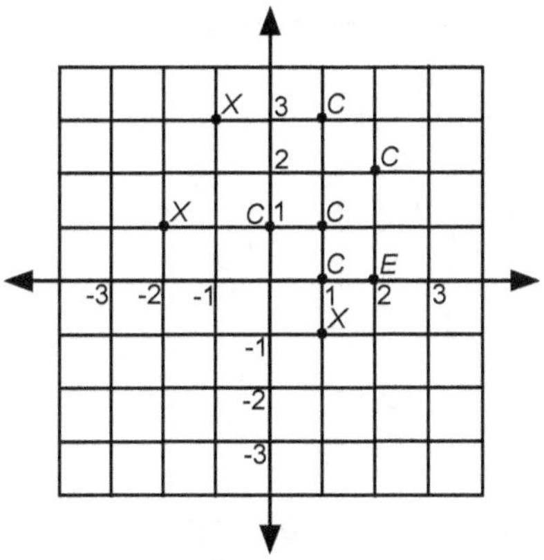

BTP 32

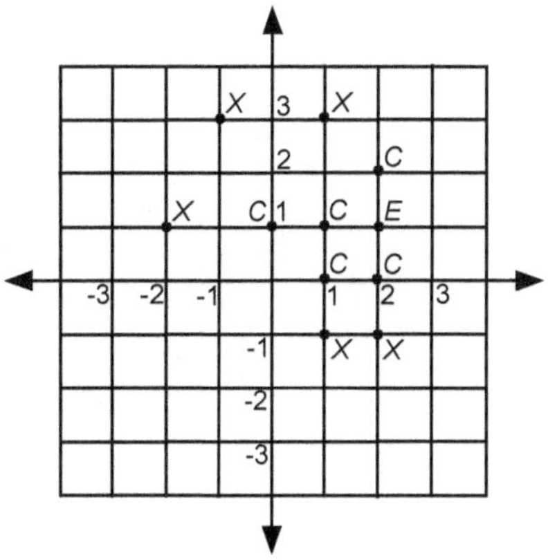

BTP 33

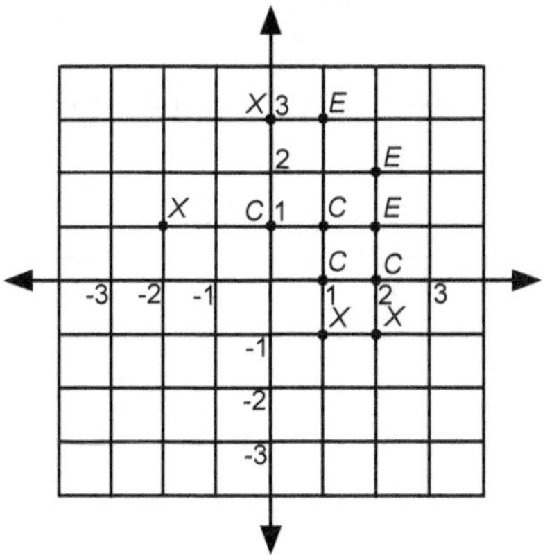

BTP 34

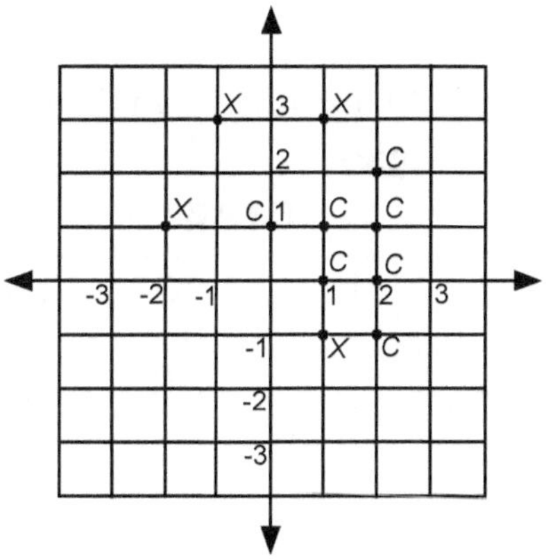

Chapter 2.9

In Chapter 1 you saw a few examples of pentominoes arranged into 6×10 rectangles. In puzzles 35–38 all 12 pentominoes have been arranged into 6×10 rectangles but they are all completely or partially hidden. The 12 pentominoes are identified by the letters shown below. These letters are given as clues. If the letter *T*, for example, is in a square, then the *T*-pentomino covers that square. Use logical reasoning to determine the location of all the pentominoes in each puzzle below.

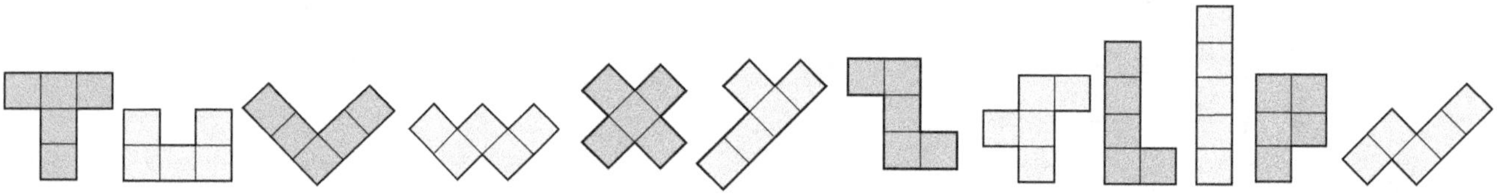

T U V W X Y Z F L I P N

BTP 35

V									Y
	F							Y	
		F	Z	Z	L	L	L		
		X	T	N	N	N	W		
	X							W	
U									W

BTP 36

				T	T				
			Y	Y	T	N			
		X	Y			N	Z		
	X	F					P	P	
V	F	F					P	P	I
				L	L				

BTP 37

				T					
		X					P		
U					P				F
V				N					F
		Y					N		
					I				

BTP 38

All pentominoes touch outer edge.

		U							
	X			L			Z		
V			Y			N			
		F			W				

All 12 pentominoes can also be arranged into a 5×12 rectangle. There are over a thousand arrangements not counting rotations and reflections. One such arrangement is shown to the right.

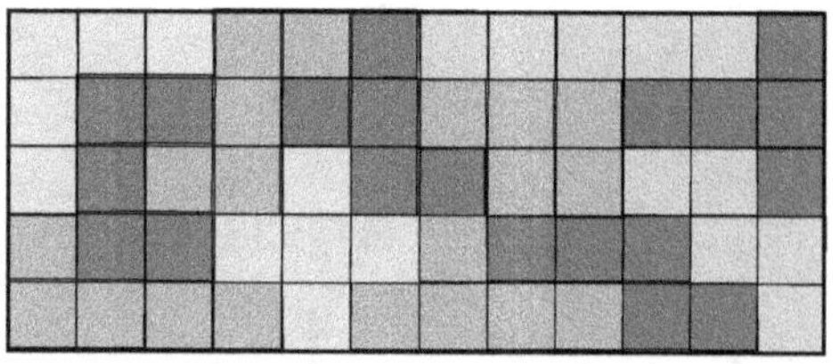

In puzzles 39 and 40, use logical reasoning to determine the locations of all 12 pentominoes in both 5×12 rectangles.

BTP 39

U						P			T		
		U			P			W			
										T	
	F						N		V		
			L		N						

BTP 40

T			I					Z			N
									F		
				U			Z				
			Y								V
					Y			X			

2.10 Pirate Treasure with Coordinate Geometry

In this section you will use your coordinate geometry skills to locate pirate treasure on ten different tropical isles. You may wish to review some properties of Cartesian coordinate geometry before you begin. Each island map has a coordinate grid overlay but the origin is hidden. Your first task will be to solve a mini-puzzle to locate the origin on the island (not in the sea). Then use your coordinate geometry skills to locate the buried treasure.

1. Buried Treasure on Cayman Key

- Place the origin at the anagram of "gotermane."
- From Cutlass Clifts send one pirate mate moving in a "south-westerly" direction at a slope of 2/3.
- Send a second mate from position (-4, 11) moving in a "south-easterly" direction at a slope of -1.
- The treasure is buried where the mates' paths cross.
- What are the coordinates of the treasure's location?

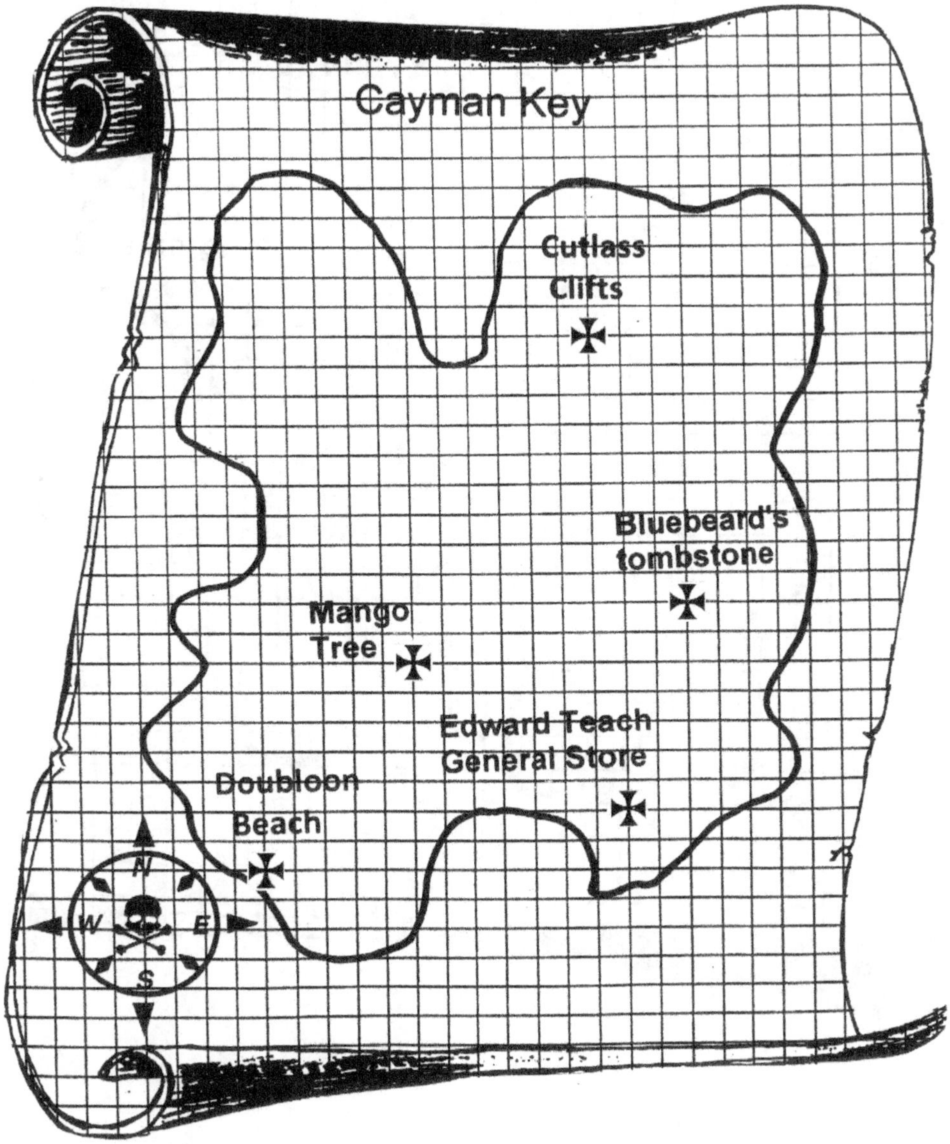

2. Buried Treasure on Barbossa Island $\hbar$

- Place the origin at the anagram of "peter lam."
- Locate the midpoint between Crocodile Skull Rock and Hangman's Tree and label it A.
- Locate the midpoint between (0, 2) and the Flying Dutchman Shipyard and label it B.
- The treasure is at the midpoint of $\overline{AB}$.
- What are the coordinates of the treasure's location?

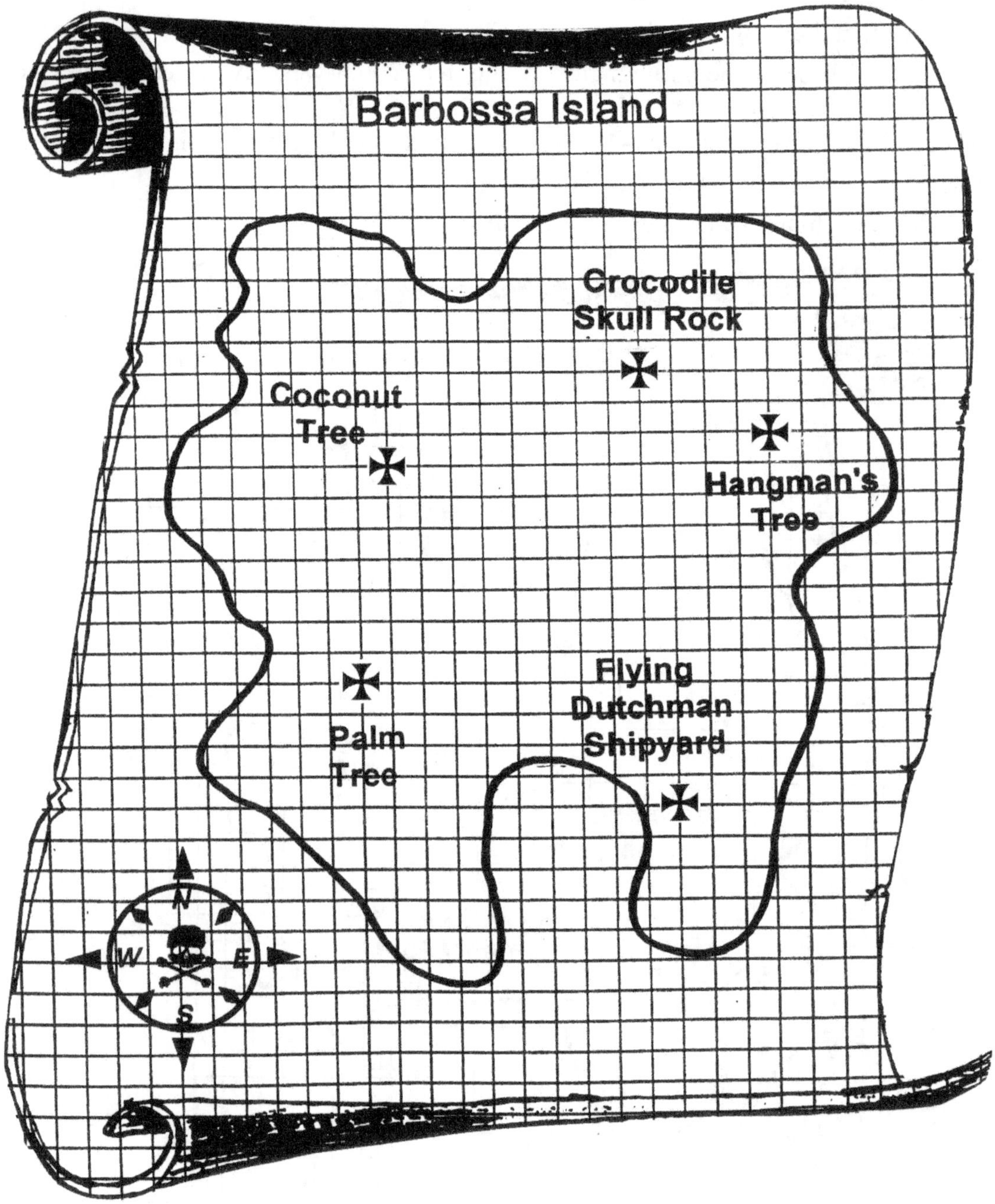

3. Buried Treasure on Isla Sirena *h*

- The pentominoes shown below right can be arranged into the 5×12 rectangle so that the letters form four math terms: circumcenter, dodecahedron, intersection, and trigonometry. One of the pentominoes has already been correctly placed. When all 12 are positioned correctly into the 5×12 rectangle the location of the origin will be revealed.

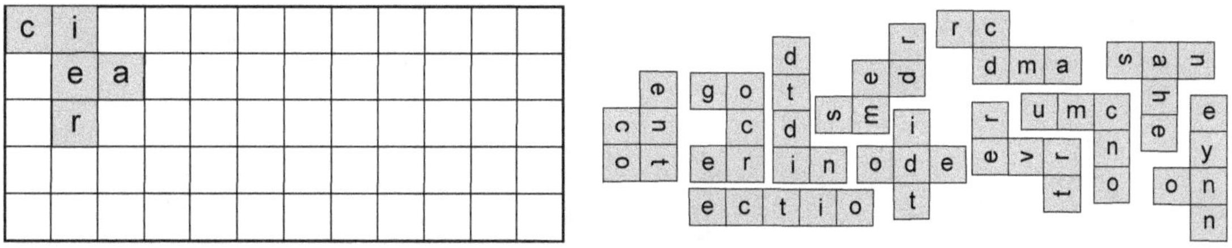

- Locate the midpoint between Devil's Spout and the point (12, 4) and label it *A*.
- The treasure is located at a point that forms a parallelogram with point *A*, Jack's Seagoing Supplies, and Dead Man's Cove.
- What are the coordinates of the treasure's location?

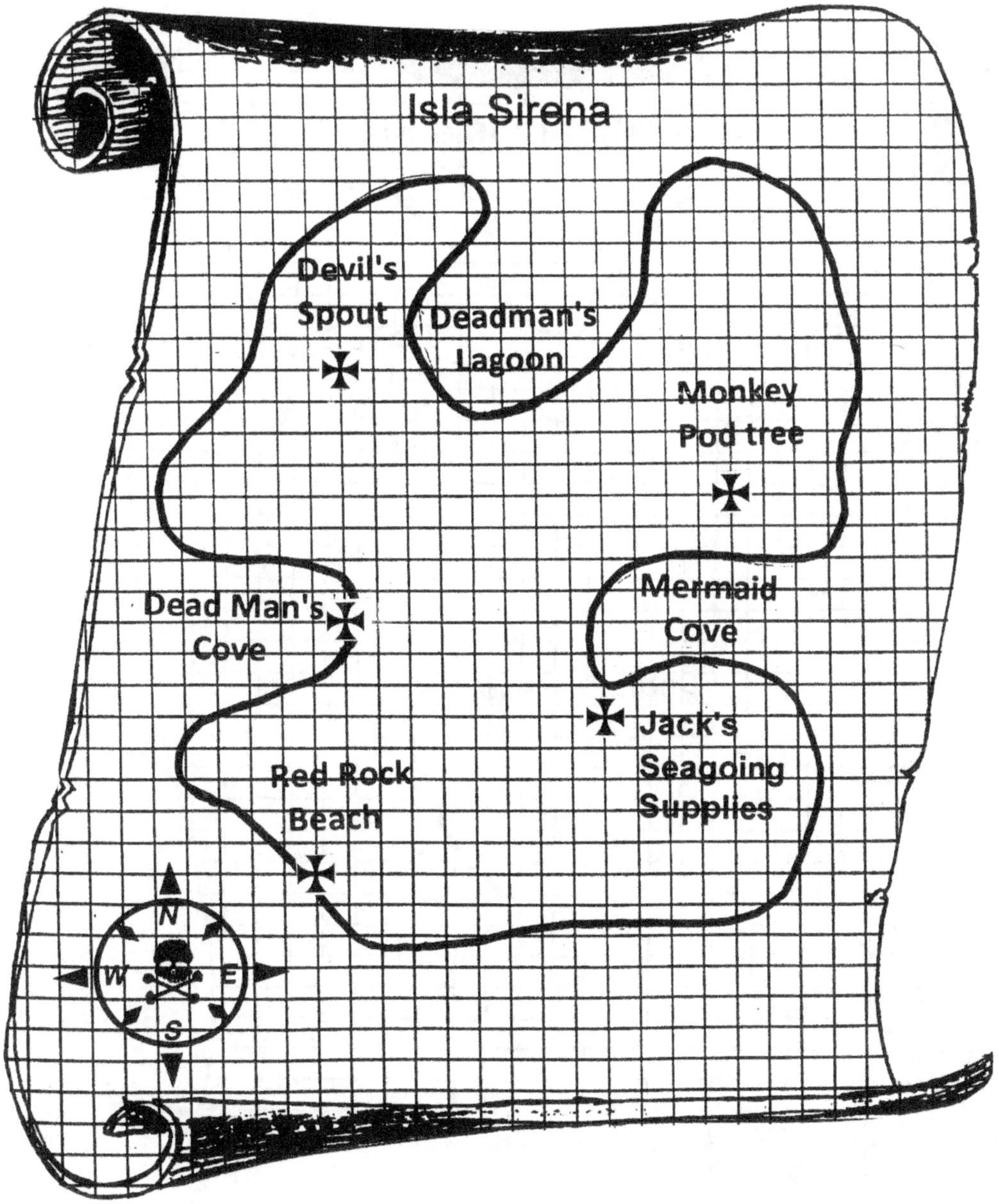

4. Buried Treasure on Blackbeard Island *ћ*

- The pentominoes shown below right can be arranged into the 6×10 rectangle. Four of the pentominoes have already been correctly placed. When all 12 are positioned correctly into the 6×10 rectangle the location of the origin will be revealed.

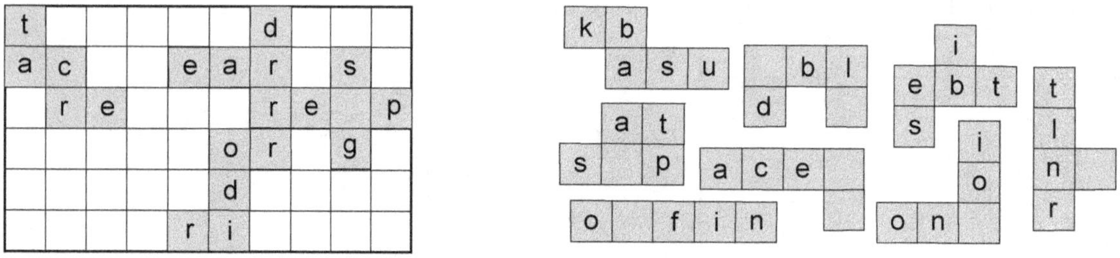

- Find the equation of line *A* through Jack Sparrow Saloon and (-6, 1).
- Find the equation of line *B* through Blackbeard's tombstone and (-1, -5).
- The treasure is located at the intersection of lines *A* and *B*.
- What are the coordinates of the treasure's location?

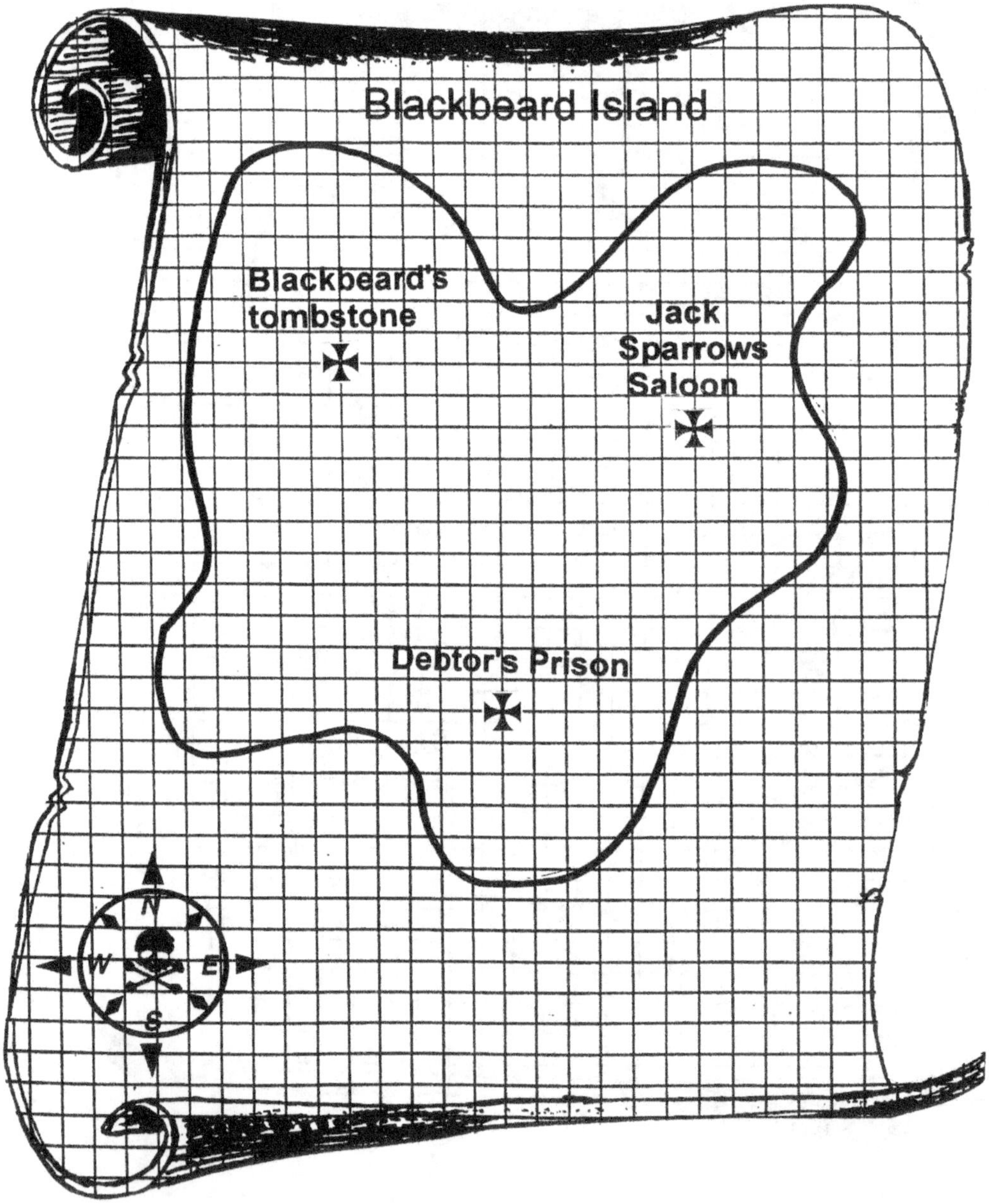

5. Buried Treasure on Haunted Isle

- The location of the origin is hidden in this 4×5 grid. It may be read in a zig-zag manner.
- Find the perpendicular bisector of the segment connecting Pirate's Graveyard and Skeleton Boulder. Label it line *A*.
- The treasure is located at the intersection of line *A* and the line $x = 3$.
- What are the coordinates of the treasure's location?

o	i	g	e
r	i	d	a
n	t	d	d
a	m	s	o
a	n	c	k

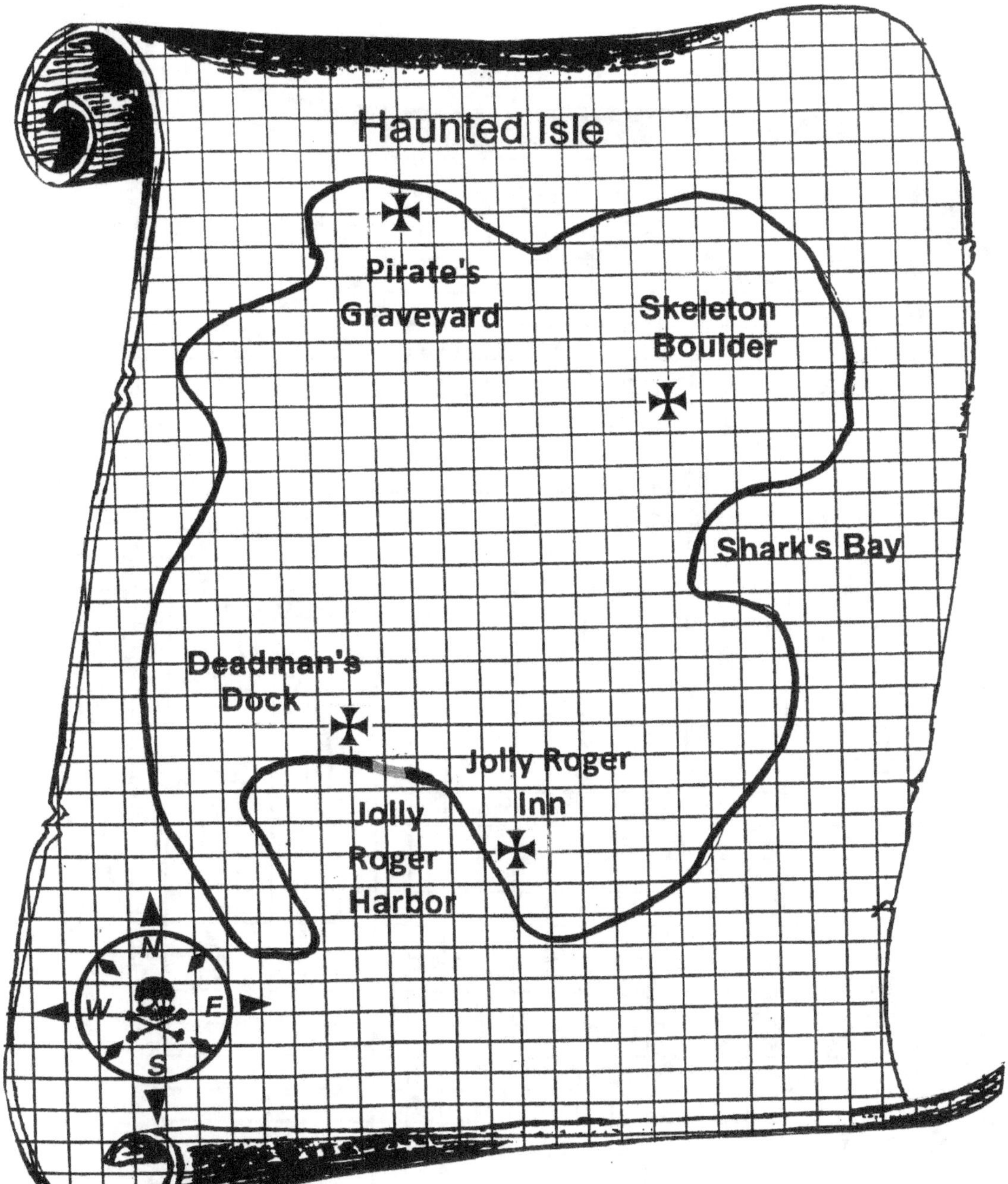

6. Buried Treasure on Skeleton Key *h*

- The location of the origin is found by arranging the letters in each column in the lower 5×8 grid into the blank squares of each corresponding column in the upper 5×8 grid so that a message may be read horizontally.
- The treasure is buried on the line $y = 9$ and is equally distant from the Henry Morgan grave and the Shiver Me Timbers Saloon.
- What are the coordinates of the treasure's location?

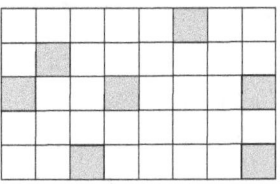

b	a	a	a	d	e	e	h
e	l	e	c	e	f	e	n
i	r	o	r	i	g	i	u
P	t	t	t	r	h	r	
				t		t	

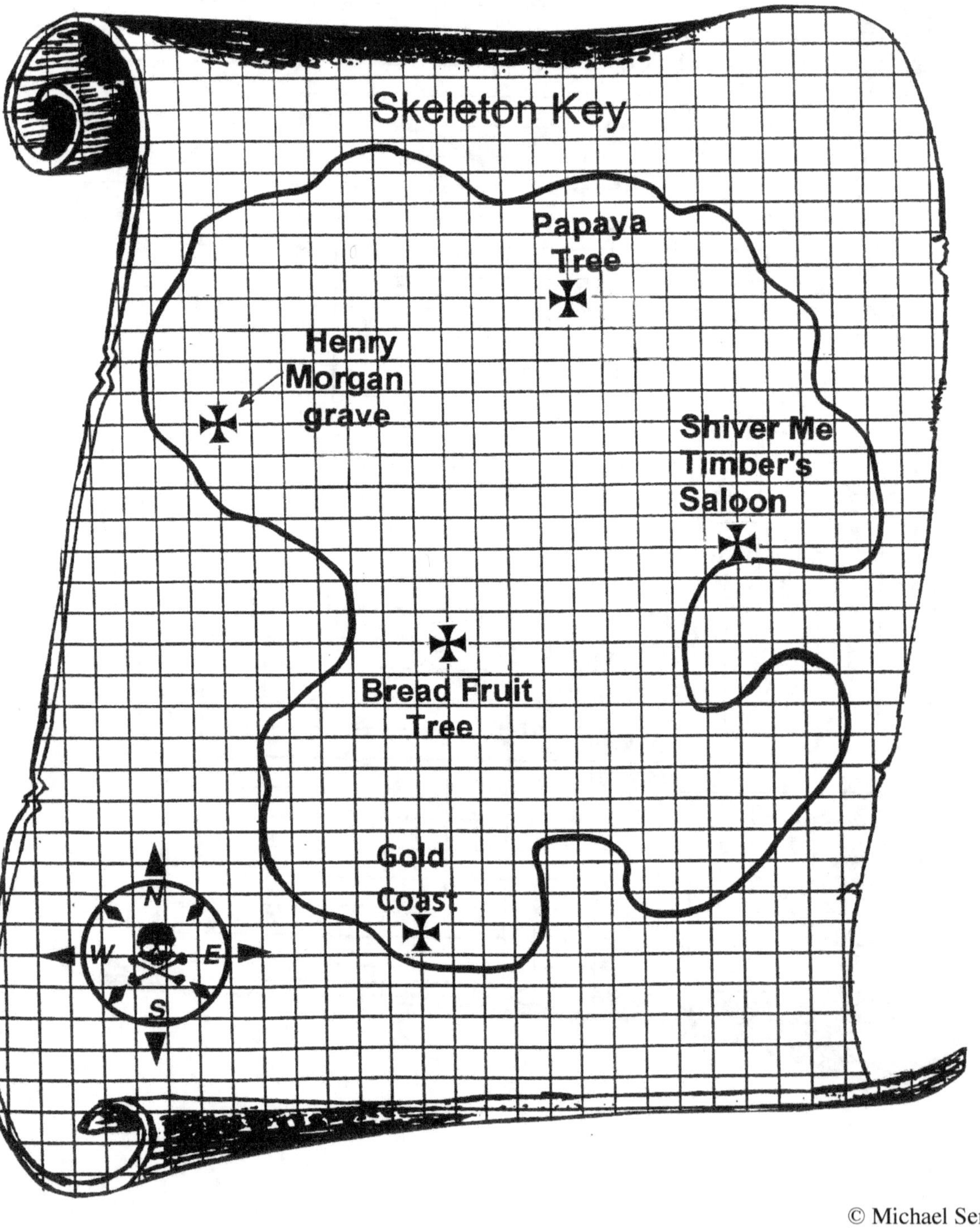

7. Buried Treasure on Doubloon Island $\hbar$

- The location of the origin is hidden in the 4×9 grid at right. It may be read horizontally or vertically.
- The location of the treasure is equally distant from Hornswaggle Inn, Doubloon Saloon, and the point (-4, 8).
- What are the coordinates of the treasure's location?

	g	i	a	t	r	n	e	l
T	i	n	c	e	o	s	l	n
h	r	i	o	d	H	w	g	n
e	o	s	l	a	t	a	g	

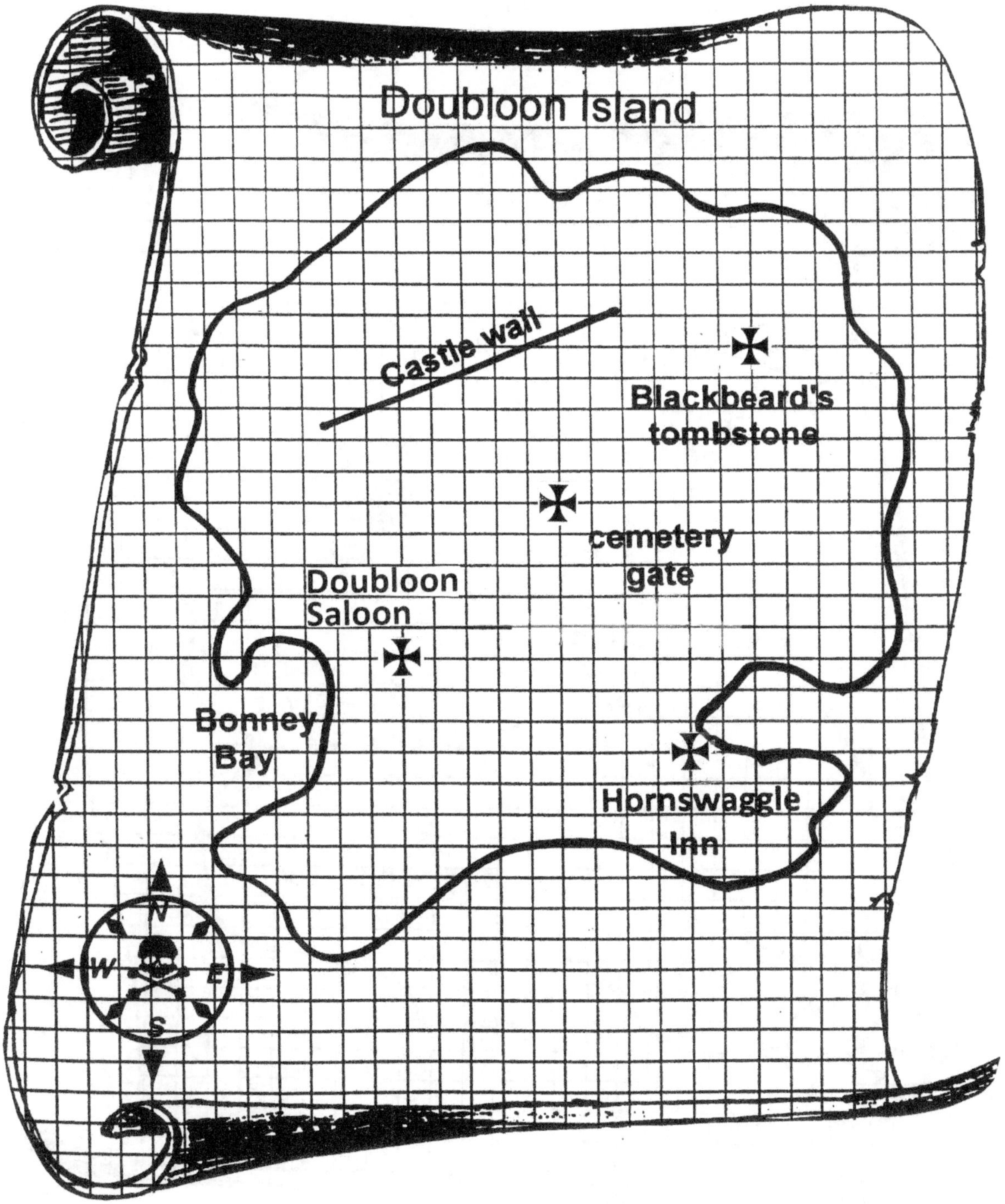

8. Buried Treasure on Skull Island ℏ

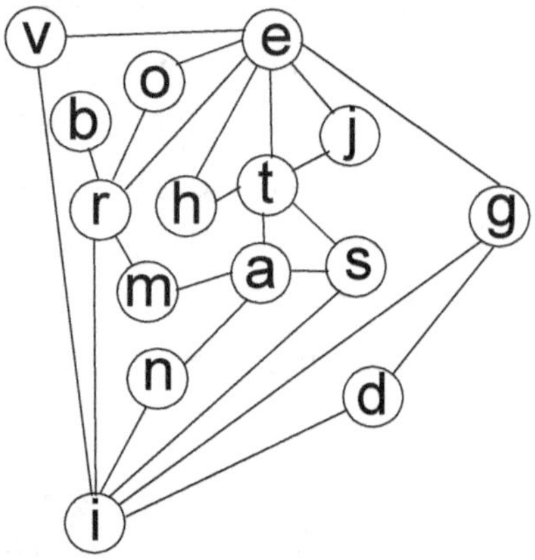

- The location of the origin is found in the network shown at right. Begin at the letter *t* and move along the segments from letter to letter forming a sentence. Letters may be used more than once.
- The treasure is located at the intersection of the line through Leaping Lizard's Saloon and Hangman's Tree and the line $x + 2y = 7$.
- What are the coordinates of the treasure's location?

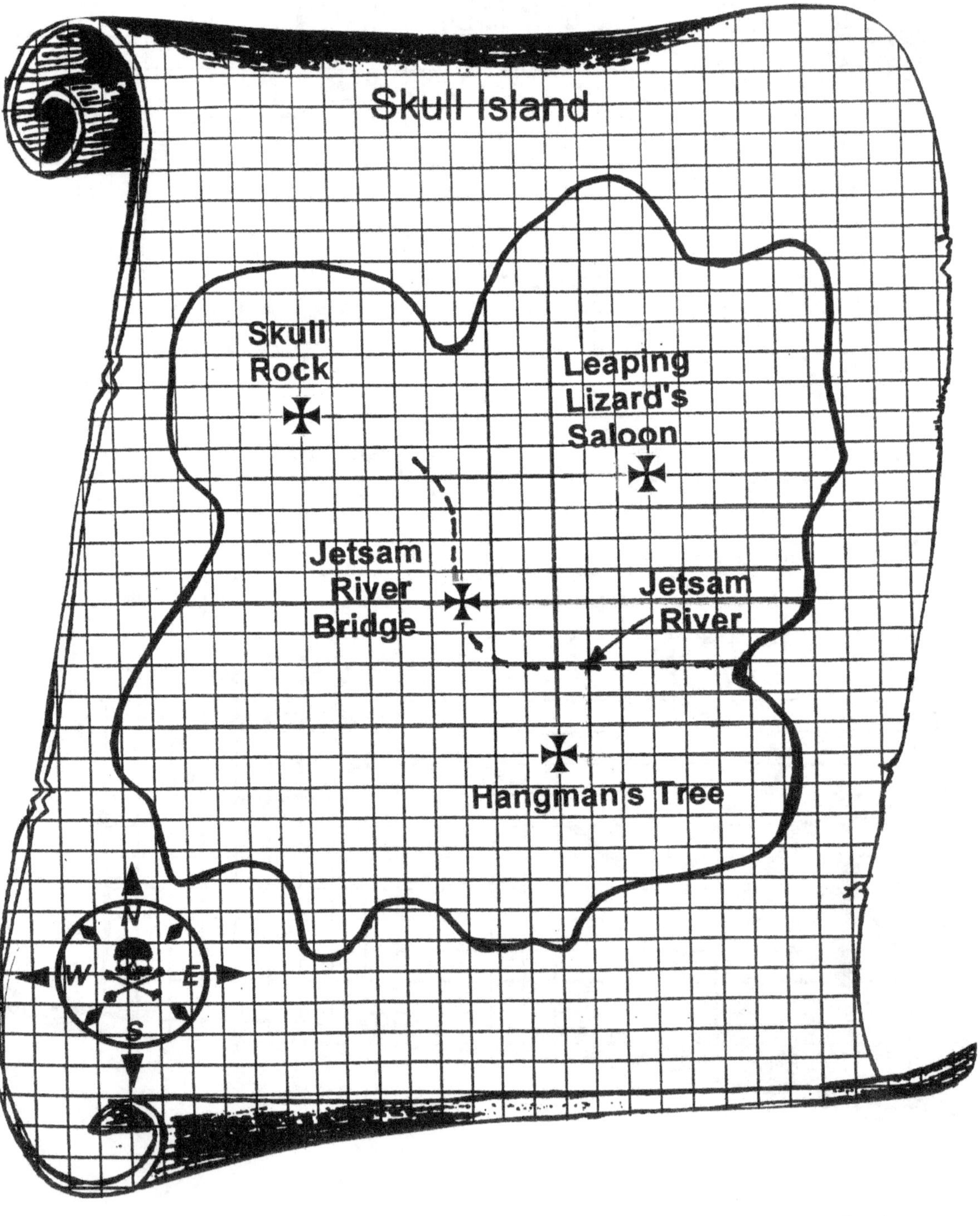

9. Buried Treasure on Demon Island *h*

- Cross out all the math terms (containing three or more letters) in the 10×10 grid to the right. The words are arranged horizontally and vertically forward and back. Some letters are used in more than one word. All but eight letters will be crossed out. Arrange those letters into a word to determine the origin for the coordinate system on Demon Island.
- The treasure is located at the orthocenter of the triangle with vertices at the cemetery gate, Hangman's Tree, and a point on the coast at (1, 7).
- What are the coordinates of the treasure's location?

a	l	g	o	r	i	t	h	m	e
l	e	l	l	a	r	a	p	u	t
g	e	o	m	e	t	r	y	l	a
e	o	c	a	x	i	s	r	t	n
b	n	u	t	w	o	e	t	i	i
r	i	s	h	s	r	m	e	p	d
a	a	r	r	s	e	i	m	l	r
t	m	y	a	r	z	r	m	y	o
l	o	g	i	c	f	p	y	e	o
e	d	o	m	e	n	i	s	o	c

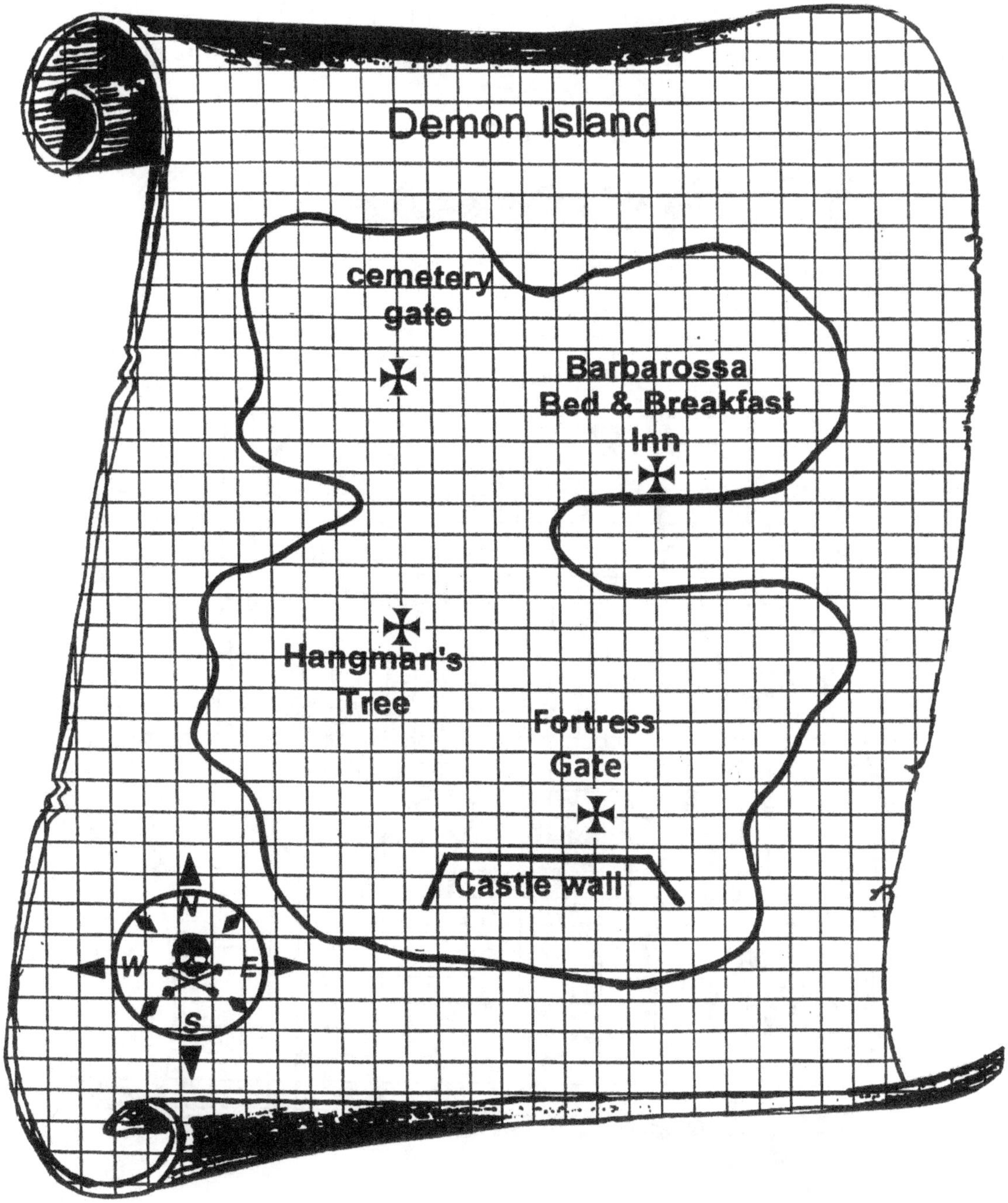

10. Buried Treasure on Isla Tortuga ℏ

- Each of the following sets of words has in common a fifth word that can be added to form a new word or two-word phrase. For example, in the set {bug, cover, flower, fellow} the word that can be attached either before or after each word is "bed." After filling in the blanks and boxes for each of the six words, arrange the nine letters in the boxes into two words to reveal the origin of the coordinate grid on Isla Tortuga.

{style, jacket, love, wild}:	☐ ___ ___ ___
{bitter, potato, tooth, talk}:	☐ ___ ___ ___ ___
{contest, mark, sleeping, shop}:	___ ___ ___ ☐ ___ ___
{walk, cup, beef, hot}:	☐ ___ ☐ ___
{hound, slide, bed, sham}:	☐ ☐ ___ ☐
{bird, sick, true, seat}:	☐ ___ ___ ___
Therefore the origin is located at	☐ ☐ ☐ ☐ ☐ ☐ ☐ ☐ ☐.

- The treasure is located at the circumcenter of the triangle formed by Turtle Rock, the Gallows, and the point (8, -1).
- What are the coordinates of the treasure's location?

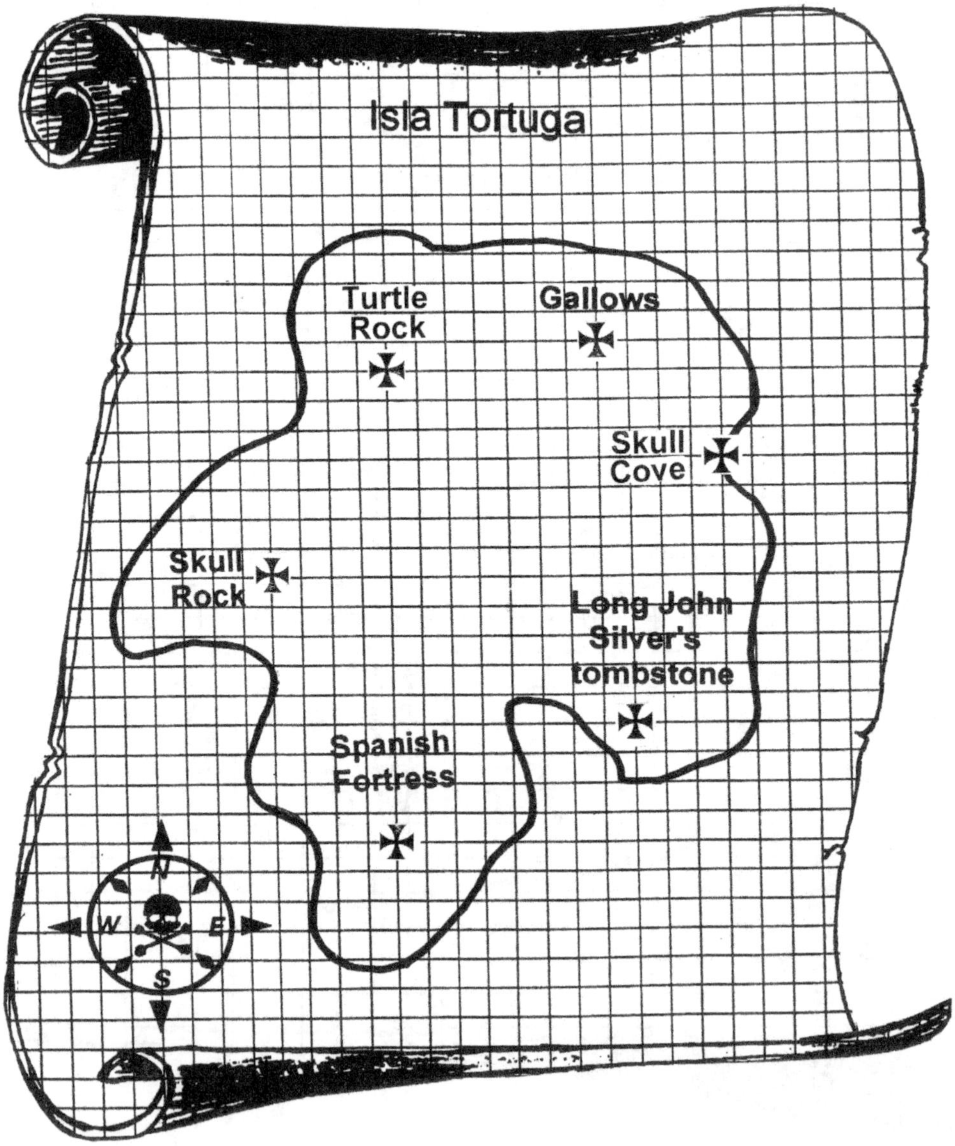

Chapter 3 Polar Buried Treasure

Only the most foolish of mice would hide in a cat's ear.
But only the wisest of cats would think to look there.
—Andrew Mercer

3.1 The Polar Coordinate System

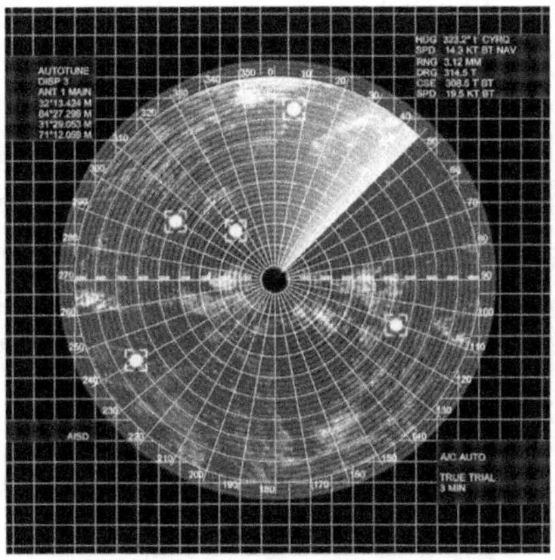

In Chapter 2 you played Buried Treasure using a rectangular coordinate system. In this chapter you are going to learn about another type of coordinate system used in advanced mathematics. If you have ever watched a movie that takes place on a submarine or in an airplane, you may have seen this coordinate system in action. The radar screen is one example of a different type of coordinate system.

In a rectangular coordinate system you locate a point with an ordered pair of numbers. The two numbers represent distances in the horizontal and vertical directions from the origin. In some mathematical applications it is useful to describe a location by its distance from a point of origin and an amount of rotation about that point. This system is called a **polar coordinate system**. Polar coordinates are also ordered pairs of numbers, but have the form (r, θ), where r represents the distance from the origin (think r as radius) and θ represents the angle of rotation counterclockwise from a horizontal line. The polar coordinates (3, 105°) identify a point 3 units from the origin and rotated 105° counterclockwise from the "zero" horizontal.

Example A

The coordinates of point A are (6, 285°). What are the coordinates of points B and C?

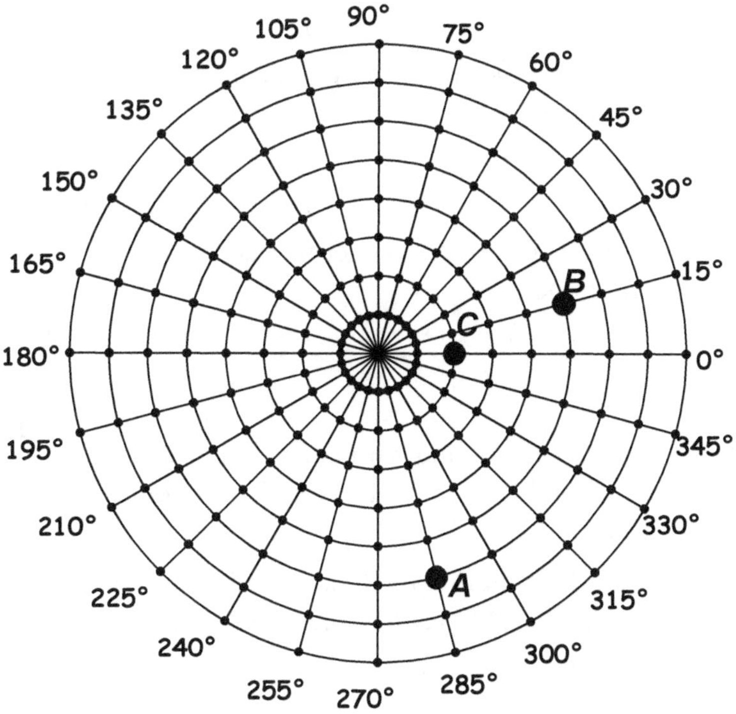

Solution

To find the polar coordinates of B, count out 5 units from the origin to point B. It is on the 15° ray, so the polar coordinates are (5, 15°). To find the polar coordinates of C, count out 2 units from the origin to point C. It is on the 0° ray, so the polar coordinates are (2, 0°).

Exercises in the Polar Coordinate System

Locate the following points on the polar coordinate grid shown to the right.

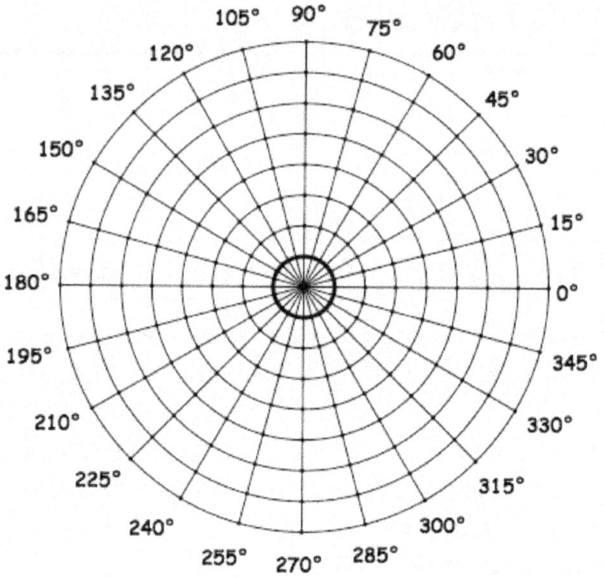

1. Point D is (5, 90°)
2. Point E is (2, 150°)
3. Point F is (7, 270°)
4. Point G is (0, 330°)
5. Point H is (8, 180°)

In the next section you are going to play Polar Buried Treasure. You will locate buried treasure on a polar coordinate grid the same way you did on a rectangular grid. The treasure looks different in Polar Buried Treasure because the grid is made of concentric circles instead of squares.

The Polar Buried Treasure grid on the right shows four different pentomino buried treasures. Notice the apparent size of a "treasure" depends on its distance from the origin. The points (3, 90°), (4, 90°), (3, 165°), and (4, 165°) are four of the 12 points that would locate or "dig up" the I-pentomino treasure.

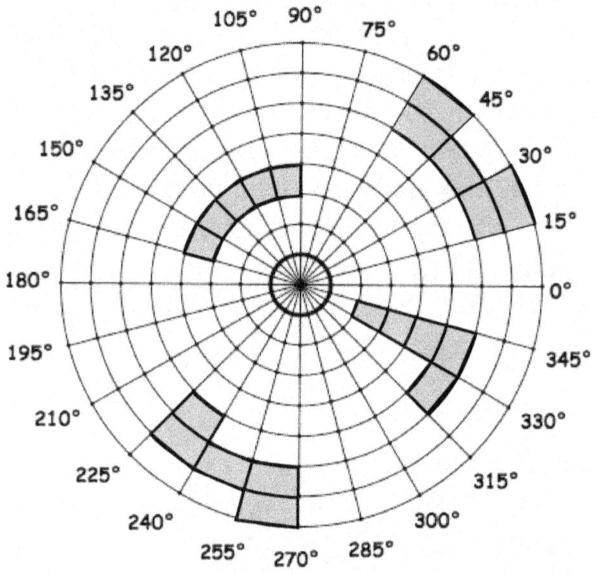

6. Name five of the eight corner points on the U-pentomino.

   (,), (,), (,),
   (,), (,)

7. Name five of the six corner points on the L-pentomino.

   (,), (,), (,),
   (,), (,)

8. Name five of the eight corner points on the Z-pentomino.

   (,), (,), (,),
   (,), (,)

9. Sketch a T-pentomino with indented corners at (5, 180°) and (5, 165°) and a regular corner at (6, 150°).

10. Sketch a U-pentomino with indented corners at (5, 75°) and (5, 90°) and regular corners at (6, 105°) and (6, 60°).

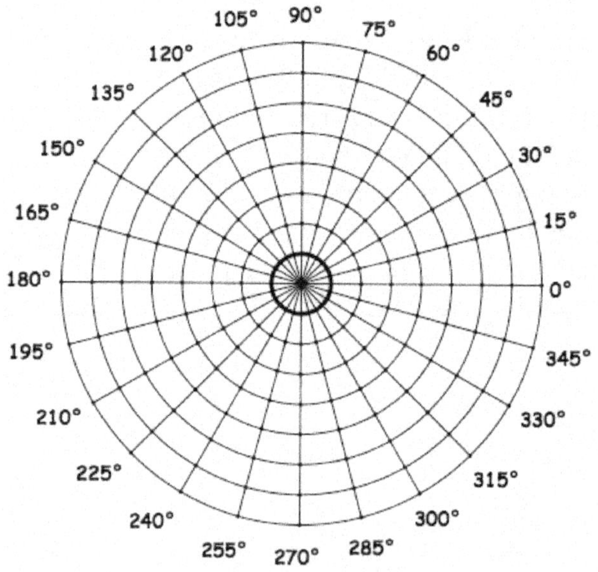

3.2 Polar Buried Treasure

Level 1A In this first Polar Buried Treasure game both teams are trying to be the first to locate the other team's buried treasure. The game begins with both teams hiding the same shape treasure (the *I*-pentomino) on their polar grids. It can look different depending on its location, as shown to the right. However, it will always have twelve points that can be *hit*. Determine which team plays first by flipping a coin or rolling a die.

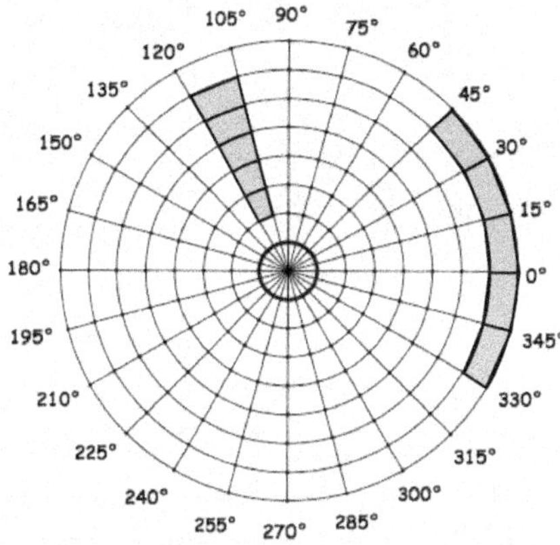

Our Team's Buried Treasure
This is where you hide your treasure and record where the other team digs for it.

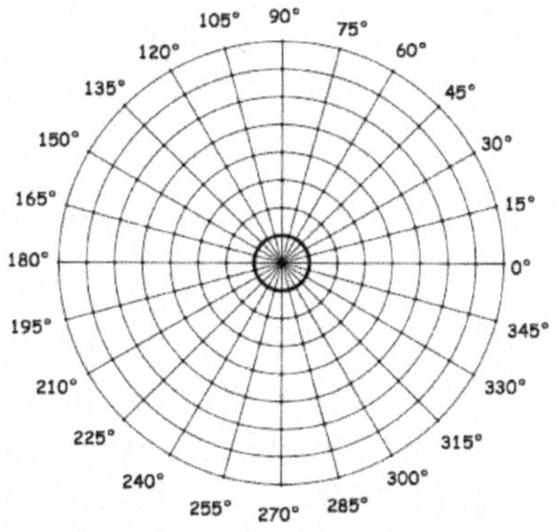

Other Team's Buried Treasure
This is where the other team hides their treasure and record where your team digs for it.

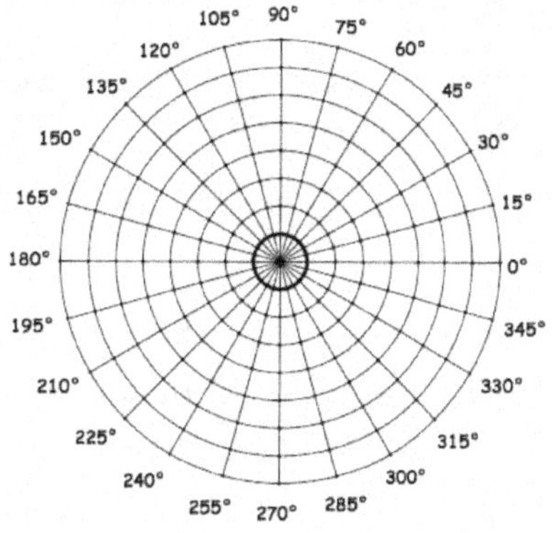

Rules for Level 1A:

1. The first team to "dig for treasure" calls out three sets of ordered pairs, or *digs*. Teammates record all ordered pairs on the dig table and record the digs on the grid labeled **Other Team's Buried Treasure.**
2. The second team responds after each guess whether the ordered pair is a hit or a miss. If it is a hit, they tell the first team whether it is one of the corners or an edge of the *I*-pentomino.
3. Then it is the second team's turn to take three digs. Continue taking turns with three digs at a time.
4. When one team has located at least two of the four corners of the pentomino with their digs then that team may guess the location of the treasure. Guessing the location of the treasure must happen when it is your turn but before you have taken your three digs. To guess, sketch on your grid where you think the *I*-pentomino is hidden and show it to the other team. If a team guesses correctly, they win and the game is over. If a team guesses incorrectly, they lose and the game is over. If the team that has located two corners is not ready to guess where the treasure is located, the game continues.

3.3 Variations on Polar Buried Treasure

Level 1B In this variation, each team selects *any* one of the 12 pentominoes and hides it on their game sheet labeled **Our Team's Buried Treasure**. Since teams do not know the pentomino shape chosen by the other team, the task will be more challenging than in Level 1A. We will also not use the origin (no values of zero for the first number in the ordered pair). Determine which team plays first by flipping a coin or rolling a die.

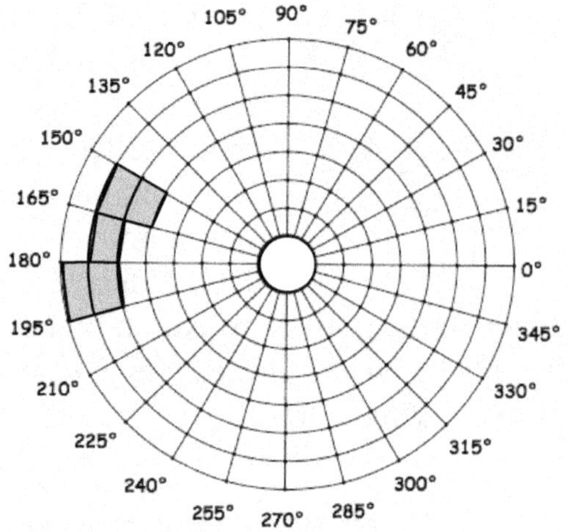

Rules for level 1B:

1. The first team to "dig for treasure" calls out three sets of ordered pairs, or *digs*. Teammates record all ordered pairs on the dig table and record the digs on the grid labeled **Other Team's Buried Treasure**.
2. The second team responds after each guess whether the ordered pair is a hit or a miss. If it is a hit, they tell the first team whether it is one of the corners or an edge of the pentomino.
3. Then it is the second team's turn to take three digs. Continue taking turns with three digs at a time.
4. When one team has located at least three of the corners of the pentomino with their digs then that team may take a guess at the location of the remaining corners. Guessing the location of the treasure must happen when it is your turn but before you have taken your three digs. Shade in the other team's pentomino shape on the grid labeled **Other Team's Buried Treasure**. Show it to the other team. If correct, you win. However, if you guess incorrectly, you lose. If the team that has located three corners does not wish to guess yet the game continues until one team is ready to take a guess on the treasure location.

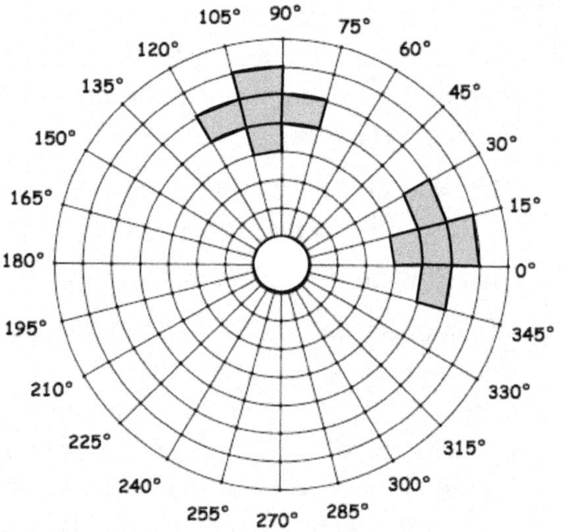

Level 1C

- Each team hides two identical pentominoes.

Level 1D

- Each team hides two different pentominoes.

For Levels 1E through 1H, each team hides two different polyominoes (hexominoes or smaller).

Level 1E

- Each team takes five digs but no information is given about hits or misses until after all five ordered pairs are given.

Level 1F

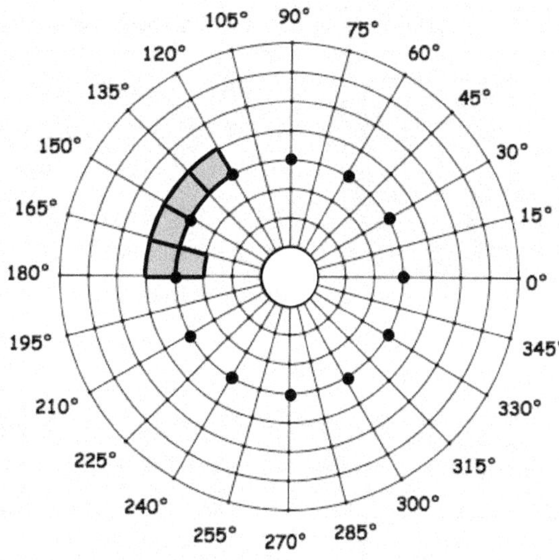

- Each team takes five digs but no information is given about hits or misses until after all five ordered pairs are given. Or, three times during the game:
- Each team selects a radius (for example $r = 4$) and chooses all the angles that are a multiple of 30° for twelve digs. No information is given about hits or misses until after all 12 ordered pairs are given.

  Team A: "(4,0°), (4,30°), (4,60°), (4,90°), (4,120°), (4,150°), (4,180°), (4,210°), (4,240°), (4,270°), (4,300°), (4,330°)"

  Team B: "You hit my pentomino three times. You hit two edges and one corner."

Level 1G

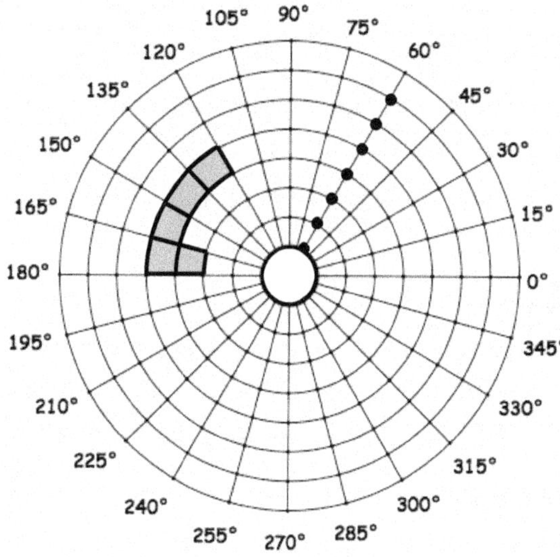

- Each team takes five digs but no information is given about hits or misses until after all five ordered pairs are given. Or, three times during the game:
- Each team selects an angle (for example $\theta = 60°$) and chooses all seven radii for the seven digs. No information is given about hits or misses until after all seven ordered pairs are given.

  Team A: "(1,60°), (2,60°), (3,60°), (4,60°), (5,60°), (6,60°), (7,60°)"

  Team B: "You missed."

Level 1H

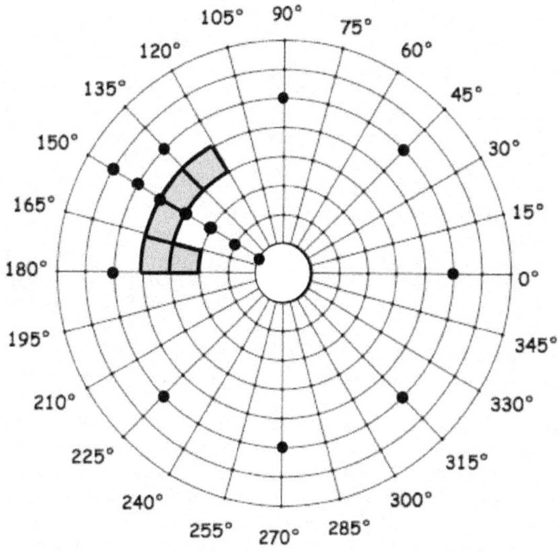

- Each team selects an angle (for example $\theta = 150°$) and chooses all seven radii for the seven digs. No information is given about hits or misses until after all seven ordered pairs are given. Or,
- Each team selects a radius (for example $r = 6$) and chooses all the angles that are multiples of 45° (eight digs). No information is given about hits or misses until after all eight ordered pairs are given.

3.4 Polar Buried Treasure Using Negative Angles

Angles greater than 360° can occur with polar coordinates. A rotation of 360° is one complete turn. An angle of rotation of 420° is the same as a complete rotation of 360° and an additional 60°. Thus an angle of rotation measuring 420° is the same as an angle of rotation measuring 60°.

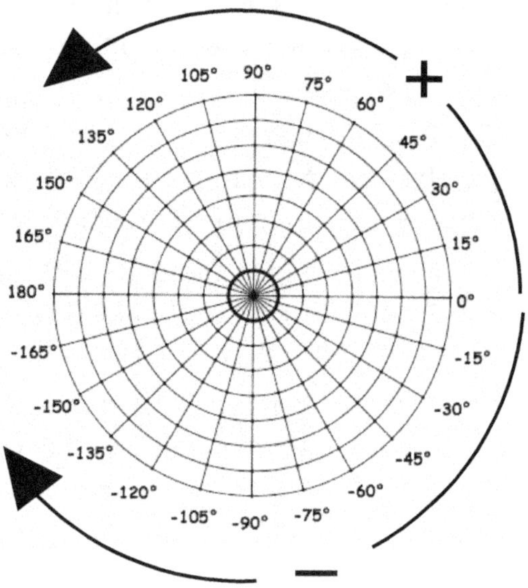

An angle of rotation can be negative. When the rotation is counterclockwise, the angle of rotation is a positive number of degrees. When rotated clockwise, however, the angle of rotation is a negative measure.

Notice that the location (3, 270°) is the same as (3, -90°) and (7, -135°) is the same as (7, 225°).

For Exercise 1, locate the following points on the polar coordinate grid above right.

1. A(2, -30°), B(4, -120°), C(7, 735°), and D(8, -300°)

Level 2A This variation uses the same rules as Polar Buried Treasure Level 1A (hiding one of the twelve pentominoes) and same size Polar Buried Treasure playing field, except you may use positive and negative angles.

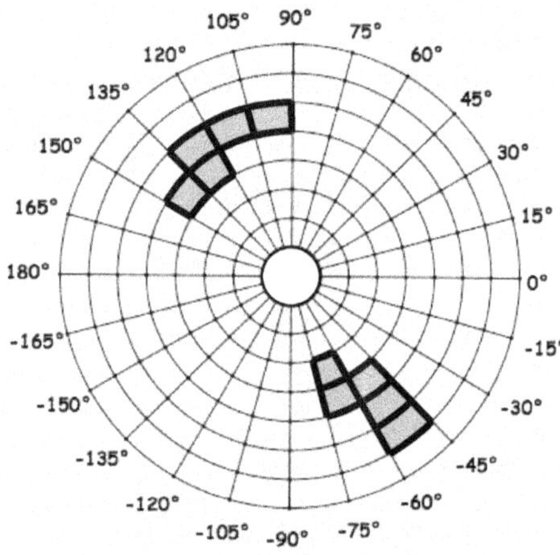

Level 2B

- You are hiding two identical pentominoes.

Level 2C

- You are hiding two different pentominoes.

Level 2D

- You are hiding two different polyominoes (from domino to hexomino).

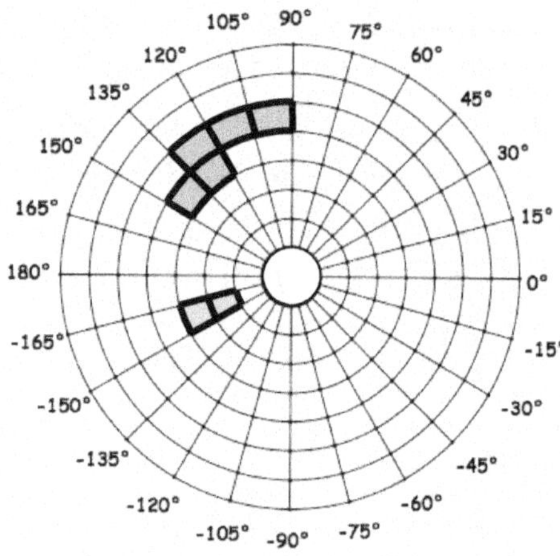

3.5 Polar Buried Treasure with Equations

Equations in polar form can be quite beautiful, as shown below.

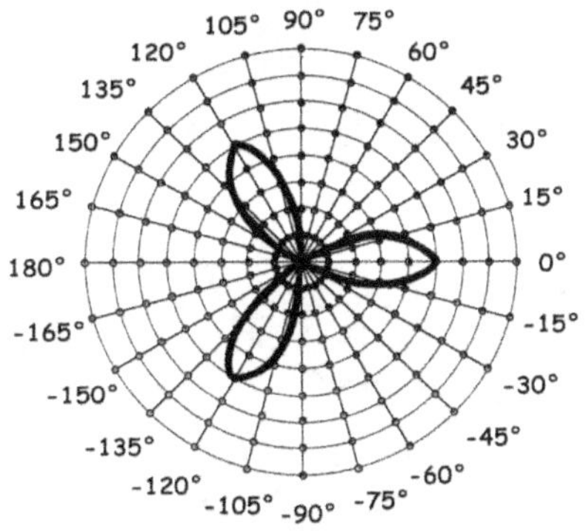

3-Petal Rose
$r = 5\cos(3\theta)$

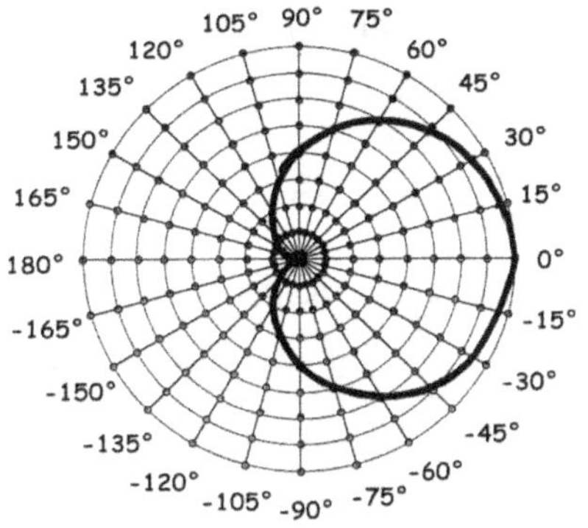

Cardioid
$r = 4 + 4\cos\theta$

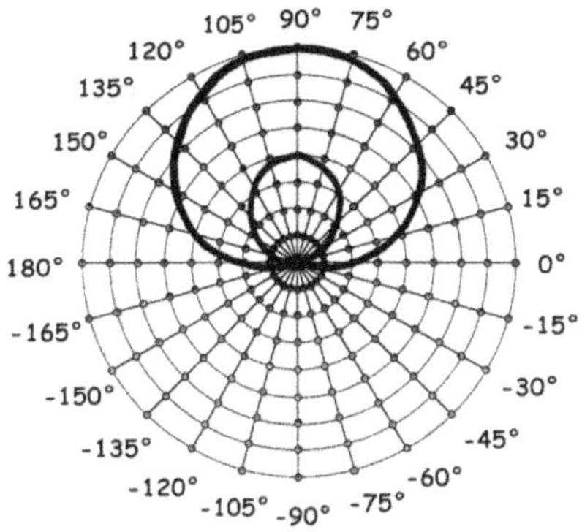

Limaçon
$r = 2 + 6\sin 3\theta$

When you graph a simpler polar equation such as $r = 5$ on a polar grid, you get a circle with a radius of 5. (The equation says: the angle can be anything but the radius is always 5.) When you graph a simpler equation such as $\theta = 60°$, you get a line through the origin at a 60° angle from the horizontal. (The equation says: the radius can be anything but the angle is always 60°.) See the table of values and the graphs below.

r	5	5	5	5	5	5	5	5	5
θ	15°	30°	45°	60°	75°	90°	105°	120°	135°

r	-5	-4	-3	-2	-1	0	1	2	3	4	5
θ	60°	60°	60°	60°	60°	60°	60°	60°	60°	60°	60°

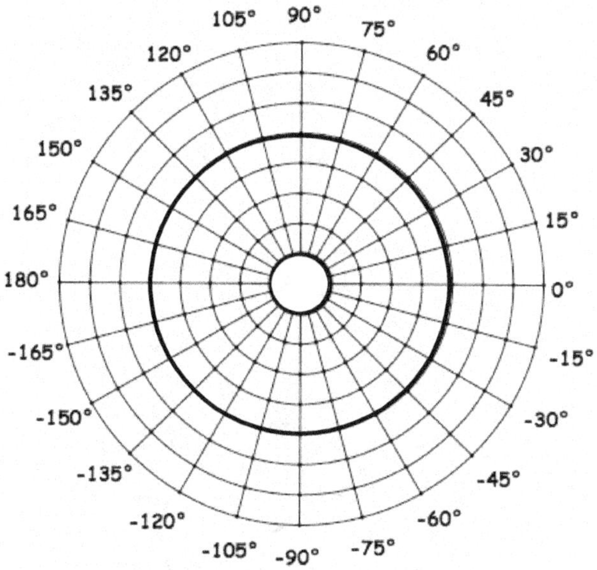

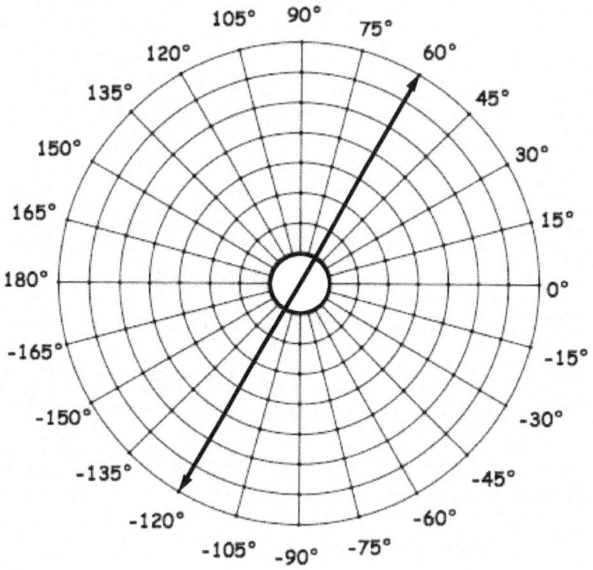

Level 3A In this level you are going to use just circles ($r = a$) and lines ($\theta = b°$) to search for your opponent's buried treasure. You will hide any one of the 12 pentominoes and you have two options for digs.

- You may take three individual digs, or
- You may call out a polar equation (either a circle, $r = a$, or a line, $\theta = b$). For example,

  Team A: "$r = 5$"

  Team B: "You missed."

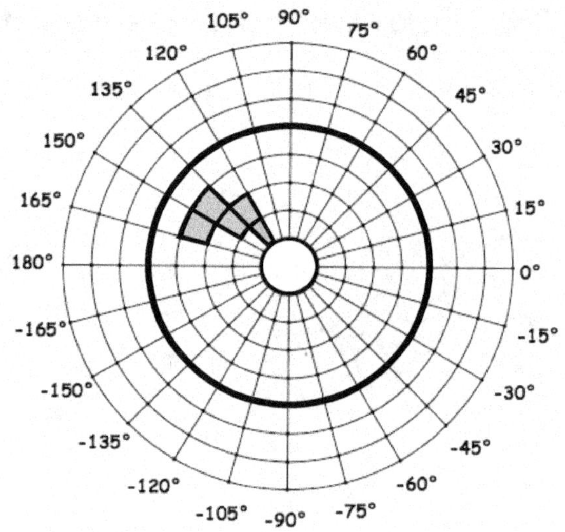

Level 3B In this level you will hide two identical pentominoes and you have two options for digs.

- You may take four individual digs, or
- You may call out either one polar equation of a circle, $r = a$, or one polar equation of a line, $\theta = b$. For example,

  Team A: "$\theta = 165°$"

  Team B: "You hit one treasure."

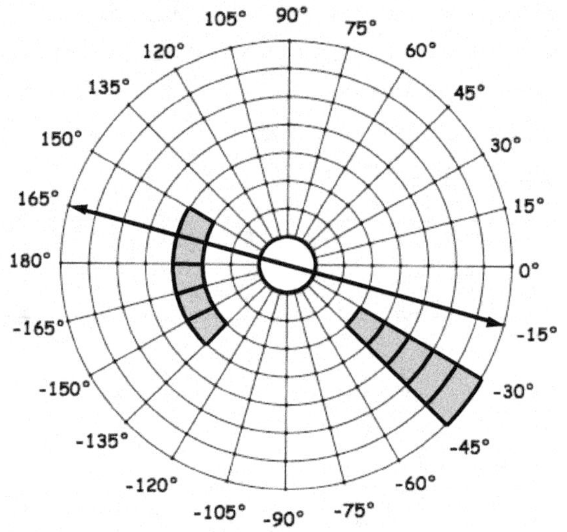

Level 3C In this level you will hide two different pentominoes and you have three options for digs.

- You may take five individual digs, or
- You may call out one polar equation of a circle, $r = a$, and one polar equation of a line, $\theta = b$. Or,
- You may call out three polar equations of lines, $\theta = b$. For example,

  Team A: "$r = 4$" "$\theta = 150°$"

  Team B: "You hit two different treasures."

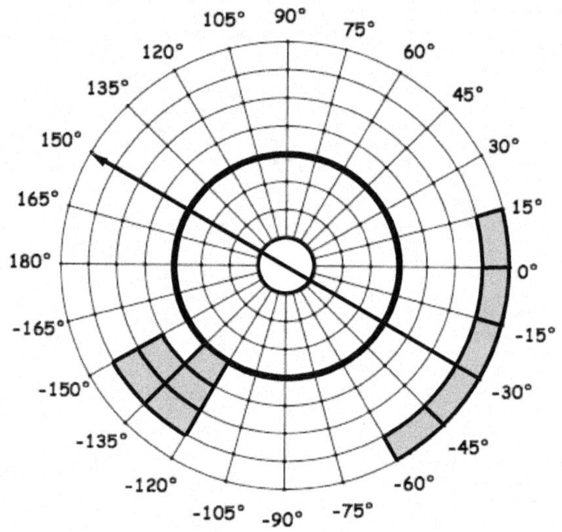

3.6 Polar Buried Treasure Puzzles

In this first set of polar buried treasure puzzles one pentomino has been hidden in the polar grid. Some points in the grid have been identified as a corner, an edge, or an interior point of the pentomino. Other points are identified as misses. Use the clues: corner (*C*), edge (*E*), interior (*I*), and miss (*X*) to determine the locations of the hidden pentominoes. Because of the tight space around the origin there are no pentomino treasures touching the origin (0, 0). Some puzzles may have more than one solution.

PBTP 1

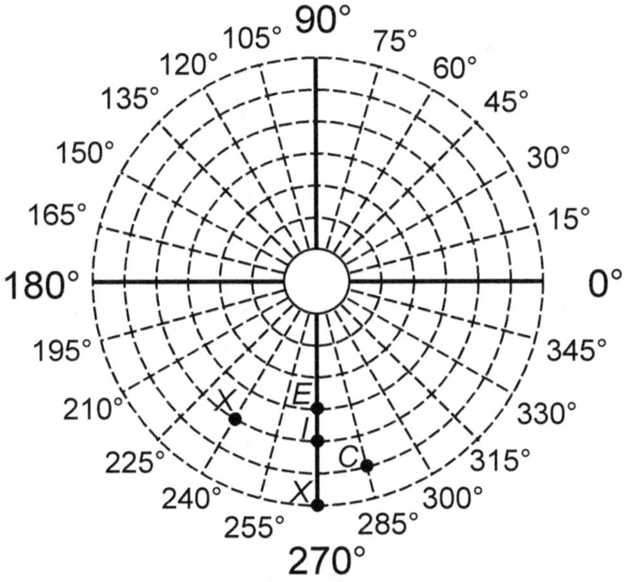

PBTP 2

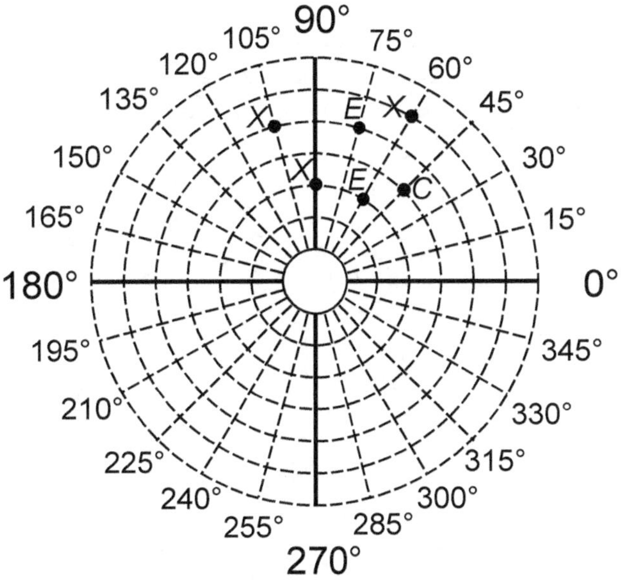

PBTP 3

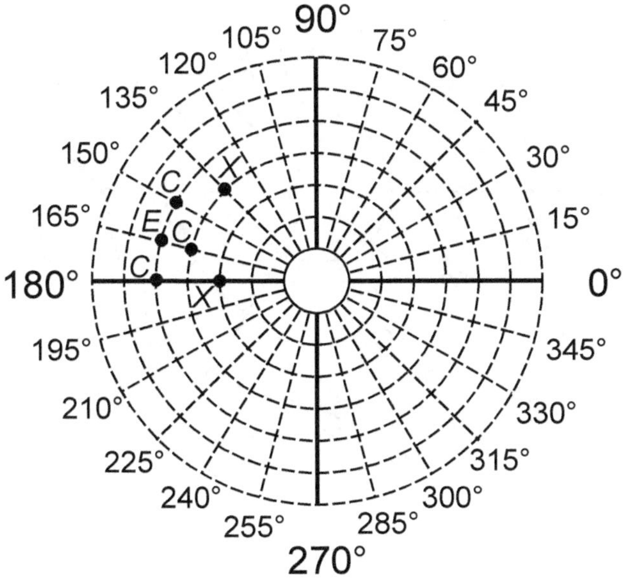

PBTP 4

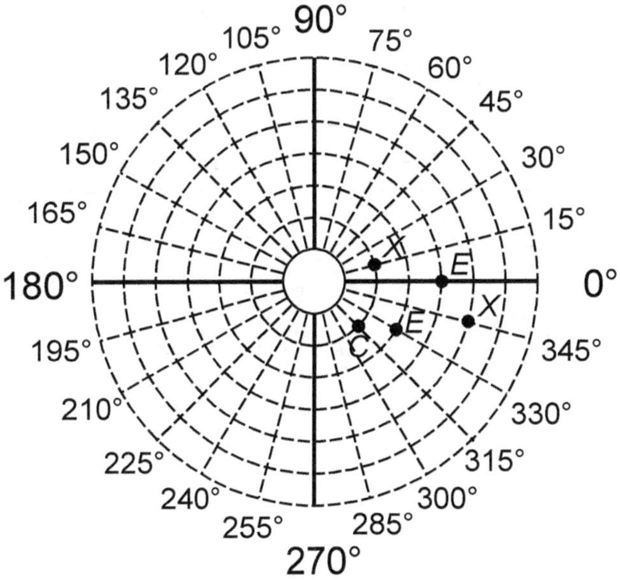

Chapter 3.6

In this second set of polar buried treasure puzzles all five tetrominoes have been hidden in the polar grid. No two tetrominoes share an edge or a corner. Some points in the grid have been identified as a corner, an edge, or an interior point of the tetromino. Other points are identified as misses. Use the clues: corner (*C*), edge (*E*), interior (*I*), and miss (*X*) to determine the locations of the hidden tetrominoes. Because of the tight space around the origin there are no tetromino treasures touching the origin.

PBTP 5 *h*

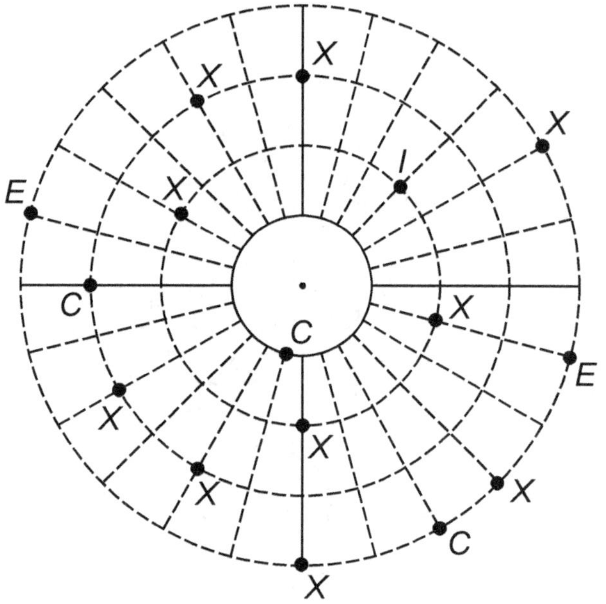

PBTP 6

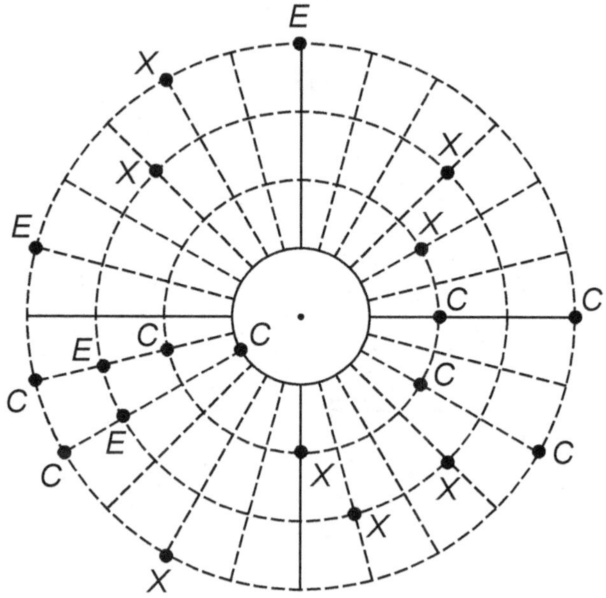

PBTP 7 *h*

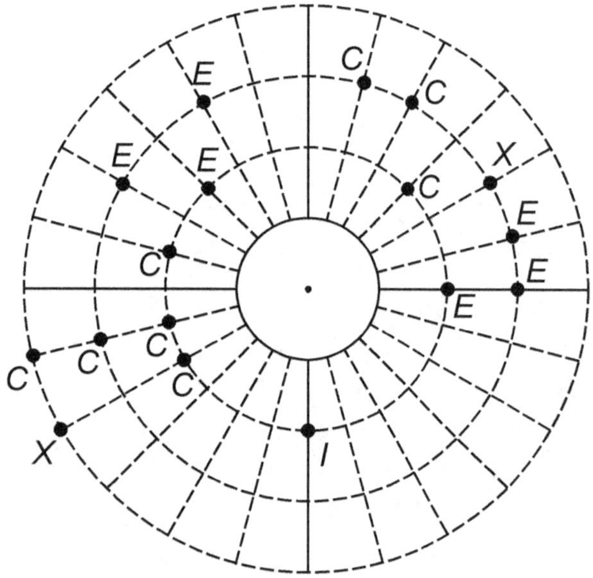

PBTP 8

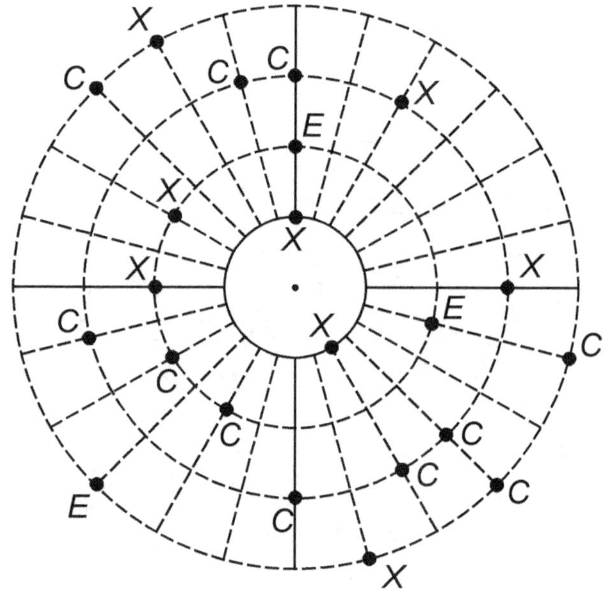

In this next set of polar buried treasure puzzles your task is to locate all five tetrominoes in the 5×10 circular grid. Some tetrominoes are given. Sketch in the remaining tetrominoes so that no two are touching, even at the corners.

PBTP 9 *h*

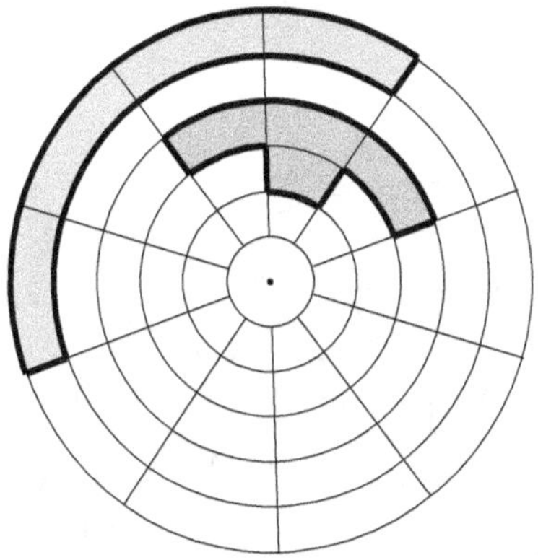

PBTP 10

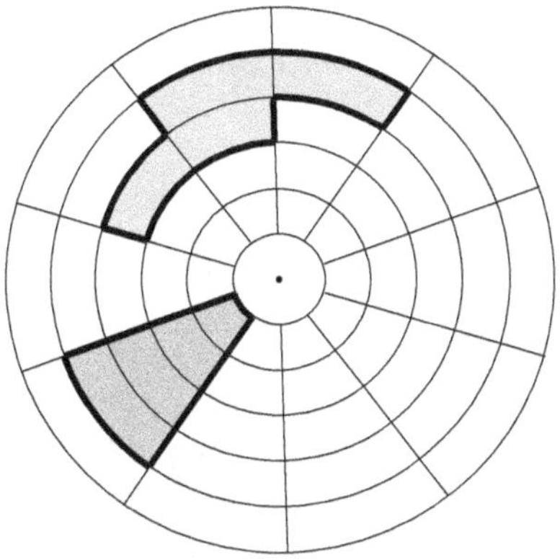

PBTP 11

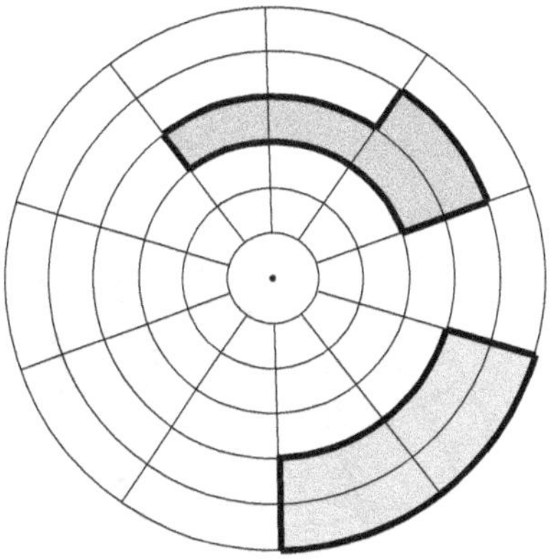

In this next set of polar buried treasure puzzles your task is to locate all 12 pentominoes in the 7×24 circular grid. Sketch in the remaining pentominoes so that no two are touching, even at the corners. Eight pentominoes are given in Puzzle 12 but only three pentominoes are given in Puzzle 13.

PBTP 12 *h*

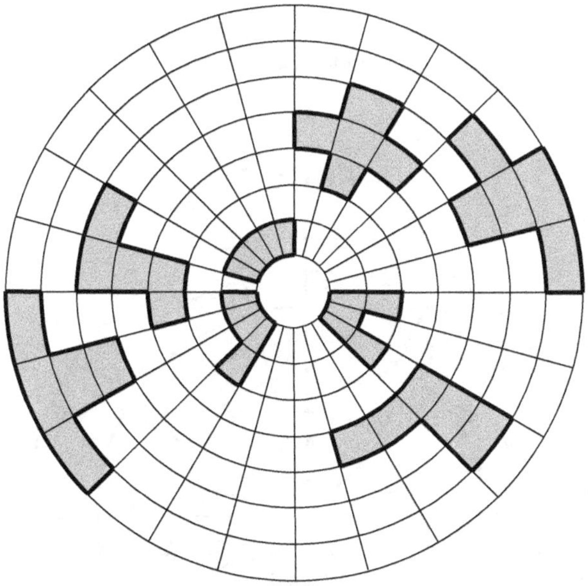

TUVWXYZFLIPN

PBTP 13

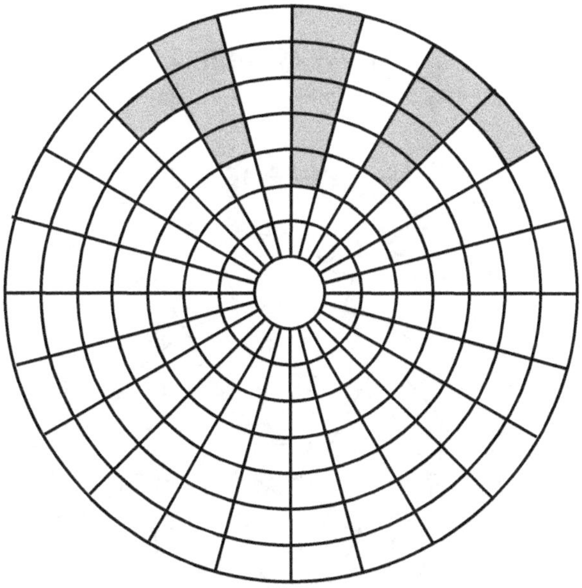

TUVWXYZFLIPN

Chapter 3.6

In this set of polar buried treasure puzzles your task is to locate all 12 pentominoes in the 7×24 circular grid with no two pentominoes touching, even at the corners. The 12 pentomino shapes are identified by the letters *T, U, V, W, X, Y, Z, F, L, I, P,* and *N*. These letters, representing the 12 shapes, are given as clues. If the letter *T*, for example, is in a region then the *T*-pentomino covers that region. Use logical reasoning to determine the location of all the pentominoes.

PBTP 14

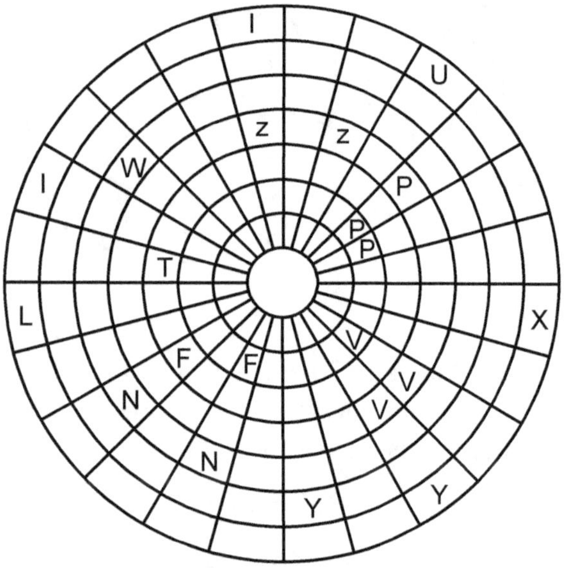

TUVWXYZFLIPN

PBTP 15

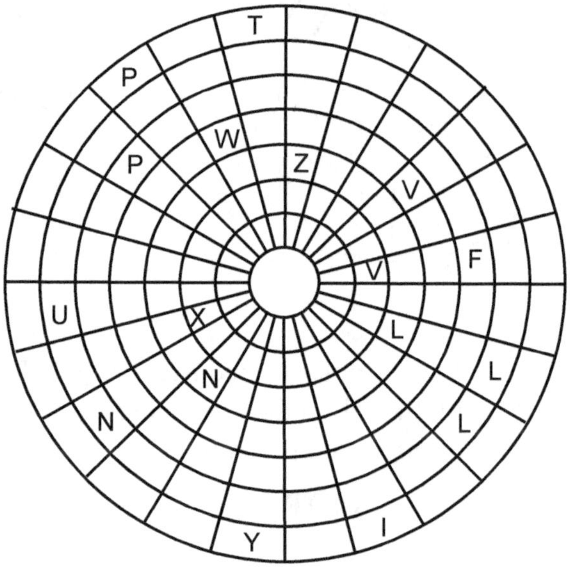

TUVWXYZFLIPN

PBTP 16

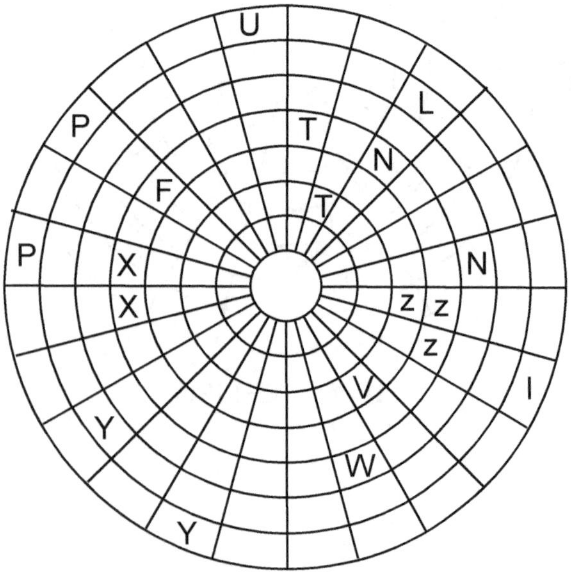

TUVWXYZFLIPN

PBTP 17

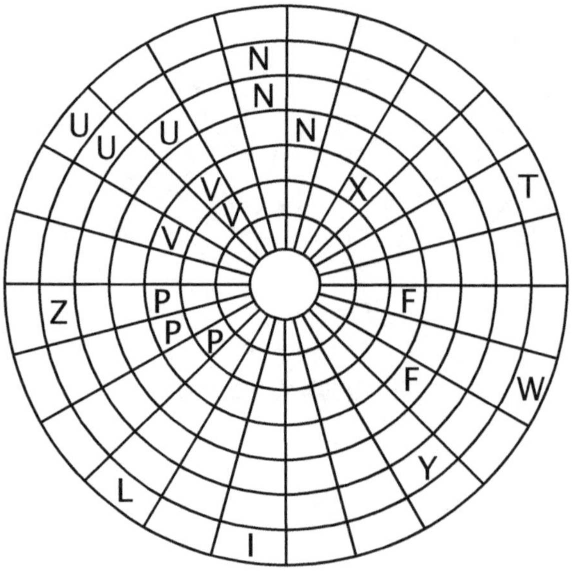

TUVWXYZFLIPN

In Chapter 1 you saw how all 12 pentominoes can be arranged into a 5×12 rectangle. One is shown below left. If you wrap the left vertical edge of the 5×12 rectangle around to meet the right vertical edge you get the 12 pentominoes filling a polar grid as shown to the right.

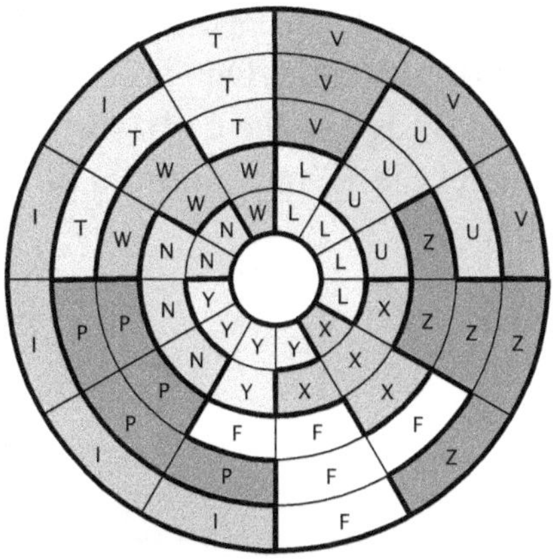

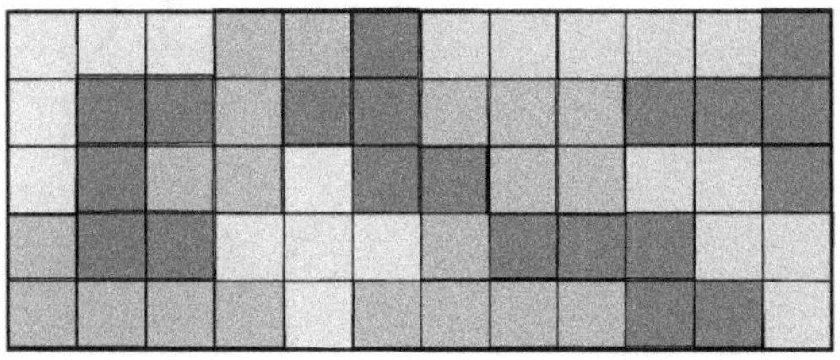

In this set of polar buried treasure puzzles, all 12 pentominoes have been hidden in the 5×12 polar grid. As in the example above, there are no gaps. The 12 pentomino shapes are identified by the letters *T*, *U*, *V*, *W*, *X*, *Y*, *Z*, *F*, *L*, *I*, *P*, and *N*. These letters, representing the 12 shapes, are given as clues. If the letter *T*, for example, is in a region then the *T*-pentomino covers that region. Use logical reasoning to determine the location of all the pentominoes.

PBTP 18

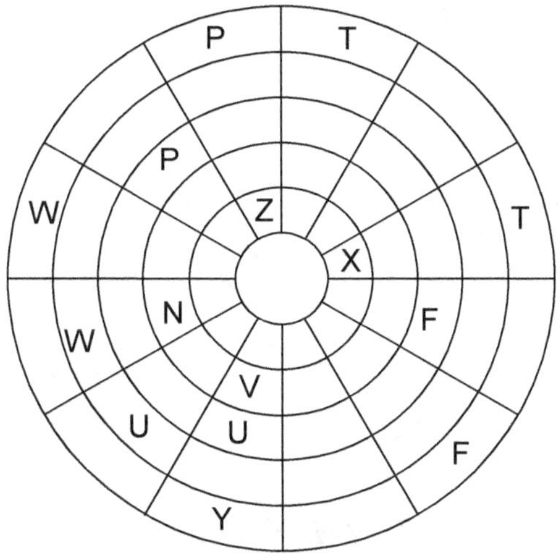

TUVWXYZFLIPN

PBTP 19

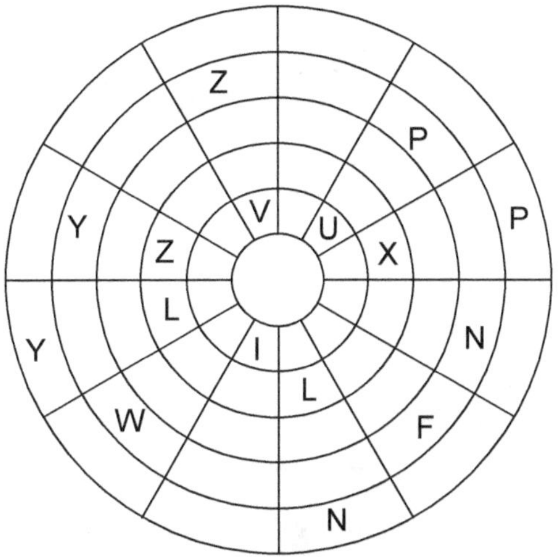

TUVWXYZFLIPN

PBTP 20

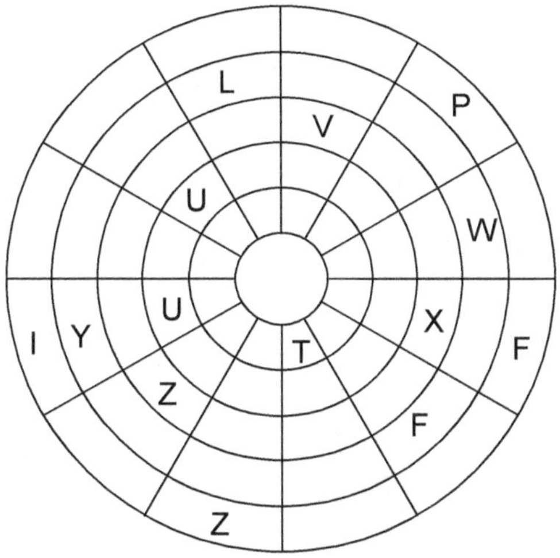

TUVWXYZFLIPN

PBTP 21

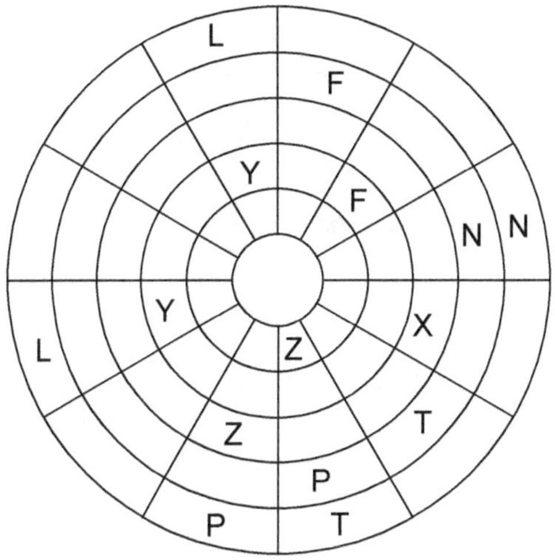

TUVWXYZFLIPN

Chapter 3.6

In Chapter 1 you saw that all 12 pentominoes can be arranged into a 6×10 rectangle. One is shown below left. If you wrap the left vertical edge of the 6×10 rectangle around to the right vertical edge you get the 12 pentominoes filling a polar grid as shown to the right.

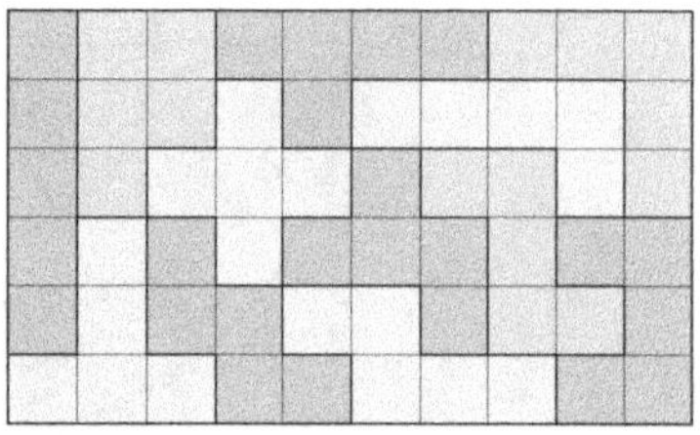

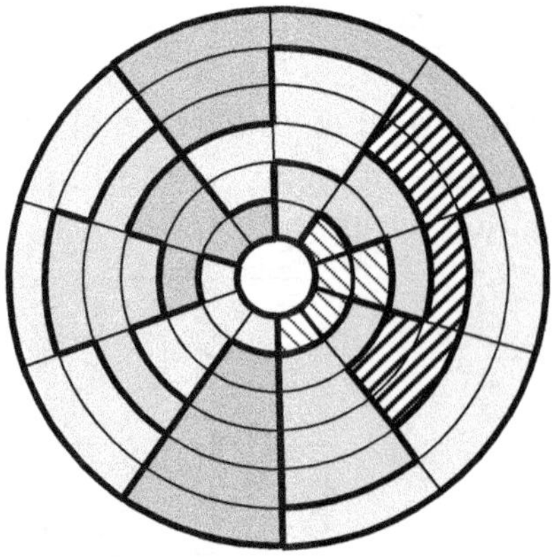

In this set of polar buried treasure puzzles, 6×10 rectangles of all 12 pentominoes have been transformed into polar grids. Use logical reasoning to determine the location of all the pentominoes in each polar grid.

PBTP 22

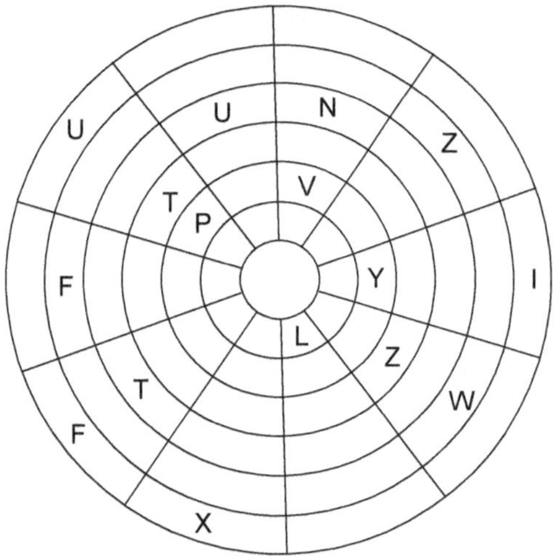

TUVWXYZFLIPN

PBTP 23

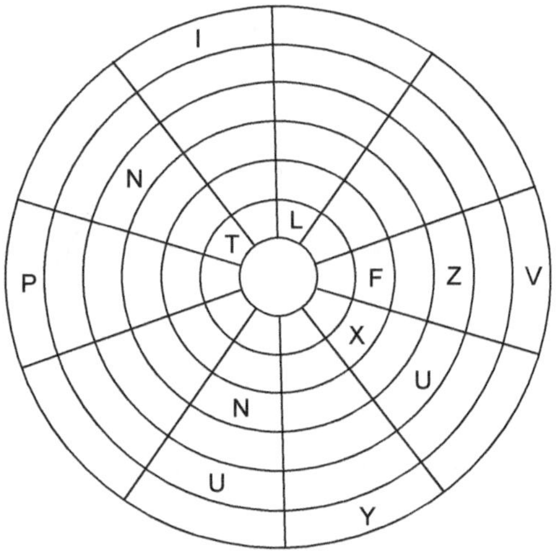

TUVWXYZFLIPN

PBTP 24

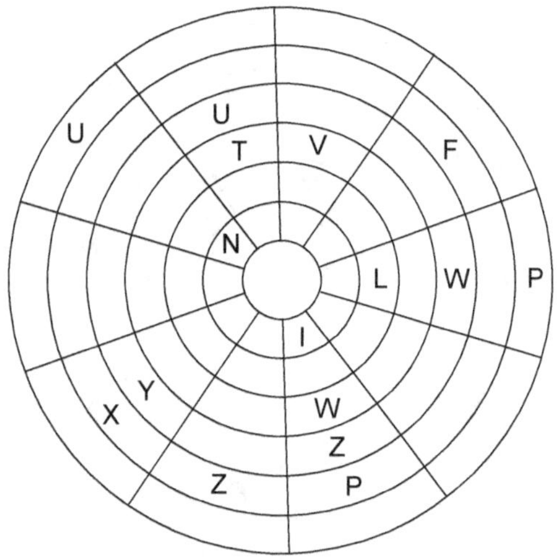

TUVWXYZFLIPN

PBTP 25

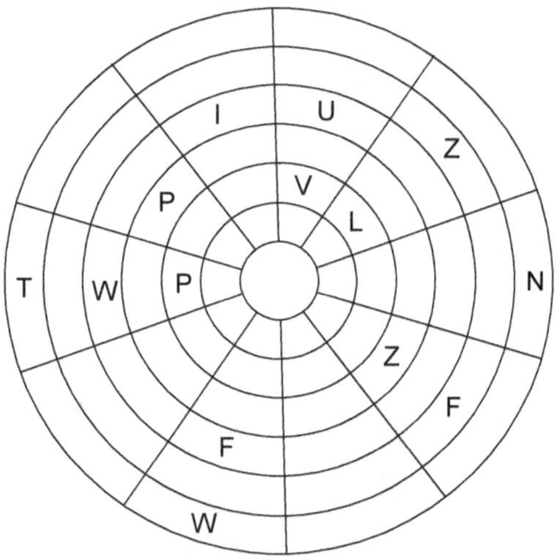

TUVWXYZFLIPN

3.7 Pirate Treasure with Polar Coordinates

In this section, you will be using your polar coordinate and geometry skills to locate pirate treasure on ten different tropical isles. You might want to review some properties of polar coordinates and geometry (Chapter 6) before you begin. Each island map has a polar grid overlay with the origin located at the gallows. The concentric circles are each ten paces apart. Your first task is to solve a mini-puzzle to locate the starting point. Next, use your polar coordinate skills to locate the buried treasure on the island (not in the sea).

1. Buried Treasure on Emerald Island

- The starting point of your treasure hunt is at the anagram of "rent o game."
- From your starting point send one pirate mate moving 45° clockwise staying the same distance from the Gallows. Drive a stake in the ground.
- From your starting point send a second mate 40 paces due south, then move 135° counterclockwise staying the same distance from the Gallows. Drive a stake in the ground.
- The treasure is buried midway between the two pirate mates.
- What are the coordinates of the treasure's location?

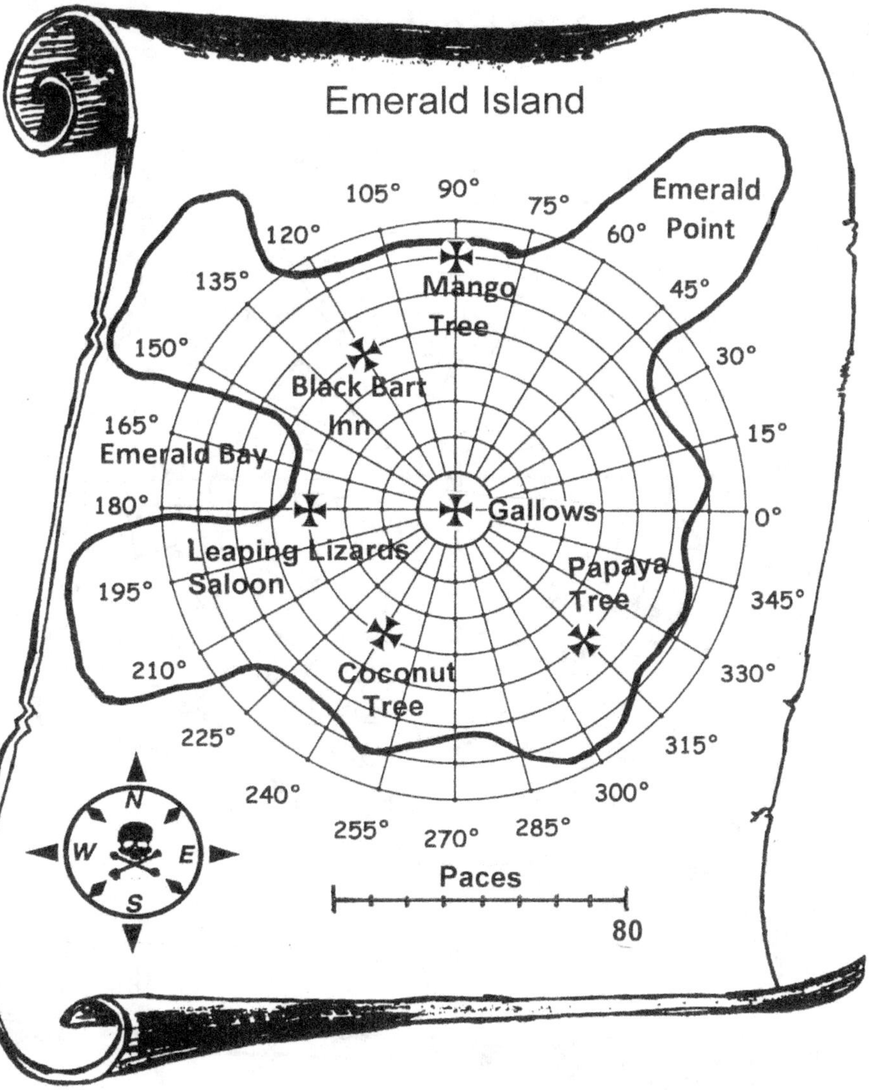

2. Buried Treasure on Rum Reef Key ħ

- The pentominoes shown below right can be arranged into the 6×10 rectangle so that the letters form six pirate terms. Two of the terms are *gangplank* and *man-o-war*. Three of the pentominoes have already been correctly placed. When all 12 are positioned correctly into the rectangle one of the pirate terms is the location of the treasure hunt starting point.
- Position your first mate at the starting point and your second mate at the Gallows. Instruct your first mate to walk 45° counterclockwise staying the same distance from the second mate. The treasure is buried 50 paces from the Gallows and collinear with the two mates but not between them.
- What are the coordinates of the treasure's location?

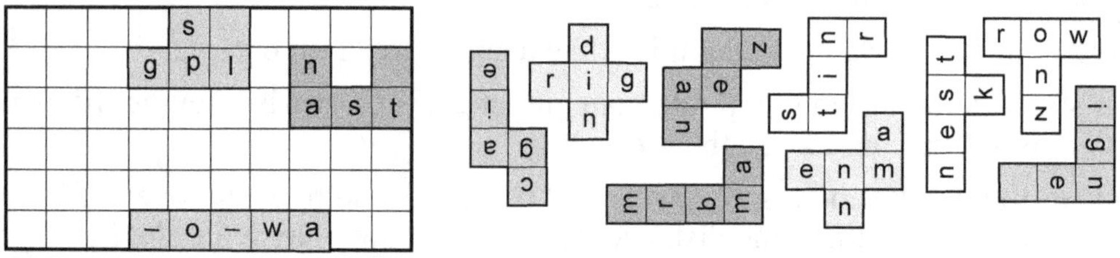

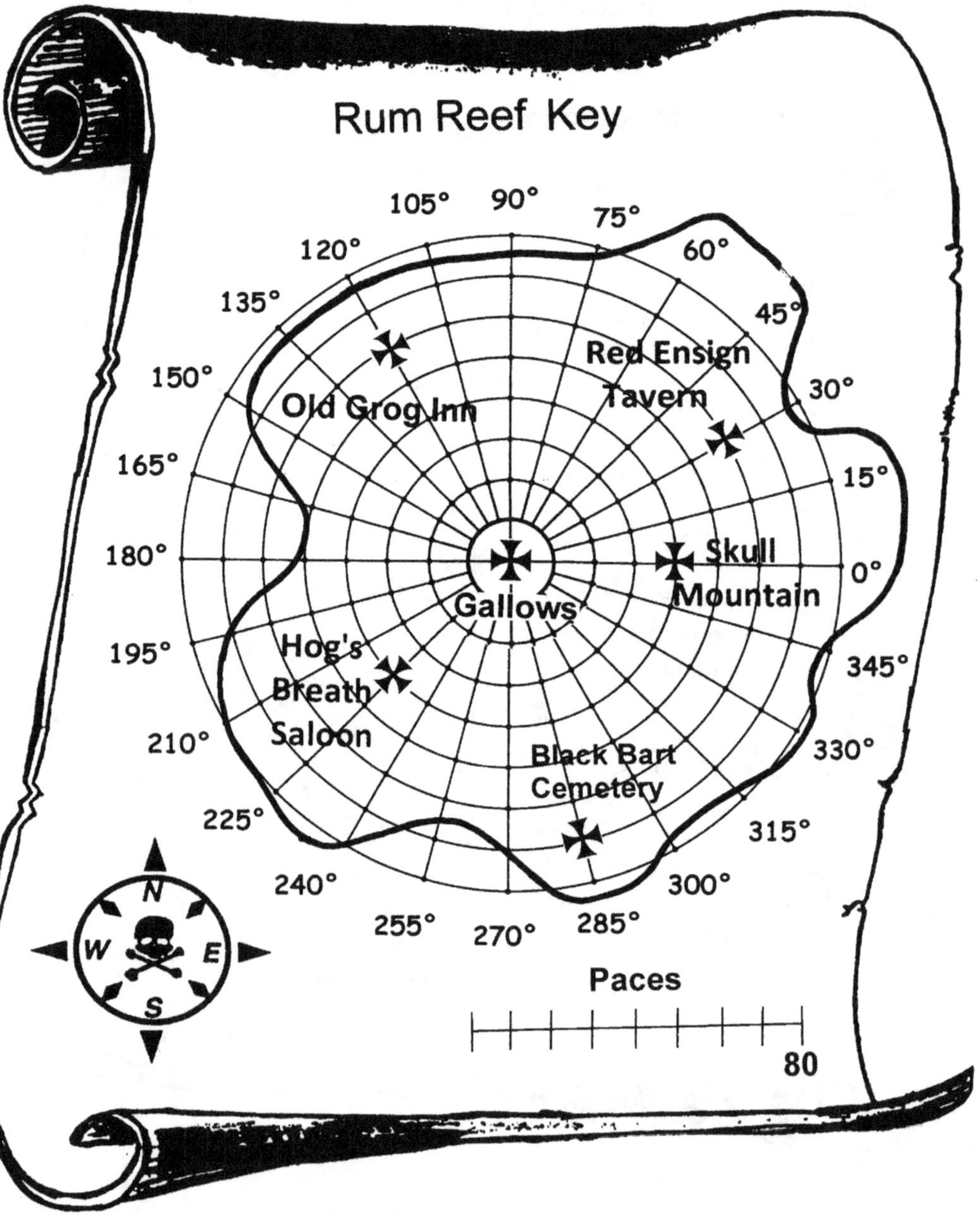

3. Buried Treasure on Scallywag Island *ℏ*

- The pentominoes shown below can be arranged into the 4×15 rectangle. Four of the pentominoes have already been correctly placed. When all 12 are positioned correctly into the rectangle the treasure hunt starting point will be revealed.
- From the starting point send your first mate in the direction of the Gallows, counting the number of paces. Continue past the Gallows pacing off the same number of steps. Next, turn right and walk for 45° keeping the same distance from the Gallows. Avast matey, ye treasure lie beneath!
- What are the coordinates of the treasure's location?

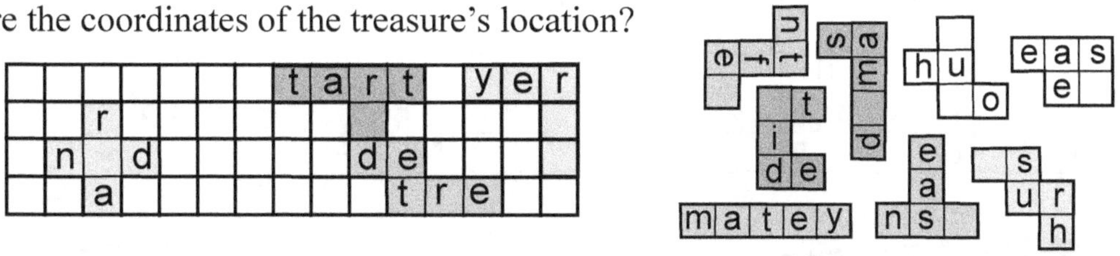

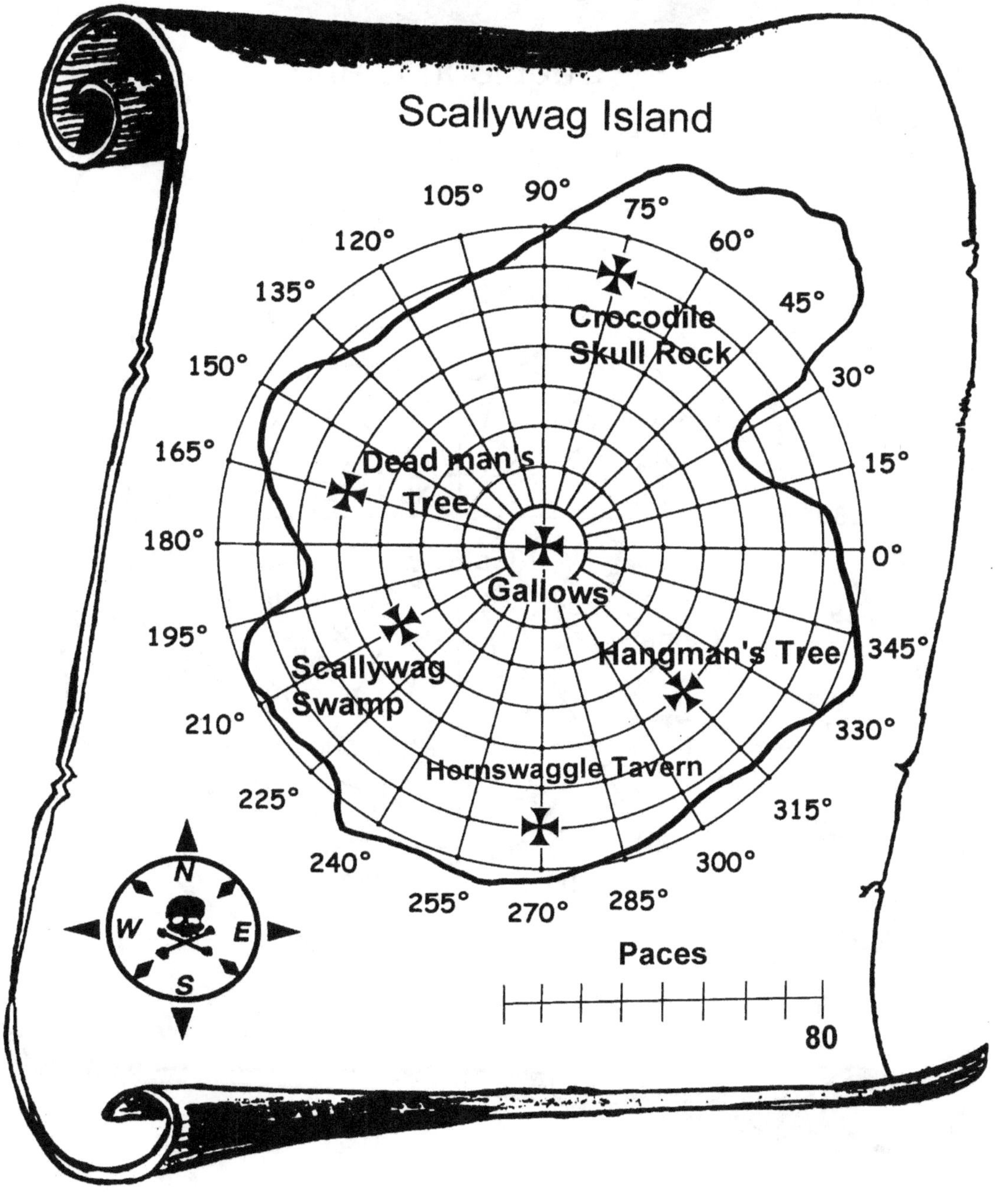

4. Buried Treasure on Doubloon Island *ℏ*

- The pentominoes shown below can be arranged into the 3×20 rectangle. Three of the pentominoes have already been correctly placed. When all 12 are positioned correctly into the rectangle the treasure hunt starting point will be revealed.
- Place your first mate at the starting point. Instruct your second mate to go to the Gallows. The treasure is buried 50 paces from the two mates.
- What are the coordinates of the treasure's location?

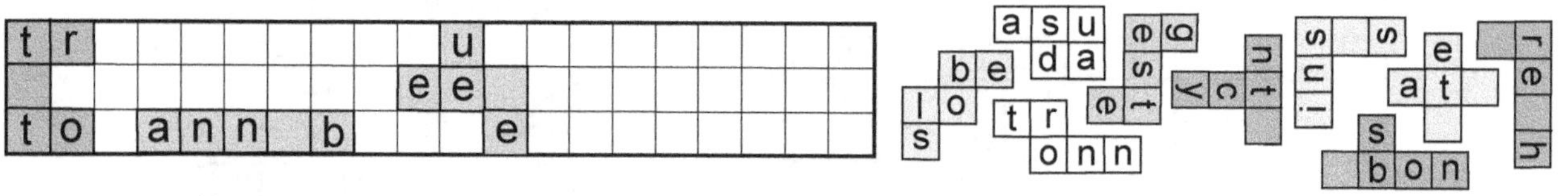

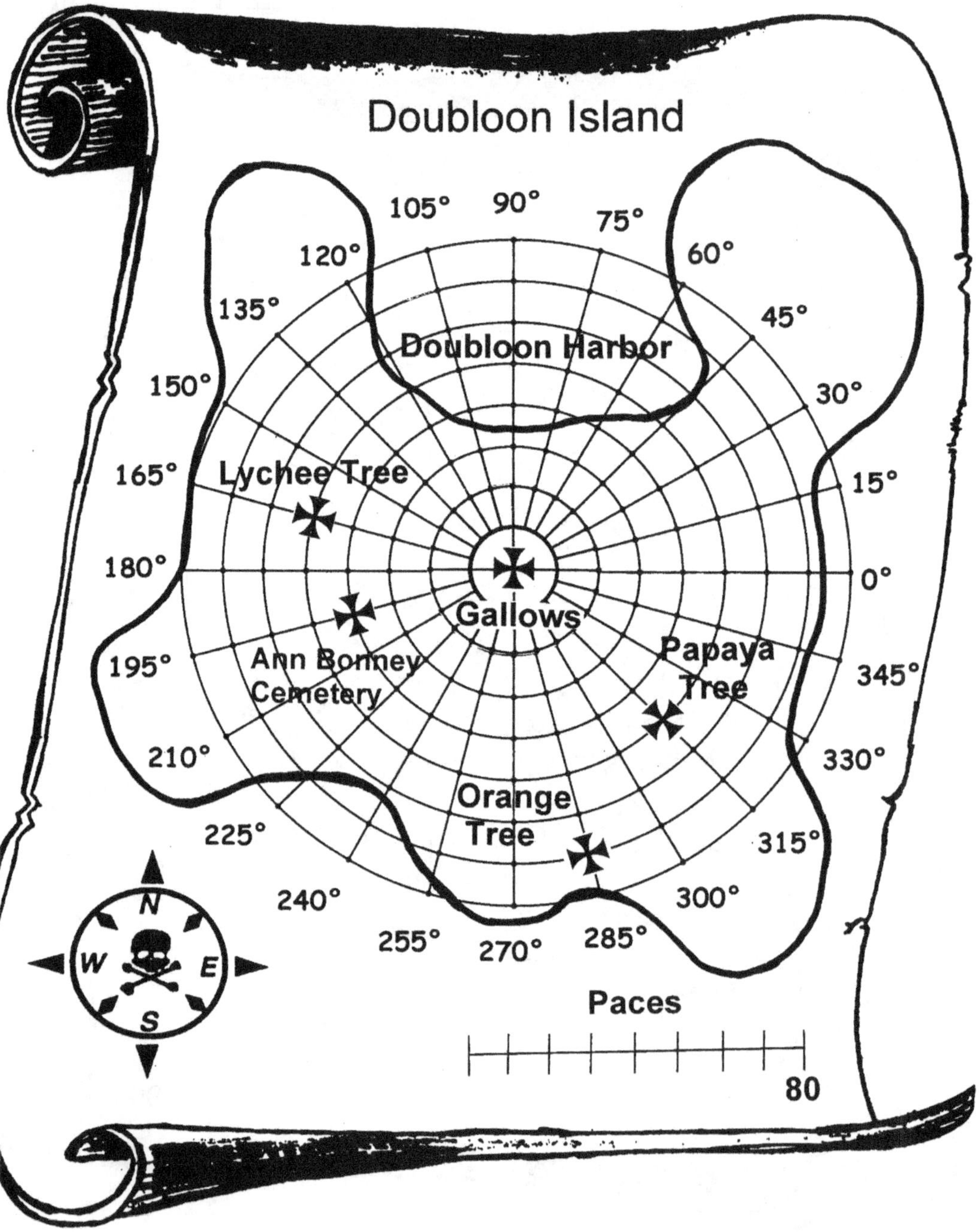

5. Buried Treasure on Shipwreck Island ℏ

- The starting point of your treasure hunt is hidden in a pattern in the 5×5 grid to the right. It may be read horizontally, vertically, or diagonally.
- From the starting point send one pirate mate moving 90° clockwise staying the same distance from the Gallows. Drive a stake in the ground and label the point *P*.
- From the starting point send a second mate 20 paces in the direction of the Gallows. Then move 90° counterclockwise staying the same distance from the Gallows. Drive a stake in the ground and label the point *Q*.
- The treasure is buried at a point *T* such that *P*, *T*, and *Q* are collinear and $PT/TQ = 1/2$.
- What are the coordinates of the treasure's location?

D	A	I	A	U
R	P	N	T	I
Y	S	C	N	F
H	H	G	L	H
M	D	Y	E	T

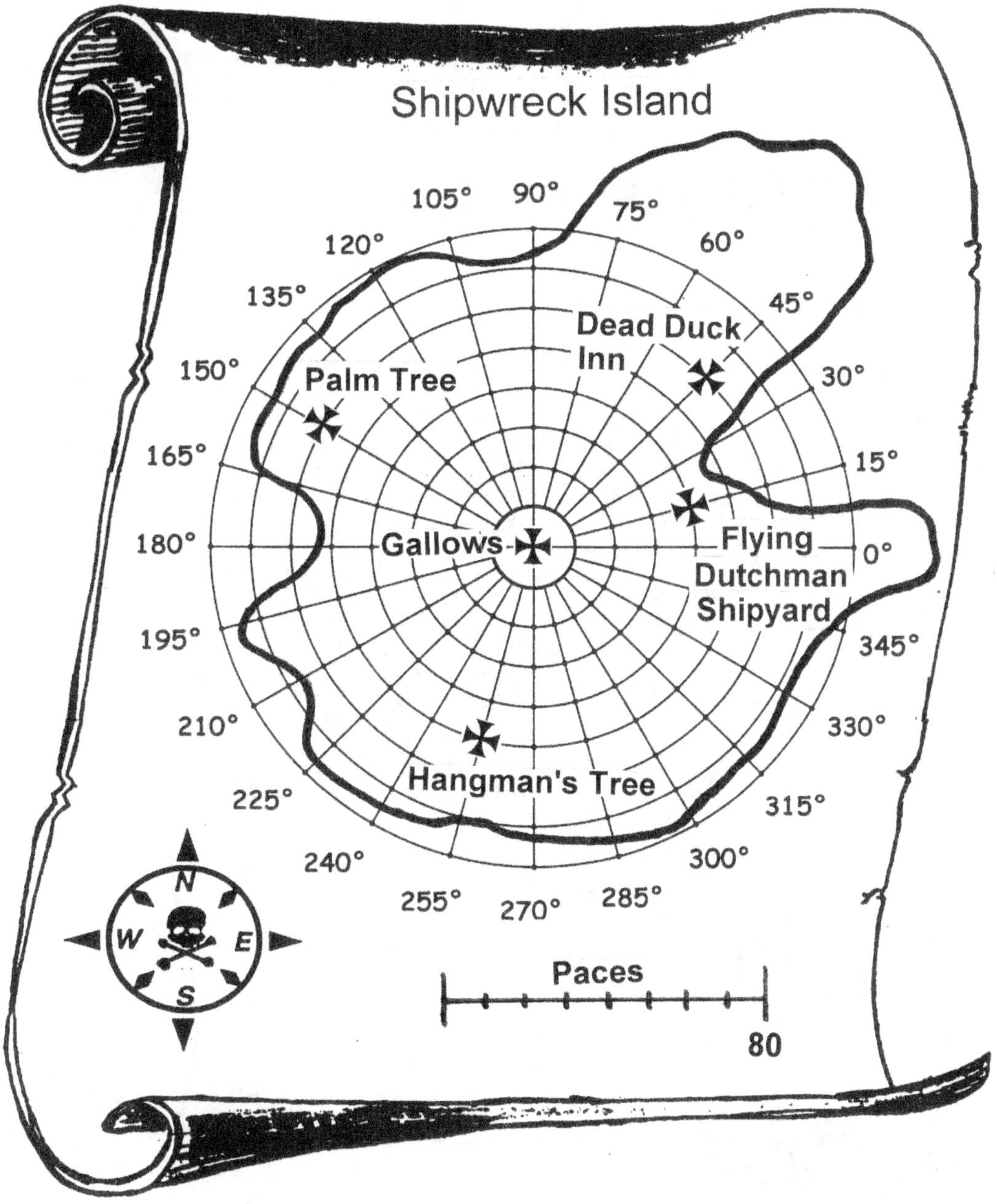

6. Buried Treasure on Albatross Island

- For each pair of words below there is another word that can be added to form familiar pirate words or phrases with each of the two given words.

  Example: CROWS ____ ____ ____ ____ EGG

  The word that can be placed after "CROWS" and before "EGG" is "NEST," giving you crows nest and nest egg.

  CAT ____ □ ____ □ THE PLANK

  FLAG □ ____ □ ____ SHAPE

  CHARTER □ ____ □ ____ SWAIN

  SPY ____ □ ____ □ ____ CEILING

  AUTO ____ ____ □ ____ □ WHALE

  WEIGH ____ ____ ____ □ □ □ MAN

  After filling in the blanks and boxes for each of the six words, arrange the 13 letters in the boxes to find the starting point for the treasure hunt on Albatross Island.

- The starting point for the hunt is □□□□□□□□□□□□□□□.
- Find a second point on the island that is the same distance to both the starting point and the Gallows as the starting point is to the Gallows. Arrr, at that point ye find the treasure!
- What are the coordinates of the treasure's location?

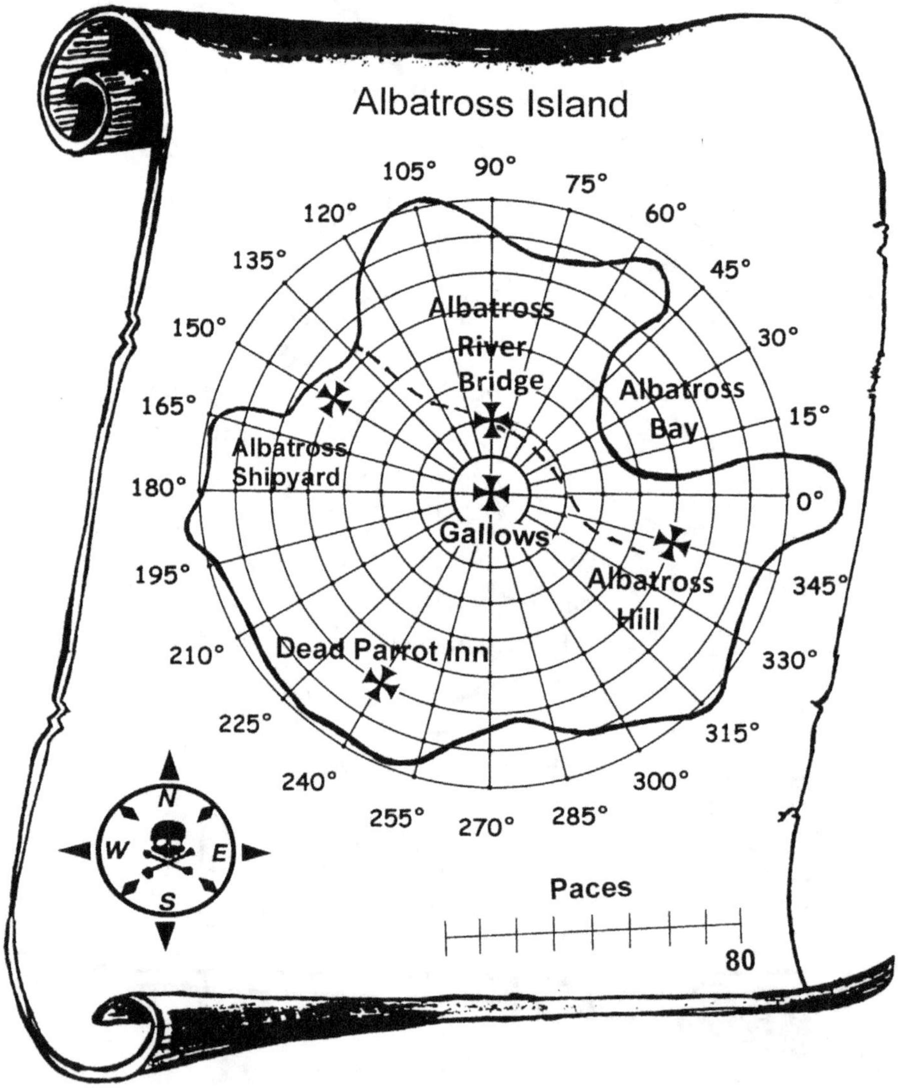

7. Buried Treasure on Isla Plata *h*

- The location of the starting point is found by arranging the letters in each column in the lower 7×6 grid into the empty squares of each corresponding column in the upper 7×6 grid and then reading the message horizontally.
- From the starting point send one pirate mate walking in the direction of the Gallows for 90 paces. Drive a stake in the ground and label the point *P*.
- From point *P* move 30° clockwise staying the same distance from the Gallows. Drive a stake in the ground and label the point *Q*.
- The treasure is buried 60 paces from the Gallows and at a point *T* such that *PT* = *QT*.
- What are the coordinates of all the possible treasure locations?

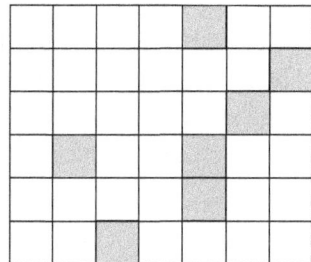

a	i	a	c	a	c	a
c	k	c	i	n	g	a
l	o	i	n	t	j	e
p	o	t	o		s	i
s	r	u	r		v	t
y			t			

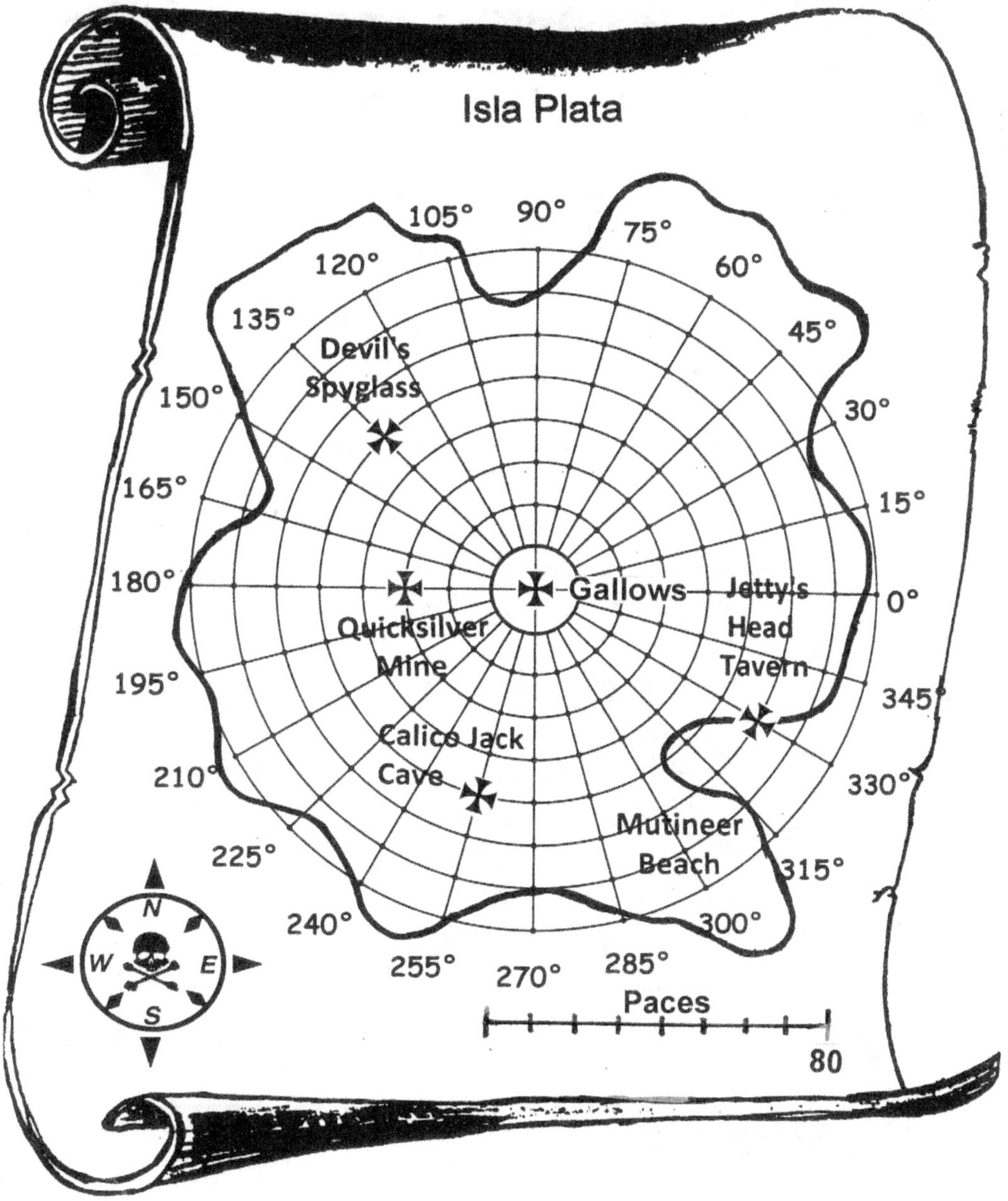

8. Buried Treasure on Isla de Oro *h*

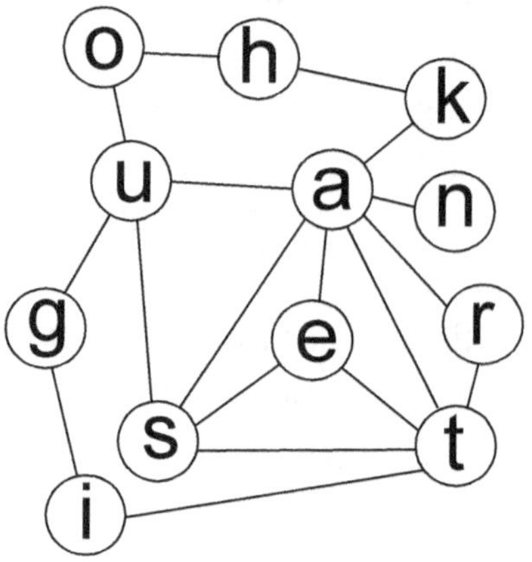

- The location of the starting point is found in the network shown at right. Begin at the letter *s* and move along the segments from letter to letter forming a sentence. Letters may be passed over more than once.
- From your starting point send one pirate mate walking in the direction of the Gallows for 80 paces. Turn right and walk clockwise for 75° staying the same distance from the Gallows. Drive a stake in the ground and label the point *P*.
- Drive a stake in the ground at (40, 330°) and label the point *Q*.
- The treasure is buried on the island 70 paces from the Gallows and at a point *T* such that $PT = QT$.
- What are the coordinates of all the possible treasure locations?

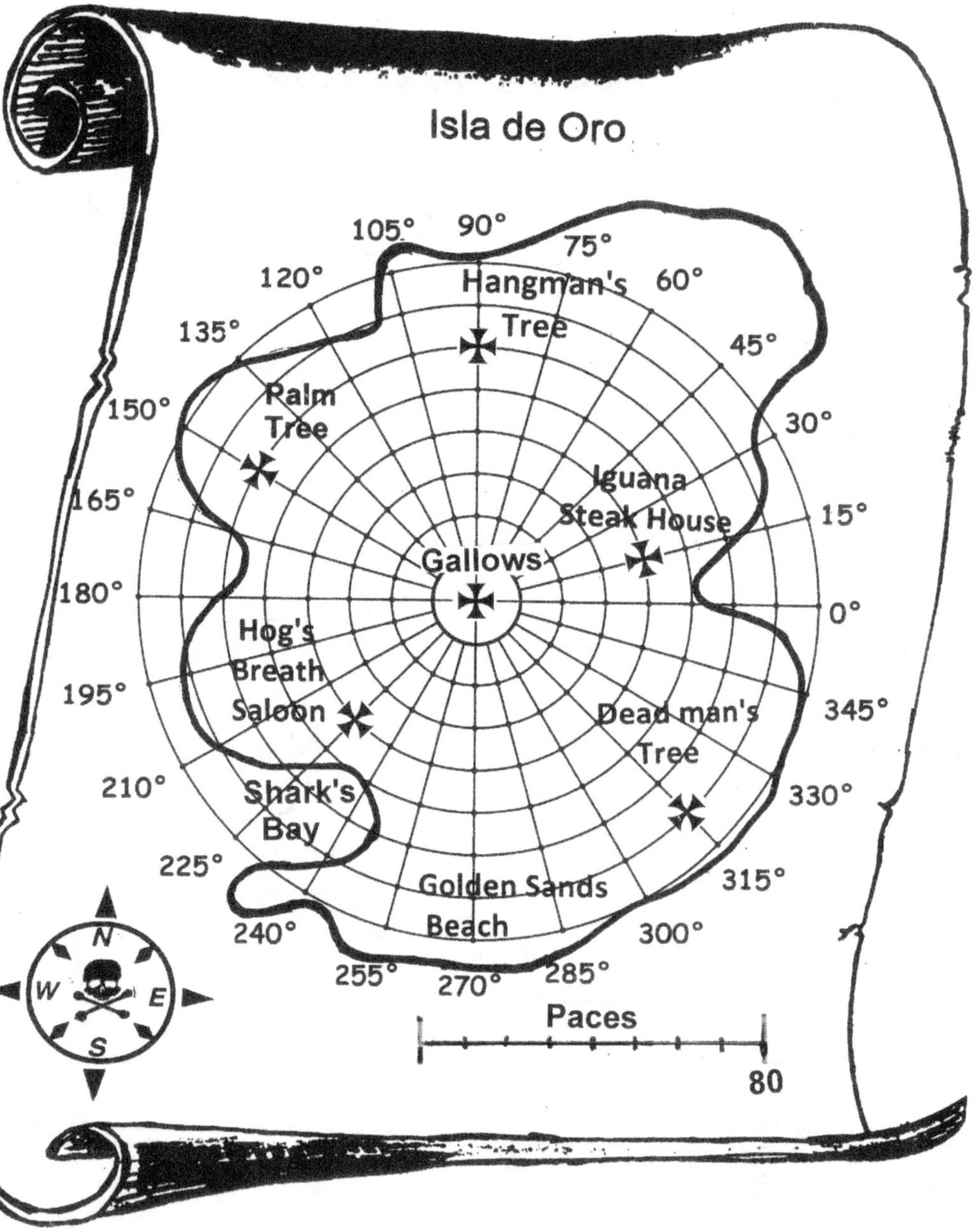

9. Buried Treasure on Isla de los Muerto *h*

- Each superhero listed below is also known by a different name. For example, Tarzan's real name is the Earl of Greystoke. Fill in the blanks and boxes for the "real" names of the following fictional characters. After finding the six names, arrange the letters in the boxes to reveal the treasure hunt starting point.

Superman: □ _ □ _ _   _ _ _ □

Batman: _ □ _ _ □   _ _ □ _ _

Spiderman: □ _ _ □ _   _ _ _ _ □ _

Ironman: _ _ _ _   _ □ _ □ _

The Saint: _ □ _ _ _   _ _ □ _ _ _ □

Captain America: _ _ _ □ □   _ _ _ □ _ _

Thus the starting point is: □ □ □ □ □ □ □ □ □ □ □ □ □ □ □ □ □

- From your starting point send one pirate mate walking in the direction of the Gallows for 100 paces. Turn left and walk counterclockwise for 45° staying the same distance from the Gallows. Drive a stake in the ground and label the point *P*.
- Drive a stake in the ground at (40, 165°) and label the point *Q*.
- The treasure is buried 60 paces from the Gallows and on the line containing the bisector of the angle with the vertex at the origin passing through points *P* and *Q*.
- What are the coordinates of all the possible treasure locations?

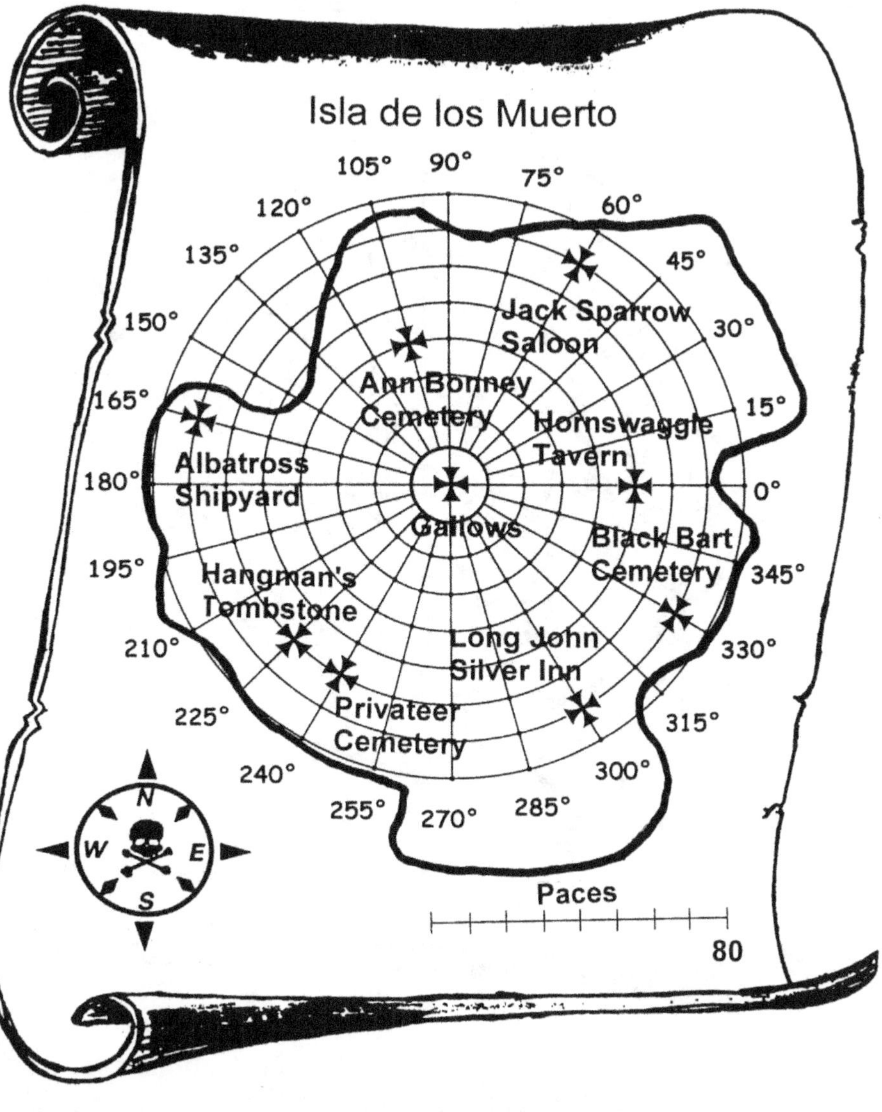

10. Buried Treasure on Isla de Sangria ℏ

For this treasure hunt the pirate treasure is buried at one of the vertices of a polar grid pentomino. The values for the coordinates of nine of the ten vertices are found by researching the answers to the following:

a = Five less than five times the number of the day in September in which Bilbo Baggins was born.

b = Ten times the sum of the digits in the zip code of the White House.

c = Five times the number of amendments ratified to the U.S. Constitution as of January 1, 2014.

d = Five times the number of bones in the human hand.

e = Five times the number of faces on a dodecahedron.

f = Ten times the number of countries bordering Bolivia.

g = Ten times the sum of the number of rooms and suspects in the board game Clue™.

- Nine of the ten vertices of the pentomino are *N*(60, ***a***°), *O*(***b***, 105°), *P*(70, ***c***°), *Q*(60, ***d***°), *R*(***e***, 150°), *S*(***f***, ***g***°), *U*(***b*** – 30, ***a***°), *L*(40, 2***e***°) and *M*(***e***, 2***e***°).
- The remaining vertex of the pentomino is the treasure's location.
- What are the coordinates of the treasure's location?

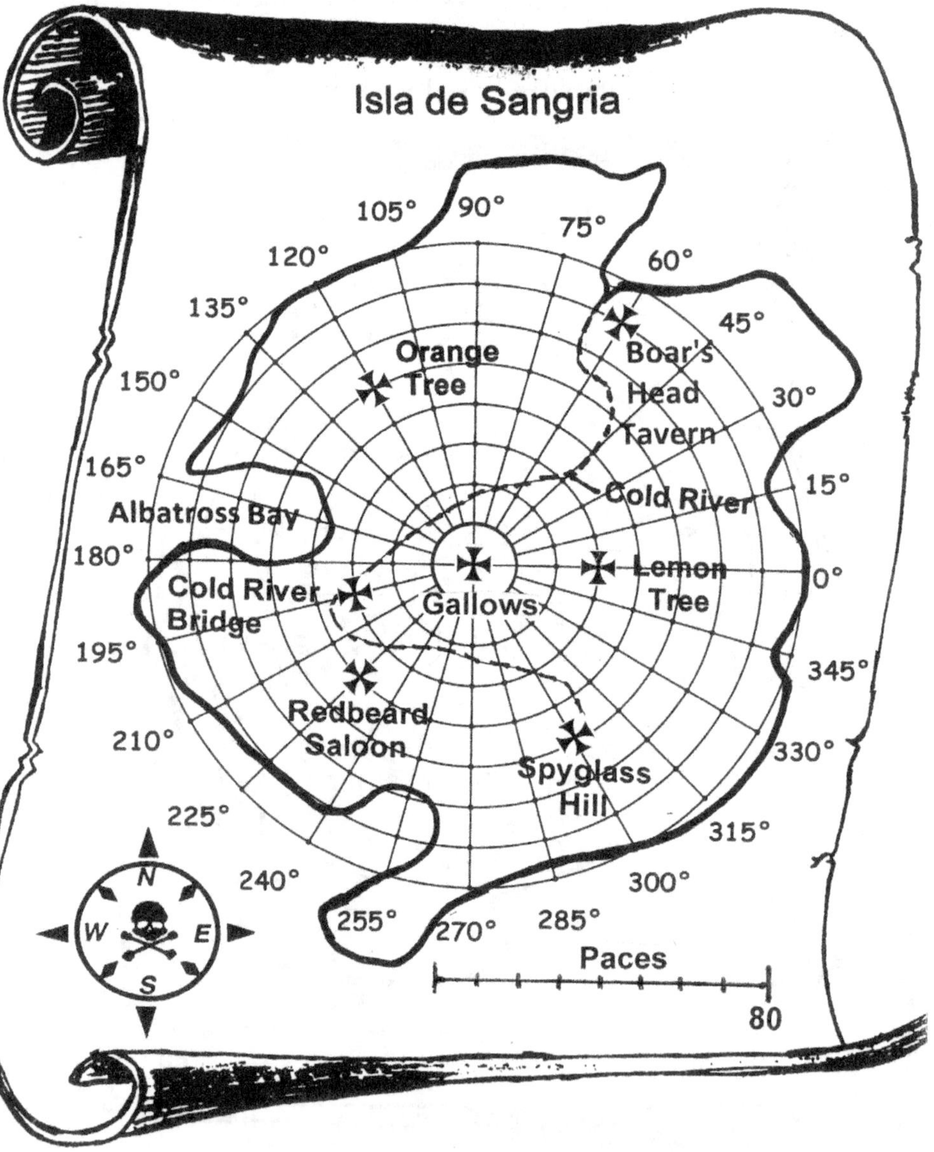

Education is not the filling of a pail, but the lighting of a fire.
—Plutarch (Greek philosopher)

4.1 The Coordinate System on a Sphere

In Chapter 2 you played Buried Treasure using a rectangular coordinate system. In Chapter 3 you played Buried Treasure using a polar coordinate system. In this chapter you will play using coordinates on a globe. Perhaps we should call it "Sunken Treasure" since water covers approximately 70 percent of the earth's surface.

If you have ever tried to find a city or country on a globe or atlas, you have used a spherical coordinate system. In order to identify locations on a globe, **cartographers** (map makers) created a coordinate grid, just as mathematicians did on a flat surface. First they ran a series of horizontal circles called **lines of latitude** around the globe. Lines of latitude are also known as **parallels** because they are parallel and run in the same direction as the Equator. The lines of latitude are not the same length or circumference. The **Equator** is the line of latitude with the greatest circumference and is numbered 0° latitude.

Lines of latitude

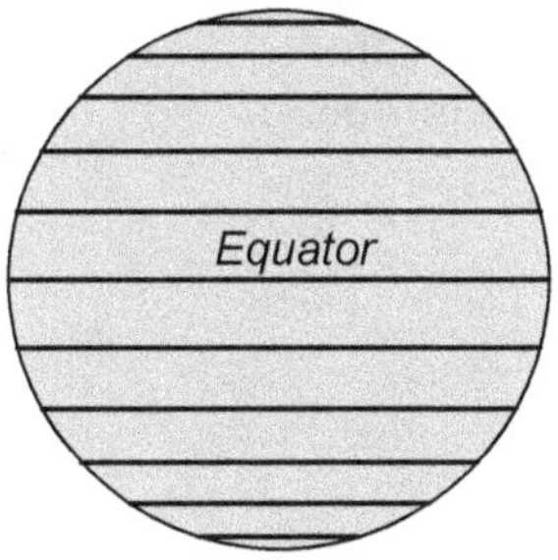

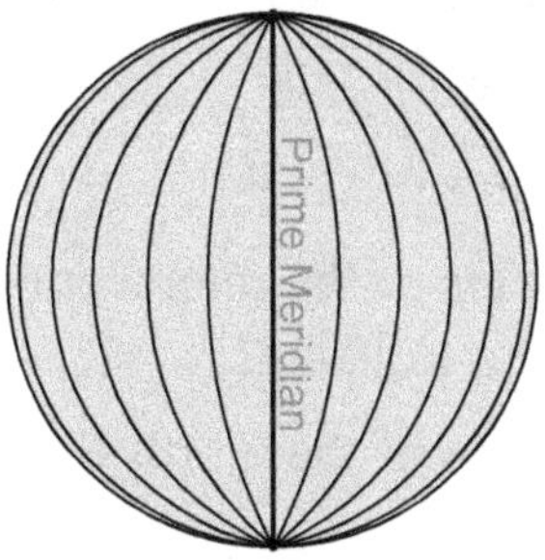

Lines of longitude

Next, cartographers ran a series of vertical circles around the globe, passing through the North and South Poles. The lines that run between the two poles, dividing Earth like the sections of an orange, are called **lines of longitude**, or **meridians**. All the lines of longitude are great circles. A **great circle** of a sphere is the intersection of the sphere with a plane passing through the center of the sphere. (The Equator is the only line of latitude that is a great circle.) All the lines of longitude are approximately the same length (the average circumference of the earth). The line at zero degrees longitude runs through the Royal Observatory in Greenwich, England and is called the **Prime Meridian**. The **International Date Line** is the line of longitude located 180° from the Prime Meridian. San Francisco, California is about 122° west of the Prime Meridian and approximately 38° north of the Equator. This is expressed as the ordered pair (38° N, 122° W).

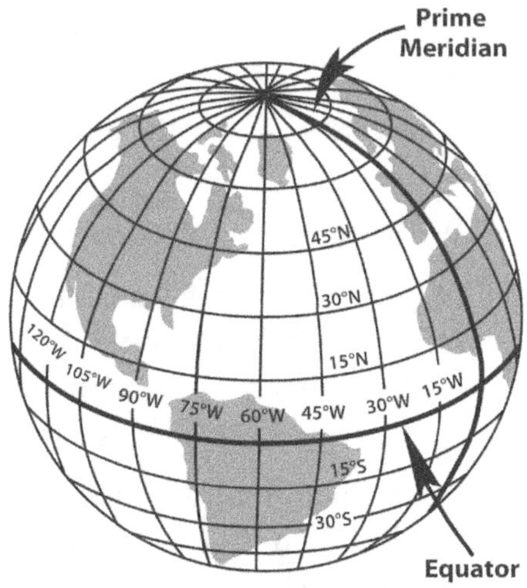

Degrees, Minutes, and Seconds

For greater accuracy in locating positions on the globe, each degree can be broken into 60 minutes (60') and each minute can be divided into 60 seconds (60"). A set of coordinates for the Transamerica Pyramid in San Francisco is (37° 47' 43" N, 122° 24' 9" W).

Example A

What are the coordinates of a point at the intersection of the International Date Line and the Equator?

Solution

The Equator is 0° (North or South) and the International Date Line is 180° (East or West). Therefore, one way of expressing the coordinates is (0°N, 180°W).

Example B

What are the coordinates of point A?

Solution

Point *A* is one 15° latitude line north of the Equator so it is 15° N. Point *A* is two 15° longitude lines east of the Prime Meridian so it is 30° E. Thus the coordinates of point *A* are (15° N, 30° E).

The longitude and latitude lines are set 15° apart.

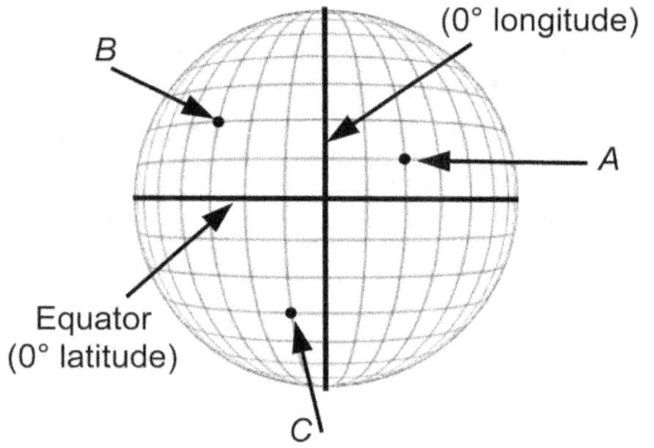

Exercises in the Coordinate System on a Sphere

For Exercises 1–4 use the globe shown at right.

1. What are the coordinates of *B*?
2. What are the coordinates of *C*?
3. What are the coordinates of the intersection of the Prime Meridian and the Equator?
4. What are the coordinates of the North Pole?

The globe at right shows the earth from above the Equator, with the Prime Meridian off to the right. The latitude and longitude lines are 15° apart.

For Exercises 5–7 use the globe shown to the right.

5. What are the coordinates of *W*, *X*, *Y*, and *Z*?
6. Ingleside, Ontario, Canada has coordinates (45° N, 75° W) and point *X*, on the coast of Peru, also has the same longitude. How many degrees between them?
7. What fraction of the earth's circumference is it between Ingleside, Ontario and point *X* on the coast of Peru? ɦ

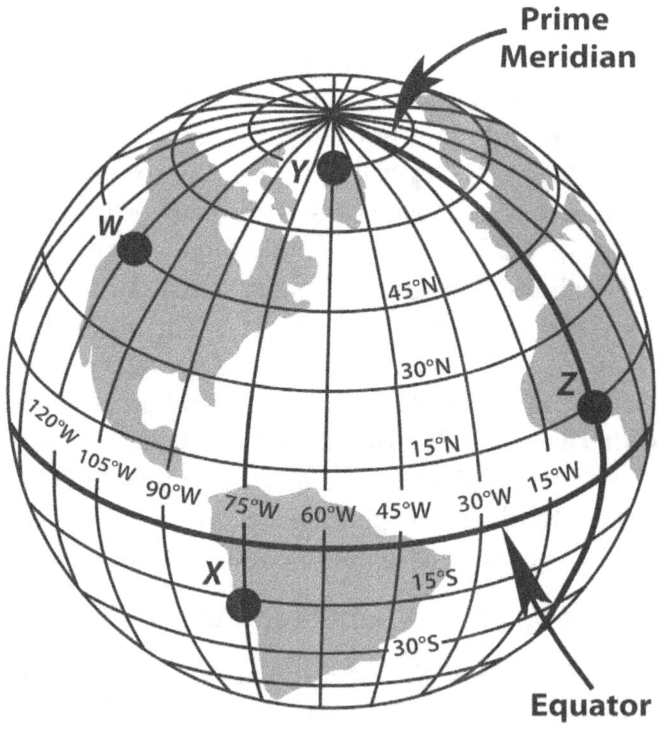

For Exercises 8–13, use an atlas, globe, or map found on the Internet to best match the U.S. cities with their coordinates.

8. Honolulu, Hawaii	A. (65° N, 148° W)
9. Key West, Florida	B. (32° N, 111° W)
10. Denver, Colorado	C. (25° N, 82° W)
11. Fairbanks, Alaska	D. (21° N, 158° W)
12. Montgomery, Alabama	E. (40° N, 105° W)
13. Tucson, Arizona	F. (32° N, 86° W)

For Exercises 14–21, match the coordinates of these famous architectural sites with their images.

A. (40° N, 79° W)	B. (37° N, 4° W)	C. (27° N, 79° E)	D. (13° N, 104°E)
E. (35° N, 136° E)	F. (3° N, 102° E)	G. (45° N, 12° E)	H. (34° S, 151°E)

14. ħ

15. ħ

16. ħ

17.

18. ħ

19. ħ

20. ħ

21.

For Exercises 22–29, match the coordinates with the city that is best associated with the famous mathematicians pictured below.

A. (49° N, 2° E) B. (53°N, 1° W) C. (36° N, 59° E) D. (56° N, 38° E)

E. (37° N, 15° E) F. (10°N, 78° E) G. (45° N, 9° E) H. (31° N, 30° E)

22. Euclid ℏ 23. Archimedes ℏ 24. S. Kovalevskaya ℏ 25. Omar Khayyám ℏ

26. G. Cardano ℏ 27. S. Germain ℏ 28. G. Boole ℏ 29. S. Ramanujan ℏ

Distances Measured on a Line of Longitude

The circumference of the earth about the Equator is approximately 24,900 miles. The distance between the North and South Poles is half that, or 12,450 miles. The distance from either pole to the Equator would be one fourth the circumference, or approximately 6,225 miles.

If two cities are along the same line of longitude, or both on the equator, and you know that the average circumference of the earth is approximately 24,900 miles, then you can calculate the distance between them.

Example C

Memphis, Tennessee, USA is located approximately (35° N, 90° W) and Merida, Mexico is located approximately (21° N, 90° W). How far apart are they in miles?

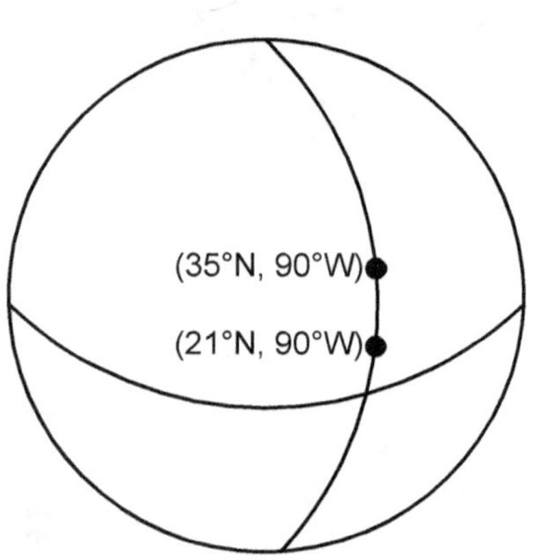

Solution

Memphis and Merida are approximately 14° apart along the 90° longitude line (35° – 21°). If we take the average circumference of the earth to be 24,900 miles, then the distance between them is (14/360) × 24,900 miles, or a little more than 968 miles.

In general: the fraction formed by the degrees between two points on the same line of longitude divided by 360° will equal the fraction formed by the miles between the two points divided by 24,900, the circumference of the earth.

For Exercises 30–32, use 24,900 miles as the average circumference of the earth. Find the distance between the following pairs of cities.

30. Anchorage, Alaska is approximately (61° N, 150° W) and Papeete, French Polynesia is approximately (18° S, 150° W).

31. Quito, Ecuador is approximately (0° N, 79° W) and Kismayo, Somalia is approximately (0° S, 43° E).

32. Atlanta, Georgia is approximately (34° N, 84° W) and San Jose, Costa Rica is approximately (10° N, 84° W).

Distances Between Two Random Locations on the Globe

Finding distances between two points on a sphere requires us to recognize that the shortest distance that appears on a flat map is not necessarily the shortest distance on the sphere.

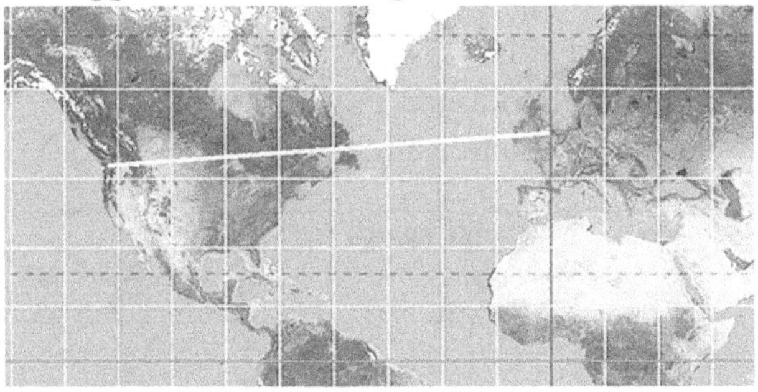

To demonstrate this, use a piece of string and a globe. Holding one end of the string at Seattle and the other end at London, carefully pull the string tight. The shortest path the string takes is along the arc of a great circle. To find the actual distance between two points on the globe, navigators use the *Spherical Law of Cosines.*

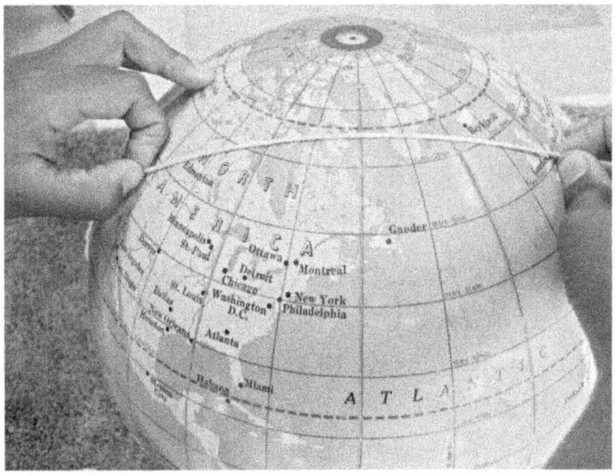

You can get a rough estimate for the distance between two cities on a globe using string. First you must know the average circumference of the earth (24,900 miles). Using string, measure the circumference of your globe and the distance between the two cities. You can set up a proportion and calculate the approximate distance between the two cities.

For Exercises 33–35, use a globe and string to find a rough approximation for the distance between the following pairs of cities that do not lie on the same line of longitude.

33. What is the approximate distance between San Francisco, California and London, England?

34. What is the approximate distance between San Francisco, California and Sydney, Australia?

35. What is the approximate distance between London and Sydney?

A Brief History of Time Zones[7]

The lines of longitude, in addition to being a part of a coordinate system for determining locations on the globe, serve another function. Lines of longitude establish time zones. For more on time zones, see Footnotes, Chapter 4, footnote 7.

4.2 Spherical Buried Treasure

Level 1A Once you have built or purchased your globes, you are ready to play Spherical Buried Treasure. For more on purchasing or building your globes see Appendix 3. You will need four globes for each game, two for each team. You will also need small pieces of paper or tape to represent buried treasure. Record the location of digs on your globes using either erasable markers or small stickers such as Sticky Dots. Determine which team plays first by flipping a coin or rolling a die.

Rules for Level 1A:

1. For this first level you will hide one *I*-pentomino as your buried treasure. Place it on the globe so at least one of the four corners is on a land mass. No part of the treasure may be above 75° N latitude or below 75° S latitude.
2. The first team to play may ask the other team a yes/no question. For example, "Is some part of the treasure hidden north of the Equator?" or, "Is some part of the treasure hidden on an island?" The second team must answer with either a *yes* or *no*. Then the second team may ask a question and the first team must answer with either a *yes* or a *no*. Only two yes/no questions about the location may be asked during the game by each team.
3. The first team to "dig for treasure" calls out three sets of ordered pairs (digs). Each ordered pair shall always be north or south with some multiple of 15° or 30° followed by east or west and some multiple of 15° or 30°. For example, (N45°, E30°) would be a location near the western shore of the Black Sea. Teammates on both teams record the digs on their globes and on the appropriate table (see diagram at right).

SPHERICAL BURIED TREASURE GAME

Our Team's Digs			Other Team's Digs		
	"Digs" (°latitude, °longitude)	X, E, C		"Digs" (°latitude, °longitude)	X, E, C
1			1		
2			2		
3			3		
4			4		
5			5		
6			6		
7			7		
8			8		
9			9		
10			10		
11			11		
12			12		
13			13		
14			14		
15			15		
16			16		
17			17		
18			18		
19			19		
20			20		
21			21		
22			22		
23			23		
24			24		
25			25		

4. The second team responds after each guess whether it is a hit or miss. If it is a hit, they tell the first team whether it is one of the corners or an edge of the pentomino.
5. Then it is the second team's turn to take three digs. Continue taking turns with three digs at a time. Both teams are responsible for recording all digs on the spheres as well as on the recording table. Continue in this way, taking turns with three digs at a time.
6. When one team has located at least two of the four corners of the *I*-pentomino, then that team may take a guess as to the location of the other two corners. Guessing the location of the other corners of the treasure must happen when it is your turn but before you have taken your three digs. If correct, they win. However, if they guess incorrectly, they lose. If the team that has located two corners does not wish to guess, the game continues until one team is ready to guess the treasure's location.

4.3 Variations on Spherical Buried Treasure

Level 1B At this level each team selects any one of the five tetrominoes and hides it on their globe so at least one of the four corners is on a land mass. No part of the treasure may be above 75° N latitude or below 75° S latitude. Determine which team plays first by flipping a coin or rolling a die.

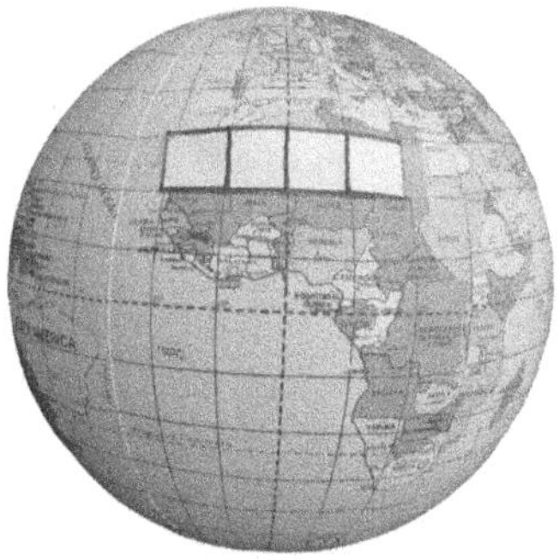

Rules for Level 1B:

1. Teams may ask each other a yes/no question. For example, "Is some part of the treasure hidden north of the Equator?" The other team must answer with either a *yes* or *no*. Only two yes/no questions about the location may be asked during the game by each team.
2. The first team to "dig for treasure" calls out three sets of ordered pairs (digs). Each ordered pair shall always be north or south with some multiple of 15° or 30° followed by east or west and some multiple of 15° or 30°. Teammates on both teams record the digs on their globes and on their game sheet.
3. The second team responds after each guess whether it is a hit or miss. If it is a hit, they tell the first team whether it is one of the corners or an edge of the tetromino.
4. Then it is the second team's turn to take three digs. Continue taking turns with three digs at a time. Both teams are responsible for recording all digs on the spheres as well as on the recording table. Continue in this way, taking turns with three digs at a time.
5. When one team has located at least three corners of the tetromino then that team may take a guess as to the type and location of the hidden tetromino. Tape a copy of the tetromino on the globe. Show the globe to the other team. If correct, you win. However, if you guess incorrectly, you lose. Guessing the location of the treasure must happen when it is your turn but before you have taken your three digs. If the team that has located three corners does not wish to guess yet, the game continues until one team is ready to take a guess.

Level 1C

- Each team hides *two identical* tetrominoes.

Level 1D

- Each team hides *two different* tetrominoes.

Level 1E

- Each team hides *three* different tetrominoes.
- Each team takes *four* digs and the other team responds after each dig.

Level 1F

- Each team hides *three* different polyominoes (pentominoes or smaller).
- Each team takes *five* digs but no information is given about hits or misses until after all five ordered pairs are given.

Level 1G

- Each team hides *four* different tetrominoes. One tetromino must touch North America. One tetromino must touch South America. One tetromino must touch Africa. One tetromino must touch Asia.
- Each team takes *five* digs but no information is given about hits or misses until after all five ordered pairs are given.

4.4 Spherical Buried Treasure Puzzles

In this set of spherical buried treasure puzzles your task is to locate the buried treasure tetromino on each globe below. A *C* represents a corner hit, an *E* represents an edge hit, an *I* represents an interior hit, and an *X* represents a miss. The tetromino is located completely on the half of the globe shown.

SBTP 1

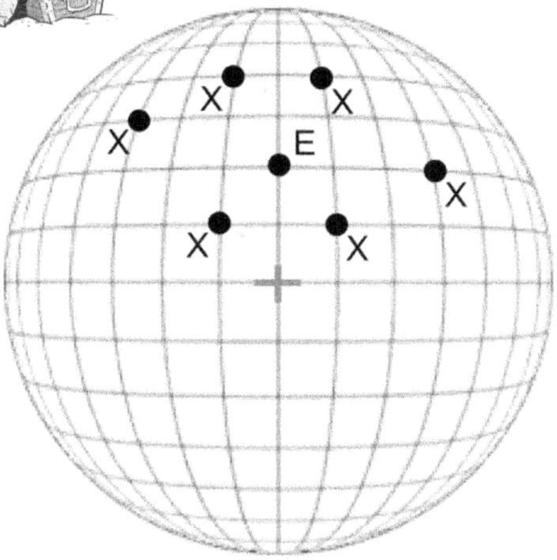

SBTP 2

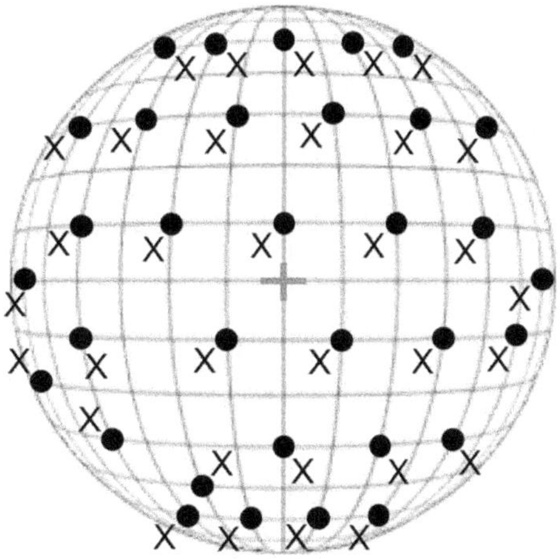

SBTP 3

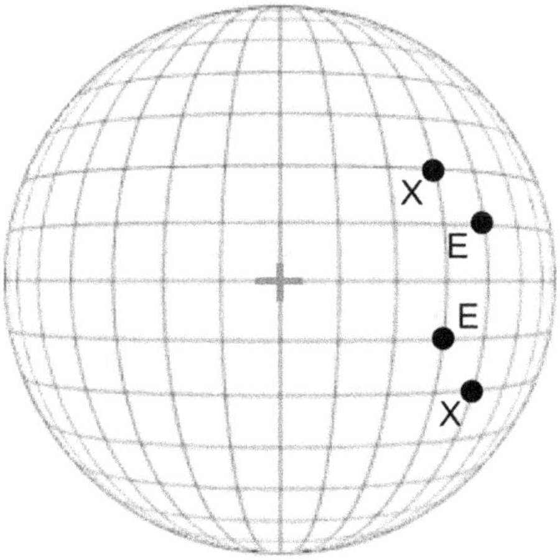

SBTP 4

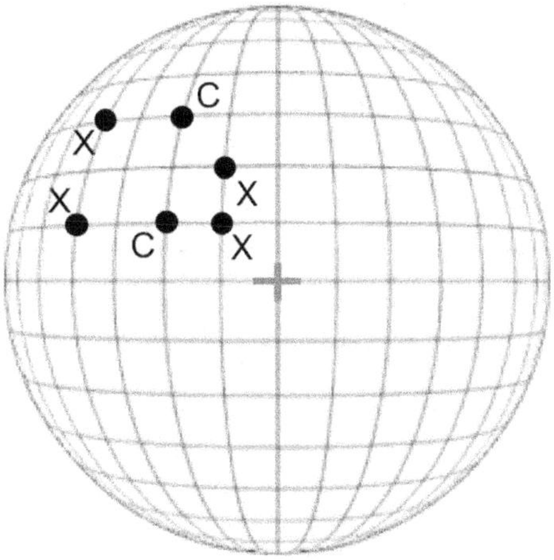

SBTP 5

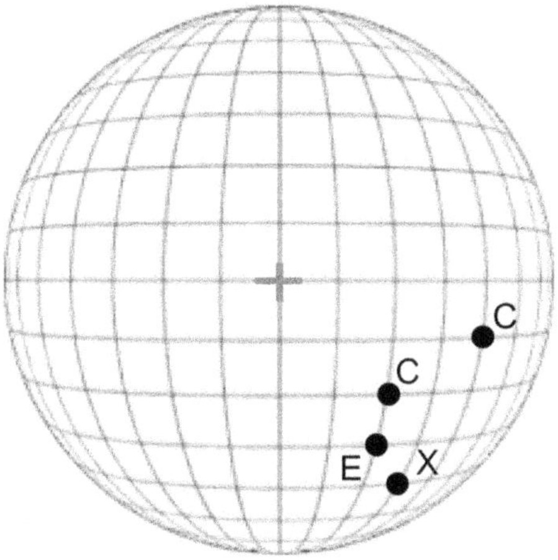

SBTP 6

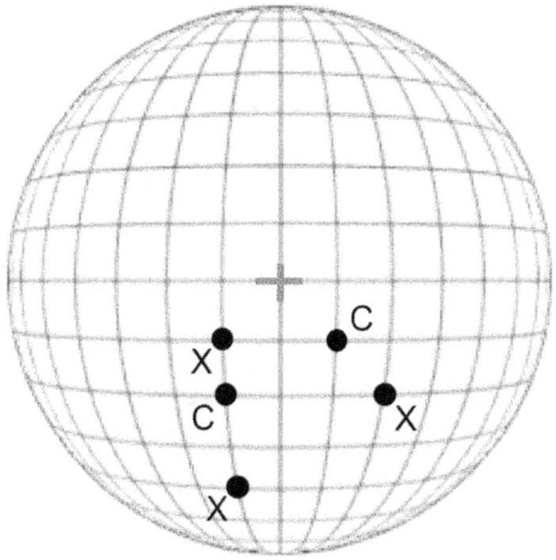

Chapter 4.4

In this set of spherical buried treasure puzzles your task is to locate two identical buried treasure tetrominoes on the globe given. The two tetrominos are reflections of each other. They are reflected over either the heavy longitude or latitude lines. The two do not touch. A *C* represents a corner hit, an *E* represents an edge hit, an *I* represents an interior hit, and an *X* represents a miss. The tetrominoes are located completely on the half of the globe shown.

SBTP 7 *h*

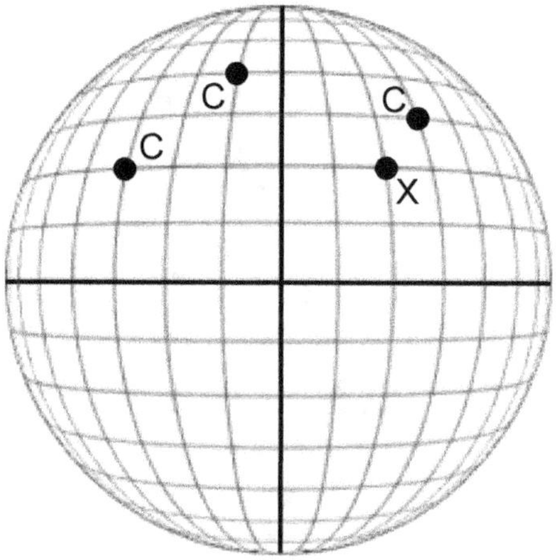

SBTP 8

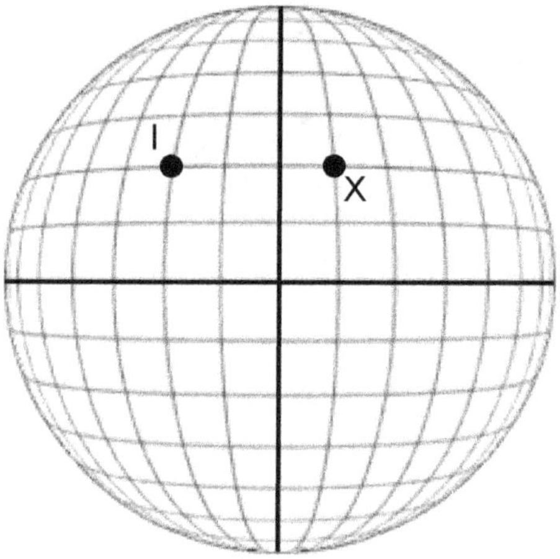

SBTP 9

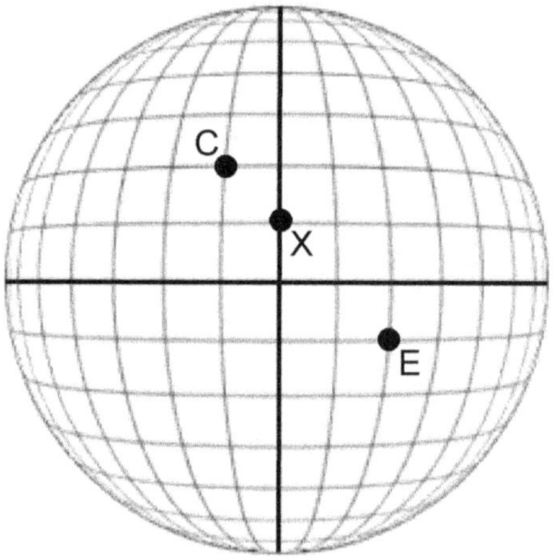

SBTP 10

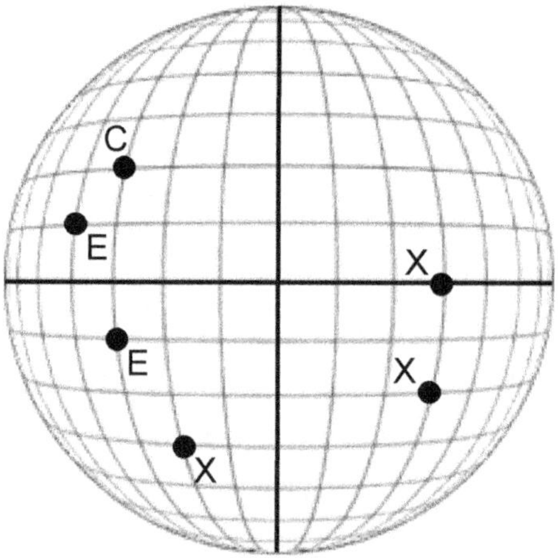

SBTP 11

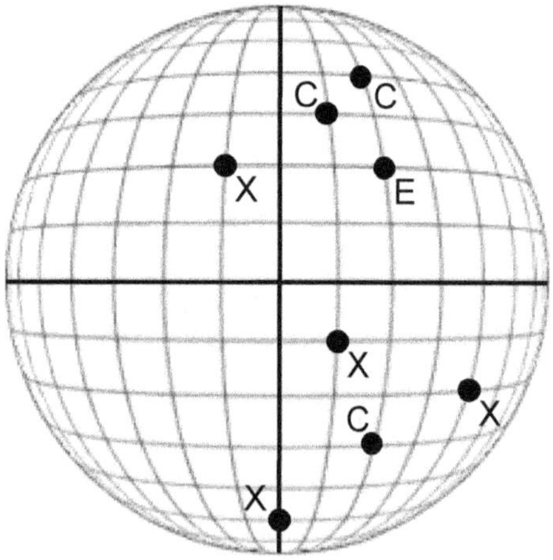

SBTP 12

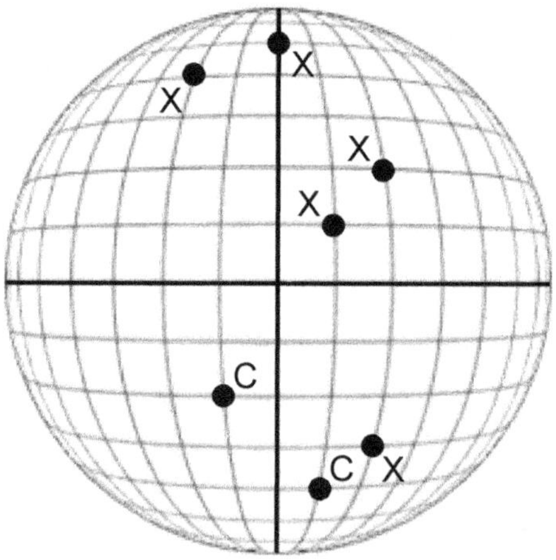

4.5 Discovering Sunken Treasure

In 2007, Odyssey Marine Exploration announced the discovery of one of the greatest sunken treasures ever found. Over 17 tons of silver and hundreds of gold coins were recovered from the Atlantic Ocean. Evidence suggested the wreckage was *Nuestra Señora de las Mercedes*[8], a Spanish ship that sank in 1804. The Spanish government laid claim to the treasure, as did individuals whose ancestors were transporting goods on the *Mercedes*. The case was dismissed and the coins were turned over to Spain. The estimated $500 million in coins arrived in Madrid in 2012, 208 years after the ship's fateful journey.

Another, more recent operation by Odyssey was the salvage of the *SS Gairsoppa*, a British cargo ship sunk by a German U-boat during World War Two. By 2013, over 110 tons of silver had been recovered, making it the largest sunken treasure recovery in history.

Sunken treasure salvage has become a big enterprise with occasional big rewards. In the early 1980's, Tommy Thompson and Bob Evans formed the Columbus-America Discovery Group. They enlisted the help of mathematician Dr. Lawrence D. Stone, who set up a data correlation matrix to narrow the search for the sunken *SS Central America*, which sank in a hurricane off the North Carolina Coast. In 1988, the shipwreck was located and more than 7,000 coins from the San Francisco Mint were recovered. After ten years of legal battles, the Columbus-America Discovery Group was awarded 92 percent of the treasure.

Prior to the sunken treasure finds mentioned earlier, the biggest discovery was made by Mel Fisher. A treasure-hunting pioneer, Fisher improved shipwreck salvage by inventing a device called a "mailbox" which sends clear water from the surface downward so divers are able to see better. In 1985, he located the Spanish galleon *Nuestra Señora de Atocha*, which sank in a hurricane off the Florida Keys in 1622. The treasure was a reported $400 million in coins and other valuables.

All money is ever good for is to start another treasure hunt.
—Mel Fisher

The search for sunken ships and their treasures continues, although dangerous and often filled with legal challenges. In the Caribbean alone there are many sites of recovered and undiscovered riches[9]. The International Registry of Sunken Ships currently has a database listing more than 117,000 individual wrecks.

Sunken Treasure Puzzle

In July 1733, a plate fleet of 15 ships carrying silver coins, gold, and jewelry left Havana for its return voyage to Spain. The fleet included two armed escorts; a flagship at the front, *Capitana*; and and a vice-flagship, *Almiranta*, sailing at the rear. After the Spanish ships sighted the Florida Keys, they encountered a tropical storm. By the next day, the storm had become a hurricane. Most of the ships sank or were swamped along 80 miles of the Florida Keys.

Ships that could not be refloated and towed back to Havana were burned to the waterline in order to conceal the wrecks from pirates. Spanish officials in Havana sent nine ships out to rescue surviving crew and recover the treasures. The salvage work continued for years until most of the treasure was recovered.

These sunken treasure sites eventually faded from memory and the remains of the 1733 Spanish plate fleet were left undisturbed for more than 200 years. By the 1960's, professional salvage teams used new techniques to recover treasure and historical artifacts from these shipwrecks.

The location of shipwreck *Sueco de Arizón* is recorded as (24° 47'N, 80° 53'W) and the location of shipwreck *Capitana* is recorded as (24° 56'N, 80° 32'W). The location of *Almiranta* was recorded to be on a line between *Sueco de Arizón* and *Capitana*. In addition, the location of the *Almiranta* wreckage was twice as far from *Capitana* as it was from *Sueco de Arizón*.

1. Give an approximate location (?° ?' N, ?° ?' W) for the wreckage of *Almiranta*.

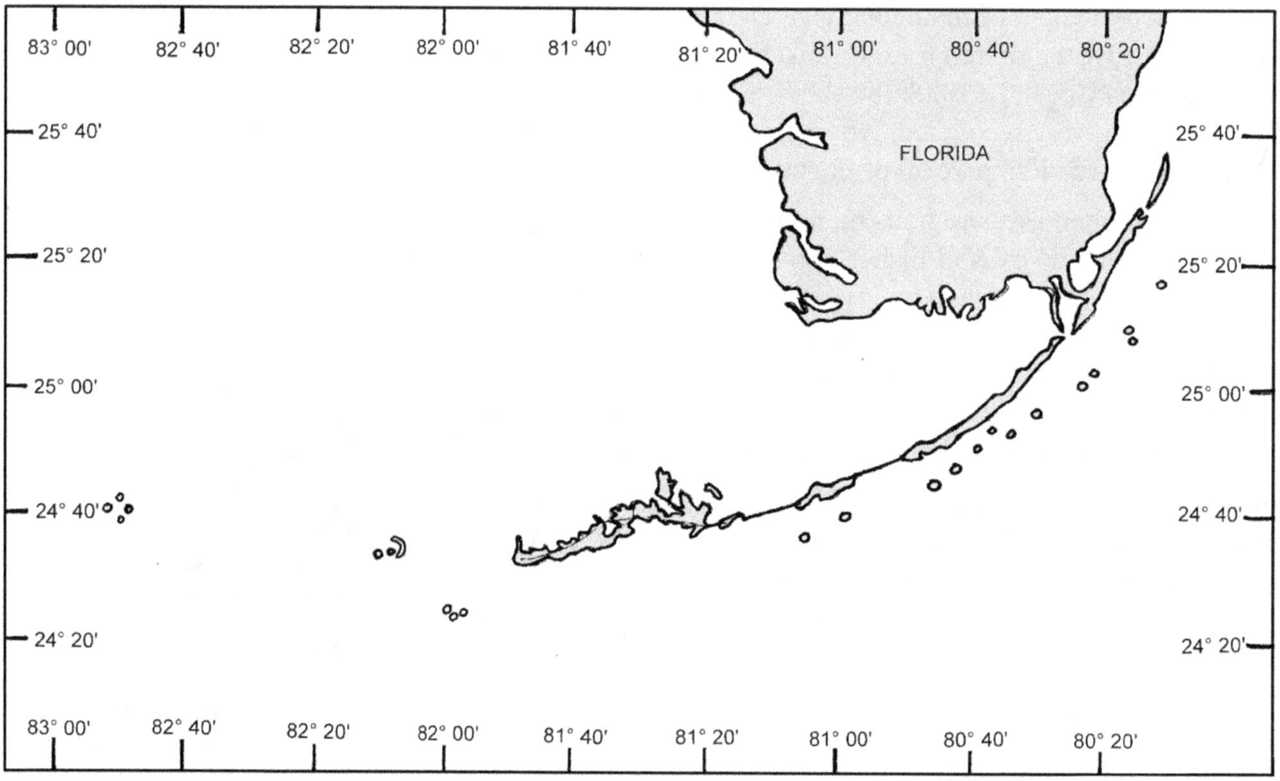

The road to wisdom?
Well, it's plain
and simple to express:
Err and err and err again
but less and less and less.
—Piet Hein

In earlier chapters you played Buried Treasure using a rectangular coordinate system, a polar coordinate system, and a coordinate system on a sphere. In this chapter we are going to extend the rectangular coordinate system to three dimensions and play 3-D Buried Treasure.

5.1 The 3-D Coordinate System

When archaeologists record locations of objects found during their digs they use a three-dimensional (3-D) coordinate system. The first two numbers locate a position on the surface and the third number locates how far down from the surface the object was found.

When marine biologists record the location of whales by their clicking sounds they also use a three-dimensional coordinate system. The first two numbers locate latitude and longitude and the third number is the sea depth.

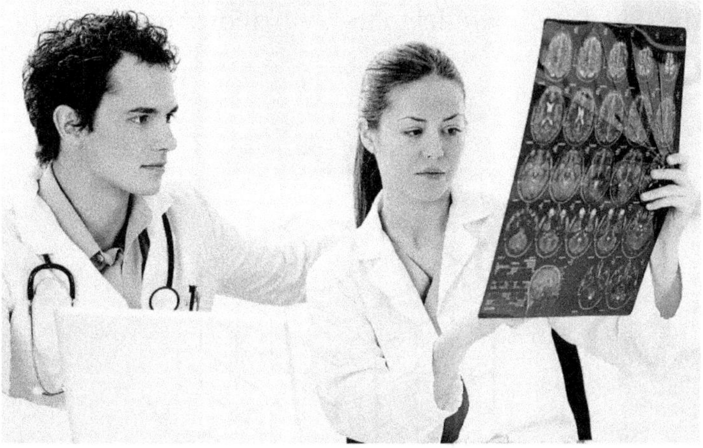

Neuroscientists create maps of the brain (called brain atlases) with the help of three-dimensional coordinates. With these brain atlases scientists are attempting to understand the complex functions of the brain. Hopefully this research will lead to better understanding of Alzheimer's disease, Parkinson's disease, autism, and schizophrenia.

To help visualize points in three dimensions (3-space) on a piece of paper (2-space), we can slice the three dimensions into levels. When doctors take a brain scan (CT[10], PET[10], or MRI[10]) they create two-dimensional slices of the three-dimensional brain.

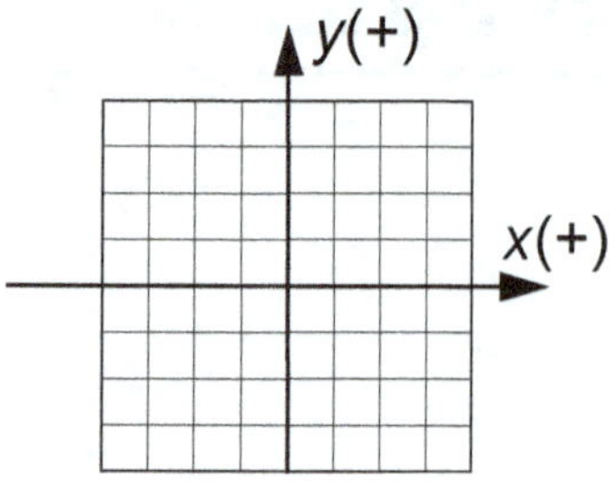

A line is one-dimensional thus one number locates a point on a line. A plane is two-dimensional, so an ordered pair of numbers locates a point in a plane. We live in a three-dimensional space. To locate a point in space requires three numbers, an **ordered triple**.

In the two-dimensional *xy*-coordinate plane, you locate points by their positive and negative distances from the *x*- and *y*-axes. These axes are placed at right angles to each other.

To create a third dimension we add a *z*-axis at right angles to both the *x*- and *y*-axes. The most common way to do this is to lay the *xy*-plane down, rotate it, and show the *z*-axis pointing straight up and down.

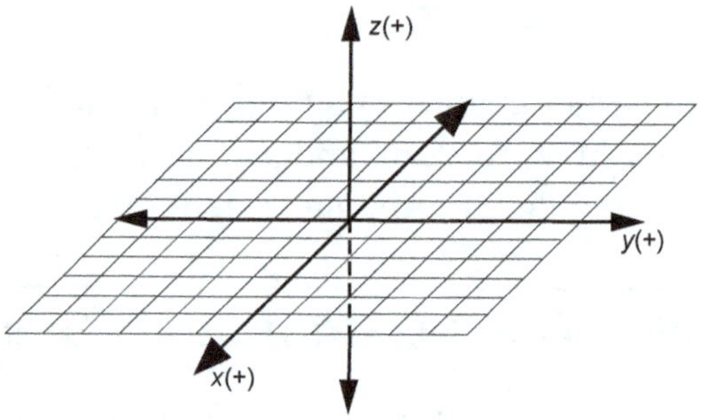

Locating a point in 3-space requires an ordered triple such as (2, -3, 1). The 2 is in the positive *x* direction, the -3 is in the negative y direction, and the 1 is in the positive *z* direction.

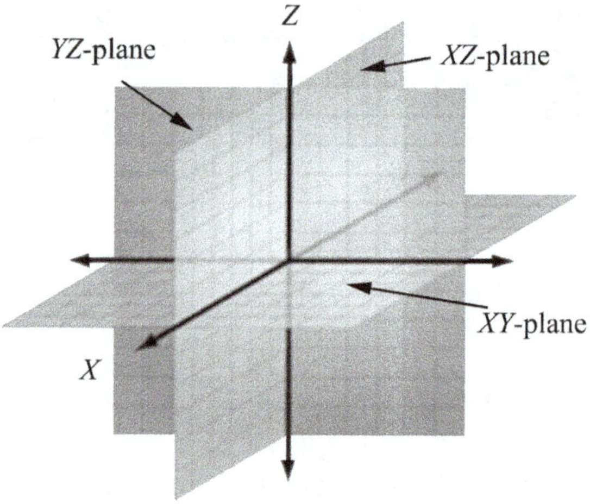

The *x*-, *y*-, and *z*- axes create three planes: the *xy*-plane, *xz*-plane, and *yz*-plane. Just as the *x*- and *y*-axes divide the coordinate plane into four quadrants, these three planes divide space into eight octants.

To help visualize points in three-dimensional space (3-space) we can slice the three dimensions into levels and arrange them in a column. For example, the three-dimensional coordinate system shown below has *x*-, *y*-, and *z*- values that range from -2 to 2. The third dimension along the *z* direction has been sliced into its five levels (all parallel to the *xy*-plane) shown below right.

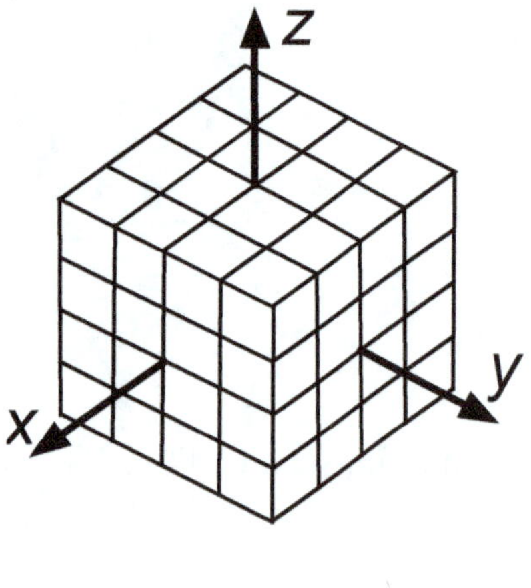

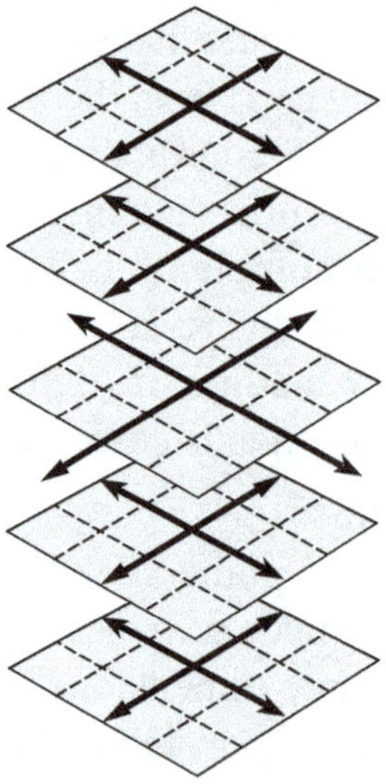

Exercises in Visualizing 3-D Coordinates

Determine the coordinates of the vertices of the rectangular prism sitting in the corner of the first octant (where all coordinates are positive).

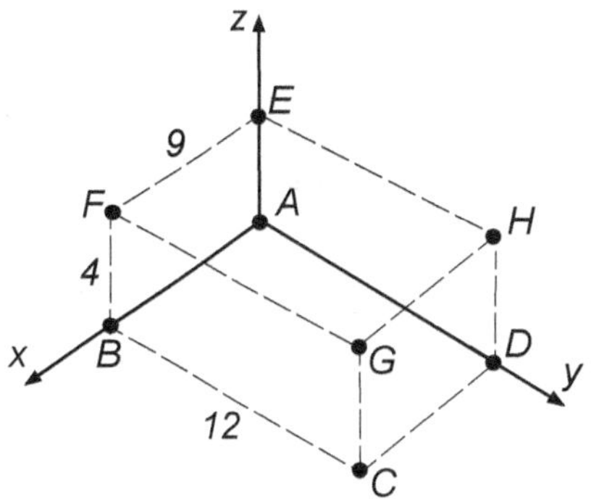

1. Point A (, ,) ɦ
2. Point B (, ,)
3. Point C (, ,)
4. Point D (, ,)
5. Point E (, ,)
6. Point F (, ,)
7. Point G (, ,)
8. Point H (, ,)

Determine the coordinates of the vertices of the rectangular prism floating in the top four octants (where all the z-coordinates are positive). The coordinates for point S are (2,3,1).

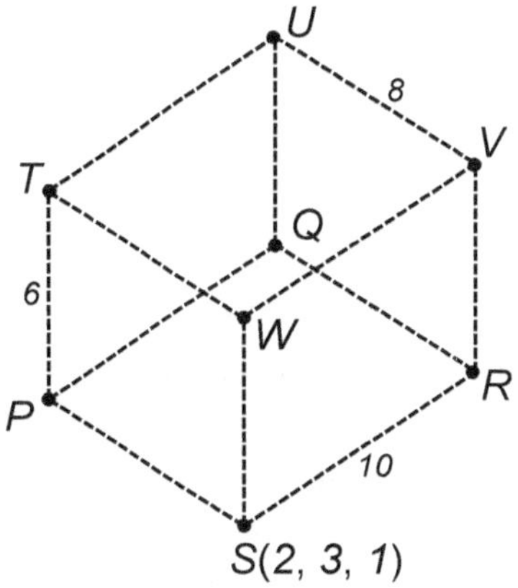

9. Point P (, ,) ɦ
10. Point Q (, ,)
11. Point R (, ,)
12. Point T (, ,)
13. Point U (, ,)
14. Point V (, ,)

Name the coordinate plane or axis in which each point below is located.

15. (1, 0, 3) ɦ
16. (2, -3, 0)
17. (0, -2, -3)
18. (0, 0, 3)
19. (-3, 0, 0)
20. (0, -4, 0)

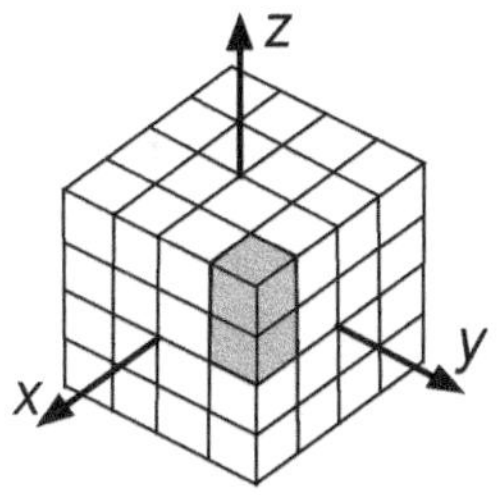

21. Find the coordinates of the eight corners of the shaded 1×1×2 rectangular prism in the three-dimensional coordinate system on the right. ɦ

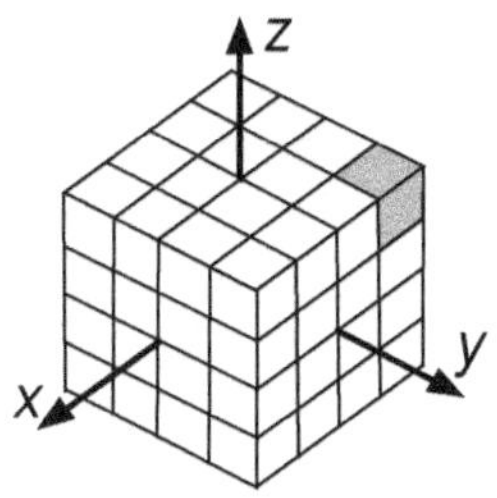

22. Find the coordinates of the eight corners of the shaded cube embedded in the three-dimensional coordinate system on the right.

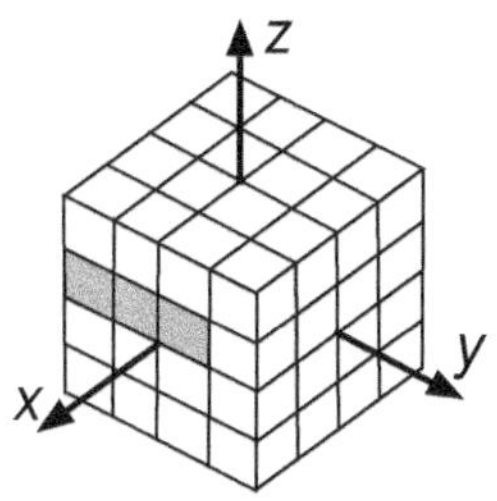

23. Find the coordinates of the eight corners of the shaded 1×1×3 rectangular prism embedded in the three-dimensional coordinate system on the right.

The 3-D coordinate system below has been sliced horizontally (parallel to the *xy*-plane) along the *z*-axis into five layers of (*xy*-planes) and is shown to the right. These are isometric views of the cube and its slices.

24. Locate points *A*, *B*, *C*, *D*, and *E* on their slices.

25. Locate points *F*(1, 1, -1), *G*(-1, -2, -2), and *H*(0, -1, 1) on their slices.

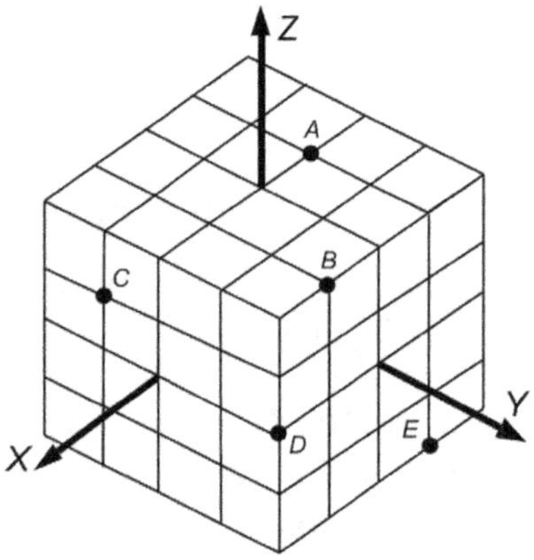

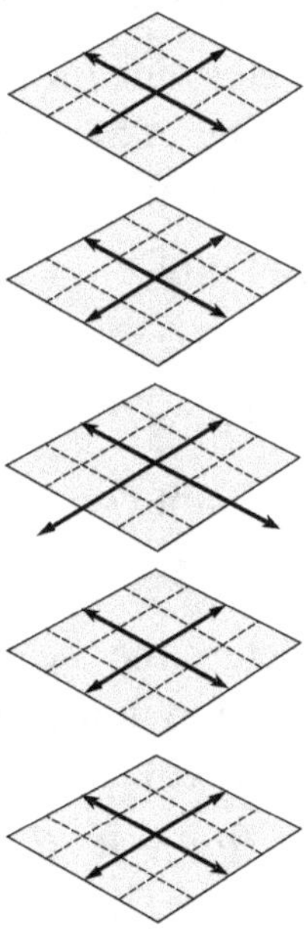

A 1×1×4 rectangular prism is embedded in the coordinate system below. The 3-D coordinate system has been sliced horizontally (parallel to the *xy*-plane) along the *z*-axis into five layers and is shown to the right. The points on the corners and edges of the 1×1×4 rectangular prism are shown by dots. The regions in each plane are shaded.

26. From the points shown on the grid to the right, shade in the location of the 1×1×4 rectangular prism on the 3-D grid below by shading the faces of the prism that are visible.

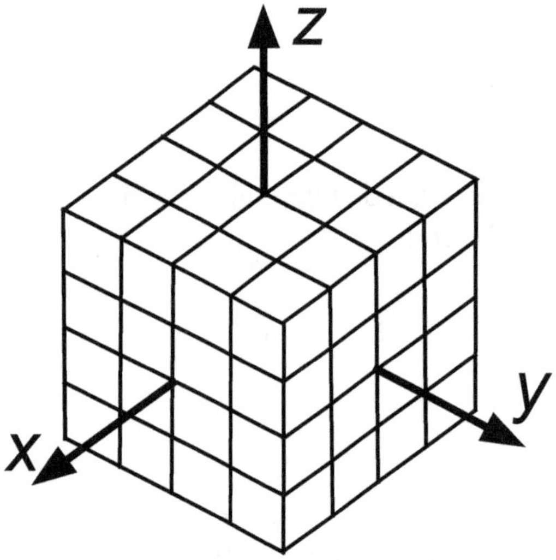

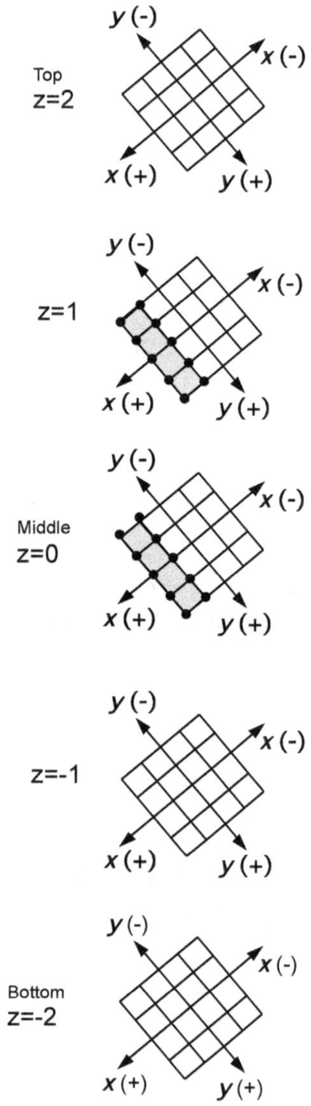

5.2 Sketching 3-D Polyominoes

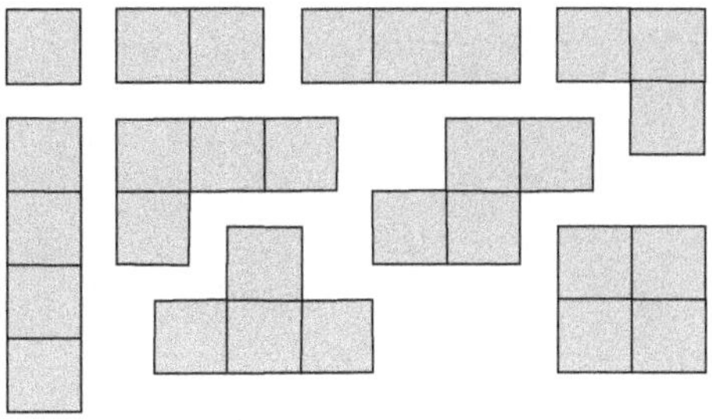

To the right are the smaller polyominoes: the monomino, the domino, both trominoes, and all five tetrominoes. Instead of arranging squares to form polyominoes, what if you arranged cubes to form solid polyominoes? Just like polyominoes, there is only one 3-D monomino (one cube), and one 3-D domino (two cubes), but there are two 3-D trominoes (three cubes).

Two-dimensional drawings of the 3-D monomino, the 3-D domino, and both 3-D trominoes (straight and bent) are shown below. These drawings are called **isometric drawings**.

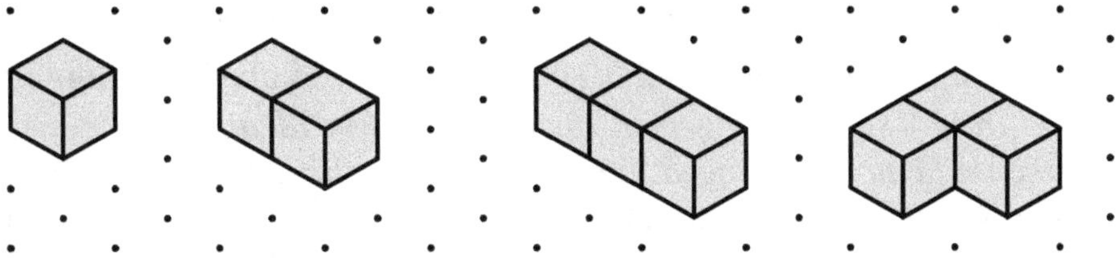

Figure 1 **Figure 2** **Figure 3** **Figure 4**

Although there are only five tetrominoes, there are more than five 3-D tetrominoes. Below are drawings of the five 3-D tetrominoes where all the cubes lie in the same plane (they are **planar**). In Exercises 1–4 you will practice your 3-D visual thinking.

1. Sketch each of the planar 3-D tetrominoes in the isometric grid below each example.

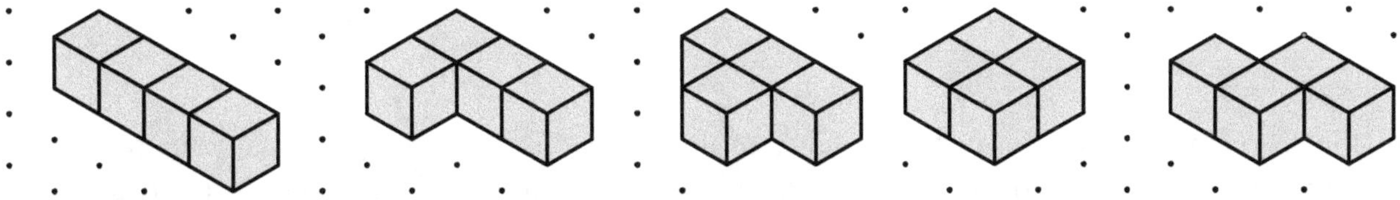

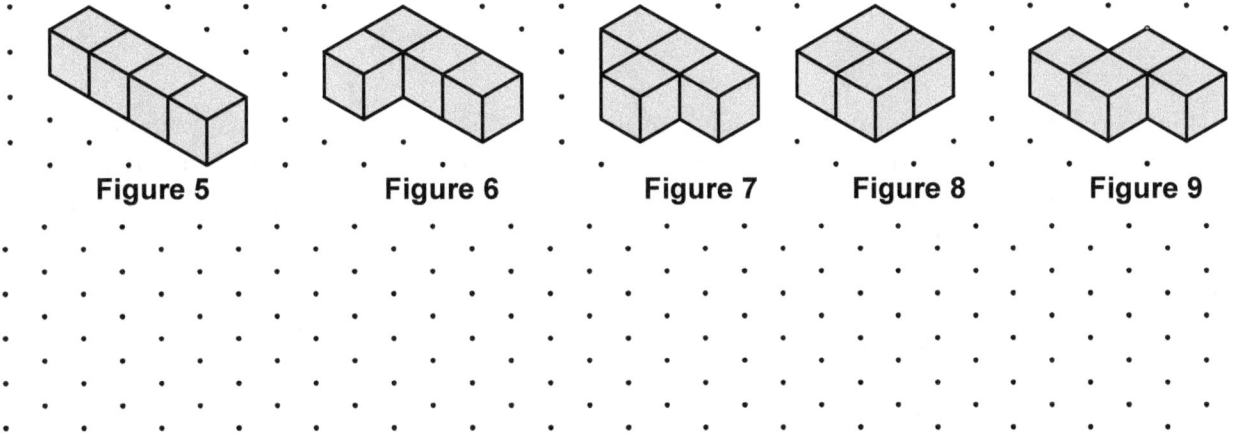

Figure 5 **Figure 6** **Figure 7** **Figure 8** **Figure 9**

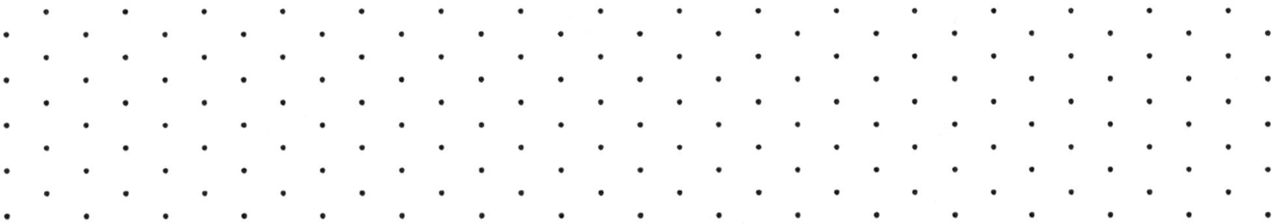

There are eight 3-D tetrominoes. For the remaining three 3-D tetrominoes, all the cubes do not lie in the same plane (they are **non-planar**). Two-dimensional isometric drawings of two of the three remaining 3-D tetrominoes are shown below.

2. Sketch a copy of each of the two 3-D non-planar tetrominoes shown.

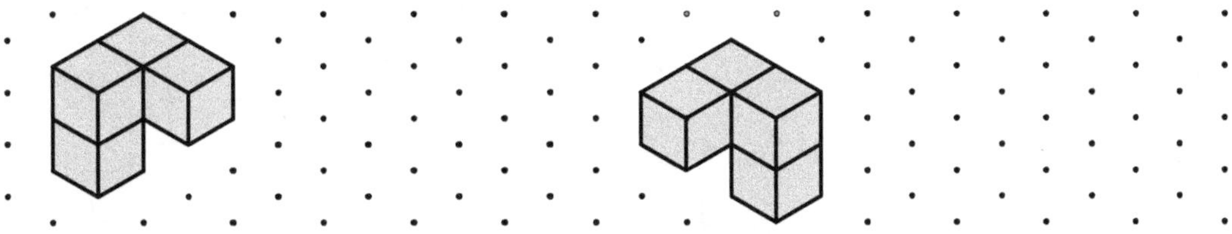

Figure 10 **Figure 11**

3. Sketch the remaining non-planar 3-D tetromino in the isometric grid below left.

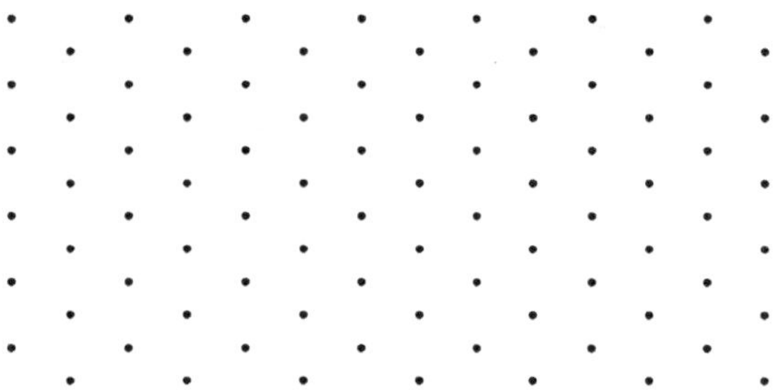

Figure 12

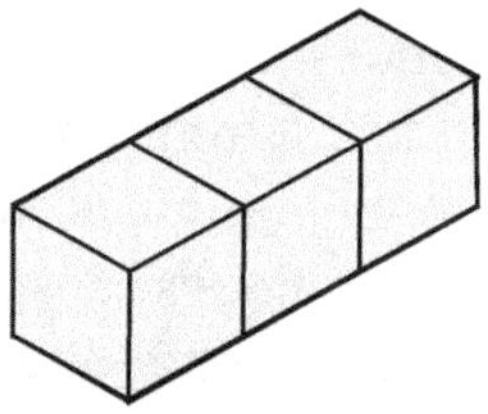

Convex

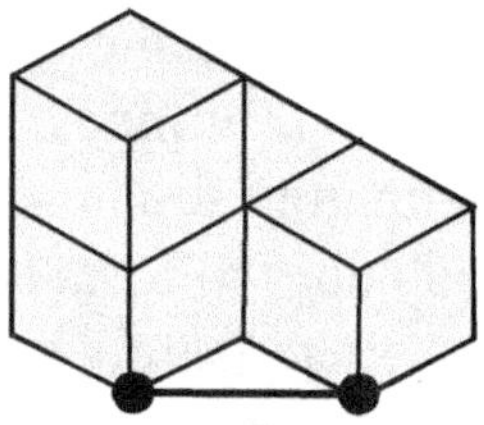

Non-convex

Figures 4, 6, 7, 9, 10, 11, and 12 are **non-convex** solids because for each of these solids it is possible to find two corners that can be connected by a segment outside of the solid.

4. Danish poet, scientist, and designer Piet Hein (1905–1996) posed the following visual thinking puzzle: *What are all the possible arrangements of four or fewer identical cubes arranged full face against full face that can be arranged into non-convex solids?* Six of them are shown on the previous page (Figures 4, 6, 7, 9, 10, and 11) and the seventh is the solution to Exercise 3 above (Figure 12). Sketch all possible arrangements on the isometric grid below.

Now that you have the isometric grid sketches of the seven possible arrangements, you are ready for the next rather amazing discovery. These seven pieces consisting of 27 cubes (six sets of four cubes and one set of three cubes) can be arranged to form a 3×3×3 cube. In 1969, Parker Brothers, Inc. produced Piet Hein's puzzle and called it the **Soma Cube**.

5. In this exercise, build the seven pieces of the Soma Cube by following these steps:
   - Use wood cubes and wood glue to build one set of the seven pieces of the Soma Cube. Be very careful and exact in positioning the cubes. Use tape to hold the pieces in position while drying.
   - When the pieces have dried, assemble them into the Soma Cube, shown below left.
   - The pieces can be arranged into other shapes. Can you create the Bed? The Multiple Staircase?

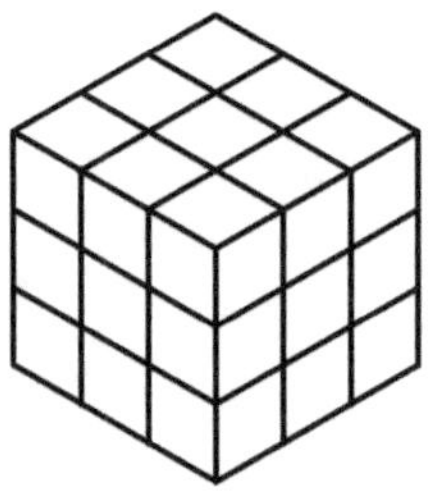

Bed

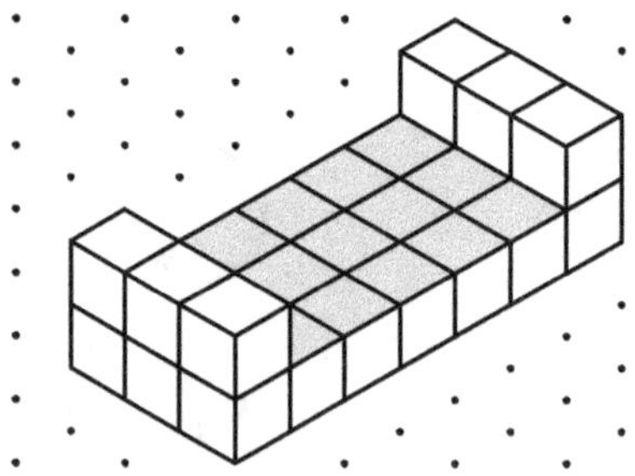

Multiple Staircase

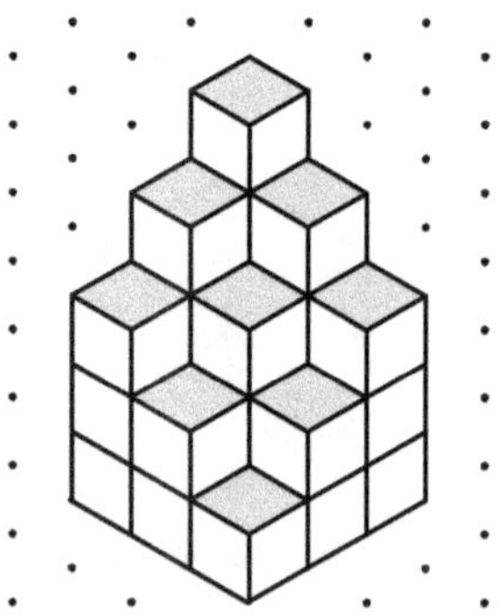

5.3 3-D Polyominoes in a 3-D Coordinate Grid

A bent 3-D tromino is embedded in the coordinate system below. The 3-D coordinate system has been sliced horizontally (parallel to the *xy*-plane) along the *z*-axis into five layers. The five slices are shown to the right. The points on the corners and edges of the 3-D tromino are shown by dots. The regions in each plane are shaded. Try this exercise.

1. From the points on the slices, sketch the location of the bent tromino on the 3-D grid below by shading the faces that are visible.

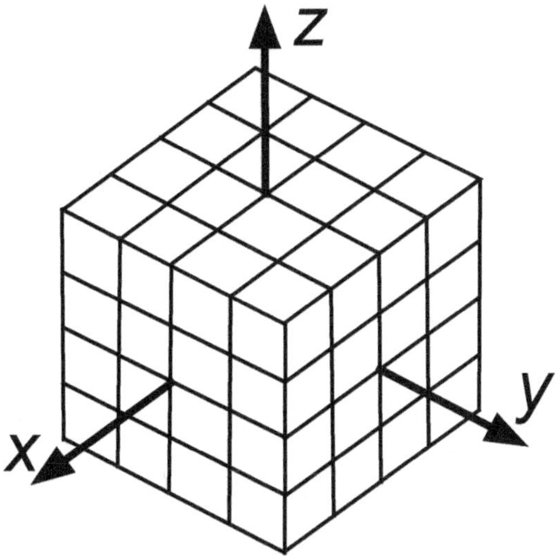

Top
$z=2$

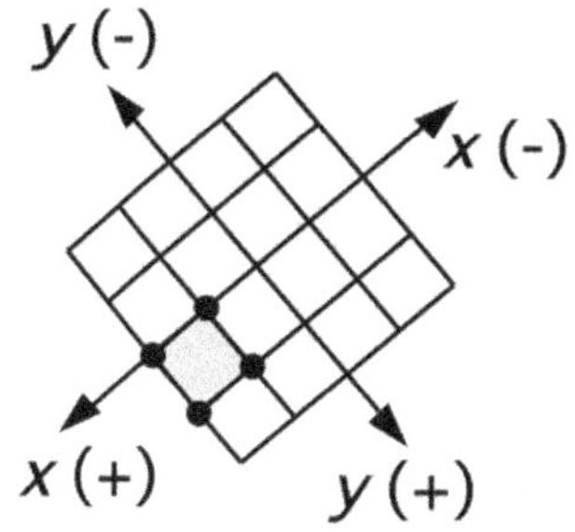

$z=1$

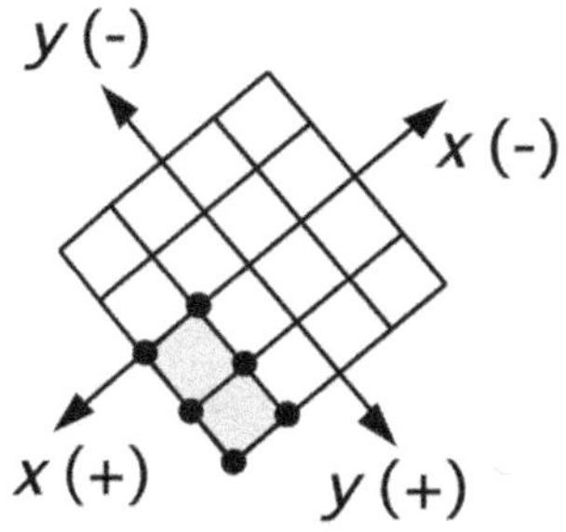

Middle
$z=0$

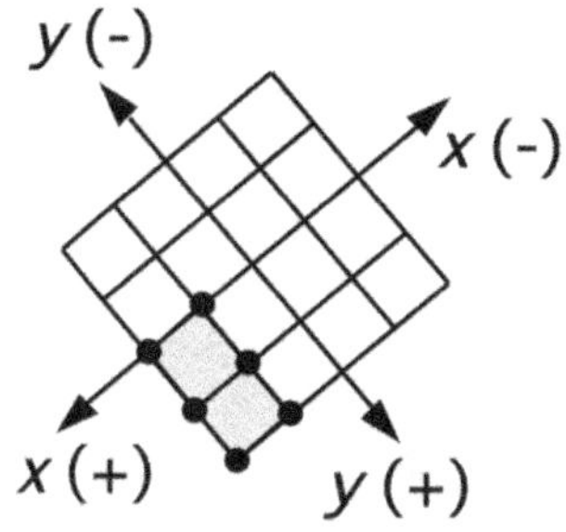

$z=-1$

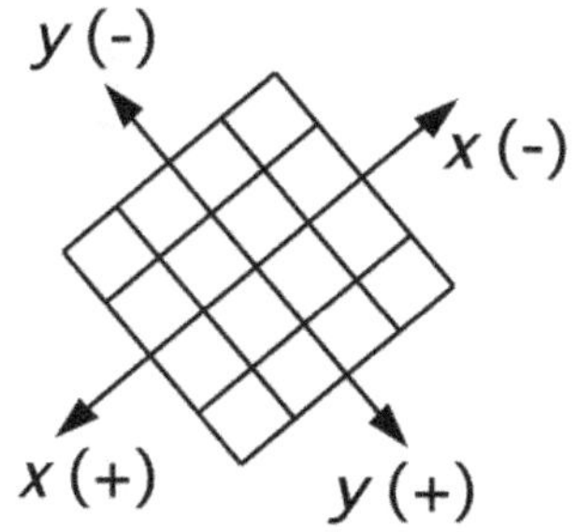

Bottom
$z=-2$

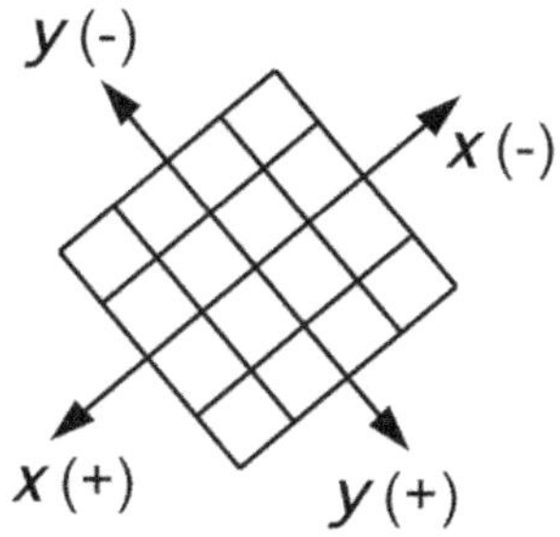

The 3-D coordinate system below has been sliced horizontally (parallel to the *xy*-plane) along the *z*-axis into seven levels of *xy*-planes, shown to the right. Try this exercise.

2. A portion of one of the non-planar 3-D tetrominoes is shaded in the 3-D coordinate system below. Shade the squares in each level the solid occupies.

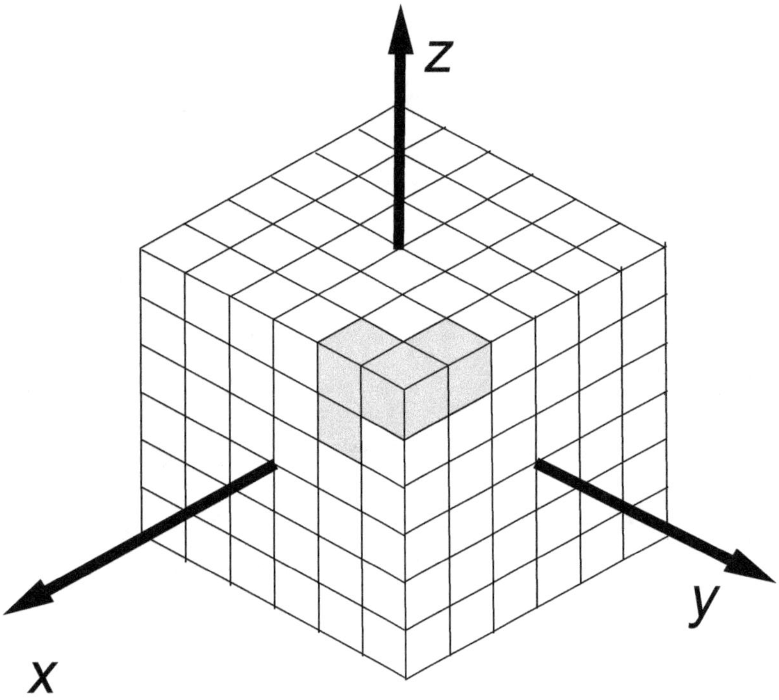

z = 3

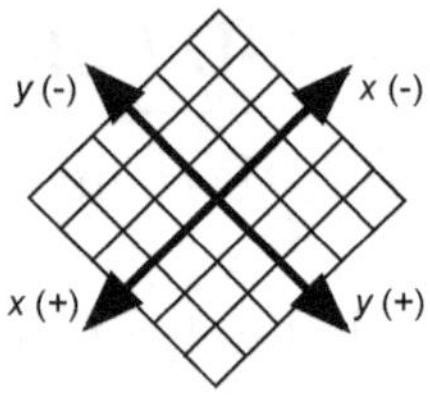

z = 2

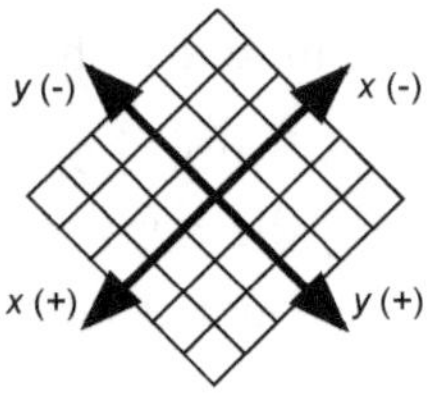

z = 1

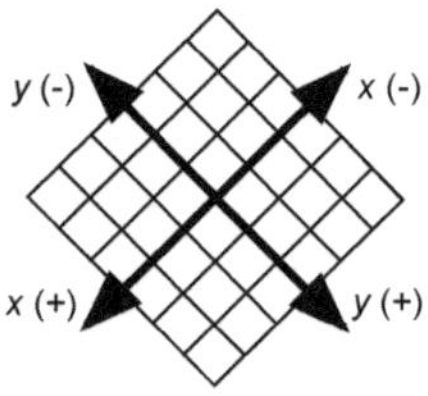

z = 0

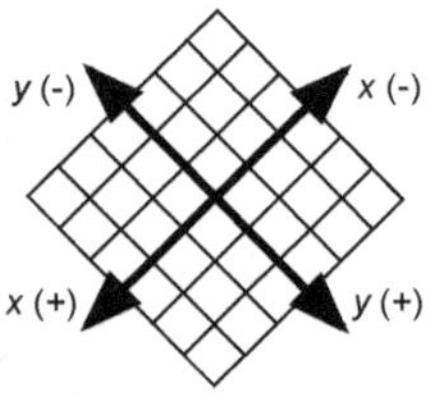

z = -1

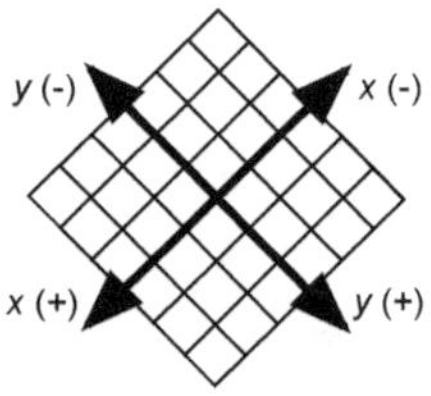

z = -2

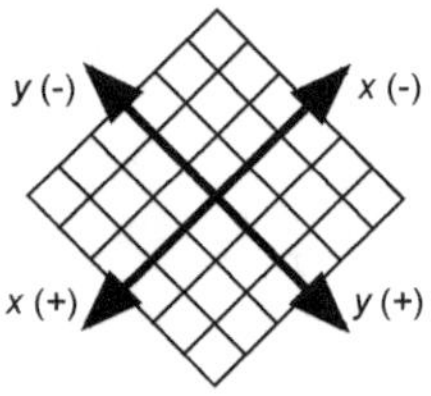

z = -3

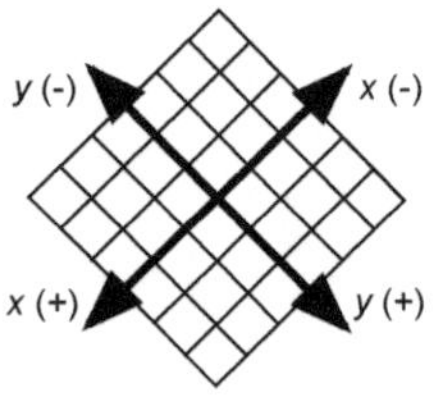

5.4 3-D Buried Treasure

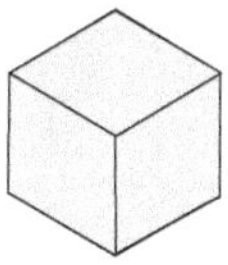

Level 1A 3-D Buried Treasure is played in a 4×4×4 three-dimensional coordinate grid where the *x*-, *y*- and *z*- values range from -2 to 2. However, the 3-D space has been sliced into five layers all parallel to the *xy*-plane. Play takes place on the five layers displayed. There is one buried treasure to be found, a cube (3-D monomino). To help visualize play in three dimensions see Appendix 3 on building 3-D models.

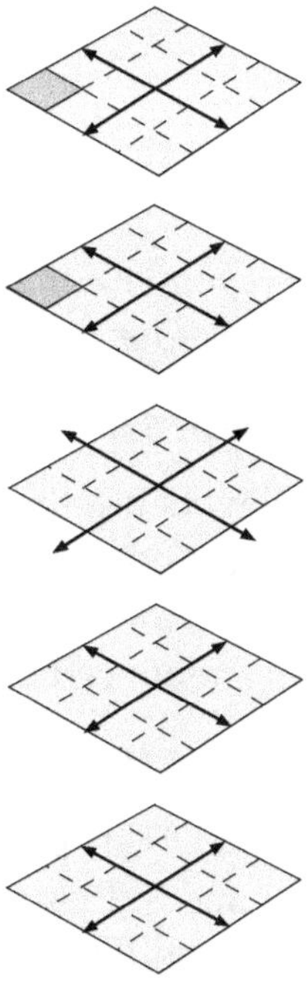

To hide your buried treasure cube, shade the squares in two of the slices. For example, if your buried treasure is located as shown in the 3-D diagram below, you shade the squares as shown on the layers to the right. The eight corners of the cube are (2, -2, 1), (2, -2, 2), (2, -1, 1), (2, -1, 1), (1, -2, 1), (1, -2, 2), (1, -1, 1), and (1, -1, 2).

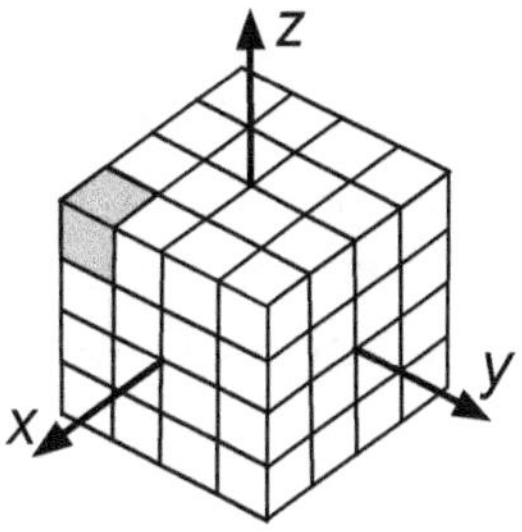

Rules for Level 1A:

1. To play, each team tries to locate the other team's buried treasure by taking turns calling out 3-D coordinates, or *digs*. Each turn consists of three digs.
2. If the first team calls out a point on a corner of one of the second team's buried treasure, the second team says, *hit*. If the first team misses, then the second team says, *miss*.
3. Teams should record their digs and their opponent's digs in the table as ordered triples as well as points on the slices to the right of the table (shown below right).
4. The second team responds after each guess whether it is a hit or miss. Then it is the second team's turn to take three digs. Continue taking turns with three digs at a time.
5. When one team has located at least three of the eight corners of the cube, then that team may take a guess as to the location of the other corners. Guessing the location of the other corners of the treasure must happen when it is your turn but before you have taken your three digs. If correct, they win. However, if they guess incorrectly, they lose. If the team that has located three corners does not wish to guess, the game continues until one team is ready to guess the treasure location.

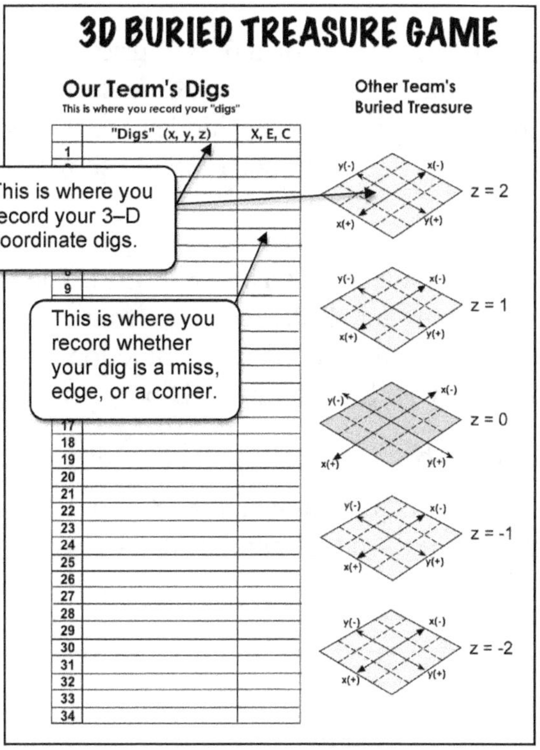

5.5 Variations on 3-D Buried Treasure

Level 1B This variation uses the same rules and $4\times4\times4$ three-dimensional coordinate grid as Level 1A, but teams hide two buried treasures; one is a cube, the other is a straight 3-D tromino (a $1\times1\times3$ rectangular prism). The two 3-D polyominoes cannot share a face, edge, or vertex. If the dig is a *hit*, you tell the other team if it is a corner point (*C*) or edge point (*E*).

Level 1C

Players use the same rules and $4\times4\times4$ grid, and hide the same two treasure pieces, but each player takes *four* digs at a time.

Level 1D

Players use the same rules and $4\times4\times4$ grid, and hide the same two treasure pieces, and each player takes four digs at a time. However, nothing is said about hit or miss until the completion of the four digs. No response is given for any one individual dig. After all four digs, the total number of misses is announced and the number of hits on each solid is announced.

Level 1E

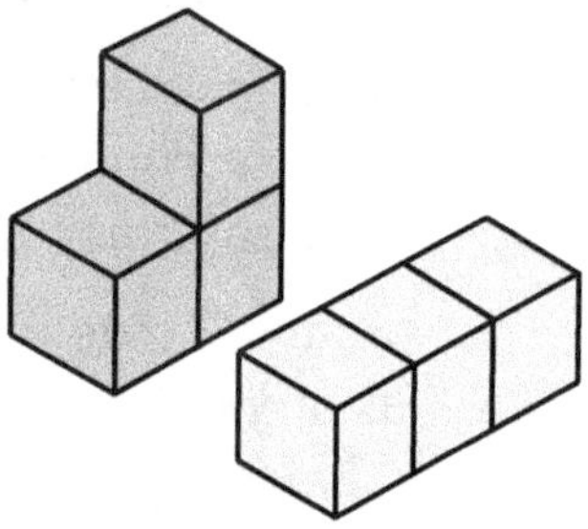

Level 1E is played on a $6\times6\times6$ grid. The values for x, y, and z are between -3 and 3. Players takes four digs at a time but nothing is said about hit or miss until the completion of the four digs. Two treasures are hidden: a straight 3-D tromino, and a bent 3-D tromino. They are shown on the right.

Level 1F

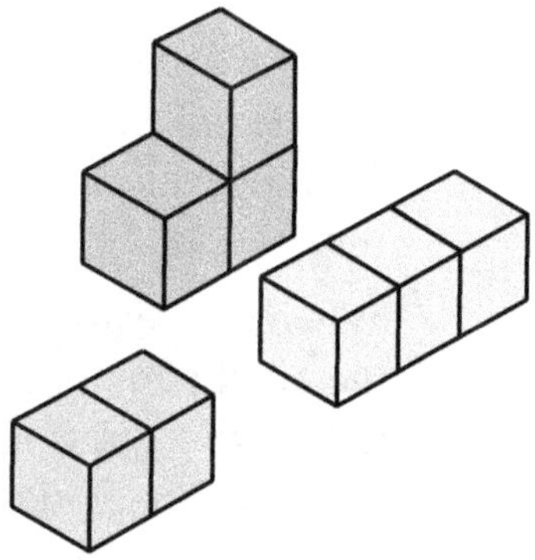

Level 1F is played on a $6\times6\times6$ grid. Players takes four digs at a time but nothing is said about hit or miss until the completion of the four digs. Three treasures are hidden: a 3-D domino, a straight 3-D tromino, and a bent 3-D tromino. They are shown on the right.

Level 1G

Level 1G is played on a $8\times8\times8$ grid. The values for x, y, and z are between -4 and 4. Players takes four digs at a time but nothing is said about hit or miss until the completion of the four digs. Three *different* treasures are hidden (any 3-D polyomino with three cubes or less).

Level 1H

Level 1H is played on a $8\times8\times8$ grid. Players takes four digs at a time but nothing is said about hit or miss until the completion of the four digs. Four treasures are hidden (any 3-D polyomino with four cubes or less).

5.6 3-D Buried Treasure Puzzles

In these 3-D Buried Treasure puzzles your task is to locate the 3-D tromino in the 5×5×5 grid. A *C* represents a corner hit, an *E* represents an edge hit, and an *X* represents a miss. Shade in the tromino in each level and sketch the tromino showing its orientation in the isometric grid below.

3-DBTP 1

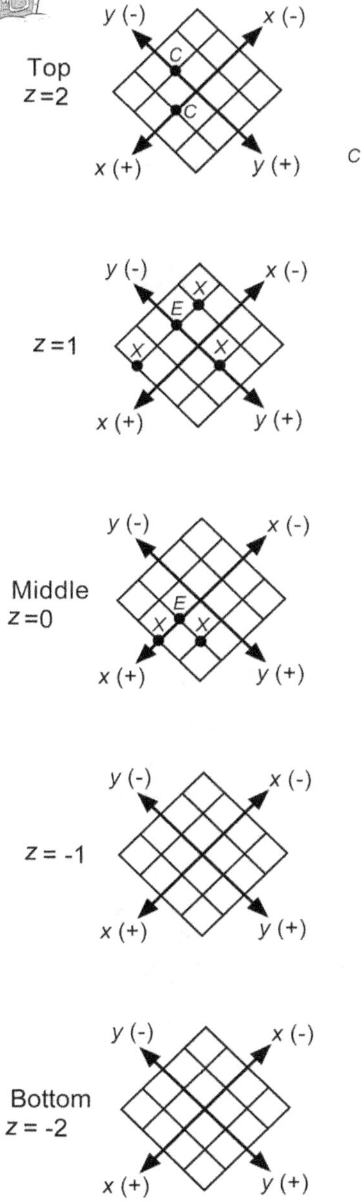

3-DBTP 2

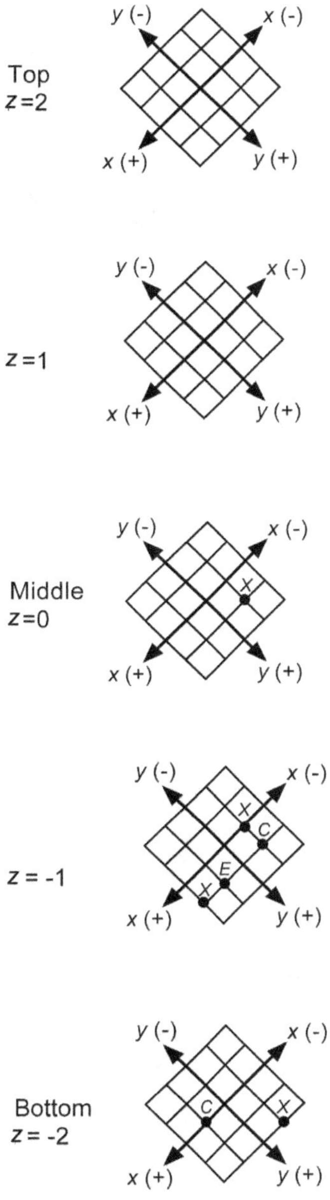

3-DBTP 3

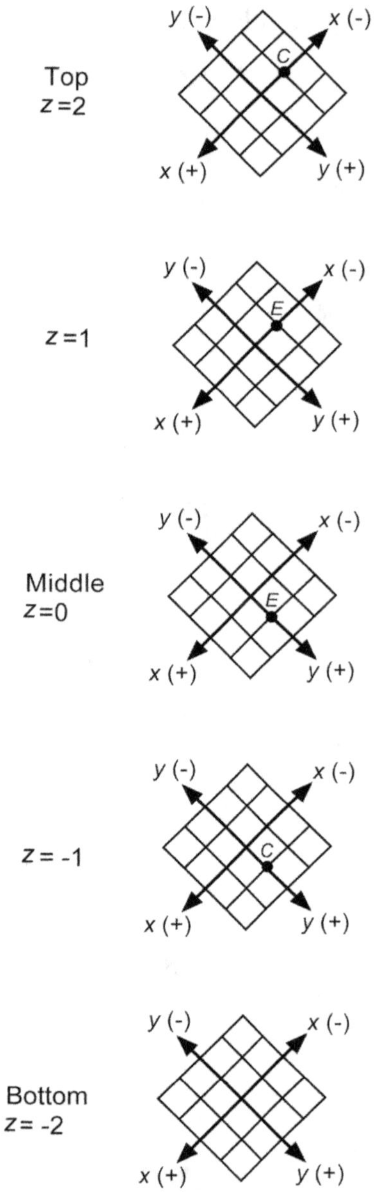

3-DBTP 4

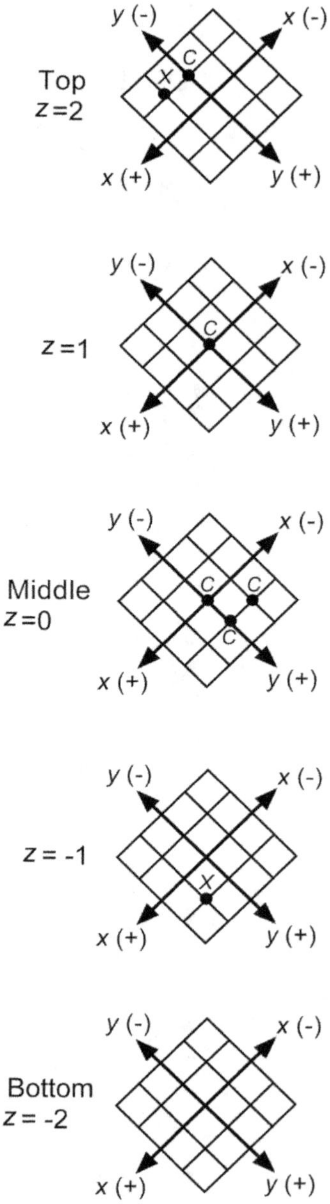

In Puzzles 5 and 6 locate the 3-D tetromino. A *C* represents a corner, an *E* an edge, and an *X* indicates a miss. Shade in the tetromino in each level and sketch it in the isometric grid below.

3-DBTP 5

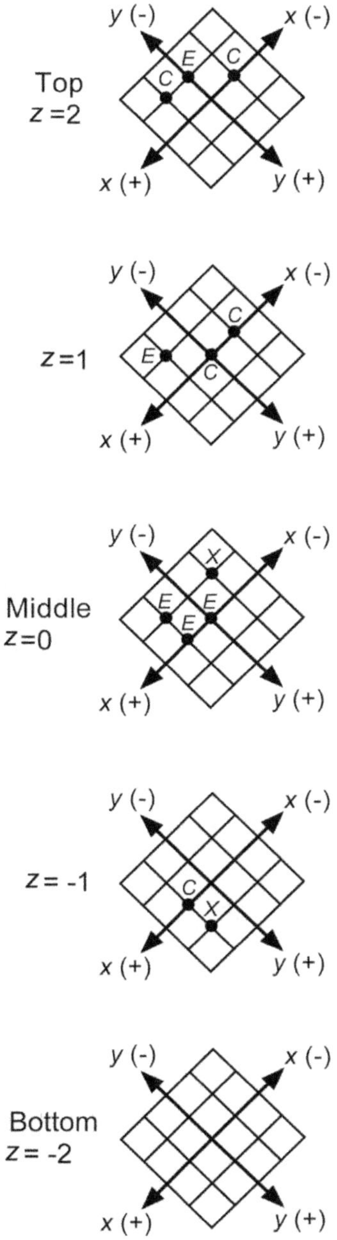

3-DBTP 6

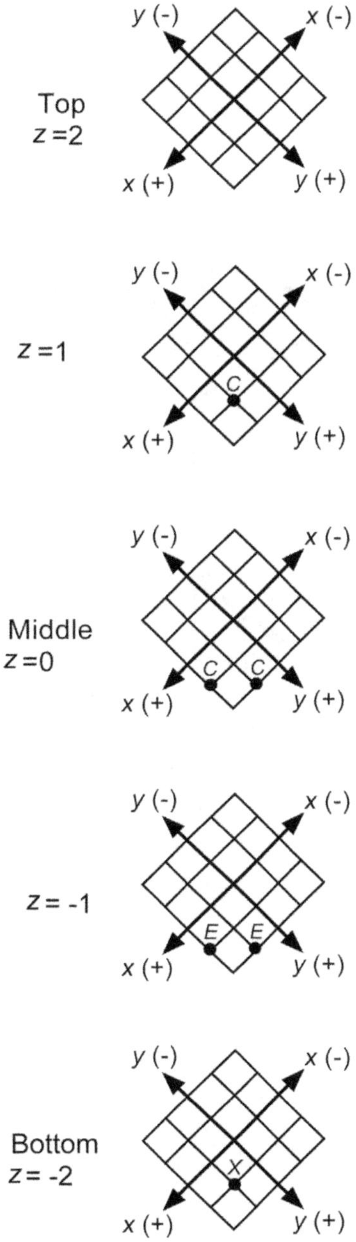

In Puzzle 7 locate the 3-D pentomino. Four of the five cubes are on the outer surface as shown below left. Only one guess (an *X* indicating a miss) was necessary to locate the fifth cube. Shade in the 3-D pentomino in each level and sketch it showing all five cubes in the isometric grid below.

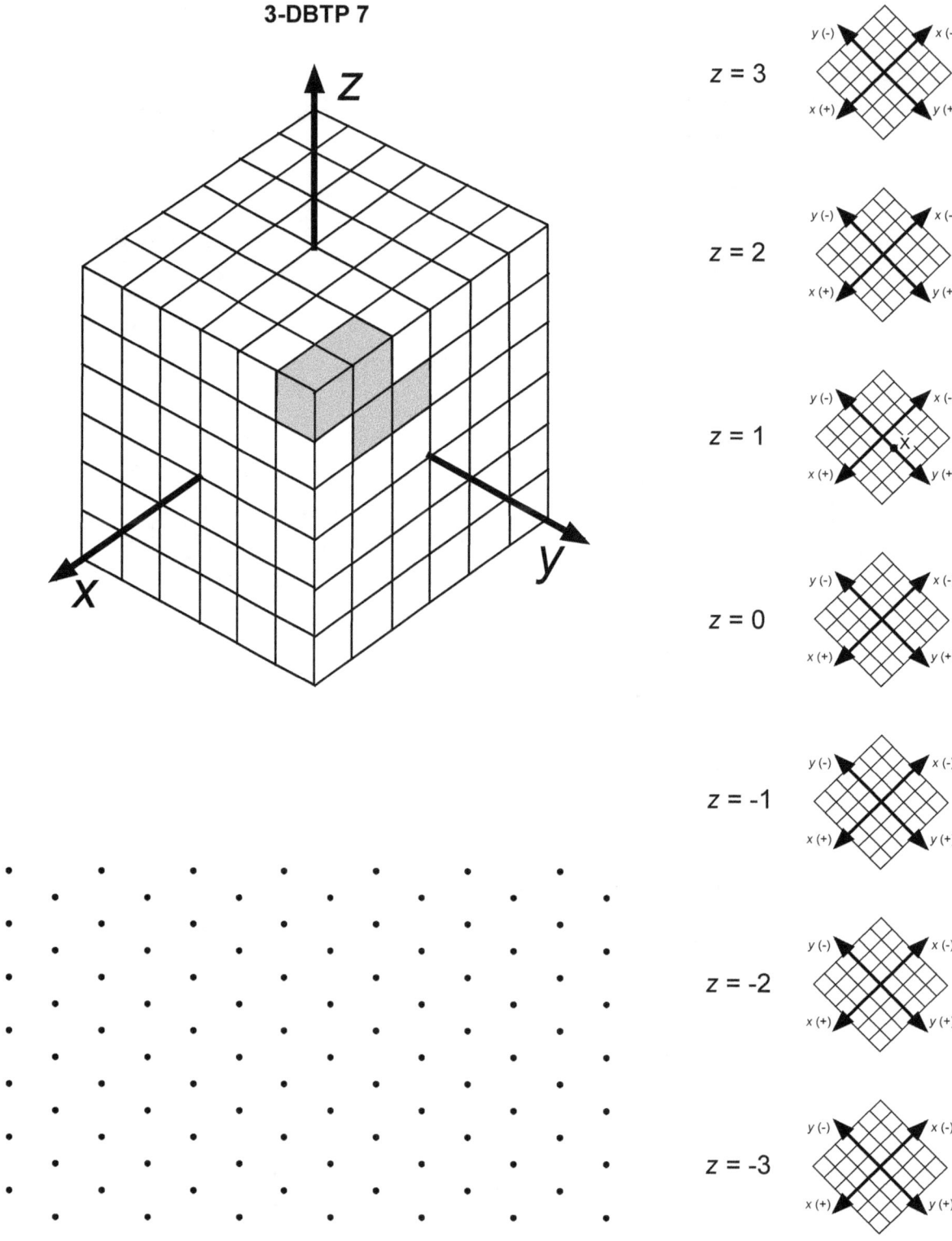

3-DBTP 7

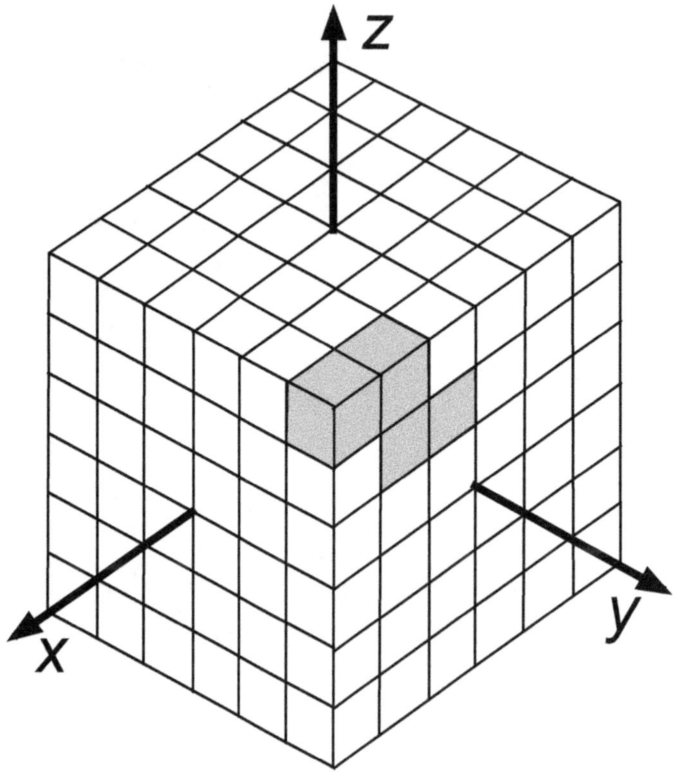

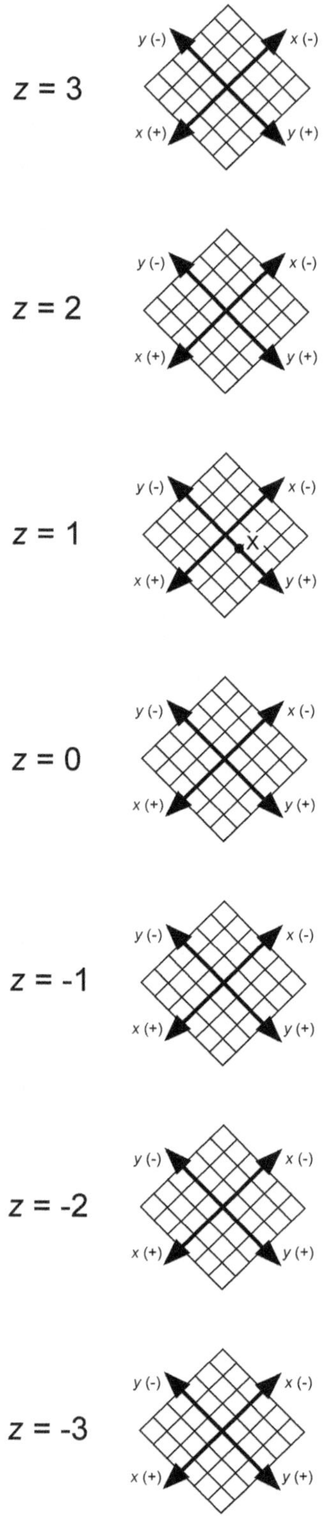

Not all treasure is silver and gold, mate.

—Captain Jack Sparrow
Pirates of the Caribbean:
Curse of the Black Pearl

6.1 Pirate Geometry

In this chapter you will use geometry to locate pirate treasure buried on sun-drenched tropical islands. You will need a compass, straightedge, ruler, and protractor. You may also need patty paper or tracing paper. You can review some properties of geometry shown below.

Geometric Constructions

During the Golden Age, Greek mathematicians made a game of geometry. They explored what they could create with a compass and straightedge. These creations are called geometric constructions. In his 13-book treatise, *Elements*, Euclid established the rules for this game of constructions. The geometry we traditionally study in school today is based on these rules and is called Euclidean Geometry. You should familiarize yourselves with the following compass and straightedge constructions:

To duplicate a given segment

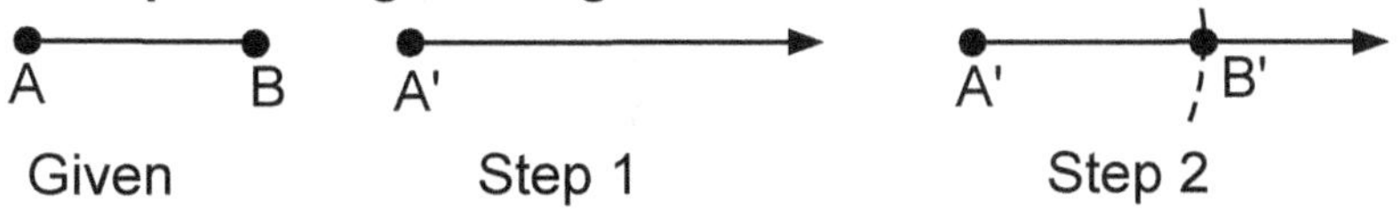

To duplicate a given angle

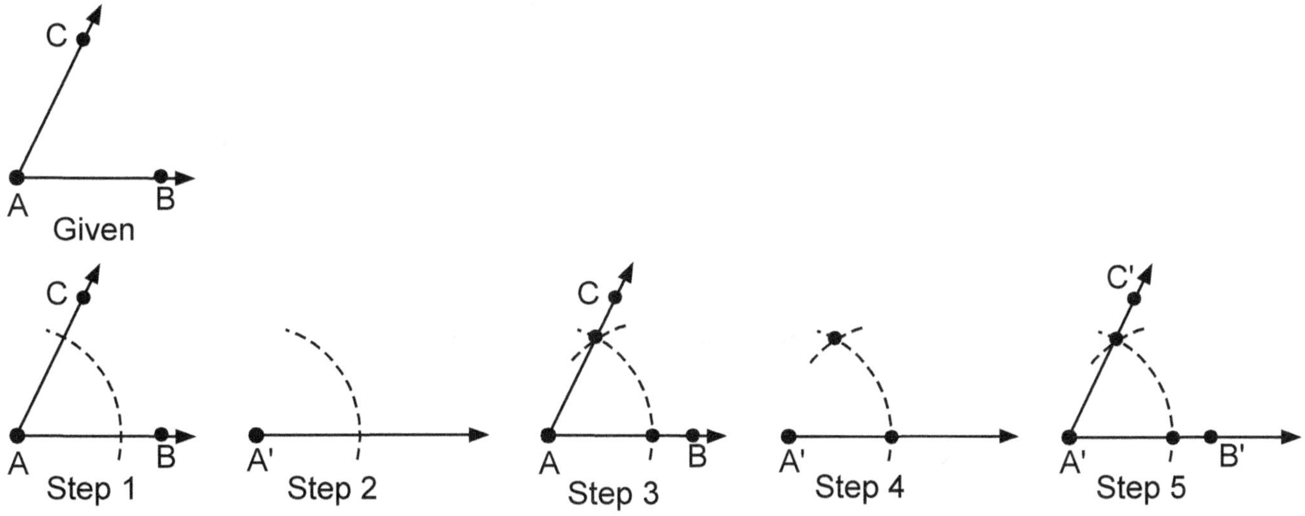

To construct the bisector of an angle

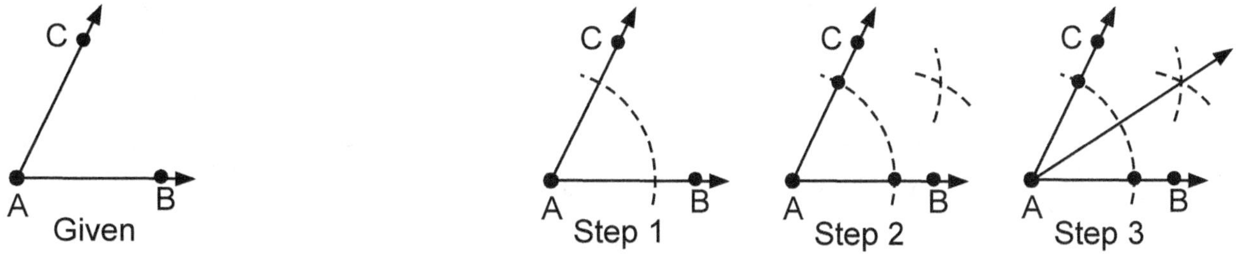

Chapter 6.1

To construct a perpendicular bisector of a given segment

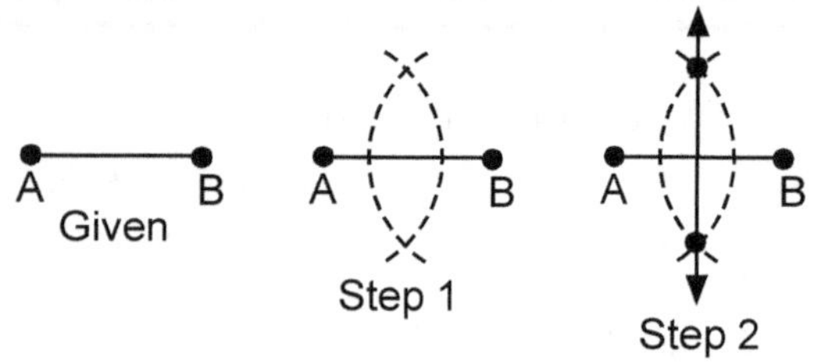

To construct a perpendicular from a point to a line

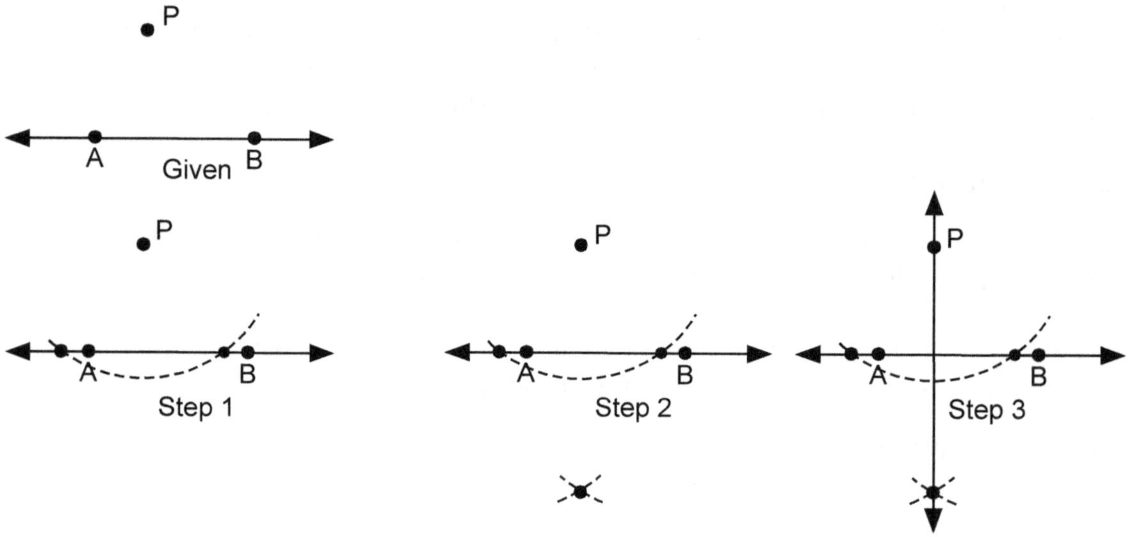

To construct a perpendicular through a point on a line

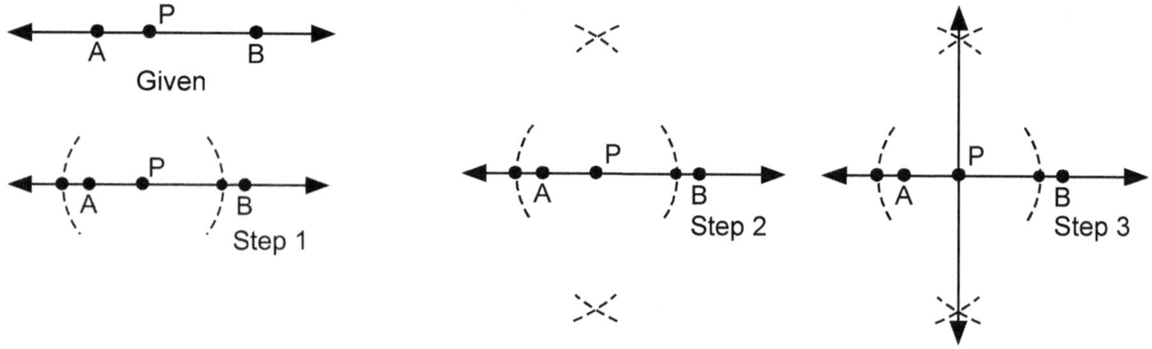

To construct a line through a given point parallel to a given line

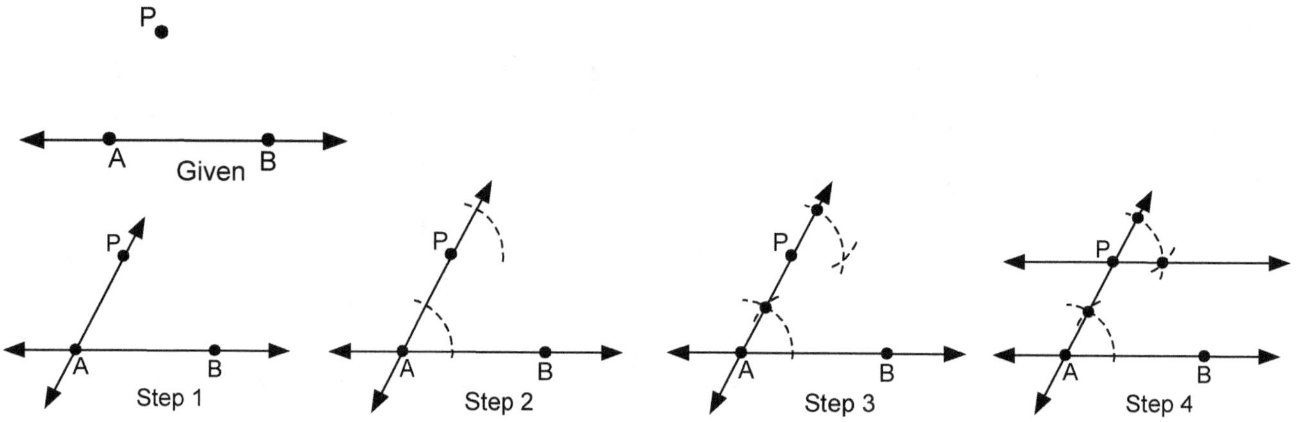

Triangle Congruence Shortcuts

Two polygons are congruent if and only if the sides and angles of one polygon are congruent to the corresponding sides and angles of the other polygon. However, because of the rigidity of triangles, there are four shortcuts to determining if two triangles are congruent. You should familiarize yourselves with the following triangle congruence shortcuts:

SSS: If the three sides of one triangle are congruent to three sides of another triangle, then the two triangles are congruent.

SAS: If two sides and the included angle of one triangle are congruent to the corresponding two sides and the included angle of another triangle, then the two triangles are congruent.

ASA: If two angles and the included side of one triangle are congruent to the corresponding two angles and the included side of another triangle, then the two triangles are congruent.

AAS: If two angles and the non-included side of one triangle are congruent to the corresponding two angles and non-included side of another triangle, then the two triangles are congruent.

Chapter 6.1

Points of Concurrency

The incenter, circumcenter, centroid, and orthocenter are the four points of concurrency commonly found in geometry textbooks.

Incenter. The three angle bisectors of the angles of a triangle are concurrent in a point called the *incenter*. It is a point that is equally distant to the three sides of the triangle and is the center of a circle inscribed in the triangle (it is tangent to each of the three sides).

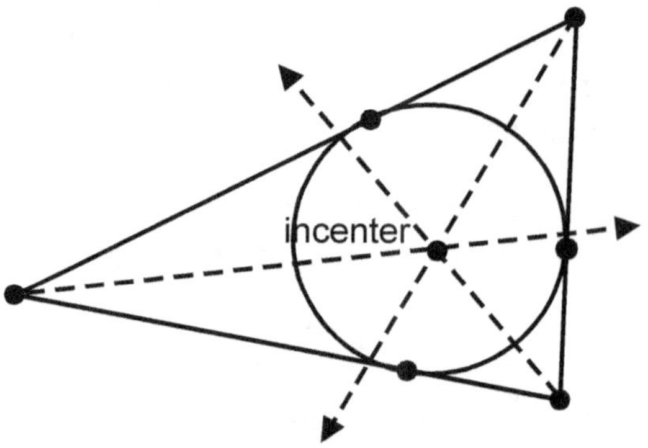

Circumcenter. The three perpendicular bisectors of the sides of a triangle are concurrent in a point called the *circumcenter*. It is a point that is equally distant to the three vertices of the triangle and is the center of a circle that circumscribes the triangle (the circle passes through the three vertices of the triangle).

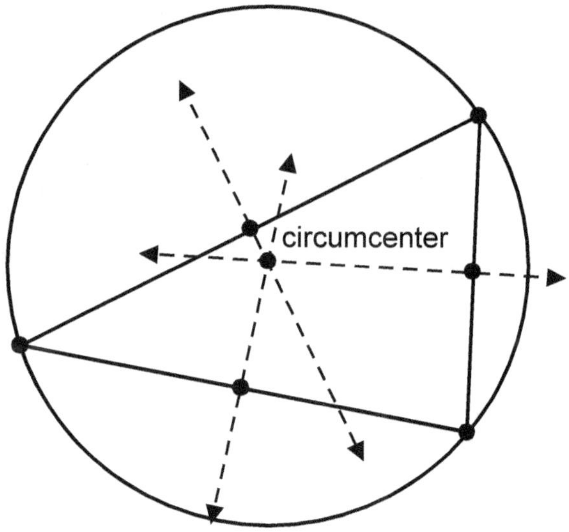

Centroid. The three medians of a triangle are concurrent in a point called the *centroid*. The centroid is the center of gravity of the triangle. The centroid divides each median into two segments such that the smaller segment is half the length of the larger segment.

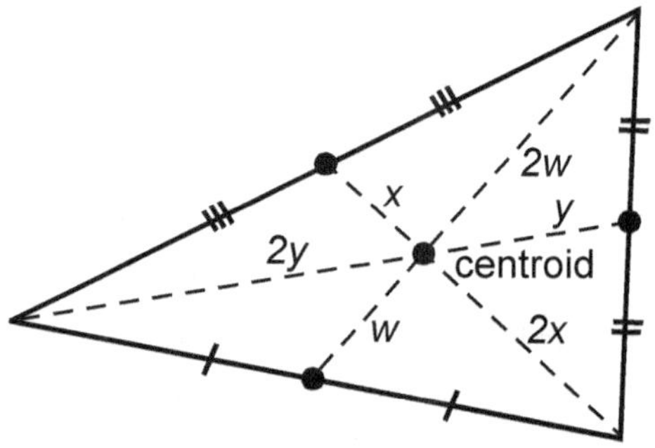

Orthocenter. The three altitudes of a triangle are concurrent in a point called the *orthocenter*.

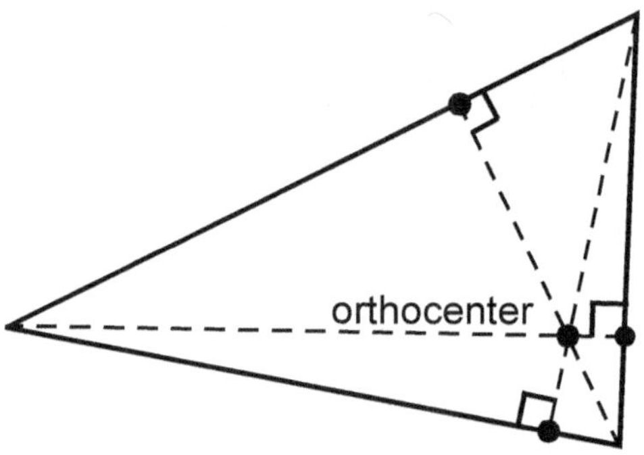

6.2 Pirate Treasure with Geometry

1. Buried Treasure on Freebooter Island *h*

You find an old map of Freebooter Island. After breaking the secret code scribbled on the back of the map you learn clues to the location of a treasure chest buried on the island (not in the sea). The map shows two important locations that will help you find the treasure, Hangman's Tree and a giant boulder in the shape of a human skull. The treasure is located 300 meters from Hangman's Tree and 500 meters from Skull Rock. Do you have enough information to find the treasure? How many places do you need to dig to locate the treasure? Where is the treasure?

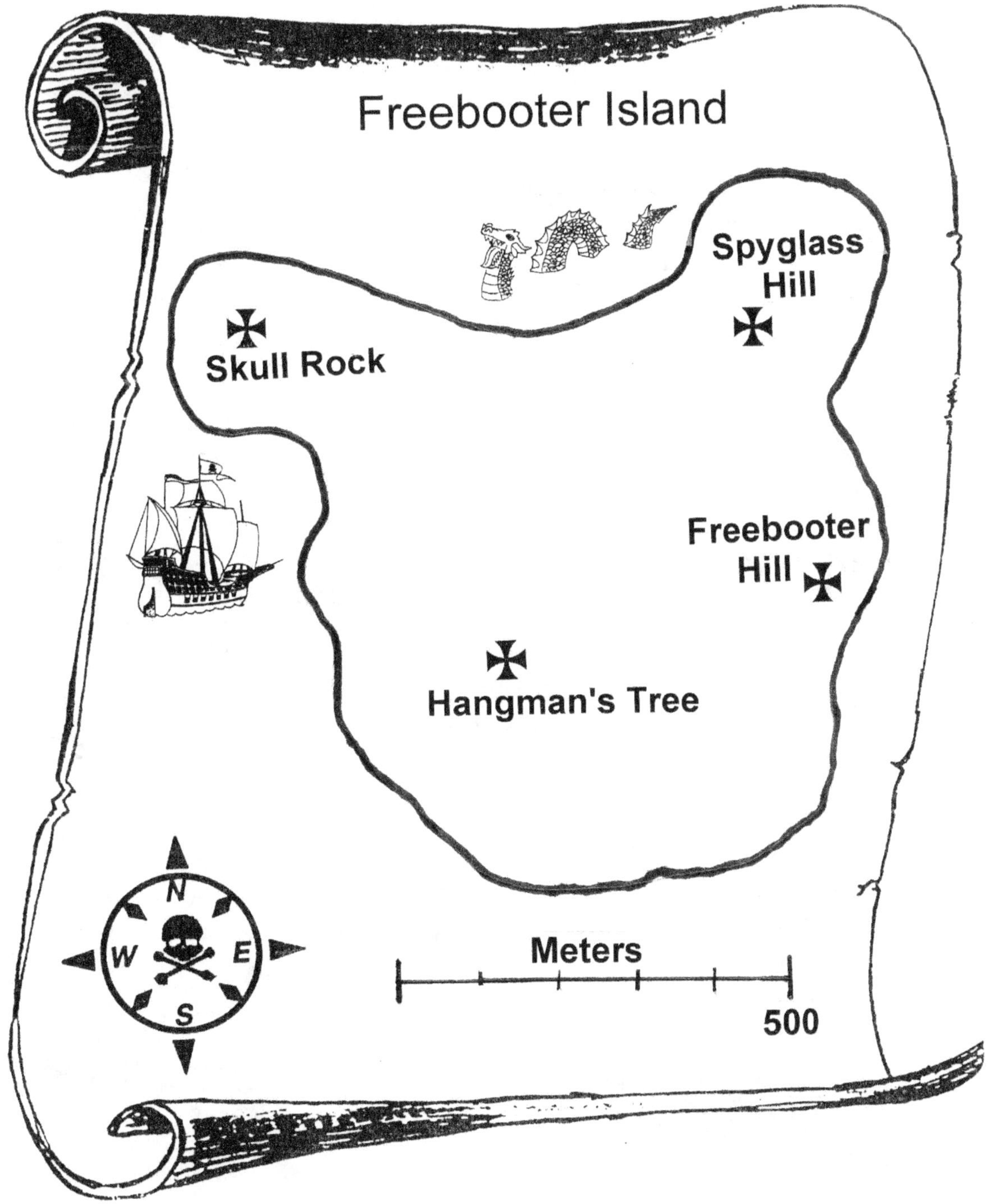

2. Buried Treasure on Turtle Island

At the bottom of an old trunk you discover what appears to be a treasure map with clues written on the back of it leading to the location of a treasure chest buried on Turtle Island. The map shows two important locations that will help you find the treasure, an old oak tree and a giant boulder at the entrance to the Davey Jones Cemetery. The treasure is located 300 meters from the old oak tree. When standing at the base of the oak tree, the angle between the location of the treasure and the line of sight to the giant boulder is 40°. Do you have enough information to find the treasure? How many places do you need to dig to locate the treasure? Find the treasure

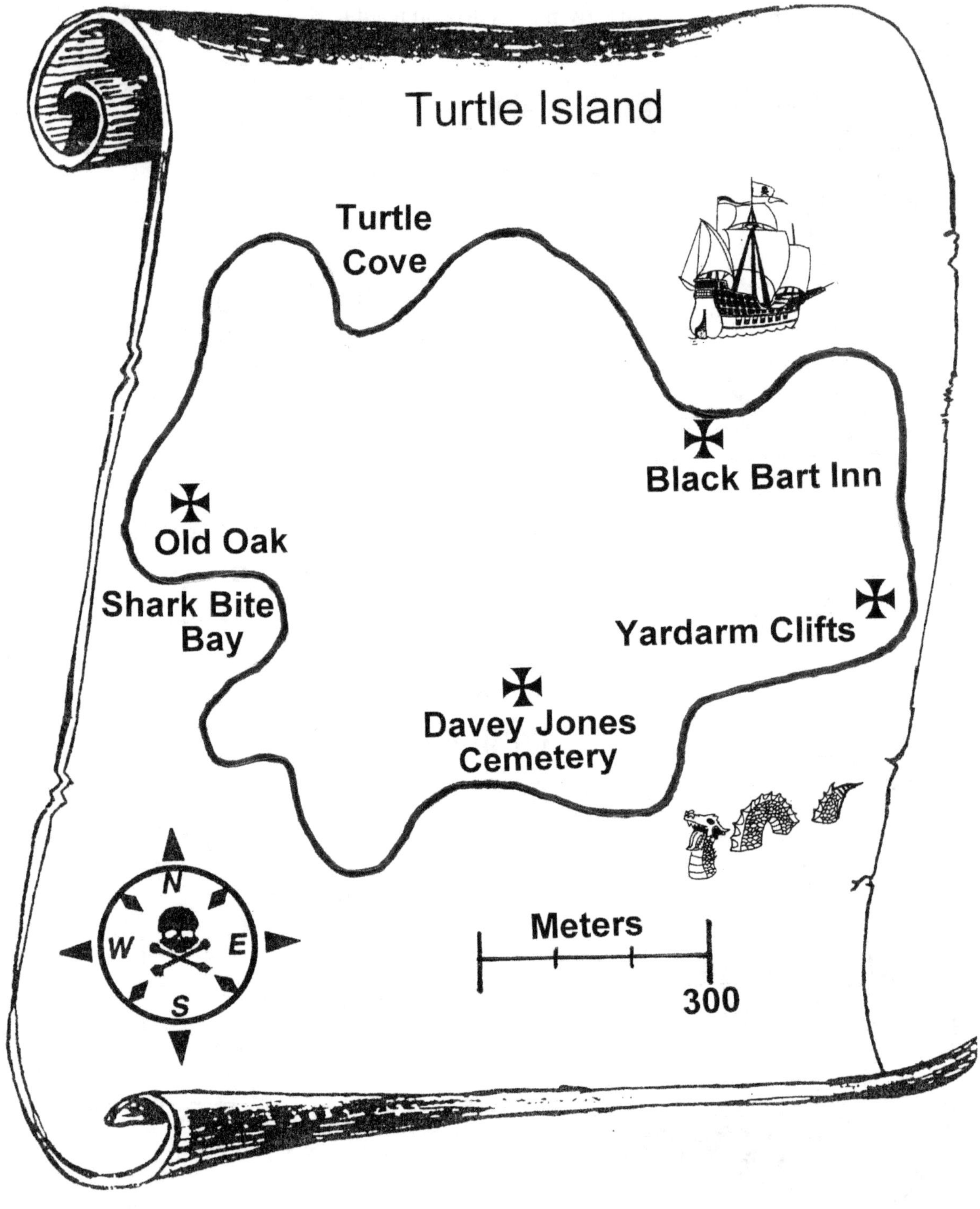

3. Buried Treasure on Calico Island

Walking on the beach you find an old rum bottle with a rolled up map inside. It appears to be a treasure map with instructions on the back of it hinting at the location of a treasure chest buried on Calico Island. The map shows two important locations you will need to find the treasure. The first is the side entrance to the Gallows Inn. The second location is Calico Jack's Cave, where the rocks are in the shape of a human skull. You enter Calico Jack's Cave through the mouth of the giant skull. When standing at the side entrance to Gallows Inn the angle between the location of the treasure and the line of sight to Calico Jack's Cave entrance is 50°. When standing at the base of Calico Jack's Cave entrance the angle between the location of the treasure and the line of sight to the Gallows Inn is 60°. Do you have enough information to find the treasure? How many places do you need to dig to locate the treasure? Find the treasure.

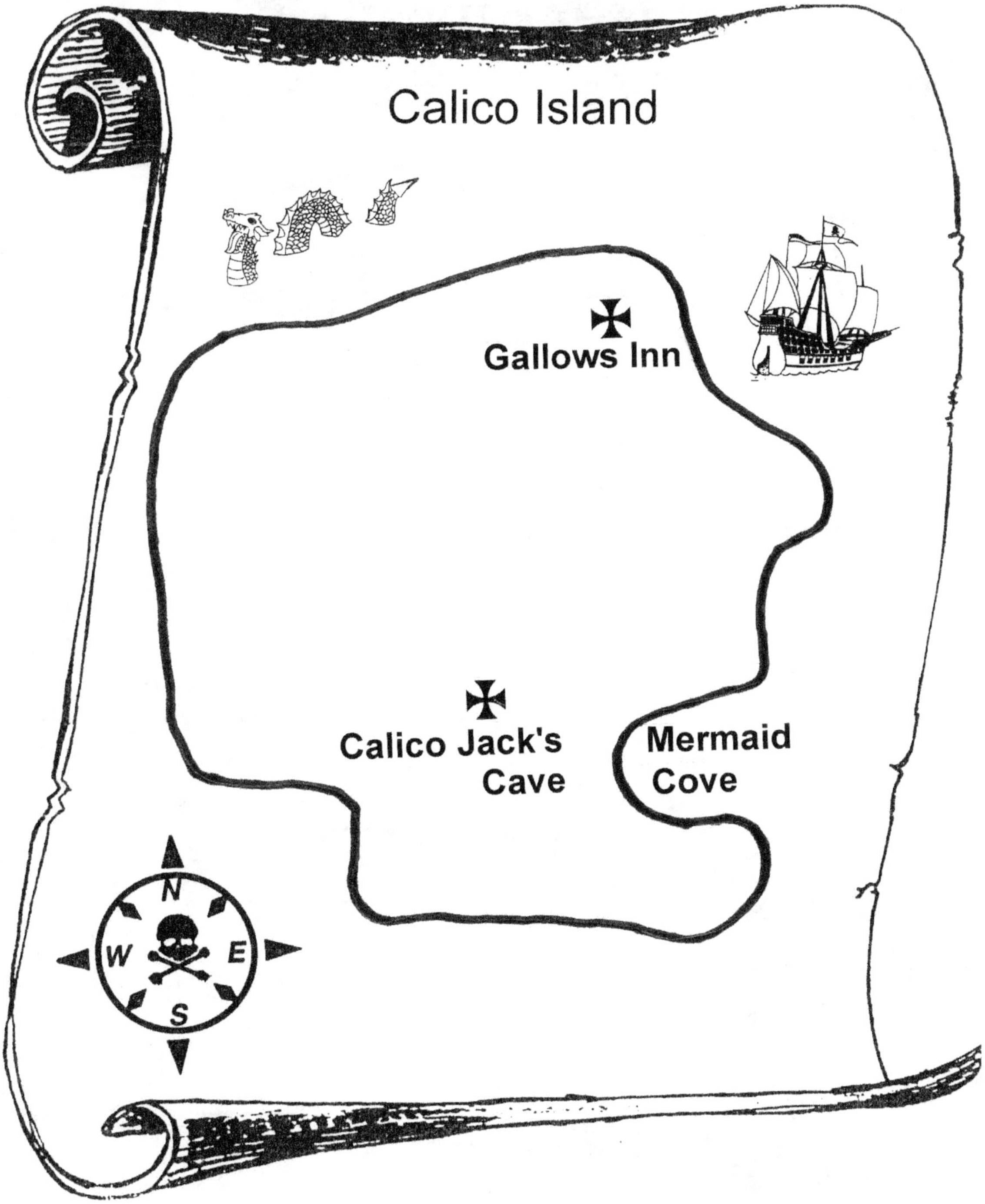

4. Buried Treasure on Swashbuckler's Island

You find an old treasure map with writing on the back. The scribbles on the back appear to be clues to the location of pirate treasure buried on Swashbuckler's Island. The map shows two important locations you will need to find the treasure. The first is the swinging door entrance to The Flying Dutchman Inn. The second location, due north of the Inn, is the central tombstone in the Pauper's Graveyard. When standing at the swinging door entrance to The Flying Dutchman Inn, the angle between the location of the treasure and the line of sight to the central tombstone in the Pauper's Graveyard is 55°. When standing at the central tombstone in the Pauper's Graveyard, the treasure is due east. Do you have enough information to find the treasure? How many places do you need to dig to locate the treasure? Find the treasure.

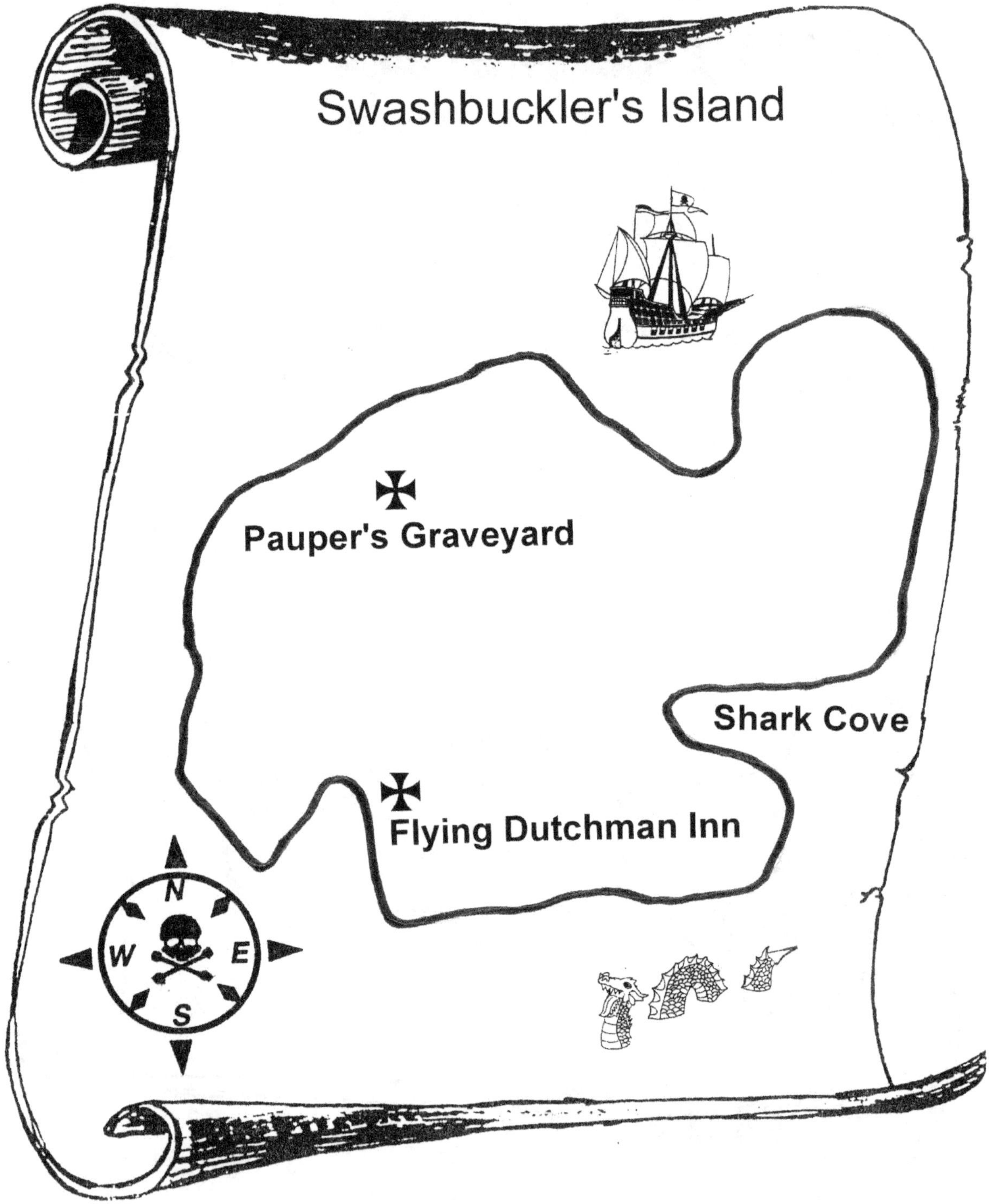

5. Buried Treasure on Isla Mauritia

While replacing the frame of an old painting, you discover a piece of paper tucked behind the canvas. It appears to be an old treasure map. The back of the map gives clues to the location of a treasure chest buried on Isla Mauritia. The map shows two important locations you will need to locate the treasure. The first is the back door entrance to the Jack Ketch Tavern. The second location, due south of the tavern, is Hangman's Tree. The treasure is due west of Hangman's Tree and 600 meters from the back door to Jack Ketch Tavern. Do you have enough information to find the treasure? How many places do you need to dig to locate the treasure? Find the treasure.

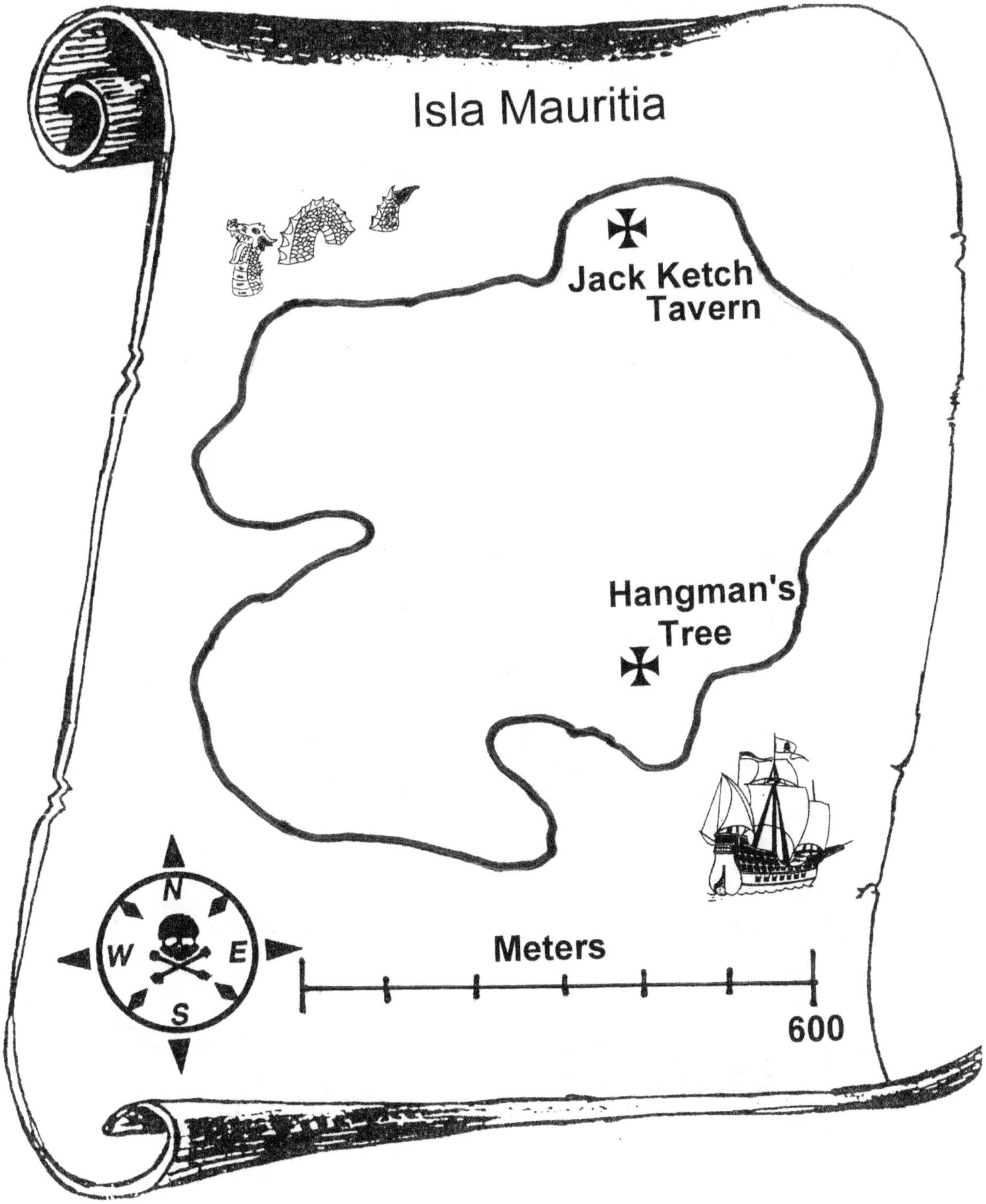

6. Buried Treasure on Barbossa Island

You find an old treasure map that gives clues to the location of a buried treasure chest on Barbossa Island. The map shows a eucalyptus tree, a giant boulder in the shape of a cannon, and Captain Barbossa's Tombstone. According to the note the treasure is located at the incenter of the triangle formed by the Eucalyptus Tree, the Giant Cannon Boulder, and the Barbossa Tombstone. Find the treasure.

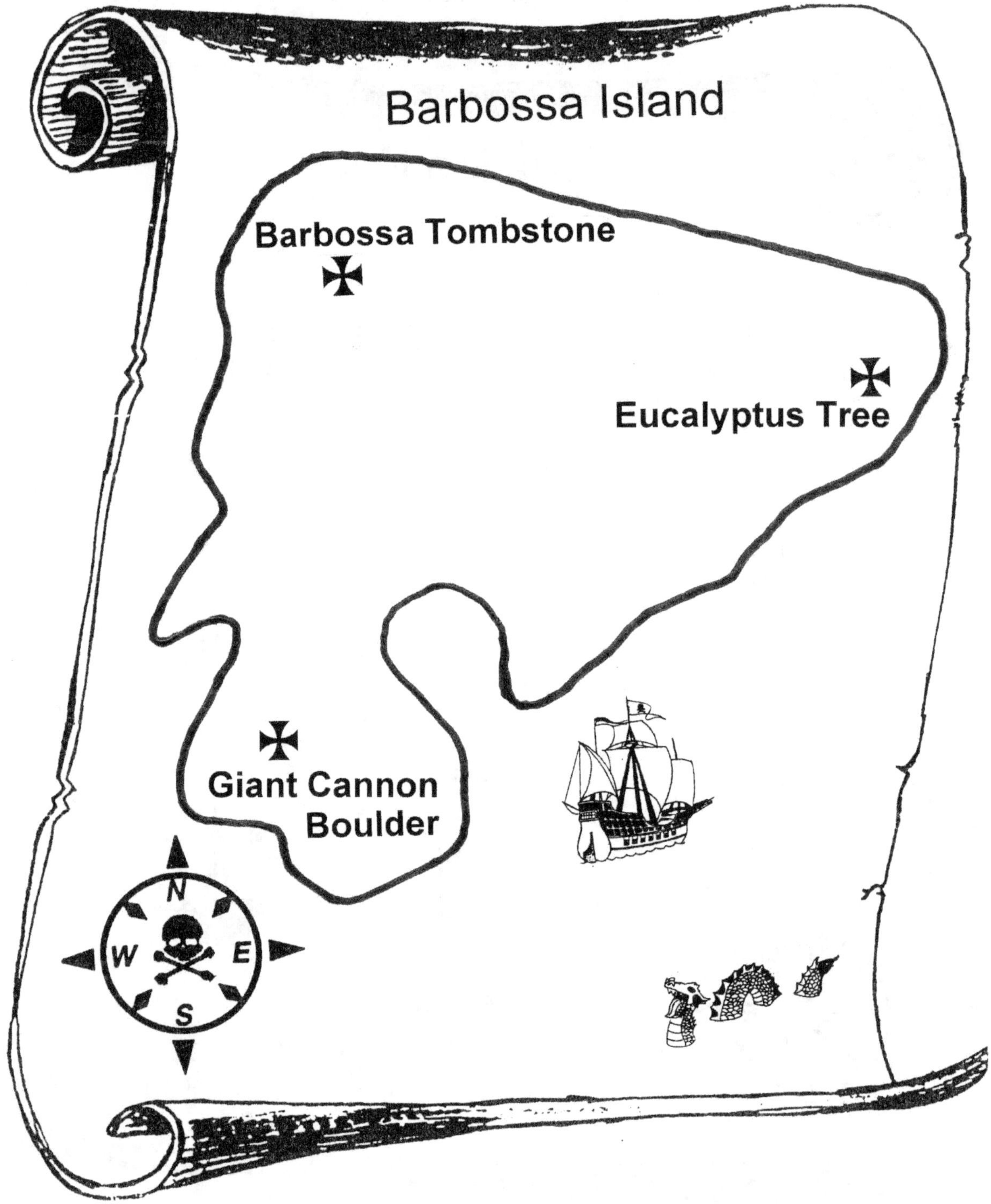

7. Buried Treasure on Crocodile Key

At the Blackbeard Tavern an old sailor offers to sell you a map showing the location of buried treasure on Crocodile Key. You pay up and as he hands you the map he whispers, “On this island you will find a giant palm tree, a small boulder in the shape of a crocodile skull, and a sign announcing the entrance to the Sulfur Bog. Find the point midway between the Bog and Crocodile Skull and drive a stake in the ground. Go to the palm tree and walk toward the stake while counting your steps. When you reach the stake, stop and record the number of steps. Continue walking along the same straight line for the same number of steps. The treasure is located at that point. Good Luck.” Find the treasure.

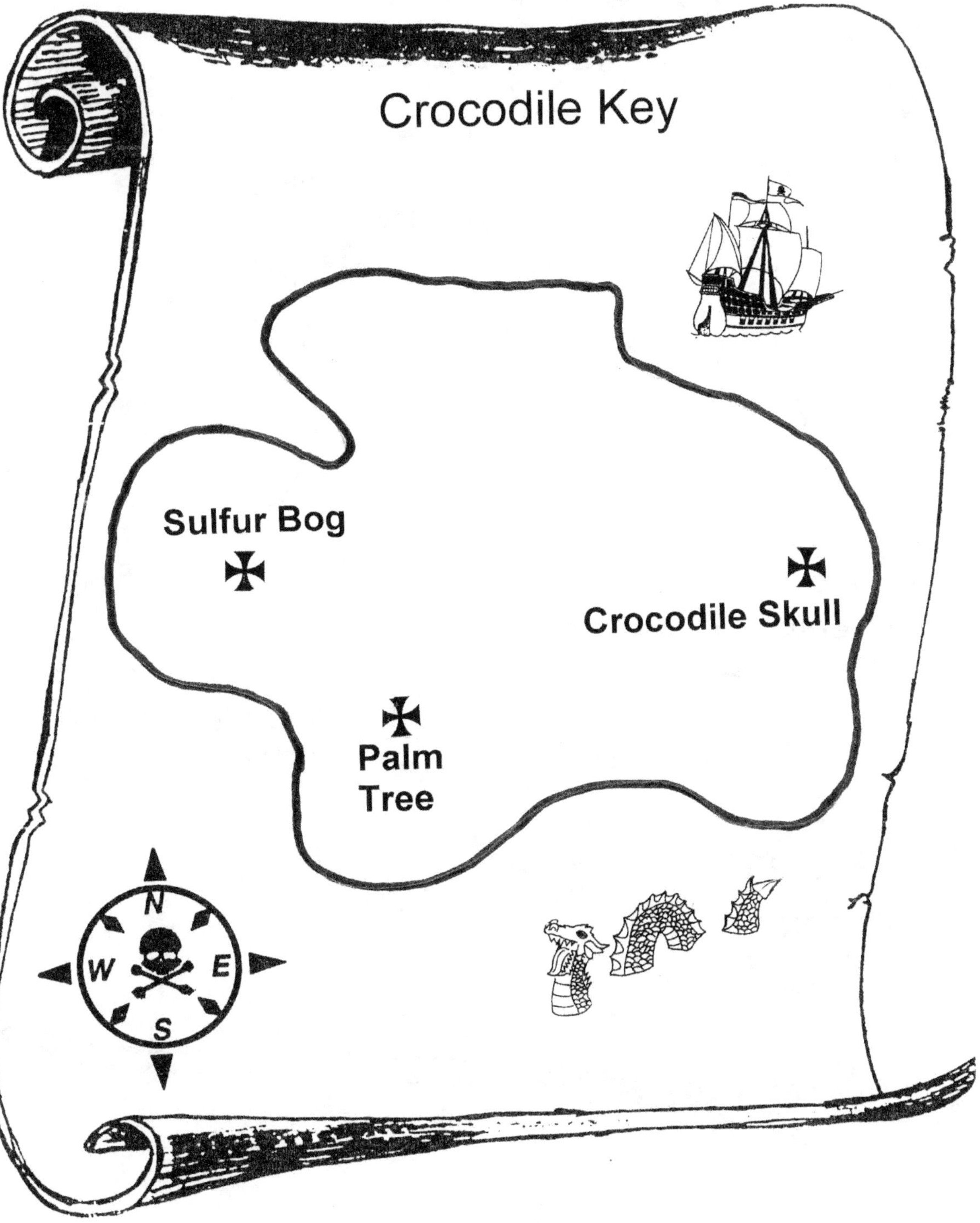

8. Buried Treasure on Isola Diavolo

You find an old treasure map with clues written on the back leading to the location of a treasure chest buried on Isola Diavolo. The map shows the Debtor's Prison and a giant boulder in the shape of a devil. The treasure is located at a point that forms an isosceles right triangle with the Debtor's Prison gate and the Devil's Boulder. Find the treasure.

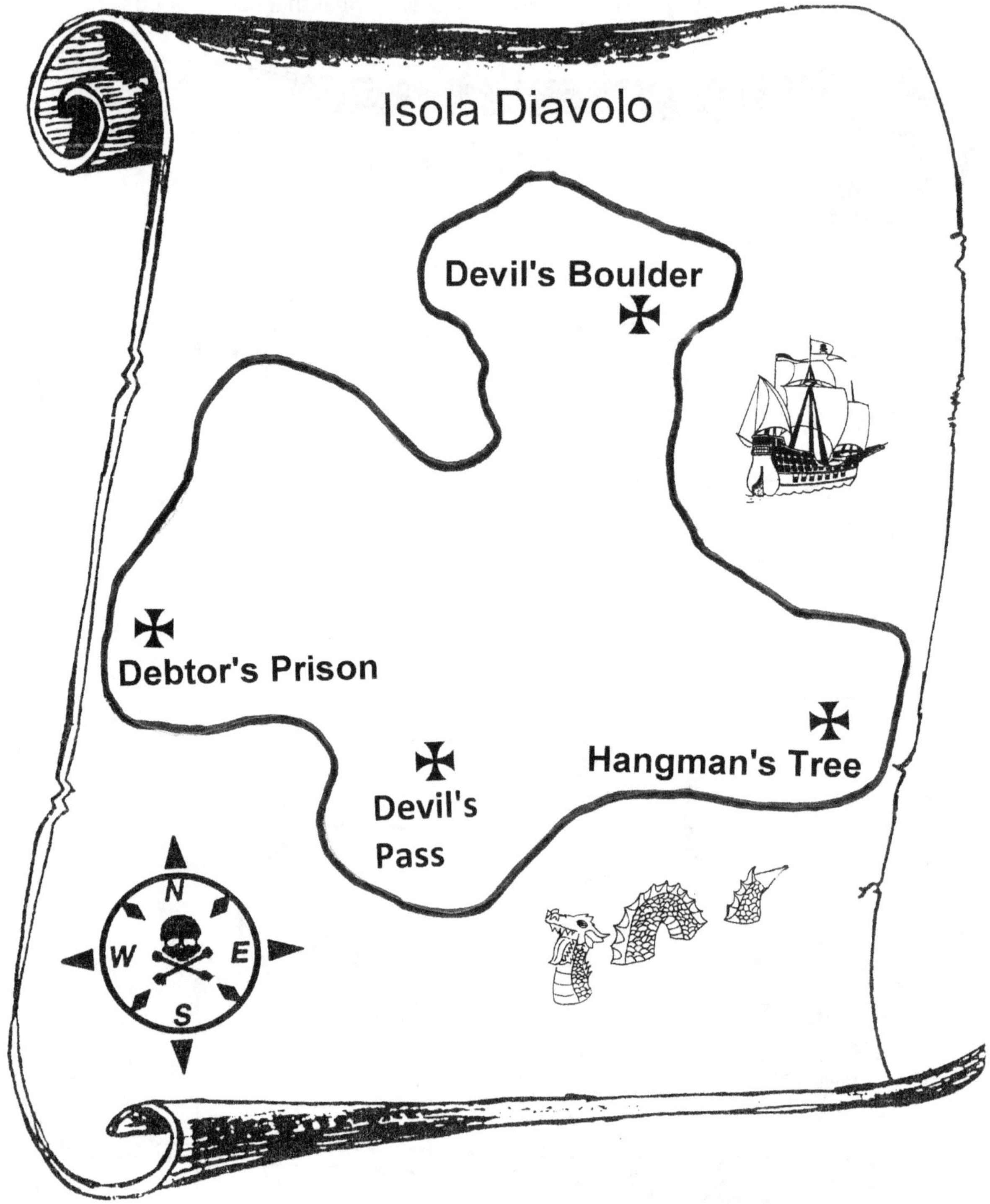

9. Buried Treasure on Torture Island

At the Torquemada Tavern an old sailor offers to sell you a map showing the location of a buried treasure on Torture Island. You pay up and as he hands you the map he whispers, "On this island you will find a giant boulder in the shape of a human skull and the Gallows. Find a point that forms an equilateral triangle with the Gallows and the Skull Boulder. Drive a stake in the ground at this point. From Captain Morgan's Tombstone walk 50 meters in the direction of the stake (you may pass the stake), then dig three feet down. The treasure will be yours." Find the treasure.

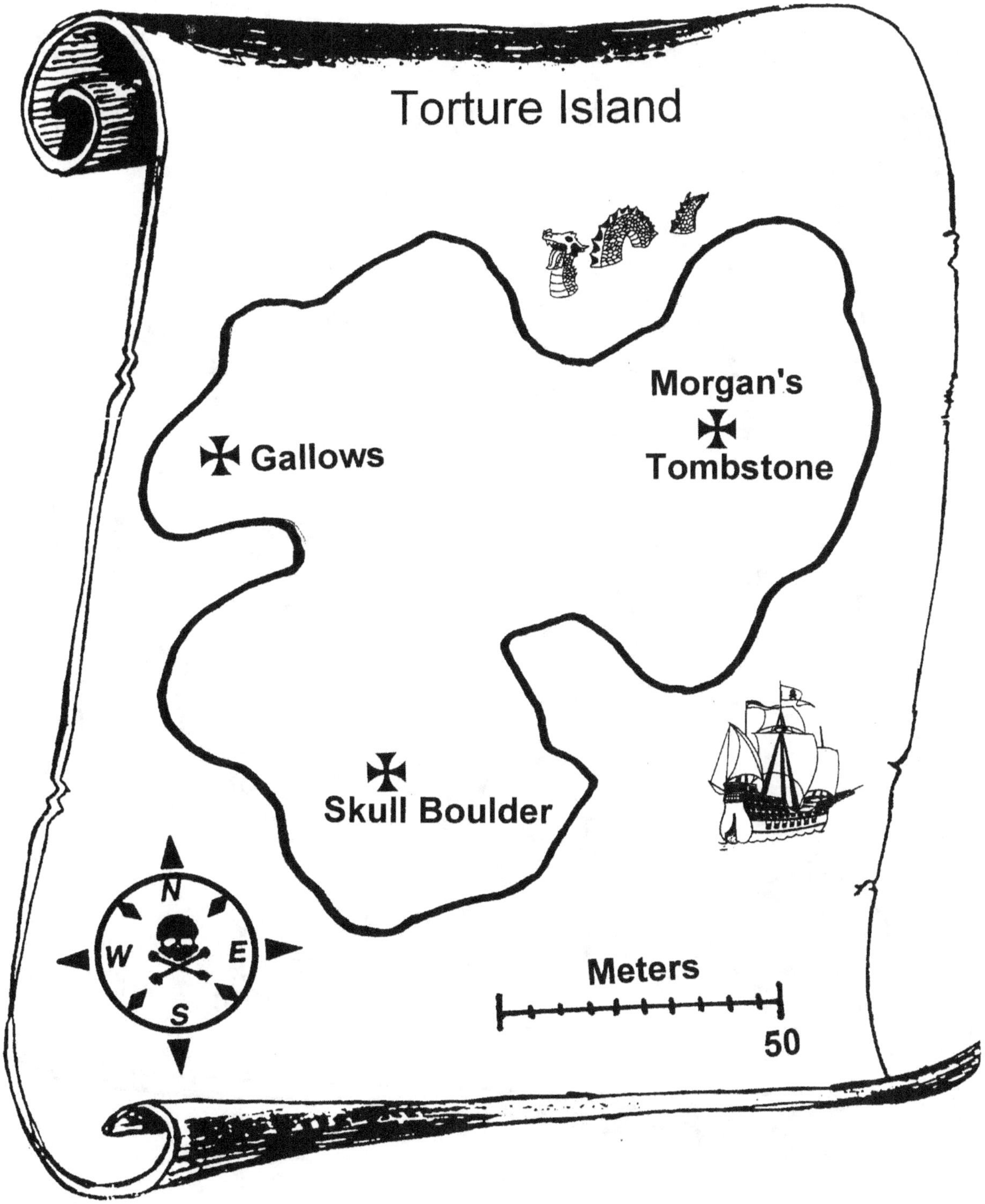

10. Buried Treasure on Isla Serpiente *h*

You find an old treasure map. Scribbled on the back in blood-red ink are clues to the location of a treasure chest buried on Isla Serpiente. The map shows a breadfruit tree, a giant boulder in the shape of a coiled snake, and a quicksand bog. The treasure is located equally distant between the boulder and bog and 300 meters from the breadfruit tree. Do you have enough information to find the treasure? How many places do you need to dig to locate the treasure? Find the treasure.

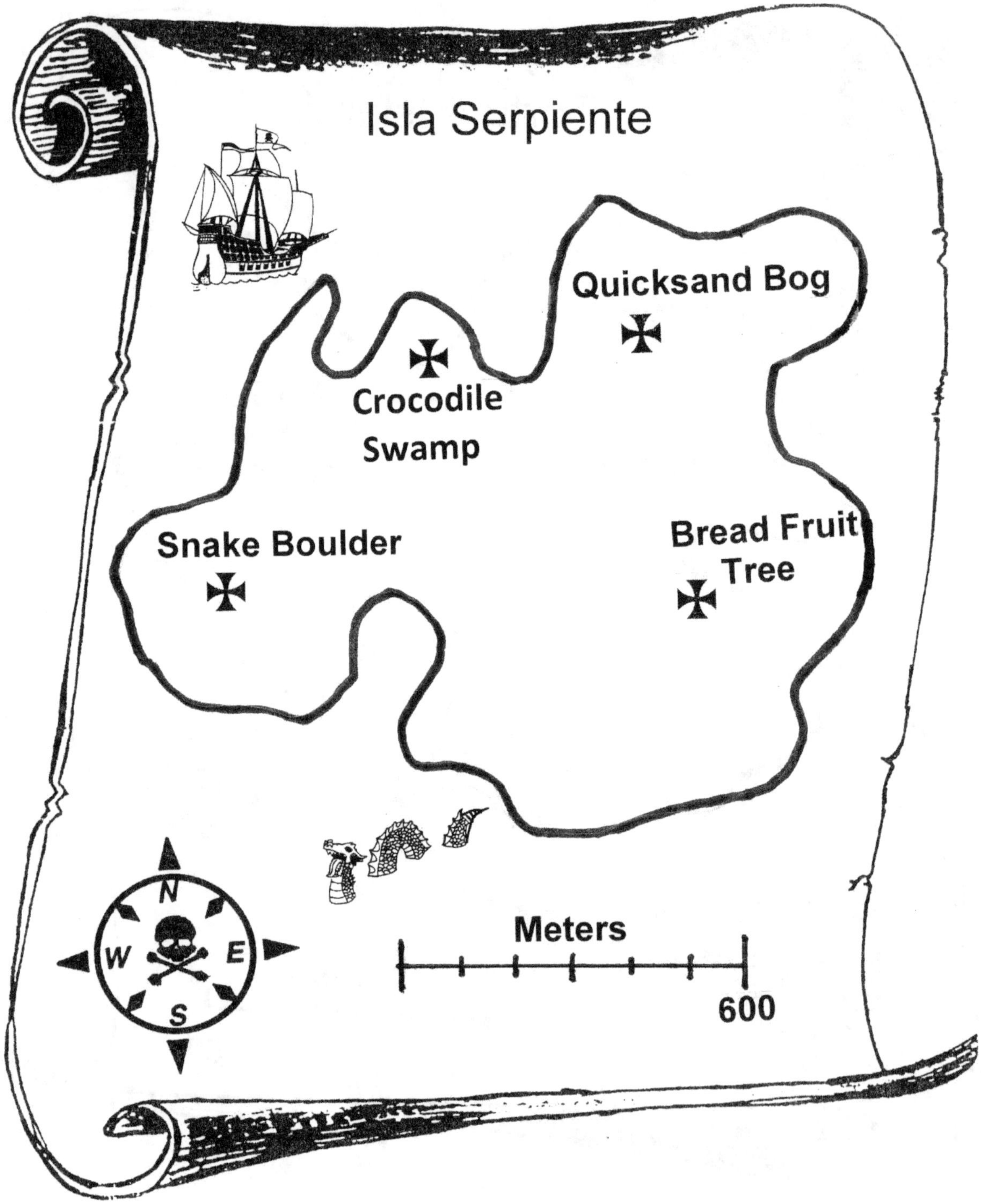

11. Buried Treasure on Isla Tortuga

While rifling through some old pictures at an antique store, you find what appears to be a treasure map. The back of the map gives clues to the location of pirate treasure buried on Isla Tortuga. The map shows a coconut tree, a giant boulder in the shape of a tortoise, a rope bridge across Jetsam River, and a stone path between the Tortoise Boulder and the rope bridge. The treasure is located on the stone path equally distant between the Tortoise Boulder and the Coconut Tree. Find the treasure.

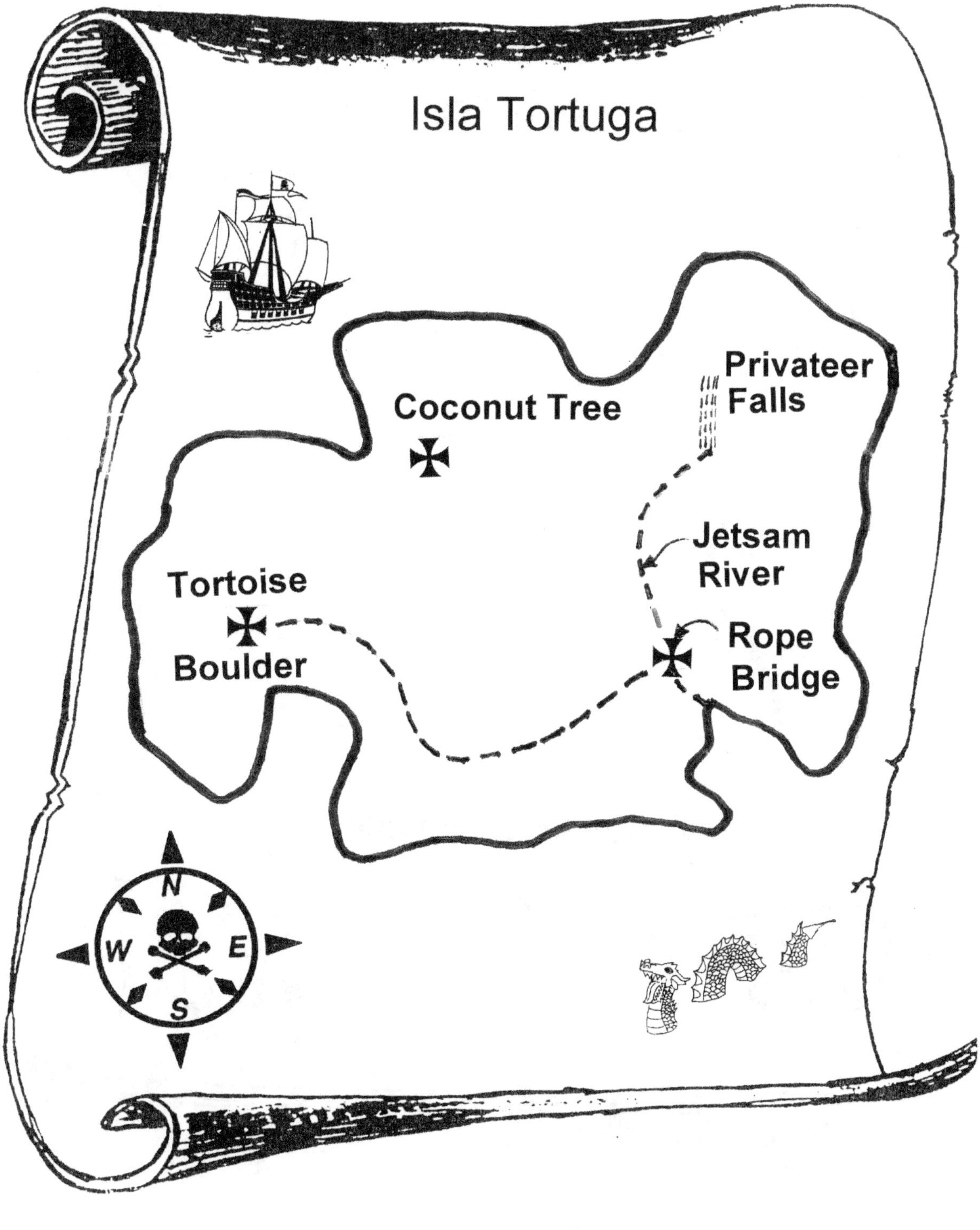

12. Buried Treasure on Spyglass Island

You find an old treasure map. The back of the map gives clues to the location of pirate treasure buried on Spyglass Island. The map shows a banyan tree, a giant boulder in the shape of a telescope, and the midpoint of a rope bridge across Vulture Valley. The treasure is located equally distant between the boulder and the banyan tree. As you stand atop the giant telescope boulder and look towards the banyan tree, swing your gaze towards the bridge over Vulture Valley. The treasure is located along the bisector of the angle. Find the treasure.

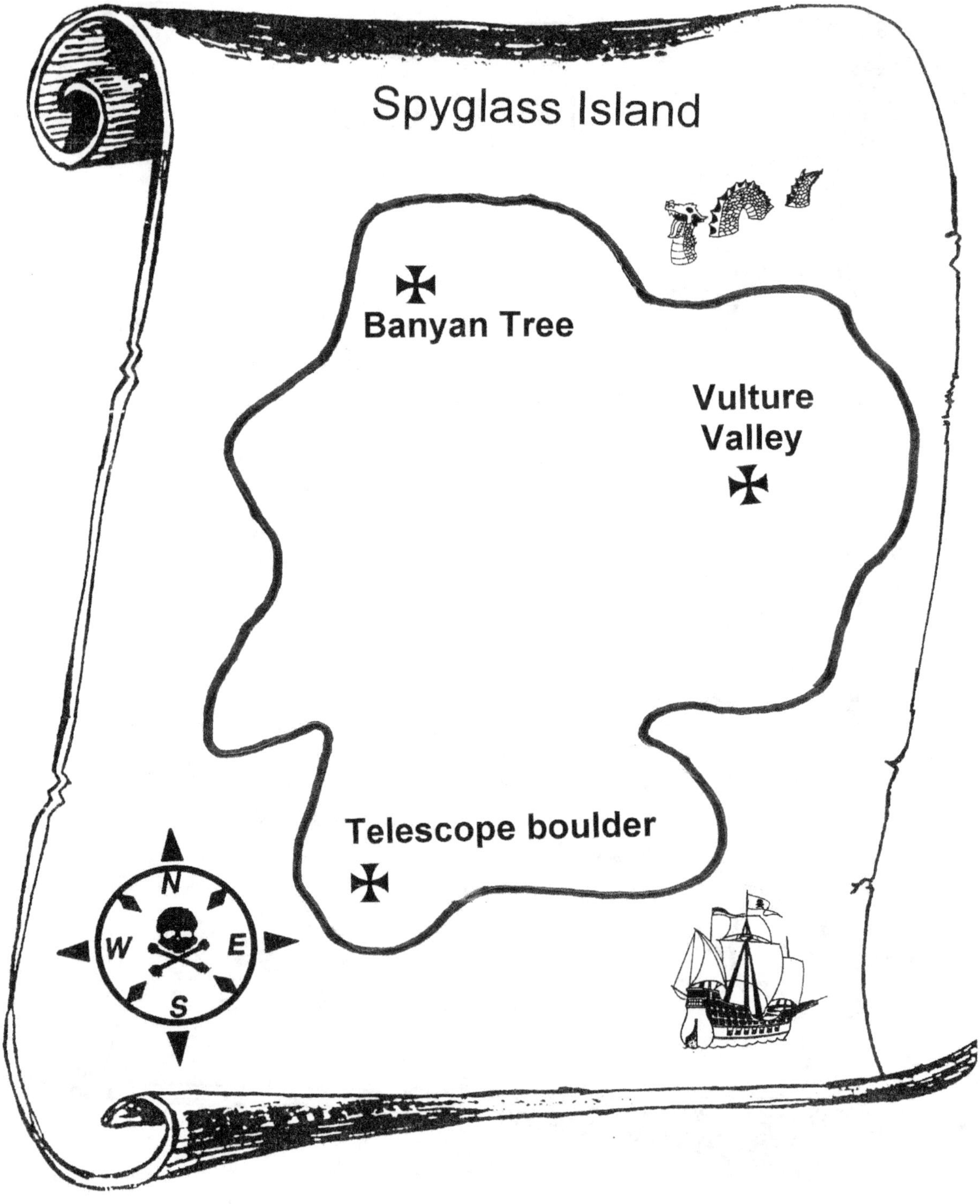

13. Buried Treasure on Mono Key

While browsing in a used bookstore you find an old treasure map that gives clues to the location of pirate treasure buried on Mono Key. The map shows a mango tree, a giant boulder in the shape of a monkey, and the treacherous entrance to Deadman's Marsh. According to the note written on the back of the map, the treasure is located equally distant between the boulder and the mango tree, and 100 meters from the line which contains the path connecting the entrance to Deadman's Marsh and the mango tree. Do you have enough information to find the treasure? How many places do you need to dig to locate the treasure? Find the treasure.

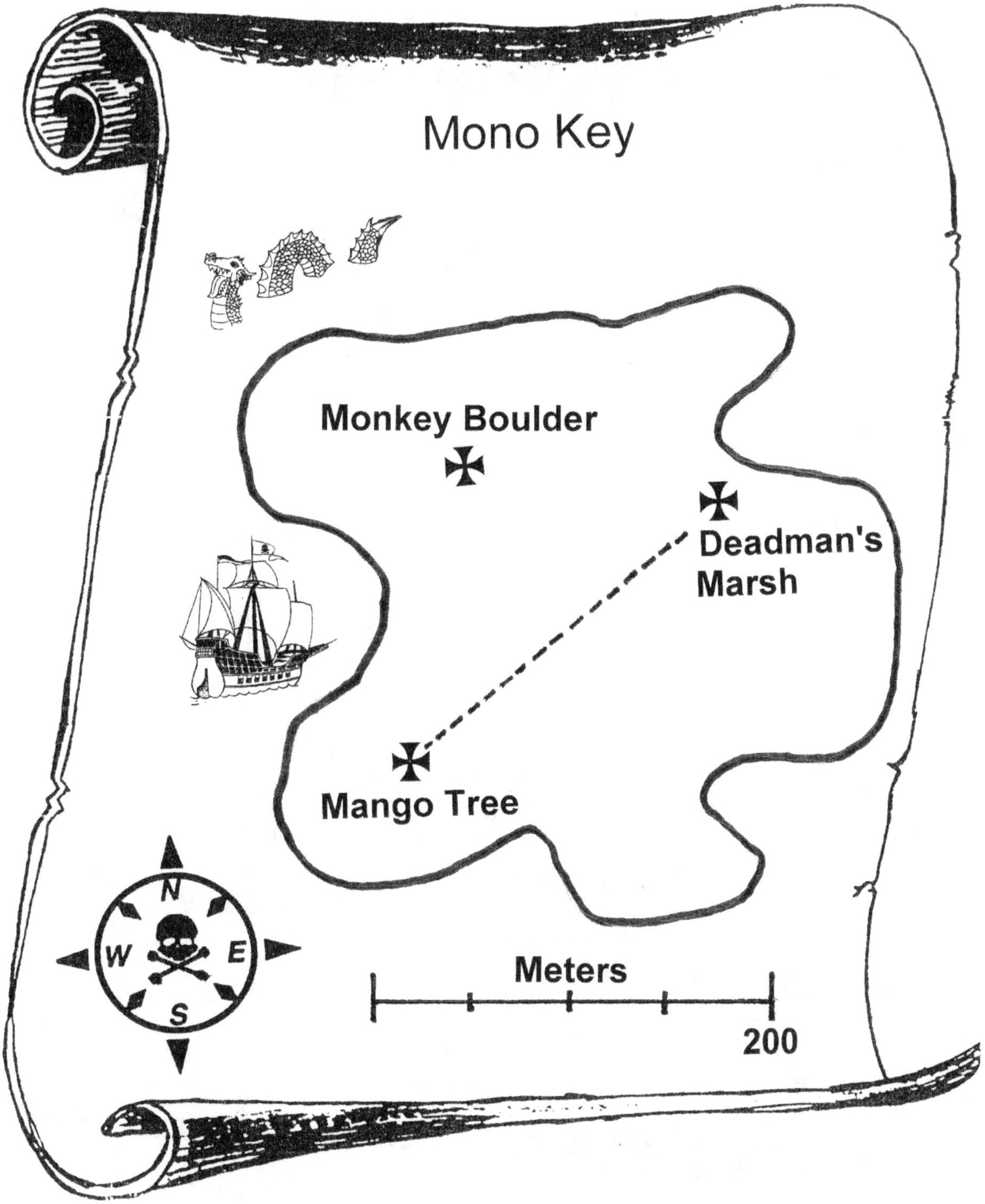

14. Buried Treasure on Isla Garuda

At the Ship Ahoy tavern, an old sailor offers to sell you a map showing the location of a buried treasure on Isla Garuda. You pay up and as he hands you the map he whispers, "On this island you will find Calico Jack Tavern, a boulder in the shape of a human skull, and a tombstone marked Calico Jack. The treasure is located equally distant from all three." When you open the map you immediately notice that a small portion of it has been burned away. No Calico Jack Tavern appears on the map! However, there are paths leading from the skull-shaped boulder and the tombstone to the hole in the map. You conjecture that the two paths must have met at Calico Jack Tavern. With a bit of geometry you should be able to find the location of the treasure.

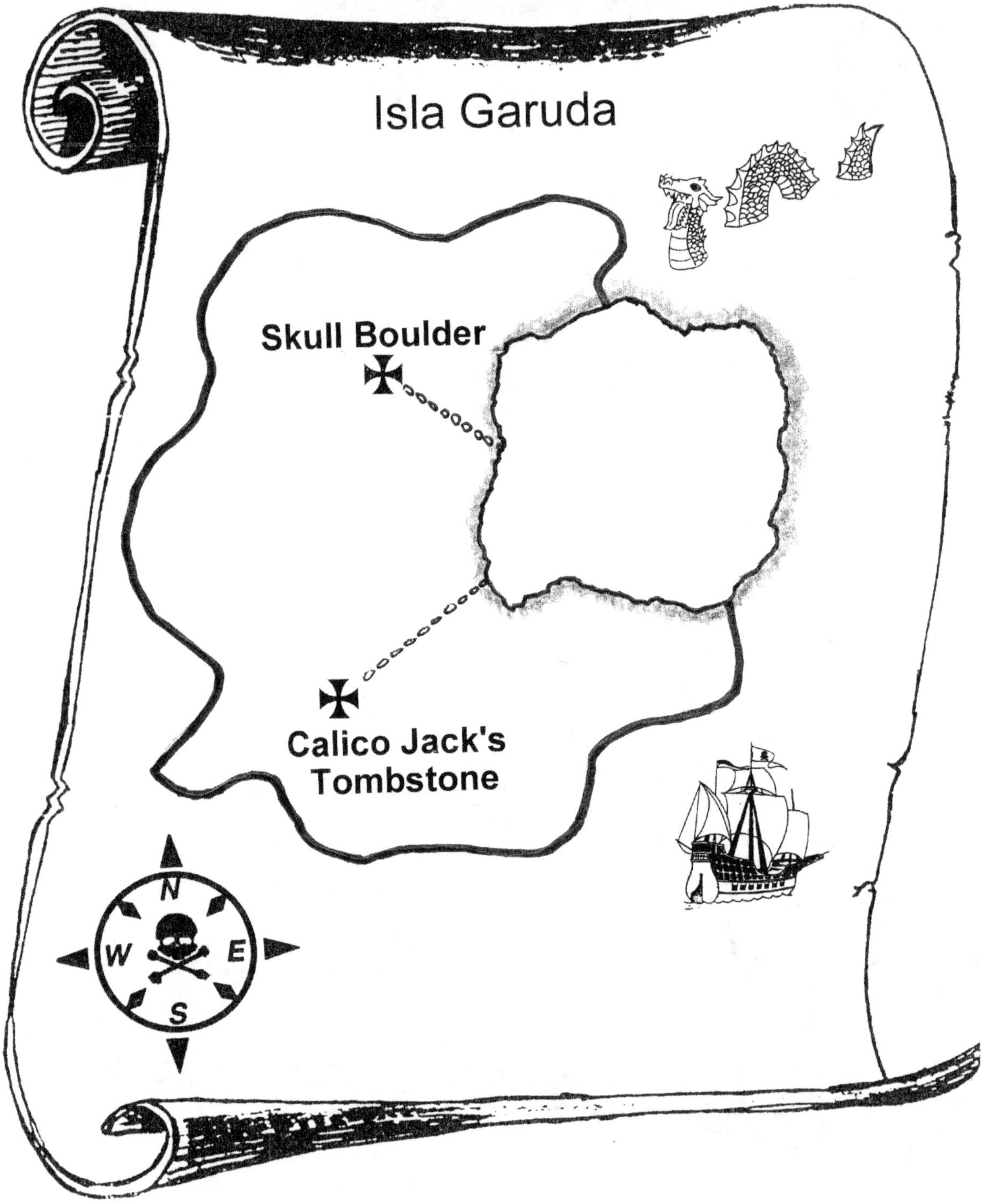

15. Buried Treasure on Long John Island

At the Shiver Me Timbers bar, a man dressed in black offers to sell you a map showing the location of a treasure buried on Long John Island. You pay up and as he hands you the map he whispers, "On this island you will find a tombstone marked "Peg-Leg" and a stone wall. This is all that remains of a British fort. The treasure is 150 meters from the wall and 200 meters from the tombstone. With a bit of geometry you should be able to find the location of the treasure." How many places do you need to dig to locate the treasure? Find the treasure.

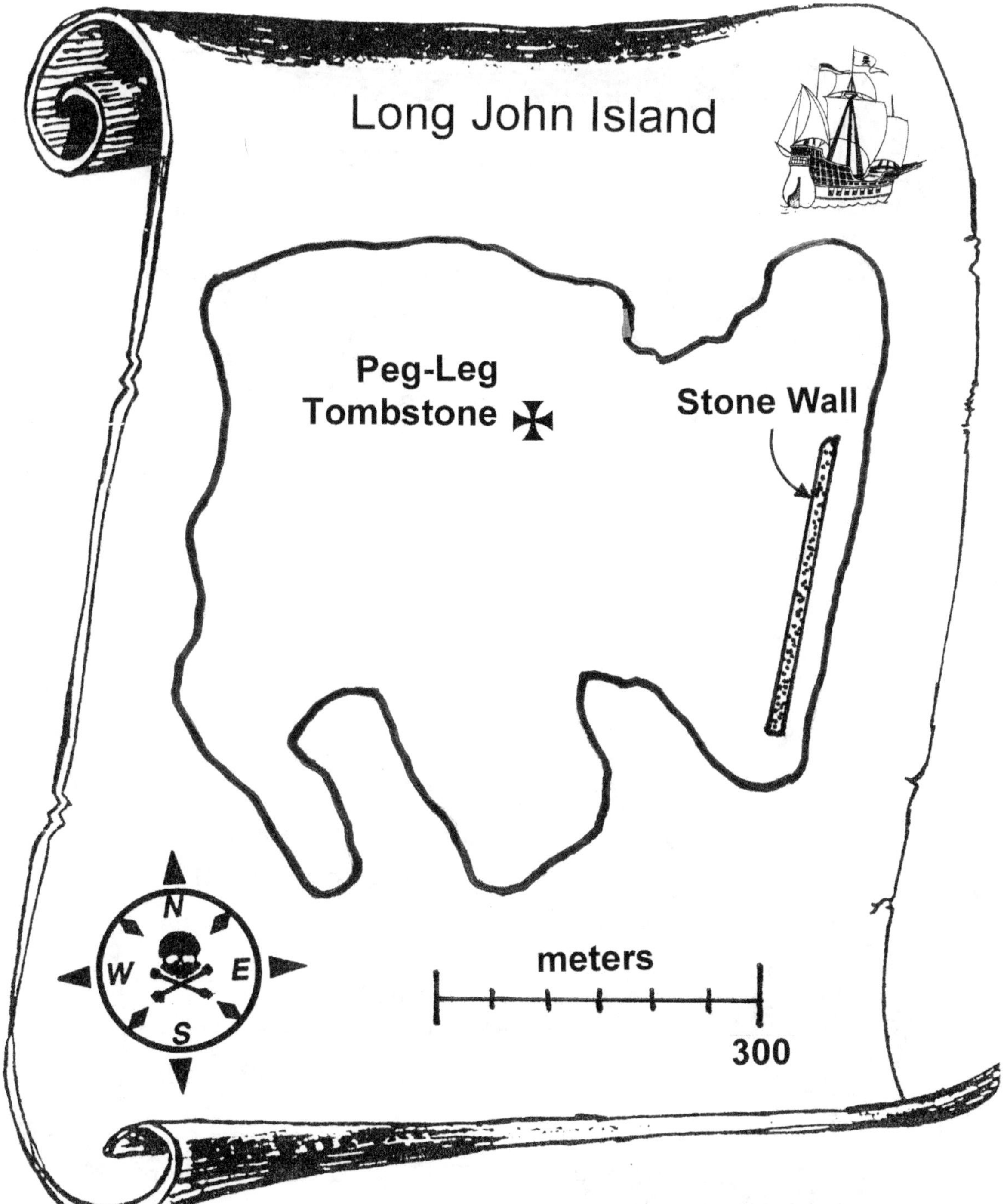

16. Buried Treasure on Parrot Island

You find an old treasure map with scribbled directions on the back pointing to a treasure chest on Parrot Island. The directions state you will find a palm tree, a portion of a stone wall with a Roman arch opening, and a gallows on the island. You are to start at the Gallows and walk toward the Palm Tree while measuring your distance. After 30 meters, stop, turn 90 degrees to the left and walk 15 meters. At that spot drive a stake. Return to the Gallows and walk toward the opening in the stone wall while measuring your distance. After 30 meters, stop, turn 90 degrees to the left and walk 15 meters. At that spot drive a stake. Find the midpoint between the two stakes and dig to locate the buried treasure.

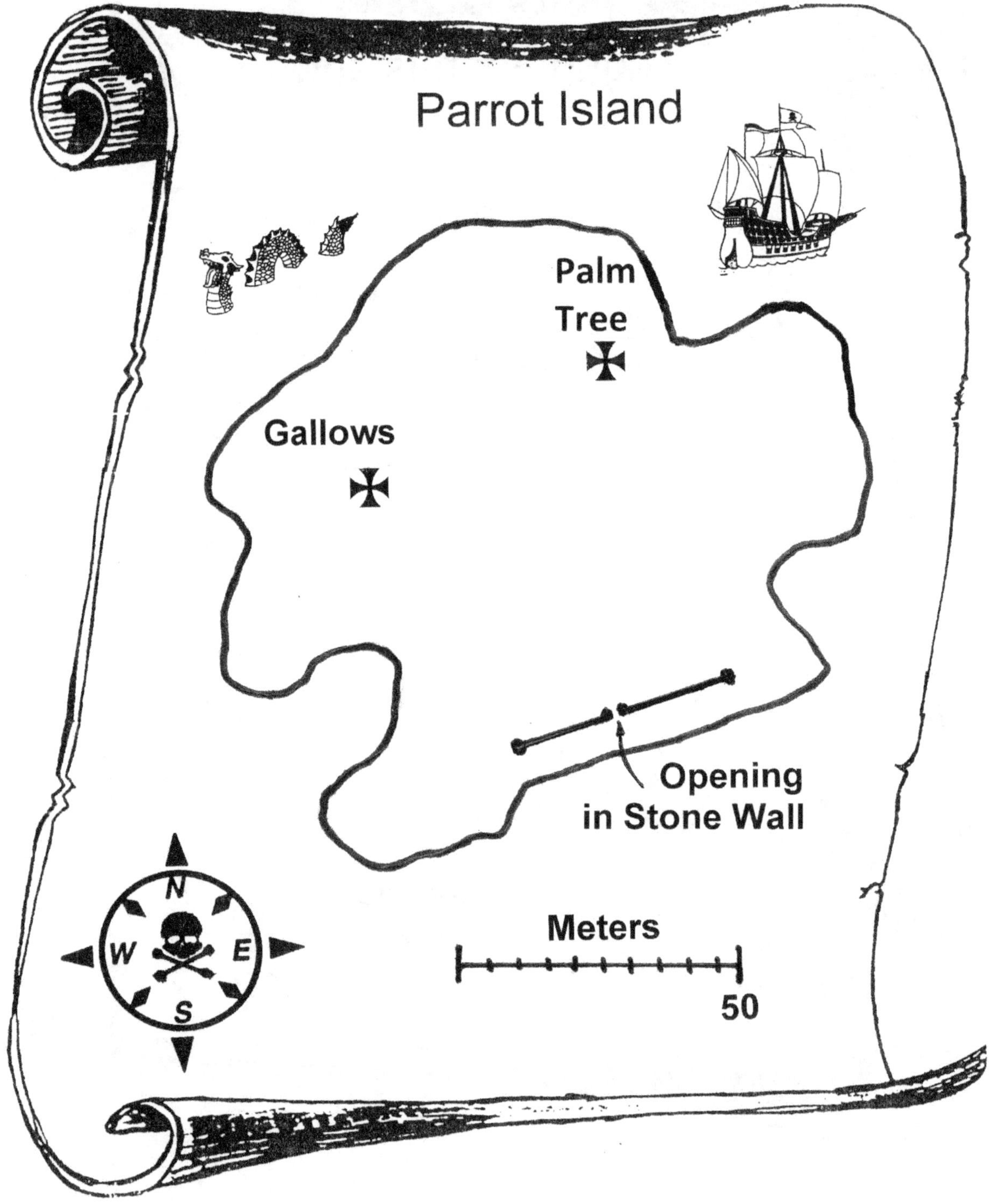

17. Buried Treasure on Cayman Key *ℏ*

At a garage sale you find an old treasure map that gives clues to the location of a treasure chest buried on Cayman Key. The map shows the locations of a giant papaya tree, a small boulder in the shape of a sleeping lizard, and a sign marking the entrance to a sulfur marsh. According to the note written on the back of the map, when lines are drawn from the treasure to each of the three locations they divide the triangle formed by all three locations into three triangles that have equal areas. Find the treasure.

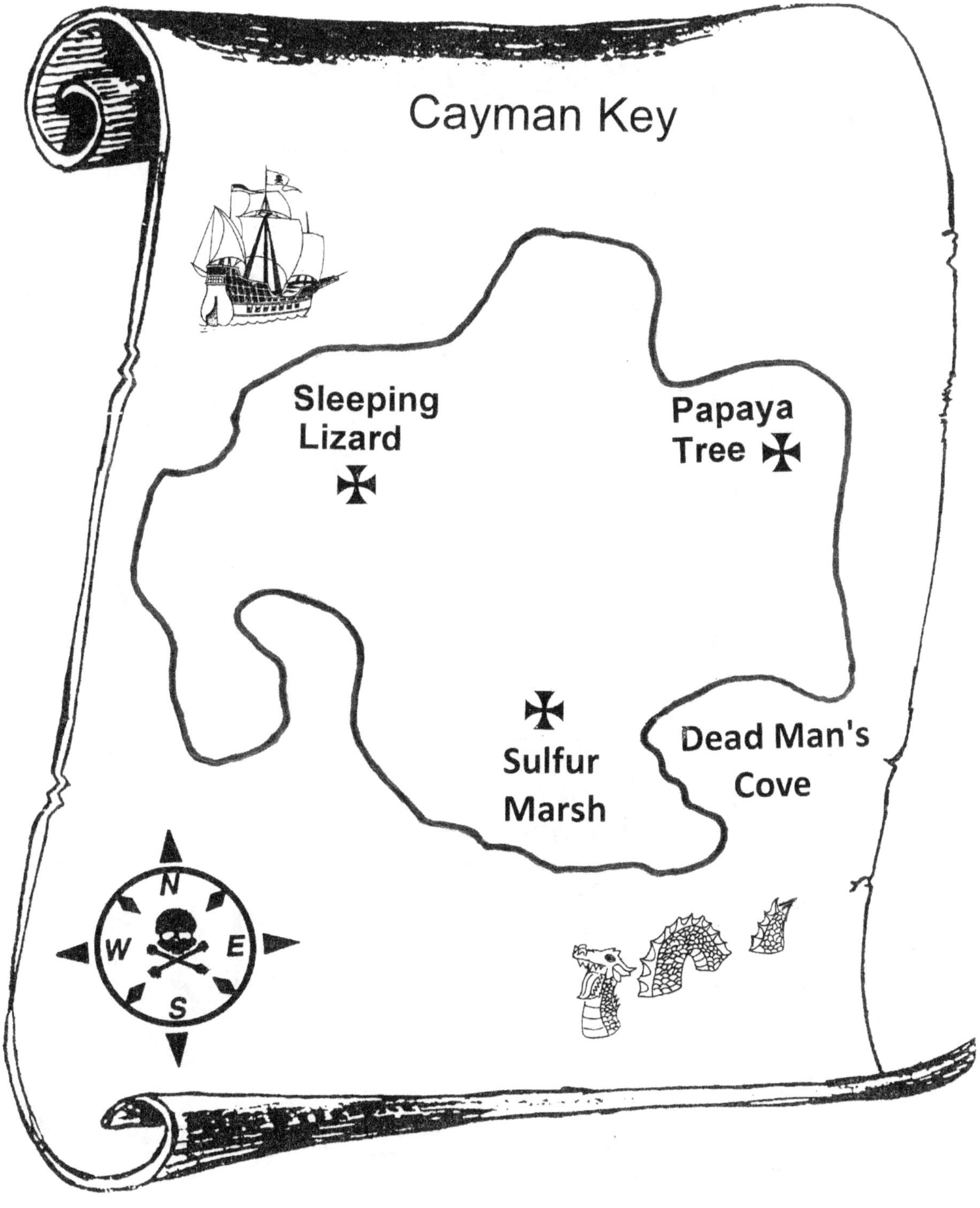

18. Buried Treasure on Skeleton Island *h*

You purchase an old treasure map that gives clues to the location of a treasure chest buried on Skeleton Island. According to the note tucked inside the map, the map shows the locations of a giant lychee tree, a small boulder in the shape of a skeleton, a hangman's tree, and the Jolly Roger Inn. The four locations form a parallelogram. The treasure chest is buried at the intersection of the two diagonals. However someone has burned a hole in the map and the location of the hangman's tree is no longer visible. Do you have enough information to find the treasure? If not explain why not. If you do, find the treasure.

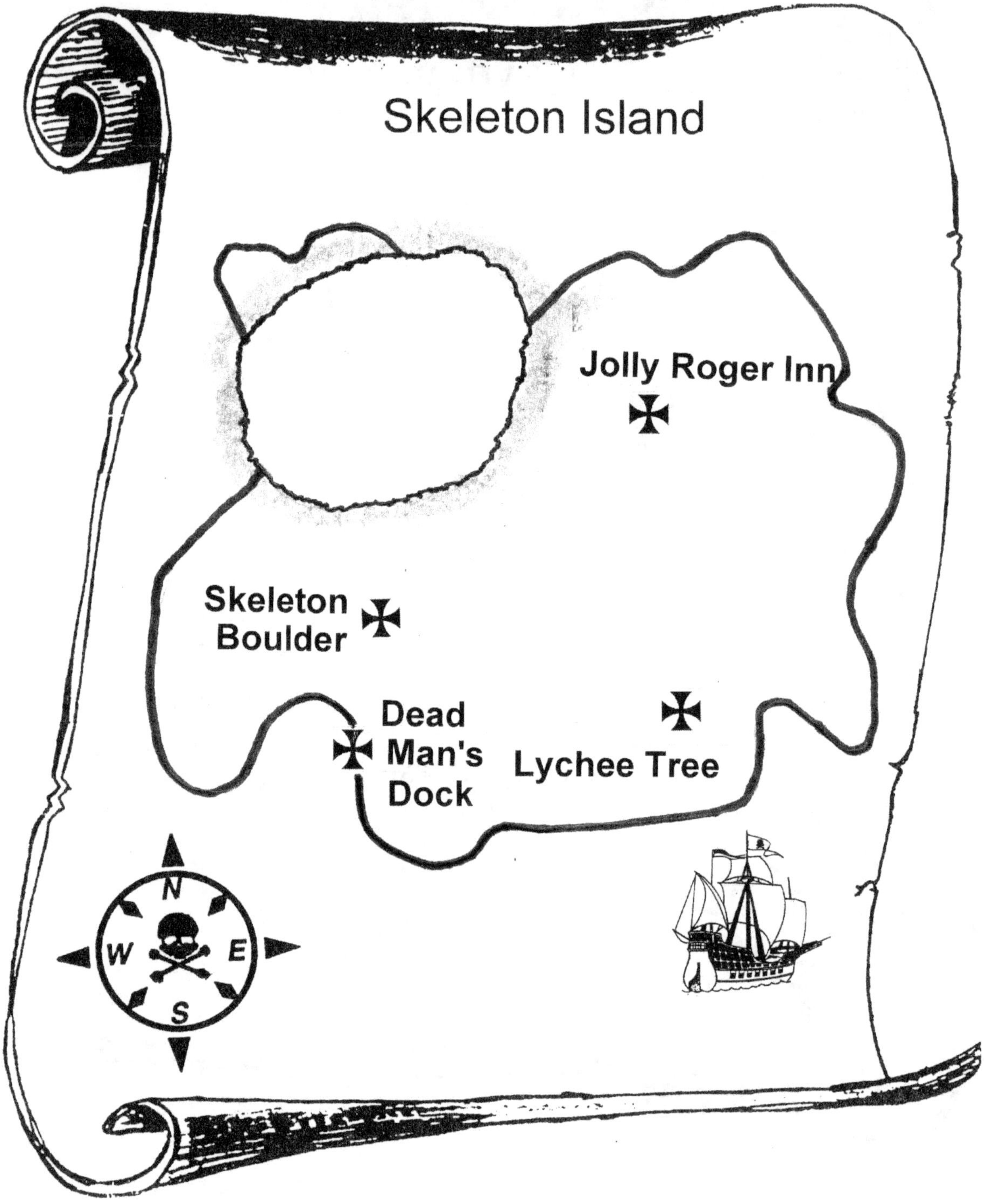

19. Buried Treasure on Buccaneer Island $\hbar$

In an attic trunk you discover what appears to be a treasure map. The back of the map gives clues to the location of a treasure chest filled with gold buried on Buccaneer Island. The original map showed the locations of the Albatross Tavern, the Dead Duck Inn, and Boot Hill Bog. The treasure, along with the other three locations, formed a rectangle. However, someone has burned a number of holes in the map and the location of the Albatross Tavern is no longer visible. Records show, however, that the distance between the Albatross Tavern and the Dead Duck Inn was half the distance between the Dead Duck Inn and Boot Hill Bog. Do you have enough information to find the treasure? If not, explain why not. If you do, find the treasure. How many places do you need to dig?

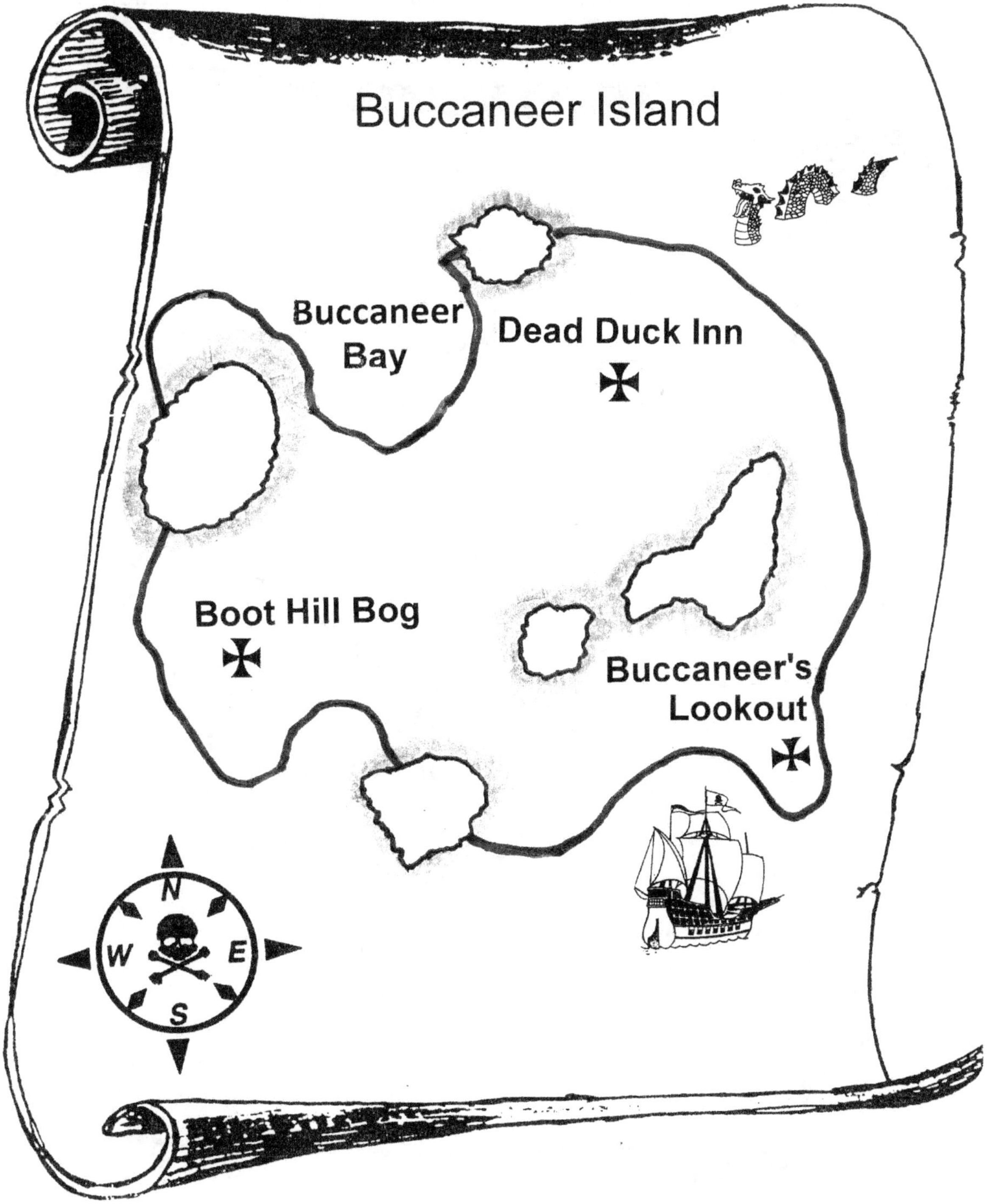

20. Buried Treasure on Grand Doubloon Island *h*

At the Yo-Ho-Ho and a Bottle of Rum Tavern an old sailor offers to sell you a map showing the location of a treasure buried on Grand Doubloon Island. You pay up, and as he hands you the map, he whispers, "This map shows that on this island there is a star fruit tree, a palm tree, and a gallows. Start at the gallows and walk toward the Palm Tree while counting your steps. When you reach the Palm Tree, stop, turn 90 degrees to the left and walk the same number of steps. At that spot drive a stake. Then return to the gallows and walk toward the Star Fruit Tree, again measuring your steps. When you get to the Star Fruit Tree, turn 90 degrees to the right and walk the same number of steps, then drive a stake at that spot. Then find the midpoint between the two stakes and dig." Unfortunately, when you unroll the map you discover there is a hole in it and the location of the gallows is missing. Do you have enough information to find the treasure? Where are you going to dig?

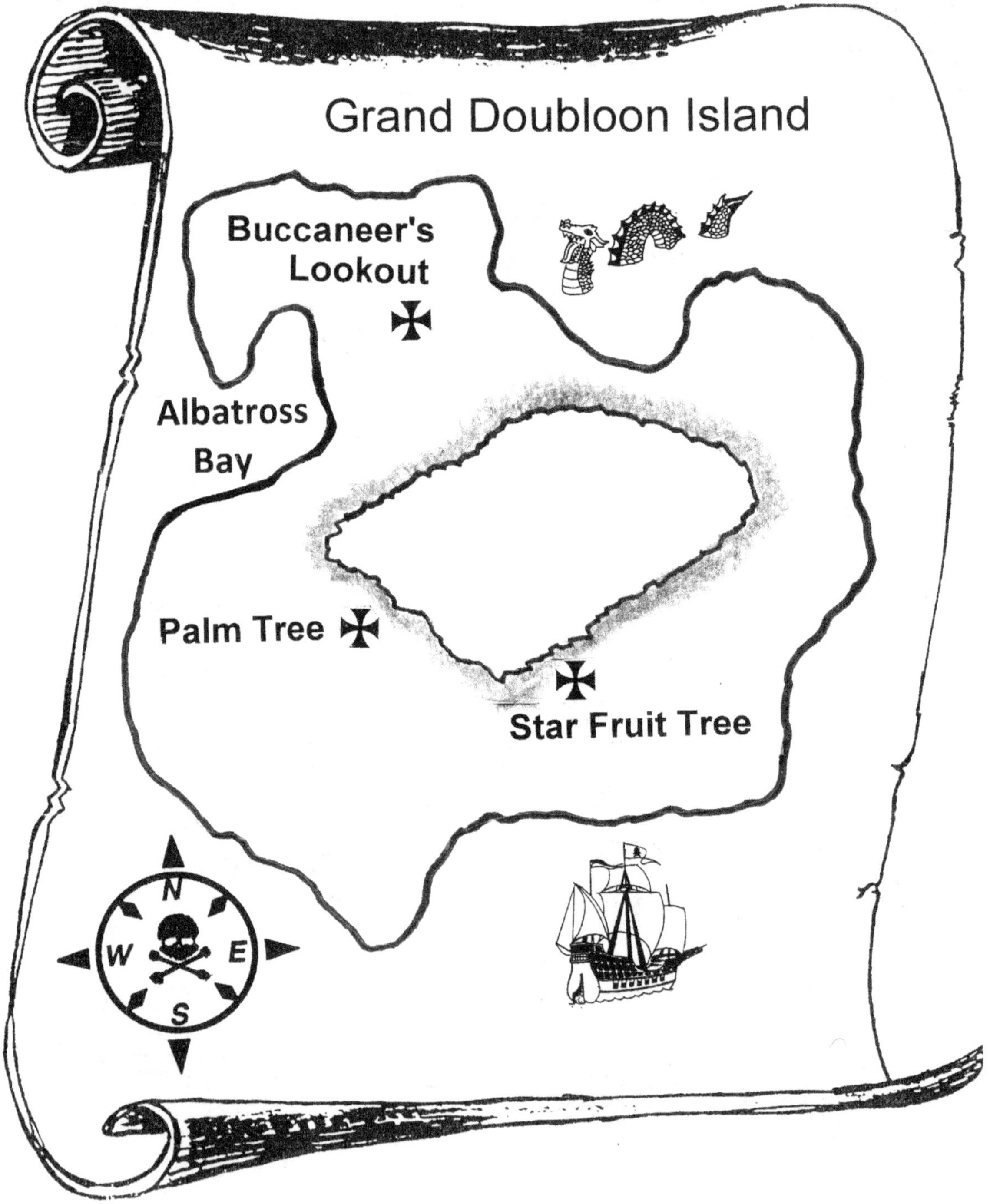

Chapter 7 Pirate Treasure with Cryptography

When cryptography is outlawed, bayl bhgynjf jvyy unir cevinpl
—Kevin McCurley

7.1 Cryptography

Cryptography is the science of writing secret messages. Cryptography dates back to about 1900 B.C.E., when an Egyptian scribe used special hieroglyphs to disguise a message. Secret communication also developed in ancient cultures of other countries, including China, India, and Japan.

The Roman poet Ovid suggested lovers communicate in code or use "invisible ink" so that others could not read their love poetry. Scholars during the Middle Ages and the Renaissance used secret writing to hide their work because it threatened those in power; Galileo was one of the more famous examples. Leonardo da Vinci hid his ideas by writing in reverse (mirror writing) so the writing made sense only by reading it in a mirror.

According to legend, Julius Caesar used a simple letter substitution method to send secret messages to his military leaders. Caesar replaced each letter of his message with the letter that followed it by three positions in the Roman alphabet. For example, in English, the letter "a" would be replaced by "D", the letter "t" would be replaced by "W", and "x" would be replaced by "A." Thus, the English phrase "strike at dawn" would be transformed to "VWULNH DW GDZQ." This technique of sending secret messages, no matter the size or direction of the shift used for the substitution, is called a **Caesar cipher**.

Plaintext	a	b	c	d	e	f	g	h	i	j	k	l	m	n	o	p	q	r	s	t	u	v	w	x	y	z
Ciphertext	D	E	F	G	H	I	J	K	L	M	N	O	P	Q	R	S	T	U	V	W	X	Y	Z	A	B	C

The process of creating a secret message is called **encryption**; it is what the sender does to hide the message. The process of translating the secret message is called **decryption**; it is what the receiver does to reveal the original message. The original message is known as the **plaintext** and the encrypted plaintext is called the **ciphertext**.

Creating and breaking ciphers has a long and fascinating history. Mary Queen of Scots was accused of plotting to assassinate Queen Elizabeth of England and was put on trial for treason. Sir Francis Walsingham had discovered Mary's coded letters to fellow plotters. Mary thought even if they found the secret messages, nobody would be able to find out what was being planned because they were encrypted. She was wrong. Walsingham, England's spymaster, decrypted the messages, and Mary was found guilty of treason and beheaded.

By the late 1700's, many European nations had "secret agents." These agents occasionally intercepted couriers carrying encrypted diplomatic correspondence. The agents turned the messages over to cryptologists, who would decrypt the messages. The agents would return the encrypted correspondence and the unsuspecting couriers would deliver the messages without knowing the mission had been compromised.

Although the terms are often used interchangeably, ciphers are different from codes. When you substitute one word for another word or sentence, like using a foreign language, you are using a code. When you mix up or substitute existing letters, you are using a cipher. Nathan Hale failed as a spy because he used a simple Latin translation of a message as a code. The British captured him, translated the message, and he was hanged. Navajo code talkers, on the other hand, using a code system based on their native language, were instrumental in the Marines' success at Iwo Jima during World War Two.

Type of Airplane	Navajo Word	Literal Translation
dive bomber	gini	chicken hawk
fighter plane	da-he-tih-hi	hummingbird
patrol plane	ga-gih	crow
transport	atsah	eagle

To keep confidential information from enemy eyes, our military and diplomatic forces have used codes and ciphers for hundreds of years. In World War Two, cryptography became so vital to the war effort computers were invented to aid in the creating and breaking of encrypted messages.

Ciphers have also appeared in fiction. In Sir Arthur Conan Doyle's *The Valley of Fear*, Sherlock Holmes receives a cipher without the decryption key. He uses his powers of deduction to decipher the message. In A. Conan Doyle's *The Adventure of the Dancing Men*, the encrypted message used a series of dancing stick men. A portion of the encrypted message is shown below.

Ciphers are broken into two main categories, **substitution ciphers** and **transposition ciphers**. Substitution ciphers replace letters in the plaintext with other letters, but the order in which the symbols occur remains the same; the Caesar cipher is one example. Sometimes symbols other than letters have been substituted, as they were in the cipher from *The Adventure of the Dancing Men*. In transposition ciphers the letters may remain the same but the arrangement or transposition has changed. One of the earliest known examples of a transposition cipher was the scytale[11] created by the ancient Egyptians and Greeks. Substitution ciphers are easier to use but also easier to break, while transposition ciphers are not as easy to use but may be more difficult to decrypt without the key. Let's look at some examples.

7.2 Substitution Ciphers

Substitution ciphers replace letters in the plaintext with other letters or symbols, but the order in which the symbols occur remains the same. The Caesar cipher table below has a shift forward of 8. Let's call this key **CCS8** (*Caesar cipher shift 8*). Sometimes a Caesar cipher may shift the letters backward rather than forward.

Plaintext	a	b	c	d	e	f	g	h	i	j	k	l	m	n	o	p	q	r	s	t	u	v	w	x	y	z
Ciphertext	S	T	U	V	W	X	Y	Z	A	B	C	D	E	F	G	H	I	J	K	L	M	N	O	P	Q	R

Subtitution Cipher Exercises

1. Try your hand at encryption. Encrypt the plaintext: "Blackbeard is in Jamaica" using CCS8.

b	l	a	c	k	b	e	a	r	d		i	s		i	n		j	a	m	a	i	c	a

2. Using CCS8, decrypt the ciphertext: "LZW LJWSKMJW AK TMJAWV GF KCMDD AKDSFV."

L	Z	W		L	J	W	S	K	M	J	W		A	K		T	M	J	A	W	V		G	F		K	C	M	D	D		A	K	D	S	F	V

A substitution cipher may include numbers. In the cipher wheel to the right there are 26 letters of the alphabet plus 10 numerals {0, 1, ...8, 9} for a total of 36 substitutions. Sometimes it is easier to use a cipher wheel rather than a shifting table. The substitution cipher wheel to the right is set for a shift of 4. Let's call this key **CCNS4** (*Caesar cipher with numbers shift 4*).

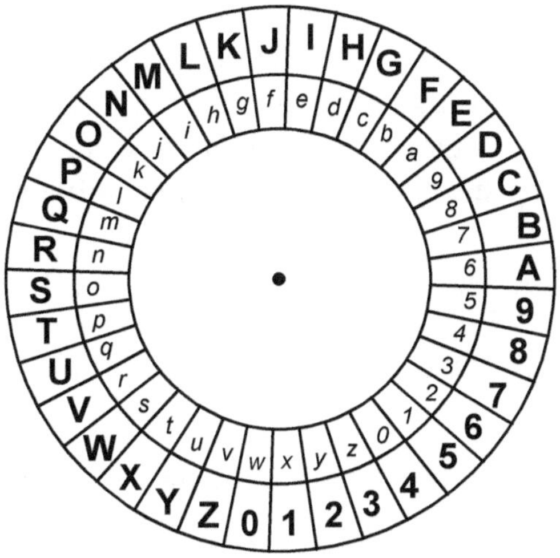

3. Encrypt the message: "Take 36 paces north towards the oak."

   Ciphertext: ______________________________

   ______________________________.

4. Use the cipher wheel above (CCNS4) to decrypt the message: "HMK 6 QIXIVW HS0R."

   Plaintext: ______________________________

Instead of letters a substitution cipher might use numbers {0, 1, 2, ... 23, 24, 25} substituted for the letters of the alphabet then shifted as done with a Caesar cipher. This is shown in the cipher table **NS2** (*Cipher with numbers shift 2*) below.

Plaintext	a	b	c	d	e	f	g	h	i	j	k	l	m	n
Ciphertext	24	25	0	1	2	3	4	5	6	7	8	9	10	11

Plaintext	o	p	q	r	s	t	u	v	w	x	y	z
Ciphertext	12	13	14	15	16	17	18	19	20	21	22	23

5. Use the cipher table above (**NS2**) to decrypt the message:

   "4.12.9.1. 6.16. 6.11. 17.5.2. 0.5.2.16.17."

   Plaintext: ______________________________

Another popular and very clever substitution cipher is the **keyword cipher**. A word or phrase is selected as the keyword. It is placed beneath the alphabet with any repeats of the letters removed. The rest of the unused letters of the alphabet are then added in order, omitting those already used. For example if the keyword is "pirate" then we create the cipher table **KW.Pirate** (*keyword pirate*).

a	b	c	d	e	f	g	h	i	j	k	l	m	n	o	p	q	r	s	t	u	v	w	x	y	z
P	I	R	A	T	E	B	C	D	F	G	H	J	K	L	M	N	O	Q	S	U	V	W	X	Y	Z

6. Use the keyword cipher table **KW.pirate** to decipher the ciphertext:

   SCT SOTPQUOT DQ WDSC APVTY FLKTQ

   Plaintext: ______________________________

Tic-Tac-Toe Cipher

A substitution cipher found in children's books and beginning cryptography texts is the **Tic-Tac-Toe cipher**, sometimes called the **Pigpen cipher** (the letters are put in pens like pigs). A variation of this cipher is used in the computer game *Assassin's Creed II*. This is an example of a substitution cipher called a **diagrammatic cipher**.

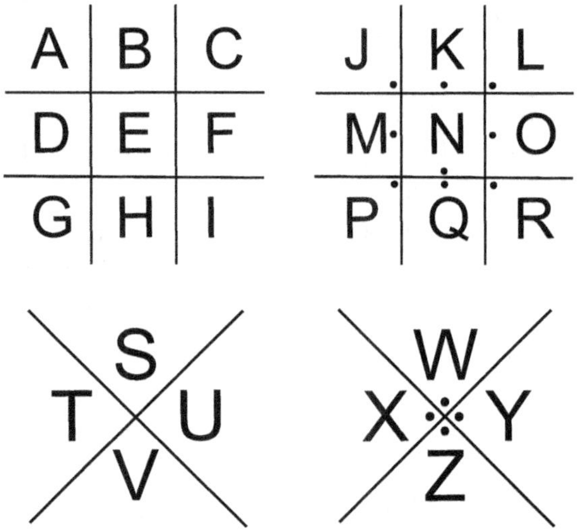

The phrase: "The parrot knows" would be encrypted as:

7. Use the Tic-Tac-Toe cipher **TTTC.H** (*Tic-Tac-Toe cipher horizontal*) to decipher the ciphertext:

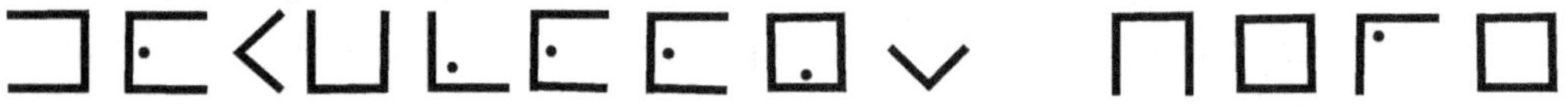

   Plaintext: ______________________________

Grid Cipher

The **grid cipher** is another diagrammatic cipher. The digits 1 through 6 are arranged along the left side and across the top of a 6×6 grid and the 26 letters of the alphabet plus the ten digits are arranged horizontally in the 36 squares. The plaintext: "X marks the spot" would be encrypted as:

46. 31.11.36.25.41. 42.22.15. 41.34.33.42.

	1	2	3	4	5	6
1	A	B	C	D	E	F
2	G	H	I	J	K	L
3	M	N	O	P	Q	R
4	S	T	U	V	W	X
5	Y	Z	0	1	2	3
6	4	5	6	7	8	9

8. Use the 6×6 cipher grid **6×6G.H** (*6 by 6 grid cipher arranged horizontally*) to decrypt the ciphertext: 14.23.21. 55.53. 34.11.13.15.41. 32.33.36.42.22.

   Plaintext: ____

Simple one-step substitution ciphers are easy to use but also easy to break. If you add complexity to the substitution, breaking the cipher becomes more difficult. To add an additional layer of complexity to the cipher we turn to mathematics, clock arithmetic in particular.

Clock Arithmetic

If it is 5 o'clock, then 6 hours later it will be 11 o'clock (5 + 6 = 11). However, if it were 8 o'clock, then 6 hours later would the time be 14 o'clock (8 + 6 = 14)? Well, perhaps on a 24-hour military clock but not on a 12-hour clock. On a regular 12-hour clock 8 + 6 is 2. Every time we pass 12 o'clock we start counting over at 1. This type of arithmetic is called **clock arithmetic**, or more formally, **modular arithmetic**. On a clock you can add any two numbers and the sum is always one of the numbers 1–12.

A clock with only five hours or positions is shown to the right. If the hand is on the 2, then four hours later where will the hand be pointing? The hand will be on the 1. (On this clock 2 + 4 = 1)

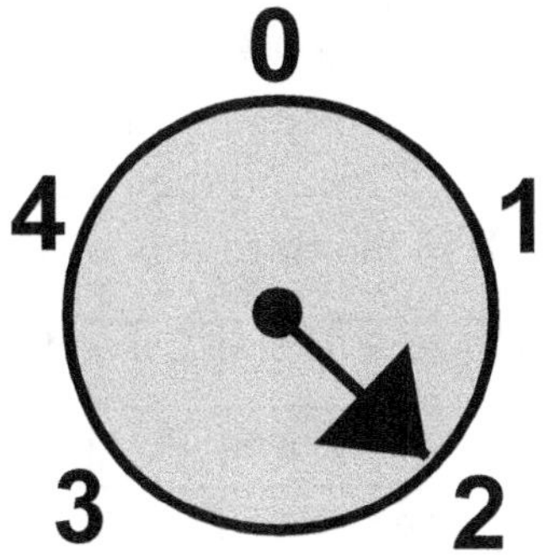

Notice that when you add any two numbers on a clock with only five numbers (0, 1, 2, 3, 4), the sum is always one of the numbers 0–4. The sum 3 + 4 = 7, but 7 on this clock is really 2, so 3 + 4 = 2. In modular arithmetic this is written $7 \equiv 2 \bmod 5$ ("7 is congruent to 2 modulo 5").

9. Complete the table showing all possible results of adding 0, 1, 2, 3, or 4 on this clock (The mod 5 table). Some of the answers have been filled in for you. For example: 1 + 1 = 2, 3 + 2 = 0, 2 + 4 = 1.

+	0	1	2	3	4
0	0	1	2	3	4
1	1	2			
2	2				1
3	3		0		
4	4				

If you add 39 + 218 the sum is 257. On the 5-hour clock going around 39 hours and then another 218 hours would put you at the 2-position. How does that work? Since every five hours is one complete revolution, you divide 257 by 5. The division gives an answer of 51 and a remainder of 2. The whole number (51) tells you that you have gone around the clock 51 times. The remainder (2) is how much more you still move on the clock. So the remainder is your position on the clock.

10. If you add 134 + 568 what would be the sum in mod 5?

11. If you had a clock with eight positions (0–7, which is mod 8), what is 2,081 in mod 8?

12. If you had a clock with 26 positions (0–25, which is mod 26), what is 285 in mod 26?

Affine Cipher

What does this have to do with cryptography? Well, with the ability to reduce any number to one of the numbers in mod 26 {0, 1, 2, 3, ... 23, 24, 25} we can create a more complex substitution for the 26 letters of the alphabet. This cipher system is called an **affine cipher**. In an affine cipher each letter of the alphabet is converted to its numerical equivalent by a mathematical function using mod 26. Here is a closer look at the process.

STEP 1: Begin by listing the alphabet and assigning a number, {0, 1, 2, 3, ... 23, 24, 25} to each letter.

a	b	c	d	e	f	g	h	i	j	k	l	m	n	o	p	q	r	s	t	u	v	w	x	y	z
0	1	2	3	4	5	6	7	8	9	10	11	12	13	14	15	16	17	18	19	20	21	22	23	24	25

STEP 2: Select a multiplier. For this cipher let's multiply by 7 (the multiplier must not contain a factor of 26) and then add 11. Multiply each number in the table by 7 then add 11 and place the result in the third row of your table.

alphabet	a	b	c	d	e	f	g	h	i	j	k	l	m
convert to numbers	0	1	2	3	4	5	6	7	8	9	10	11	12
X by 7 then +11	11	18	25	32	39	46	53	60	67	74	81	88	95

alphabet	n	o	p	q	r	s	t	u	v	w	x	y	z
convert to numbers	13	14	15	16	17	18	19	20	21	22	23	24	25
X by 7 then +11	102	109	116	123	130	137	144	151	158	165	172	179	186

STEP 3: Reduce each number in the third row to mod 26 and place in the fourth row of the table.

alphabet	a	b	c	d	e	f	g	h	i	j	k	l	m
convert to numbers	0	1	2	3	4	5	6	7	8	9	10	11	12
X by 7 then +11	11	18	25	32	39	46	53	60	67	74	81	88	95
convert to mod 26	11	18	25	6	13	20	1	8	15	22	3	10	17

alphabet	n	o	p	q	r	s	t	u	v	w	x	y	z
convert to numbers	13	14	15	16	17	18	19	20	21	22	23	24	25
X by 7 then +11	102	109	116	123	130	137	144	151	158	165	172	179	186
convert to mod 26	24	5	12	19	0	7	14	21	2	9	16	23	4

STEP 4: Convert each number in the fourth row to the corresponding letter of the alphabet and place in the fifth row of the table.

alphabet	a	b	c	d	e	f	g	h	i	j	k	l	m
convert to numbers	0	1	2	3	4	5	6	7	8	9	10	11	12
X by 7 then +11	11	18	25	32	39	46	53	60	67	74	81	88	95
convert to mod 26	11	18	25	6	13	20	1	8	15	22	3	10	17
convert to alphabet	L	S	Z	G	N	U	B	I	P	W	D	K	R

alphabet	n	o	p	q	r	s	t	u	v	w	x	y	z
convert to numbers	13	14	15	16	17	18	19	20	21	22	23	24	25
X by 7 then +11	102	109	116	123	130	137	144	151	158	165	172	179	186
convert to mod 26	24	5	12	19	0	7	14	21	2	9	16	23	4
convert to alphabet	Y	F	M	T	A	H	O	V	C	J	Q	X	E

Now we have our key **AC.M7.A11** (*affine cipher multiply by 7 then add 11*).

a	b	c	d	e	f	g	h	i	j	k	l	m	n	o	p	q	r	s	t	u	v	w	x	y	z
L	S	Z	G	N	U	B	I	P	W	D	K	R	Y	F	M	T	A	H	O	V	C	J	Q	X	E

Thus "pirate treasure" is encrypted as "MPALON OANLHVAN."

13. Use the cipher table **AC.M7.A11** to decrypt the ciphertext:

    WLZD HMLAAFJ IPG OIN OANLHVAN

    Plaintext: ______________________________

In the previous example you converted each letter of the alphabet to a number 0–25, then multiplied that number by 7 and added 11. You then converted each number back to a number less than 26 (mod 26), and finally converted that number back to a letter.

Here is an example where we multiply by 11, then add 9, then convert to mod 26, then convert back to the alphabet. We'll call this cipher table **AC.M11.A9** (*affine cipher multiply by 11 add 9*).

alphabet	a	b	c	d	e	f	g	h	i	j	k	l	m
convert to numbers	0	1	2	3	4	5	6	7	8	9	10	11	12
multiply by 11	0	11	22	33	44	55	66	77	88	99	110	121	132
add 9	9	20	31	42	53	64	75	86	97	119	119	130	141
convert to mod 26	9	20	5	16	1	12	23	8	19	4	15	0	11
convert to alphabet	J	U	F	Q	B	M	X	I	T	E	P	A	L

Complete the table for the rest of the alphabet.

alphabet	n	o	p	q	r	s	t	u	v	w	x	y	z
convert to numbers	13	14	15	16	17	18	19	20	21	22	23	24	25
multiply by 11	143	154	165										
add 9	152	163											
convert to mod 26	22	7											
convert to alphabet	W												

14. Encrypt "pirate treasure" using the table.

    Ciphertext: ______________________________

15. Use your cipher table **AC.M11.A9** to decrypt the ciphertext: QTX IBOB MHO XHAQ

    Plaintext: ______________________________

Date Cipher

With the date cipher, or date-shift cipher, a unique letter does not replace each letter of the plaintext. Instead, a plaintext message is written out and then a pattern of repeating numbers is placed beneath. In the classic date cipher the repeating numbers represent a date such as someone's birthday or a special event. For example, September 6, 1955 would be 090655. Then each letter is shifted to the right in the alphabet according to the number below it to create the ciphertext. You would send the receiver a key, "Angie's birthday" for example, and the receiver would know that the repeating set of numbers would be 090655.

The pattern of repeating numbers doesn't have to be a date. Repeating decimals generated by simple fractions work just as well. For example, the fractions 1/7, 2/7, 3/7, ..., n/7, ... all have repeating numbers in their decimal representation (all the same digits but they are just shifted).

1/7 = 0.142857142857142857 with the 142857 repeating forever.

2/7 = 0.285714285714285714 with the 285714 repeating forever.

3/7 = 0.428571428571428571 with the 428571 repeating forever. And so on.

Thus you can send an encrypted message that is a bit more secure than a simple substitution cipher and the key is a simple fraction. Here are the steps in detail.

STEP 1: Write out the message you wish to encrypt ("gold ten paces west") in a table.

g	o	l	d	t	e	n	p	a	c	e	s	w	e	s	t

STEP 2: Pick a pattern. For example, 1/7 as a repeating decimal is 0.142857142857142857... and so on. Your key then is 1/7. Place this pattern of repeating numbers below each of the letters in your message.

g	o	l	d	t	e	n	p	a	c	e	s	w	e	s	t
1	4	2	8	5	7	1	4	2	8	5	7	1	4	2	8

STEP 3: Have the alphabet written out in order left to right. Keep it nearby.

a	b	c	d	e	f	g	h	i	j	k	l	m	n	o	p	q	r	s	t	u	v	w	x	y	z

g	o	l	d	t	e	n	p	a	c	e	s	w	e	s	t
1	4	2	8	5	7	1	4	2	8	5	7	1	4	2	8

STEP 4: To create the ciphertext, shift each letter of the message (plaintext) the number of spaces to the right in the alphabet indicated by the number below it. For example: the "g" has a "1" below it, so the "g" is shifted one space to the right in the alphabet and becomes "H." The "o" has a "4" below it, so the "o" is shifted four spaces in the alphabet to become "S." The "t" at the end of the message has an "8" below it, so it is shifted eight spaces to the right and becomes "B" (the alphabet wraps around as we did in the simple substitution ciphers).

a	b	c	d	e	f	g	h	i	j	k	l	m	n	o	p	q	r	s	t	u	v	w	x	y	z

g	o	l	d	t	e	n	p	a	c	e	s	w	e	s	t
1	4	2	8	5	7	1	4	2	8	5	7	1	4	2	8
H	S	N	L	Y	L	O	T	C	K	J	Z	X	I	U	B

Notice that the same letters in the plaintext do not necessarily go to the same new letter in the ciphertext. The letter "e" became "L" in one case, "J" in another case, and "I" in a third case.

To decipher the encrypted message you need to place the repeating number pattern beneath the encrypted message (ciphertext). Then shift each letter of the ciphertext the number of spaces to the left in the alphabet indicated by the number below it. "H" goes one space to the left to become "g" and so on.

H	S	N	L	Y	L	O	T	C	K	J	Z	X	I	U	B
1	4	2	8	5	7	1	4	2	8	5	7	1	4	2	8
g	o	l	d	t	e	n	p	a	c	e	s	w	e	s	t

16. Decipher the encrypted message below using this date cipher **DC.1/7** (*date cipher key 1/7*).

Ciphertext: EEXMD QPRGA MHT XJM YYFEUCWL

Plaintext: ______________________________

1	4	2	8	5	7	1	4	2	8	5	7	1	4	2	8	5	7	1	4	2	8	5	7
E	E	X	M	D	Q	P	R	G	A	M	H	T	X	J	M	Y	Y	F	E	U	C	W	L

7.3 Code Breaking

When cryptographers do not have the key, how do they break a cipher? What tools do they use? Mathematics is the short answer. Given enough ciphertext, patterns begin to appear with substitution ciphers. Just as many serious Scrabble™ players learn all the one-, two- and three-letter words, cryptographers catalogue their relative frequency in common English text. Cryptographers collect data about the relative frequencies of not only words, but also the relative frequencies of letters, and two- and three-letter combinations. See the frequency tables below. The highest frequency letter or word is on the left in each list.

Frequency of single letters: e t o a n i r s h d l c ...

Frequency of one-letter words: a, I

Frequency of two-letter words: of, to, in, it, is, be, as, at, so, we, he, by, or, on, do, if, me, my, up, an, go, no, us, am...

Frequency of three-letter words: the, and, for, are, but, not, you, all, any, can, had, her, was, one, our, out, day, get, has, him, his, how, man, new, now, old, see, two, way, who, boy, did, its, let, put, say, she, too, use...

Frequency of four-letter words: that, with, have, this, will, your, from, they, know, want, been, good, much, some, time, very, when, come, here, just, like, long, make, many, more, only, over, such, take, than, them, well, were...

Frequency of two-letter combinations: th er on an re he in ed nd ha at en es of or nt ea ti to it st io le is ou ar as de rt ve

Frequency of three-letter combinations: the and tha ent ion tio for nde has nce edt tis oft sth men

Frequency of most common doubles: ss ee tt ff 11 mm oo

Order of frequency of initial letters: t o a w b c d s f m ...

Order of frequency of final letters: e s t d n r y f l ...

Code breaking often begins by finding the most common letter in a ciphertext and replacing each occurrence of that letter with the letter "e" ("e" being the most common letter). If that doesn't seem to work, replace the most common letter in the ciphertext with the next most common letter ("t" or "o" or "a").

The next strategy is to look for the one-letter terms in the ciphertext. These one-letter terms can be replaced by either "a" or the letter "i" since the words "a" and "I" are the only one-letter words in English. Repeat this strategy for two- and three-letter terms in the ciphertext. If a three-letter word starts some ciphertext sentences, then the three-letter term is probably "the" which gives you a few more substitutions. If you are fortunate enough to have ciphertext that contains words such as ZXC'G then you know the letter following the apostrophe (') is either the letter "s" or "t" in the plaintext.

7.4 Transposition Ciphers

In transposition ciphers the letters remain the same but the arrangement has changed (transposed) according to a system. The secret word "treasure" rewritten as "steareur" would be an example of a transposition. People who are good with anagrams might prefer to encrypt their messages by transposition.

Rail Fence Cipher

T	L	U	5	R	T	E	M	R
H	D	R	M	S	O	H	A	E
E	I	I	E	W	F	A	N	E
G	S	E	T	E	T	N	S	X
O	B	D	E	S	H	G	T	X

The rail fence cipher is a classic transposition cipher. A simple rail fence cipher features a message written in columns. When the message reaches the bottom of one column, the next letter of the message floats back up to the top of the next column. For example, you could arrange the plaintext "The gold is buried 5 meters west of the hangman's tree" in columns of five terms as shown at right. This plaintext has 43 terms so we arrange them into five rows (rails) of nine terms and fill in the remaining two positions with anything (X's in this case).

To create the ciphertext, list the terms horizontally, organizing the terms in equal-sized groups. Since there are 45 terms altogether we could pick groups of 3, 5, 9, or 15. With groups of five the ciphertext is: TLU5R TEMRH DRMSO HAEEI IEWFA NEGSE TETNS XOBDE SHGTX. Let's call this cipher key **RFV.5.5** (*rail fence vertical 5 rails grouped in 5's*).

To decipher the message you must know the number of rails, in this case five. Since there are 45 terms (43 in the message and two X's) you create five rails of nine terms each. Then read the message in the columns. Graph paper is also helpful with rail fence ciphers.

Transposition Cipher Exercises

1. Decrypt the following ciphertext using the cipher key **RFV.6.4**: DESO OTDE ISIM SFCR TASY GEOT OEHS YYFT UHNE EUOY IETE UATR UYVR HCTN RERY

   Plaintext: ______________________________

   ____

A common rail fence cipher features text that is written in a diagonal pattern instead of vertical columns. For example, the plaintext "doubloons beneath coconut tree" is arranged in a diagonal pattern. The plaintext has 27 terms. If we use four rails then we could use a rectangle of 4×28 as shown below.

d						o						e						c						r			
	o				o		n				n		a				o		o				t		e		
		u		l				s		e				t		c				n		t				e	
			b						b						h						u						x

To encrypt the message, you rewrite it by reading across the rails and organizing the letters in equal-sized groups. With groups of seven the ciphertext is: DOECROO NNAOOTE ULSETCN TEBBHUX. Let's call this cipher key **RFD.4.7**, (*rail fence diagonal 4 rails grouped in 7's*).

2. Decrypt the following ciphertext using the cipher key RFD.5.5: FBGWO TEEAW UELHL SREOT LWFWO

   Plaintext: ______________________________

Chapter 7.4

Route Cipher

A similar transposition cipher, the **route cipher**, weaves the plaintext through patterns in a rectangular grid. For example, the plaintext "Calico Jack's coffin contains gold and jewels" is spiraled in a counter-clockwise pattern in the 5×8 rectangle shown below.

This plaintext written in a counter-clockwise spiral in the 5×8 rectangle is then rearranged left to right into groupings of five to create the cipher text: CATNO CNIAI EWEJD FLNLS XXNFI SGOLD AOCOJ ACKSC. The remaining two cells are filled in with X's. Let's call this cipher key **RC.CCS.5.5** (*route cipher counterclockwise spiral 5 rails grouped in 5's*).

c	a	t	n	o	c	n	i
a	i	e	w	e	j	d	f
l	n	l	s	x	x	n	f
i	s	g	o	l	d	a	o
c	o	j	a	c	k	s	c

3. Decrypt the following ciphertext using the cipher key **RC.CS.6.4** (*route cipher clockwise spiral 6 rails grouped in 4's*) DWIT HTEL VECR IIWR AERS WSPA UNIA TSBS IERU.

   Plaintext: ______________________________

Grille Cipher

Another transposition cipher, the **grille cipher**, positions the ciphertext in a square grid. The cipher key is a square grid with cut-out squares called the grille. To decipher the message you place the grille over the ciphertext square grid and read off the letters showing through the cut-out squares as they appear, left to right top to bottom. Next, you rotate the grille 90° clockwise and read the letters again. Rotate the grille 180° and repeat. Finally, rotate the grille 270° and repeat.

For example, the message "dig here 3 feet down" when encrypted looks like the 4×4 grid to the near right. The grille is shown to the far right.

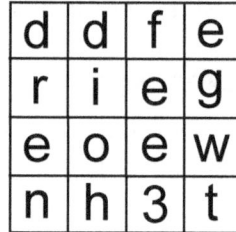

When the grille is placed over the ciphertext the beginning of the message is revealed "digh." When the grille is rotated 90° clockwise the message continues when "ere3" is revealed.

d	d	f	e
r	i	e	g
e	o	e	w
n	h	3	t

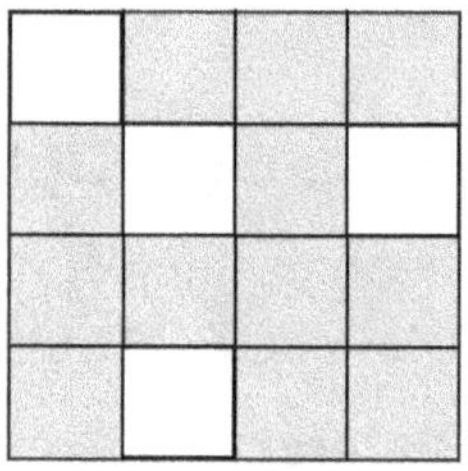

Let's call this cipher key the **GC.1.6.8.14**. (*grille cipher with holes at squares 1, 6, 8, and 14*) The four positions of the grille are shown below revealing the message.

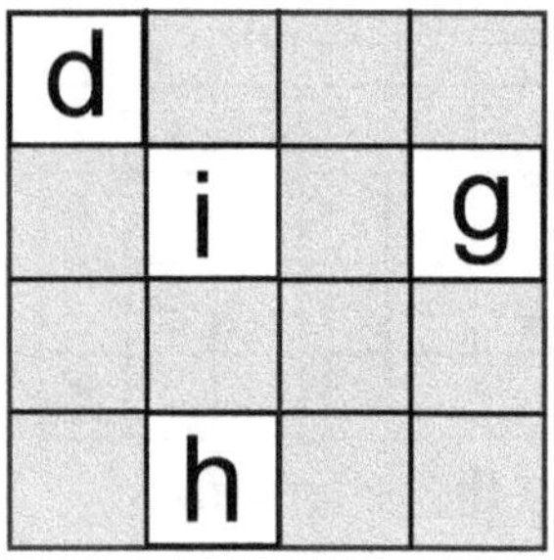

0° rotation

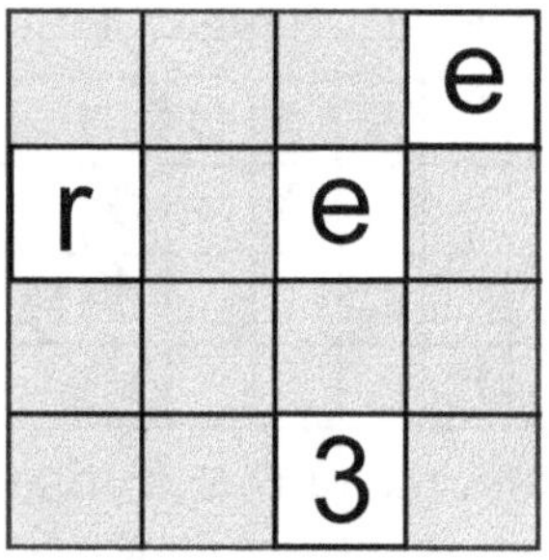

90° rotation

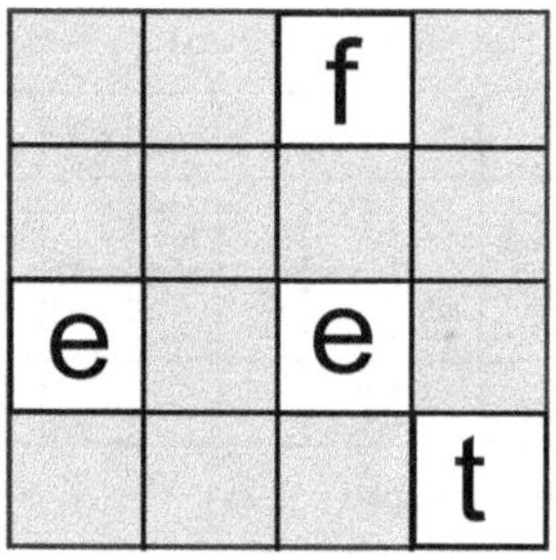

180° rotation

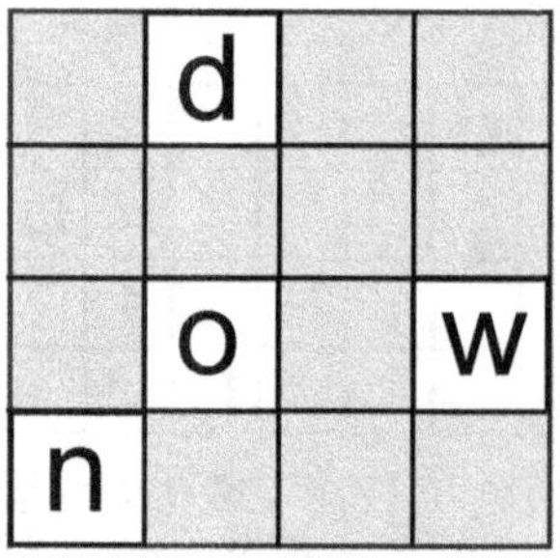

270° rotation

You might be wondering, how do you create the grille? First notice that the positions of the four holes in the grille cover all 16 squares of the 4×4 grid when the grille has been rotated into all four positions. How is that done?

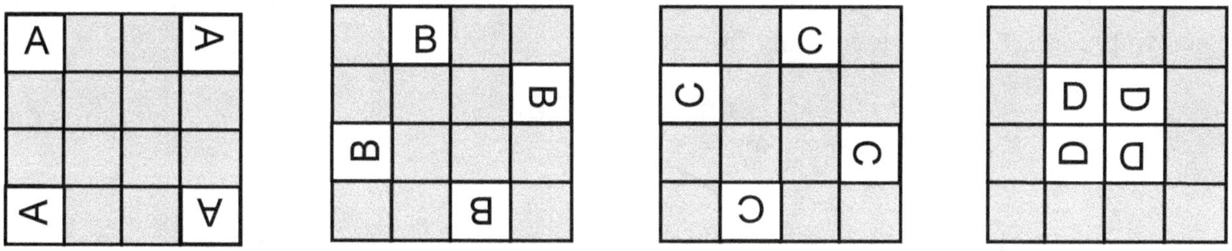

Notice that the "A" in the first upper left square will move to the other three positions after rotations of 90°, 180°, and 270°. The same is true for the "B", "C", and "D" positions.

So you select one of the "A" positions, one of the "B" positions, one of the "C" positions, and one of the "D" positions for your holes in the grille. These four positions cover all 16 squares after the rotations.

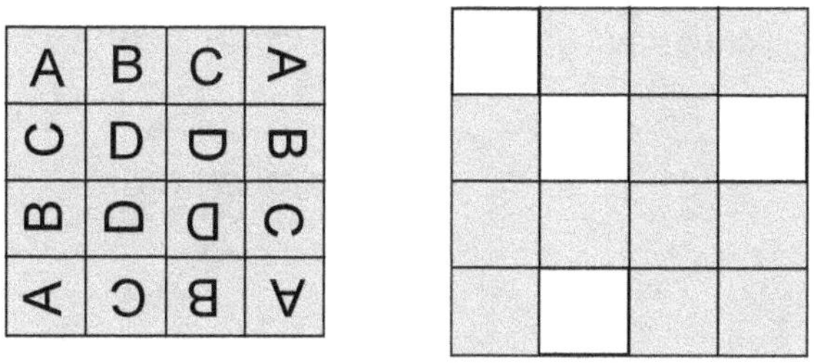

The key for the grille cipher shown to the right is **GC.1.8.10.17.20.23** (*grille cipher with holes at squares 1, 8, 10, 17, 20, and 23*). Copy the 5×5 grille to the right onto patty paper or tracing paper. Don't copy the letters. Shade in all the squares except 1, 8, 10, 17, 20, and 23.

4. Use this sheet to decipher the hidden message.

Notice that six squares are cut out (1, 8, 10, 17, 20, 23). Since each square gets rotated (each occupying four positions) the message is 24 letters or numbers. The holes never land on the center square and thus, the center square "x" is not part of the message.

g	l	o	m	e
u	t	o	t	l
e	t	x	r	r
h	d	p	e	5
e	s	m	s	a

Plaintext: ____

7.5 Modern Use of Cryptography

Today businesses send trade secrets and private financial information as encrypted data over the Internet. We use modern cryptography every time we use an ATM or a credit card. The numbers are encrypted to protect their privacy during transmission.

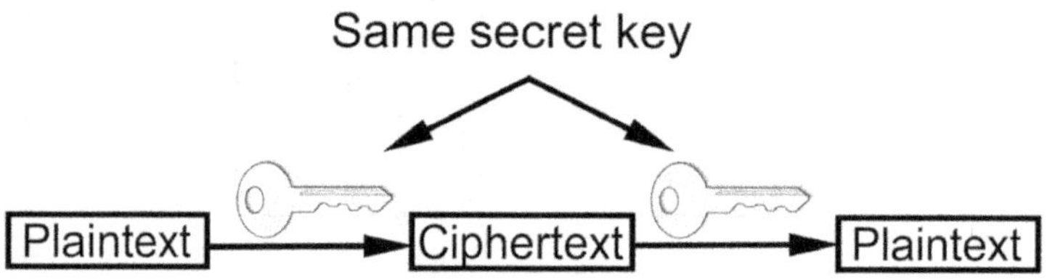

So far we have looked at **secret key cryptography** (**SKC**). SKC uses a single key (a set of rules or cipher table) for both encryption and decryption. The sender uses the key to encrypt the plaintext (secret message) and sends the ciphertext to the receiver. The receiver applies the same key to decrypt the message and uncover the plaintext.

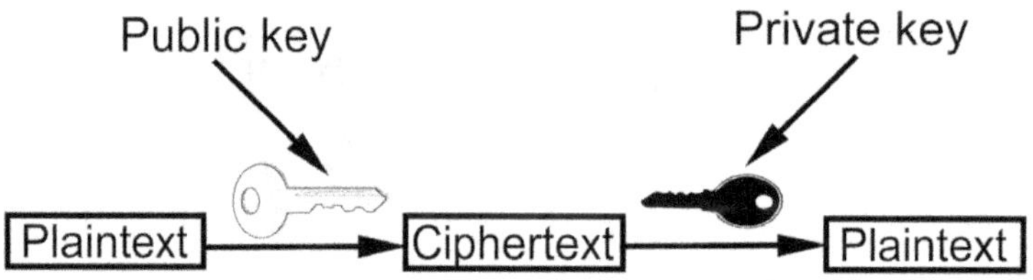

Public-key cryptography (**PKC**) uses two keys, one for encryption and another for decryption. One key is public and the other is private. The keys are related mathematically. There are so many combinations using a secure private key with a public key, the cipher is essentially secure, even with the most powerful computers.

The mathematics used involves one-way mathematical functions that are easy to compute while the inverse function is much more difficult to compute. For example, multiplying two very large primes (public key) is manageable, but factoring the product of two extremely large primes (private key) is very difficult.

A **semiprime** is a natural number that is the product of exactly two prime numbers. The first few semiprimes are 4, 6, 9, 10, 14, 15, ... It is difficult to find prime factors because mathematicians don't have a fast method. They have to try every prime up to the square root of the number. For example, multiply the primes 1987 and 1979 and you get, after a tedious bit of arithmetic, the semiprime 3,932,273. It can be done. However, if you were given the semiprime number 3,992,003, how fast can you determine that its two prime factors are 1,997 and 1999? How about factoring the semiprime 334,004,240,761? This can still be done rather quickly with a computer. For really secure encryption, cryptographers rely on semiprimes with hundreds of digits. Cryptography is a vital field in today's technological society and mathematics is the language spoken by cryptographers.

7.6 Pirate Treasure with Ciphers

You recently came across an old seaman's chest that contained 30 island maps, a document titled *Island Notes*, and another document showing a 4×11 grid filled with mysterious symbols. You believe these maps and the accompanying documents hold the secrets to finding pirate treasure buried on each of the 30 islands (not in the sea). The *Island Notes* document seems to be written in various cipher systems. You believe that when deciphered, they will each lead to pirate treasure. The document containing geometric figures and a skeleton key appears to be a table that tells which type of cipher system is used for each secret message on the *Island Notes* document. Unfortunately, dark splotches that look like spilled blood cover some of the words and symbols in the table.

It will be helpful to have read about cryptography, the science of writing secret messages, in Sections 7.1 through 7.4 before attempting the pirate buried treasure puzzles that follow.

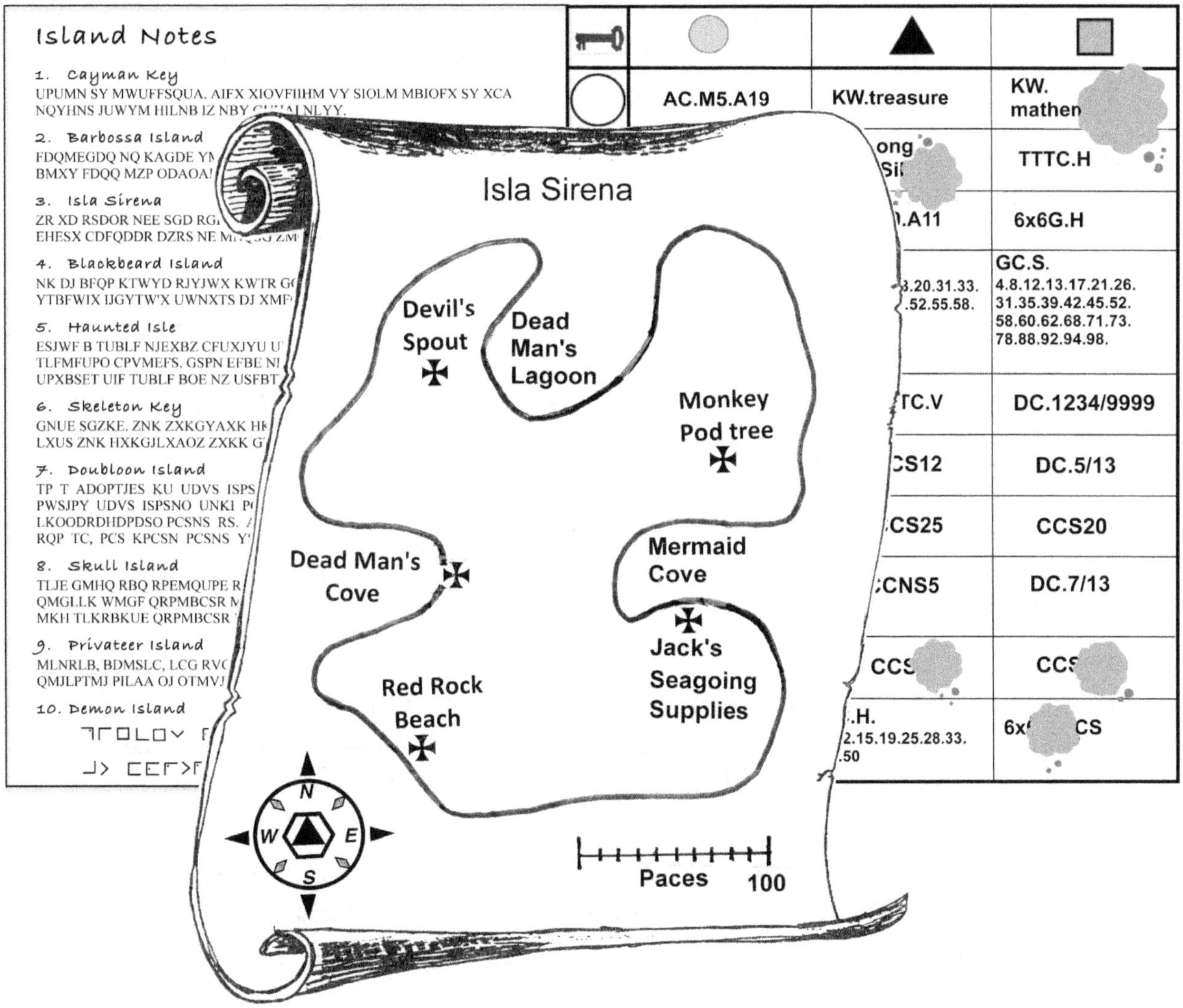

Island Notes

1. Cayman Key

UPUMN SY MWUFFSQUA. AIFX XIOVFIIHM VY SIOLM MBIOFX SY XCA NQYHNS JUWYM HILNB IZ NBY GUHAI NLYY.

2. Barbossa Island

FDQMEGDQ NQ KAGDE YMFQK UR KAG PUS YUPIMK NQFIQQZ FTQ BMXY FDQQ MZP ODAOAPUXQ EWGXX

3. Isla Sirena

ZR XD RSDOR NEE SGD RGHO ZS CDZC LZM'R BNUD VZKJ ENQSX OZBDR EHESX CDFQDDR DZRS NE MNQSG ZMC LX SQDZRTQD ZVZHSR XD.

4. Blackbeard Island

NK DJ BFQP KTWYD RJYJWX KWTR GQFHPGJFWI'X YTRGXYTSJ YTBFWIX IJGYTW'X UWNXTS DJ XMFQQ INL KTW ITZGQTTSX.

5. Haunted Isle

ESJWF B TUBLF NJEXBZ CFUXJYU UIF KPMMZ SPHFS JOO BOE TLFMFUPO CPVMEFS. GSPN EFBE NBO'T EPDL XBML UXFOUZ NFUFST UPXBSET UIF TUBLF BOE NZ USFBTVSF CF ZPVST.

6. Skeleton Key

GNUE SGZKE. ZNK ZXKGYAXK HK EUAXY YNUARJ EUA JOM 15 SKZKXY LXUS ZNK HXKGJLXAOZ ZXKK GTJ 20 SKZKXY LXUS SUXMGT'Y MXGBK

7. Doubloon Island

TP T ADOPTJES KU UDVS ISPSNO UNKI YS KHAS ETOPHS WTHH TJA PWSJPY UDVS ISPSNO UNKI PCS ESISPSNY BTPS, PWK LKOODRDHDPDSO PCSNS RS. ADB JKP RY RHTEGRSTNA'O PKIROPKJS RQP TC, PCS KPCSN PCSNS YS OCTHH UDJA IS PNSTOQNS ITPS.

8. Skull Island

TLJE GMHQ RBQ RPEMQUPE RL AE ILUKH. IPLJ GEMNBKC GBZMPH QMGLLK WMGF QRPMBCSR MQ YE AE MTPLQQ DERQMJ PBVEP APBHCE MKH TLKRBKUE QRPMBCSR ILP MKLRSEP IBIRY NMTEQ MKH HBC.

9. Privateer Island

MLNRLB, BDMSLC, LCG RVGG. YJ PILAA HVCG QDBOPQDCJP QIMJJ. BY QMJLPTMJ PILAA OJ OTMVJG JKTLAAY HMDB LAA QIMJJ.

10. Demon Island

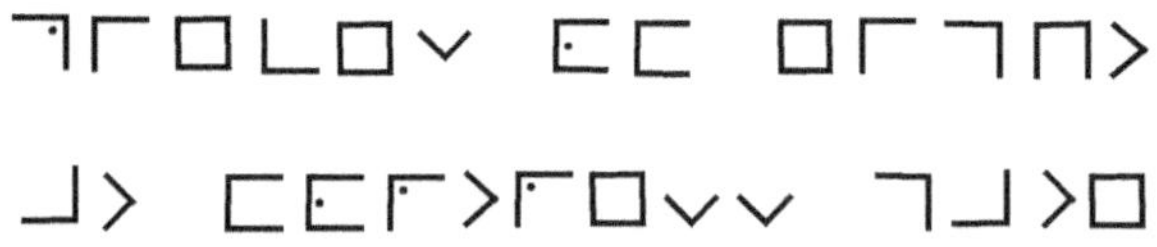

11. Isla Tortuga

12. Isla Langosta

11.41. 51.15. 41.42.15.34.41. 33.16.16. 42.22.15. 41.22.23.34. 11.42. 14.15.11.14. 31.11.32.'41. 13.33.44.15. 45.11.26.25. 16.23.16.42.51. 34.11.13.15.41. 61.53 14.15.21.36.15.15.41. 15.11.41.42. 33.16. 32.33.36.42.22. 11.32.14. 31.51. 42.36.15.11.41.43.36.15. 11.45.11.23.42.41. 51.15.

13. Parrot Island

15.51. 35.62.41.51. 24.63.51.11.14.34.63.51. 21.51. 61.33.34.23.41. 45.26. 13.51.24.51.63.14. 11.23.41. 36.35. 41.51.12.63.51.51.14. 54.51.14.24. 33.61. 14.33.34.24.22. 61.63.33.13. 31.63.33.54.14. 23.51.14.24. 24.11.44.51.63.23.

14. Silver's Island

	1	2	3	4	5	6	7	8
1	L	o	r	e	o	m	e	i
2	s	d	n	C	m	b	a	g
3	e	J	u	o	l	t	r	i
4	c	i	e	e	r	d	h	s
5	n	N	o	s	J	t	a	t
6	w	c	r	o	o	k	r	e
7	t	h	c	a	u	h	s	a
8	v	u	n	f	e	r	d	r

15. Crocodile Key

GWN GANBDJAN ZD EJAZNK DZS LNGNAD QARL GWN UBIL GANN BOK KJN ORAGW RQ GWN TBIIRPD.

16. Devil's Island

AM1N 0O3 N1U1GV0O B0 N3MNBVW P1E3 LBG9 5D N303MT B0 BU BUHG3 1A YC W3HM33T 3BT0 1A U1M0O BUW WVH NB03T WVH.

17. Isla Marsopa

EIHP UGLDX ULIA FYY BLGX AHBLIMR MLST OHYVR DVPVAVIT EHI ABVYAT EFSV RAVQR, AJIY GVEA LYM BLGX LYHAWVI EFSV RAVQR LYM AWV AIVLRJIV UV THJIR.

18. Buccaneer Island

JN LWIN KANTFPAN YN CHIING SHSKJ BNKNAF SALB KCN DNGKNA LS KCN DLWI AHUNA YAHIXN TGI KCHAKJ BNKNAF SALB KCN DNBNKNAJ ZTWW.

19. Monkey Island

YATX WUN UVIJXVI'L WANN DVMB WTDVACL LBHMM ATRB YTA 10 XNWNAL VIC WUNAN ZN LUVMM YFIC CTHGMTTIL VEMNIWZ.

20. Crescent Key

	1	2	3	4	5	6	7	8
1	T	d	b	o	w	t	s	f
2	J	t	e	r	o	a	e	n
3	n	t	c	y	a	e	k	s
4	u	R	y	a	e	c	m	s
5	e	h	r	t	e	e	g	k
6	h	a	r	a	a	l	l	s
7	l	m	o	W	t	f	e	r
8	e	s	o	i	X	t	m	n

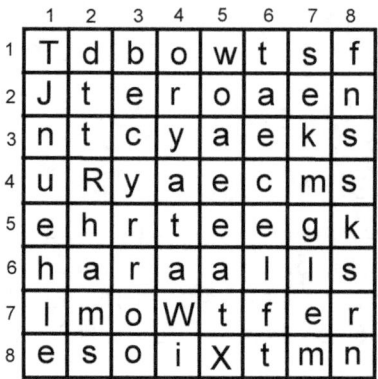

21. Isla Mariposa

26.62.65.14. 14.62.22.12.65.62.62.63.31. 11.41.15. 21.62. 12.15. 16.62.22.63.14. 46.16. 35.15. 24.11.65.66. 16.41.62.64. 21.36.15. 13.11.31.21.65.15. 26.11.21.15. 34.55.55. 61.11.13.15.31. 21.36.41.62.22.26.36. 21.36.15. 21.24.46.63. 64.62.63.62.65.46.21.36.31.

22. Mistico Island

AMJH OC9 AMJIO NO9KN JA EJGGT MJB9M DII N9I8 JI9 6P7FJ R5GFDIB DI OC9 8DM97ODJI JA NFPGG HJPIO5DI AJM WVV H9O9MN 5I8 5IJOC9M 6P7FJ JI 5 7JPMN9 OJR5M8N 75KMD7JMI KJDIO AJM 3V H9O9MN. OC9 OM95NPM9 GJ75ODJI AJMHN 5I 9LPDG5O9M5G OMD5IBG9 RDOC OC9 ORJ 6P7FJN

23. Serpent Island

LRTH HF DRCVY JK BM AGMP IZSS DWRKSJJQH AOAMQ UWGQ UTZIVJT LDBSX HQHV JUS F KCRJSJG UIZFWV BYXO WLOLZ XFOS WOYYB UIZFWV. LVOWJ D AXGLJ. GQK SJIZIC HFYZQBZ ZTXZ WZBPH IRJ UMH OMGOY EWYREJU IXUQ NJCETB MLTP.

24. Isla Tesoro

OSGA HGS FTPS UMHF ANTRCH JMNOHG SNILPY JTESO PHWTMAO ITGIJCTGB OTCHHG TGA OSGA T OSEHGA FTPS UMHF PLS ITCCHWO ONXPY JTESO PHWTMAO LHI'O LSTA PTVSMG. UNGA PLS JHNGP FNAWTY RSPWSSG PLS PWH TGA PMSTOQMS RS YS MSWTMA.

25. Isla de los Muerto

h	d	o	f	e	i	r	r	r	t	r	o
m	h	3	e	t	0	c	w	h	t	p	a
i	e	o	l	a	k	h	c	n	4	a	e
0	s	n	e	o	g	p	f	m	a	a	d
s	e	c	a	e	t	x	g	s	n	a	s
d	t	o	m	x	a	t	r	n	l	e	u
e	r	s	d	n	w	a	x	w	d	r	a
i	i	g	a	o	x	c	l	h	k	t	k
s	5	t	t	y	0	a	o	u	n	r	p
n	d	a	u	a	w	c	n	e	r	a	s
s	d	h	l	i	o	f	k	v	a	n	a
n	e	t	c	o	h	l	e	t	e	x	n

26. Shipwreck Island

QNDGF C PEUGB EU VKI NKGABA SSJPW FFVZIFP WLF ORRLGB TPF WVFG DRE VKI QCOQ UTHI GTRQ UJH LBPJQBP'V XSGH ABNN XPYDVEU BSVT PEUGB GPWQXJPJ CPWU WUGSW JH BI DQQXJPXI PP WLF UDQF FLWUCQGF AH WICOP GKQH SKFLFU EIMQZ

27. Emerald Island

NM ZI MVTDT CGZ LLPQGBWF, UVGIXBSI CEFPUW AM. YOF XTMFZVVG BNZ CYTQJK BX VPJ MPYTBM WPMPB TM B TCZFSMINWLYBQ HWWTFH DG YOF QCVLV UVGM, HVDSPCY ASIG ISK QERIDH UVGM.

28. Isla de Sangria

WZIGTZUM GNFXW WJ MPQG JI LPZQL YTEJU I FUVQGMV OO HRTH XJAHZ IWVFOTC JJXWIRZ GWRU XNF TUIRMF YUMI GOI WPI RFRRV XXFJ

29. Isla de Oro

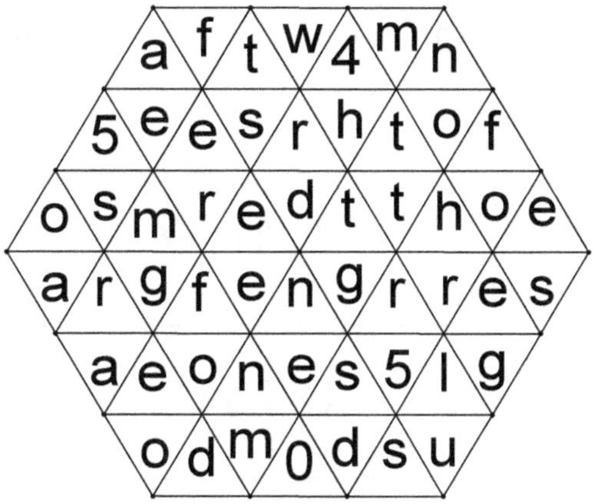

30. Isla Plata

61.64.36.41. 12.63.51. 46.64.41.16.26.64.36.12. 21.51.12.42.64.52.12. 65.51.12.12.53.'13. 63.51.11.41. 12.11.32.51.14.36. 11.36.41. 41.51.32.64.56.'13 13.16.53.62.56.11.13.13. 61.64.36.41. 12.63.51. 46.64.41.16.26.64.36.12. 21.51.12.42.64.52.12. 12.63.51. 46.26.36.66.51.53. 16.26.41. 12.14.51.51. 11.36.41. 15.22.64.31.66.13.64.56.32.51.14. 46.64.36.51. 64.61. 53.51. 61.26.56.56.26.42. 46.51. 42.26.14.41.13. 12.14.51.11.13.22.14.51. 21.51. 53.26.22.14.13. 51.52.11.31.12.56.53. 21.51.12.42.64.52.12. 12.63.51. 12.42.26. 46.64.41.16.26.64.36.12.13.

Chapter 7.6

Cipher Key Document

🔑	●	▲	■
○	AC.M5.A19	KW.treasure	KW. mathem
△	AC.M3.A1	KW.Long John Sil	TTTC.H
▽	AC.M11.A21	AC.M9.A11	6x6G.H
□	GC.S. 1.5.11.16.18.20.31.33. 36.38.43.48.52.55.58. 62.	GC.S. 1.5.11.16.18.20.31.33. 36.38.43.48.52.55.58. 62.	GC.S. 4.8.12.13.17.21.26. 31.35.39.42.45.52. 58.60.62.68.71.73. 78.88.92.94.98.
◇	6x6G.V	TTTC.V	DC.1234/9999
⬠	DC.4/7	CCS12	DC.5/13
⬡	AC.M7.A1 (mod36)	CCS25	CCS20
heptagon	6x6G.CS	CCNS5	DC.7/13
octagon	CCS[illegible]	CCS[illegible]	CCS[illegible]
nonagon	KW[illegible]sure Isla[illegible]	GC.H. 2.12.15.19.25.28.33. 47.50	6x[illegible]CS

Island Treasure Map 1 ɦ

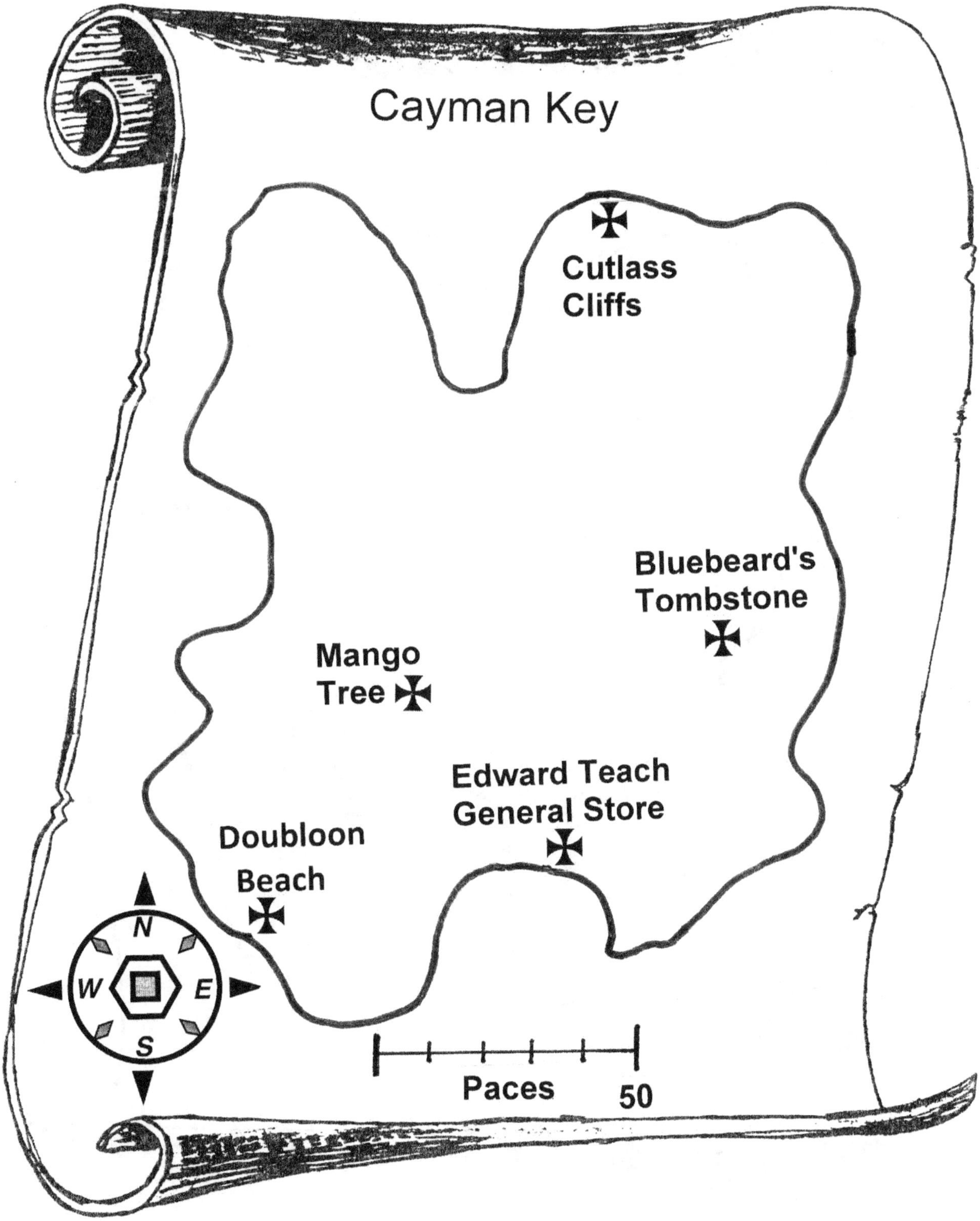

Island Treasure Map 2 h

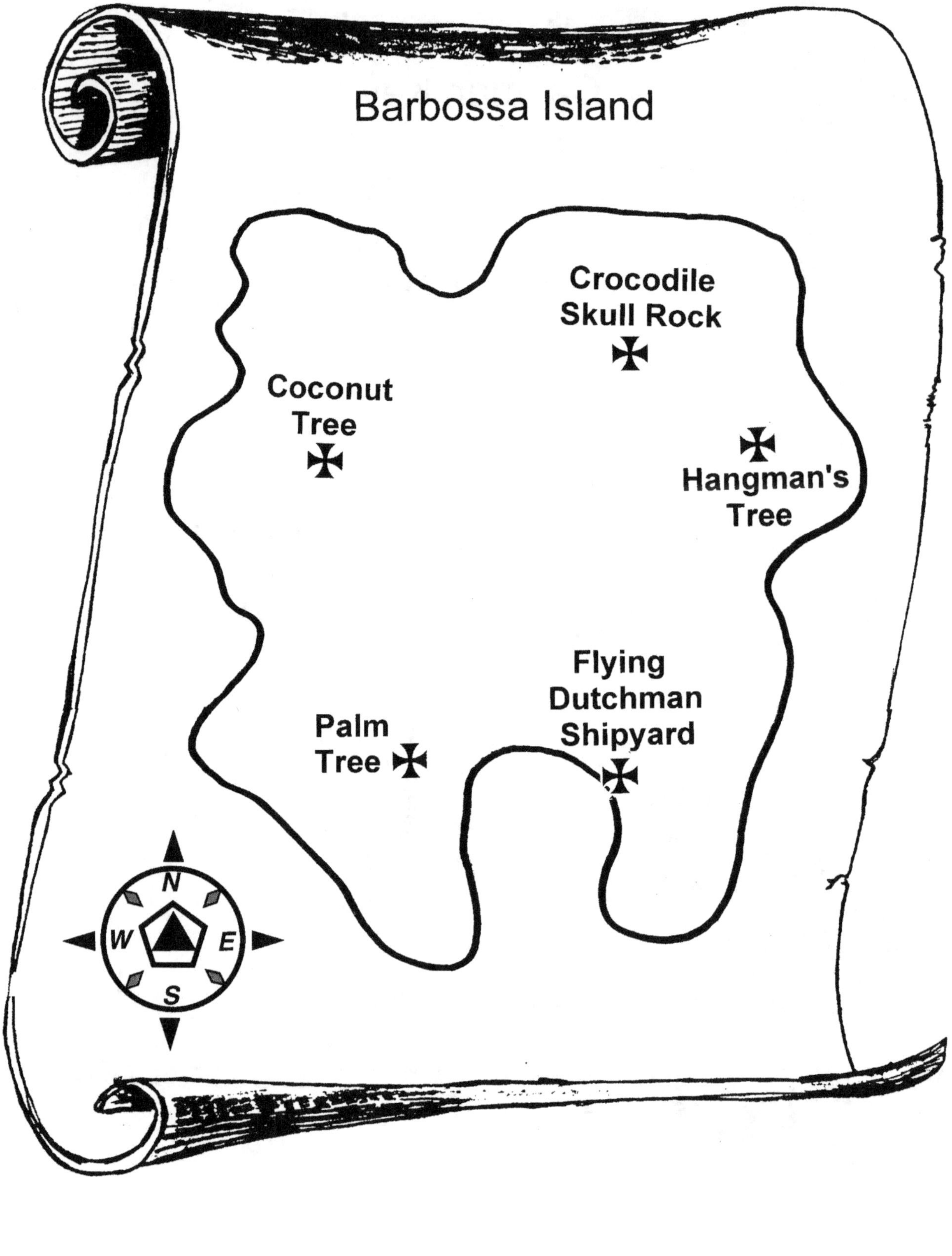

Island Treasure Map 3

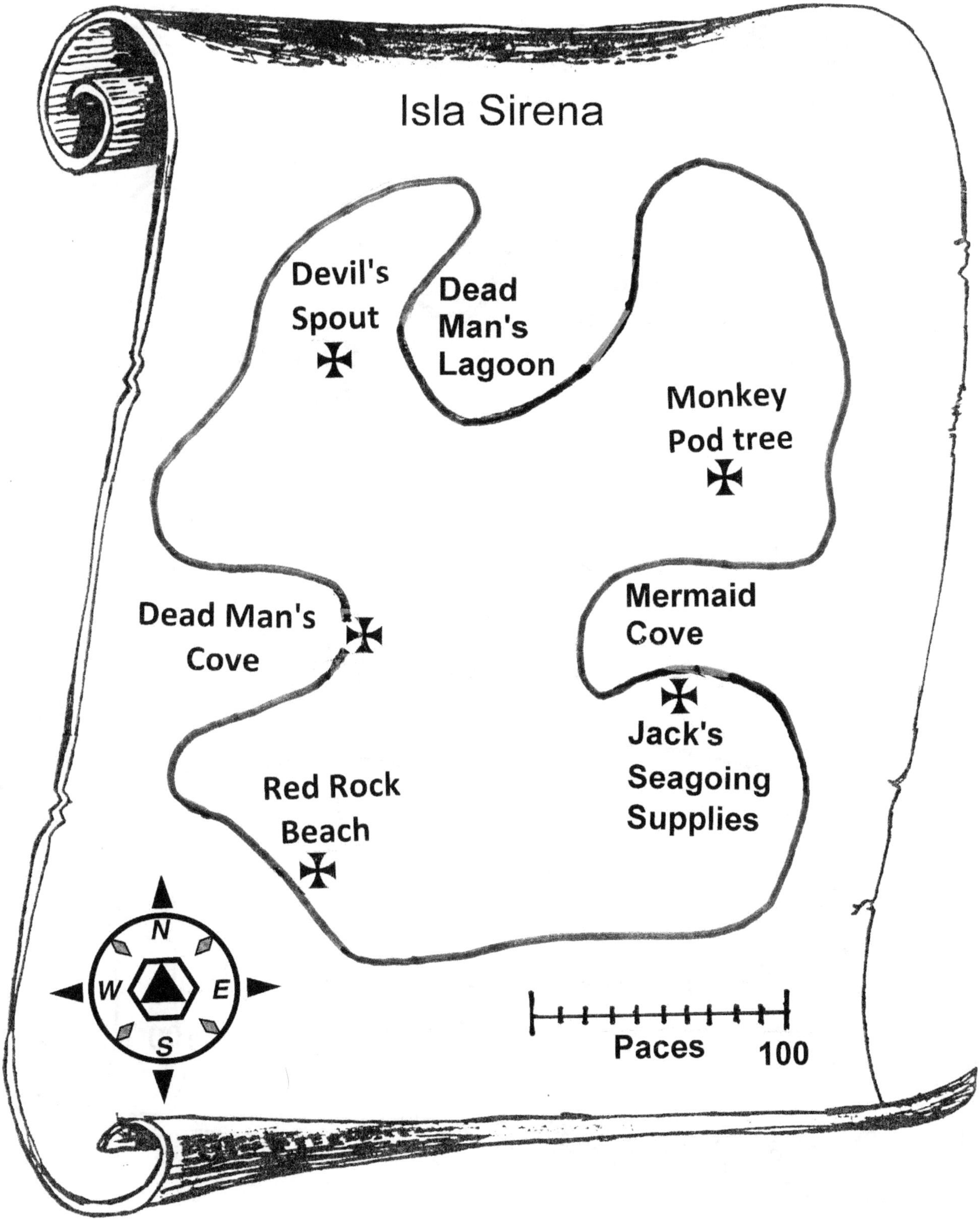

Island Treasure Map 4 ɦ

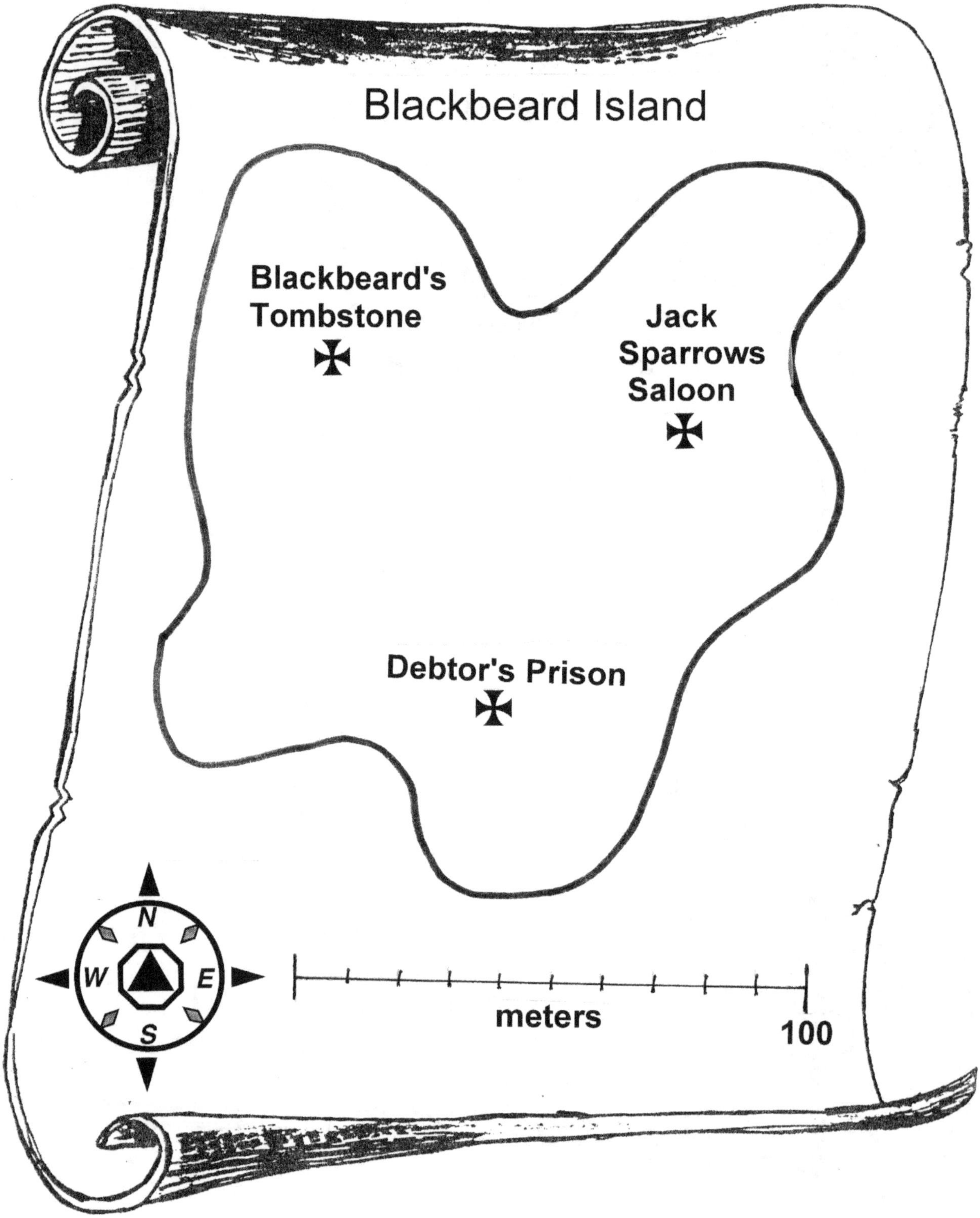

Island Treasure Map 5 *h*

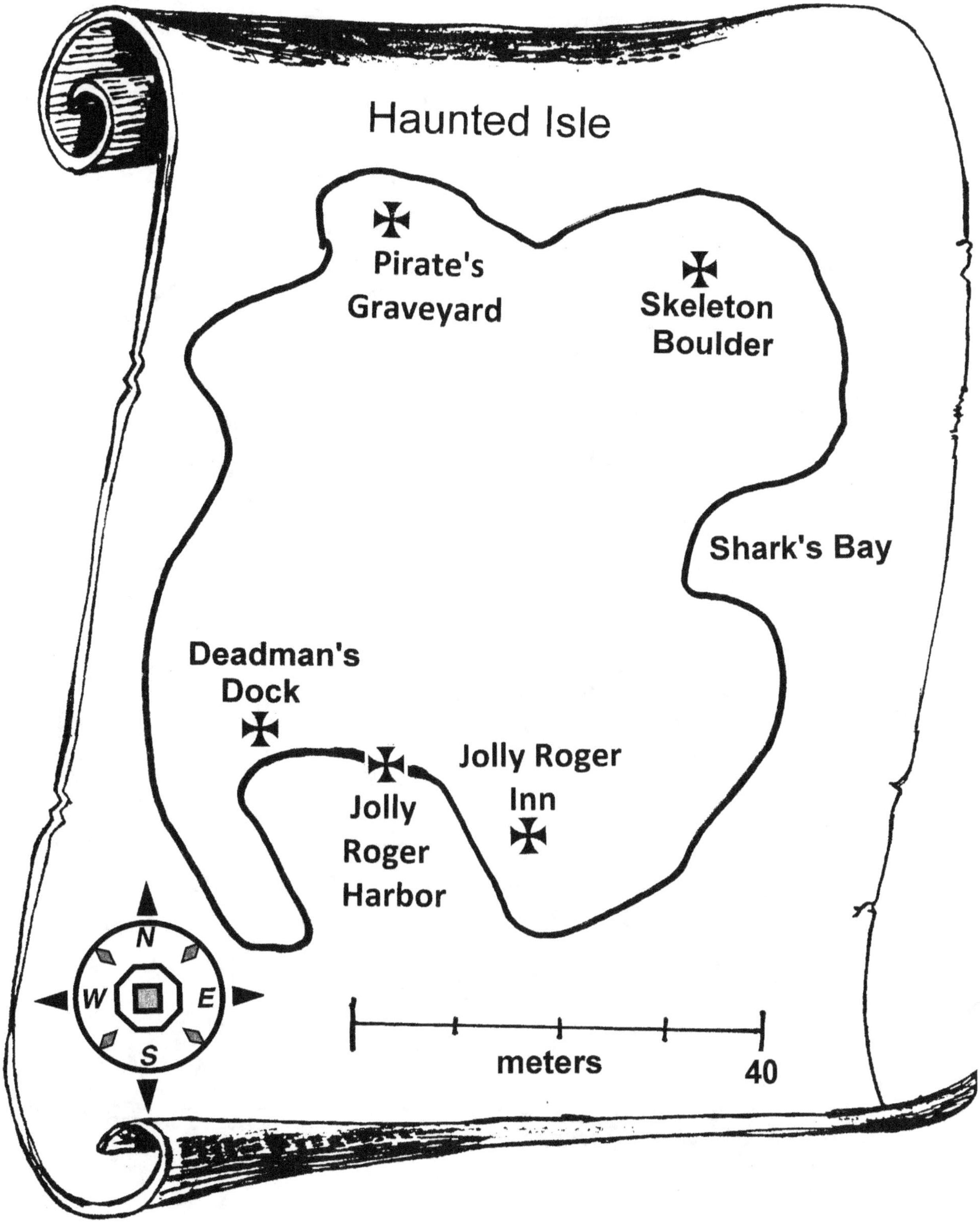

Island Treasure Map 6 h

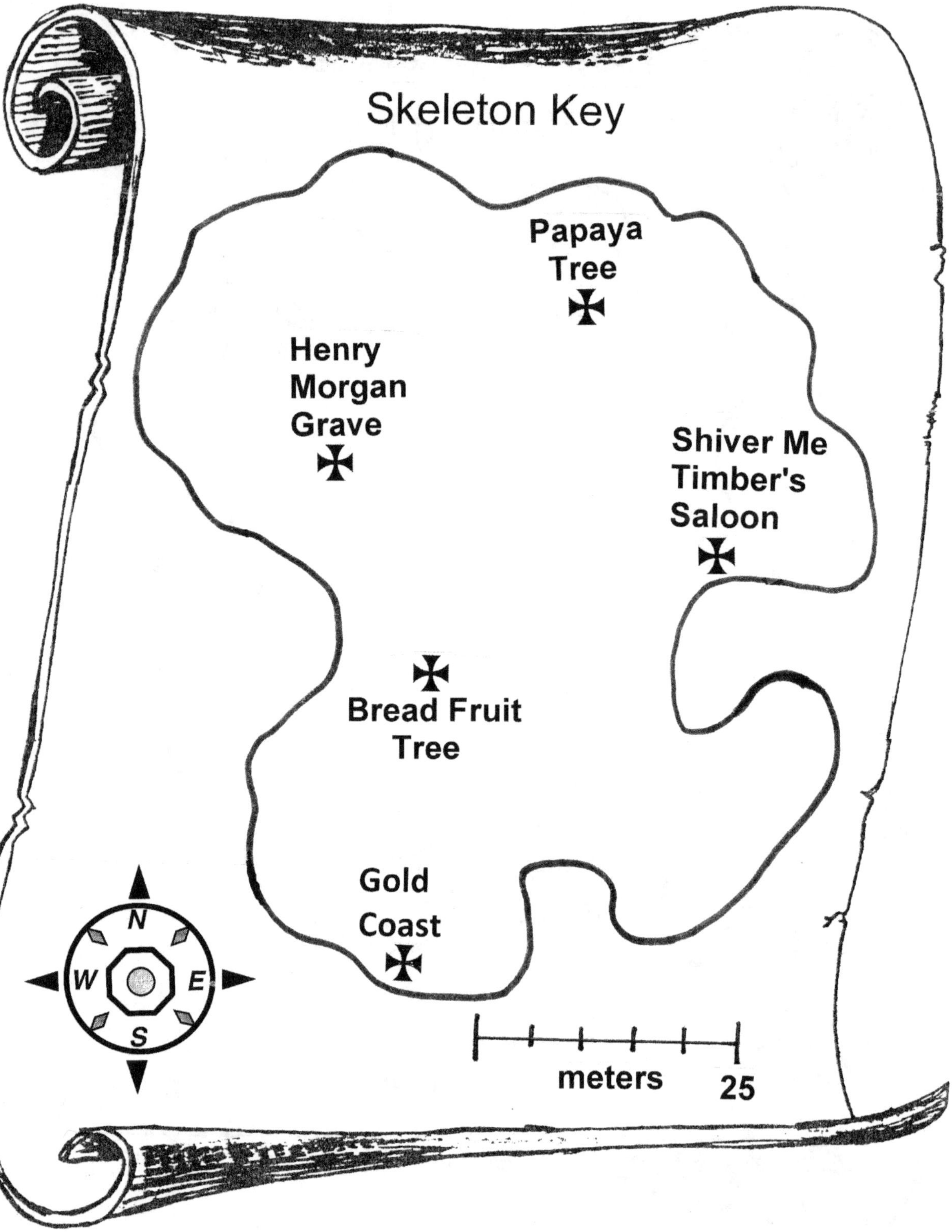

Island Treasure Map 7 ℏ

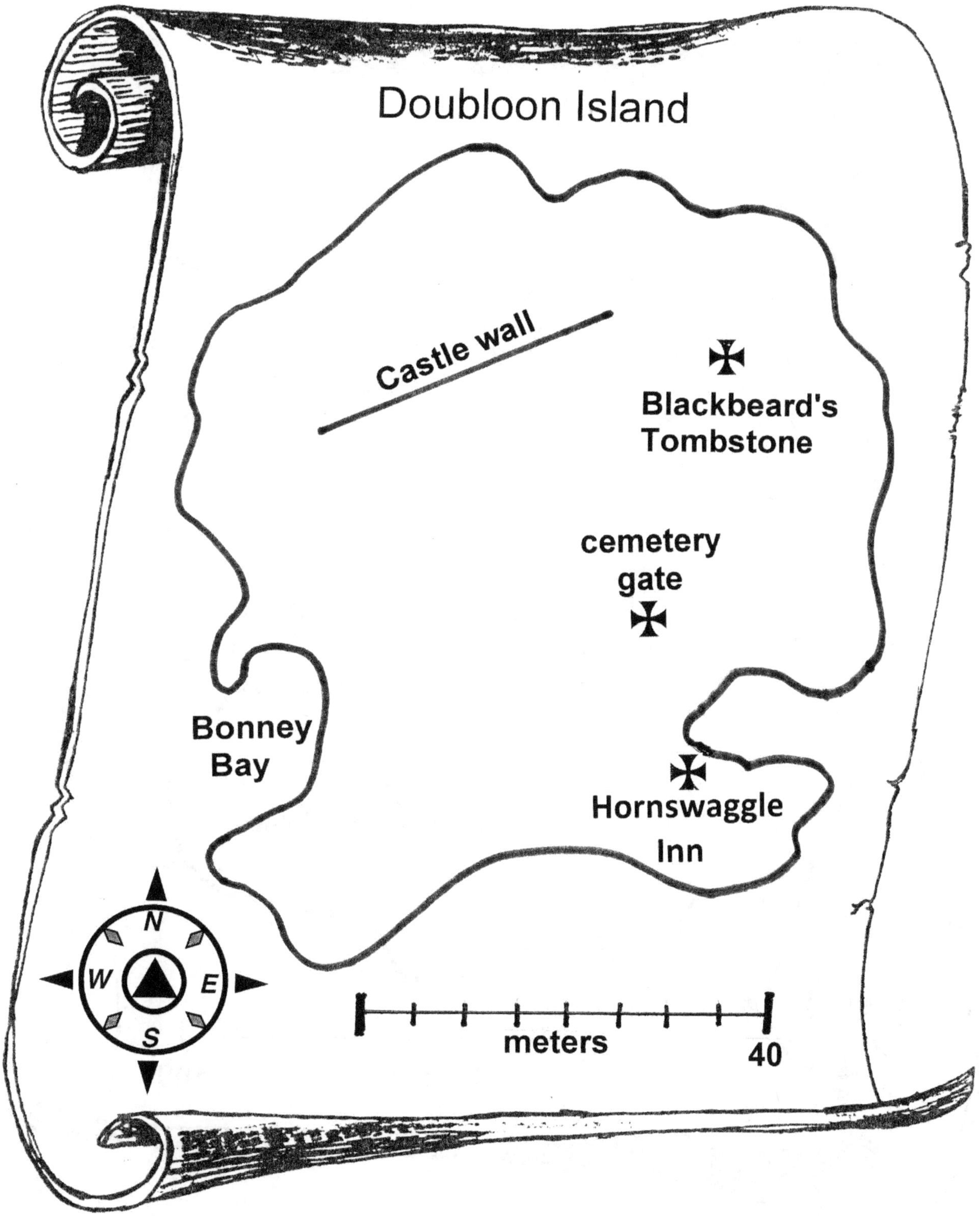

Island Treasure Map 8 h

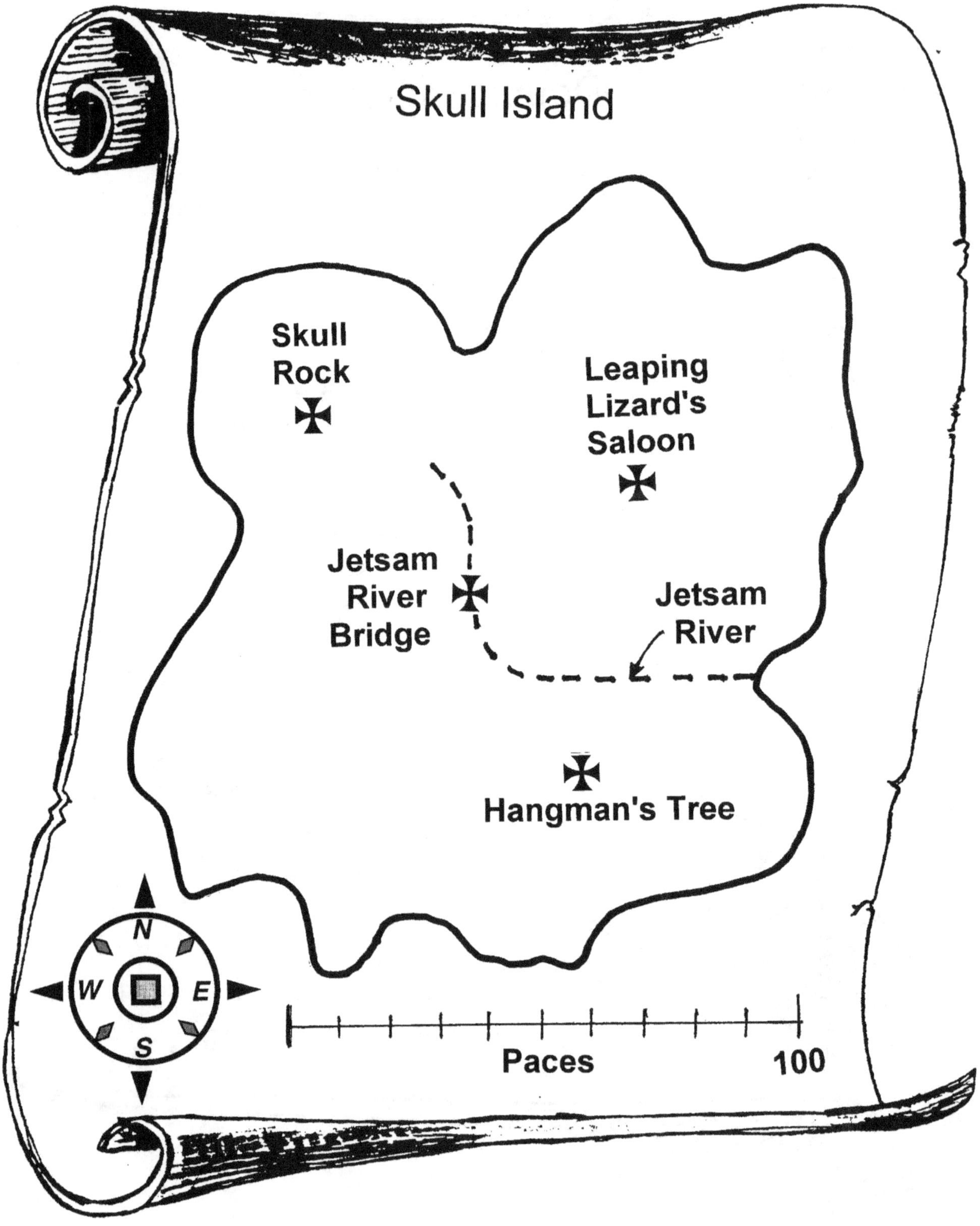

Island Treasure Map 9 h

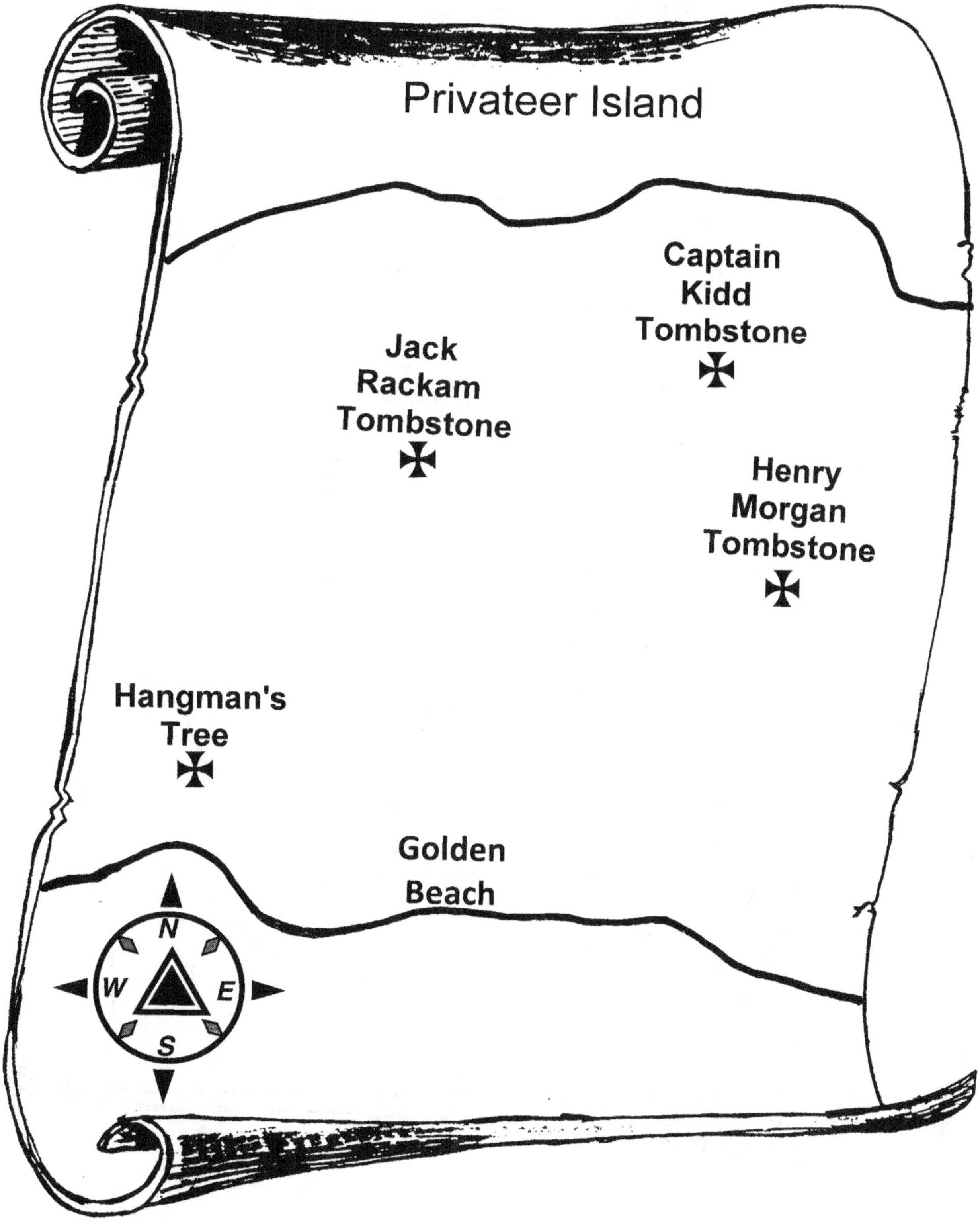

Island Treasure Map 10 h

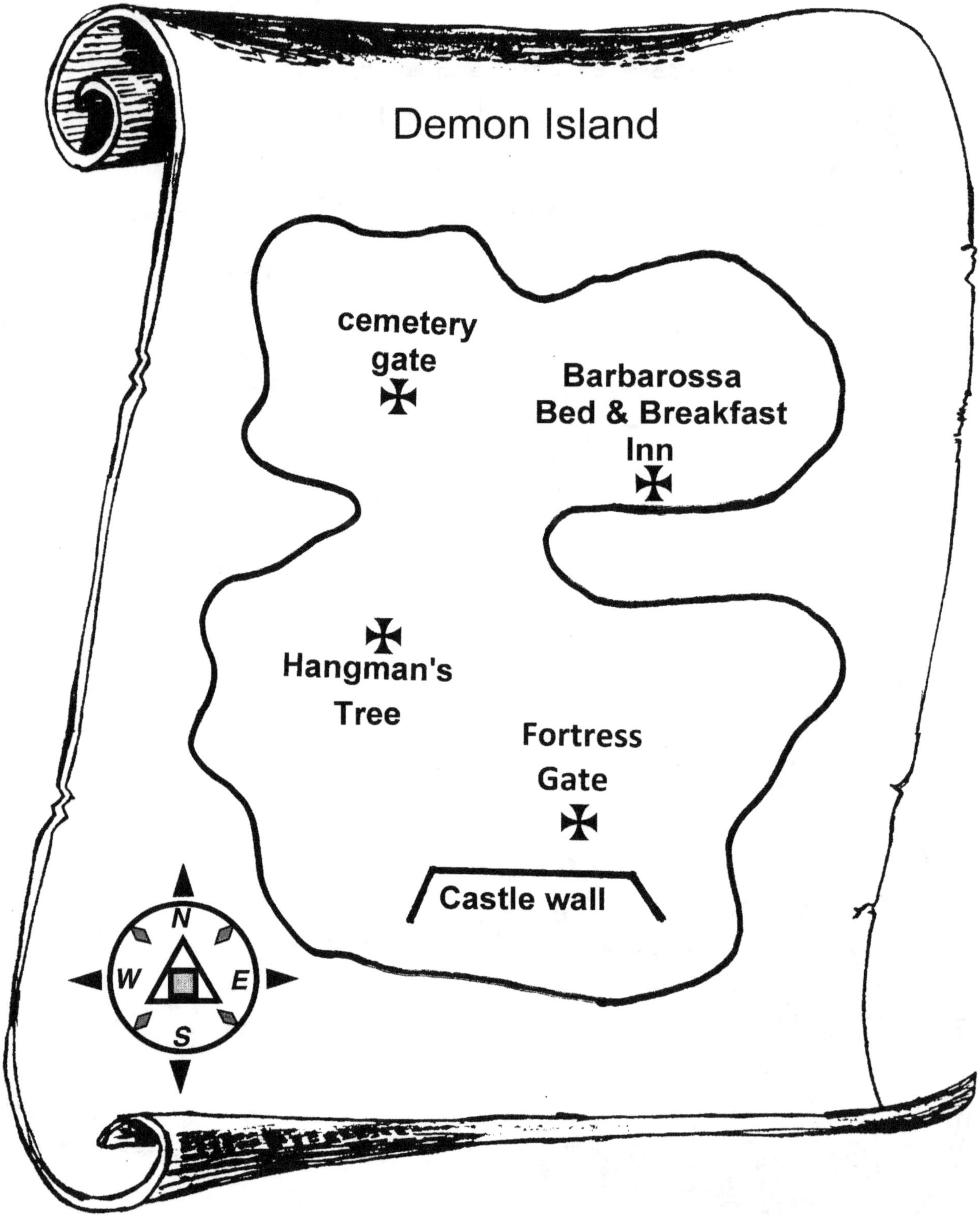

Island Treasure Map 11 ɦ

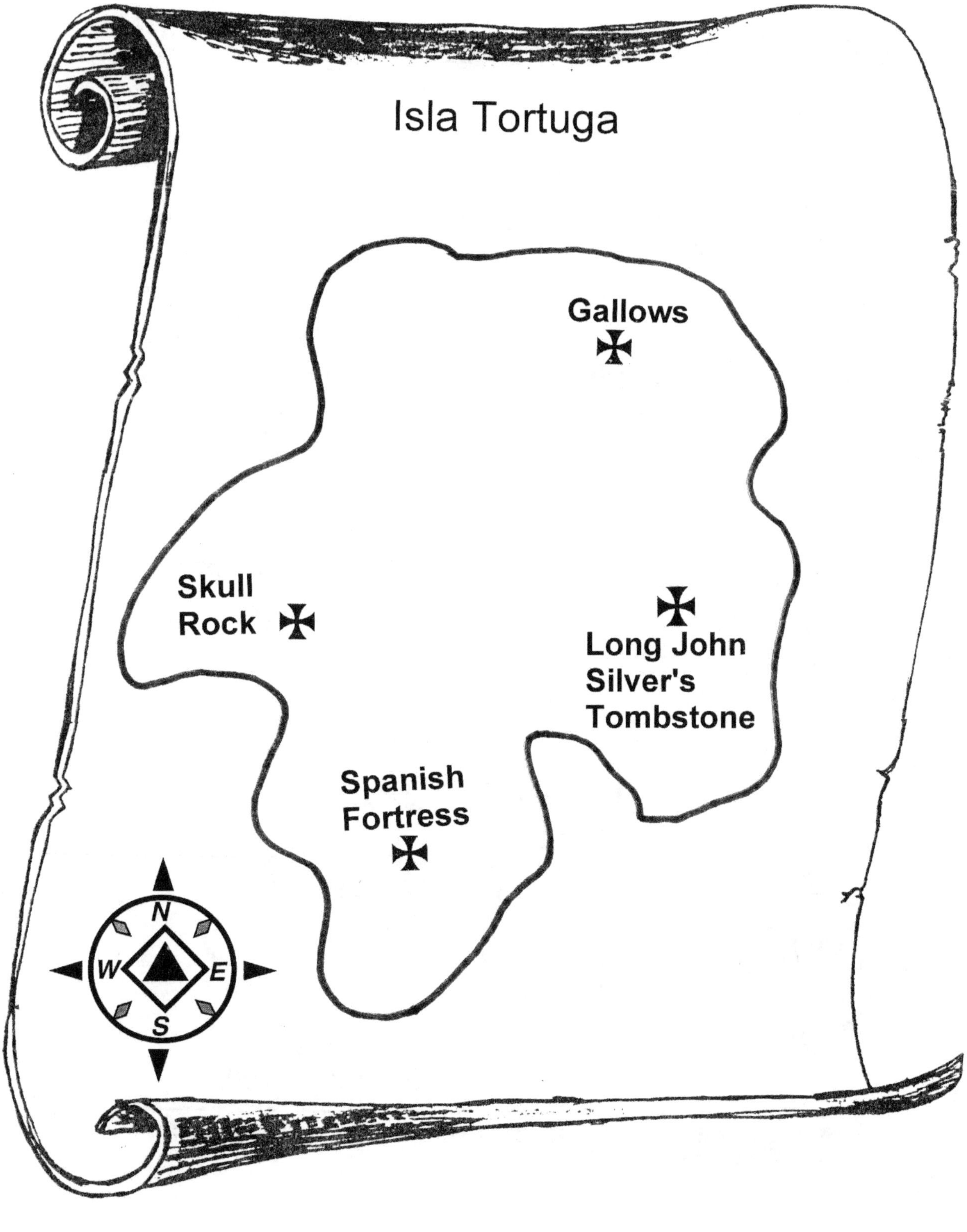

Island Treasure Map 12 *h*

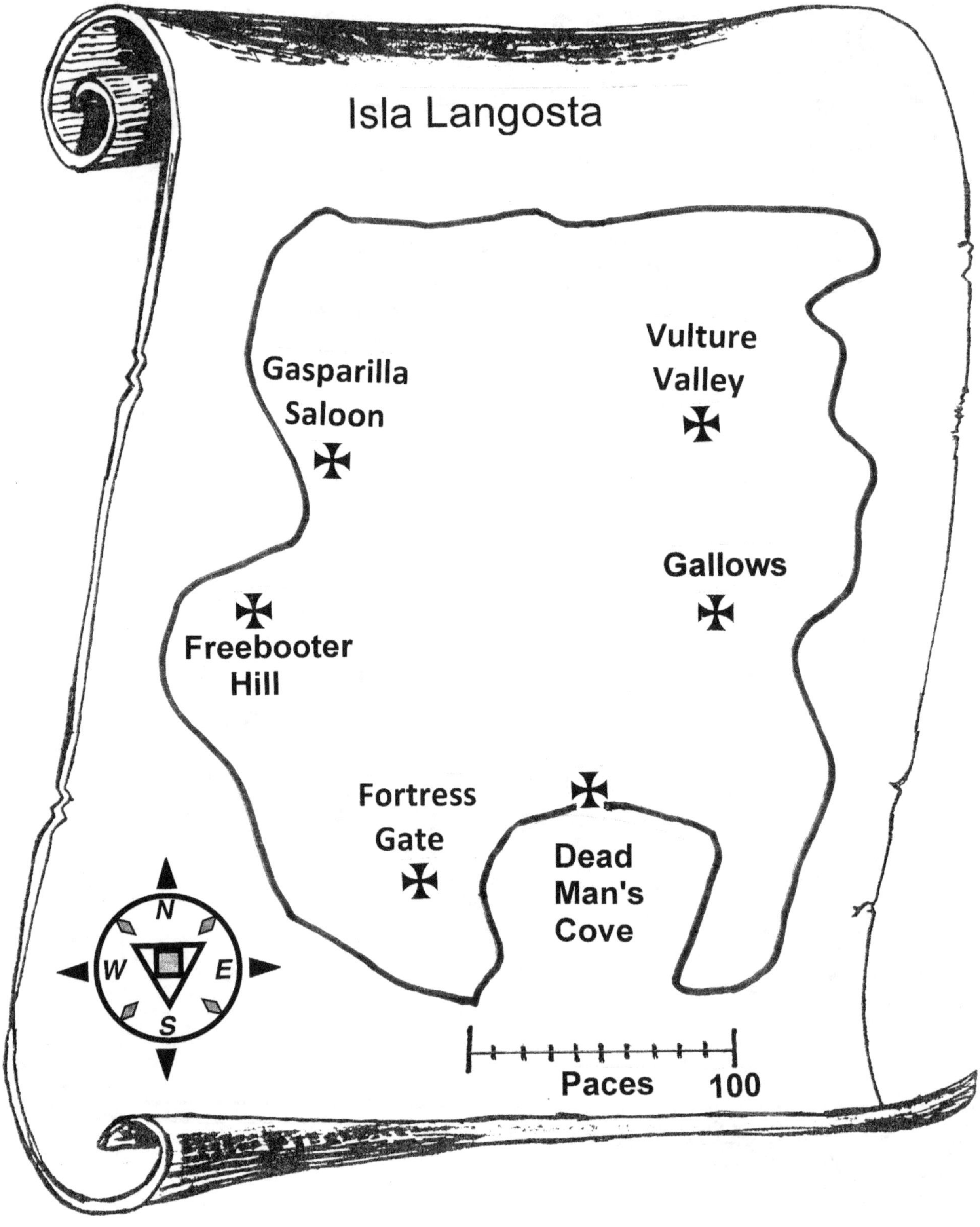

Island Treasure Map 13

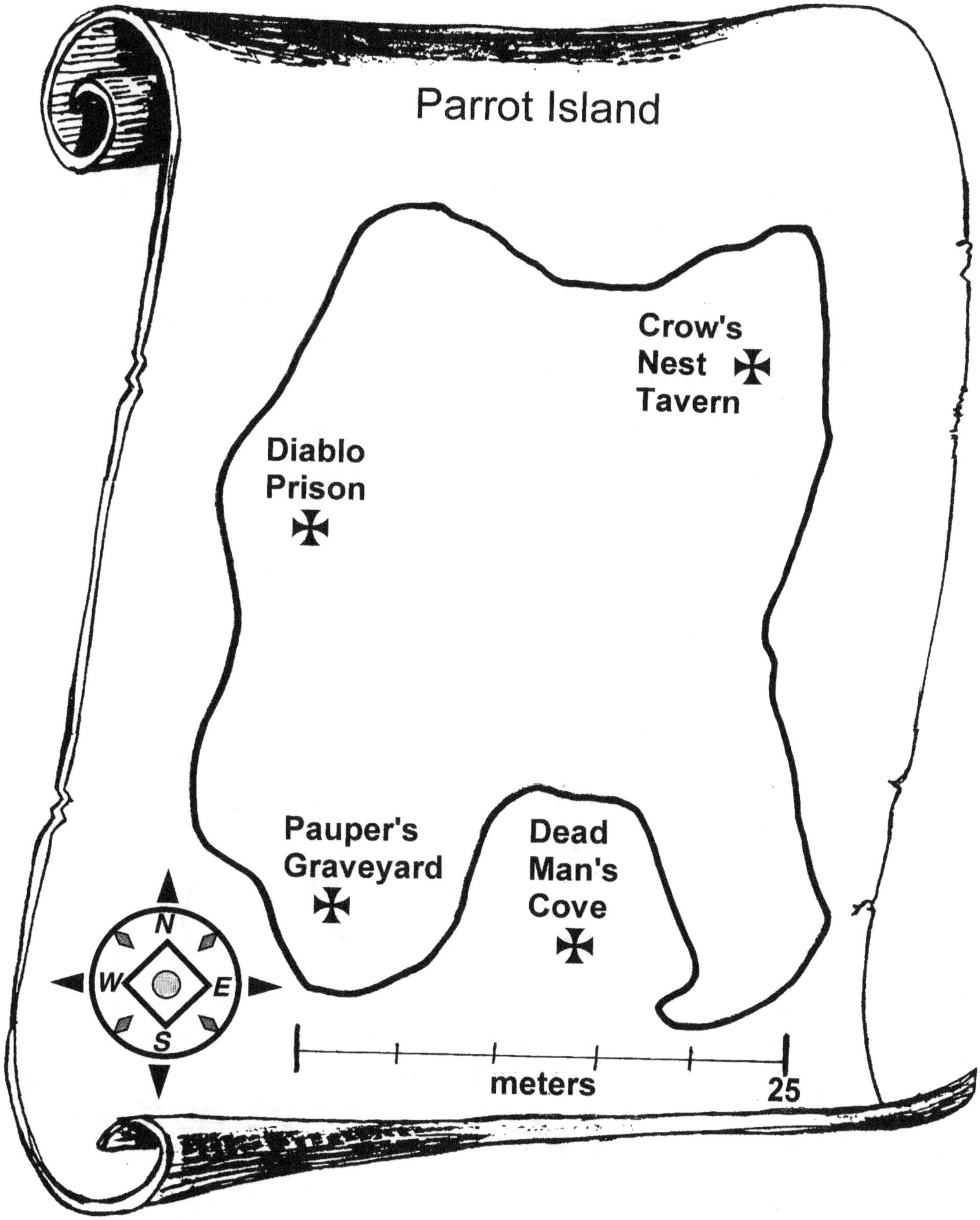

Island Treasure Map 14

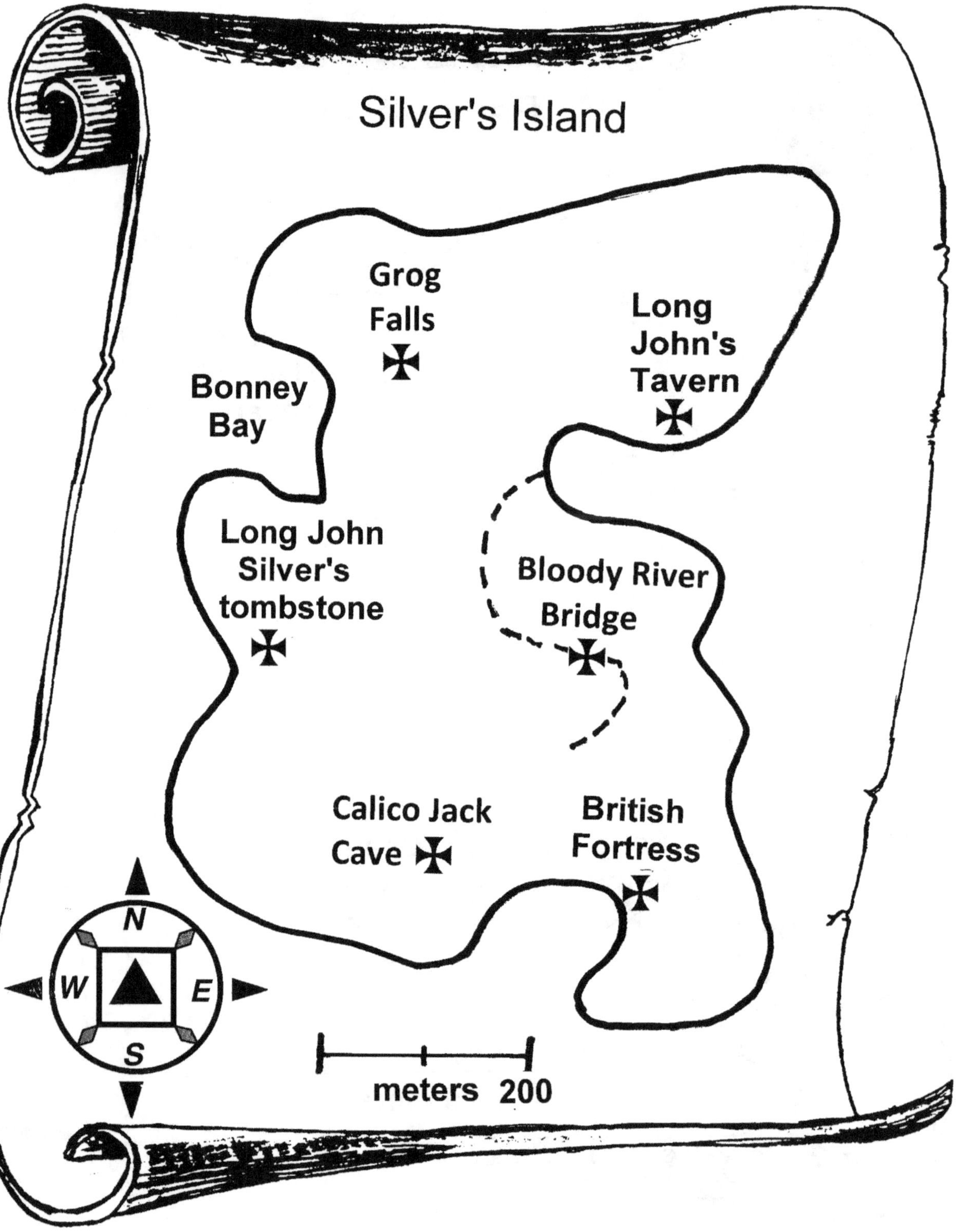

Island Treasure Map 15

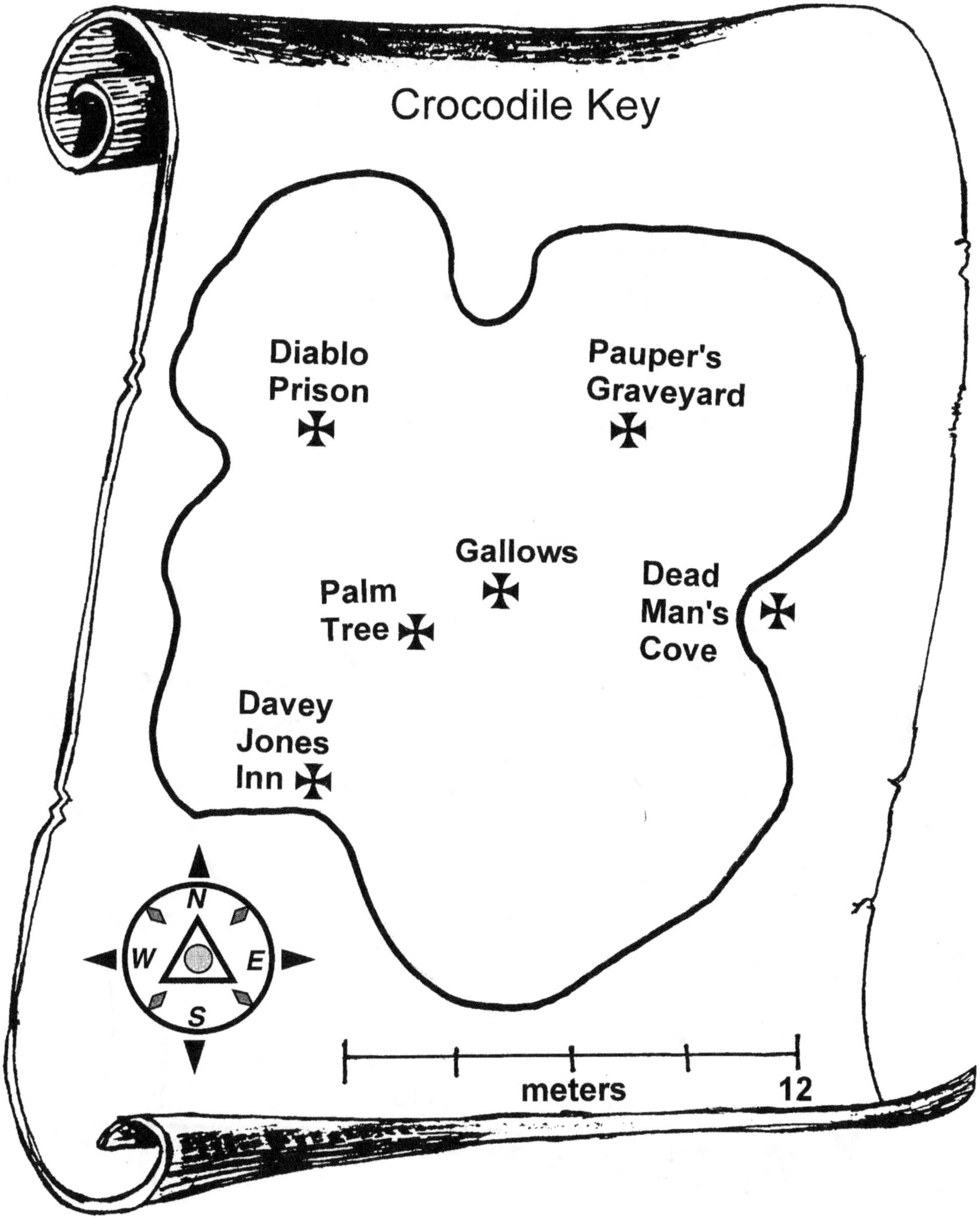

Island Treasure Map 16 ℏ

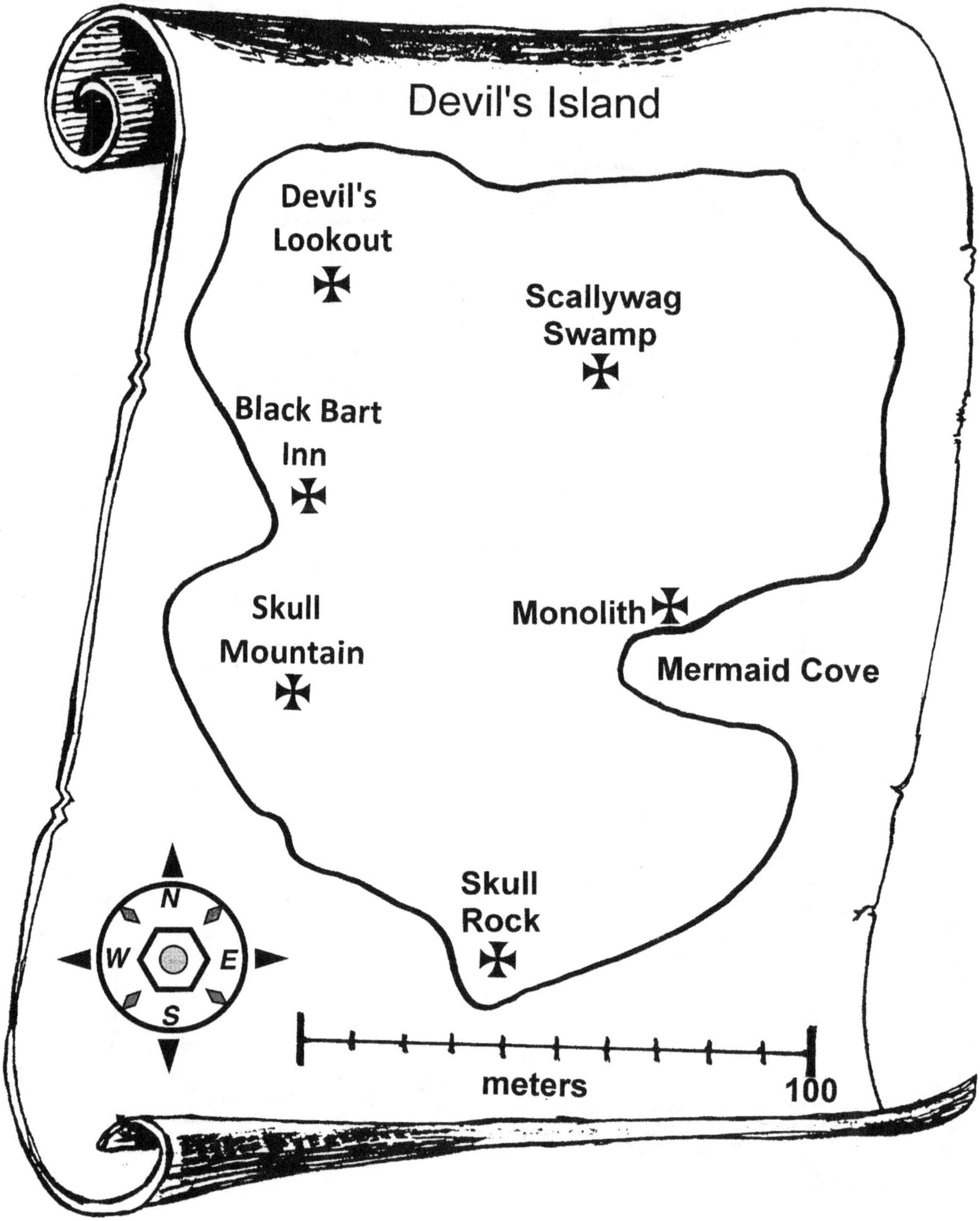

Island Treasure Map 17

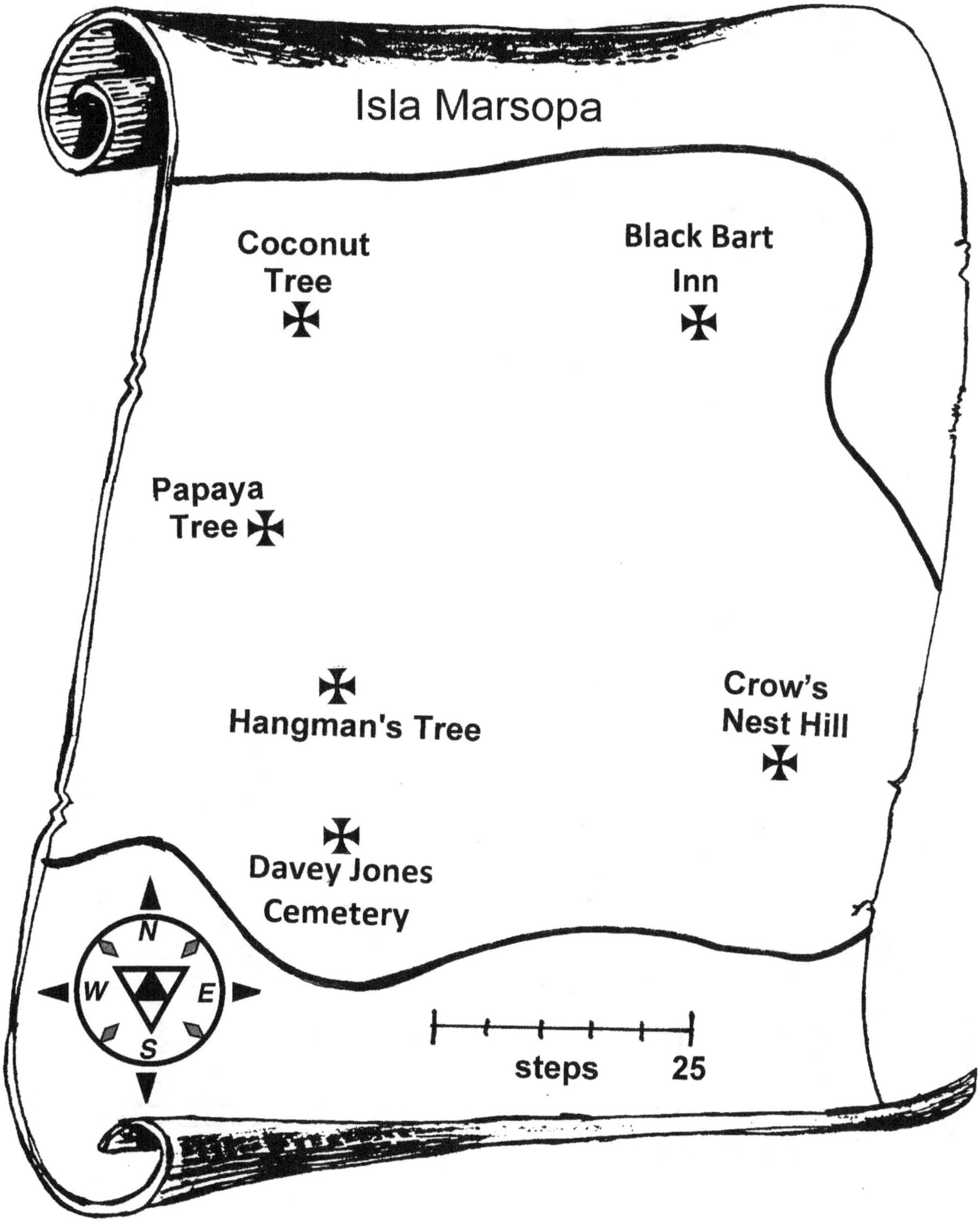

Chapter 7.6

Island Treasure Map 18 h

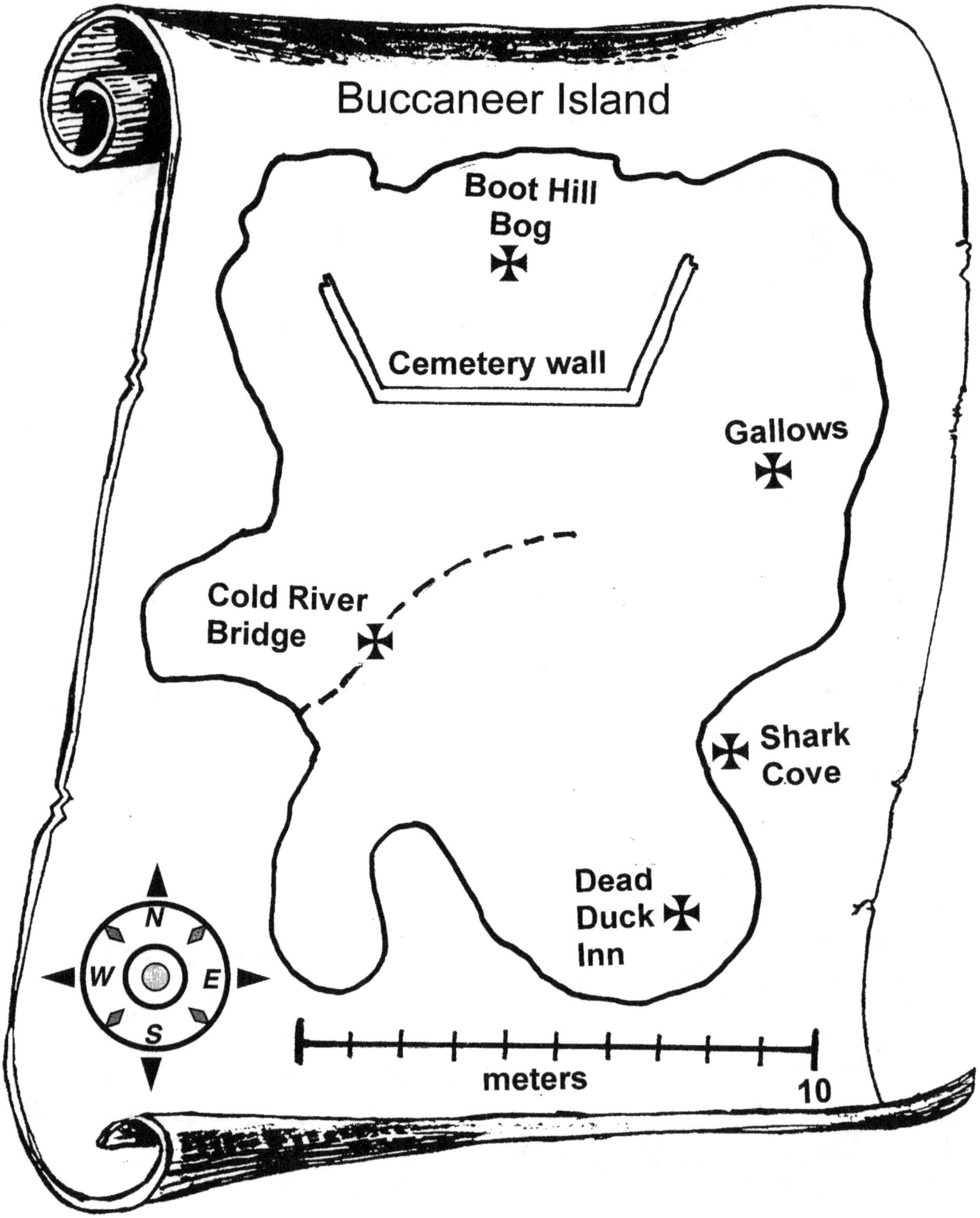

Island Treasure Map 19

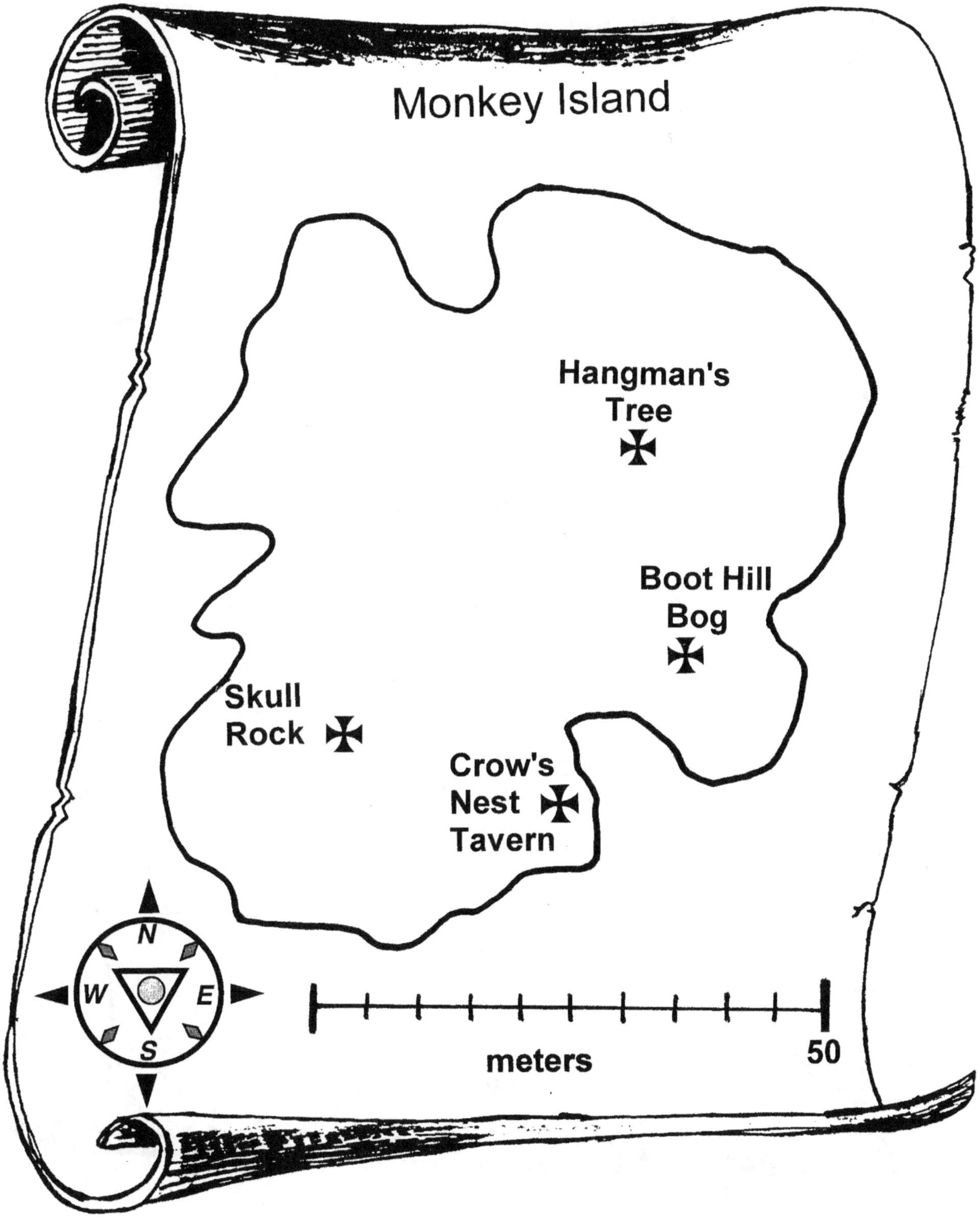

Island Treasure Map 20

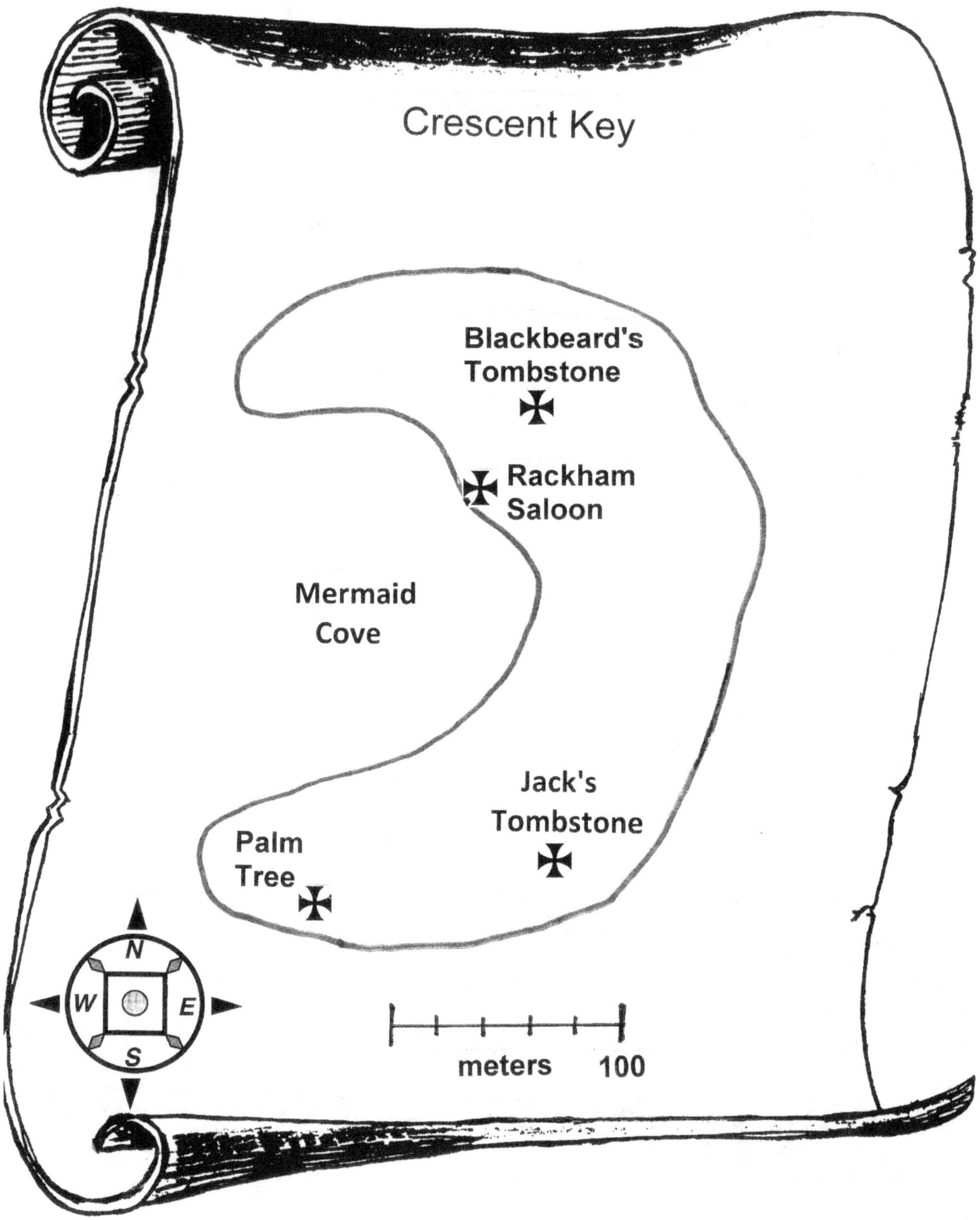

Island Treasure Map 21 h

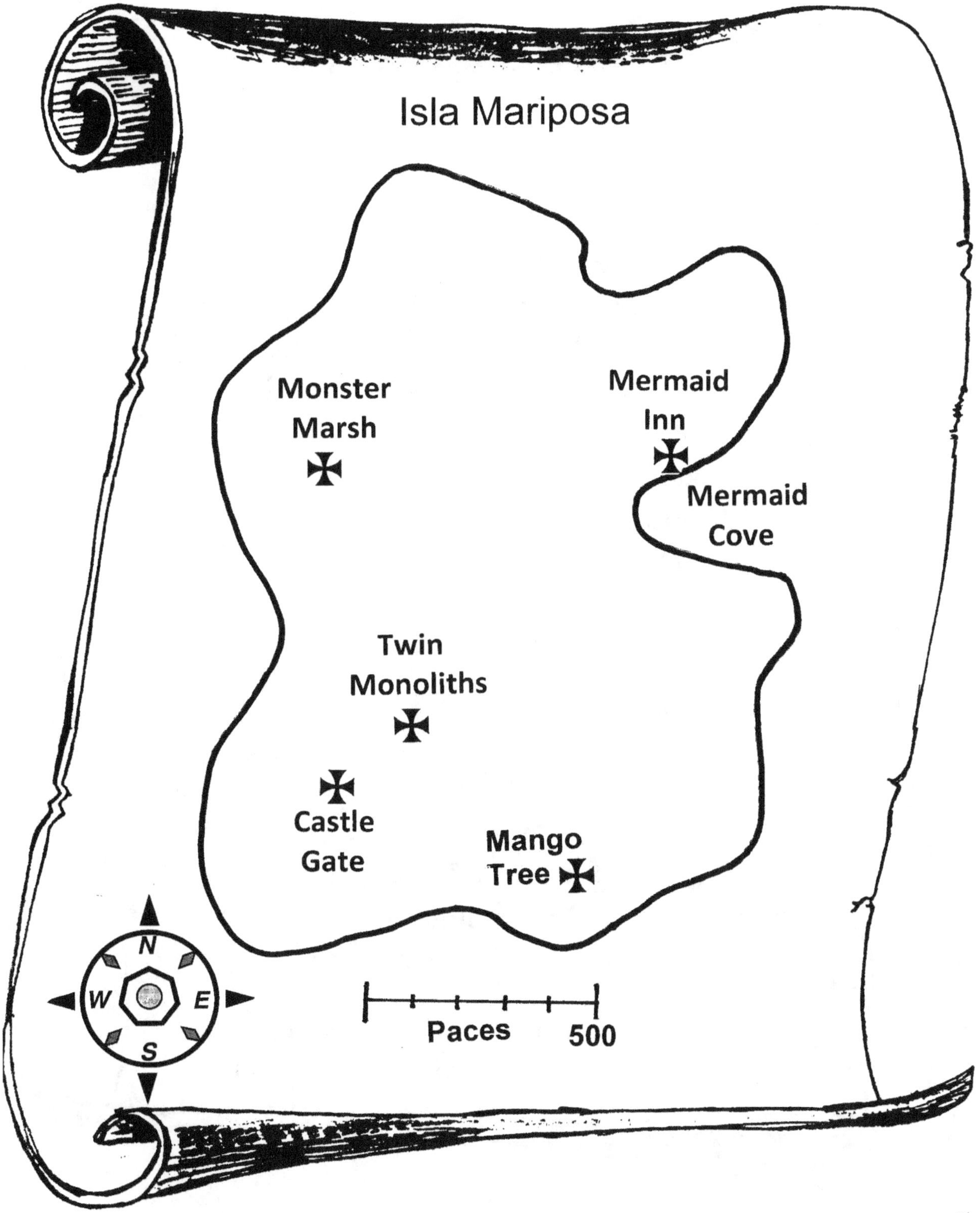

Island Treasure Map 22

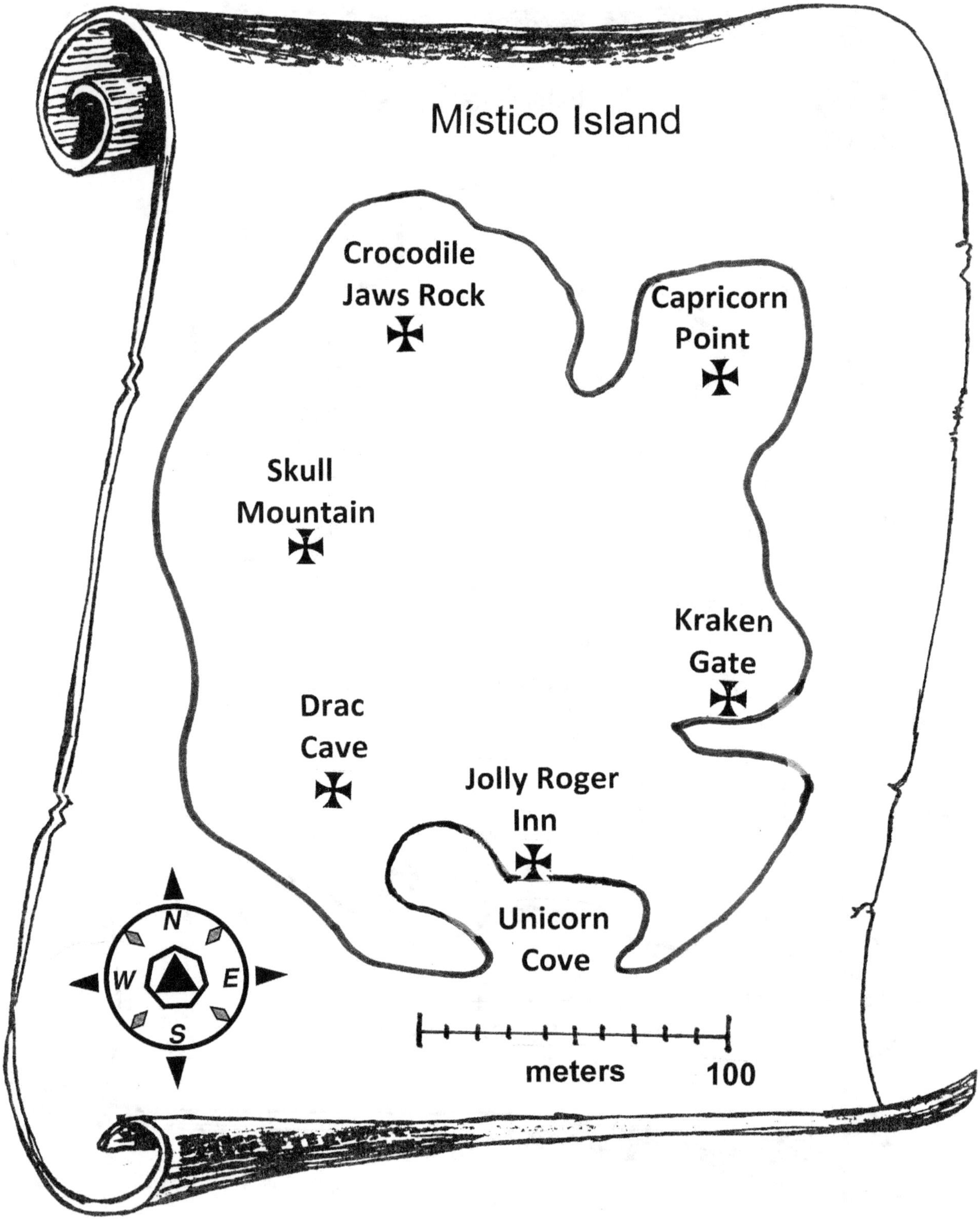

Island Treasure Map 23

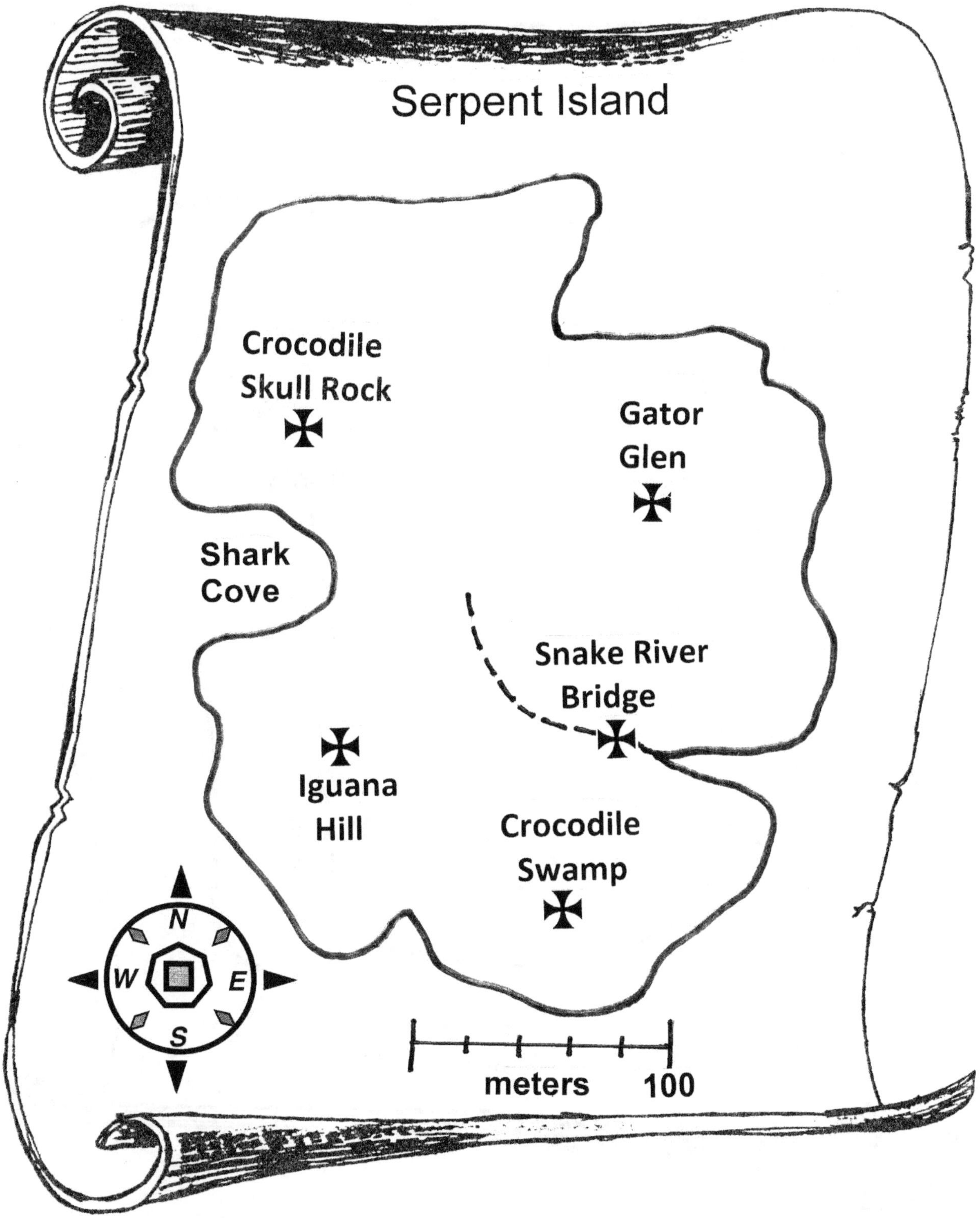

Island Treasure Map 24

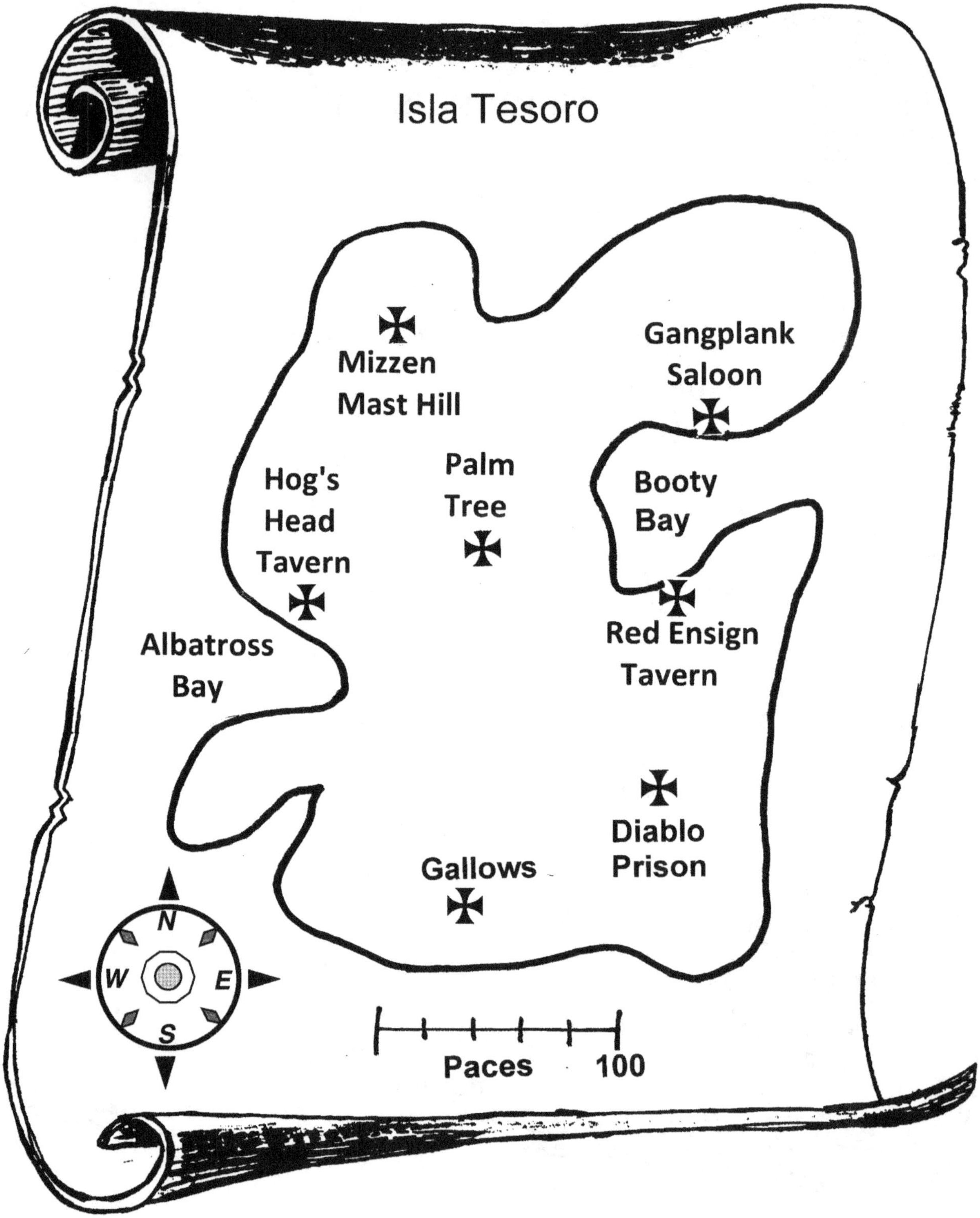

Island Treasure Map 25

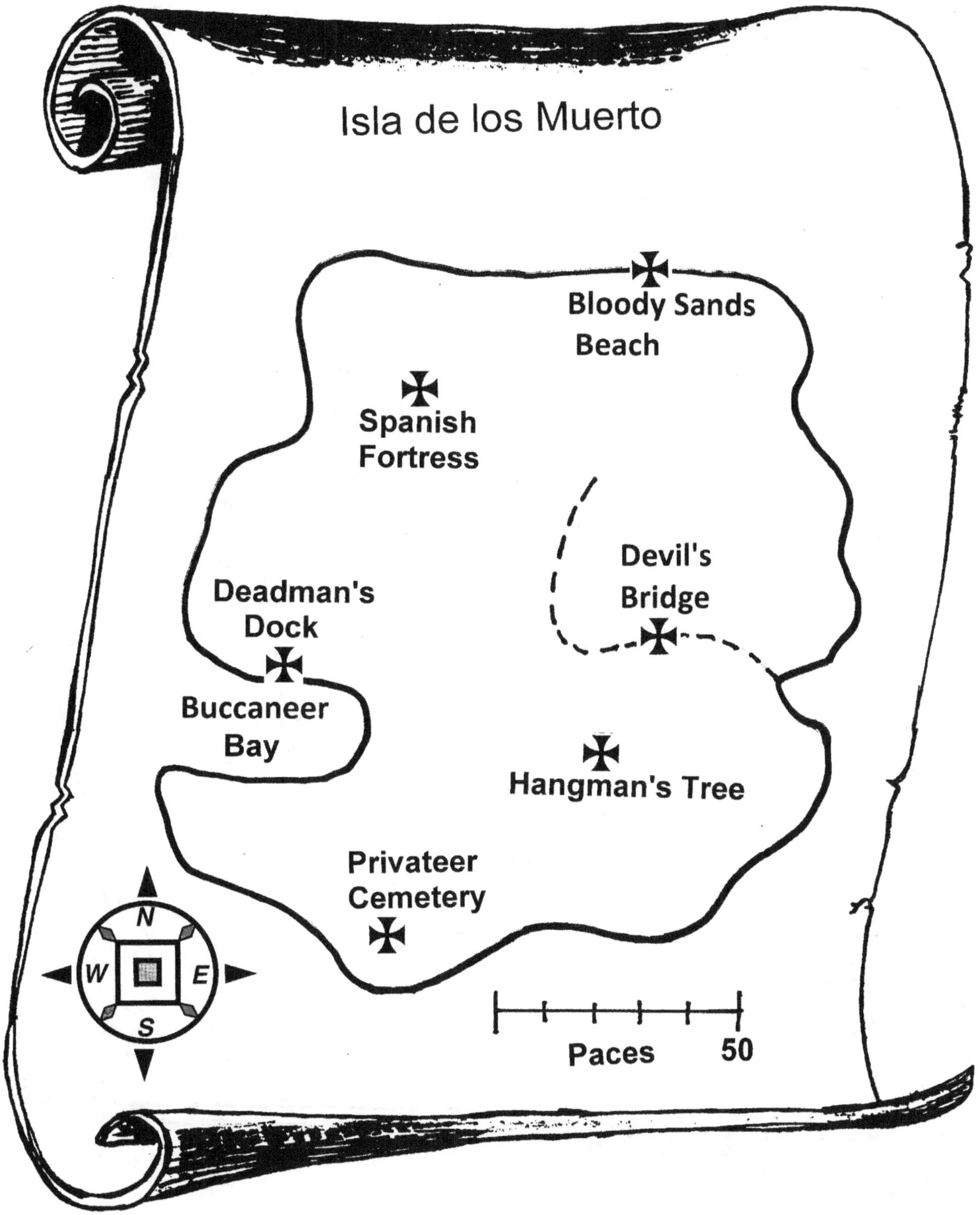

Island Treasure Map 26

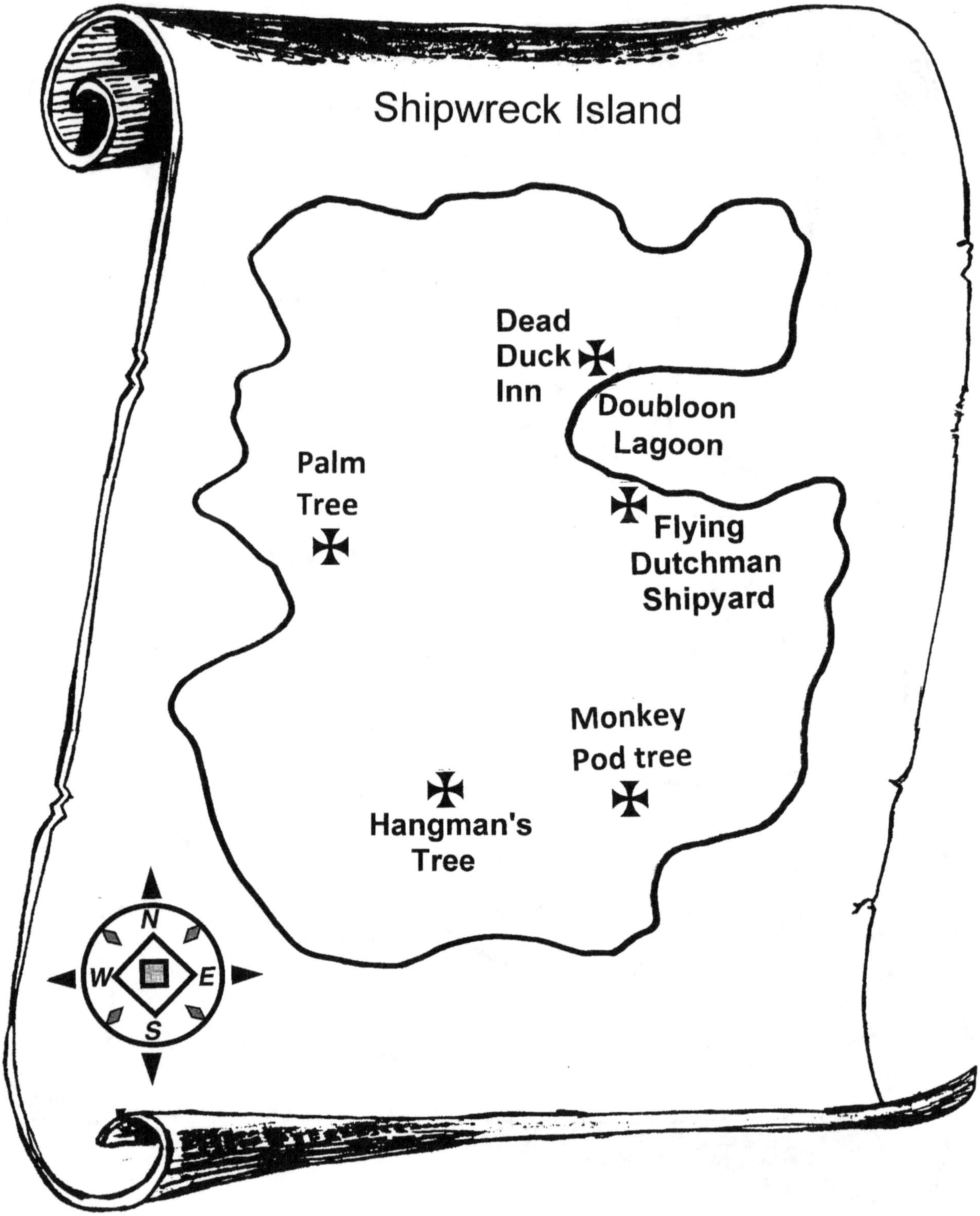

Island Treasure Map 27

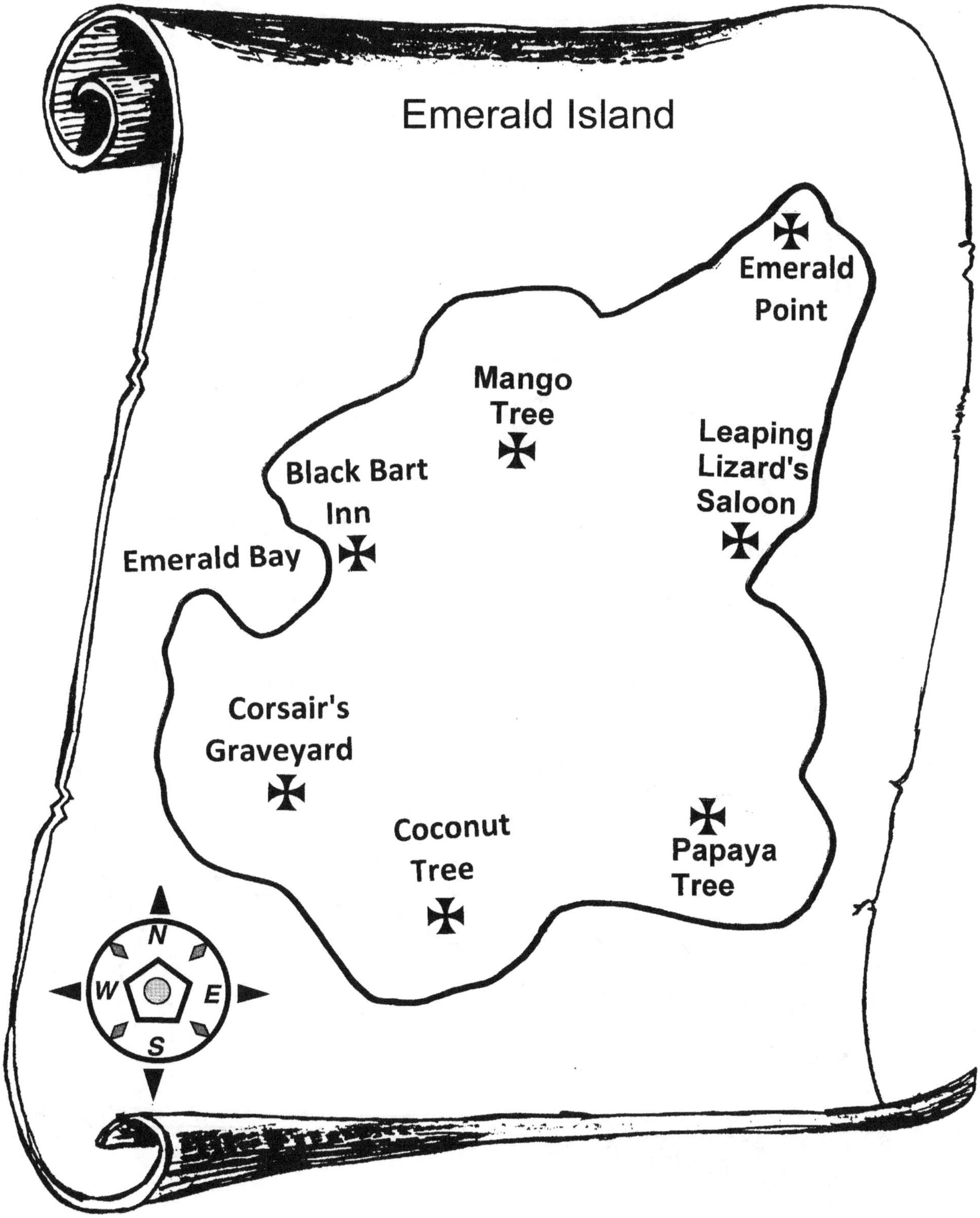

Island Treasure Map 28

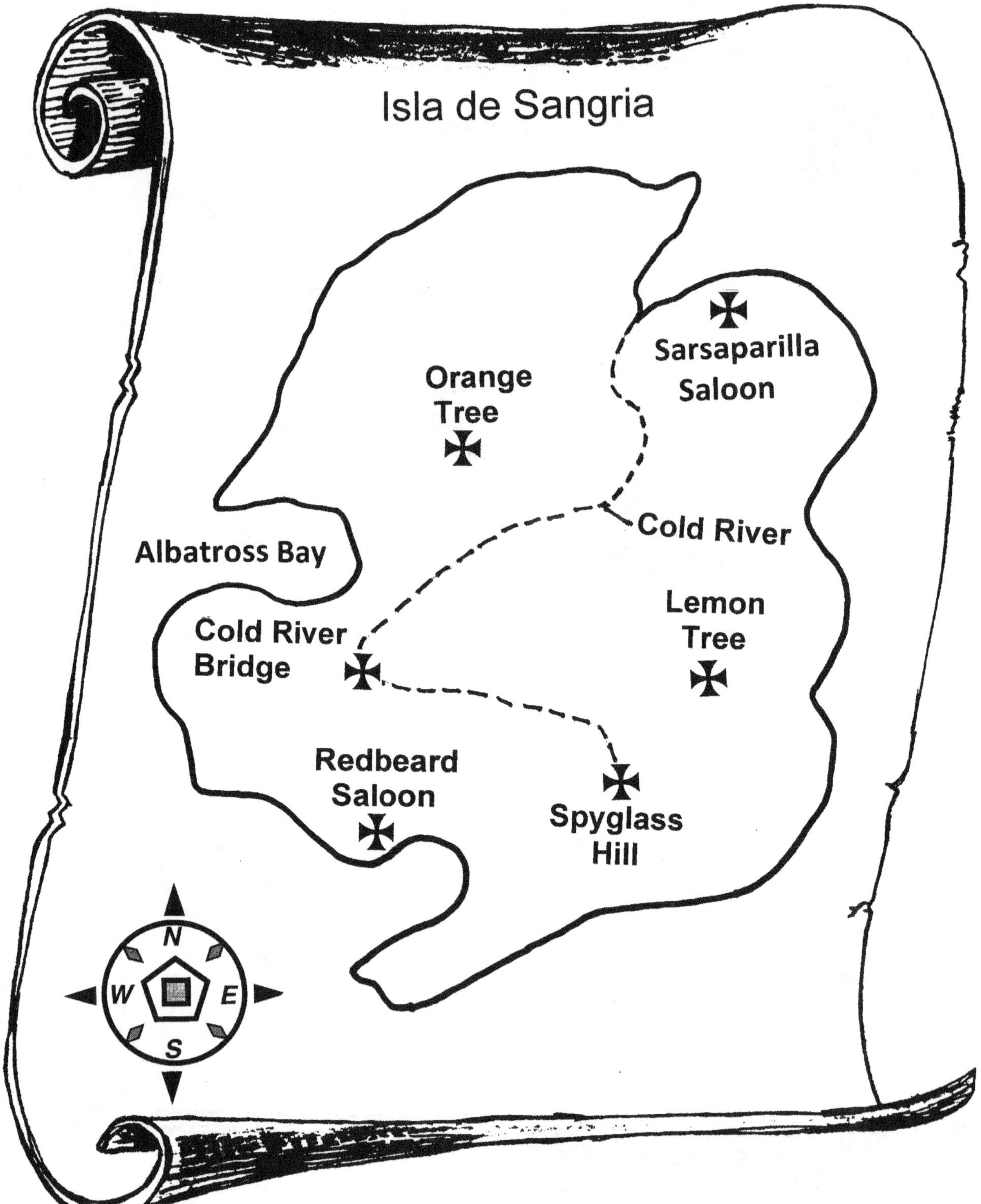

Island Treasure Map 29

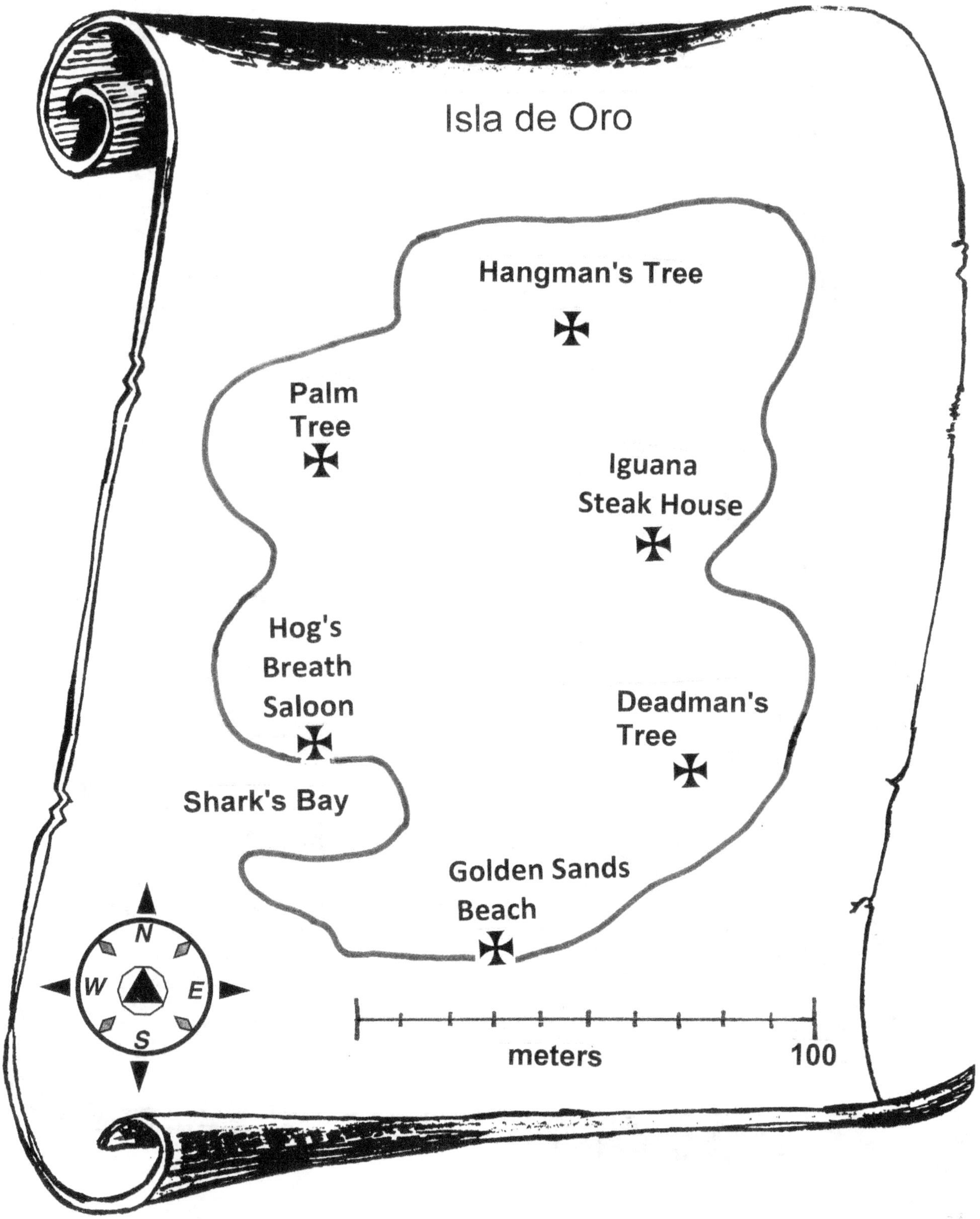

Island Treasure Map 30

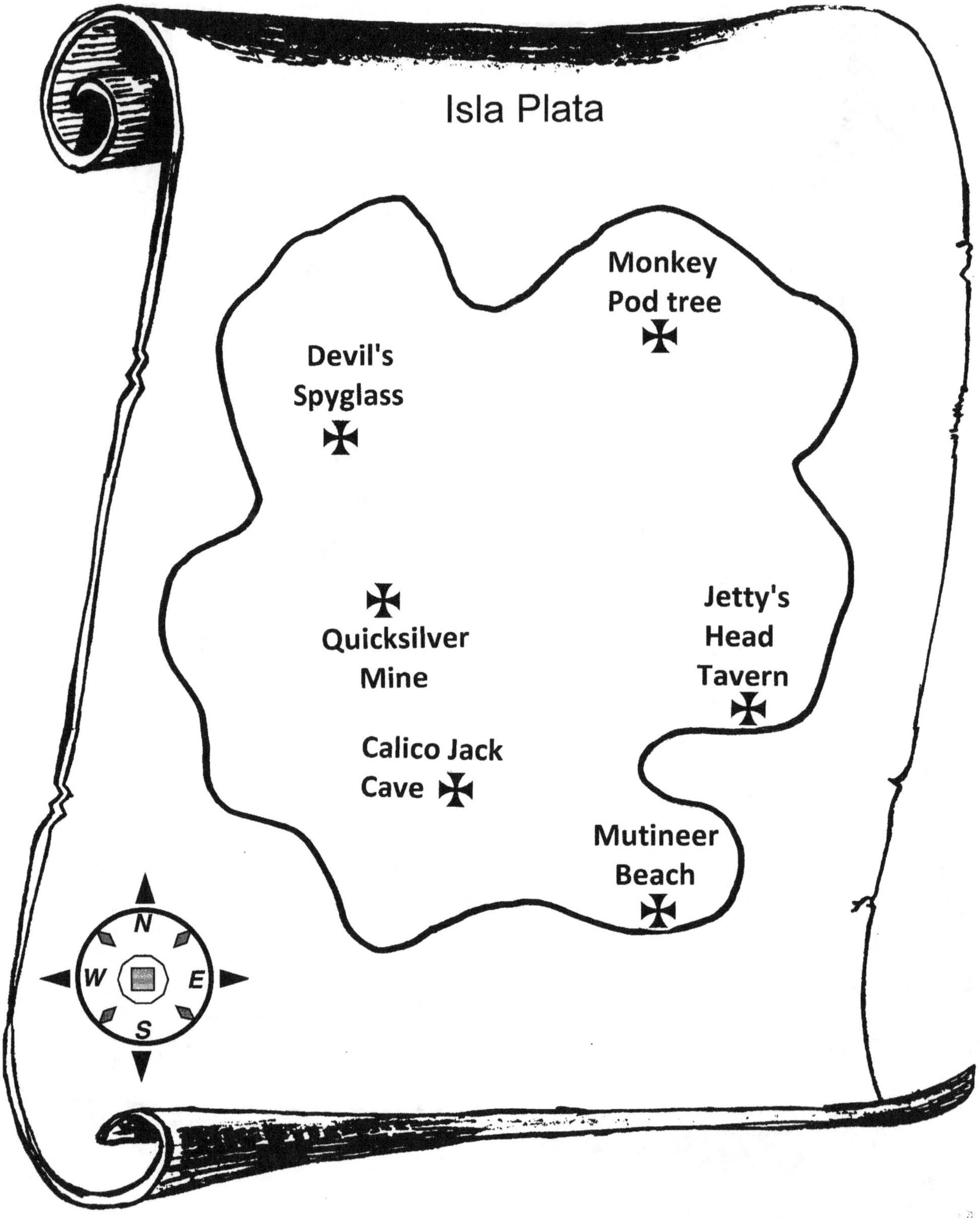

Appendices

Appendix 1 Buried Treasure Game Sheets

RECTANGULAR BURIED TREASURE GAME

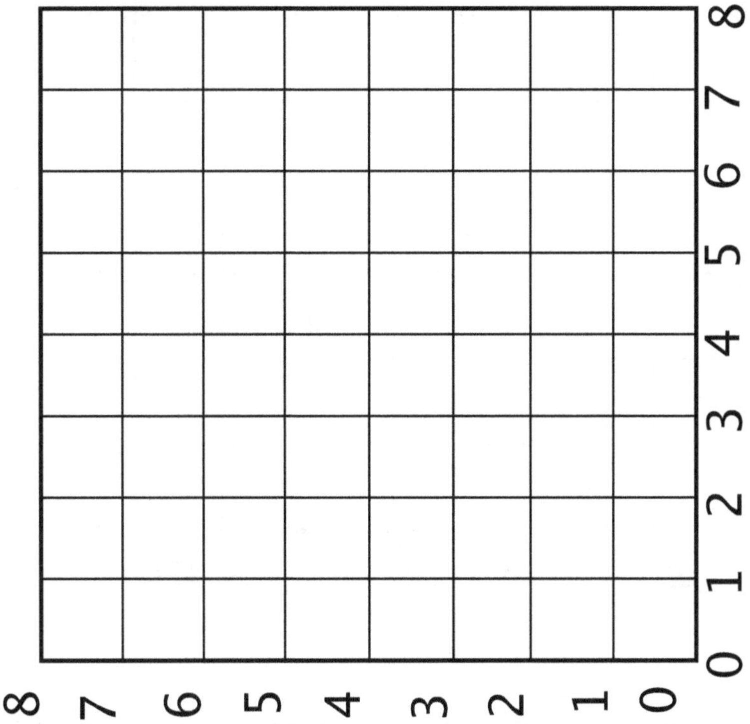

Other Team's
Buried Treasure

Our Team's Digs

This is where you record your "digs"

	"3 Digs" (x,y)	X, E, C
1		
2		
3		
4		
5		
6		
7		
8		
9		
10		
11		
12		
13		
14		
15		
16		
17		
18		
19		
20		
21		
22		
23		
24		
25		

1R

2R

RECTANGULAR BURIED TREASURE GAME

Other Team's Digs

This is where you record their "digs"

	"3 Digs" (x,y)	X, E, C
1		
2		
3		
4		
5		
6		
7		
8		
9		
10		
11		
12		
13		
14		
15		
16		
17		
18		
19		
20		
21		
22		
23		
24		
25		

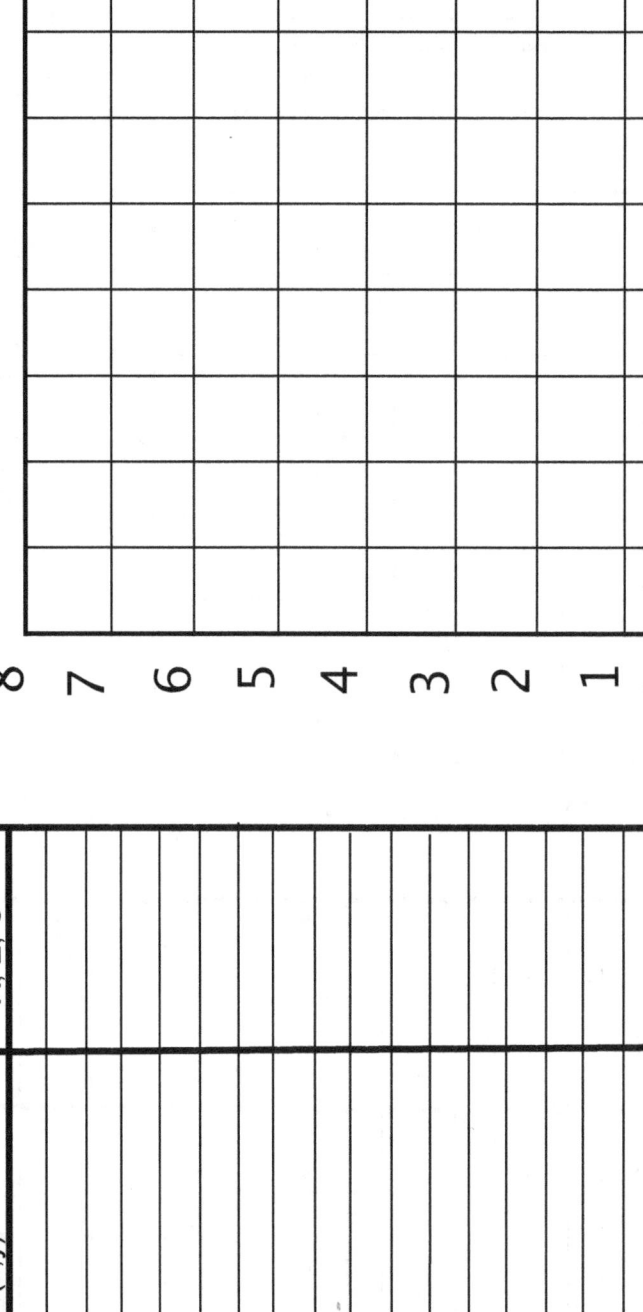

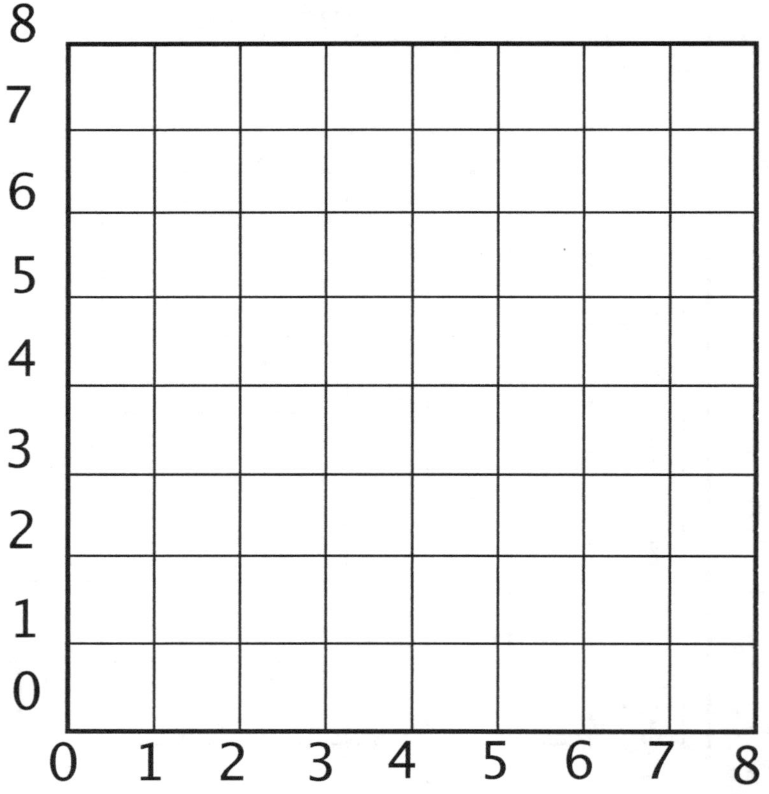

Our Team's Buried Treasure

3R

RECTANGULAR BURIED TREASURE GAME

Our Team's Digs

This is where you record your "digs"

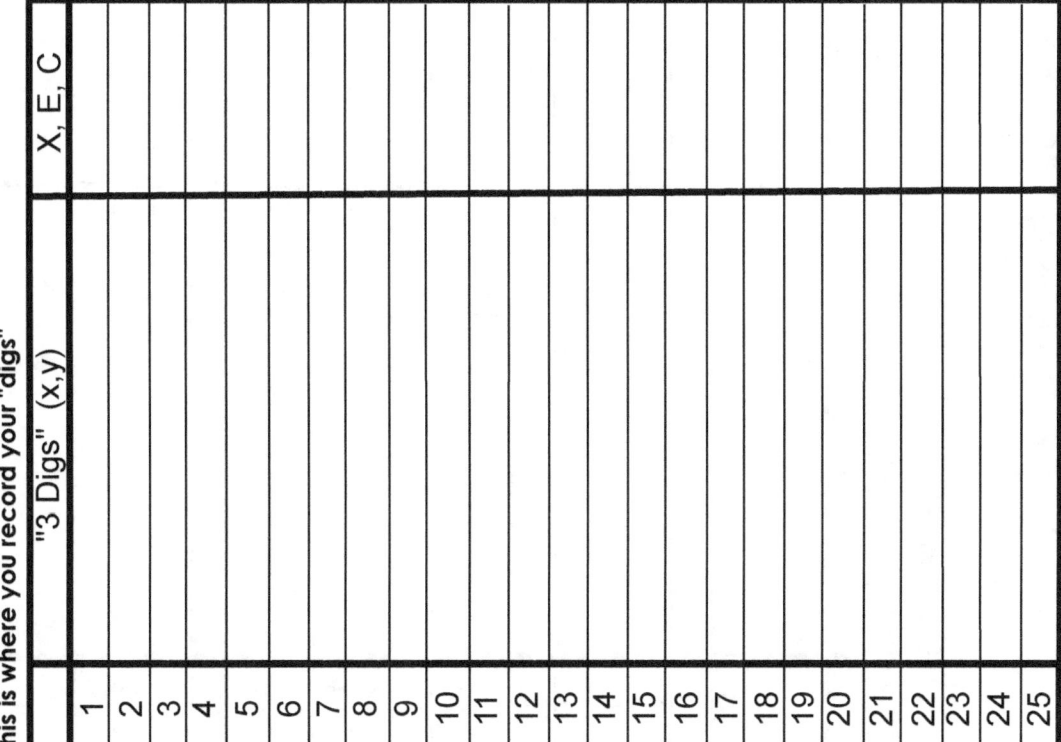

	"3 Digs" (x,y)	X, E, C
1		
2		
3		
4		
5		
6		
7		
8		
9		
10		
11		
12		
13		
14		
15		
16		
17		
18		
19		
20		
21		
22		
23		
24		
25		

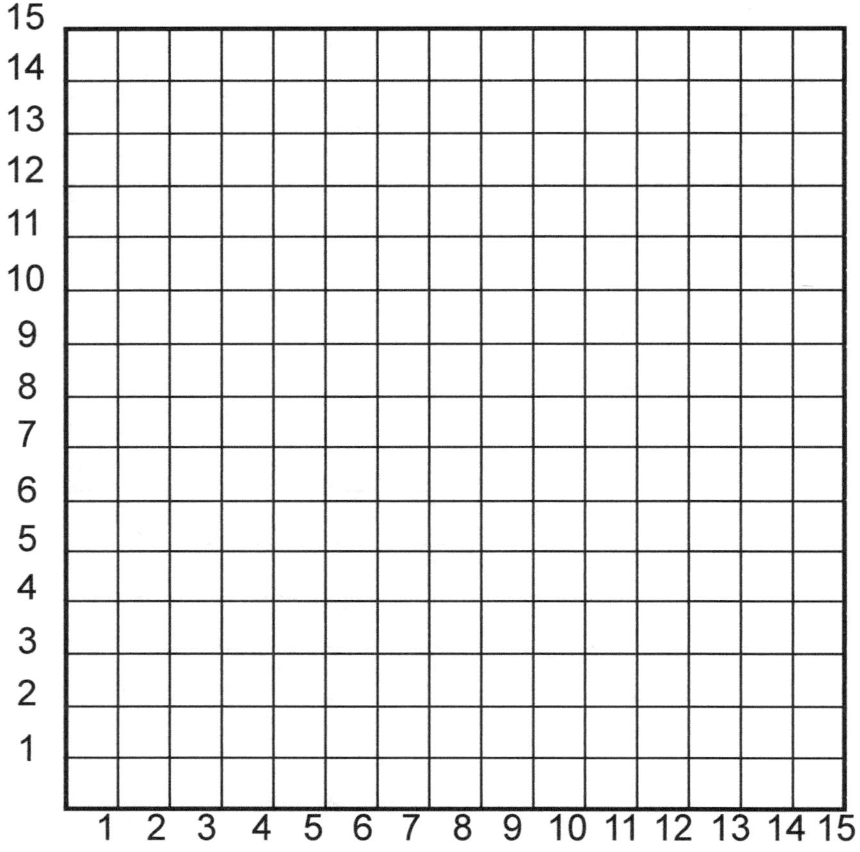

Other Team's Buried Treasure

4R

RECTANGULAR BURIED TREASURE GAME

Other Team's Digs

This is where you record their "digs"

	"3 Digs" (x,y)	X, E, C
1		
2		
3		
4		
5		
6		
7		
8		
9		
10		
11		
12		
13		
14		
15		
16		
17		
18		
19		
20		
21		
22		
23		
24		
25		

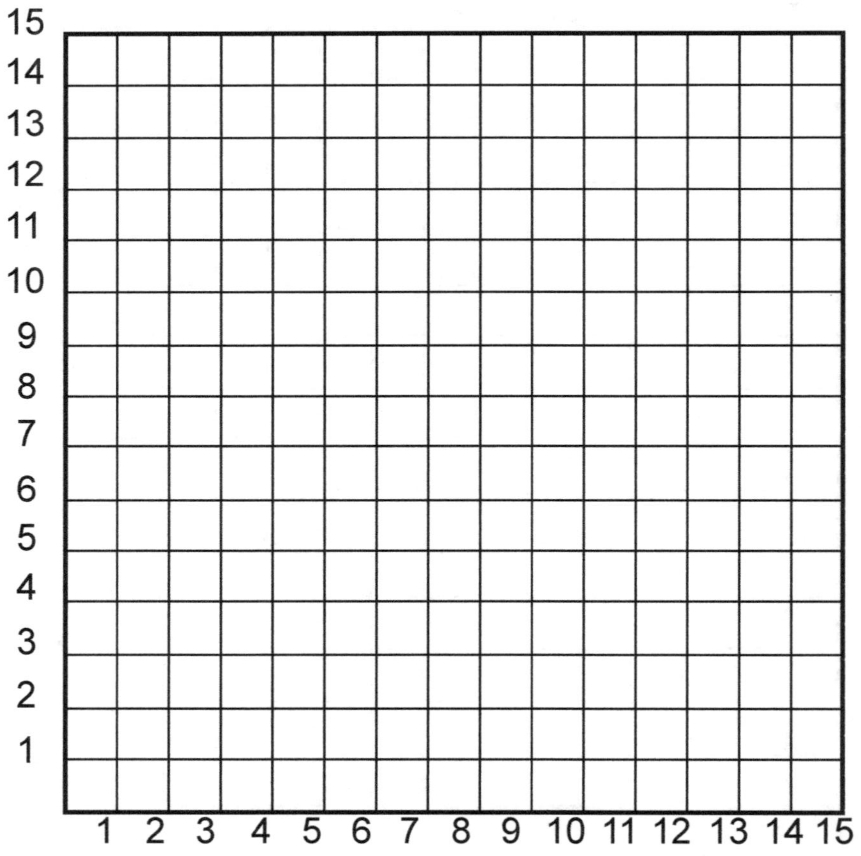

Our Team's Buried Treasure

5R

RECTANGULAR BURIED TREASURE GAME

Our Team's Digs

This is where you record your "digs"

	"Digs" (x,y)	X, E, C
1		
2		
3		
4		
5		
6		
7		
8		
9		
10		
11		
12		
13		
14		
15		
16		
17		
18		
19		
20		
21		
22		
23		
24		
25		

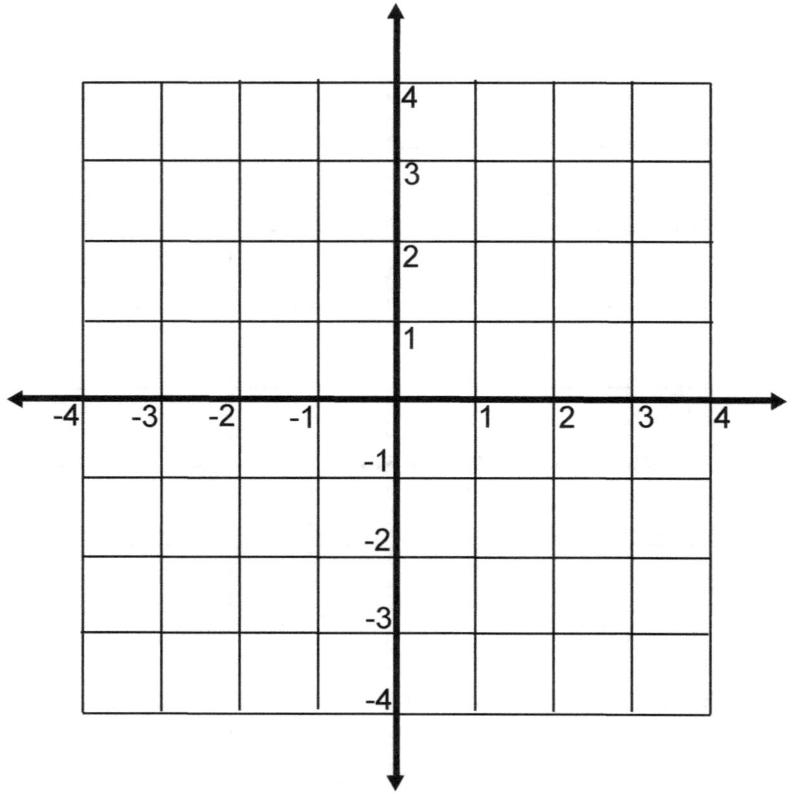

Other Team's Buried Treasure

6R

RECTANGULAR BURIED TREASURE GAME

Other Team's Digs

This is where you record their "digs"

	"Digs" (x,y)	X, E, C
1		
2		
3		
4		
5		
6		
7		
8		
9		
10		
11		
12		
13		
14		
15		
16		
17		
18		
19		
20		
21		
22		
23		
24		
25		

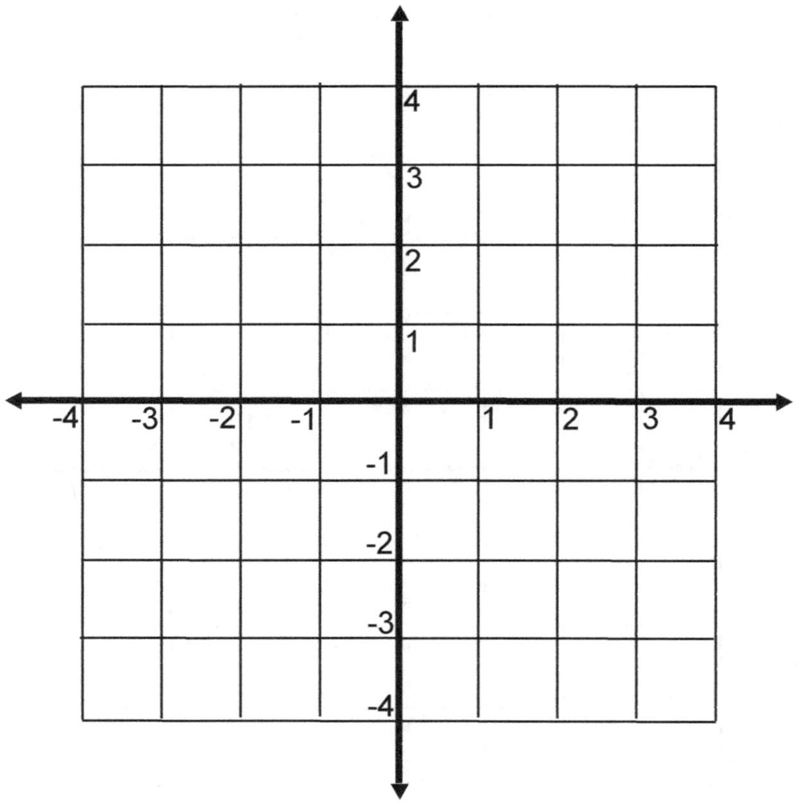

Our Team's Buried Treasure

7R

RECTANGULAR BURIED TREASURE GAME

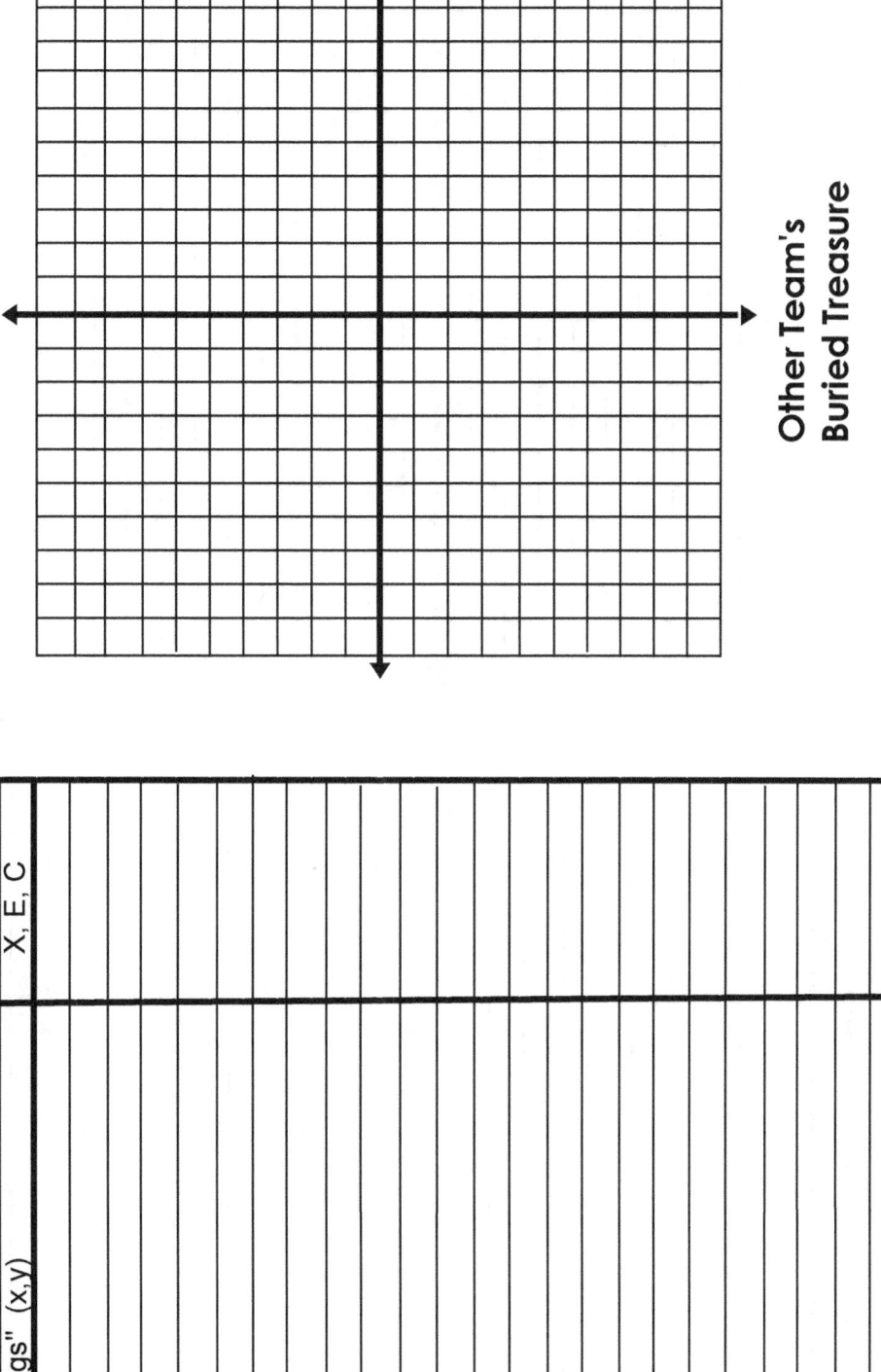

Our Team's Digs

This is where you record your "digs"

	"Digs" (x,y)	X, E, C
1		
2		
3		
4		
5		
6		
7		
8		
9		
10		
11		
12		
13		
14		
15		
16		
17		
18		
19		
20		
21		
22		
23		
24		
25		

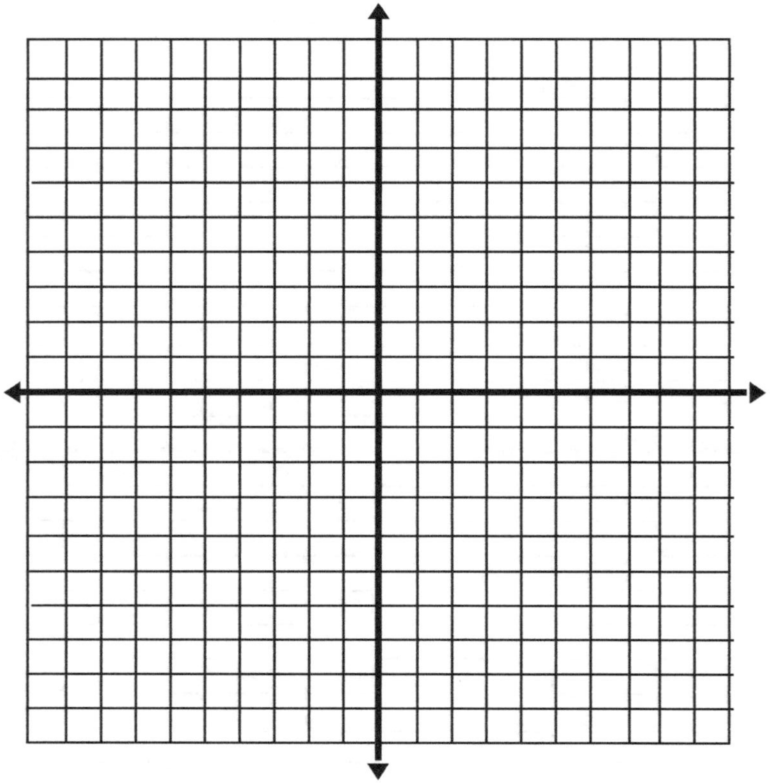

Other Team's
Buried Treasure

8R

RECTANGULAR BURIED TREASURE GAME

Other Team's Digs

This is where you record their "digs"

	"Digs" (x,y)	X, E, C
1		
2		
3		
4		
5		
6		
7		
8		
9		
10		
11		
12		
13		
14		
15		
16		
17		
18		
19		
20		
21		
22		
23		
24		
25		

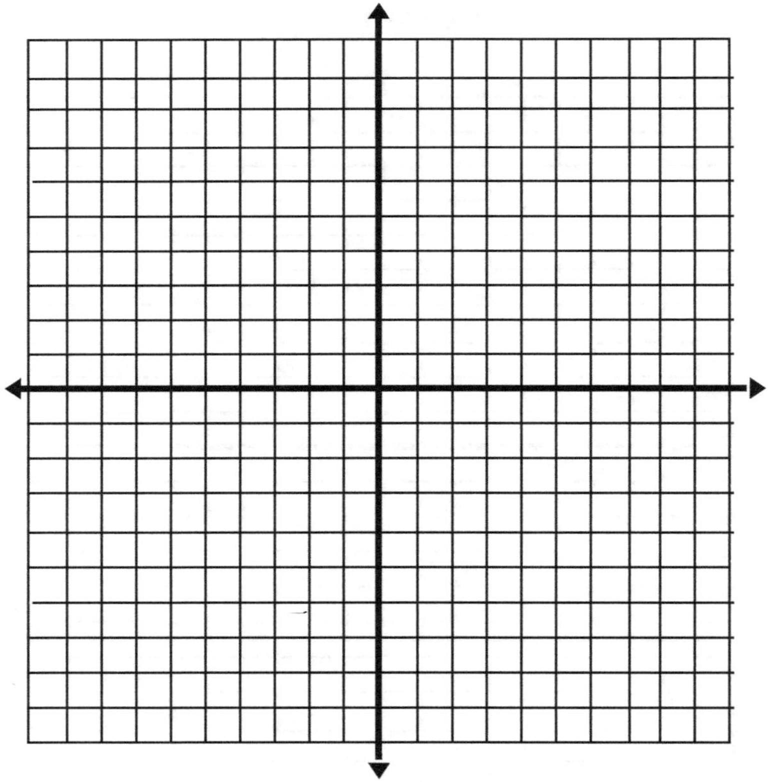

Our Team's
Buried Treasure

9P

POLAR BURIED TREASURE GAME

Our Team's Digs

This is where you record your "digs"

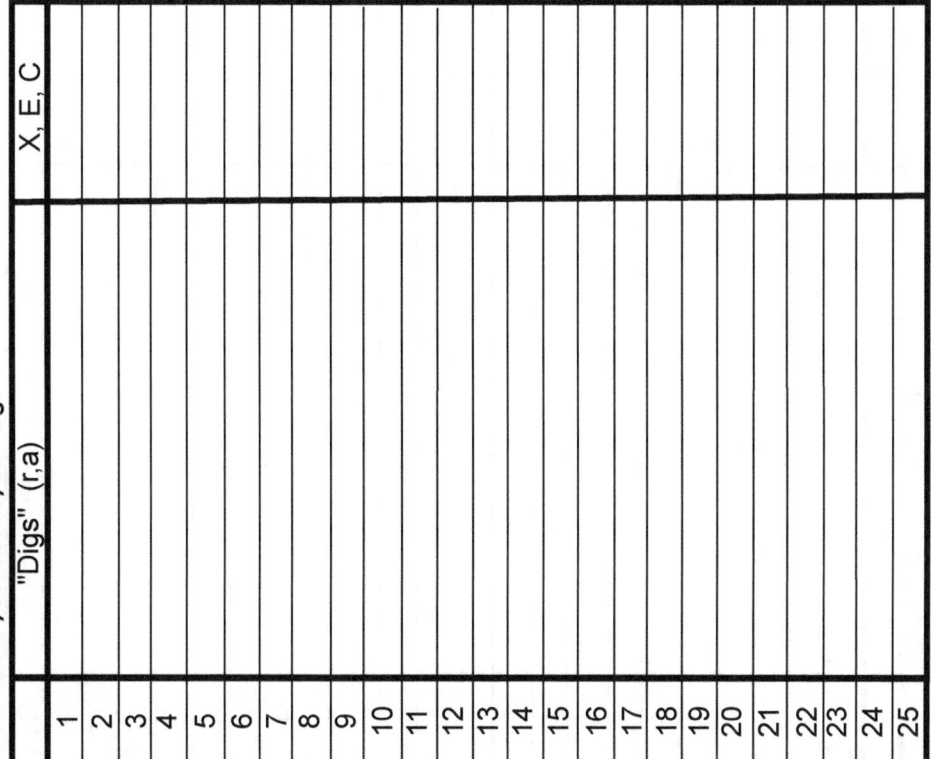

	"Digs" (r,a)	X, E, C
1		
2		
3		
4		
5		
6		
7		
8		
9		
10		
11		
12		
13		
14		
15		
16		
17		
18		
19		
20		
21		
22		
23		
24		
25		

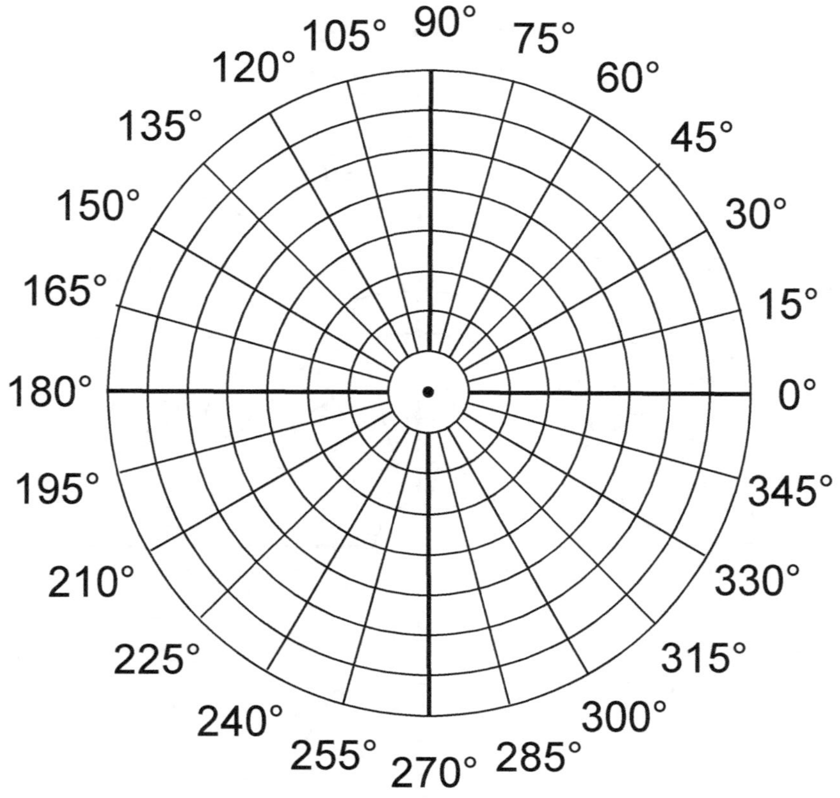

Other Team's
Buried Treasure

10P

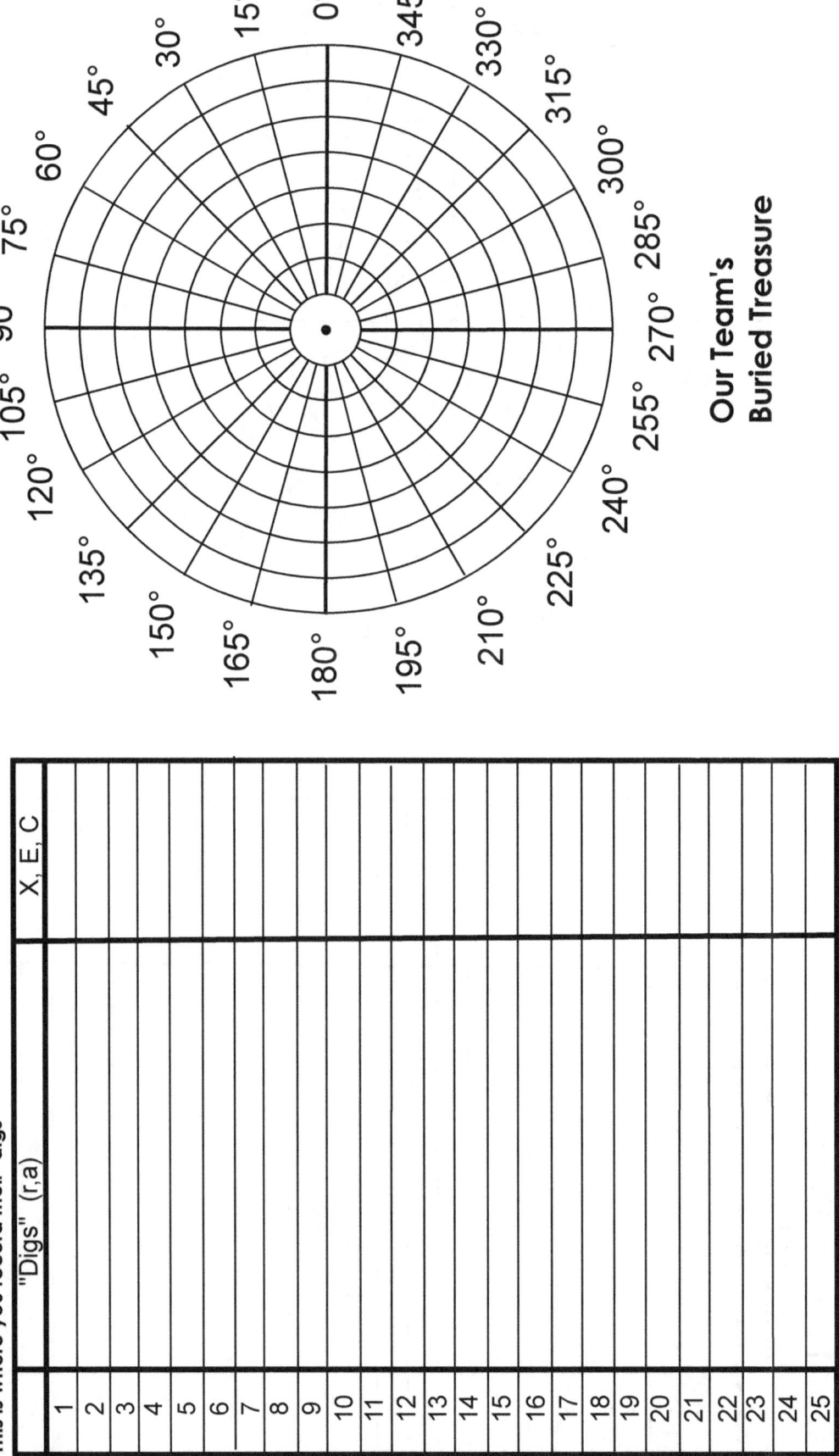

POLAR BURIED TREASURE GAME

Other Team's Digs

This is where you record their "digs"

	"Digs" (r,a)	X, E, C
1		
2		
3		
4		
5		
6		
7		
8		
9		
10		
11		
12		
13		
14		
15		
16		
17		
18		
19		
20		
21		
22		
23		
24		
25		

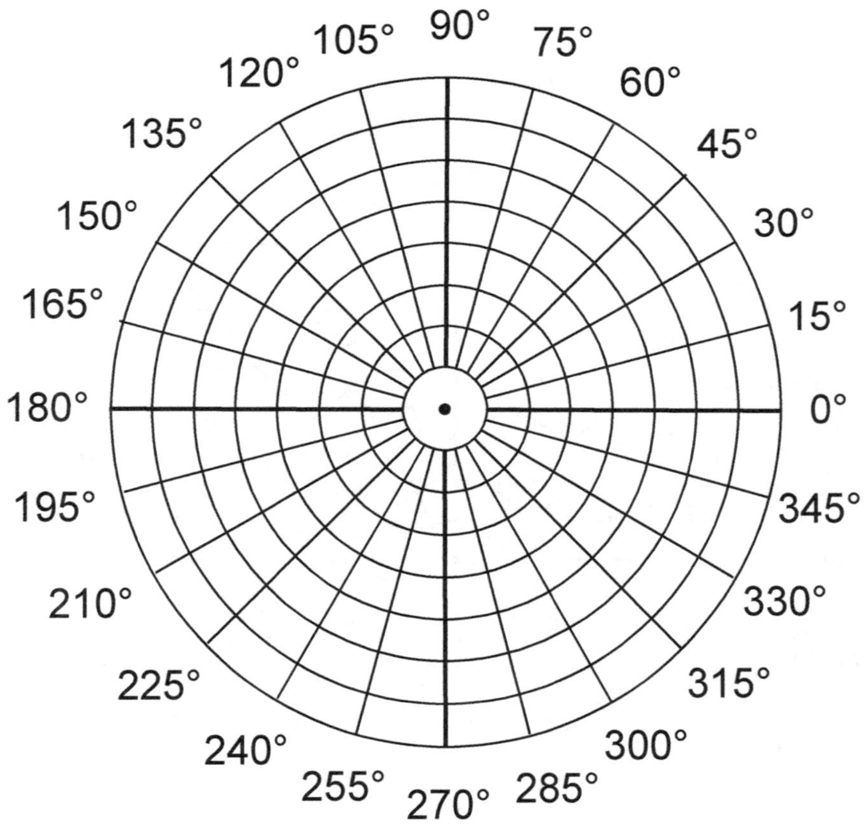

Our Team's Buried Treasure

11P

POLAR BURIED TREASURE GAME

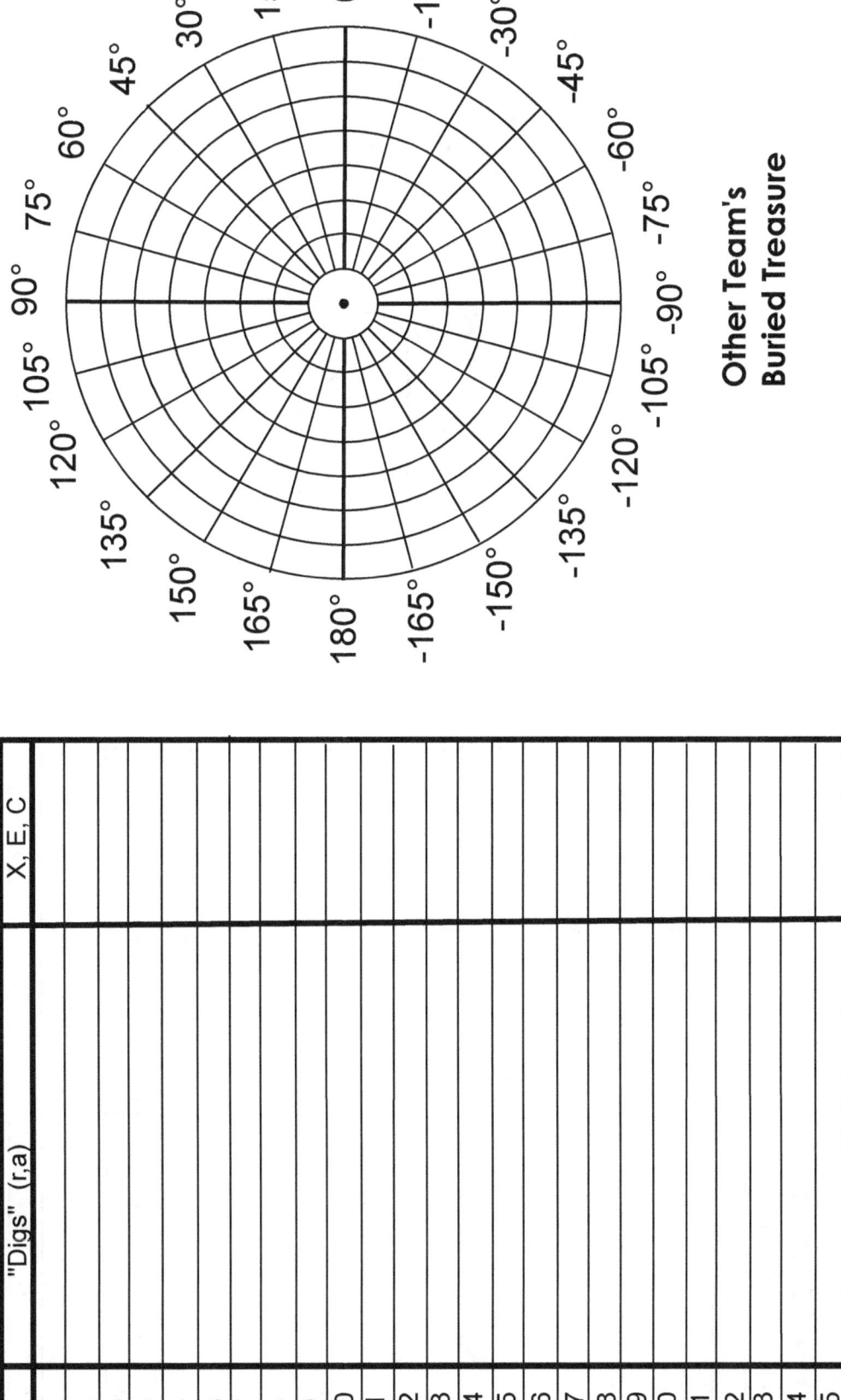

Our Team's Digs

This is where you record your "digs"

	"Digs" (r,a)	X, E, C
1		
2		
3		
4		
5		
6		
7		
8		
9		
10		
11		
12		
13		
14		
15		
16		
17		
18		
19		
20		
21		
22		
23		
24		
25		

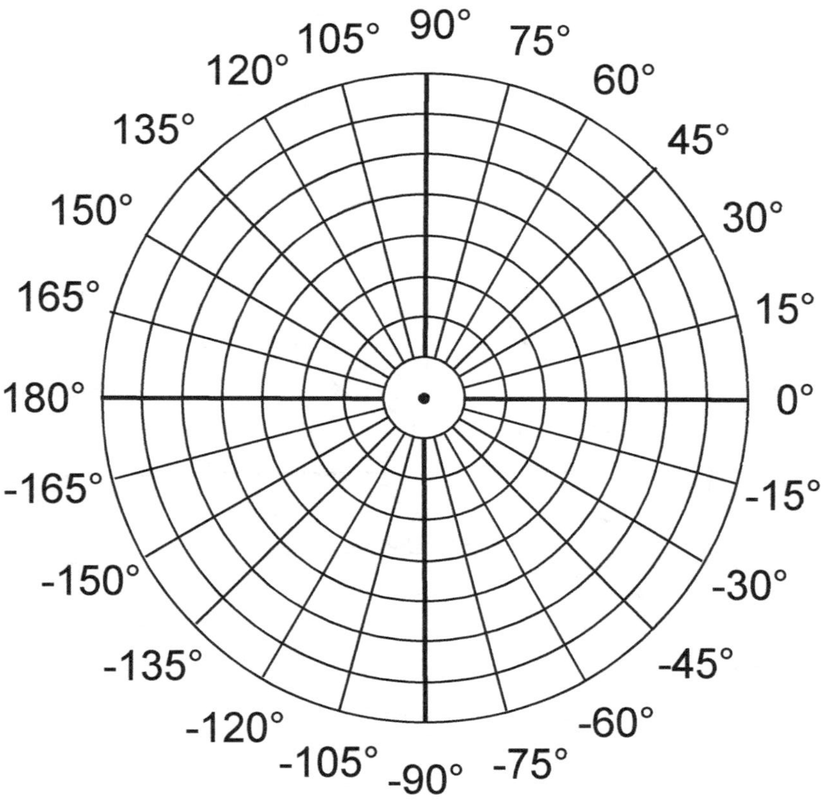

Other Team's Buried Treasure

12P

POLAR BURIED TREASURE GAME

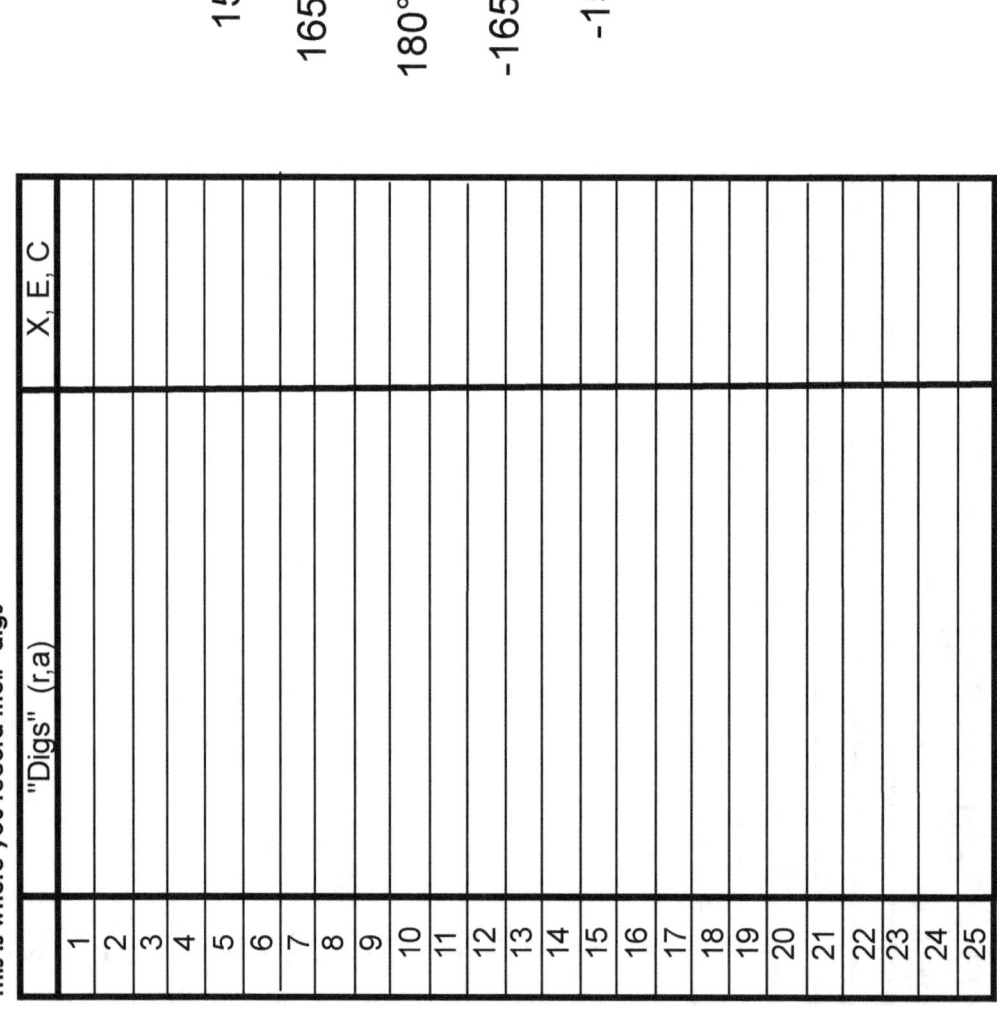

Other Team's Digs

This is where you record their "digs"

	"Digs" (r,a)	X, E, C
1		
2		
3		
4		
5		
6		
7		
8		
9		
10		
11		
12		
13		
14		
15		
16		
17		
18		
19		
20		
21		
22		
23		
24		
25		

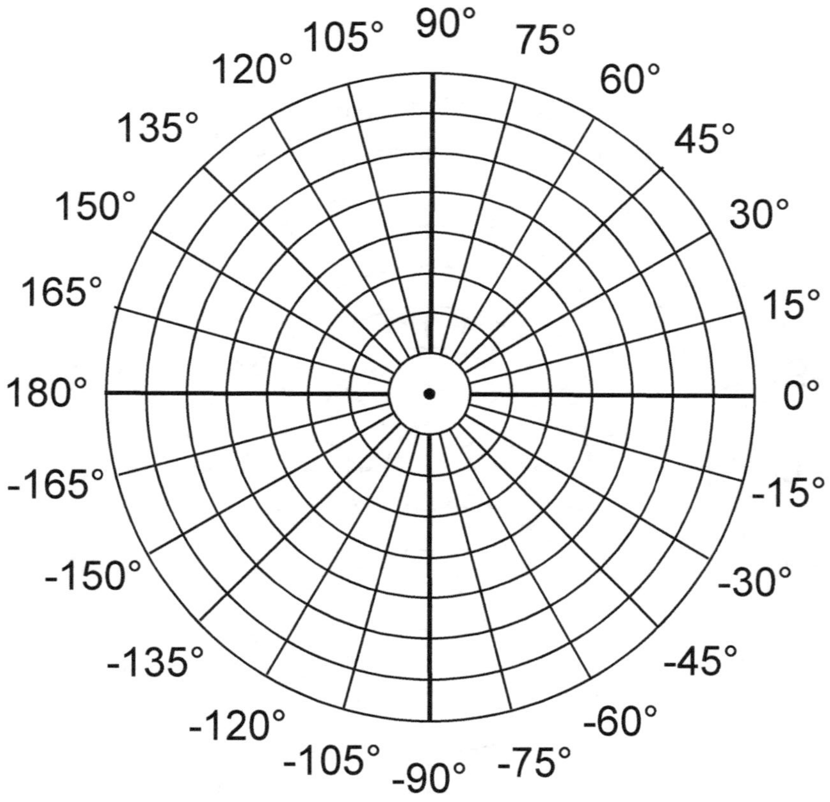

Our Team's Buried Treasure

SPHERICAL BURIED TREASURE GAME

Our Team's Digs

	"Digs" (°lattitude, °longitude)	X, E, C
1		
2		
3		
4		
5		
6		
7		
8		
9		
10		
11		
12		
13		
14		
15		
16		
17		
18		
19		
20		
21		
22		
23		
24		
25		

13S

SPHERICAL BURIED TREASURE GAME

Other Team's Digs

	"Digs" (°lattitude, °longitude)	X, E, C
1		
2		
3		
4		
5		
6		
7		
8		
9		
10		
11		
12		
13		
14		
15		
16		
17		
18		
19		
20		
21		
22		
23		
24		
25		

14S

3D BURIED TREASURE GAME

Our Team's Digs

This is where you record your "digs"

	"Digs" (x, y, z)	X, E, C
1		
2		
3		
4		
5		
6		
7		
8		
9		
10		
11		
12		
13		
14		
15		
16		
17		
18		
19		
20		
21		
22		
23		
24		
25		

Other Team's Buried Treasure

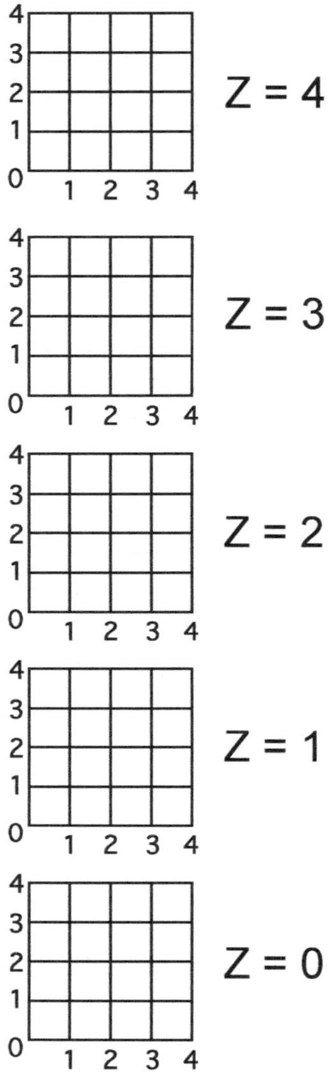

15-3D

3D BURIED TREASURE GAME

Other Team's Digs

This is where you record their "digs"

	"Digs" (x, y, z)	X, E, C
1		
2		
3		
4		
5		
6		
7		
8		
9		
10		
11		
12		
13		
14		
15		
16		
17		
18		
19		
20		
21		
22		
23		
24		
25		

Our Team's Buried Treasure

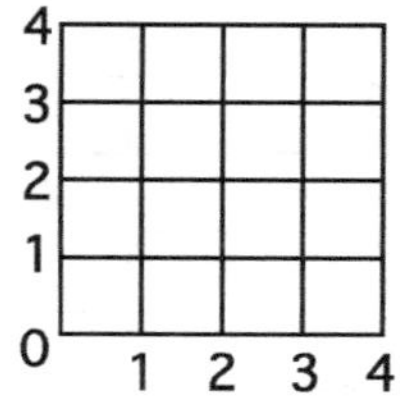

Z = 4

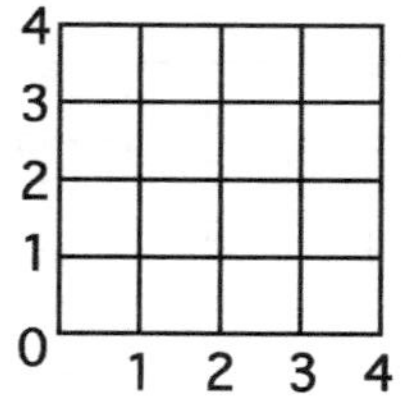

Z = 3

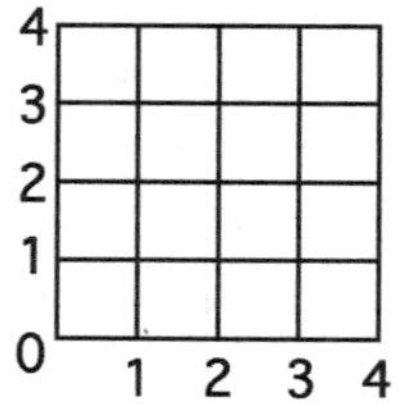

Z = 2

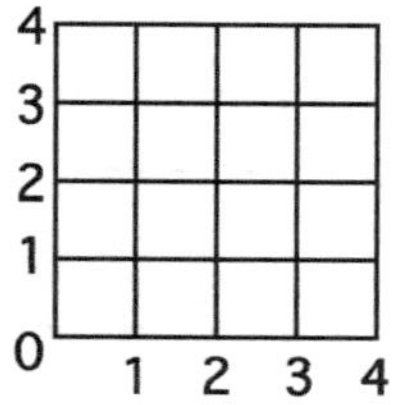

Z = 1

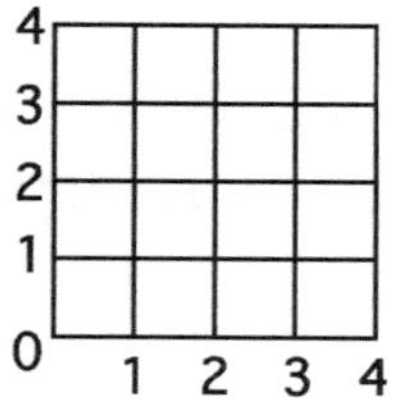

Z = 0

16-3D

3D BURIED TREASURE GAME

Our Team's Digs

This is where you record your "digs"

	"Digs" (x, y, z)	X, E, C
1		
2		
3		
4		
5		
6		
7		
8		
9		
10		
11		
12		
13		
14		
15		
16		
17		
18		
19		
20		
21		
22		
23		
24		
25		
26		
27		
28		
29		
30		
31		
32		
33		
34		

Other Team's Buried Treasure

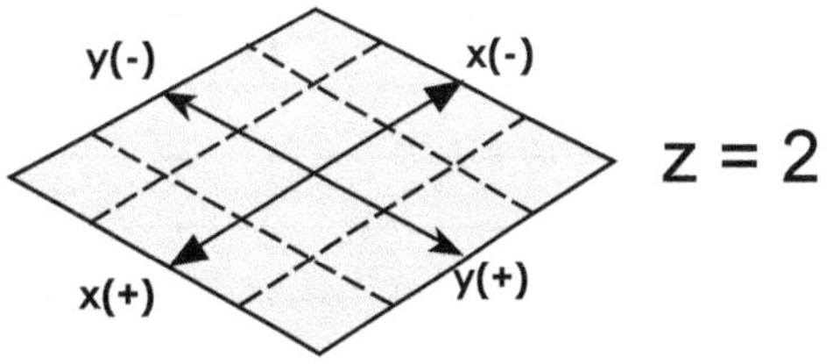

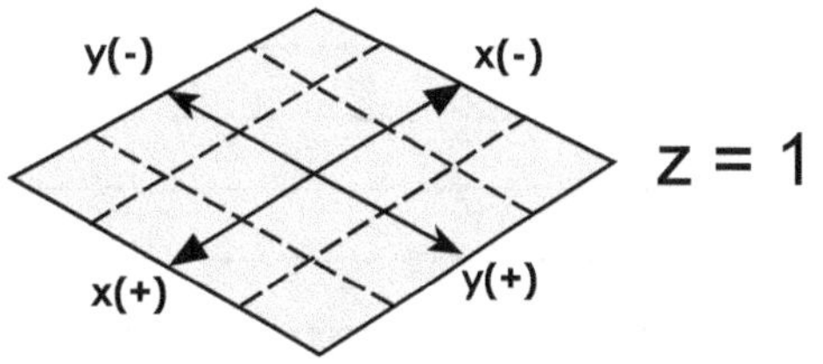

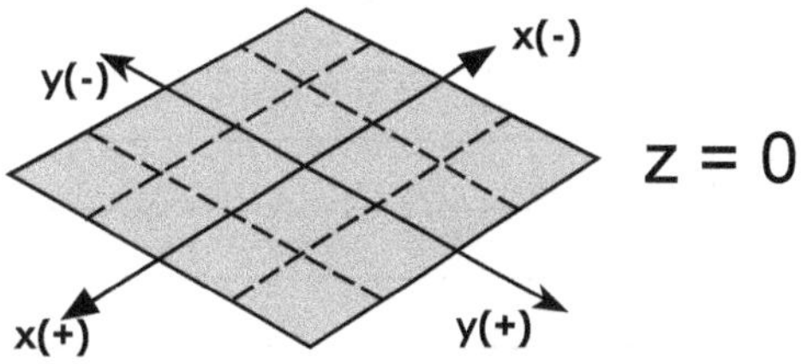

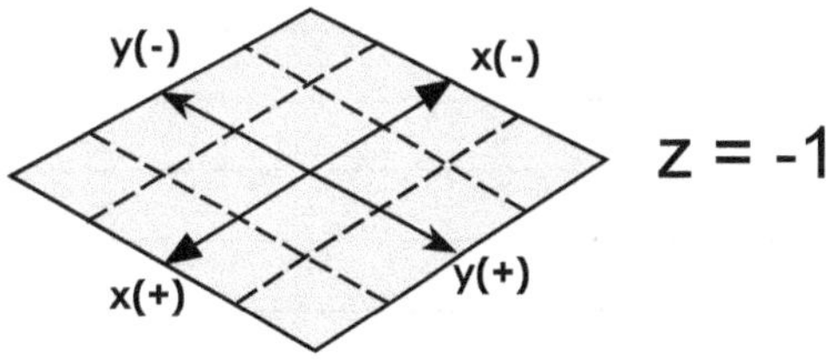

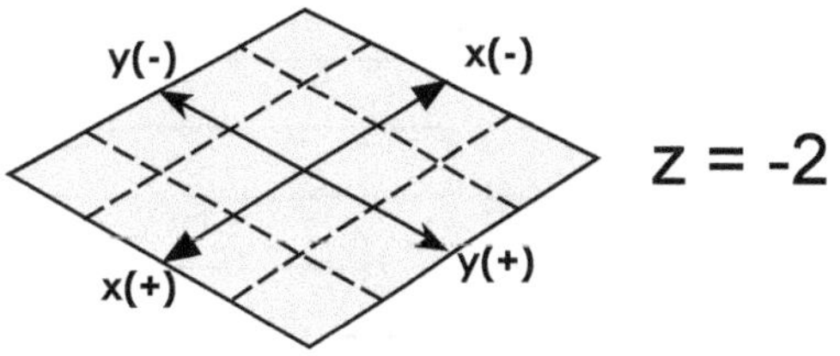

17-3D

3D BURIED TREASURE GAME

Other Team's Digs

This is where you record their "digs"

	"Digs" (x, y, z)	X, E, C
1		
2		
3		
4		
5		
6		
7		
8		
9		
10		
11		
12		
13		
14		
15		
16		
17		
18		
19		
20		
21		
22		
23		
24		
25		
26		
27		
28		
29		
30		
31		
32		
33		
34		

Our Team's Buried Treasure

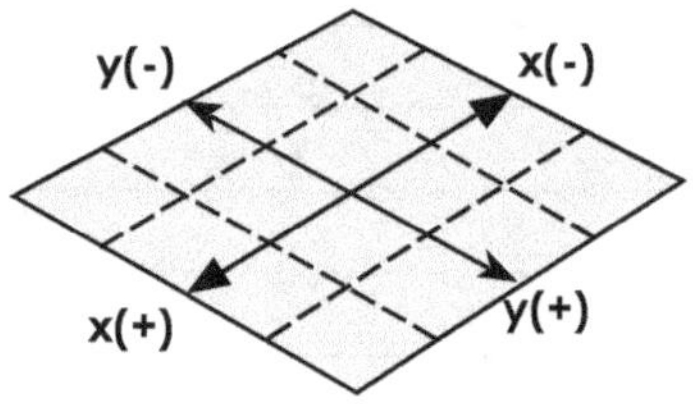

z = 2

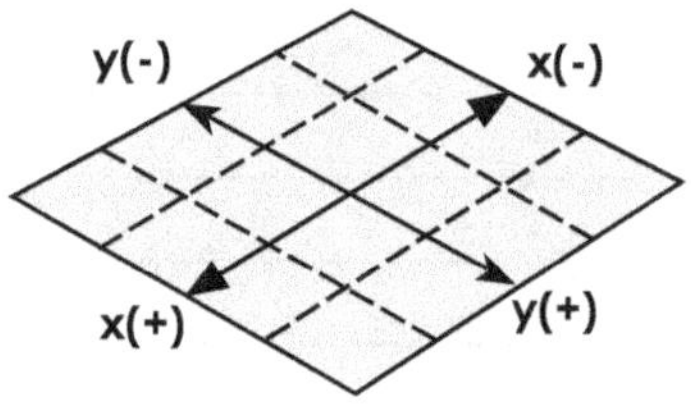

z = 1

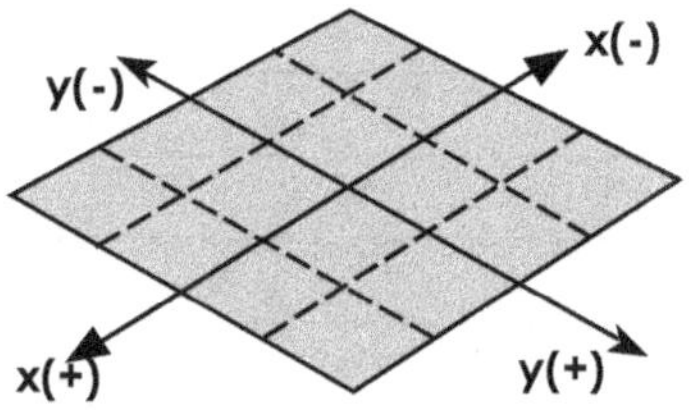

z = 0

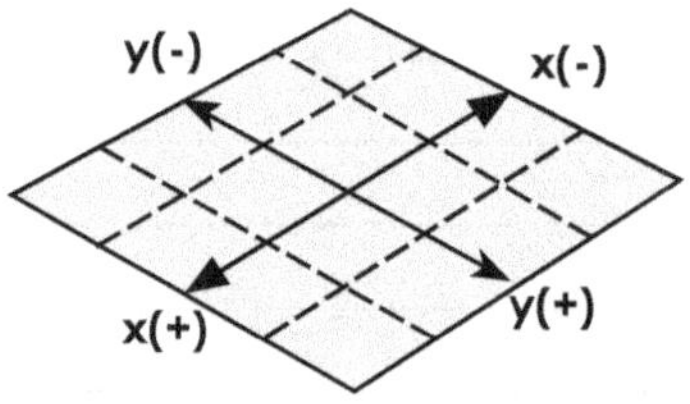

z = -1

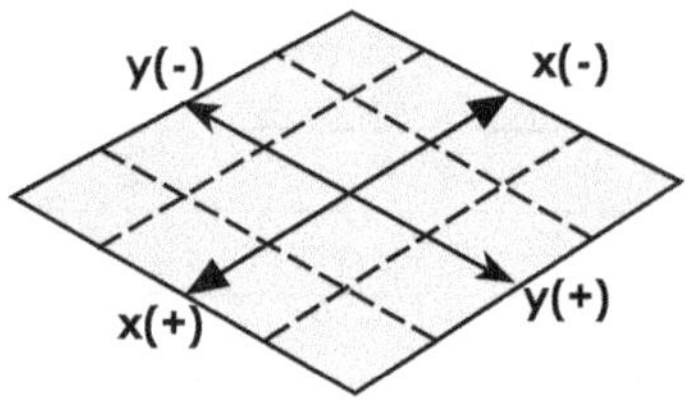

z = -2

18-3D

3D BURIED TREASURE GAME

Our Team's Digs

This is where you record your "digs"

	"Digs" (x, y, z)	X, E, C
1		
2		
3		
4		
5		
6		
7		
8		
9		
10		
11		
12		
13		
14		
15		
16		
17		
18		
19		
20		
21		
22		
23		
24		
25		
26		
27		
28		
29		
30		
31		
32		
33		
34		

19-3D

Other Team's Buried Treasure

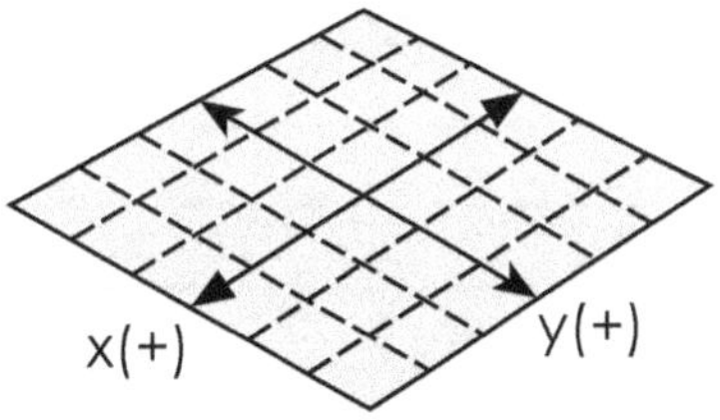

z = 3

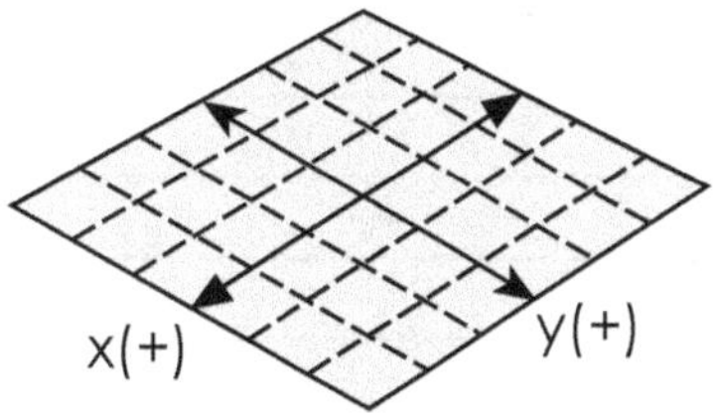

z = 2

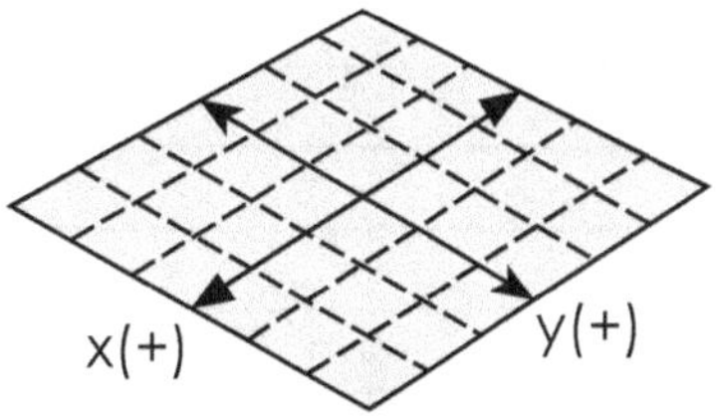

z = 1

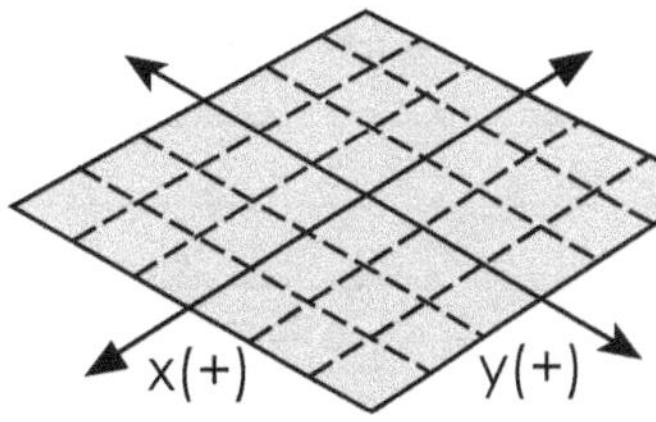

z = 0

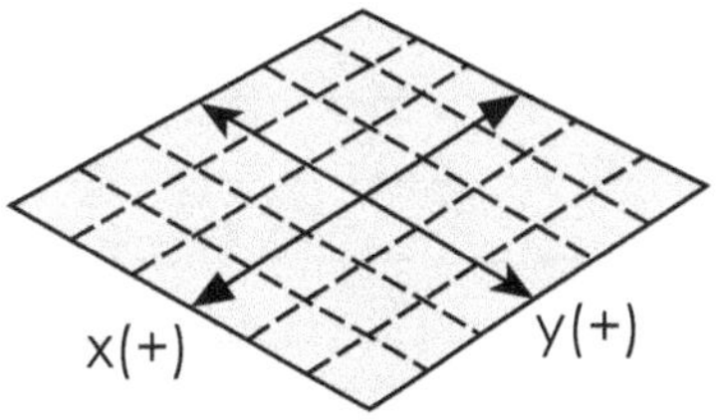

z = -1

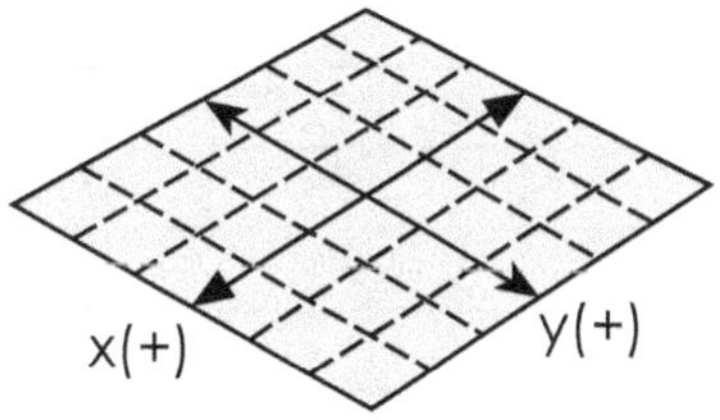

z = -2

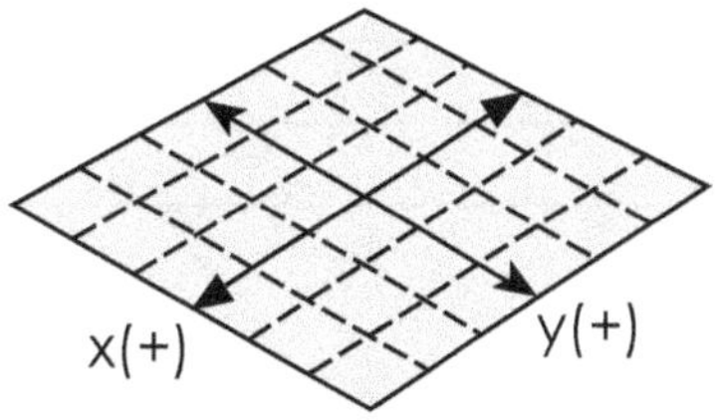

z = -3

3D BURIED TREASURE GAME

Other Team's Digs

This is where you record their "digs"

	"Digs" (x, y, z)	X, E, C
1		
2		
3		
4		
5		
6		
7		
8		
9		
10		
11		
12		
13		
14		
15		
16		
17		
18		
19		
20		
21		
22		
23		
24		
25		
26		
27		
28		
29		
30		
31		
32		
33		
34		

Our Team's Buried Treasure

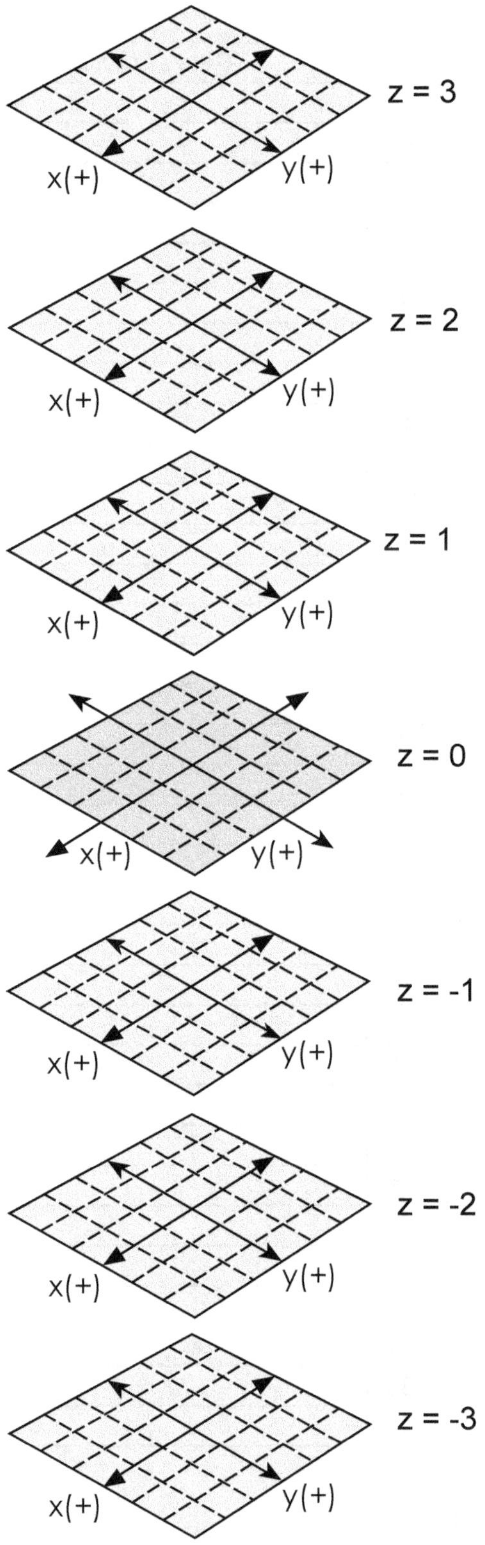

20-3D

3D BURIED TREASURE GAME

Our Team's Digs

This is where you record your "digs"

	"Digs" (x, y, z)	X, E, C
1		
2		
3		
4		
5		
6		
7		
8		
9		
10		
11		
12		
13		
14		
15		
16		
17		
18		
19		
20		
21		
22		
23		
24		
25		
26		
27		
28		
29		
30		
31		
32		
33		
34		

Other Team's Buried Treasure

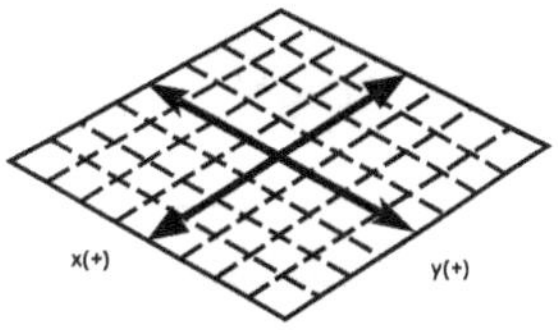

z = 4

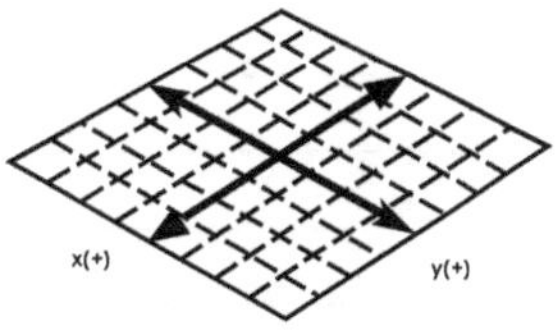

z = 3

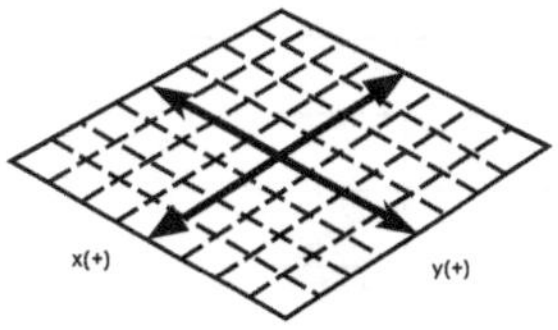

z = 2

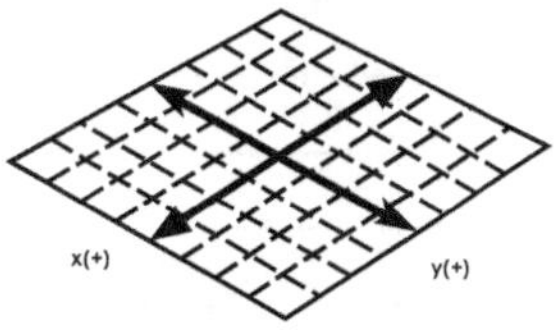

z = 1

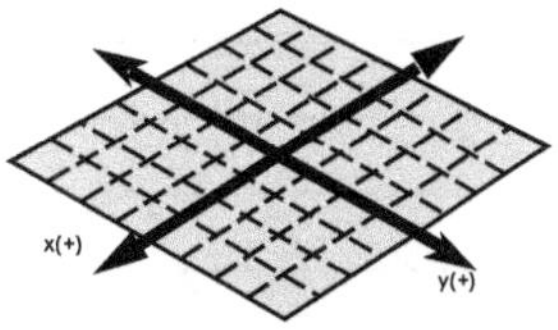

z = 0

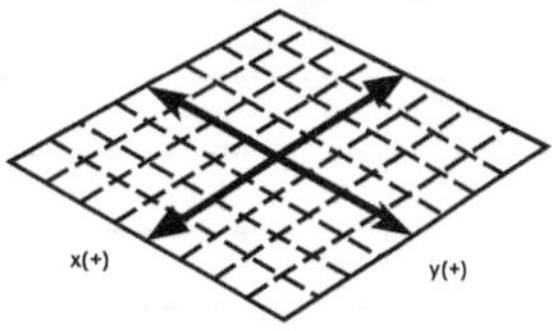

z = -1

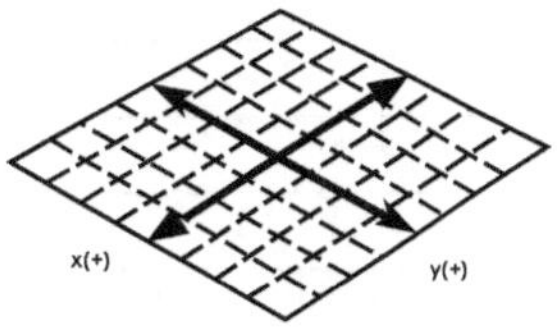

z = -2

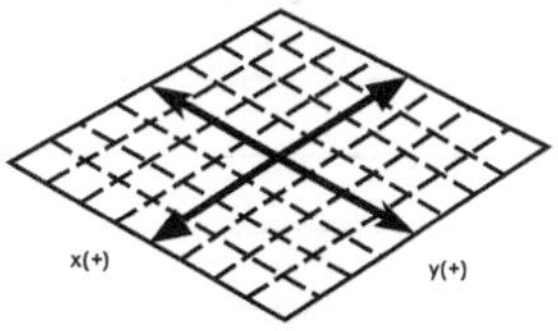

z = -3

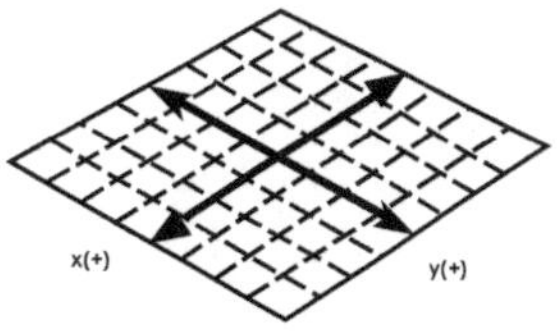

z = -4

21-3D

3D BURIED TREASURE GAME

Other Team's Digs

This is where you record their "digs"

	"Digs" (x, y, z)	X, E, C
1		
2		
3		
4		
5		
6		
7		
8		
9		
10		
11		
12		
13		
14		
15		
16		
17		
18		
19		
20		
21		
22		
23		
24		
25		
26		
27		
28		
29		
30		
31		
32		
33		
34		

Our Team's Buried Treasure

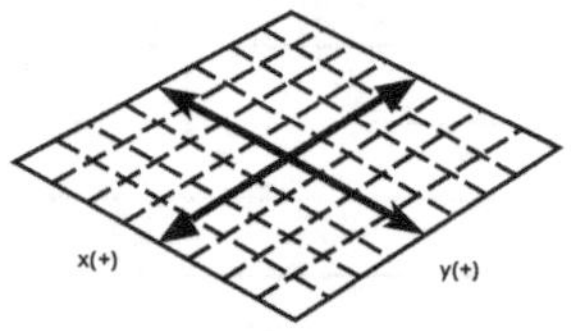

z = 4

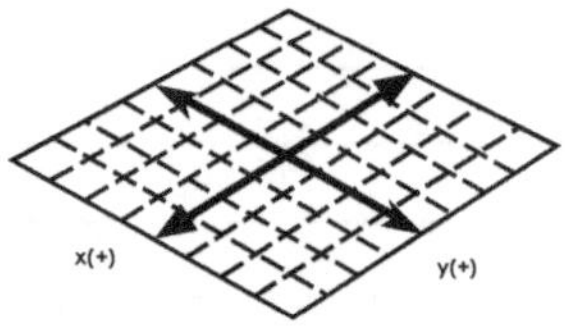

z = 3

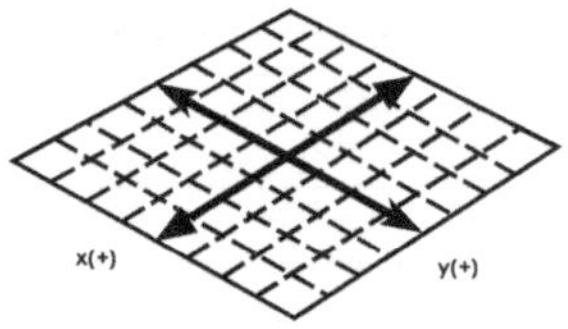

z = 2

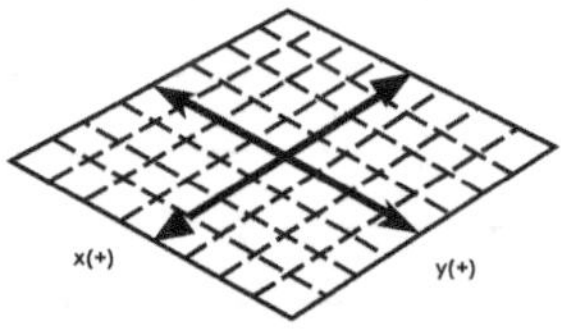

z = 1

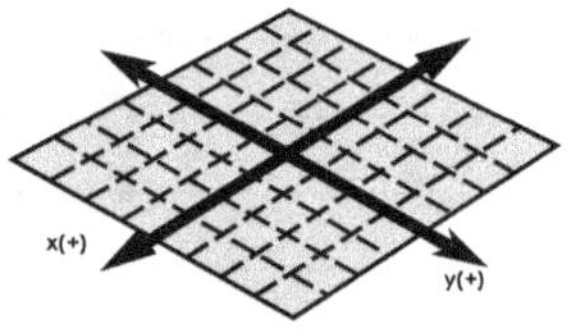

z = 0

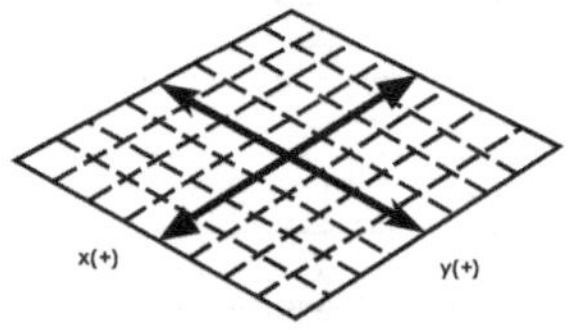

z = -1

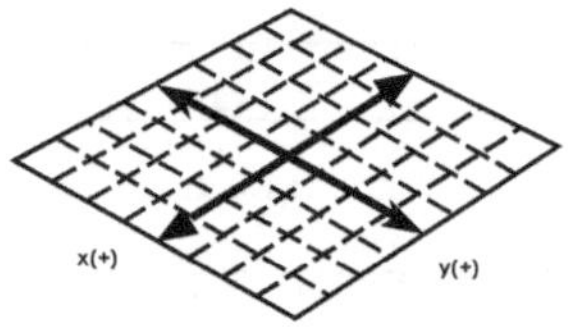

z = -2

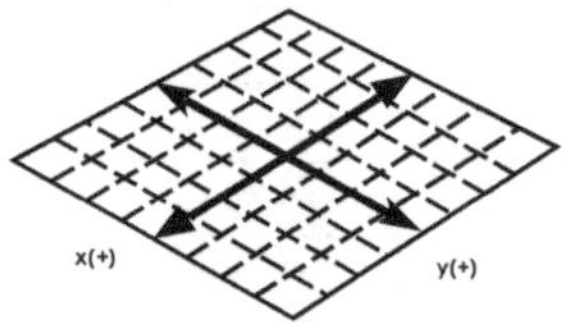

z = -3

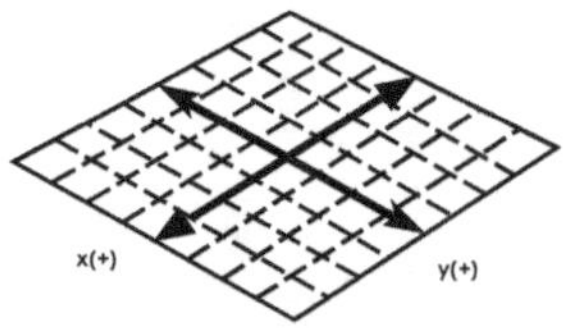

z = -4

22-3D

Appendix 2 Linear Equations

In this appendix you are going to either learn or review the graphing of linear equations. The answers to these exercises are found at the end of this appendix on pages 215 and 216.

Functions

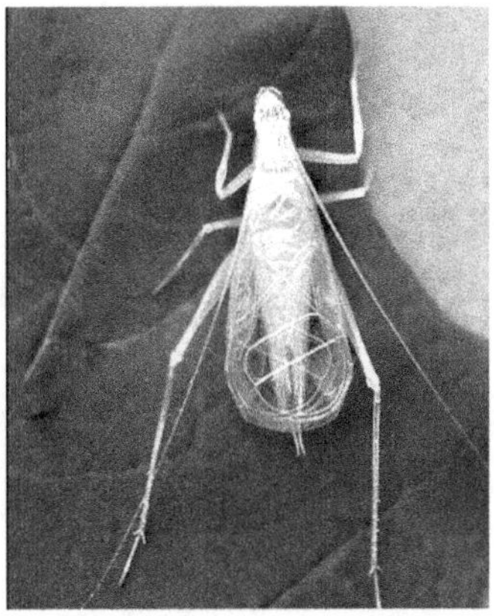

You may have heard the term "function" in everyday usage. "Good health is a function of proper diet and exercise." Biologists discovered that the rate a snowy tree cricket chirps is a function of the temperature of its environment. The pulse rate of mammals is a function of their size. In physics, the distance an object falls is a function of the time it has been falling. The length a spring is stretched is a function of the weight that is hung from it. In mathematics the circumference of a circle is a function of its radius. The area of that circle is a function of the square of its radius.

A **function** is a relationship between two sets of numbers such that each number from the first set corresponds to exactly one number in the second set.

A function can be expressed as a table of values, as an equation, or as a graph. Functions are very useful because with functions you can make predictions. For example, below is a table of values showing the relationship between the number of chirps by a snowy tree cricket every 13 seconds versus temperature in Fahrenheit (°F).

Cricket chirps every 13 seconds	15	25	30	37	40	...	C
Temperature (degrees Fahrenheit)	55	65	70	77	80	...	C + 40

With this table you can see by adding 40 to the number of cricket chirps you can determine the Fahrenheit temperature. Thus the algebraic rule for this function is

$T = C + 40$. With this rule you can predict how fast a cricket would chirp when the temperature reaches 72° or calculate the temperature when you have counted 32 chirps from the cricket in a 13 second span.

If this set of values is graphed, the points lie on a line. Thus this function is a **linear function**. The equation $T = C + 40$ is a **linear equation**.

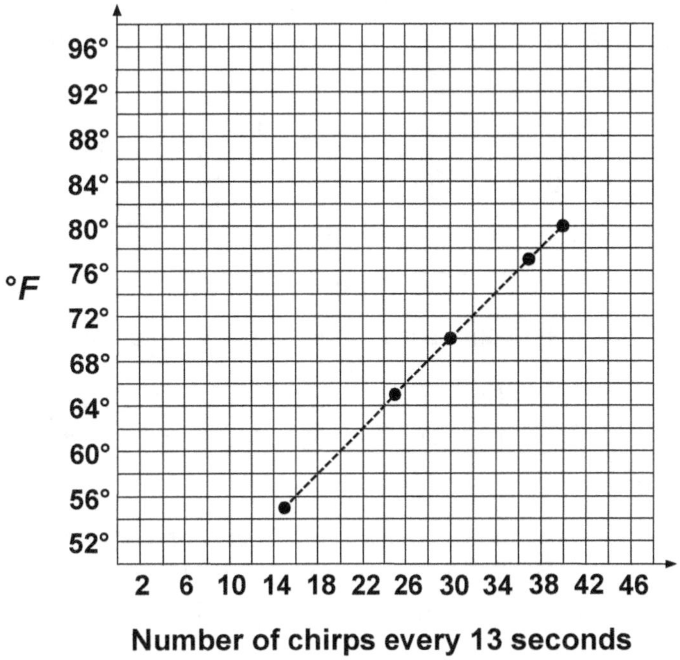

The formula to convert °*F* to °*C* is a linear equation. You use degrees Fahrenheit (°*F*) in the United States but most of the rest of the world uses degrees Celsius (°*C*). If you are traveling to Europe and are familiar with °*F* but unfamiliar with °*C* the conversion formula $°F = (9/5)C + 32$ will be helpful.

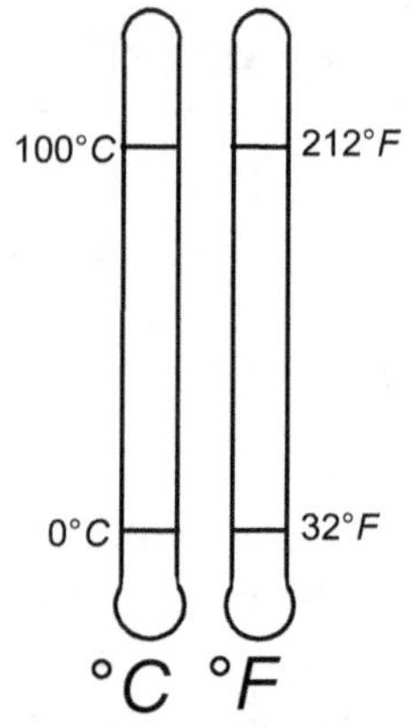

Example A *If the temperature is 30° Celsius what is that in degrees Fahrenheit?*

Solution $°F = (9/5)C + 32$

$= (9/5)(30) + 32$

$= (9)(6) + 32$

$= 86$

(A temperature of 30° Celsius is 86° Fahrenheit.)

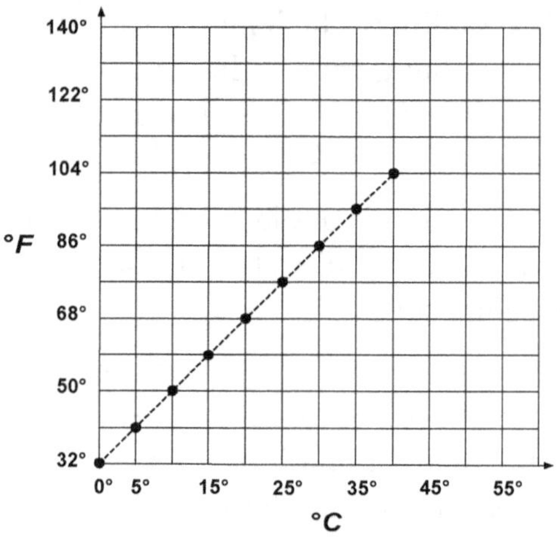

If you use the formula $°F = (9/5)C + 32$ you can find the missing temperature values in the table below. Complete the table and then check your results with the answers for Example 1 at the end of this appendix.

°C	0	5	10	15	20	25	30		
°F								95	104

If you graph these values as ordered pairs (°*C*, °*F*) the points lie on a line. There are infinitely many values you can pick for °*C*. By choosing "nice" values that are multiples of five, the arithmetic is nice and you get "nice" values for °*F*.

Example B *How do you graph the linear equation* $y = 2x + 1$?

Solution Make a table of values. Pick a value for *x* and put it into the equation in place of *x* and calculate the value of *y*.

If $x = 0$, then $y = 2(0) + 1$ or $y = 1$.

If $x = 1$, then $y = 2(1) + 1$ or $y = 3$.

If $x = 2$, then $y = 2(2) + 1$ or $y = 5$.

If $x = 3$, then $y = 2(3) + 1$ or $y = 7$.

X	0	1	2	3			
Y	1	3	5	7			

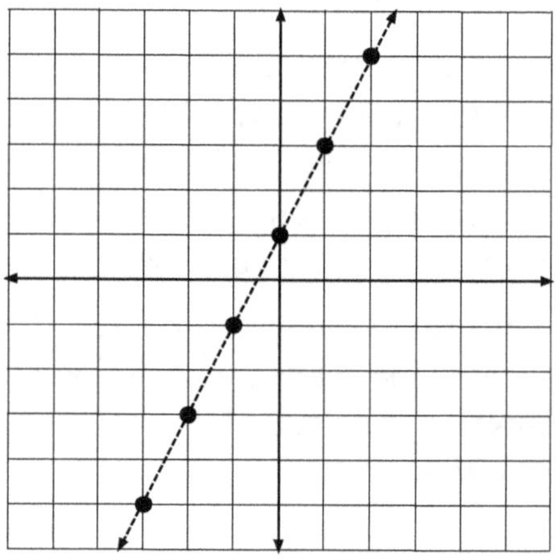

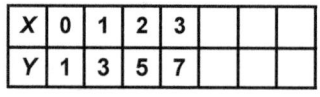

You can also choose negative numbers such as -1, -2, -3, …

If $x = -1$, then $y = 2(-1) + 1$ or $y = -1$.

If $x = -2$, then $y = 2(-2) + 1$ or $y = -3$.

If $x = -3$, then $y = 2(-3) + 1$ or $y = -5$.

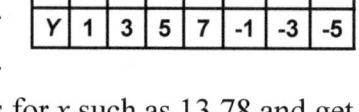

X	0	1	2	3	-1	-2	-3
Y	1	3	5	7	-1	-3	-5

Again, you can choose any numbers for *x* such as 13.78 and get a *y* value of 28.56. This ordered pair (13.78, 28.56) would also lie on the line but the arithmetic would be "not so nice."

Graphing the point (13.78, 28.56) would not be as accurate as graphing an order pair with integers such as (13, 27).

Example C *How do you graph the linear equation* $y = (2/3)x + 1$?

Solution Make a table of values. Pick a value for x and put it into the equation in place of x and calculate the value of y.

If $x = 0$, then $y = (2/3)(0) + 1$ or $y = 1$.

You can choose any number you want for x. Since you're going to multiply it by 2/3, it makes it easier if you choose numbers divisible by 3. So choose 3, 6, 9, ….

X	0						
Y	1						

If $x = 3$, then $y = (2/3)(3) + 1$; thus $y = 2 + 1$ or $y = 3$.

If $x = 6$, then $y = (2/3)(6) + 1$; thus $y = 4 + 1$ or $y = 5$.

If $x = 9$, then $y = (2/3)(9) + 1$; thus $y = 6 + 1$ or $y = 7$.

X	0	3	6	9			
Y	1	3	5	7			

You can choose negative multiples of 3, such as -3, -6, -9, ….

If $x = -3$, then $y = (2/3)(-3) + 1$; thus $y = -2 + 1$ or $y = -1$.

If $x = -6$, then $y = (2/3)(-6) + 1$; thus $y = -4 + 1$ or $y = -3$.

If $x = -9$, then $y = (2/3)(-9) + 1$; thus $y = -6 + 1$ or $y = -5$.

X	0	3	6	9	-3	-6	-9
Y	1	3	5	7	-1	-3	-5

Once you have a table of ordered pairs you can graph the points and draw a line through them.

X	0	3	6	9	-3	-6	-9
Y	1	3	5	7	-1	-3	-5

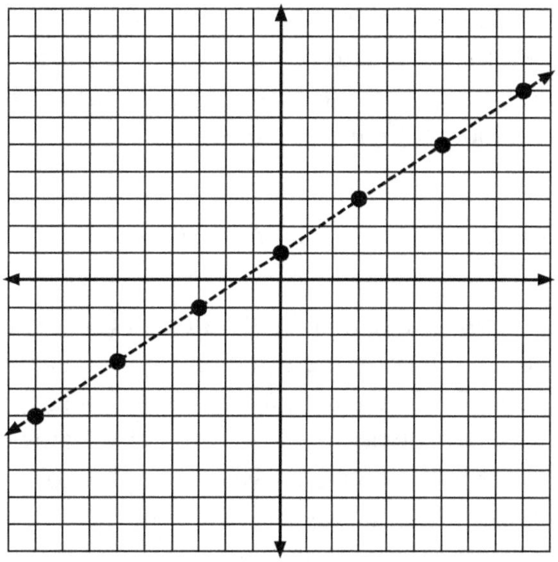

Example D *How do you graph the linear equation* $y = -(5/2)x - 3$?

Solution Make a table of values. Pick a value for x and put it into the equation in place of x and calculate the value of y.

If $x = 0$, then $y = -(5/2)(0) - 3$ or $y = -3$.

You can choose any numbers you want for x. Since you're going to multiply it by 5/2, it makes it easier if you choose numbers divisible by 2. So choose 2, 4, 6, … as well as -2, -4, -6, ….

X	0	2	4	6	-2	-4	-6
Y	-3	-8	-13	-18	2	7	12

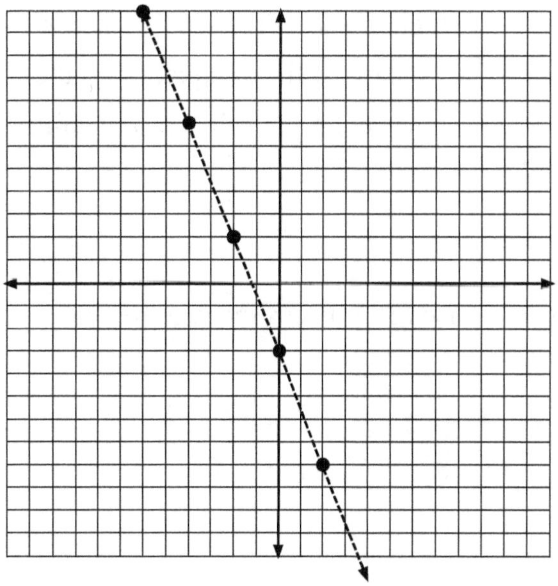

Horizontal and Vertical lines

Some lines are horizontal and some are vertical. Let's take a look at their equations. In order for a line to be horizontal, the y-coordinates of the points on the line must all be the same value.

Example E *How do you graph the linear equation* $y = 4$?

Solution Make a table of values. Pick a value for x and put it into the equation in place of x then calculate the value of y. Ah, but there is no x. What does this mean? It means, it doesn't matter what value you pick for x, the y value is always 4.

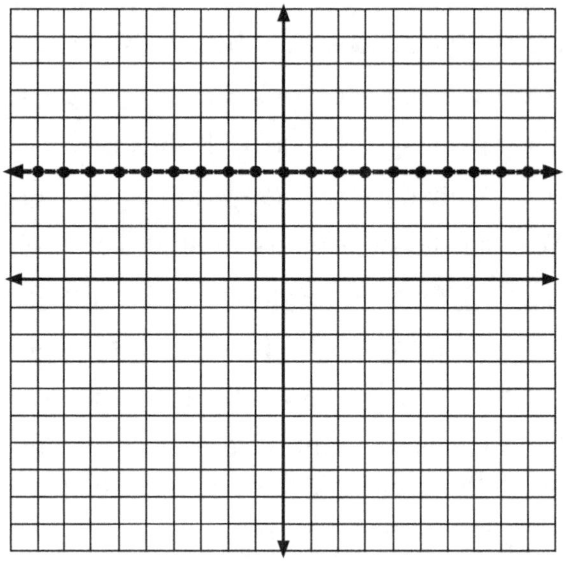

If $x = 0$, then $y = 4$. If $x = 10$, then $y = 4$.

If $x = -10$, then $y = 4$. If $x = 17.35$, then $y = 4$.

In other words, every linear equation in the form

$y = a$, has a horizontal line for its graph a units from the x-axis.

What does the equation of a vertical line look like? In order for a line to be vertical, the x-coordinates of the points on the line must all be the same value. Let's take a look at their equations.

Example F *How do you graph the linear equation* $x = -2$?

Solution Make a table of values. Pick a value for x and, ah but wait, the equation says, "x is always negative 2." You can't pick other numbers for x because x is always -2. You can pick whatever you want for y, but no matter what you pick for y in this equation, x will always be -2.

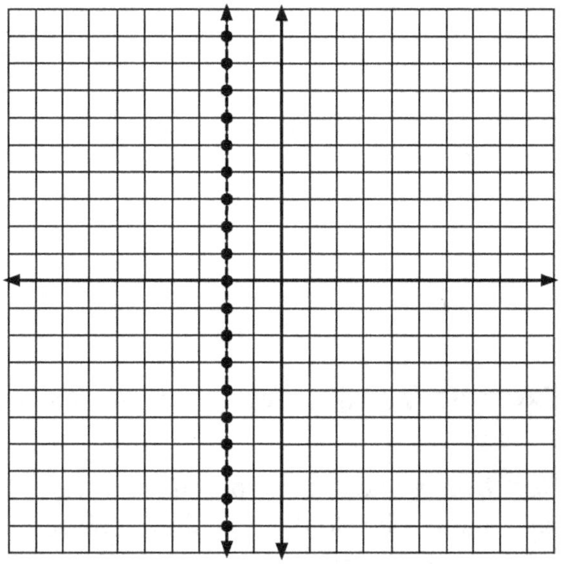

If $y = 0$, then $x = -2$. If $y = 10$, then $x = -2$.

If $y = -30$, then $x = -2$. If $y = -70.38$, then $x = -2$.

In other words, every linear equation in the form

$x = b$, has a vertical line for its graph b units from the y-axis.

For Exercises 1–4 determine whether the graphs of the equations below are vertical or horizontal lines.

1. $y = 3$
2. $x = -5$
3. $y = 0$
4. $x = 0$

Here is some practice graphing linear equations. Graph Exercises 5–8 on the coordinate grid to the right.

5. $y = 2x + 3$

X							
Y							

6. $y = 4x - 5$

X							
Y							

7. $y = -2x + 1$

X							
Y							

8. $y = -5x - 2$

X							
Y							

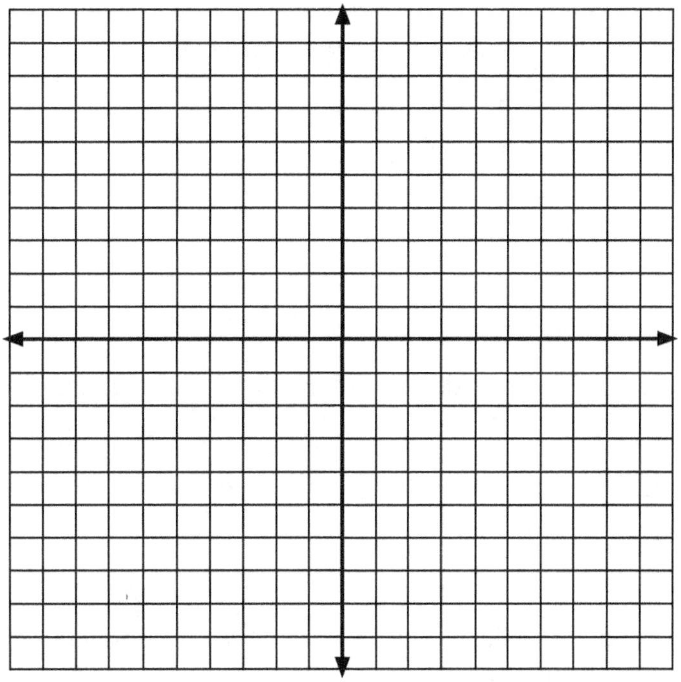

Here is some practice graphing linear equations where the number in front of the x is a fraction. Graph Exercises 9–12 on the coordinate grid to the right.

9. $y = (2/3)x + 3$

X							
Y							

10. $y = (3/4)x - 5$

X							
Y							

11. $y = -(2/5)x + 1$

X							
Y							

12. $y = -(1/2)x - 4$

X							
Y							

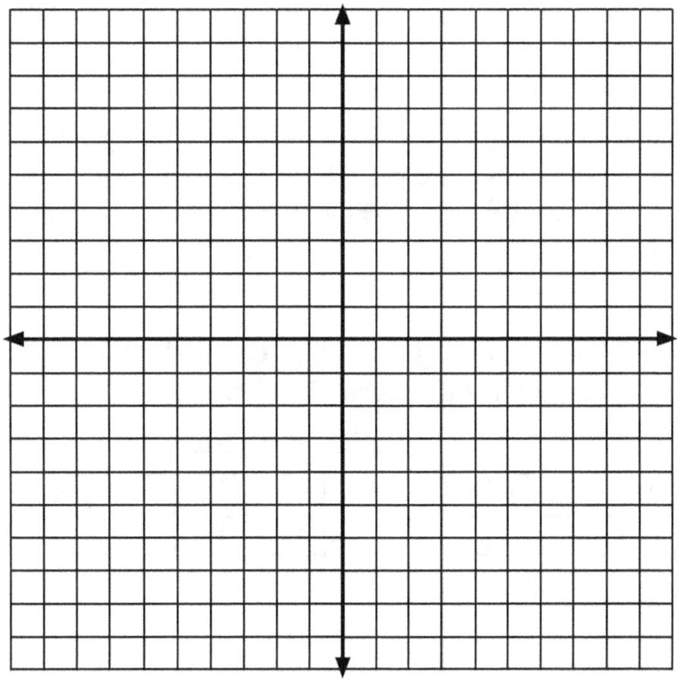

By now you may be noticing some patterns. These patterns can be used to predict what the graphs of linear equations will look like. For example, you should now be able to look at an equation and determine where the graph will cross the y-axis. This is the point where the x value of the ordered pair is zero. The point where the graph crosses the y-axis is called the ***y*-intercept**.

Example G *Find the y-intercept of these lines (the point where each crosses the y-axis). Look back on your graphs of Exercises 5–8 to confirm these answers. Check to confirm that these y-intercepts are in your table of values as well.*

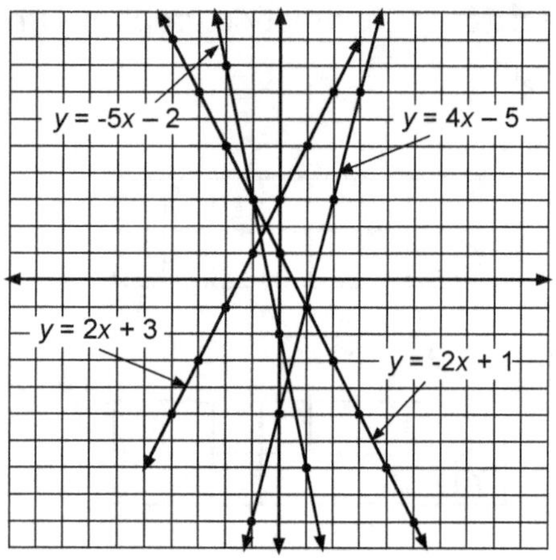

Solution

Equation	***Y*-intercept**
$y = 2x + 3$	(0, 3)
$y = -2x + 1$	(0, 1)
$y = 4x - 5$	(0, -5)
$y = -5x - 2$	(0, -2)

For Exercises 13–20 find the y-intercept for these equations by just looking at the equation:

13. $y = (2/3)x + 3$ (0,)
14. $y = (3/4)x - 5$ (0,)
15. $y = (3/2)x + 4$ (0,)
16. $y = -(2/5)x + 1$ (0,)
17. $y = -(5/3)x - 2$ (0,)
18. $y = (7/3)x$ (0,)
19. $y = -3$ (0,)
20. $x = 4$ (0,)

Are you ready to make a conjecture for the rule connecting the y-intercept with the equation of the line? Complete this statement:

21. If the equation of a line is $y = mx + b$ then the y-intercept is (0, ___).

There is another important relationship found in the equation of a line when written in the form $y = mx + b$. To discover this relationship let's look at parallel lines.

The lines $y = 2x + 3$, $y = 2x - 2$, and $y = 2x - 7$ are graphed to the right. All three lines are parallel. What do the equations of these lines have in common? They all have the same coefficient of x, namely 2.

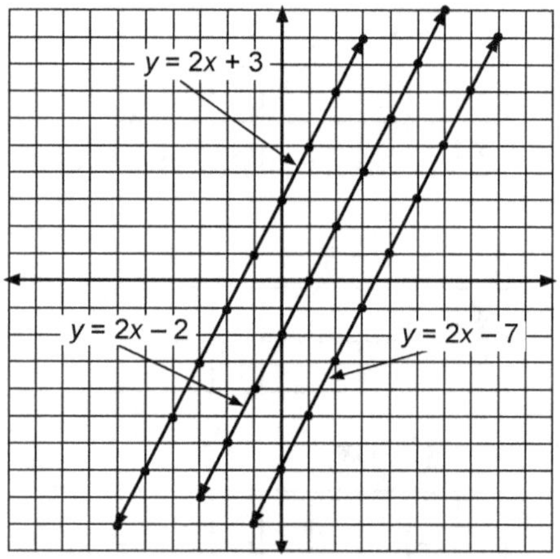

Test this with the following equations. Graph the four equations below onto the graph at right. Are they parallel?

22. $y = -(2/5)x + 7$

X	-10	-5	0	5	10
Y					

23. $y = -(2/5)x + 3$

X	-10	-5	0	5	10
Y					

24. $y = -(2/5)x - 2$

X	-10	-5	0	5	10
Y					

25. $y = -(2/5)x - 6$

X	-10	-5	0	5	10
Y					

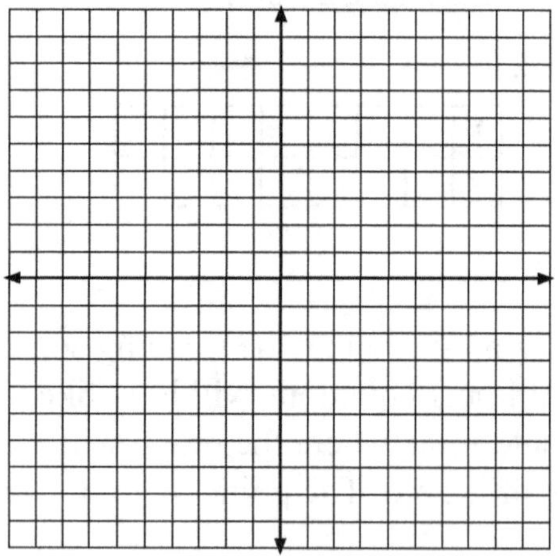

The number in front of the x in the equation, called the coefficient of x, plays a role in how the graph of the equation is slanted or tilted. This is called the slope of the line. The line $y = (3/4)x - 2$ is graphed to the right. Let's start at one of the points (-8, -8). Now move from that point to the next point (-4, -5), by first moving vertically then moving horizontally. To do this you moved 3 units vertically then 4 units horizontally. If you continue in this way, moving 3 units vertically then 4 units horizontally from (-4, -5) you land on the other points (0, -2), then (4, 1) and then (8, 4).

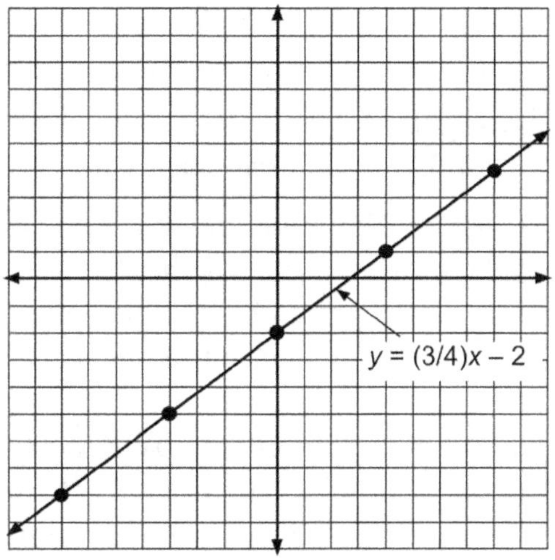

Of course you may have noticed that the number of units you move vertically, 3, and the number of units you move horizontally, 4, are also found in the equation of the line, in the coefficient of x, namely 3/4.

Let's look at two more examples to see the relationship between the slope of a line and the coefficient of x in the equation of the line.

There are two ways you can move from point to point on the line $y = (5/2)x + 1$. Starting at the lower left, you can move vertically 5 then horizontally 2, or starting at the upper right you can move vertically -5 (down 5) then horizontally -2 (back to the left 2).

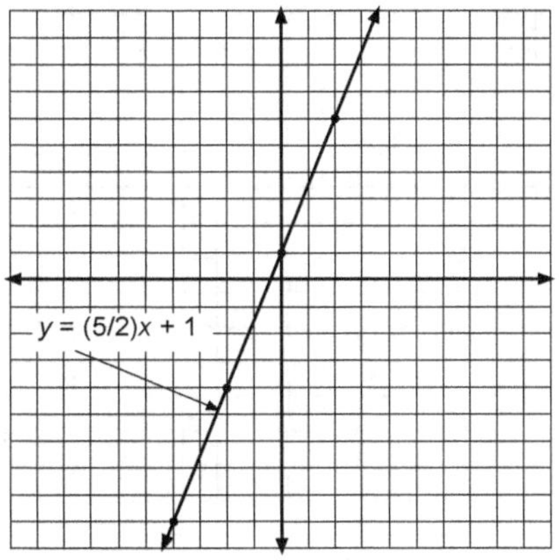

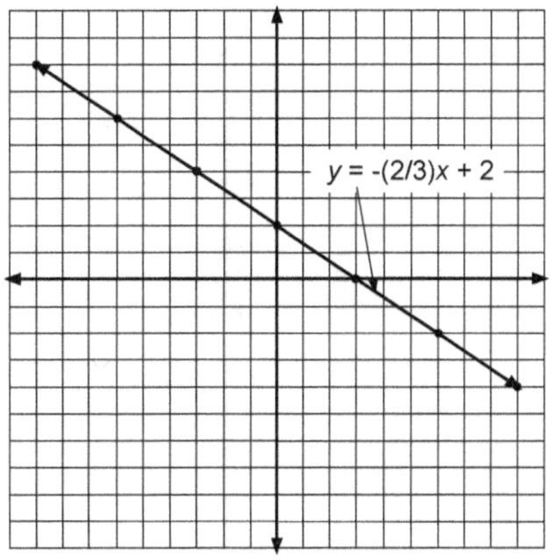

You can move from point to point on the line $y = -(2/3)x + 1$, either of two ways. Starting at the upper left, you can move vertically -2 (down 2) then horizontally 3, or starting at the lower right you can move vertically 2 then horizontally -3 (left 3).

The amount you move vertically up (+) or down (-) appears in the numerator of the fractional coefficient of x and the amount you move horizontally right (+) or left (-) appears in the denominator of the fractional coefficient of x.

This movement of vertical followed by horizontal moves from one point on a line to the next describes the slope of the line. The slope of a line is defined as a number that represents the amount of vertical movement divided by the amount of horizontal movement to move from one point on the line to another point on the line. For example, if the equation of a line is $y = (3/4)x + 5$, then the line has a slope of 3/4.

Are you ready to make a conjecture for the rule connecting the slope of a line with the equation of the line? Complete this statement:

26. If the equation of a line is $y = mx + b$ then the slope of the line is _________.

Now you know just by looking at the equation of a line where the line crosses the y-axis (the y-intercept) and you know the slope of the line.

Example H *Identify the slope and y-intercept of the line* $y = -(4/3)x - 1$ *and then graph it.*

Solution From looking at the equation, the fraction (-4/3) in front of the x is the slope and the y-intercept is (0, -1). To graph the line, begin by locating the y-intercept. Then since the line has a slope of -4/3, move down 4 units (-4) and to the right 3 units to locate the next point on the line (3, -5). Repeat this motion, down 4 units (-4), right 3, to the point (6, -9). You can also return to the y-intercept (0, -1) and use 4/-3 as your slope movement rule. Thus you move up 4 units and then left 3 units (-3) to locate another point on the line, (-3, 3), and so on.

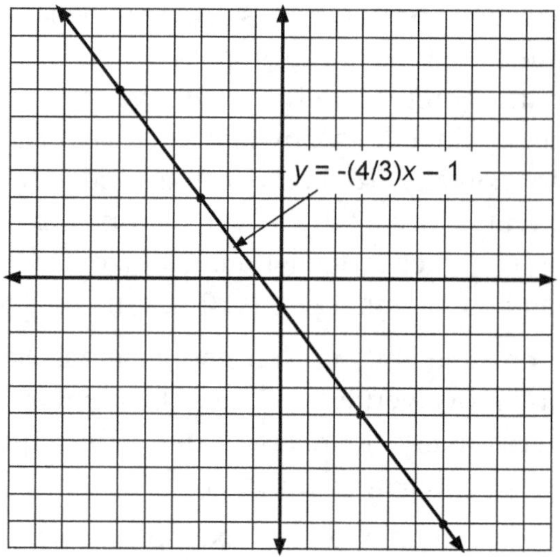

In the following exercises, determine the slope and the y-intercept of the line given the equation of the line. Then graph each line on the grid provided to the right.

Equation	**Slope**	***Y*-intercept**
27. $y = (2/3)x + 4$	$m =$ ___	(0,)
28. $y = -3x - 1$	$m =$ ___	(0,)
29. $y = -(5/3)x + 2$	$m =$ ___	(0,)
30. $y = (1/4)x - 6$	$m =$ ___	(0,)

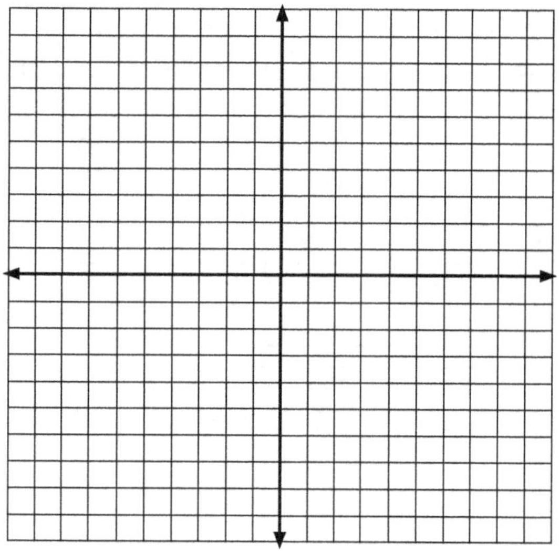

In the following exercises, determine the equation of a line, given the slope and the y-intercept of the line. Then graph each line on the grid provided to the right.

Slope	***Y*-intercept**	**Equation**
31. 3	(0, 2)	$y =$ ____$x +$ ____
32. 1/5	(0, -1)	$y =$ ____$x +$ ____
33. -(5/4)	(0, 3)	$y =$ ____$x +$ ____
34. -(2/7)	(0, -4)	$y =$ ____$x +$ ____

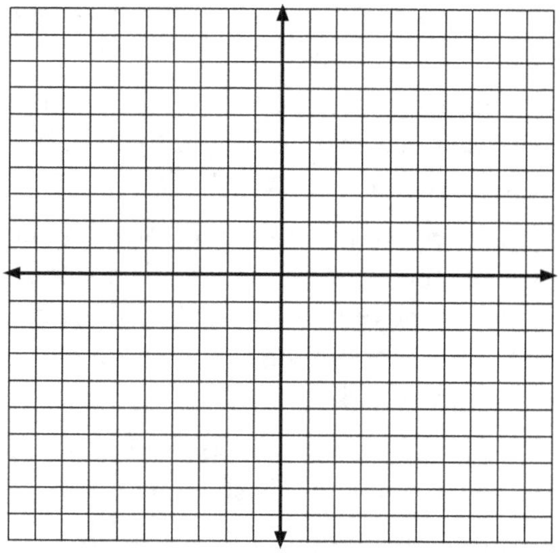

In the following exercises, determine the slope, y-intercept, and equation of a line given the graph of the line.

	Line	Slope	Y-Intercept	Equation
35.	p		(0,)	y =
36.	q		(0,)	y =
37.	r		(0,)	y =
38.	s		(0,)	y =

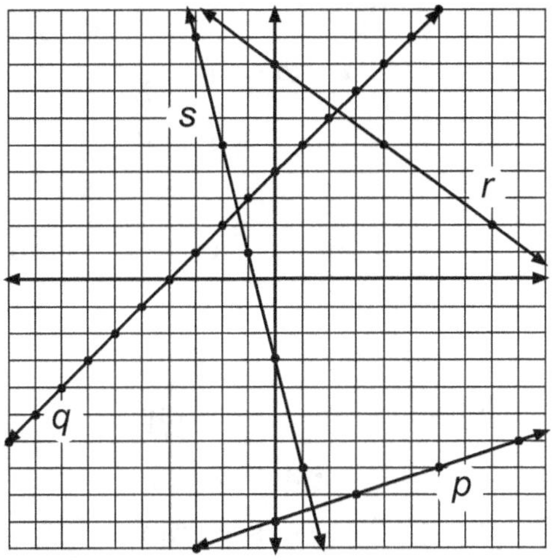

Answers for Appendix 2

Example A

°C	0	5	10	15	20	25	30	35	40
°F	32	41	50	59	68	77	86	95	104

Exercises 1–8

1. $y = 3$ horizontal
2. $x = -5$ vertical
3. $y = 0$ horizontal (x-axis)
4. $x = 0$ vertical (y-axis)
5. $y = 2x + 3$ see graph
6. $y = 4x - 5$ see graph
7. $y = -2x + 1$ see graph
8. $y = -5x - 2$ see graph

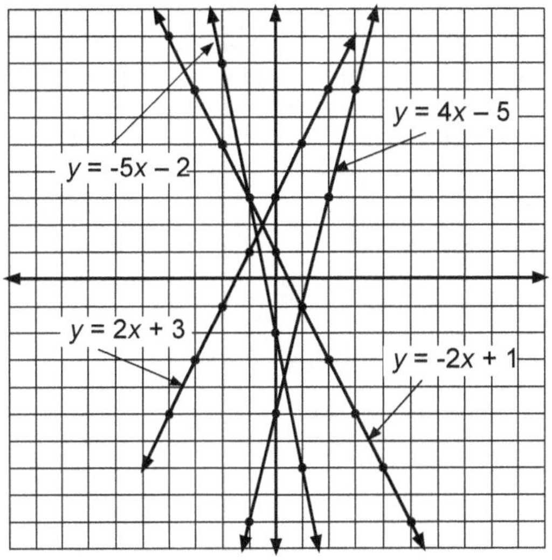

9. $y = (2/3)x + 3$ see graph
10. $y = (3/4)x - 5$ see graph
11. $y = -(2/5)x + 1$ see graph
12. $y = -(1/2)x - 4$ see graph

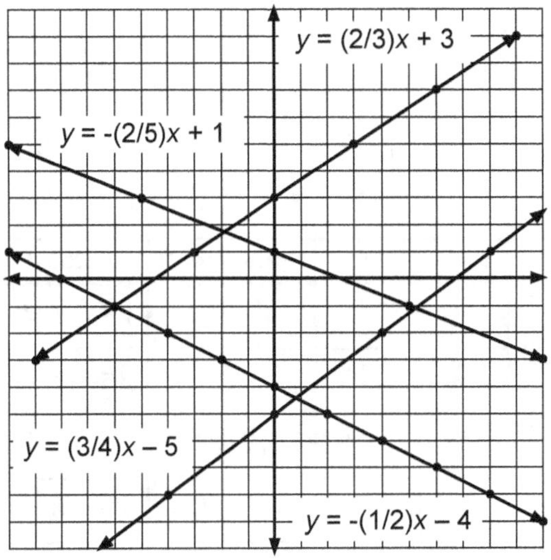

13. $y = (2/3)x + 3$	(0, 3)	14. $y = (3/4)x - 5$	(0, -5)
15. $y = (3/2)x + 4$	(0, 4)	16. $y = -(2/5)x + 1$	(0, 1)
17. $y = -(5/3)x - 2$	(0, -2)	18. $y = (7/3)x$	(0, 0)
19. $y = -3$	(0, -3)	20. $x = 4$	No y-intercept

21. If the equation of a line is $y = mx + b$ then the y-intercept is $(0, b)$.

22. $y = -(2/5)x + 7$, see graph.

23. $y = -(2/5)x + 3$, see graph.

24. $y = -(2/5)x - 2$, see graph.

25. $y = -(2/5)x - 6$, see graph.

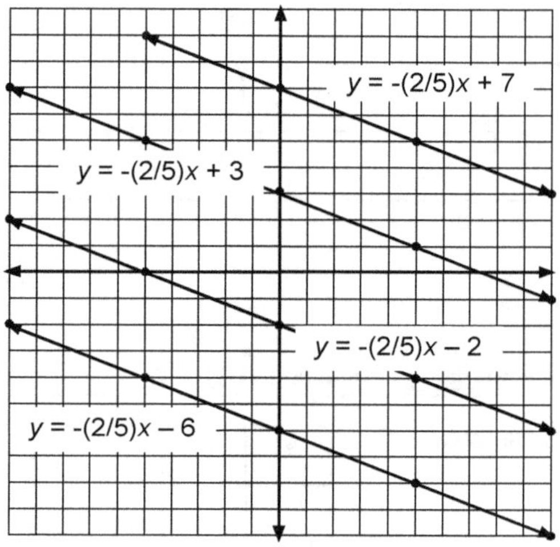

26. If the equation of a line is $y = mx + b$ then the slope of the line is m.

Equation	Slope	Y-intercept
27. $y = (2/3)x + 4$	2/3	(0, 4)
28. $y = -3x - 1$	-3	(0, -1)
29. $y = -(5/3)x + 2$	-5/3	(0, 2)
30. $y = (1/4)x - 6$	1/4	(0, -6)

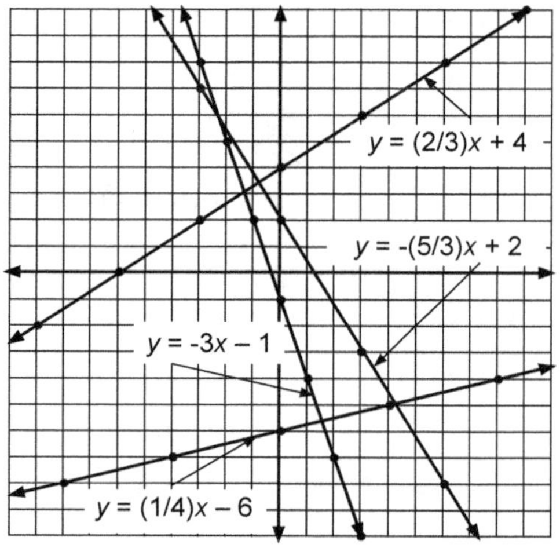

Slope	Y-intercept	Equation
31. 3	(0, 2)	$y = 3x + 2$
32. 1/5	(0, -1)	$y = (1/5)x - 1$
33. -(5/4)	(0, 3)	$y = -(5/4)x + 3$
34. -(2/7)	(0, -4)	$y = -(2/7)x - 4$

	Line	Slope	Y-Intercept	Equation
35.	*p*	*1/3*	**(0, *-9*)**	$y = (1/3)x - 9$
36.	*q*	*1*	**(0, *4*)**	$y = x + 4$
37.	*r*	*-3/4*	**(0, *8*)**	$y = -(3/4)x + 8$
38.	*s*	*-4*	**(0, *-3*)**	$y = -4x - 3$

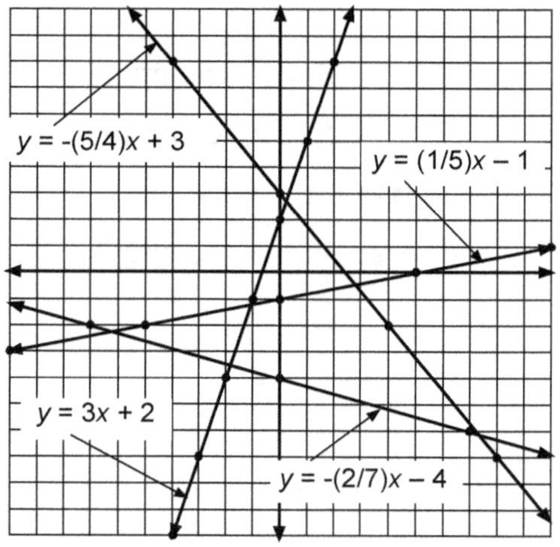

Appendix 3 Building Models for Buried Treasure Games

Building Spherical Buried Treasure Game Equipment

To play spherical buried treasure you will need globes with longitude and latitude lines. In this section we will outline a few approaches to either acquiring or building your spherical buried treasure game set.

Inflatable Earth Globes

An easy, colorful, and fun approach is to purchase inflatable Earth globes. They can be found on the Internet; one supplier is the Oriental Trading Company (www.OrientalTrading.com)[12]. You will need four globes for each game, two for each team. You will also need to find a bowl or lid to serve as a base for the globes.

Light Bulbs

One approach to building your own set of globes for spherical buried treasure is to use permanent markers on white light bulbs. The larger the light bulbs, the easier it is to use them in the game. Here are the steps:

- Carefully sketch the Equator on each bulb with a permanent marker. Let it dry until no ink rubs off.
- Sketch one of the great circles. Starting at the North Pole, draw a line down to the South Pole and around back up to the North Pole. This will be your Prime Meridian (0° Longitude) and the International Date Line (180° Longitude).
- From the intersection of the Prime Meridian and the Equator (0°, 0°), place a mark on the Equator every 15° or 30° depending on how detailed you want your globes to be.
- Do the same along the Prime Meridian and International Date Line.
- Sketch in all latitude and longitude lines.

The photos show different ways to support the light bulbs. You could purchase light sockets or Styrofoam bases (sold at hobby and craft stores) to hold them.

Lenart Spheres

Playing Buried Treasure on a Lenart Sphere is the perfect way to introduce yourself to geometry on a sphere. You can purchase a set of spheres by contacting the inventor, Istvan Lenart, at istvan.lenart@lenartsphere.com. He lives in Hungary but speaks English. You can watch his video and contact him through his website at www.lenartsphere.com.

Building Models for 3-D Coordinate Systems

To play 3-D Buried Treasure it is helpful to have models available to practice visualizing points located in three dimensions. The first step would be to turn your room or classroom into a 3-D coordinate system. Use two adjacent walls and the floor to represent the *xy*-, *xz*-, and *yz*-planes. You might also hang objects by string from the ceiling and practice identifying their coordinates. In this section we will outline a few approaches to either acquiring or building 3-D coordinate systems.

Purchase Three-Dimensional Systems

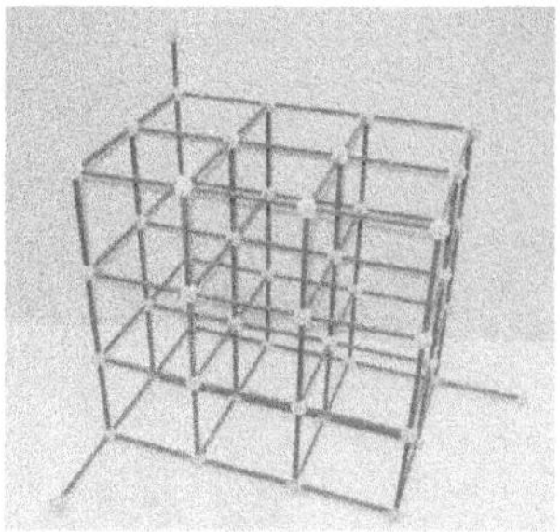

You could use a large Tinkertoy™ set to build a 3-D coordinate system. Another wonderful set for creating geometric solids is the structural system called Zometool™. A 3-D coordinate system built from Zometool™ struts is shown to the right.

Build Three Intersecting Planes

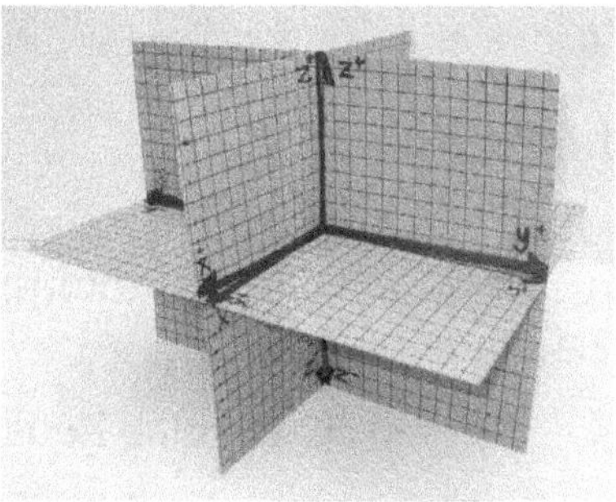

You can build a 3-D coordinate system using cardboard or heavy stock paper. First draw a square grid on both sides of three squares of heavy stock paper. On one square grid cut slits halfway. On the second square, cut one slit halfway as shown, then cut two slits at right angles, one-fourth of the way, as shown in the diagram below. Slide the two square grids together to create two planes intersecting (for example, the *xy*-plane and the *xz*-plane). Next, cut the third square (the *yz*-plane) in half and cut slits halfway into each piece. Slide the two pieces onto the first two intersecting planes and secure them with tape. You have now created a model of three planes intersecting at right angles. Use hat pins with large round ends to represent points in space.

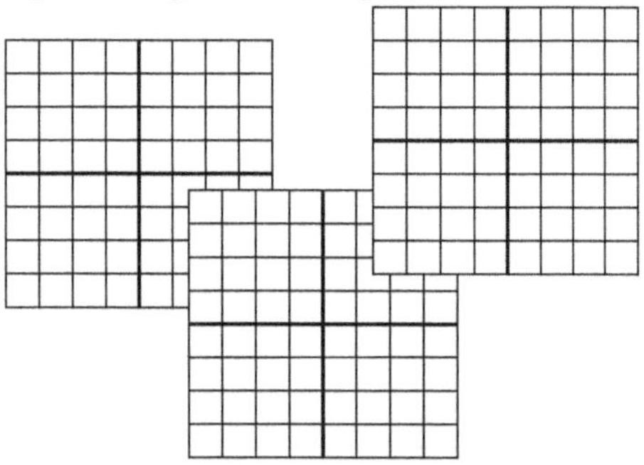

Three square grids

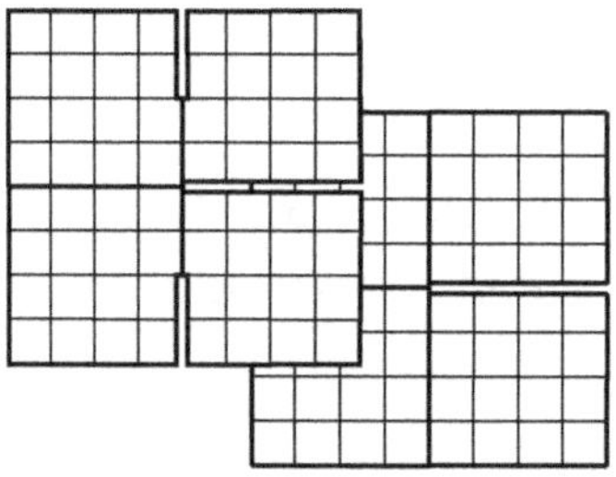

Add slits on two

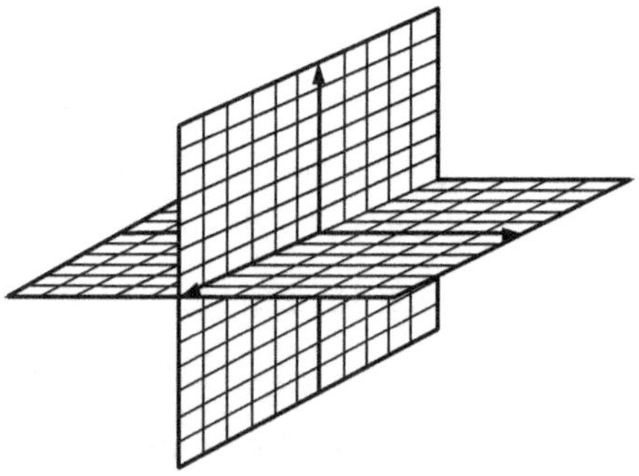

Slide squares together

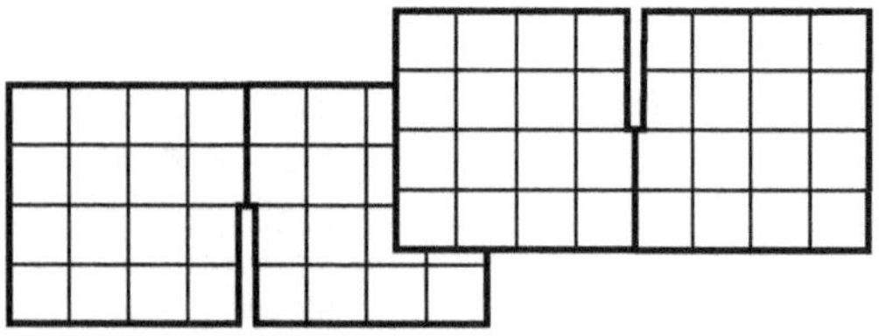

Cut third square in half and cut slits

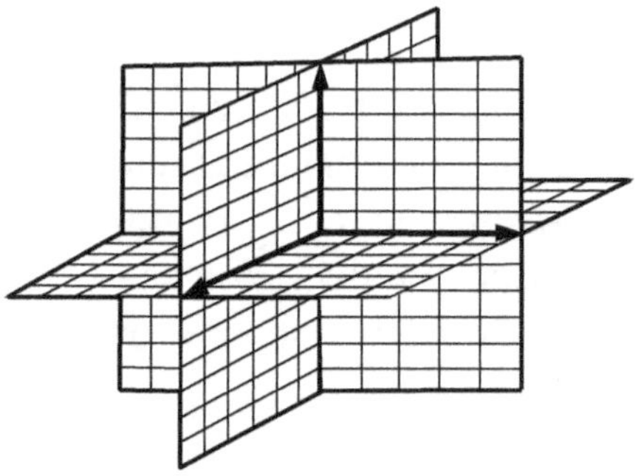

Assemble

Appendix 4 Hints to Exercises and Puzzles

Hints Chapter 1

1.3

Pentomino Puzzle 1

The pentominoes can be named by the letters *T, U, V, W, X, Y, Z*, and *F, L, I, P, N*. Most are fairly obvious but the *N* is very difficult to see. Here are five of them:

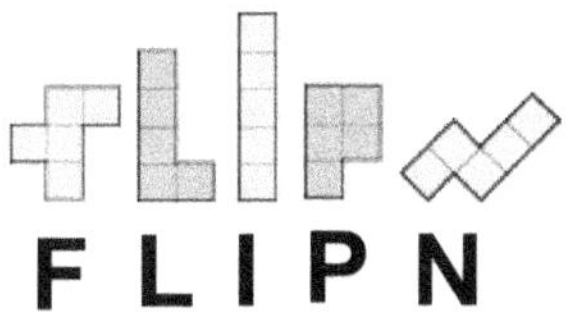

Pentomino Puzzle 2

A design has **reflectional symmetry** if you can fold it along a line of symmetry so that all the points on one side of the line exactly coincide with all the points on the other side of the line. The *U*-pentomino has one line of reflectional symmetry and the *X*-pentomino has four lines of reflectional symmetry.

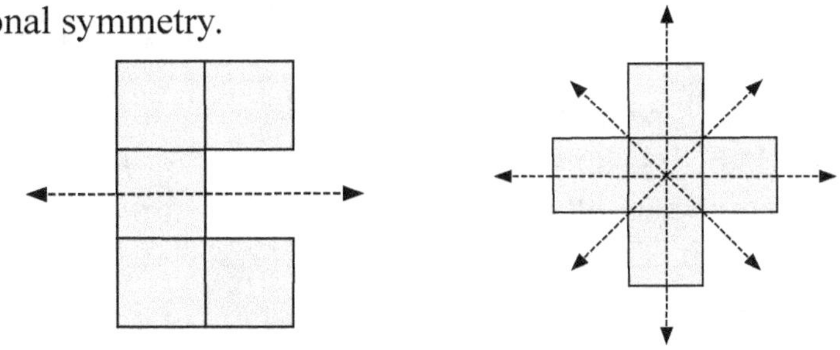

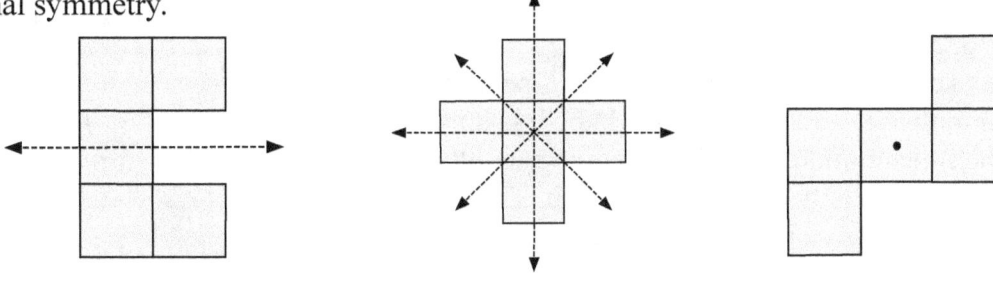

A design has **rotational symmetry** if it looks the same after you turn it around a point by less than a full circle. The number of times that the design looks the same as you turn it through a complete 360° circle determines the type of rotational symmetry. The *Z*-pentomino has one rotational symmetry of 180° and the *X*-pentomino has 90°, 180°, and 270° rotational symmetries.

Below left is an example of the eight orientations of the *P*-pentomino arranged into a pattern with 180° rotational symmetry. Below center is an example of the eight orientations of the *F*-pentomino arranged into a pattern with 90°, 180°, and 270° rotational symmetries. Below right is an example of the eight orientations of the *Y*-pentomino arranged into a pattern with one reflectional symmetry.

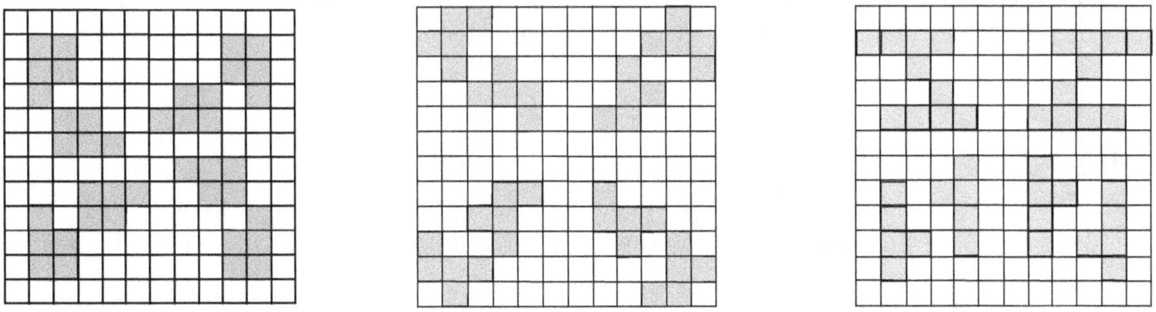

Pentomino Puzzle 3

Of the *F, L, I, P*, and *N* pentominoes, just the *F, L*, and *N* pentominoes will fold into a box without a lid. Five more will fold into a box without a lid.

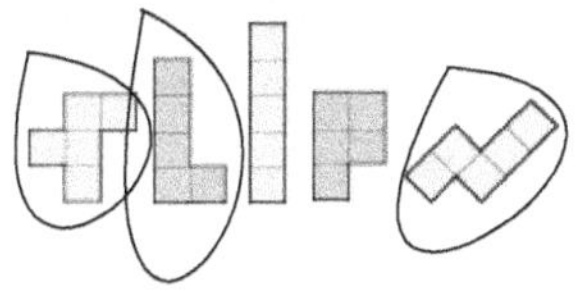

Pentomino Puzzle 4

Many possibilities. Here is one using the *P*-pentomino four times (at right).

Pentomino Puzzle 5

Many possibilities. Here is one using the *U-, Y-, L-, I-*, and *P*-pentominoes (above right).

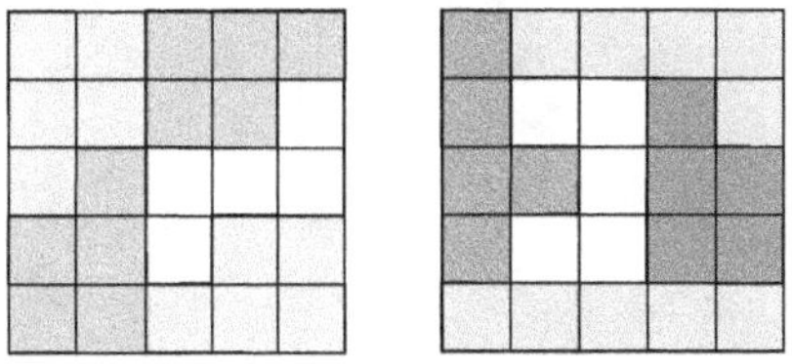

Pentomino Puzzle 6

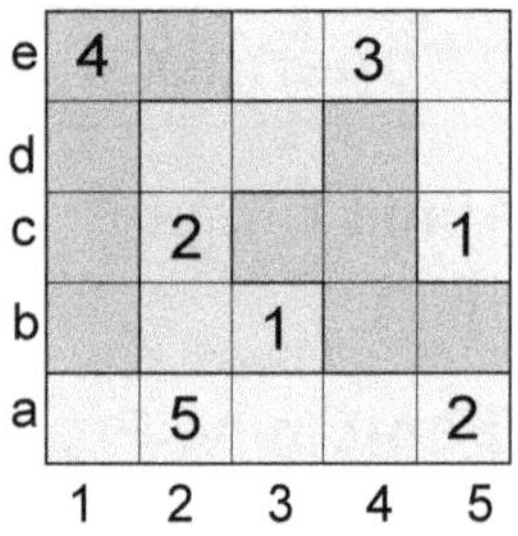

Since there is a *3* and a *4* in row e and a *1* and a *2* in column 5, then there must be a *5* in square e5.

Now there is a *3*, *4*, and *5* in row e and a *1* in column 3. So there must be a *2* in square e3.

Now there is a *2*, *3*, *5*, and *1* in the *V*-pentomino region. So there must be a *4* in square d5.

Pentomino Puzzle 10

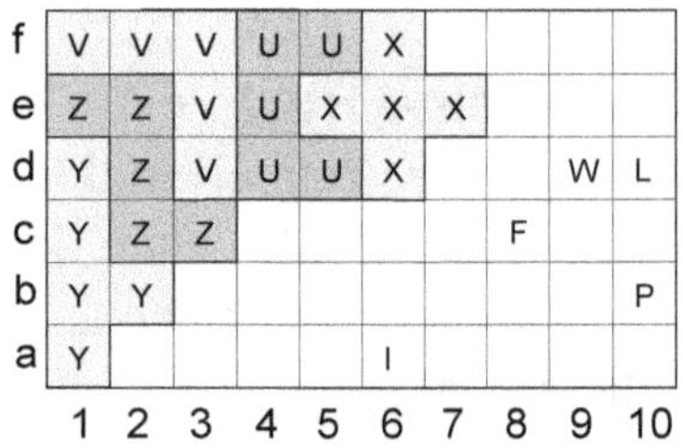

The location of the given L forces the three other L's in squares c10, e10, and f10. There is only one posibility for the remaining squares of the W: f7, f8, e8, and e9. This forces the final square of the L:f9. There must be a P in squares b9, a9, and a10.

Pentomino Puzzle 11

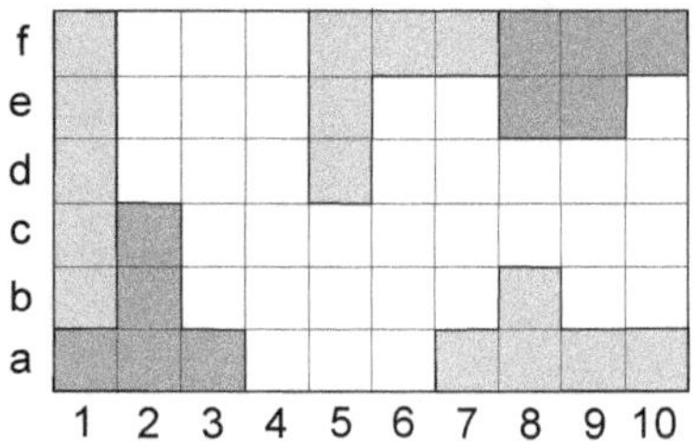

The only piece that will fit into space e10 is the *L*-pentomino. Since the *P*-pentomino is already positioned, there is only one way to place the *L*-pentomino. The *X*-pentomino cannot touch the perimeter, so there is only one place left for it. This forces the *U*-pentomino. There is only one pentomino remaining that will cover squares c9–d9.

Pentomino Puzzle 12

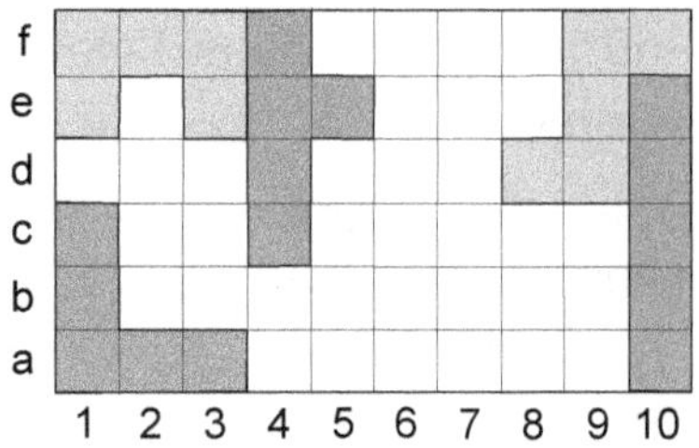

Only the *X*- and *F*- pentominoes will cover square d2. If you try covering the square d2 with the *F*-pentomino, there is no pentomino left to cover the b2 and c2 squares that can reach the perimeter. Therefore the *X*-pentomino and *F*-pentomino are forced. There is only one remaining pentomino that can cover square d5 and still reach the rectangle's perimeter. Of the remaining pentominoes, only one can cover square f5. This leaves only one pentomino to cover f8. Only one pentomino remains that can cover square c6.

1.4

Hexomino Puzzle 1

There are 35 hexominoes. One with a longest chain of six squares, three with a longest chain of five squares, 13 with a longest chain of four squares, 17 with a longest chain of three squares, and one with a longest chain of two squares.

Hexomino Puzzle 2

There are more than nine but less than 13 hexominoes that will fold into a box. Three are shown below.

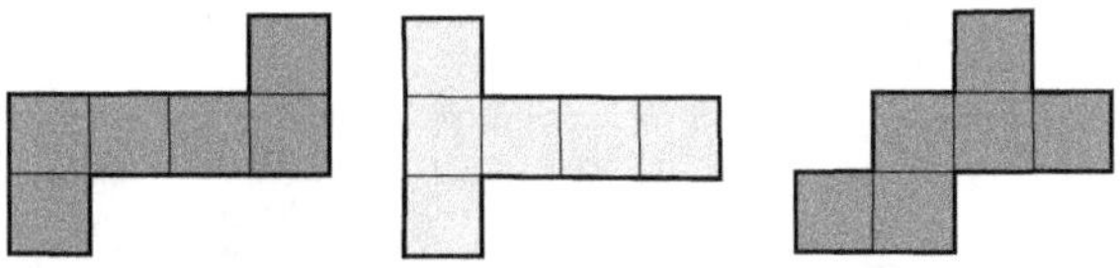

Hexomino Puzzle 3

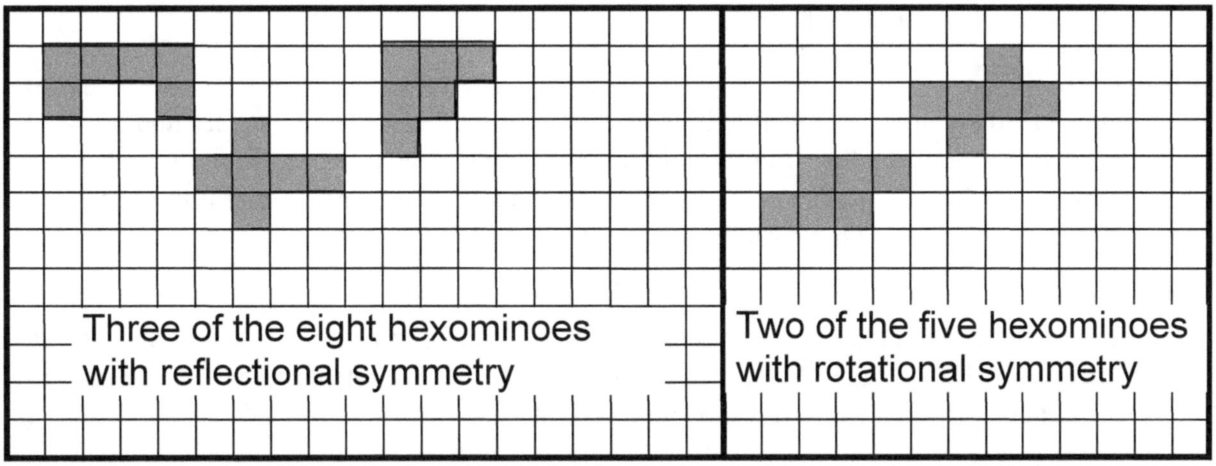

Hexomino Puzzle 4

Three of the seven hexominoes with a perimeter of 12.

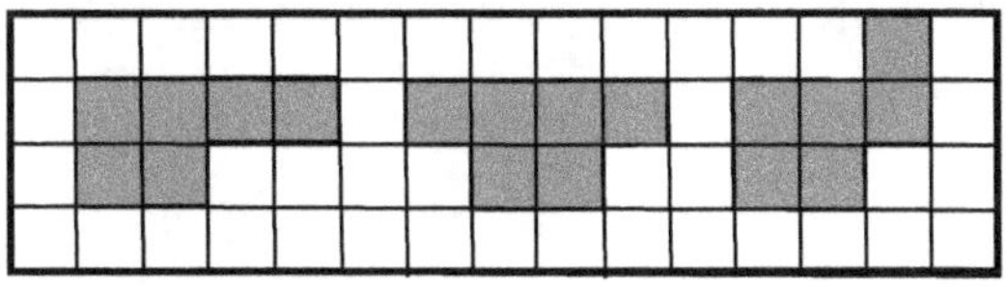

Hexomino Puzzle 5

Here is one example.

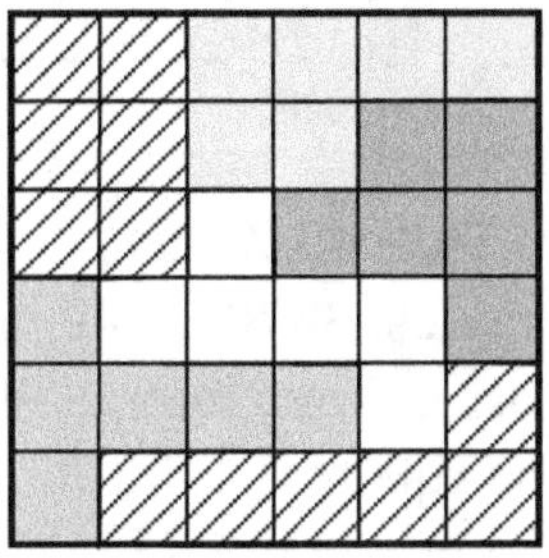

Hexomino Puzzle 6

There is a 1 in row c and column 3, so there must be a 1 in square b6. Since there is a 2 in square f2, then there must be a 2 in square b1. Since there is a 3 in square a1, then there must be a 3 in square f3.

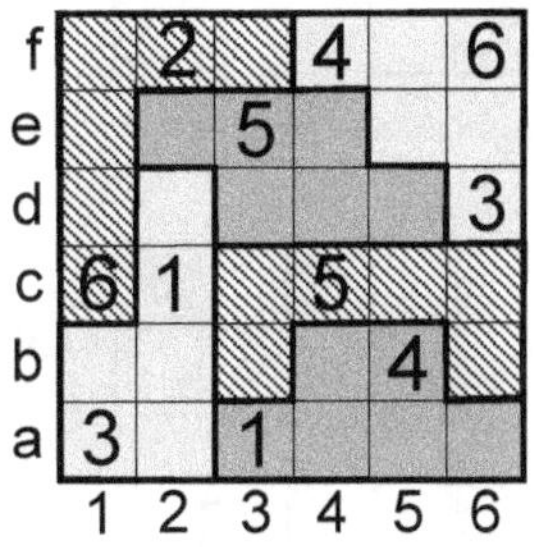

1.5

Polyomino Puzzle 1

One of the possible five is shown to the right.

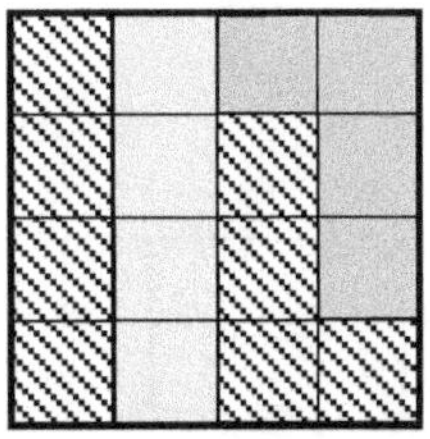

Polyomino Puzzle 2

There is only one 2-rectifiable pentomino. There are four 2-rectifiable hexominoes. One is shown to the right.

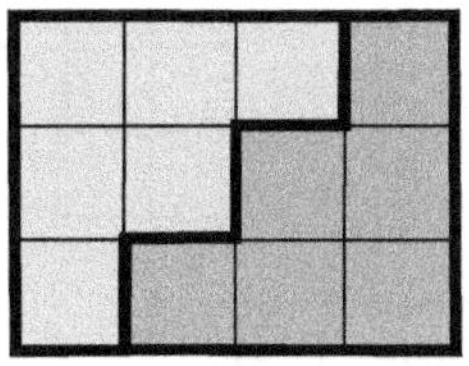

Polyomino Puzzle 4

There are ten possible deficient 8×8 boards.

Polyomino Puzzle 5

The alternating shaded squares are a visible hint. If each domino has a shaded square and an unshaded square, how many shaded squares and how many unshaded squares are there with 31 dominoes? How many shaded squares and how many unshaded squares are there on the chessboard with one pair of opposite corners removed?

Polyomino Puzzle 6

If you tile the 4×5 and 2×10 rectangles with alternating color squares you get an equal number of each color (below left). If you color the alternating squares of the five tetrominoes, do you get an equal number of each color in each tetromino (below right)?

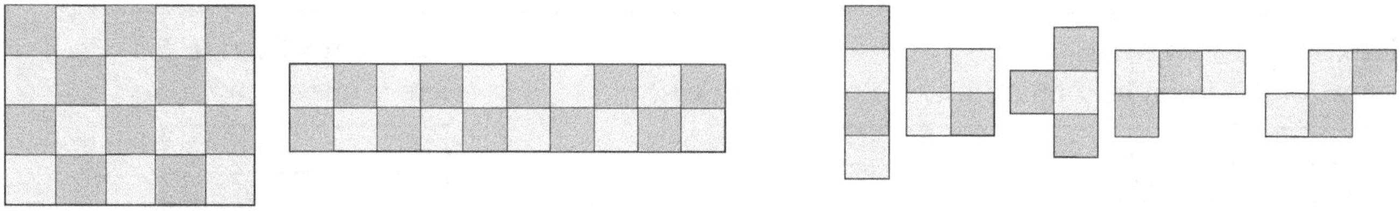

Polyomino Puzzle 7

All the rectangles: 3×70, 5×42, 6×35, 7×30, 10×21, and 14×15 have an even number of squares. If the squares are colored alternately there will always be 105 squares of each color (an odd number). If you shade the squares of the 35 hexominoes with alternating colors can you get 105 squares of each color? The 35 hexominoes are shown below with some of them shaded to get you started.

1.6

Domino Puzzle 1

Only one possibility for the (1,1), (2,2) and (3,3).

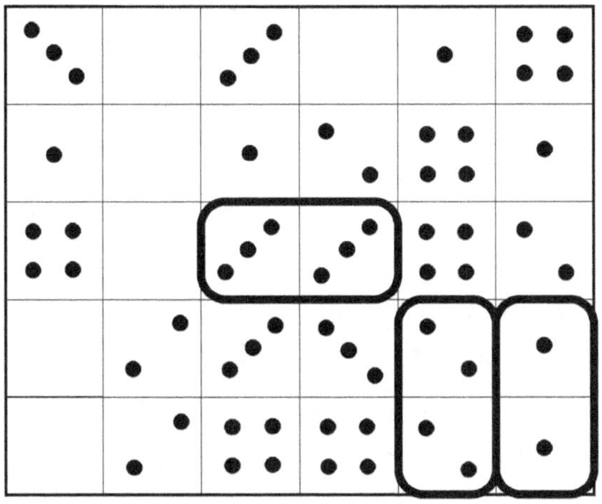

Domino Puzzle 3

Only one possibility for the (0,0), (2,2) and (3,3).

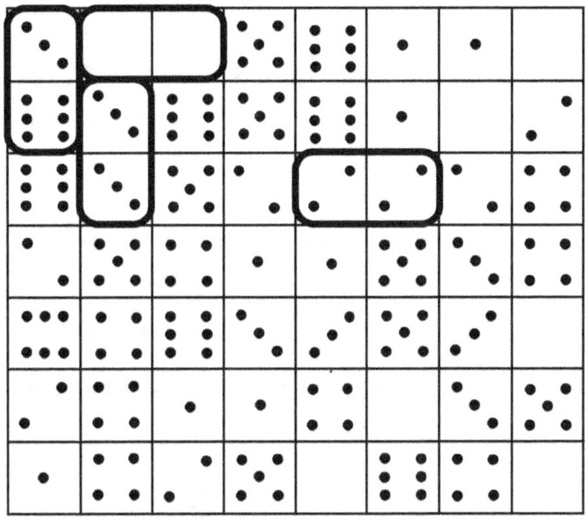

Domino Puzzle 5

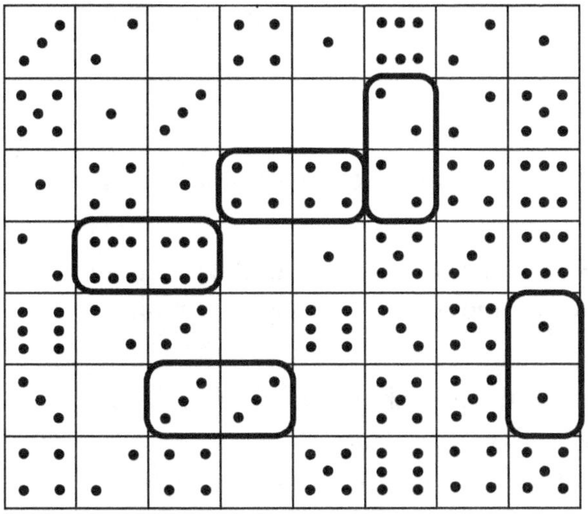

Domino Puzzle 7

0	5	6	2	5	4	5	0
0	1	1	4	0	2	3	2
6	4	2	2	3	6	1	4
3	1	0	3	3	4	5	0
4	6	1	4	1	4	3	1
3	0	3	5	6	5	5	6
6	2	1	2	5	2	0	6

Domino Puzzle 9

4	1	5	4	2	2	1	5
0	3	1	3	6	4	0	6
0	6	0	6	3	0	5	2
2	4	5	5	3	2	4	1
6	5	0	2	5	3	5	4
1	3	2	1	6	1	2	4
3	6	6	3	0	1	4	0

Domino Puzzle 11

2	4	6	6	3	5	6	0
2	3	1	0	6	5	4	2
1	1	3	0	4	1	4	2
0	2	5	4	0	6	3	3
3	1	2	1	4	6	1	6
6	5	5	5	0	3	2	2
4	5	0	0	4	3	1	5

Hints Chapter 2

2.1

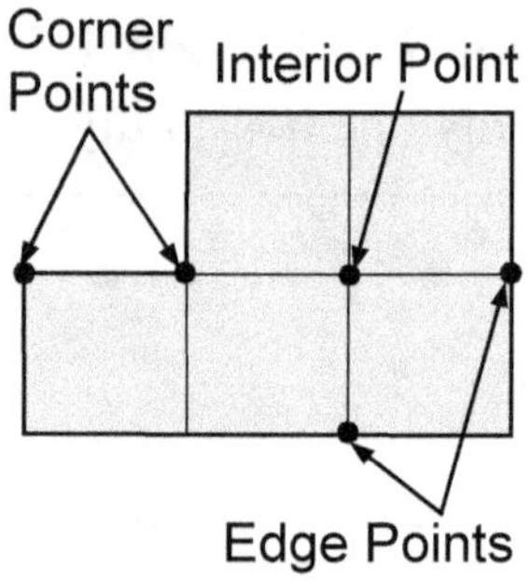

22. The *P*-pentomino is the only pentomino with an interior point.

24. The two X's tell you that there is nothing below 2 and nothing above 5. The two E's and the distance the C's are apart from each other tell you that the edge through the two E's is vertical.

2.4

16. *IJKL* is a square since all the sides and all the angles are the same.

25. Since *ABCD* is a square it is also a parallelogram. Thus the slope of $\overline{CD}$ is the same as the slope of $\overline{AB}$. The slope of $\overline{AB}$ is "down 4 and left 2" or -4/-2. From point *C* go down 4 and left 2.

31. The point (1,-1) translates to the point (-3, 2). The point (4,-4) translates to the point (0, -1).

33. The point (1,-1) reflects to the point (-1, -1). The point (4,-3) reflects to the point (-4, -3).

35. The point (1,-1) reflects to the point (1, 1). The point (3,-4) reflects to the point (3, 4).

37. A piece of tracing paper is helpful with rotations. The point (0,-1) rotates to the point (-1, 0).

38. A piece of tracing paper is helpful with rotations. The point (0,-1) rotates to the point (0, 1).

2.9

BTP 7. First eliminate the zero column and the zero row. A good first attempt would be to try putting three squares in a row for the row with a 3, and three squares next to each other for the column with a 3.

BTP 10. The zero row divides the 6×6 grid into two regions. The bottom region, the two bottom rows, contains eight tetromino squares or two tetrominoes. The top region contains four tetromino squares or one tetromino.

BTP 11. When the "zero" rows and columns are eliminated, the grid shows the four regions containing each of the four tetrominoes. The two "five" columns can be completely filled in with tetromino squares. This reveals how the tetromino pairs are reflected. See below left.

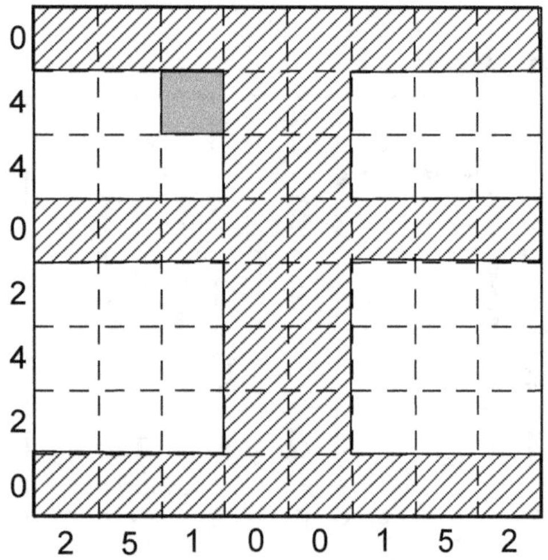

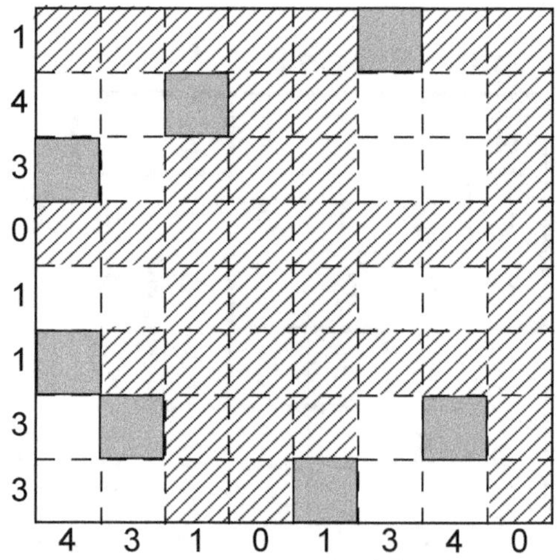

BTP 13. First eliminate the "zero" rows and columns. Then eliminate the remainder of the two "one" rows and the remainder of the two "one" columns. See above right.

BTP 15. First eliminate the "zero" row and the two zero columns. There must be one tetromino in the upper left region, one tetromino in the lower left region, one tetromino in the lower right region, and therefore two tetrominoes in the upper right region since no two tetrominoes may touch. See below left.

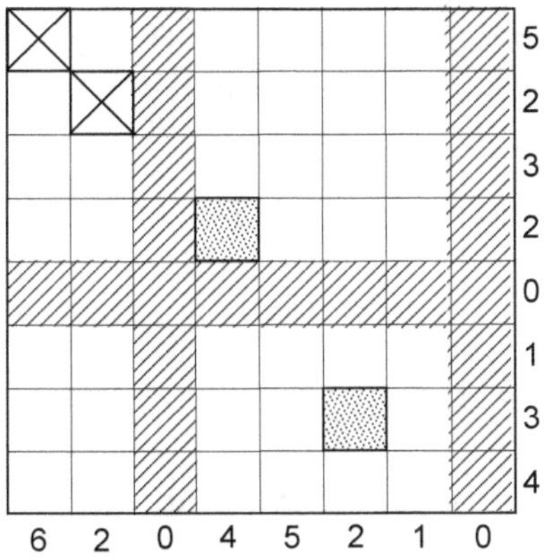

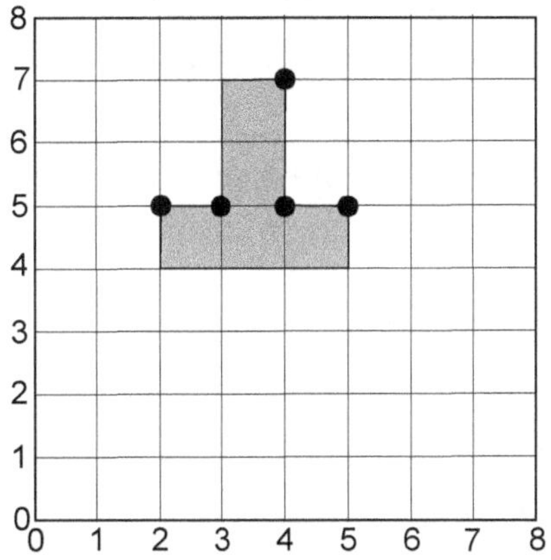

BTP 19. Here is one possible pentomino. There are at least five possible from the given points. See above right.

BTP 23. Begin by eliminating the four squares about each point labeled X. There is only one pentomino with an interior point. See below left.

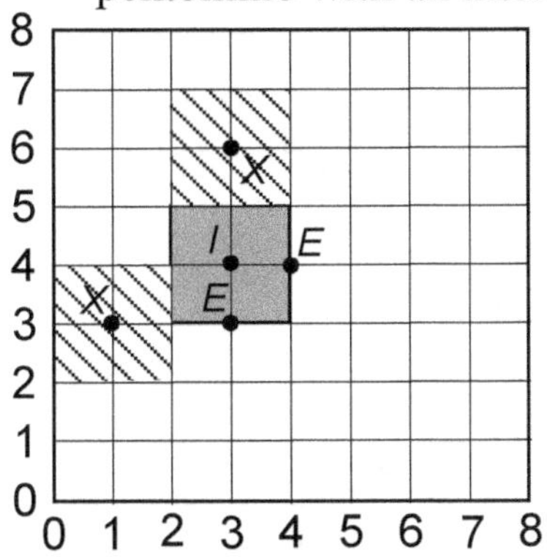

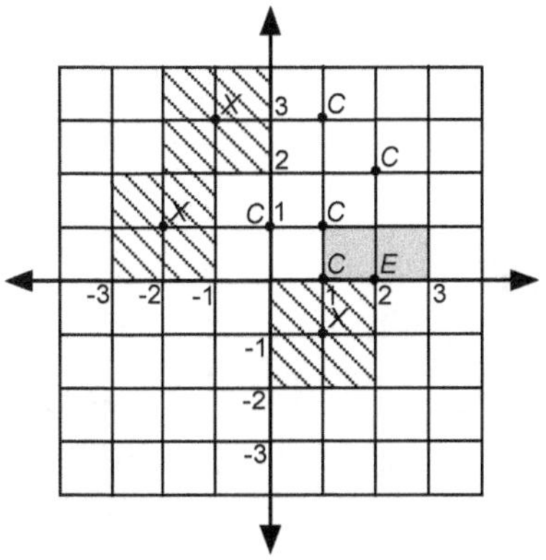

BTP 31. Begin by eliminating the four squares about each point labeled X. The point labeled E, an edge point, must indicate a horizontal edge otherwise you could never reach both the C at (0, 1) and the C at (1, 3). See above right.

BTP 35. Because of the two F's, the position of the V-pentomino is forced. The two squares beneath the given T must also contain T's. This forces the position of the X-pentomino. This forces the position of the U-pentomino. This forces the rest of the T-pentomino...

V	V	V							Y
V	F							Y	
V	X	F	Z	Z	L	L	L		
X	X	X	T	N	N	N	W		
U	X	U	T	T	T			W	
U	U	U	T						W

2.10

2. **Barbossa Island** The coordinates for A and B: $A(11,9)$ and $B(5, -1)$
3. **Isla Sirena** See right

c	i										
d	e	a									
t	r	i									
d	o	d	e								
i	n	t									

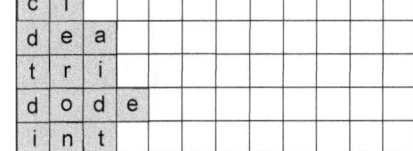

4. **Blackbeard Island** The equations for A and B: $A{:}y = (2/3)x + 5$ and $B{:}y = -4x + 9$.
6. **Skeleton Key** The beginning of the solution to the 5×8 grid: "Place the origin ..."

7. **Doubloon Island** The beginning of the solution to the 4×9 grid: "The origin is located at ..."
8. **Skull Island** The beginning of the solution to the network grid: "The origin is located" ... .
9. **Demon Island** A partial list of words that can be found in the 10×10 grid: *algebra*, *domain*, *locus*, *math*, *zero*, *prime*, *symmetry*, *multiply*, *coordinate*, *algorithm*, *parallel*, *geometry*, *axis*, *two*, *ray*, *logic*, and *cosine*. You might wish to check the meaning of *orthocenter* in Chapter 6.
10. **Isla Tortuga** A partial list of words that can be found in the six word puzzles (but not in any order): *beauty*, *cake*, *life*, and *love*. You might wish to check the meaning of *circumcenter* in Chapter 6.

Hints Chapter 3

3.6

PBTP 1

The *I* is the big clue.

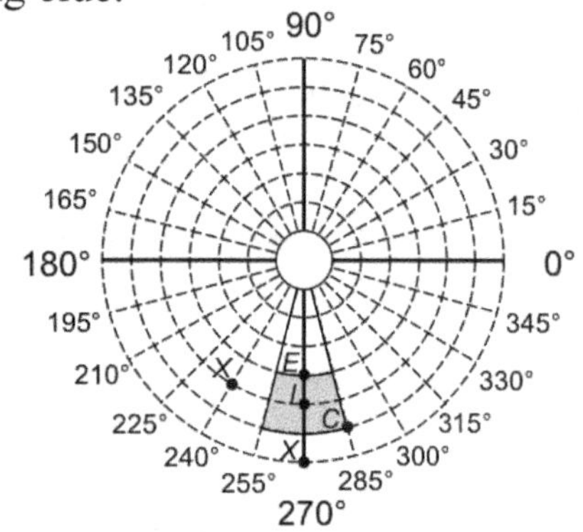

PBTP 3

First, eliminate where it can't be.

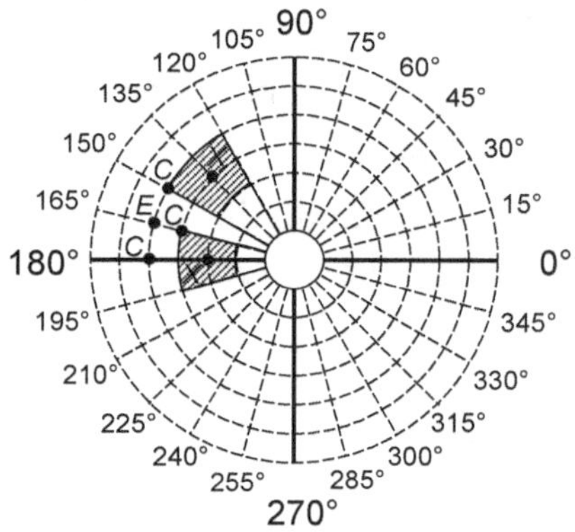

PBTP 5

First, eliminate where they can't be and where the square tetromino must be.

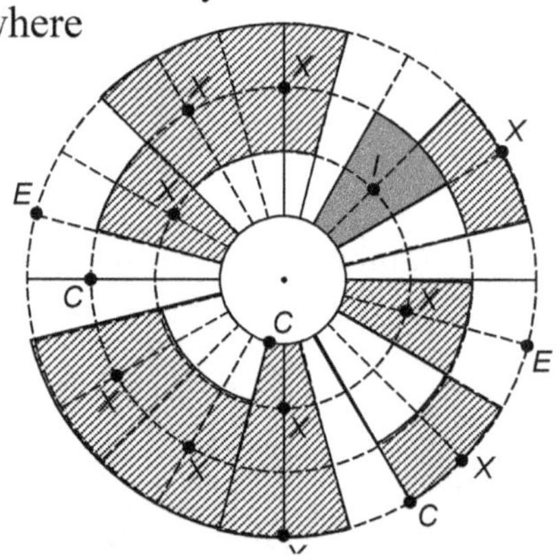

PBTP 7

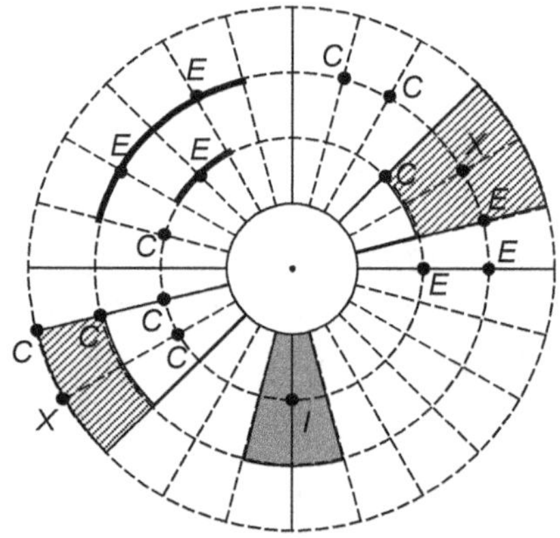

PBTP 9

Since no two may touch you can eliminate regions.

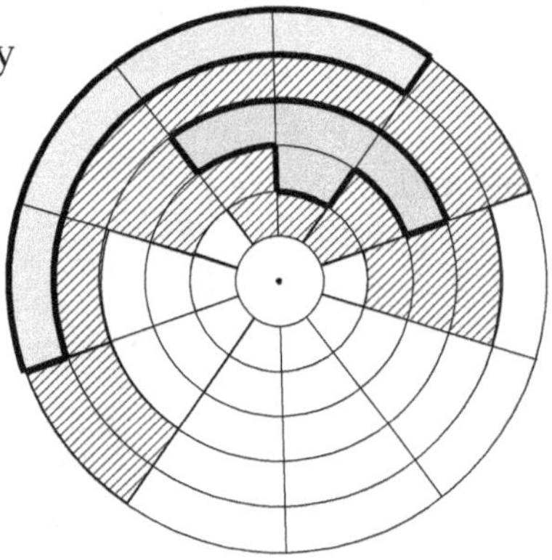

PBTP 12

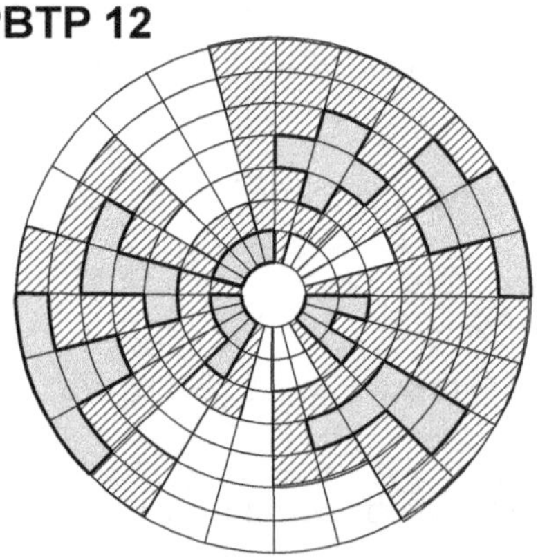

PBTP 14

The *I* and *L* pentominoes are forced.

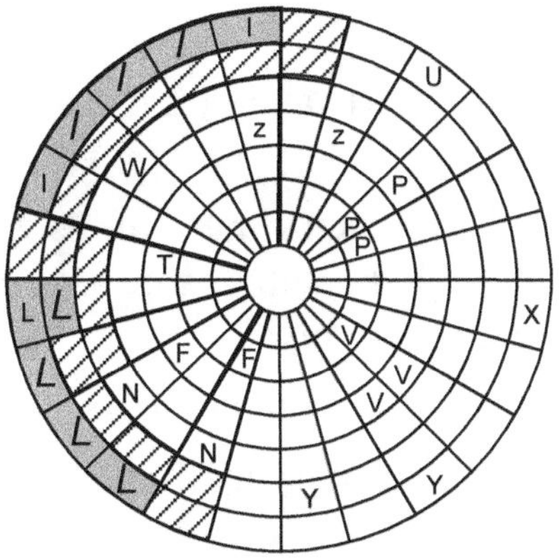

PBTP 18

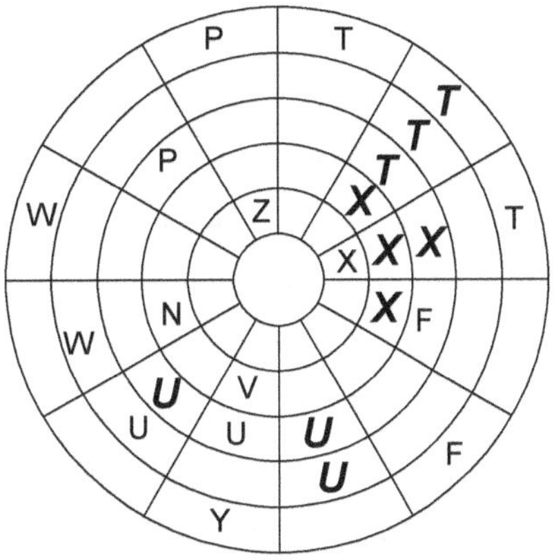

PBTP 22

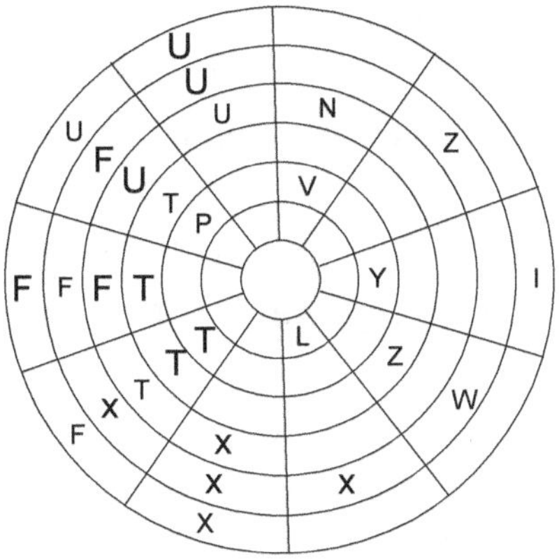

3.7

2. **Rum Reef Key** The pirate term *gangplank* can be found in row two: "... g p l ...". The pirate term *Man-o-war* can be found in the bottom row: "... - o - w a r ...". Therefore the *L*-pentomino goes in the lower left corner. The *N*-pentomino goes in the upper left corner and the *T*-pentomino goes to the right of it so that the "g a n" begins to spell *gangplank.*
3. **Scallywag Island** The first line in the 4×15 grid says: *matey start yer.*
4. **Doubloon Island** The first line in the 3×20 grid says: *treasure hunt begins.*
5. **Shipwreck Island** Start reading letters on diagonals from the lower right corner: T...H...E....
6. **Albatross Island** The first one is: CAT WALK and WALK THE PLANK.
7. **Isla Plata** The first three words in the 7×6 grid are: *your starting point.*
8. **Isla de Oro** The first two words in the network are: *start at.*
9. **Isla de los Muerto** Superman's "real name" on Earth (not his name Kal-El from his home planet Krypton) is Clark Kent. A young orphan decides to call himself Simon Templar and when he grows up becomes "The Saint."
10. **Isla de Sangria** You should be able to find all the answers for a–g via an internet search. For example, Bilbo Baggins and Frodo Baggins were both born on September 22, which has been proclaimed by the American Tolkien Society as Hobbit Day.

Hints Chapter 4

4.1

7. The fraction is the number of degrees between Ingleside Ontario and Point X divided by the number of degrees in a complete circle, 360°.

14. Moghal emperor Shah Jahan had this structure built to honor the memory of his wife, Mumtaz Jahal. This famous building was described by the poet Rabindranath Tagore as "*rising above the banks of the river like a solitary tear suspended on the cheek of time.*"

15. Fallingwater by Frank Lloyd Wright. An anagram for the nearest major city is *sturb pight.*

16. The Doge's Palace was the seat of power for this 13th–15th century maritime empire. An anagram for this city is *cenive.*

18. The Moorish rulers of the Emirate of Granada built this Islamic palace. The palace is a UNESCO World Heritage Site. An anagram for this city and country is *nada paris nag.*

19. This temple complex was built for a king in the early 12th century. An anagram for this site is *wang karot.*

20. Danish architect Jorn Utzon designed this Opera House. It won him the Pritzker Prize, architecture's highest honor. The Opera House is a UNESCO World Heritage Site. An anagram for this city and country is *trendy sausilyas.*

22. **Euclid (ca 322–275 BC)**
Euclid founded the school of mathematics at the great university in Alexandria. He was the first to prove that there are infinitely many prime numbers and he proved there are only five Platonic solids. One of his most important contributions was his recognition that the Parallel Postulate must be an axiom rather than a theorem. His math textbook, *Elements*, introduced the notions of axiom and theorem and has been used as a textbook for more than 2000 years.

23. **Archimedes (287–212 BC)**
Archimedes of Syracusa made advances in number theory, algebra, analysis, and especially geometry. He was the first to prove Heron's formula for the area of a triangle. It is reported by some historians that he visited Egypt and while there, invented a device now known as Archimedes' Screw. According to legend, during the invasion of his city by the Romans, Archimedes was so engrossed in the study of a geometric figure in the sand that he failed to respond to the questioning of a Roman soldier and the soldier killed him.

24. **Sofia Kovalevskaya (1850–1891)**
As a young Russian woman Sofia Kovalevskaya wanted to pursue studies under Karl Weierstrass. He agreed to privately tutoring her because the university did not permit women to attend. Sofia earned a Ph.D. and eventually became the first woman appointed to a full professorship in Northern Europe. Kovalevskaya once wrote "It is impossible to be a mathematician without being a poet in soul." Many of her scientific papers were groundbreaking including the important Cauchy-Kovalevskaya Theorem.

25. **Omar Khayyám (1048–1123)**
Omar Khayyám was born under Turkish rule in Nishapur in the northeastern province of Persia. The name "Khayyám" means, "tent maker." Today, Omar Khayyám is most famous for his rich poetry, the *Rubaiyat*. Perhaps his most famous line is: A Jug of Wine, a Loaf of Bread--and Thou. As a mathematician, Khayyám developed an alternate to Euclid's Parallel Postulate and then derived the parallel result using theorems based on the Khayyám-Saccheri quadrilateral.

26. **Girolamo Cardano (1501–1576)**
Girolamo Cardano studied medicine at the University of Pavia. Cardano was a physician, a gambler (he wrote a book on probability), a chess player, and an inventor. He invented a ciphering tool, the combination lock, the Cardan shaft, and helped develop the camera obscura. In mathematics, he was first to publish general solutions to cubic and quartic equations, and first to publish the use of complex numbers in calculations. Near the end of his life he moved to Rome under the patronage of Pope Gregory XIII.

27 **Sophie Germain (1776–1831)**
Sophie Germain began teaching herself mathematics using her father's books. Her parents felt that her interest in mathematics was inappropriate for a Parisian woman and did all that they could to discourage her. She attempted to hide her mathematical inquiries by studying at night. To prevent her late night studies her parents deprived her of heat and light during the night and took her clothes from her once she was in bed. Sophie Germain did first-class work in number theory. She provided a major step towards the proof of Fermat's Last Theorem by proving that if x, y, and z are integers and if $x^5 + y^5 = z^5$ then either x, y, or z must be divisible by 5.

28. **George Boole (1815–1864)**
Despite having no formal training, George Boole became one of the most respected mathematicians in England of that time. He studied Augustus de Morgan's work on symbolic logic and eventually de Morgan claimed that Boole had surpassed him in this branch of mathematics. Professor de Morgan invited Boole to study mathematics at his university but Boole couldn't afford to attend—so he was appointed a professorship instead! It is Boole's work in Boolean algebra and symbolic logic for which he is best known. This work became the foundation for the development of computer languages. Bertrand Russell spoke of Boole as the "discoverer of pure mathematics."

29. **Srinivasa Ramanujan (1887–1920)**
Born to a poor Brahmin family, Ramanujan demonstrated mathematical talent as a youngster. By the time he was 12 he was discovering theorems of his own, including independently re-discovering Euler's Identity ($e^{i\pi} + 1 = 0$). Although he had a short lifespan of 33 years, he produced 4,000 theorems or conjectures in number theory, algebra, and combinatorics. It is believed many of the proofs of Ramanujan's theorems may not have been recorded (because of poverty he used chalk and erasable slate rather than paper). Despite these limitations, Ramanujan is considered by many math historians to be among the great mathematicians of all time. Today some mathematicians achieve fame just by finding a new proof for one of Ramanujan's many results.

4.4

SBTP 1
Not in the shaded regions.

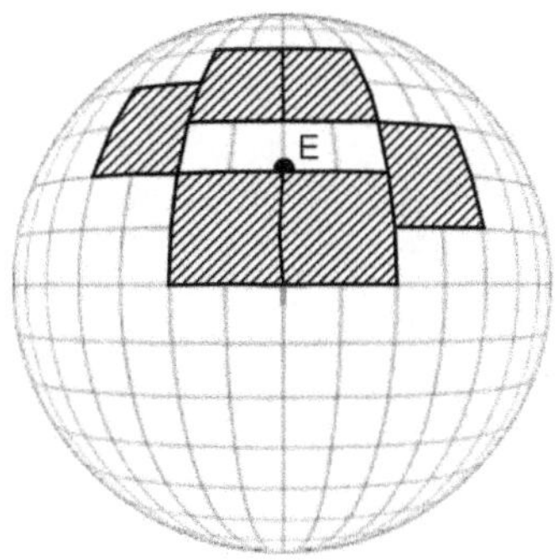

SBTP 7
Not in the shaded regions.

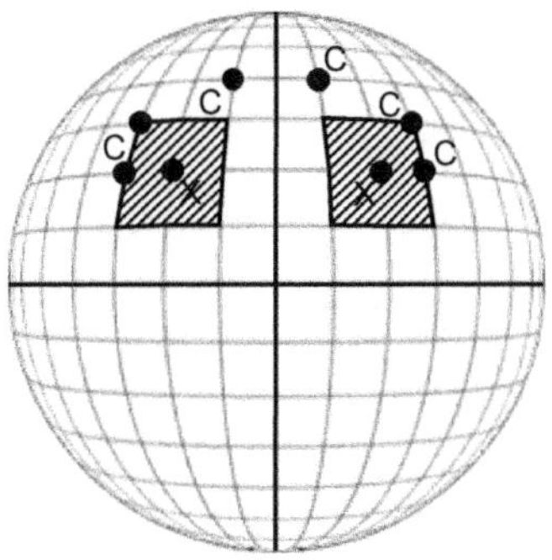

Hints Chapter 5

5.1

1. Point A is the origin (0, 0, 0).
9. Since $S(2, 3, 1)$ then the x- coordinate and z- coordinate are the same, you go back 8 units in the y direction for the y- coordinate. Therefore $P(2, -5, 1)$.
15. (1, 0, 3) is in the xz-plane.
21. Here are six of the eight: (2, 2, 0), (2, 2, 2), (2, 1, 0), (2, 1, 2), (1, 2, 0), and (1, 2, 2).
24. To the right are the locations for points A, B, C, and D. We leave E for you to locate.

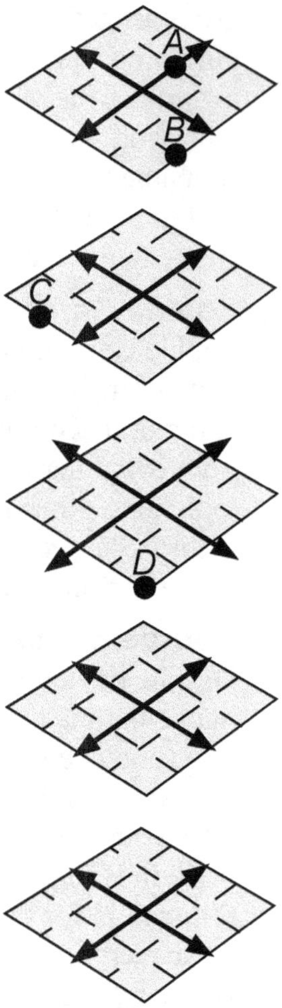

5.2

3.

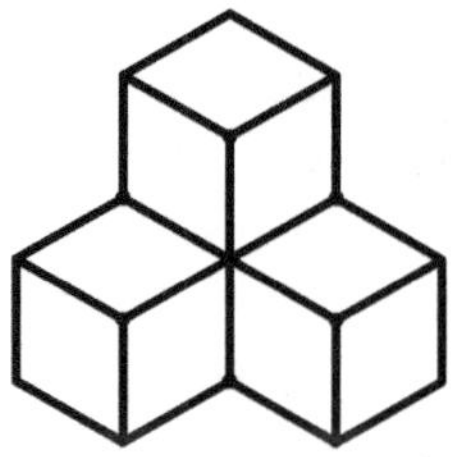

5.6

3-DBTP 1. The slices are shown to the right. The task remaining for you is to sketch the 3-D tromino in the isometric grid.

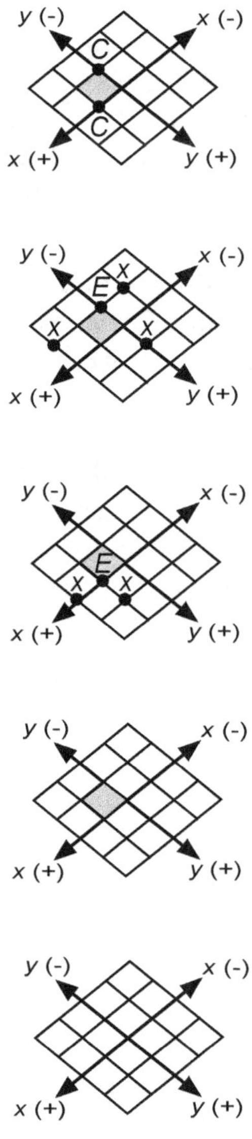

Hints Chapter 6

6.2

1. **Freebooter Island** There are two points that are 300 meters from Hangman's Tree and 500 meters from Skull Rock. One of them is in the sea and not on the island, thus that point is eliminated.

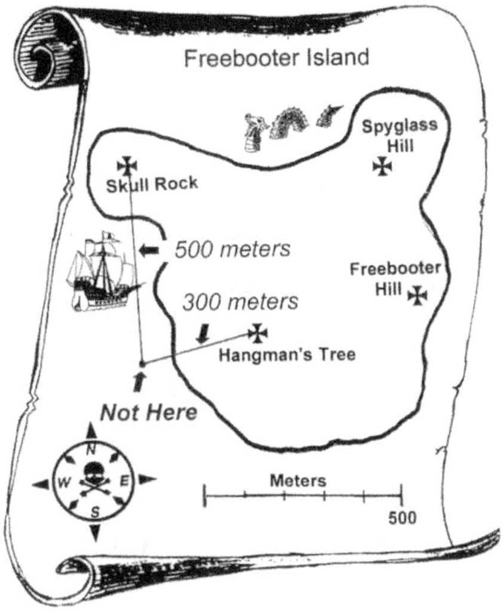

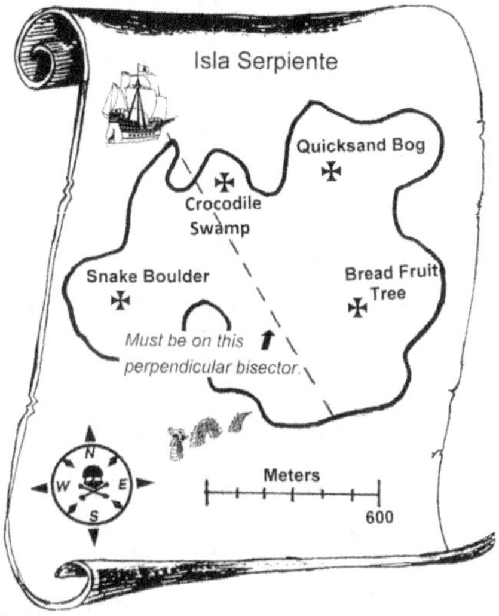

10. **Isla Serpiente** There are two possible locations for the treasure on the island.

17. **Cayman Key** It might be the circumcenter, orthocenter, centroid, or incenter. Use your geometric reasoning to determine which point of concurrency is the key to the treasure.

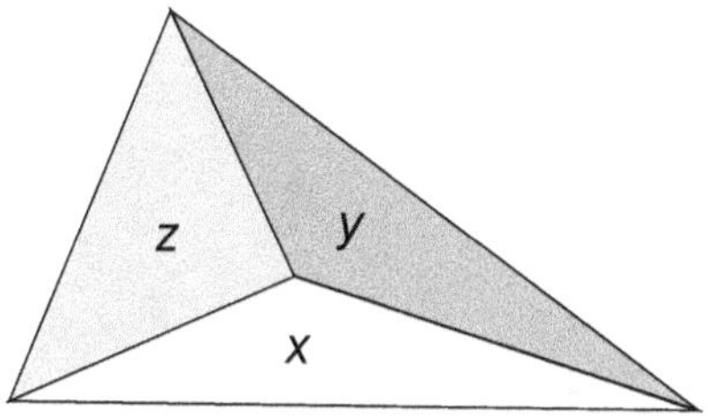

$x = y = z$

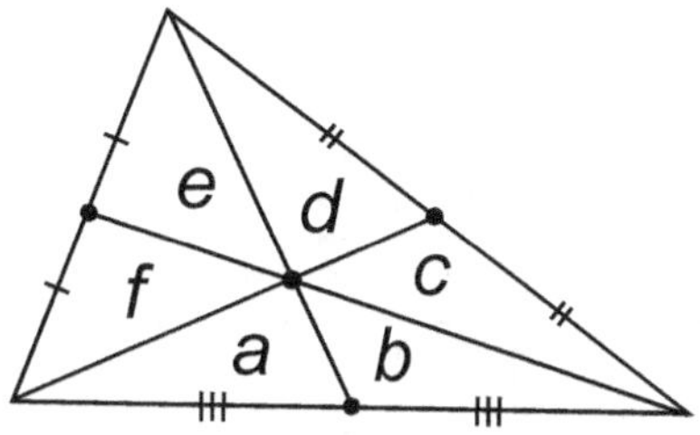

$a = b \quad c = d \quad e = f$

$a + b + c = d + e + f$

$a + b + f = c + d + e$

$b + c + d = a + f + e$

18. **Skeleton Island** What do the diagonals of a parallelogram do to each other?

19. **Buccaneer Island** There are a number of rectangles that can be formed with the given information. However, all four points must lie on the island since the Albatross Tavern and the treasure are on the island. This eliminates all but one rectangle. So our treasure is located at one of the other two points of the rectangle and the Albatross Tavern is located at the opposite point.

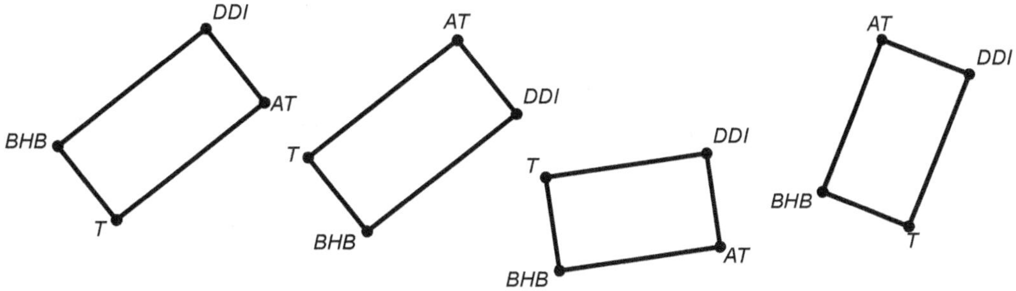

20. **Grand Doubloon Island** Pick an arbitrary point to represent the Gallows. Follow the instructions to find a point that could be the location of the treasure. Pick a second arbitrary point to represent the Gallows and again follow the instructions. If done carefully you should arrive at the same location.

Hints Chapter 7

7.6

1. **Island Treasure Map 1 Cayman Key**: CCS20. The shift may be forward or back 20.
2. **Island Treasure Map 2 Barbossa Island**: also a Caesar cipher.
3. **Island Treasure Map 3 Isla Sirena**: also a Caesar cipher.
4. **Island Treasure Map 4 Blackbeard Island**: also a Caesar cipher.
5. **Island Treasure Map 5 Haunted Isle**: also a Caesar cipher.
6. **Island Treasure Map 6 Skeleton Key**: also a Caesar cipher.
7. **Island Treasure Map 7 Doubloon Island**: a keyword cipher.
8. **Island Treasure Map 8 Skull Island**: also a keyword cipher.
9. **Island Treasure Map 9 Privateer Island**: also a keyword cipher.
10. **Island Treasure Map 10 Demon Island**: a TTT cipher.
11. **Island Treasure Map 11 Isla Tortuga**: a TTT cipher but vertical rather than horizontal.
12. **Island Treasure Map 12 Isla Langosta**: a vertical grid cipher.
16. **Island Treasure Map 16 Devil's Island**: Remember to add 0–9 at the end of the alphabet for mod 36.
18. **Island Treasure Map 18 Buccaneer Island**: AC.M5.A19

alphabet	a	b	c	d	e	f	g	h	i	j	k
convert to numbers	0	1	2	3	4	5	6	7	8	9	10
multiply by 5	0	5	10	15	20	25	30	35	40	45	50
add 19	19	24	29	34	39	44	49	54	59	64	69
convert to mod 26	19	24	3	8	13	18	23	2	7	12	17
convert to alphabet	T	Y	D	I	N	S	X	C	H	M	R

21. **Island Treasure Map 21 Isla Mariposa**: 6×6G.CS is a grid cipher arranged in a clockwise spiral. 11 is the letter *A* and 66 is the letter *K*.

Appendix 5 Answers to Investigations, Exercises, and Puzzles

Answers Chapter 1

1.2

The remaining tetromino:

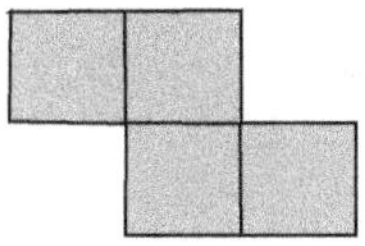

1.3

There are twelve Pentominoes. See below.

Pentomino Puzzle 1

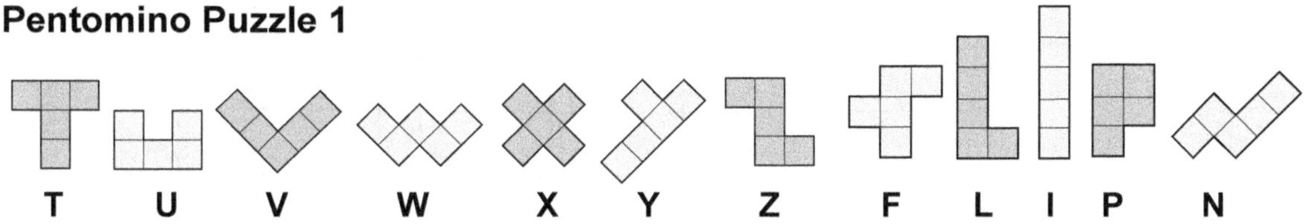

Pentomino Puzzle 2 Answers will vary.

8 Orientations of the *F*-pentomino

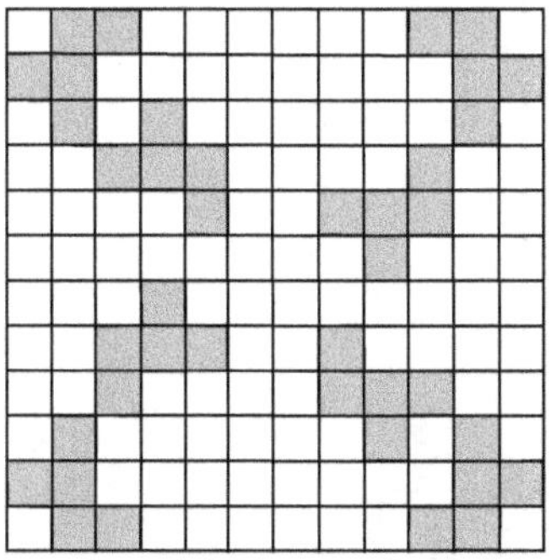

Design has 180° rotational symmetry

8 Orientations of the *P*-pentomino

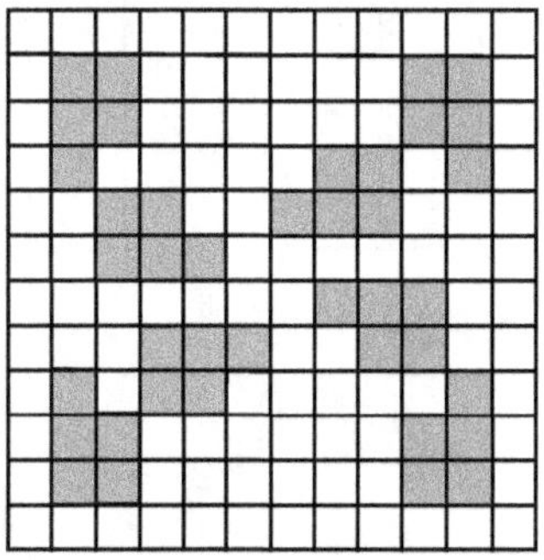

Design has 180° rotational symmetry

8 Orientations of the *Y*-pentomino

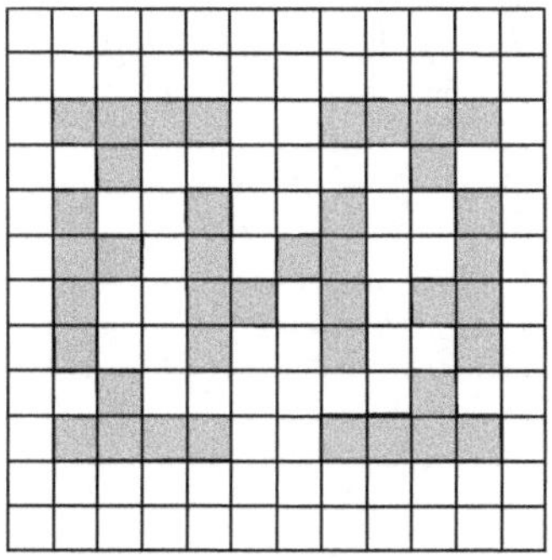

Design has 180° rotational symmetry

8 Orientations of the *N*-pentomino

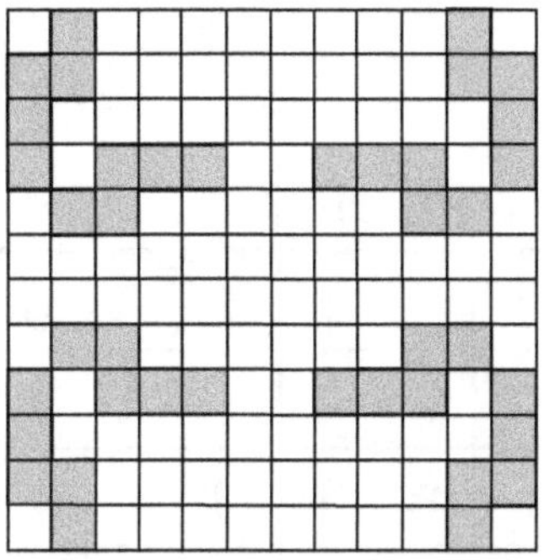

Design has 180° rotational symmetry

Pentomino Puzzle 3

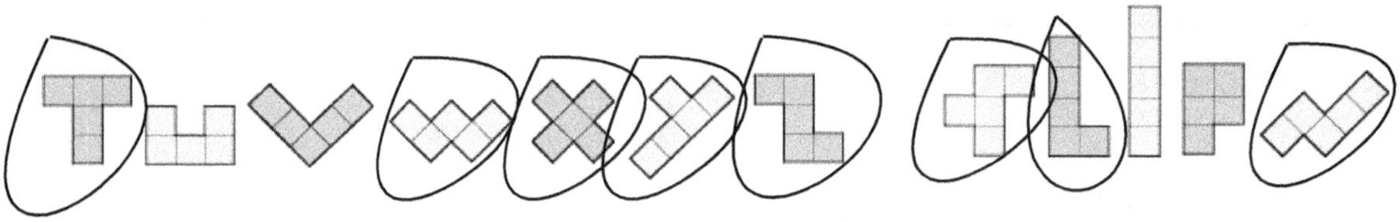

Pentomino Puzzle 4 Answers will vary.

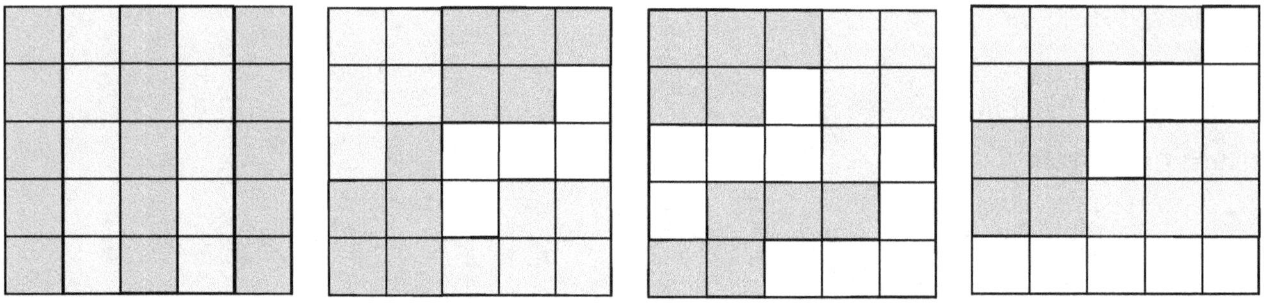

Pentomino Puzzle 5 Answers will vary.

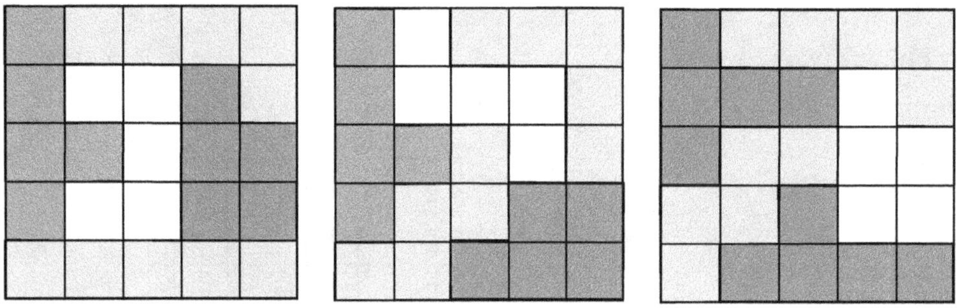

Pentomino Puzzle 6

4	6	7	2	1	8	9	5	3
1	3	2	9	6	5	8	7	4
8	9	5	4	7	3	6	1	2
7	8	4	5	9	1	2	3	6
2	5	3	7	4	6	1	9	8
6	1	9	3	8	2	7	4	5
3	4	1	6	2	9	5	8	7
9	7	6	8	5	4	3	2	1
5	2	8	1	3	7	4	6	9

4	1	2	3	5
2	3	5	1	4
3	2	4	5	1
5	4	1	2	3
1	5	3	4	2

Pentomino Puzzle 7

e	u	l	e	r	s	e	g	m	e	n	t
p	r	o	p	o	r	t	i	o	n	a	l
s	t	r	a	i	g	h	t	e	d	g	e
c	i	r	c	u	m	c	e	n	t	e	r
c	e	n	t	r	a	l	a	n	g	l	e

Pentomino Puzzle 8

p	r	o	t	r	a	c	t	o	r
h	y	p	o	t	e	n	u	s	e
c	o	o	r	d	i	n	a	t	e
h	e	m	i	s	p	h	e	r	e
o	c	t	a	h	e	d	r	o	n
c	o	n	j	e	c	t	u	r	e

Pentomino Puzzle 9

r	e	f	l	e	c	t	i	o	n
h	e	x	a	h	e	d	r	o	n
p	o	s	t	u	l	a	t	e	s
p	y	t	h	a	g	o	r	a	s
o	c	t	a	h	e	d	r	o	n
c	o	m	p	l	e	m	e	n	t

Pentomino Puzzle 10

V	V	V	U	U	X	W	W	L	L
Z	Z	V	U	X	X	X	W	W	L
Y	Z	V	U	U	X	F	F	W	L
Y	Z	Z	N	N	N	T	F	F	L
Y	Y	N	N	T	T	T	F	P	P
Y	I	I	I	I	I	T	P	P	P

Pentomino Puzzle 11

	U	U	U	V	V	V			
	U	X	U	V	N	Z			L
	X	X	X	V	N	Z	Z	Z	L
		X	F	N	N	W	W	Z	L
		F	F	N	W	W		L	L
			F	F	W				

Pentomino Puzzle 12

			Y	T	T	T	N		
	X		Y	Y	T	N	N		
X	X	X	Y	L	T	N			
	X	F	Y	L	W	N	P	P	
	F	F	F	L	W	W	P	P	
			F	L	L	W	W	P	

1.4

1.4 Investigation 1

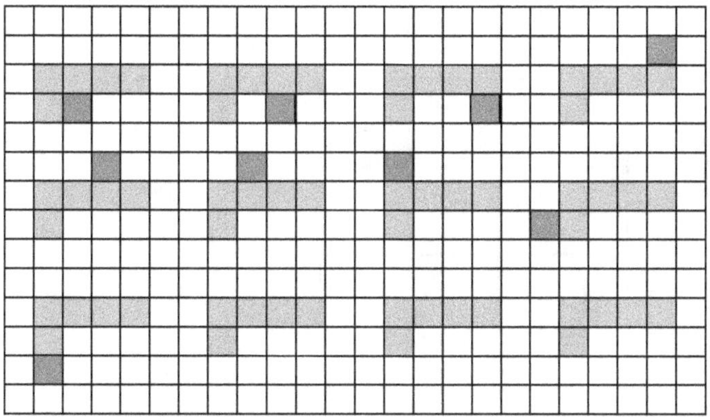

1.4 Investigation 2

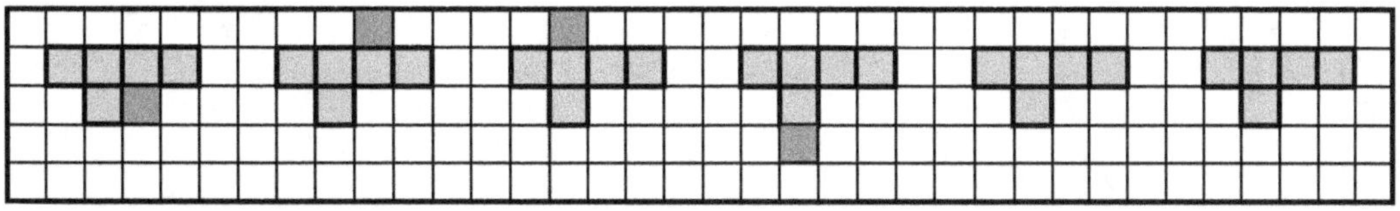

1.4 Investigation 3

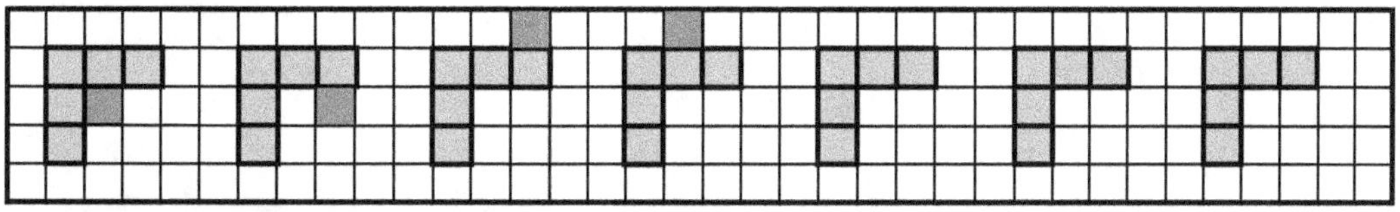

1.4 Investigation 4

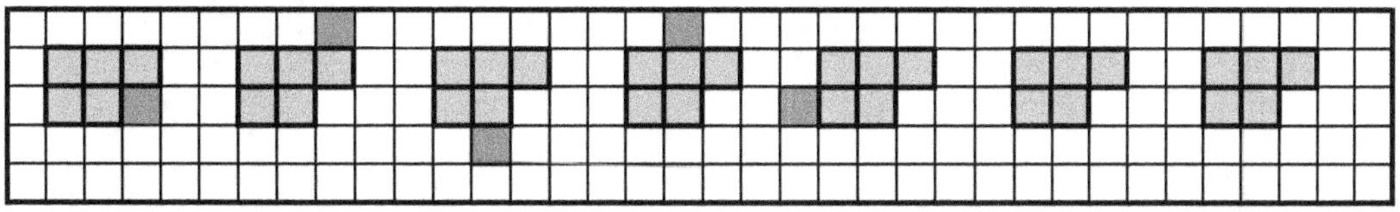

1.4 Investigation 5

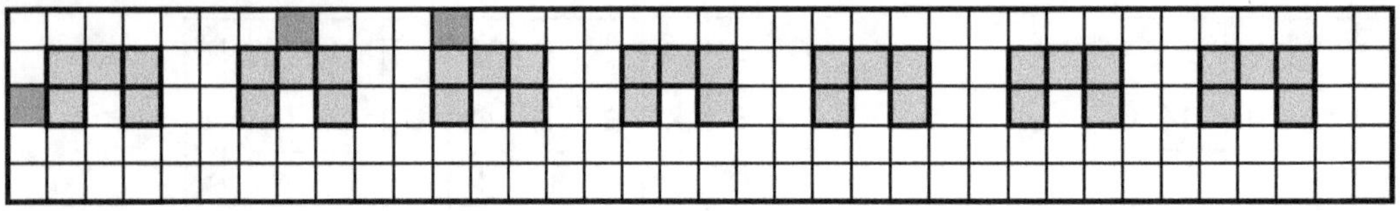

1.4 Investigation 6

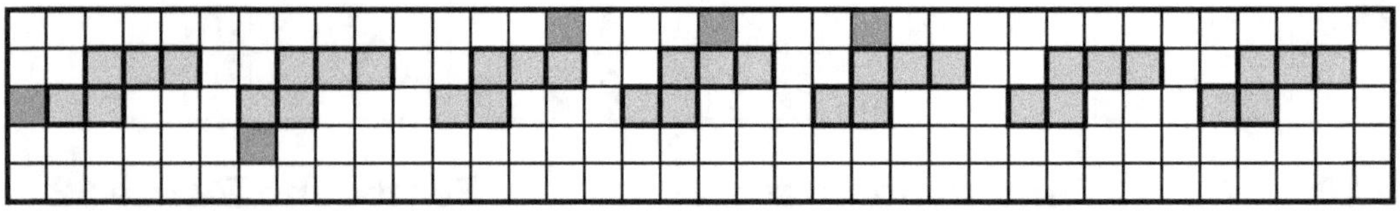

1.4 Investigation 7

No new hexominoes with a longest chain of three squares.

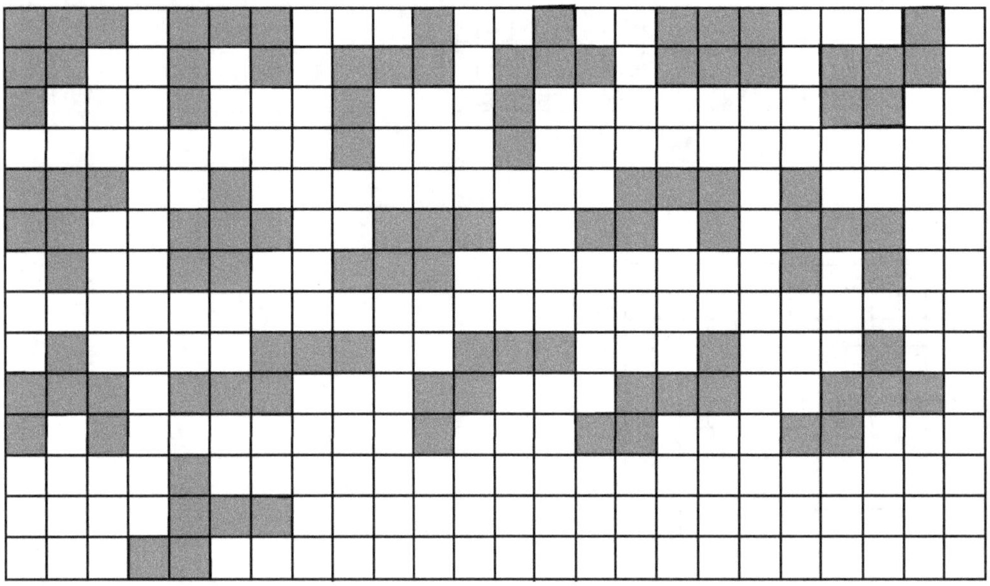

1.4 Investigation 8

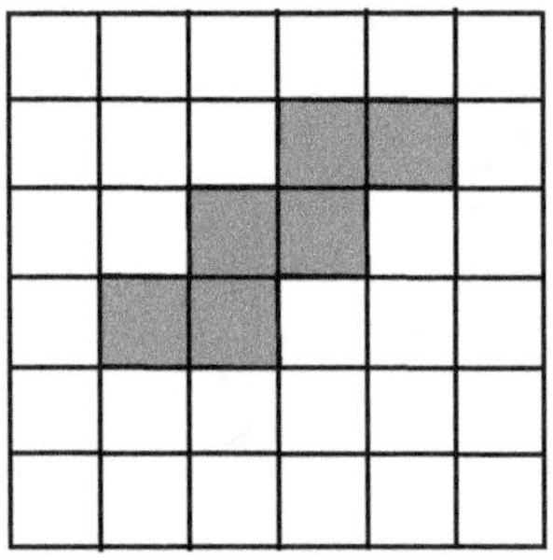

Hexomino Puzzle 1 **Hexomino Puzzle 2**

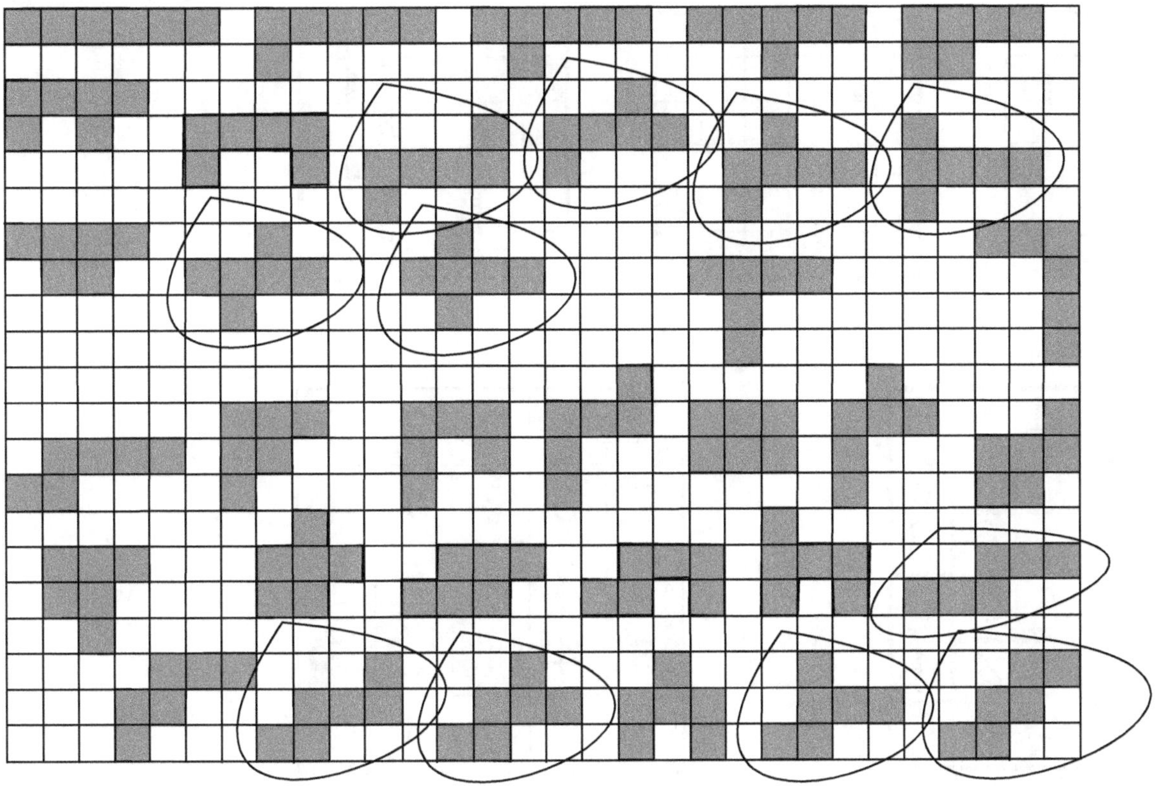

Hexomino Puzzle 3

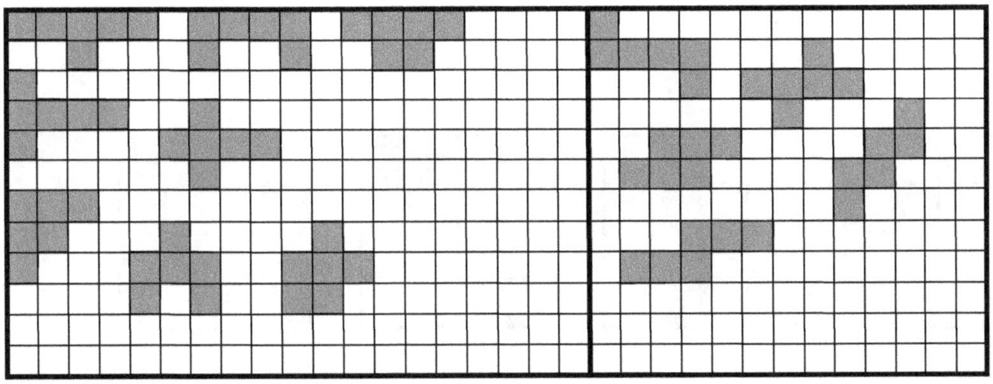

Hexomino Puzzle 4

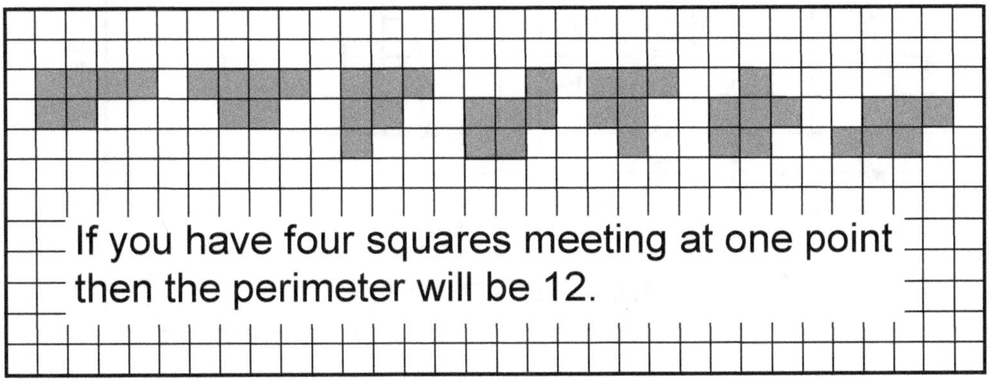
If you have four squares meeting at one point then the perimeter will be 12.

Hexomino Puzzle 5 Answers will vary.

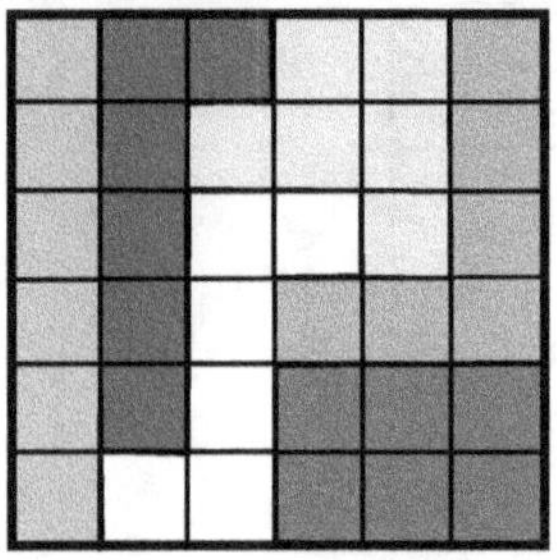
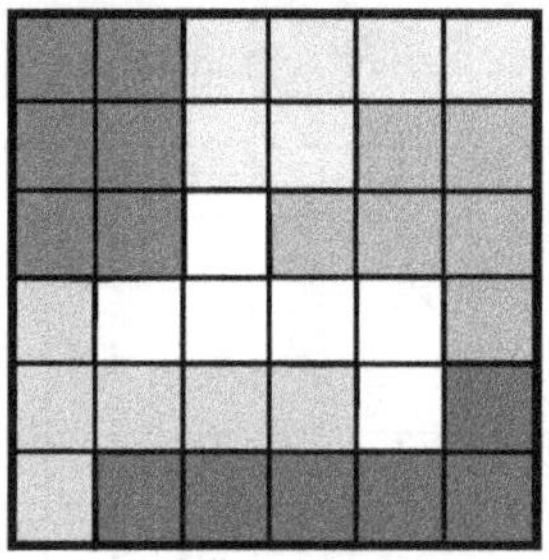
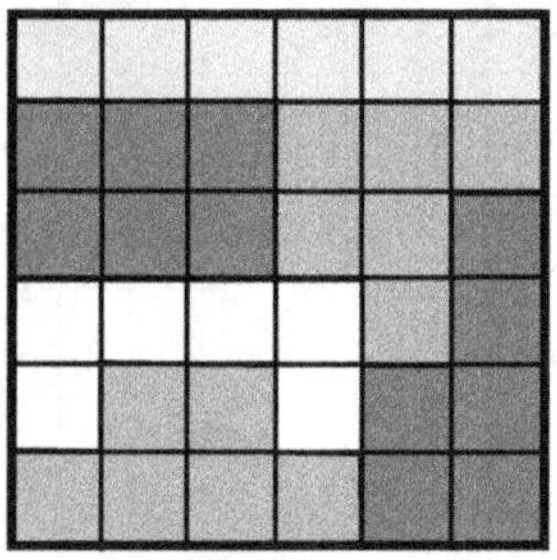

Hexomino Puzzle 6

1	2	3	4	5	6
4	3	5	6	1	2
5	6	4	1	2	3
6	1	2	5	3	4
2	5	6	3	4	1
3	4	1	2	6	5

4	1	2	3	5
2	3	5	1	4
3	2	4	5	1
5	4	1	2	3
1	5	3	4	2

1.5

Polyomino Puzzle 1

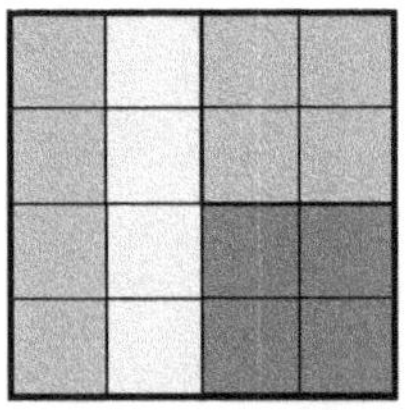
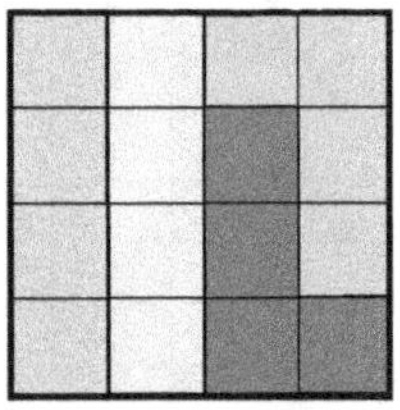
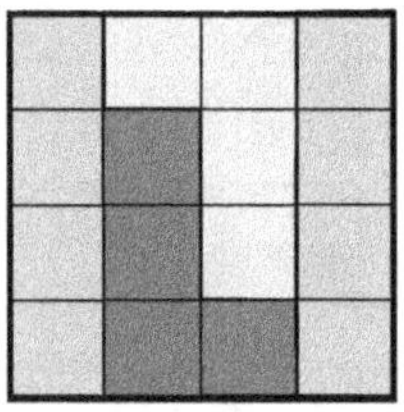
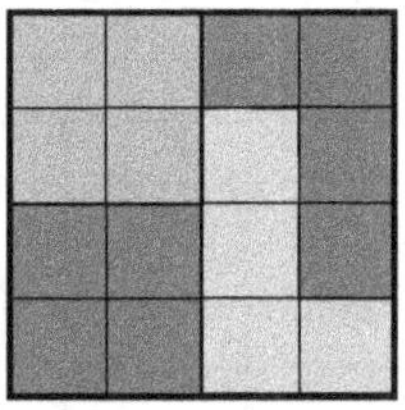
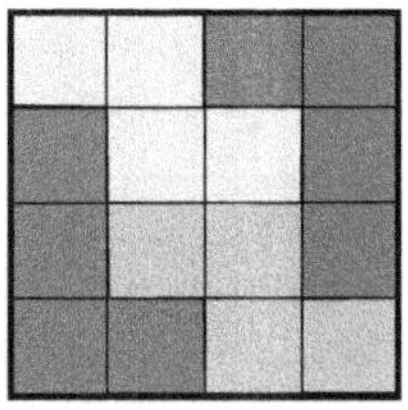

Polyomino Puzzle 2

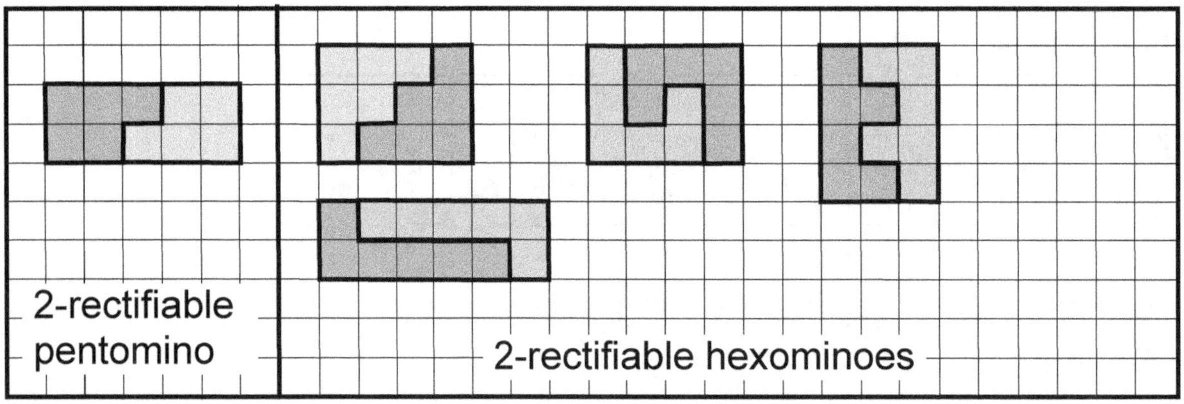

Polyomino Puzzle 3 Every pentomino can tile the plane.

Polyomino Puzzle 4

There are exactly 10 distinct 8×8 deficient boards. Each can be tiled with 21 bent trominoes.

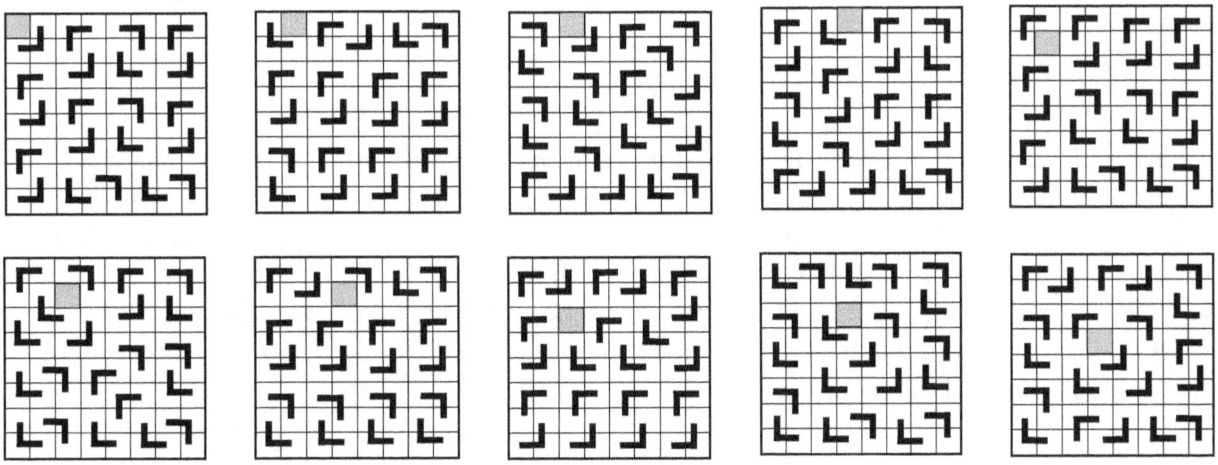

Polyomino Puzzle 5

As you may have observed with the 4×4 grid, removing the opposite corners removes the same color square. This leaves a grid with an unequal number of shaded and unshaded squares. But if you are attempting to cover the grid with dominoes (one shaded and one unshaded square) you will be unsuccessful since you will always cover an equal number of shaded and unshaded squares.

Polyomino Puzzle 6

If you tile the 4×5 and 2×10 rectangles with alternating color squares you always get an equal number of each color.

10 dark
10 light

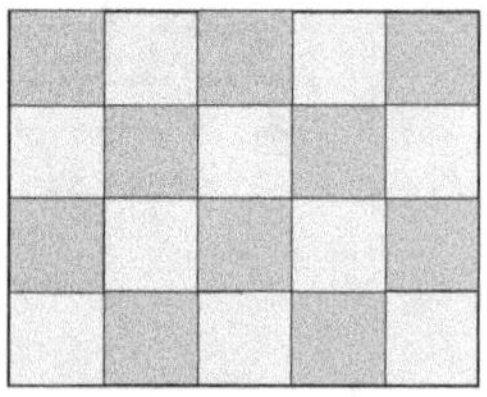

10 dark
10 light

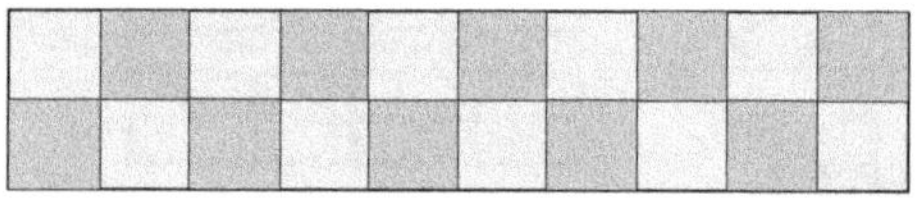

If you color the alternating squares of the five tetrominoes you get an equal number of each color in four of the tetrominoes. However in one tetromino there is always three of one color and one of the other color. Therefore there will never be an arrangement of the five tetrominoes into a 4×5 rectangle or a 2×10 rectangle.

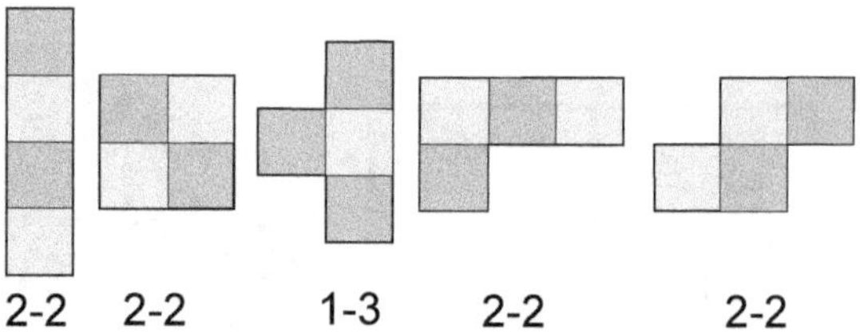

Polyomino Puzzle 7

All the rectangles: 3×70, 5×42, 6×35, 7×30, 10×21, and 14×15 have an even number of squares. Thus if the squares are colored alternately there will always be 105 squares of each color (an odd number).

There are 24 hexominoes that will always use an equal number of dark and light squares (3-3).

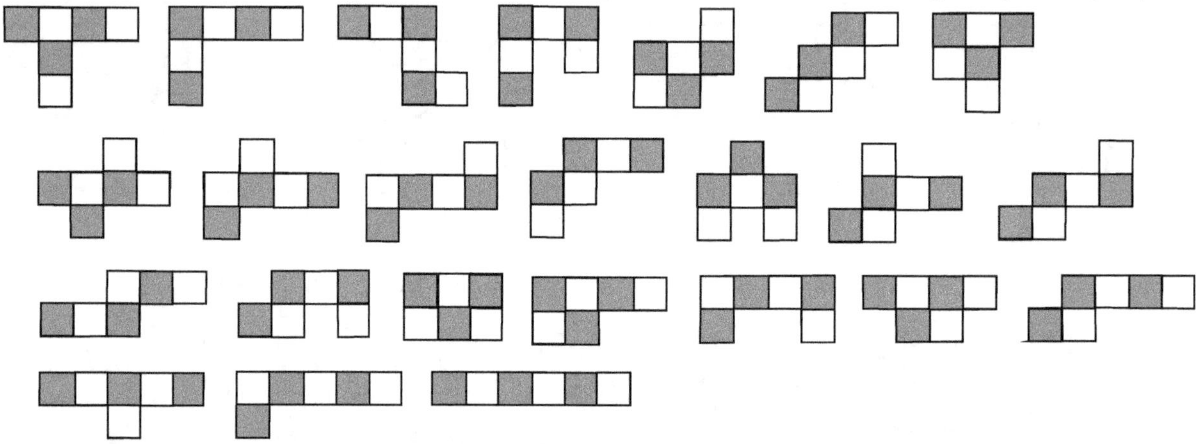

The remaining 11 hexominoes always use two squares of one color and four squares of the other color. Since there are an odd number of these hexominoes, no matter how you shade the squares there will always be an excess of one color over the other color. For example, in the shading shown below you can create five pairs that have a hexomino with four dark squares paired with a hexomino with two dark squares. This gives an equal number of dark and light squares in each pair but you are still left with one hexomino that has an unequal number of dark and light squares. Thus the 35 hexominoes cannot be used to form a rectangle.

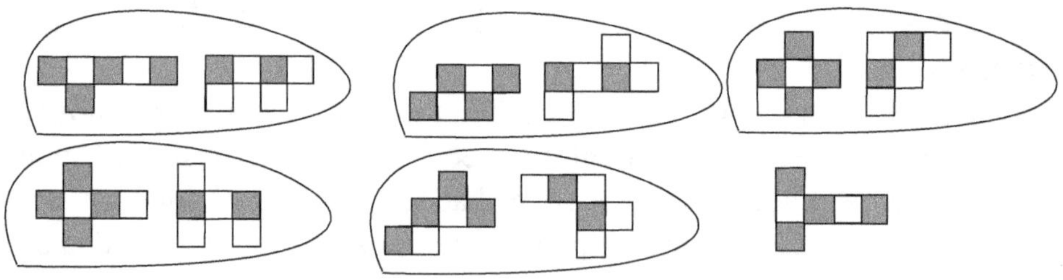

1.6

Domino Puzzle 1

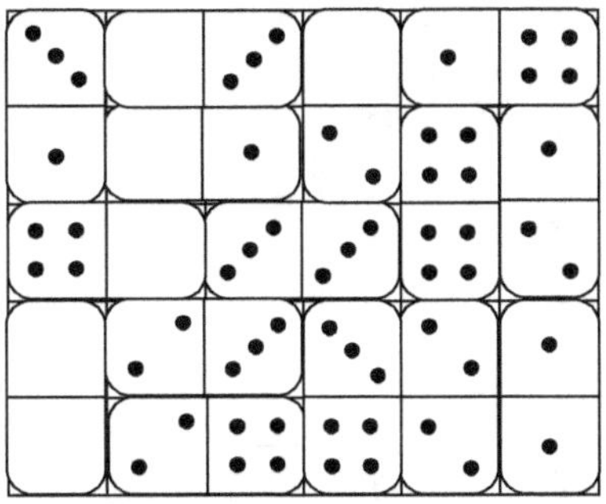

Domino Puzzle 2

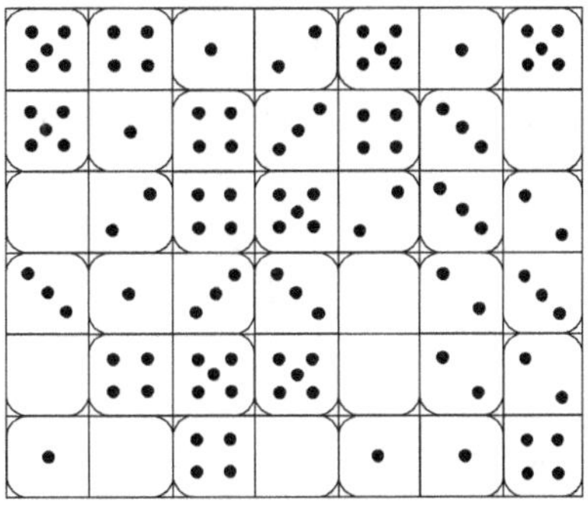

Domino Puzzle 3

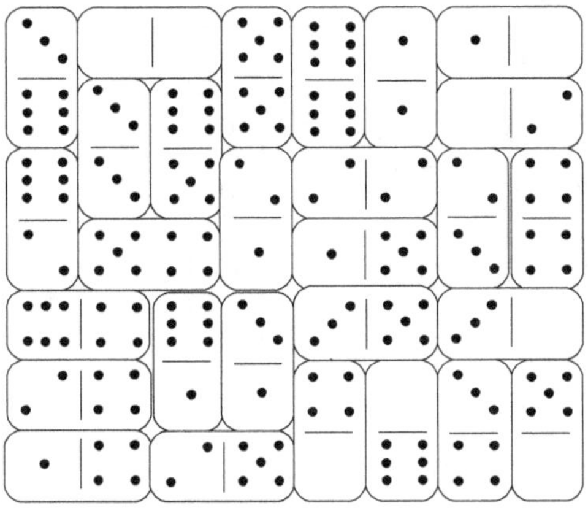

Domino Puzzle 4

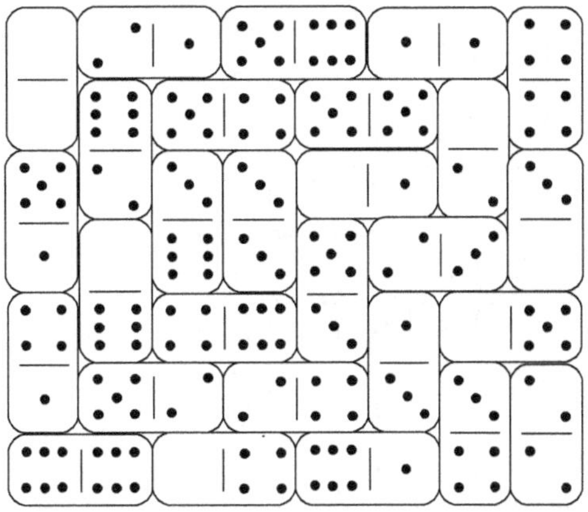

Domino Puzzle 5

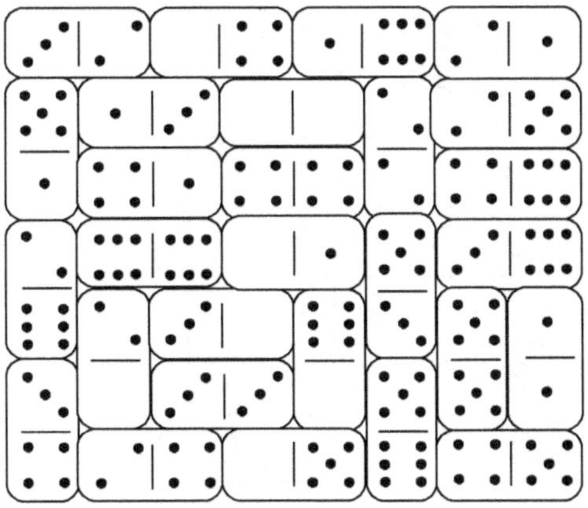

Domino Puzzle 6

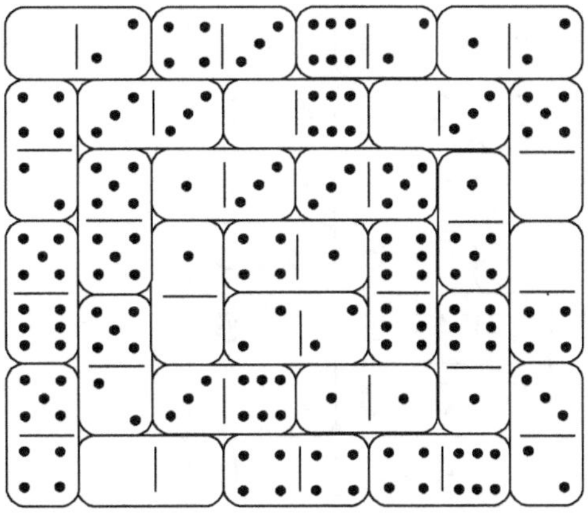

Domino Puzzle 7

0	5	6	2	5	4	5	0
0	1	1	4	0	2	3	2
6	4	2	2	3	6	1	4
3	1	0	3	3	4	5	0
4	6	1	4	1	4	3	1
3	0	3	5	6	5	5	6
6	2	1	2	5	2	0	6

Domino Puzzle 8

5	0	4	1	3	6	4	3
5	2	6	5	2	5	3	1
0	3	6	1	6	0	6	2
4	1	4	4	3	1	2	4
5	3	2	3	3	0	2	6
1	2	6	0	4	6	1	0
0	5	4	5	2	5	1	0

Domino Puzzle 9

4	1	5	4	2	2	1	5
0	3	1	3	6	4	0	6
0	6	0	6	3	0	5	2
2	4	5	5	3	2	4	1
6	5	0	2	5	3	5	4
1	3	2	1	6	1	2	4
3	6	6	3	0	1	4	0

Domino Puzzle 10

0	4	1	0	2	4	3	1
0	1	3	6	0	3	5	4
6	2	6	4	2	6	1	4
5	3	1	1	2	0	2	6
1	5	4	5	3	0	2	4
1	3	2	5	4	3	3	2
5	0	6	6	0	5	6	5

Domino Puzzle 11

2	4	6	6	3	5	6	0
2	3	1	0	6	5	4	2
1	1	3	0	4	1	4	2
0	2	5	4	0	6	3	3
3	1	2	1	4	6	1	6
6	5	5	5	0	3	2	2
4	5	0	0	4	3	1	5

Domino Puzzle 12

0	1	4	4	6	6	6	6
5	1	4	4	6	2	0	1
5	1	3	3	5	5	1	1
4	1	0	5	5	5	5	3
2	2	2	6	2	2	2	2
1	0	0	3	3	3	3	4
0	0	4	4	6	6	3	0

Answers Chapter 2

2.1

Exercises 1–6

1. Point *A* (2, 7)
2. Point *B* (7, 2)
3. Point *C* (4, 6)
4. Point *D* (8, 5)
5. Point *E* (5, 0)
6. Point *F* (0, 1)

Exercises 7–12

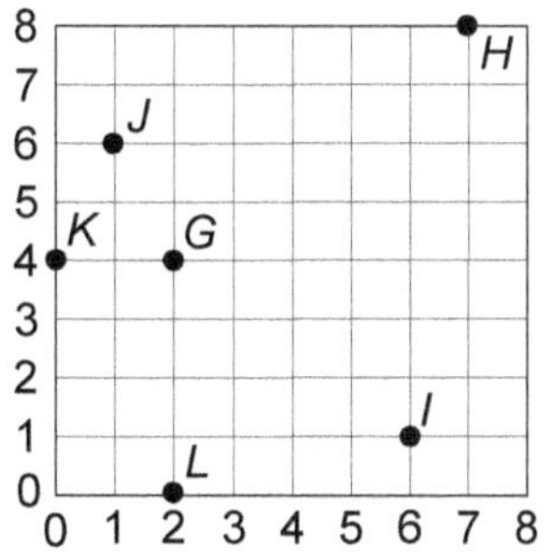

Exercise 13

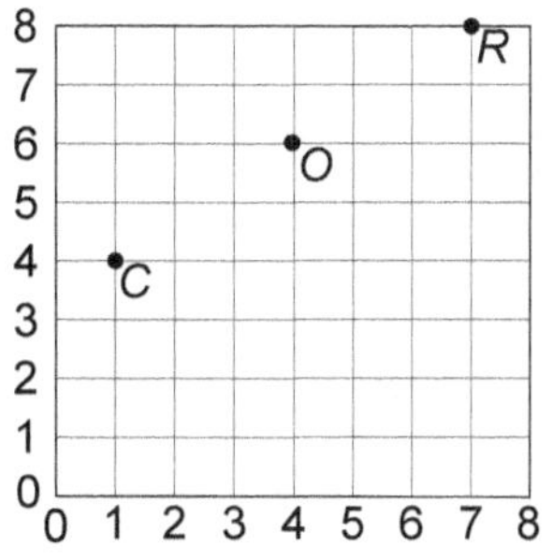

Exercise 14

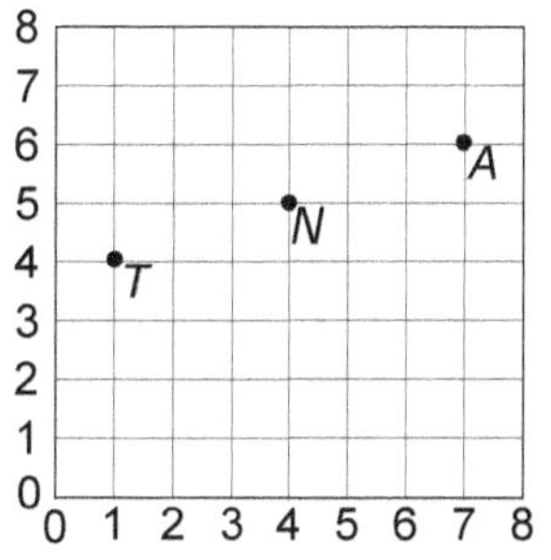

Exercises 15–16

Answers will vary. Point *N* can also be (4, 0) or (0, 8). Point *O* can also be (2, 6) or (4, 5).

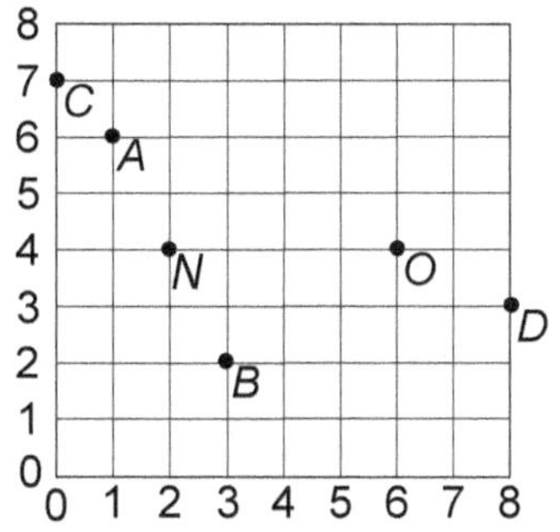

Exercise 17

(5, 5), (5, 6), (6, 4), (6, 5), (6, 6), (6, 7), (7, 4), (7, 7)

Exercise 18

(3, 1), (3, 2), (4, 0), (4, 1), (4, 2), (4, 3), (5, 0), (5, 2), (6, 2), (6, 3)

Exercise 19

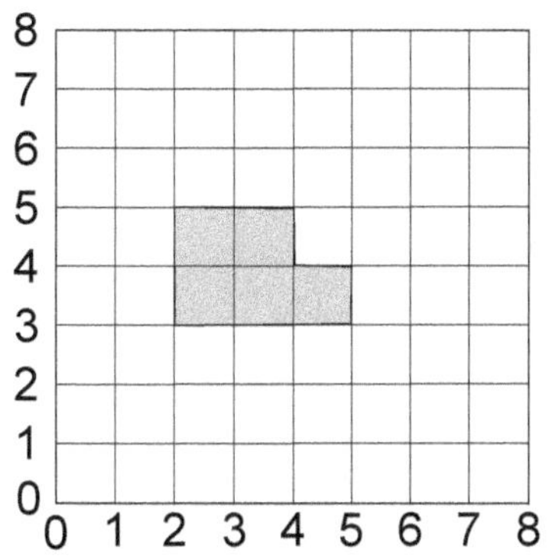

Exercise 20

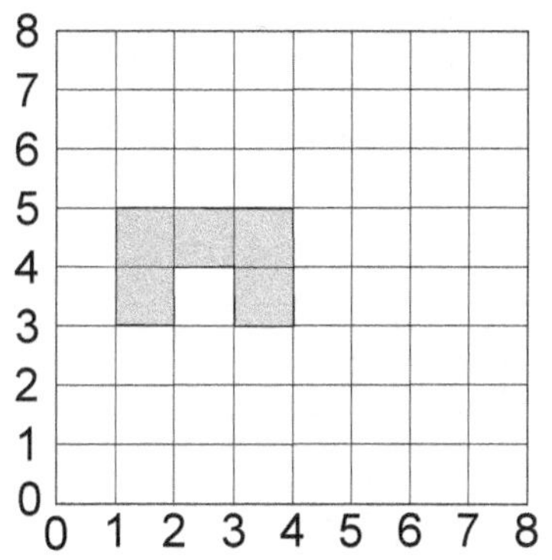

Exercise 21

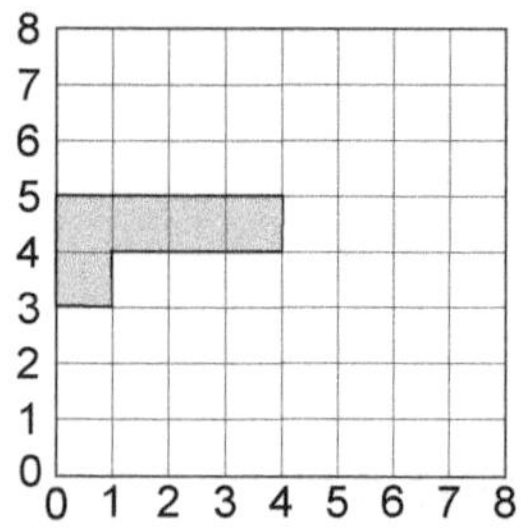

Exercise 22

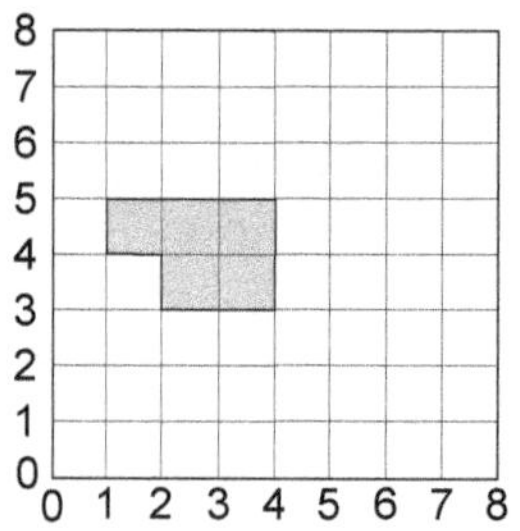

Exercise 23

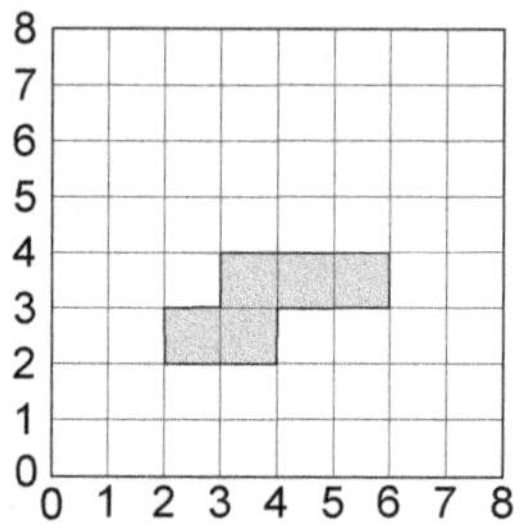

Exercise 24

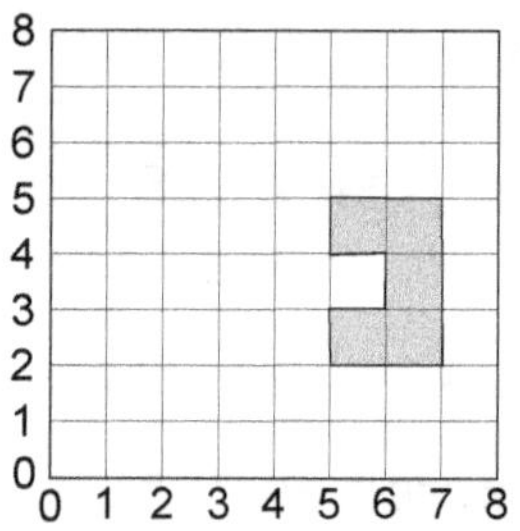

2.4

Exercises 1–6

1. Point *A* (4, 1)
2. Point *B* (-1, 2)
3. Point *C* (-2, -3)
4. Point *D* (3, -2)
5. Point *E* (3, 0)
6. Point *F* (0, 3)

Exercises 7–12

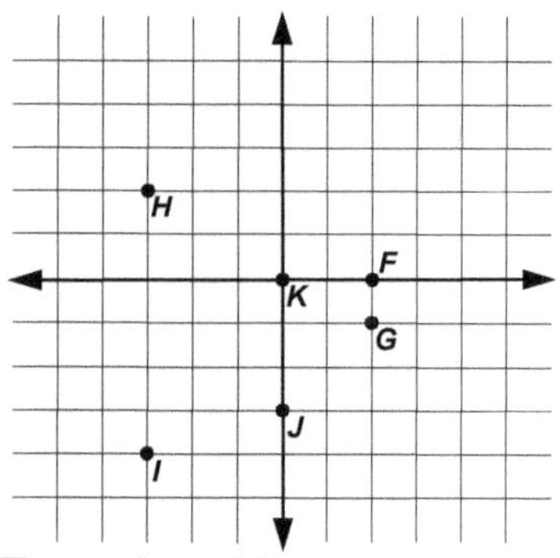

Exercise 13

A(2, 3), *B*(4, 3),
C(4, -2), *D*(2, -2)

Exercise 14

E(1, 2), *F*(4, 0),
G(3, -4), *H*(0, -2)

Exercise 15

M(-2, 1), *N*(4, -2),
O(4, 2), *P*(2, 3)

Exercise 16

IJKL is a square.
Diagonals intersect at (3, 1).

Exercise 17

QRST is a rhombus.
Diagonals intersect at (1, 0).

Exercise 18

UVWX is a kite.
Diagonals intersect at (3, 1).

Exercises 19–20

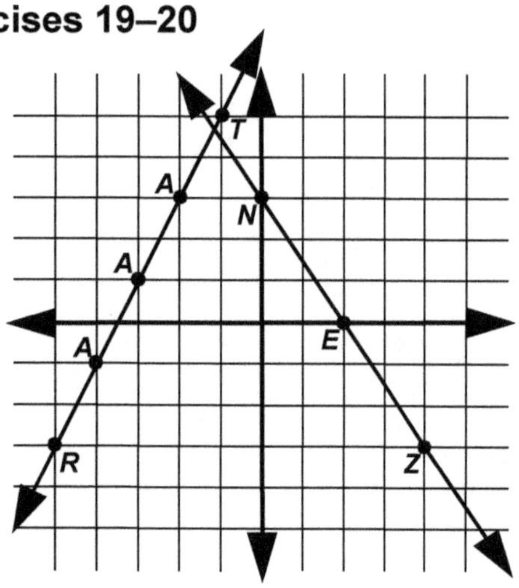

Exercises 21–24

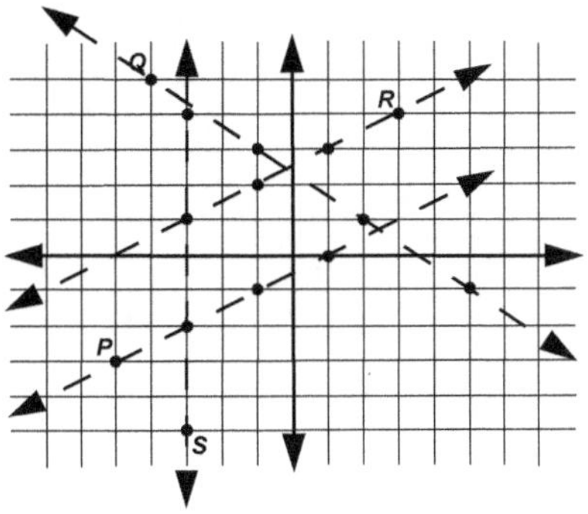

Exercise 25

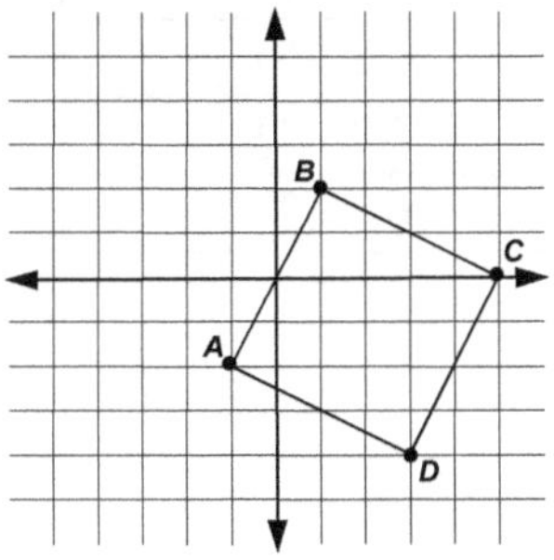

D(3, -4)

Exercise 26

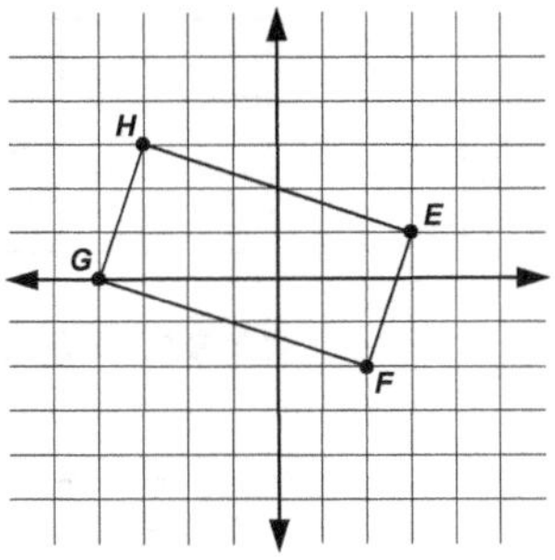

F(2, -2)

Exercise 27

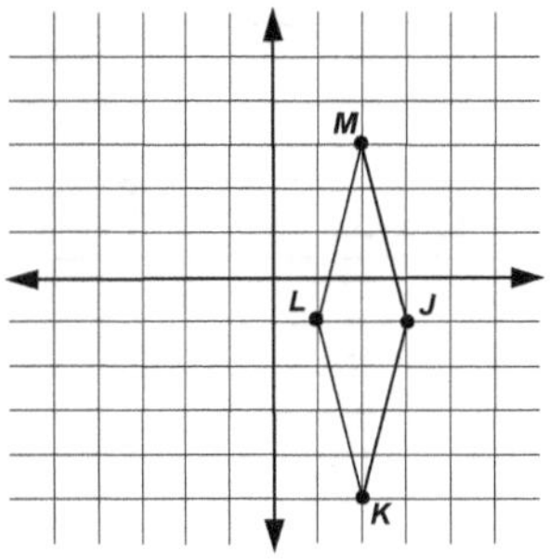

K(2, -5)

Exercise 28

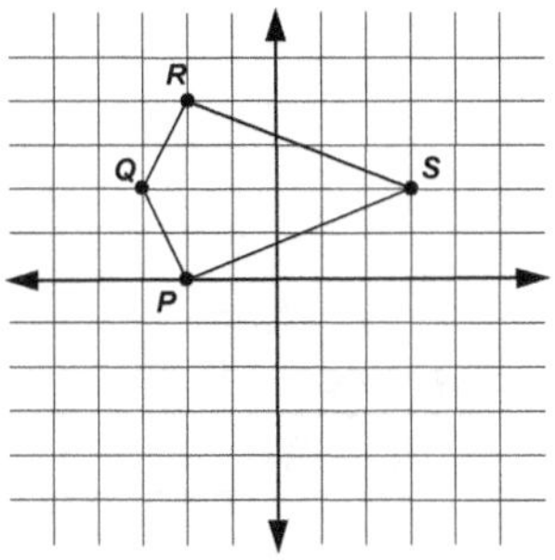

P(-2, 0)

Exercise 29

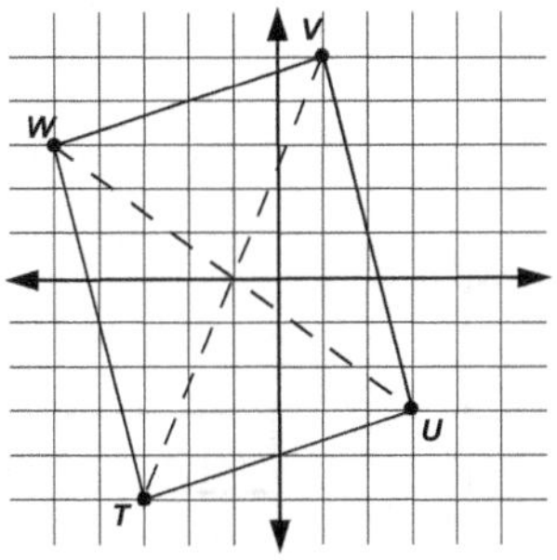

V(1, 5)
Diagonals intersect (-1, 0)

Exercise 30

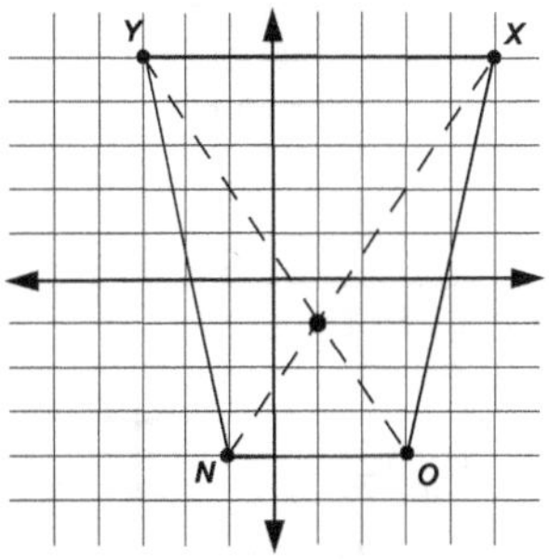

Y(-3, 5)
Diagonals intersect (1, -1)

Exercise 31

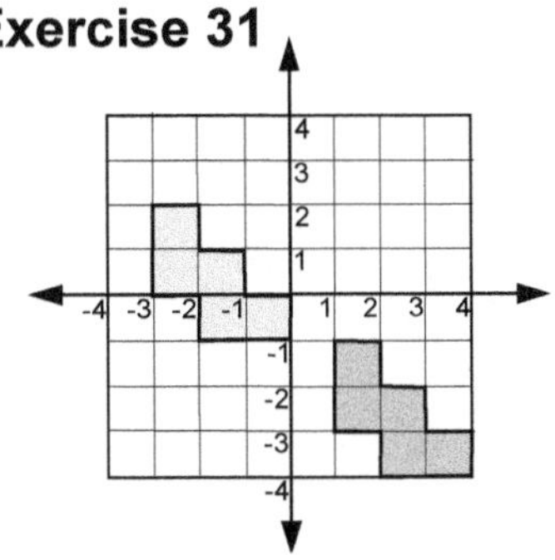

(*x*, *y*) before translation	(*x*, *y*) after translation
(2, -2)	(-2, 1)
(3, -3)	(-1, 0)
(2, -3)	(-2, 0)

Exercise 32

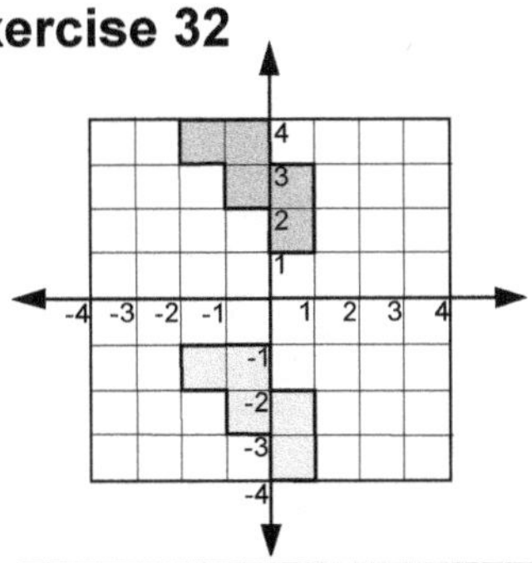

(*x*, *y*) before translation	(*x*, *y*) after translation
(-1, 3)	(-1, -2)
(0, 3)	(0, -2)
(0, 2)	(0, -3)

Exercise 33

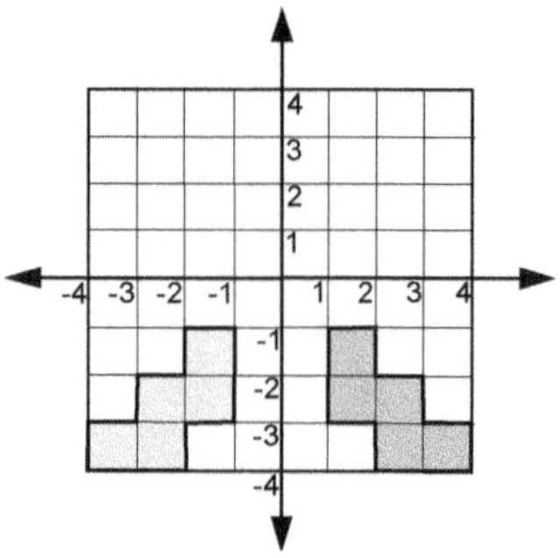

(x, y) before reflection	(x, y) after reflection
(2, -2)	(-2, -2)
(2, -3)	(-2, -3)
(3, -3)	(-3, -3)

Exercise 34

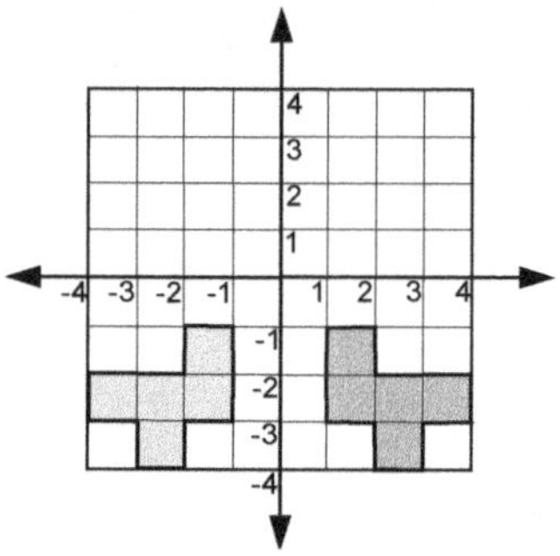

(x, y) before reflection	(x, y) after reflection
(2, -2)	(-2, -2)
(2, -3)	(-2, -3)
(3, -3)	(-3, -3)

Exercise 35

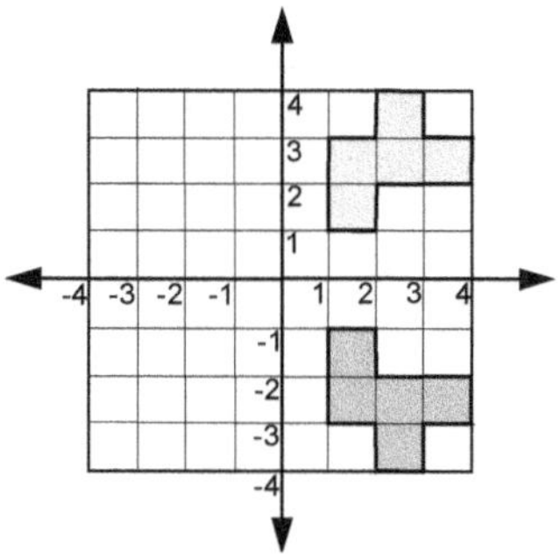

(x, y) before reflection	(x, y) after reflection
(2, -2)	(2, 2)
(2, -3)	(2, 3)
(3, -3)	(3, 3)

Exercise 36

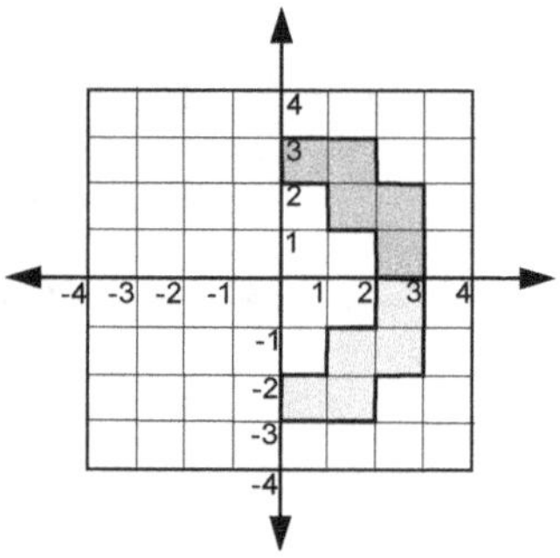

(x, y) before reflection	(x, y) after reflection
(1, 2)	(1, -2)
(2, 1)	(2, -1)
(2, 2)	(2, -2)

Exercise 37

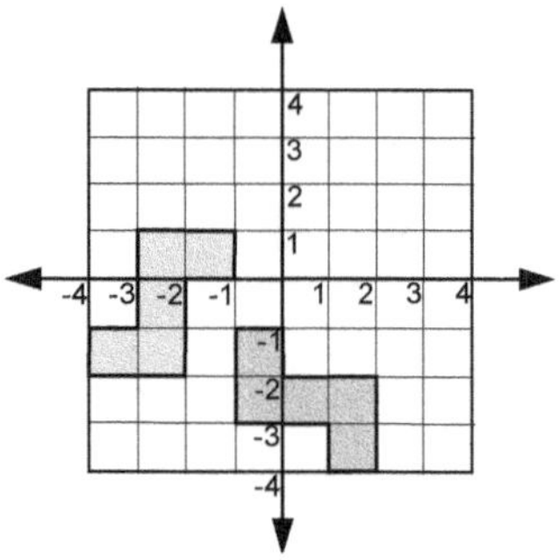

(x, y) before rotation	(x, y) after rotation
(0, -2)	(-2, 0)
(1, -3)	(-3, -1)

Exercise 38

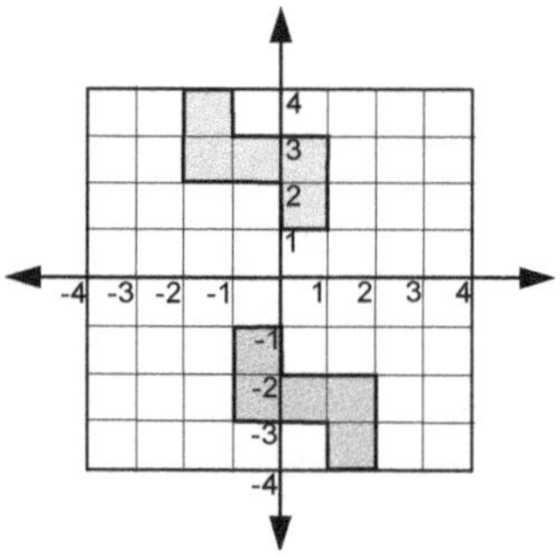

(x, y) before rotation	(x, y) after rotation
(0, -2)	(0, 2)
(1, -3)	(-1, 3)

Exercise 39

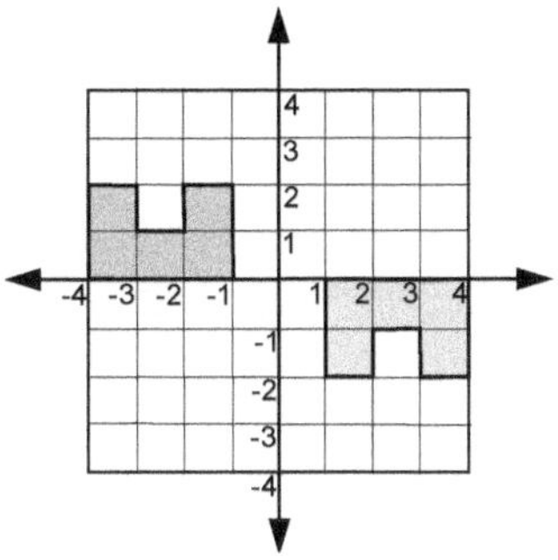

(*x*, *y*) before rotation	(*x*, *y*) after rotation
(-3, 1)	(3, -1)
(-2, 1)	(2, -1)

Exercise 40

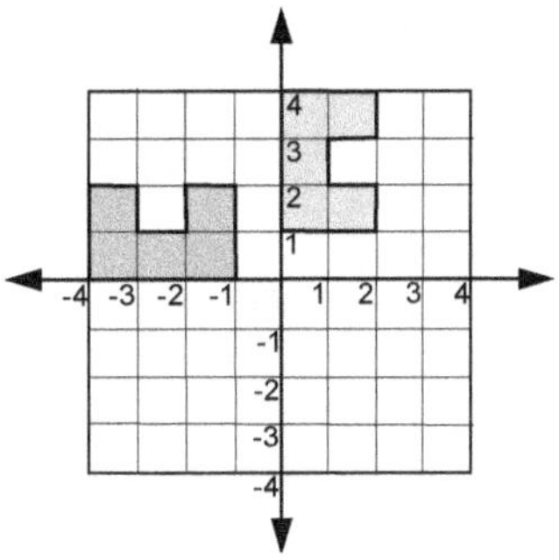

(*x*, *y*) before rotation	(*x*, *y*) after rotation
(-3, 1)	(1, 3)
(-2, 1)	(1, 2)

2.9

BTP 1

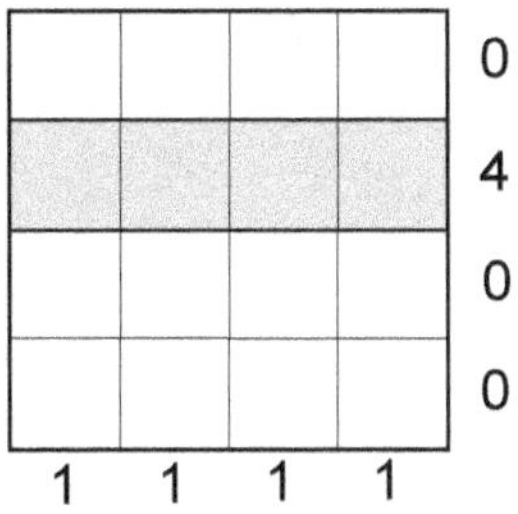

BTP 2

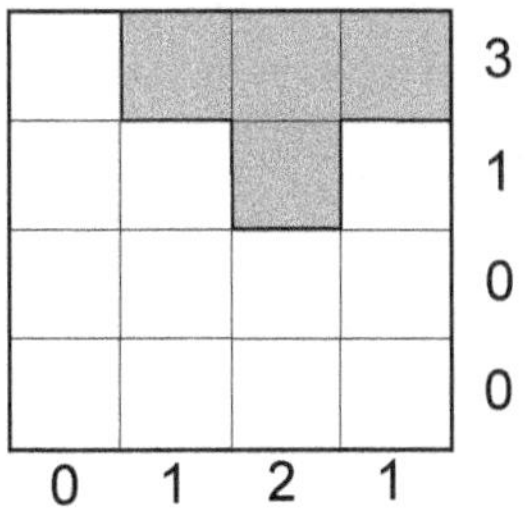

BTP 3

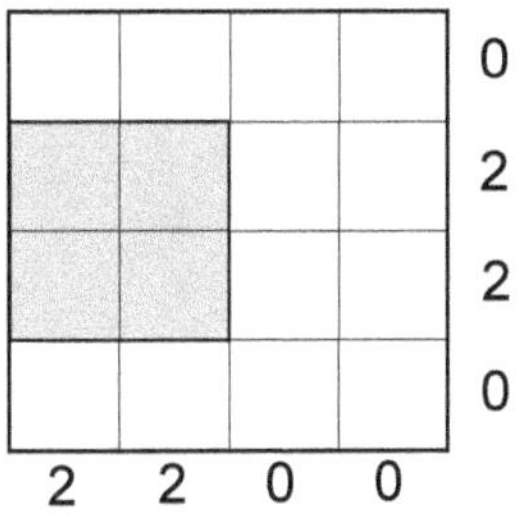

BTP4

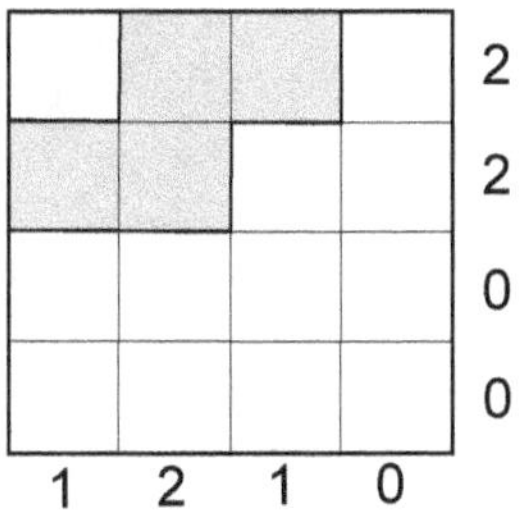

BTP 5

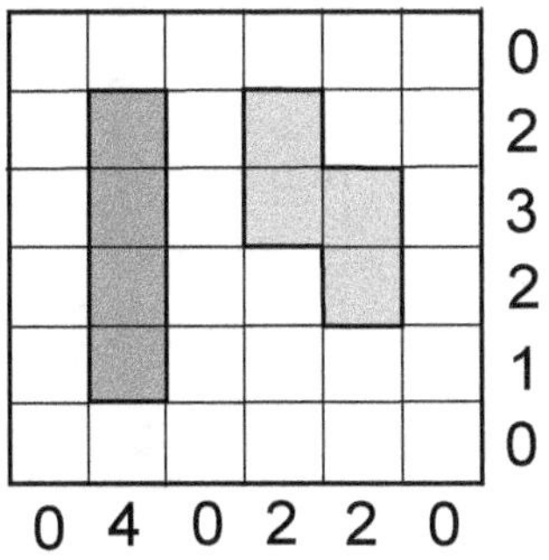

BTP 6

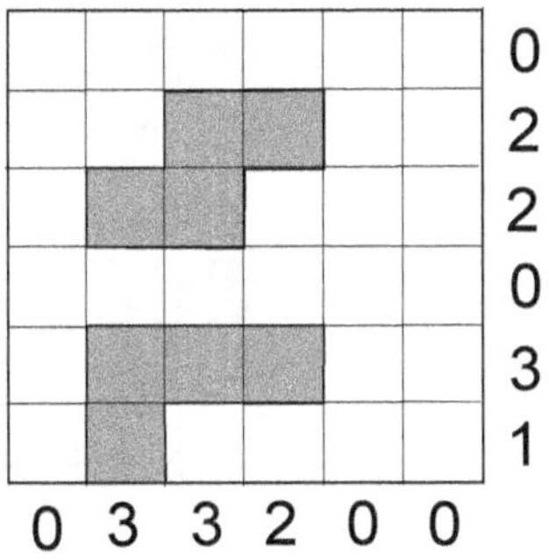

BTP 7

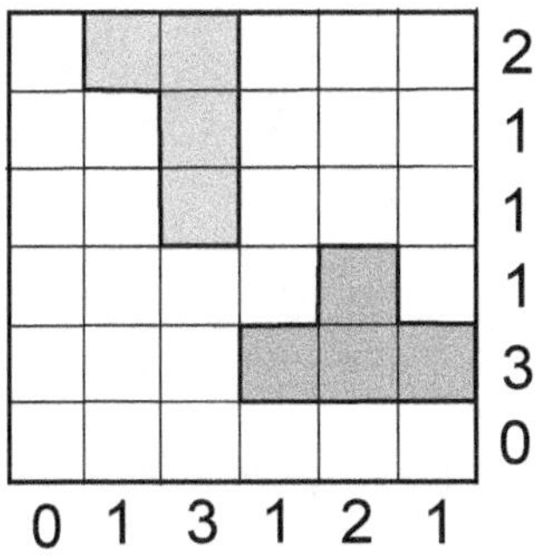

BTP 8

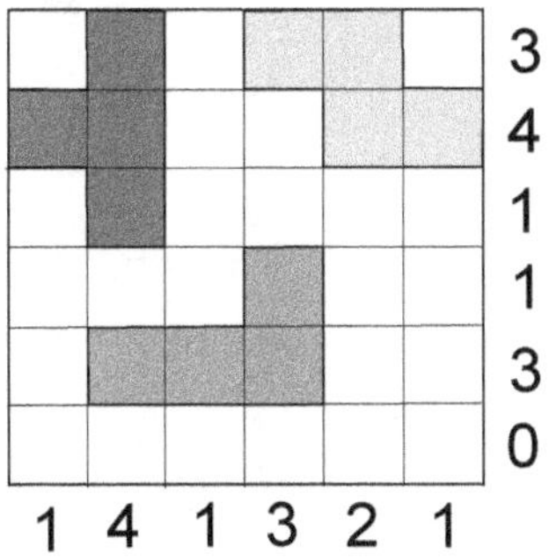

BTP 9

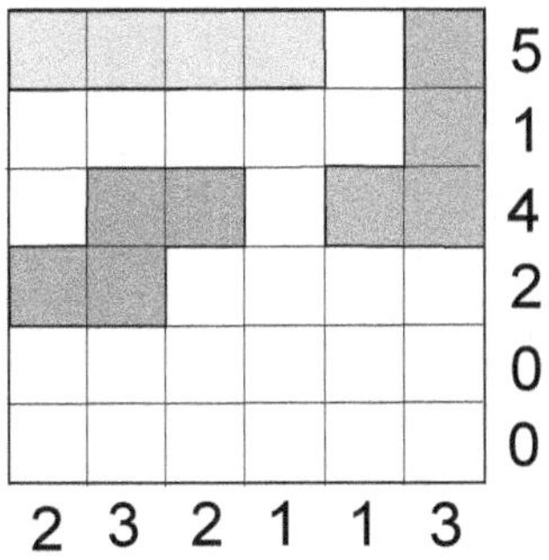

BTP 10

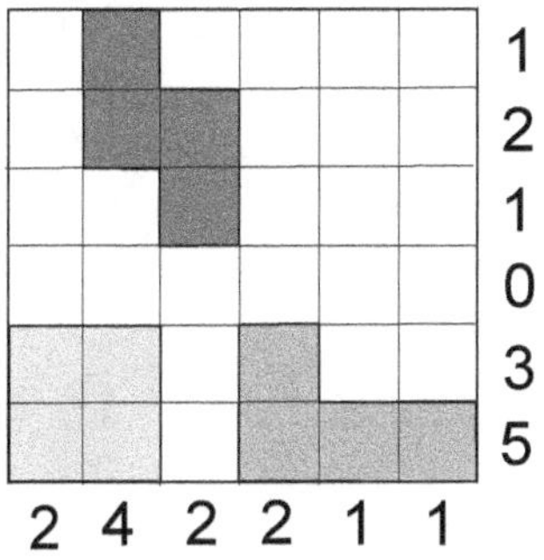

BTP 11

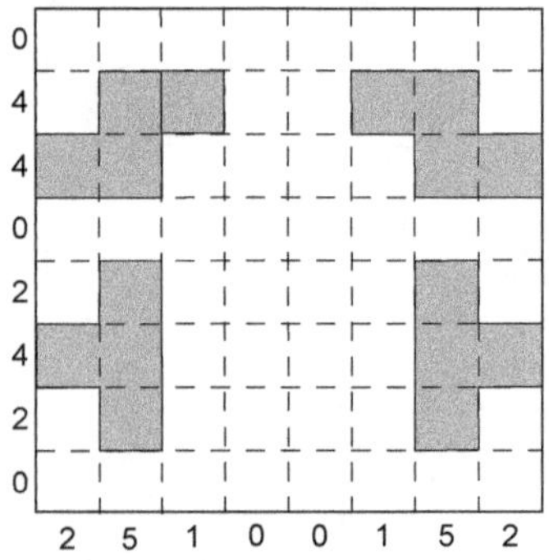

BTP 12

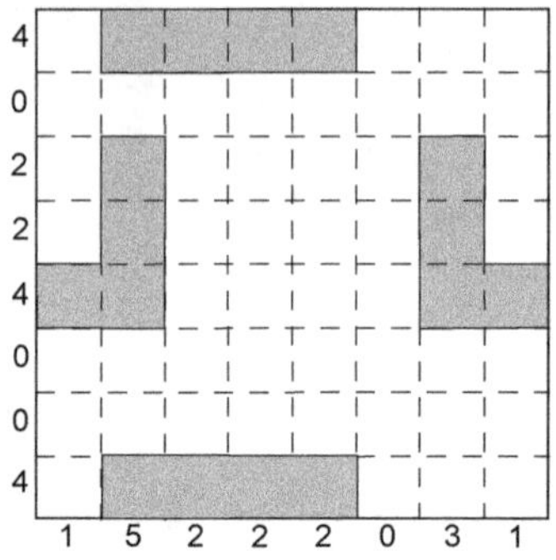

BTP 13

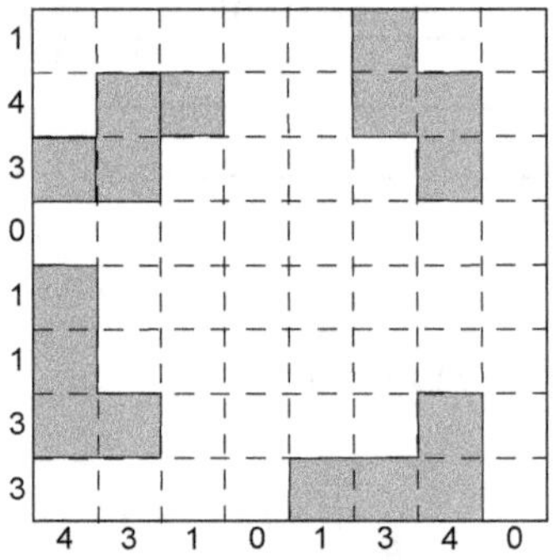

BTP 14

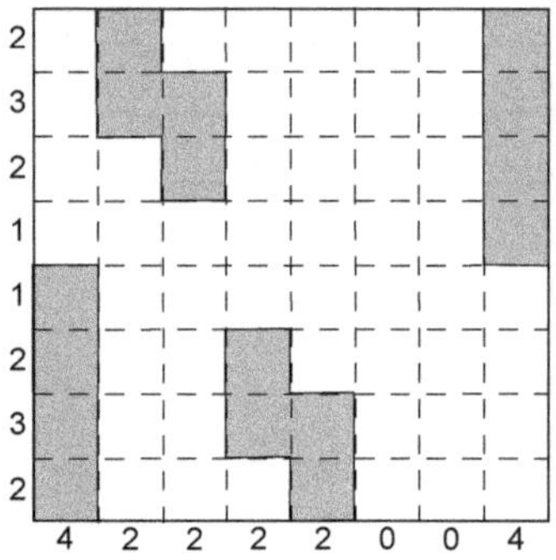

BTP 15

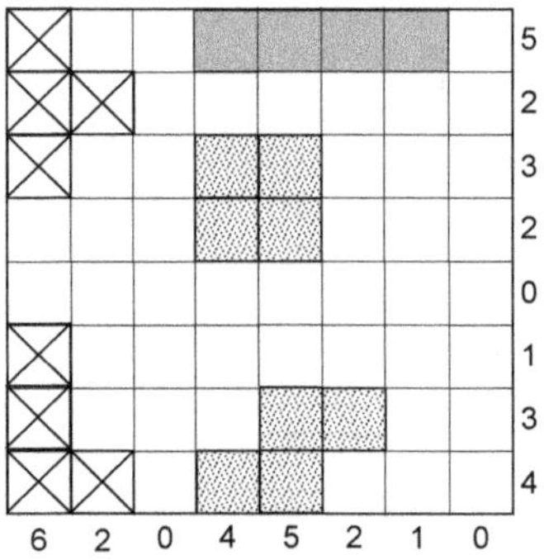

BTP 16

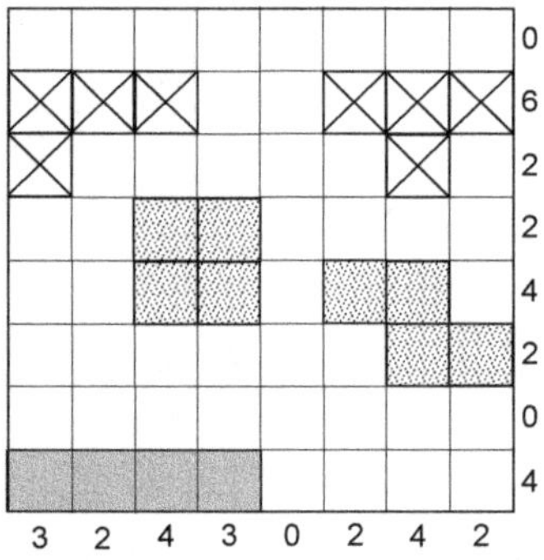

BTP 17

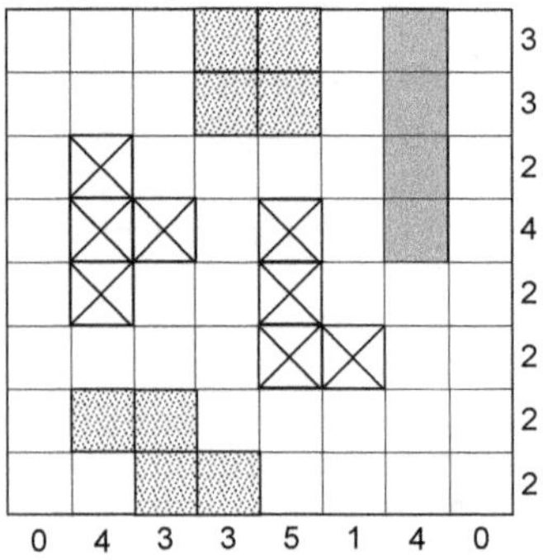

BTP 18

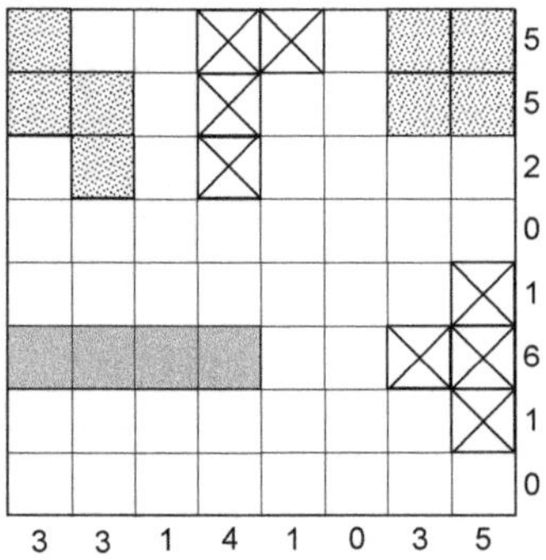

BTP 19

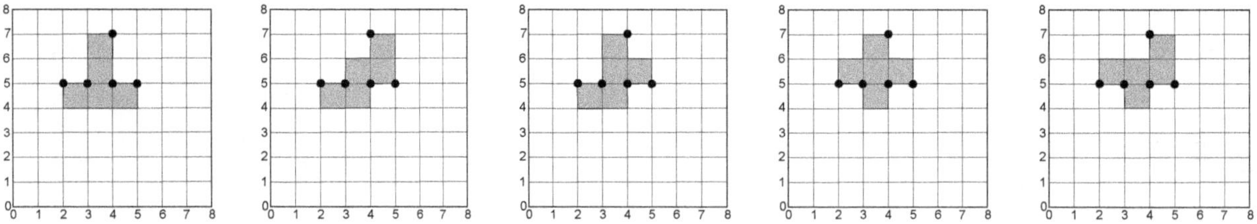

BTP 20

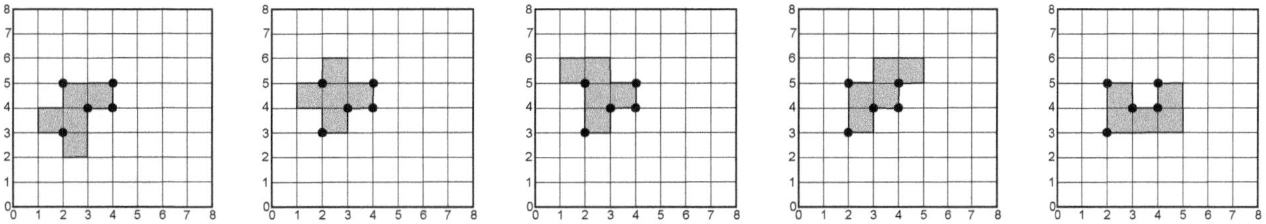

BTP 21

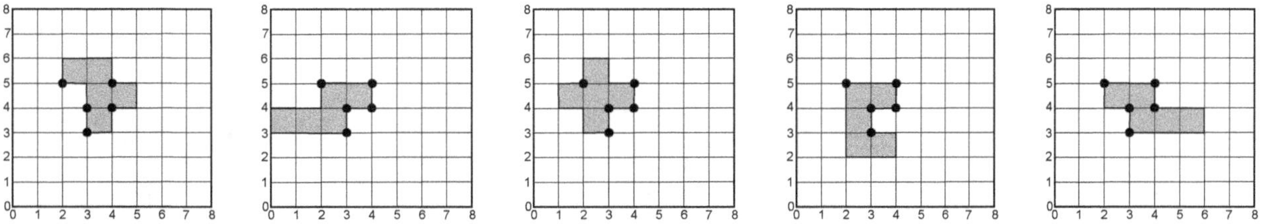

BTP 22

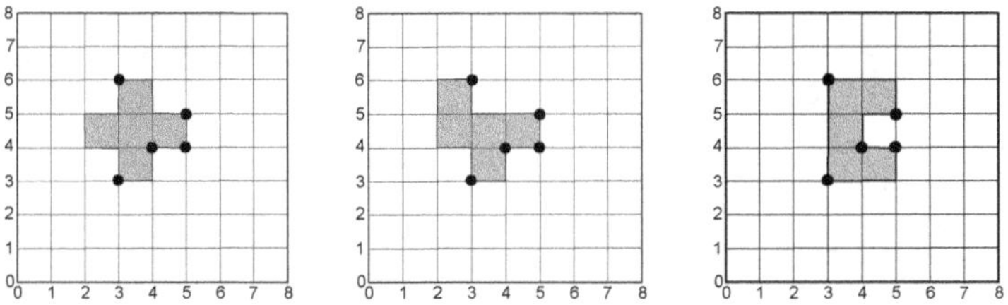

BTP 23

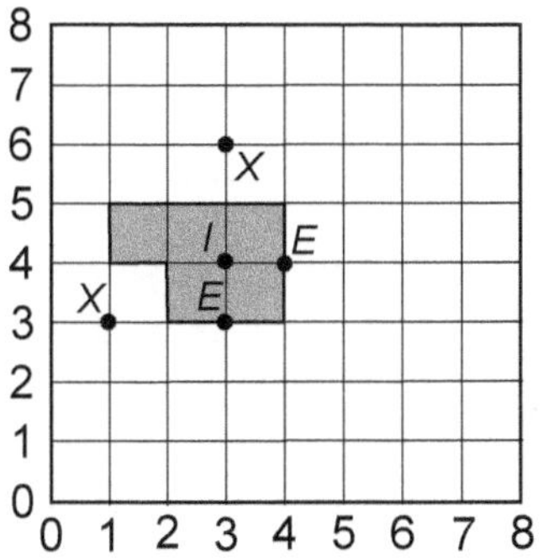

BTP 24

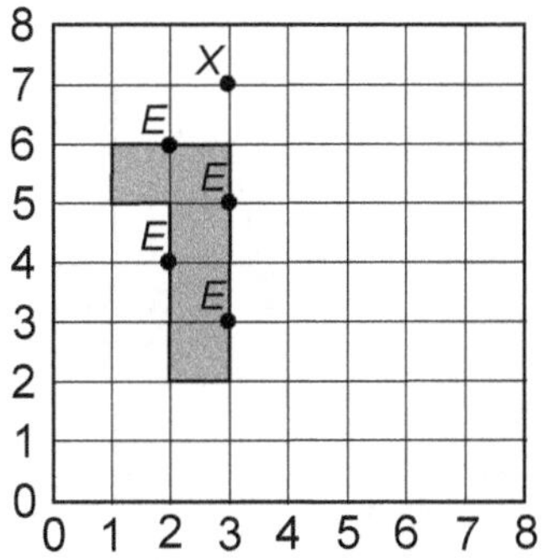

BTP 25

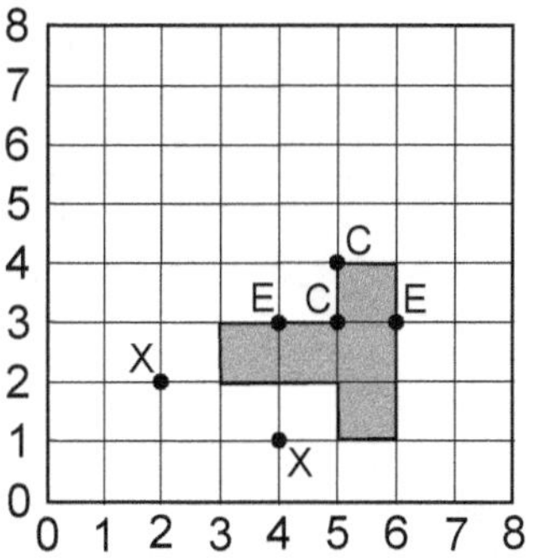

BTP 26

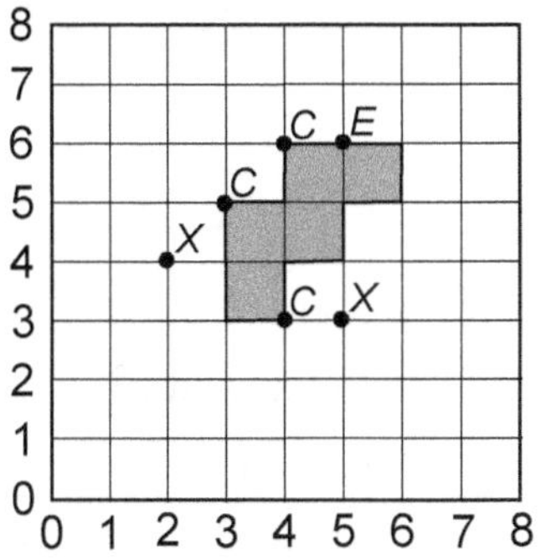

BTP 27

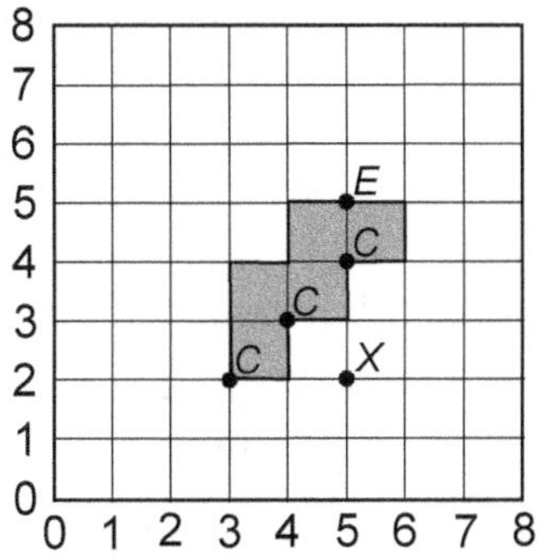

BTP 28

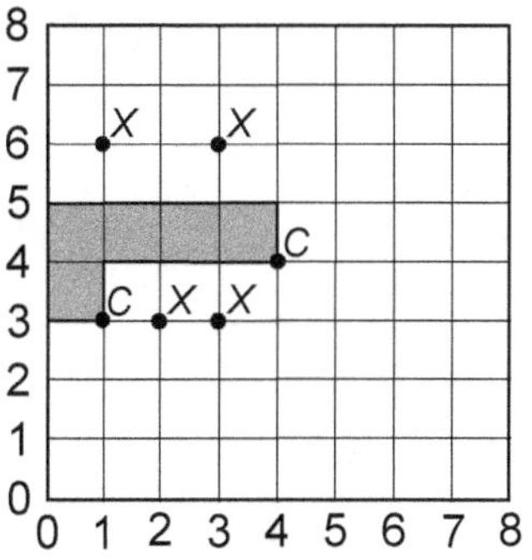

BTP 29

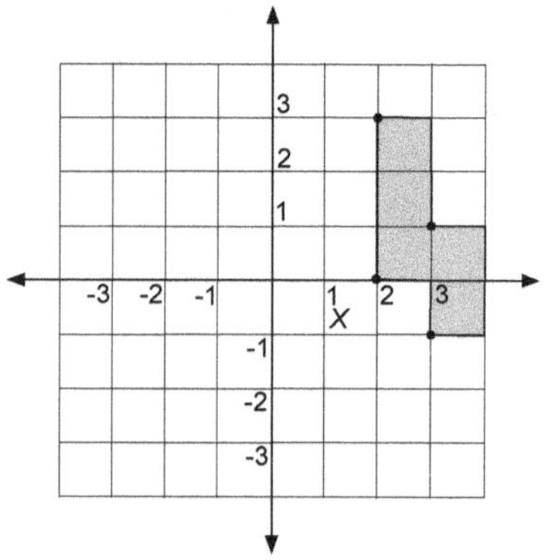

BTP 30

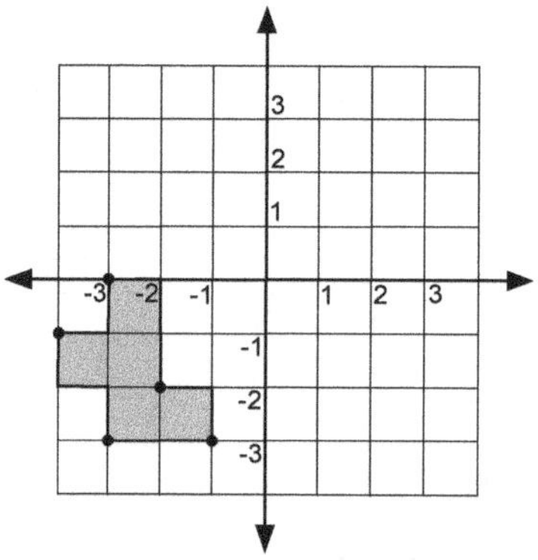

BTP 31

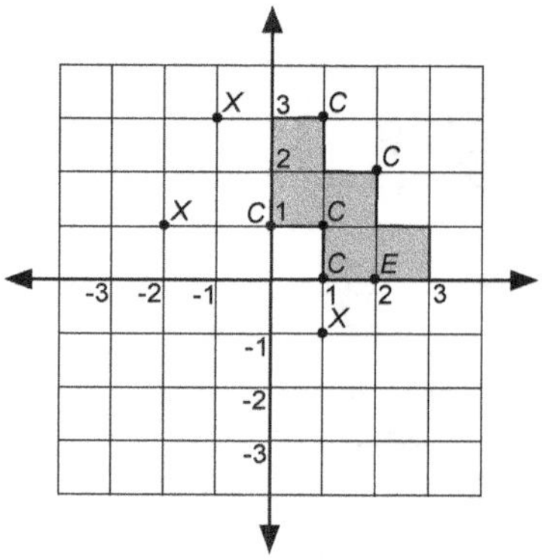

BTP 32

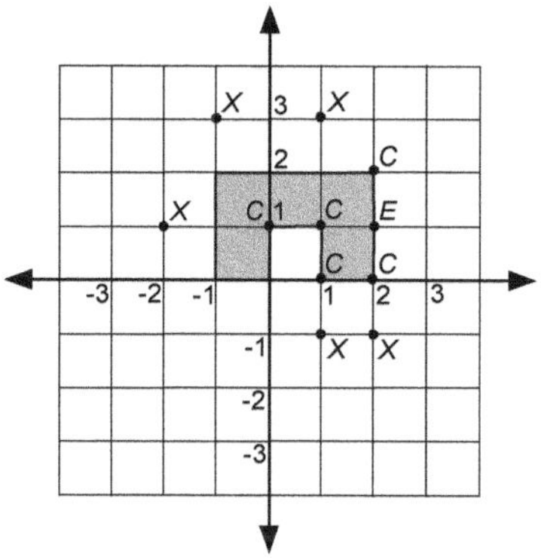

BTP 33

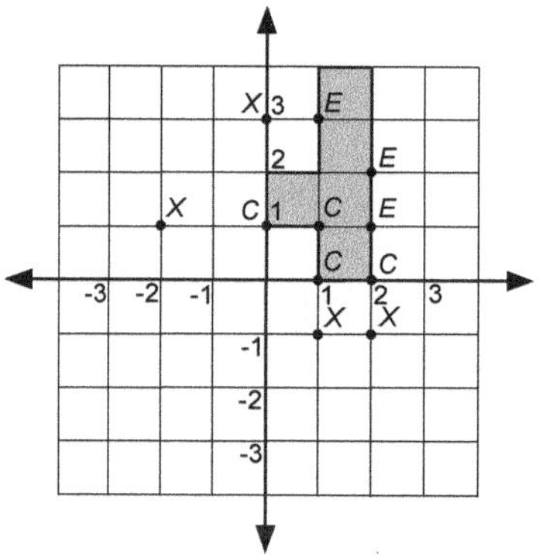

BTP 34

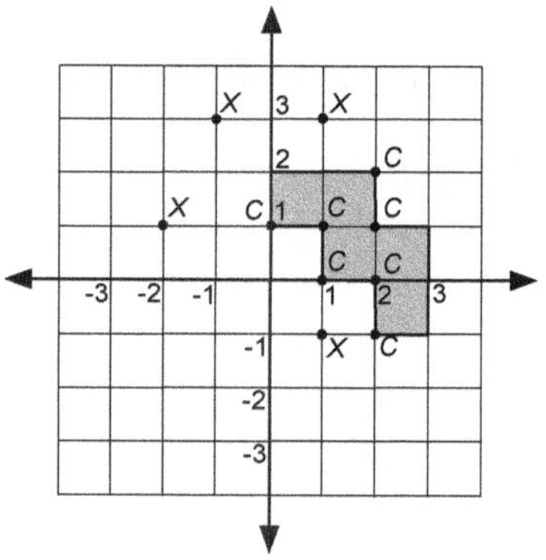

BTP 35

V	V	V	F	Z	Z	P	P	P	Y
V	F	F	F	Z	L	P	P	Y	Y
V	X	F	Z	Z	L	L	L	L	Y
X	X	X	T	N	N	N	W	W	Y
U	X	U	T	T	T	N	N	W	W
U	U	U	T	I	I	I	I	I	W

BTP 36

U	U	U	Y	T	T	T	N	Z	Z
U	X	U	Y	Y	T	N	N	Z	I
X	X	X	Y	L	T	N	Z	Z	I
V	X	F	Y	L	W	N	P	P	I
V	F	F	F	L	W	W	P	P	I
V	V	V	F	L	L	W	W	P	I

BTP 37

U	U	X	T	T	T	L	L	L	L
U	X	X	X	T	P	P	P	F	L
U	U	X	Z	T	P	P	F	F	F
V	Z	Z	Z	N	N	N	W	W	F
V	Z	Y	Y	Y	Y	N	N	W	W
V	V	V	Y	I	I	I	I	I	W

BTP 38

U	U	U	Y	T	T	T	N	Z	Z
U	X	U	Y	Y	T	N	N	Z	I
X	X	X	Y	L	T	N	Z	Z	I
V	X	F	Y	L	W	N	P	P	I
V	F	F	F	L	W	W	P	P	I
V	V	V	F	L	L	W	W	P	I

BTP 39

U	U	U	Z	Z	P	P	W	W	T	T	T
U	F	U	Z	P	P	P	Y	W	W	T	V
F	F	Z	Z	X	Y	Y	Y	Y	W	T	V
L	F	F	X	X	X	N	N	N	V	V	V
L	L	L	L	X	N	N	I	I	I	I	I

BTP 40

T	I	I	I	I	I	L	Z	Z	F	F	N
T	T	T	L	L	L	L	Z	F	F	N	N
T	P	U	U	U	W	Z	Z	X	F	N	V
P	P	U	Y	U	W	W	X	X	X	N	V
P	P	Y	Y	Y	Y	W	W	X	V	V	V

2.10

1. Cayman Key	The origin is at the Mango Tree.	The treasure is located at (0, 7).
2. Barbossa Island	The origin is at the Palm Tree.	The treasure is located at (8, 4).
3. Isla Sirena	The origin is at Dead Man's Cove.	Two locations: (-2, 9) and (2, -9).
4. Blackbeard Island	The origin is at Debtor's Prison.	The treasure is located at (-3, 3).
5. Haunted Isle	The origin is at Deadman's Dock.	The treasure is located at (3, 9).
6. Skeleton Key	The origin is at Bread Fruit Tree.	The treasure is located at (2, 9).

7. Doubloon Island	The origin is at Hornswaggle Inn.	The treasure is located at (-4, 3).
8. Skull Island	The origin is at Jetsam River Bridge.	The treasure is located at (5, 1).
9. Demon Island	The origin is at Fortress Gate.	The treasure is located at (-5, 7).
10. Isla Tortuga	The origin is at Skull Rock.	The treasure is located at (8, 4).

Answers Chapter 3

3.1

Exercises 1–5

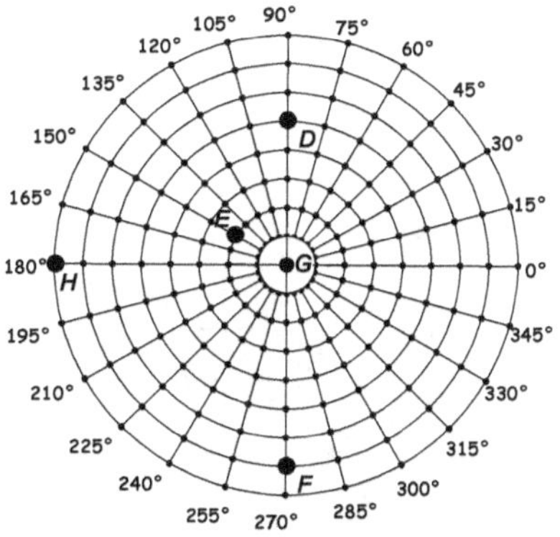

Exercises 6–8

6. (6, 15°), (8, 15°), (8, 30°), (7, 30°), (7, 45°), (8, 45°), (8, 60°), (6, 60°)
7. (2, 345°), (6, 345°), (6, 315°), (5, 315°), (5, 330°), (2, 330°)
8. (5, 225°), (7, 225°), (7, 255°), (8, 255°), (8, 270°), (6, 270°), (6, 240°), (5, 240°)

Exercises 9–10

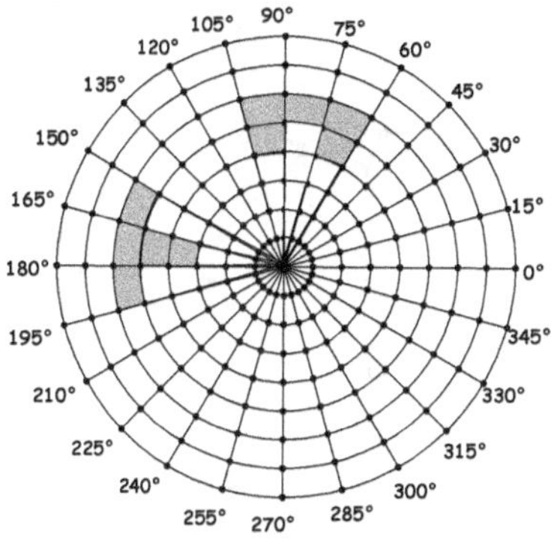

3.4

Exercise 1

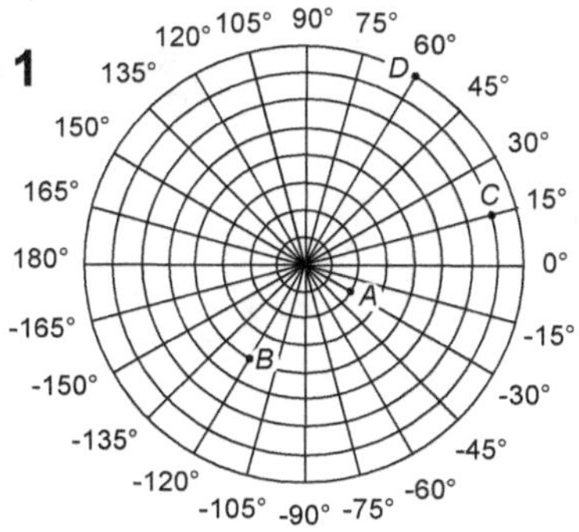

3.6

PBTP 1

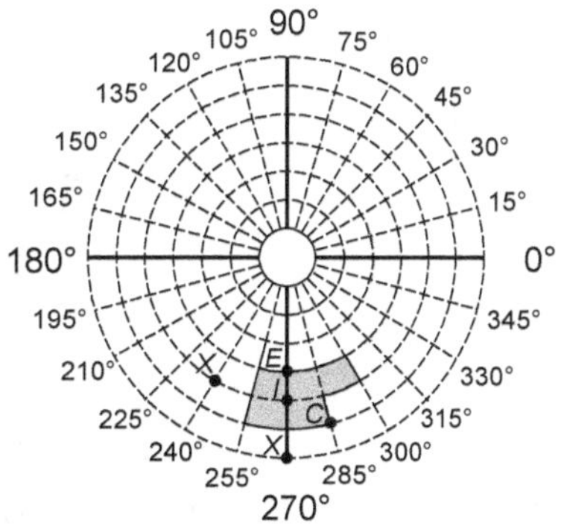

PBTP 2

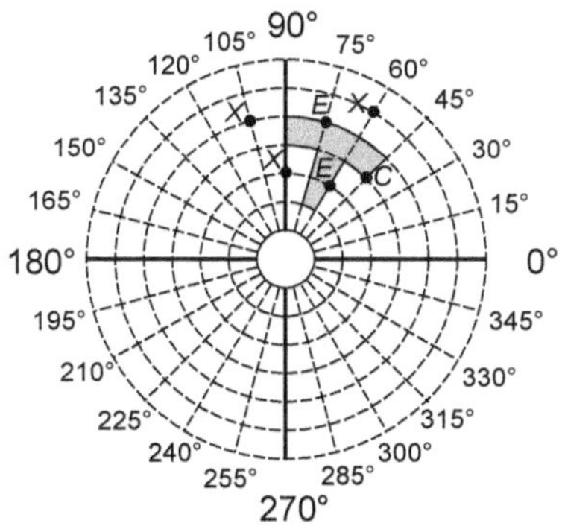

PBTP 3

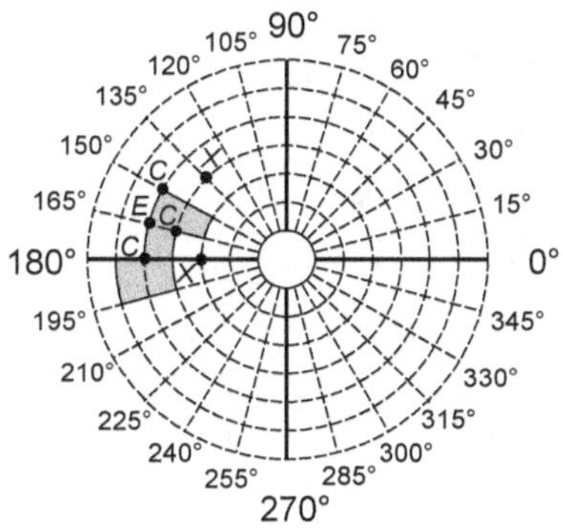

PBTP 4

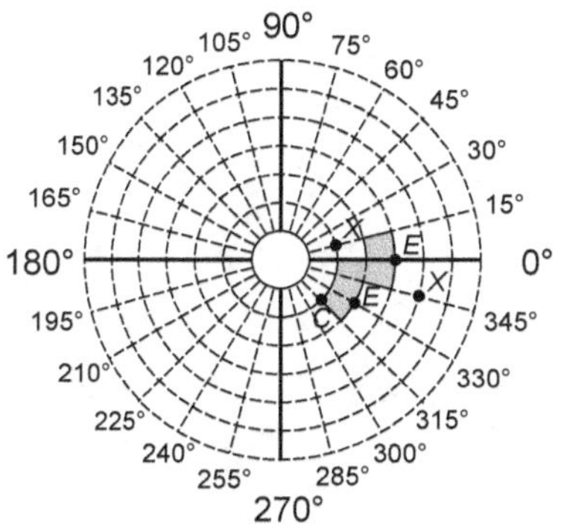

PBTP 5

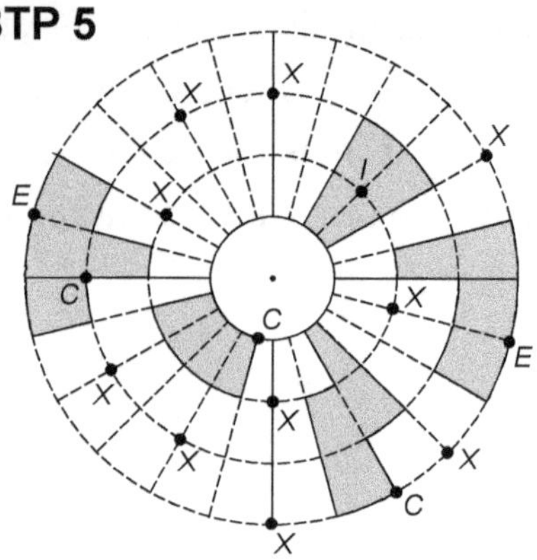

PBTP 6

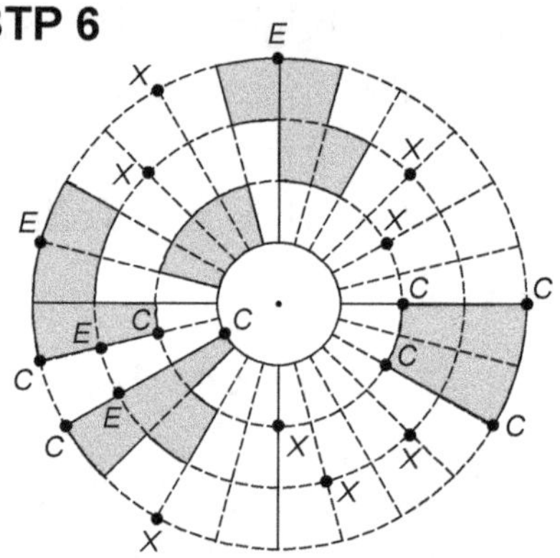

PBTP 7

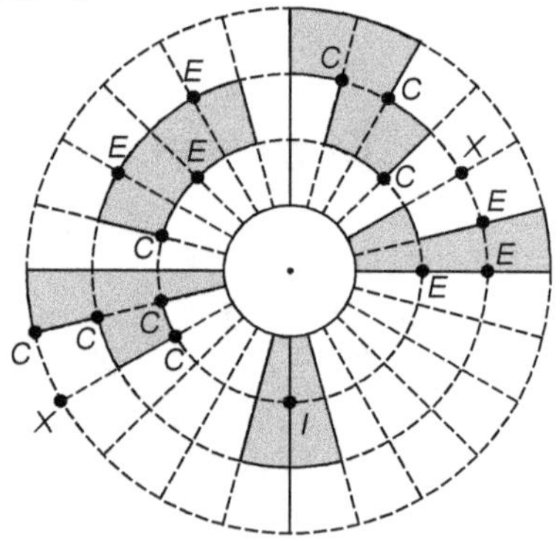

PBTP 8

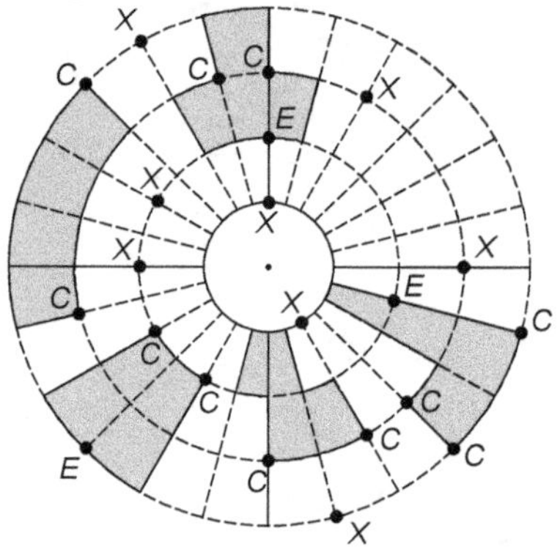

PBTP 9

Here is *one* possible solution.

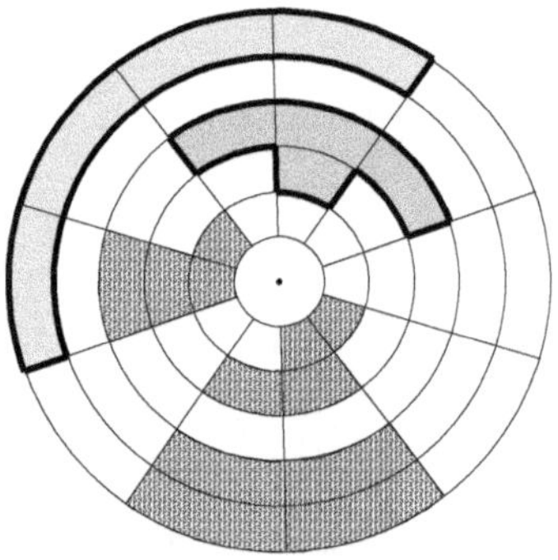

PBTP 10

Here is *one* possible solution.

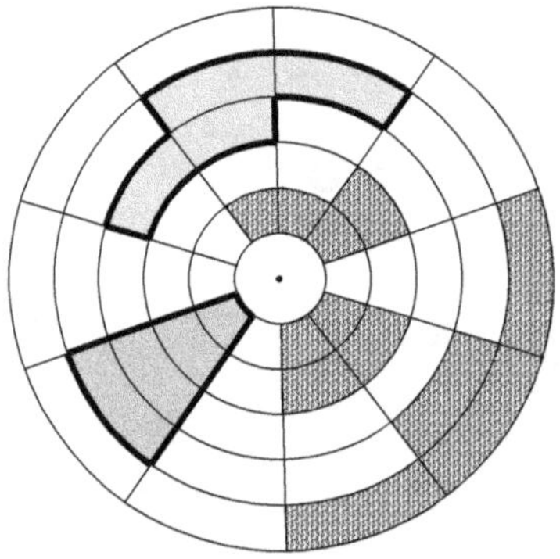

PBTP 11

Here is *one* possible solution.

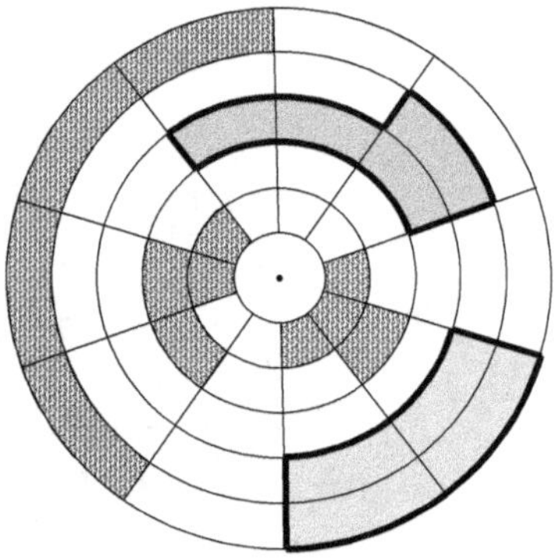

PBTP 12

Here is *one* possible solution.

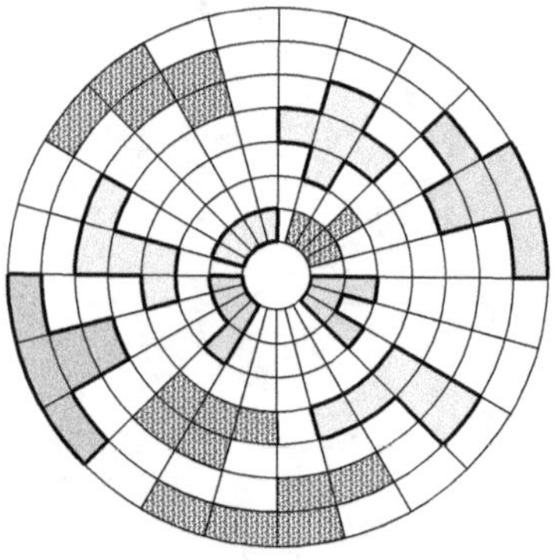

PBTP 13

Here is *one* possible solution.

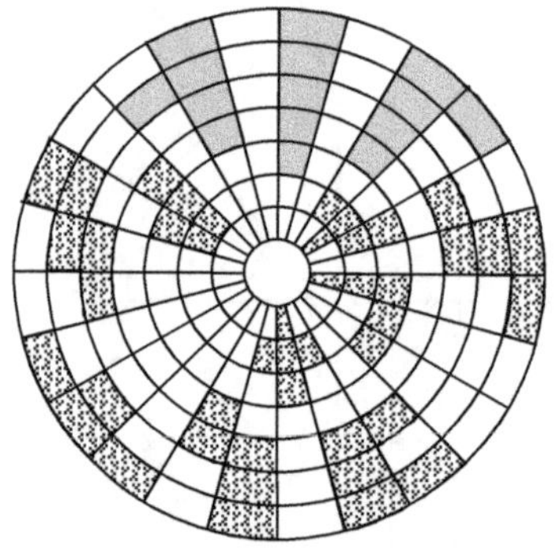

PBTP 14

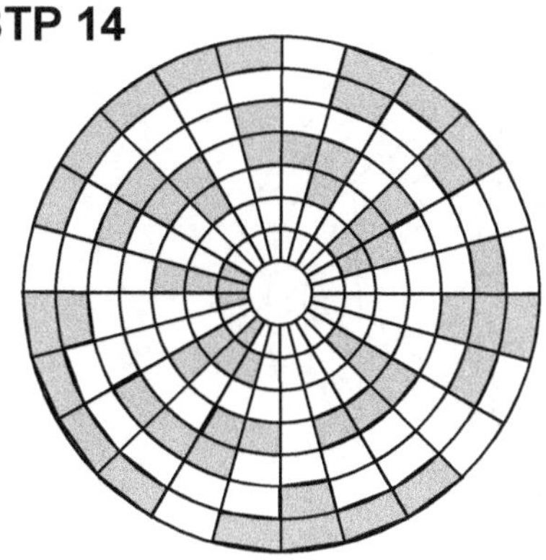

PBTP 15

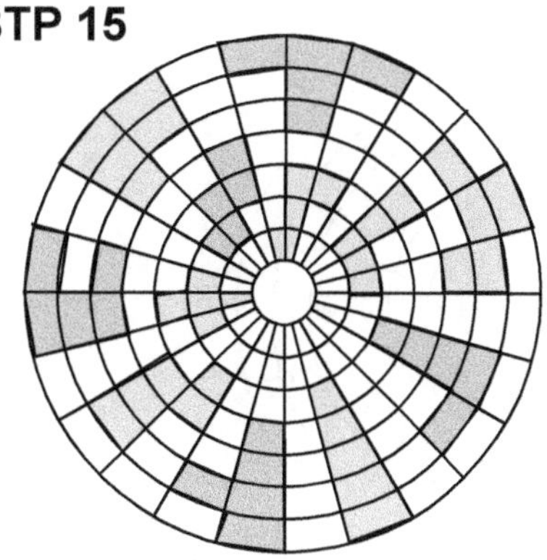

PBTP 16

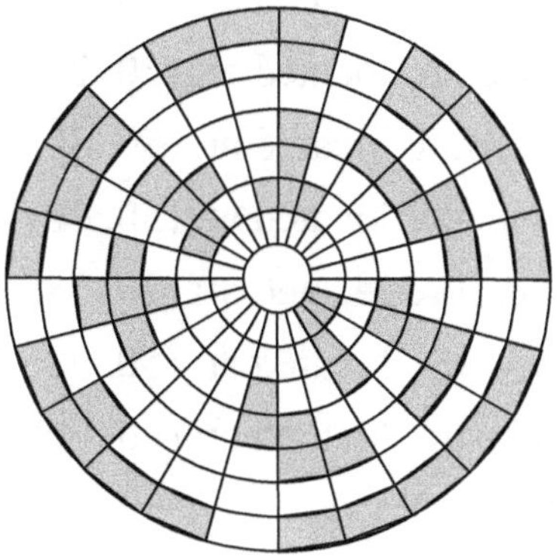

PBTP 17

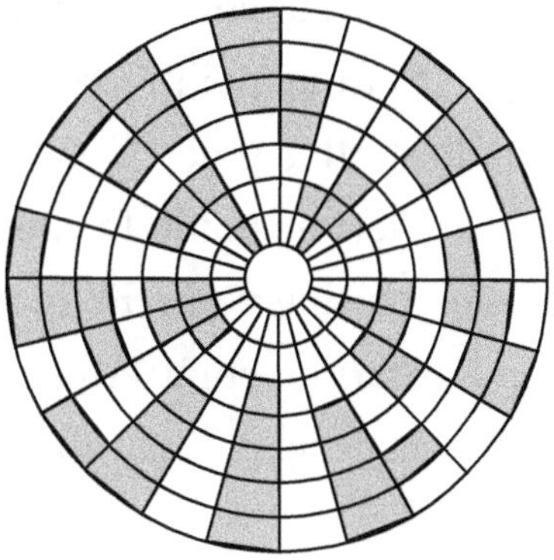

PBTP 18

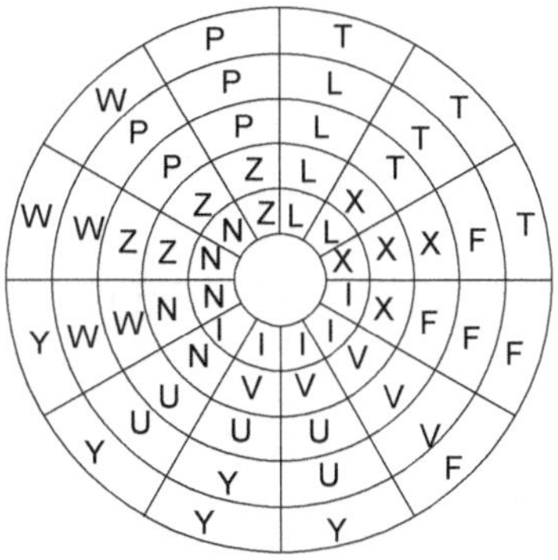

PBTP 19

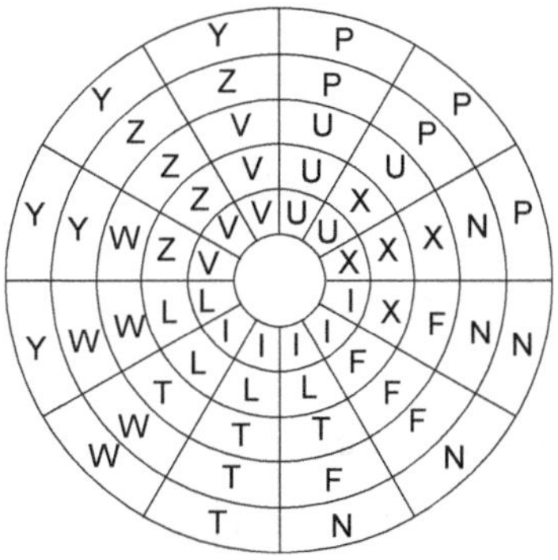

PBTP 20

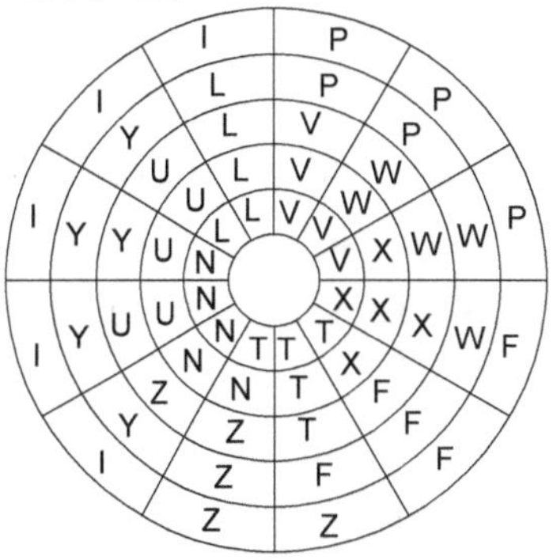

PBTP 21

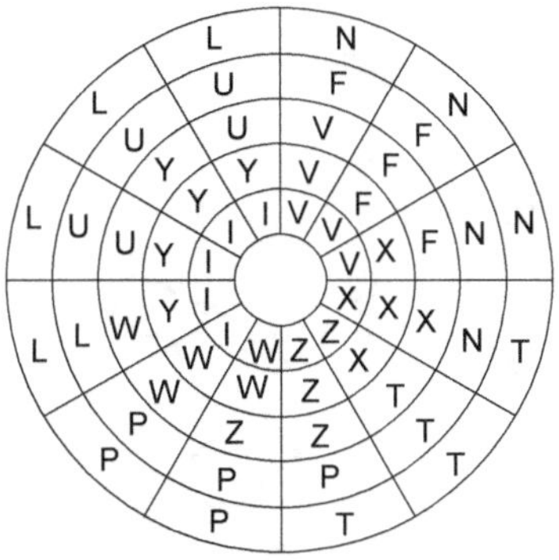

PBTP 22

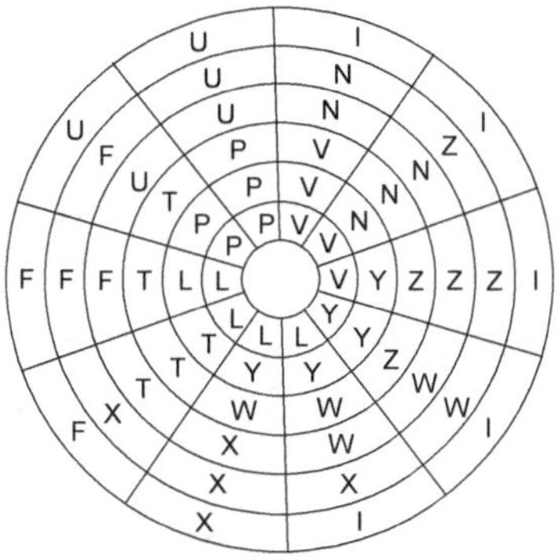

PBTP 23

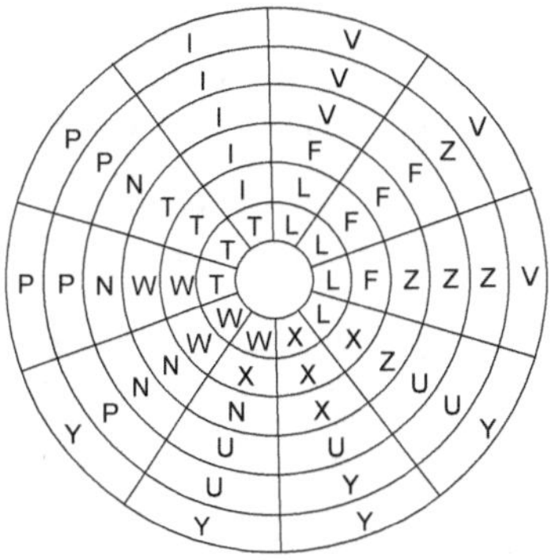

PBTP 24

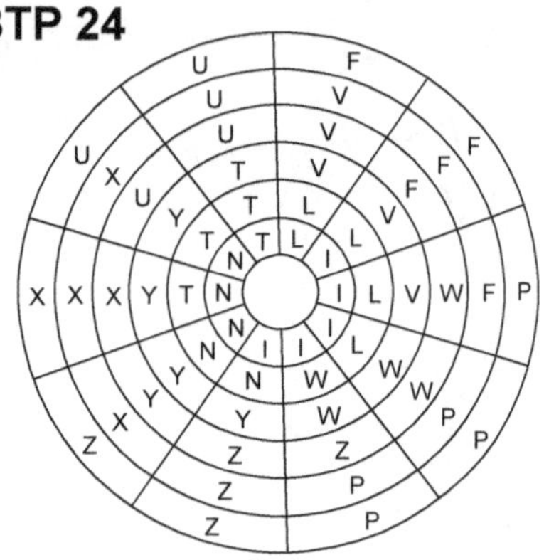

PBTP 25

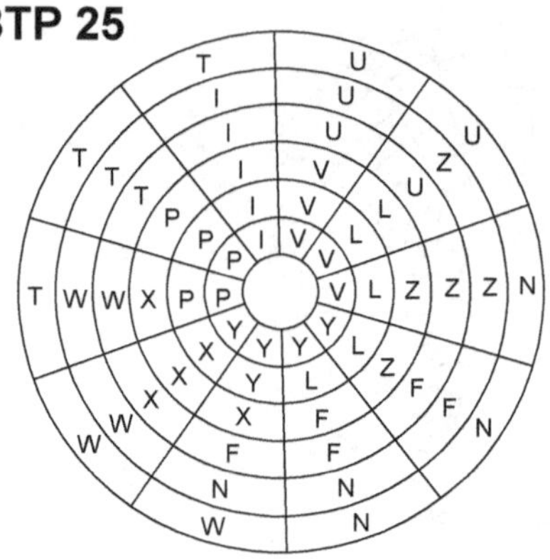

3.7

1.	Emerald island	Starting point: Mango Tree	Treasure located at: (20, 45°)
2.	Rum Reef Key	Starting point: Red Ensign Tavern	Treasure located at: (50, 255°)
3.	Scallywag Island	Starting point: Dead man's Tree	Treasure located at: (50, 300°)
4.	Doubloon Island	Starting point: Lychee Tree	Treasure located at: (50, 225°)
5.	Shipwreck Island	Starting point: Flying Dutchman Shipyard	Treasure located at: (20, 285°)
6.	Albatross Island	Starting point: Albatross Hill	Treasure located at: (50, 285°)
7.	Isla Plata	Starting point: Calico Jack Cave	Treasure located at: (60, 60°) or (60, 240°)
8.	Isla de Oro	Starting point: Iguana Steak House	Treasure located at: (70, 45°)
9.	Isla de los Muerto	Starting point: Privateer Cemetery	Treasure located at: (60, 315°)
10.	Isla de Sangria		Treasure located at: (50, 135°)

Values for *a*–*g* for Isla de Sangria

a = Five less than five times the number of the day in September in which Bilbo Baggins was born. $(5\times22 - 5 = 105)$, $a = 105$.

b = Ten times the sum of the digits in the zip code of the White House. (20500 —> $2+5 = 7$ thus $10 \times 7 = 70$), $b = 70$.

c = Five times the number of amendments to the U.S. Constitution. $(27\times5 = 135)$, $c = 135$.

d = Five times the number of bones in the human hand. $(27\times5 = 135)$, $d = 135$.

e = Five times the number of faces on a dodecahedron. $(5\times12 = 60)$, $e = 60$.

f = The number of countries bordering Bolivia times ten. $(5\times10 = 50)$, $f = 50$.

g = Ten times the sum of the number of rooms and suspects in the board game Clue™. $(10\times(9+6) = 10\times15 = 150)$, $g = 150$.

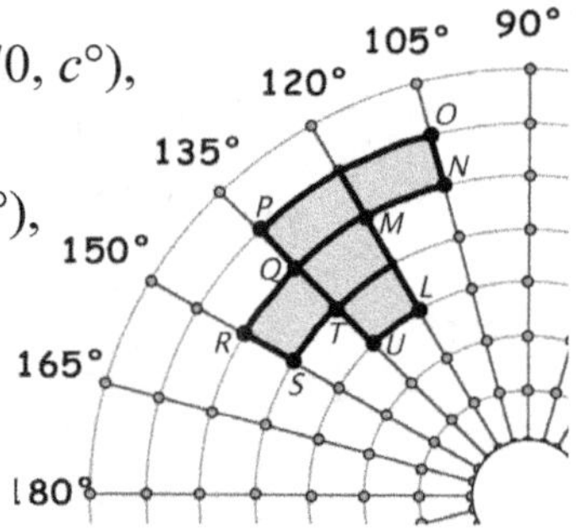

- Nine of the ten vertices of the pentomino are $N(60, a°)$, $O(b, 105°)$, $P(70, c°)$, $Q(60, d°)$, $R(e, 150°)$, $S(f, g°)$, $U(b - 30, d°)$, $L(40, 2e°)$ and $M(e, 2e°)$.
- Therefore nine of the vertices are: $N(60, 105°)$, $O(70, 105°)$, $P(70, 135°)$, $Q(60, 135°)$, $R(60, 150°)$, $S(50, 150°)$, $U(40, 135°)$, $L(40, 120)$ and $M(60, 120)$.
- The remaining vertex of the *F*-pentomino $T(50, 135°)$ is the treasure location.

Answers Chapter 4

4.1

Exercises 1–7

1. (30° N, 45° W) 2. (45° S, 15° W) 3. (0° N, 0° W) 4. (90° N, 0° W)

5. *W*(45° N, 120° W) *X*(15° S, 75° W) *Y*(75° N, 60° W) *Z*(15° N, 0° W)

6. 60° 7. 1/6

Exercises 8–29

8. D 9. C 10. E 11. A 12. F 13. B

14. C (Taj Mahal) 15. A (Fallingwater) 16. G (Doge's Palace) 17. E (Kinkaku-ji)

18. B (Alhambra) 19. D (Angkor Wat) 20. H (Sydney Opera House)

21. F (Petronas Towers)

22. H 23. E 24. D 25. C 26. G 27. A 28. B 29. F

Exercises 30–35

30. 5,400 miles 31. 8,440 miles 32. 1,660 miles

33. 5,300 miles 34. 7,400 miles 35. 10,500 miles

4.4

SBTP 1

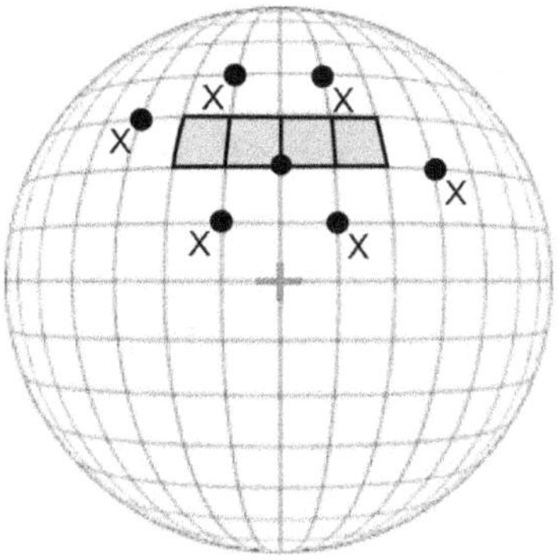

SBTP 2

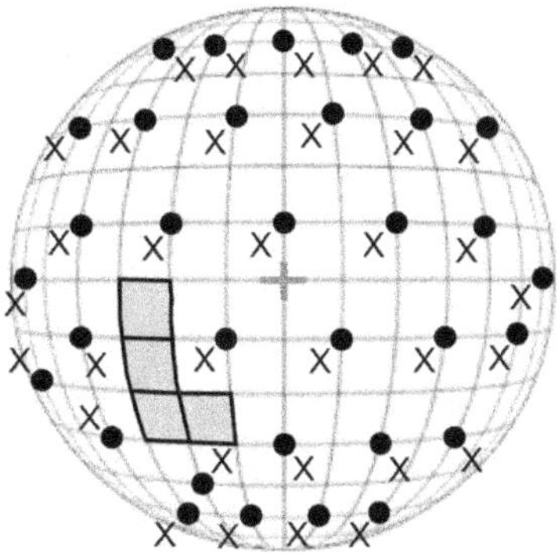

SBTP 3

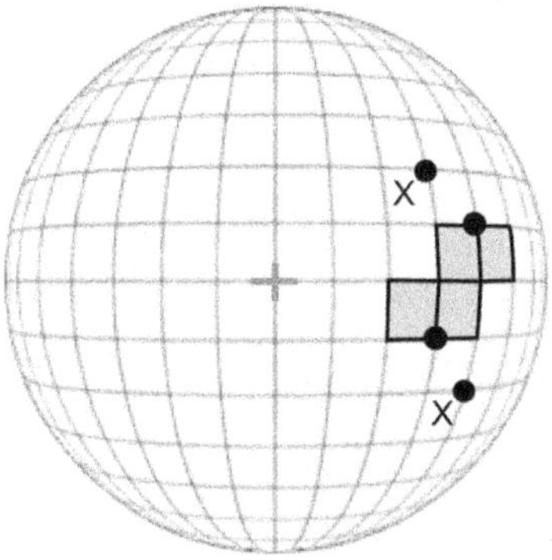

SBTP 4

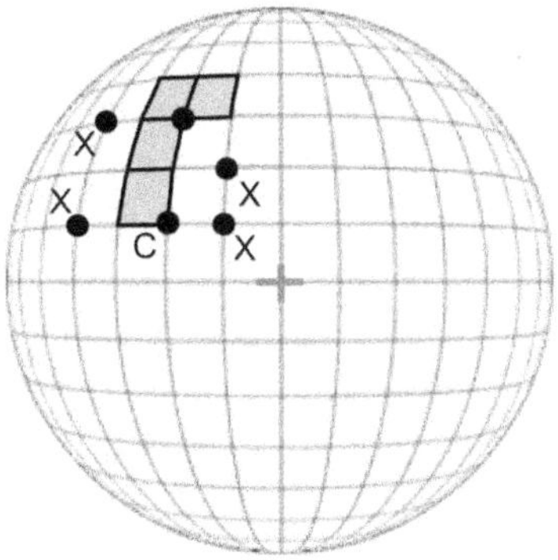

SBTP 5

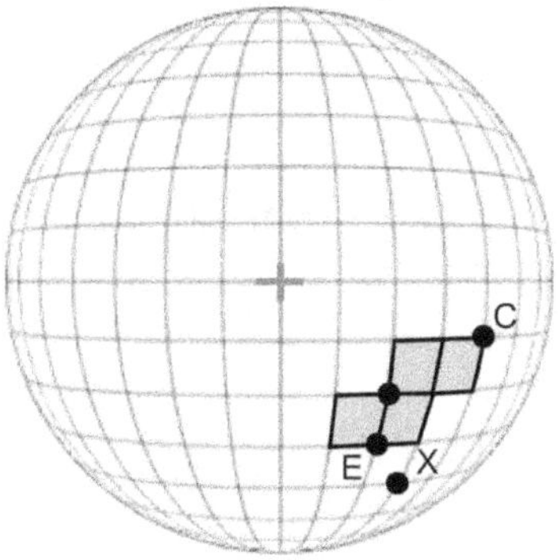

SBTP 6

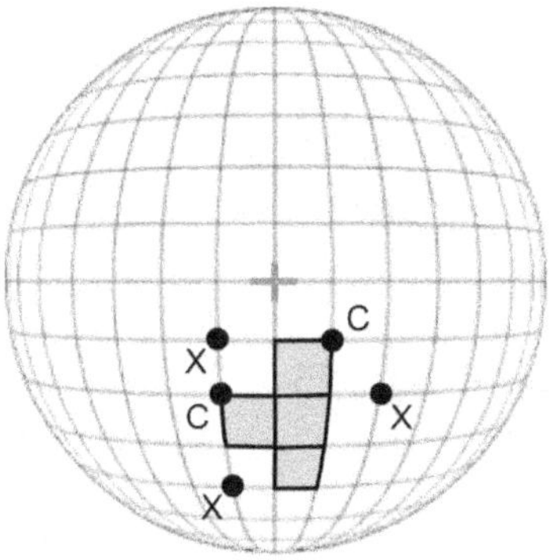

SBTP 7

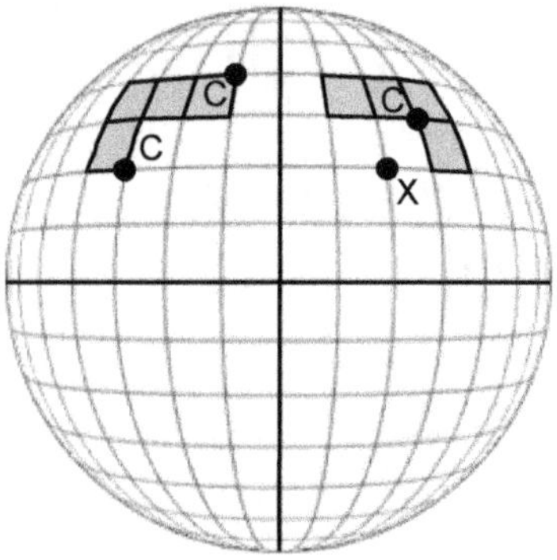

SBTP 8

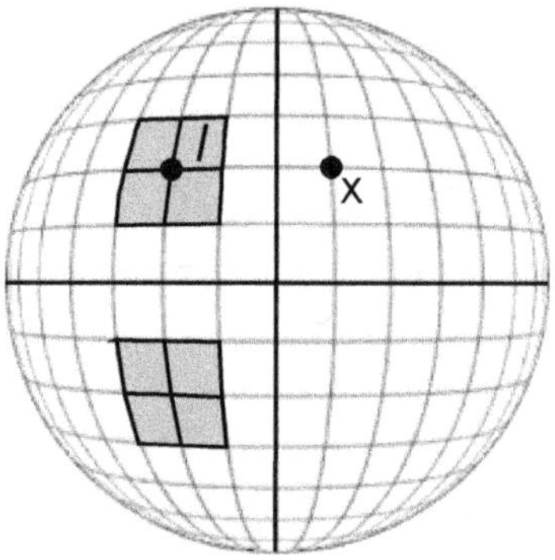

SBTP 9

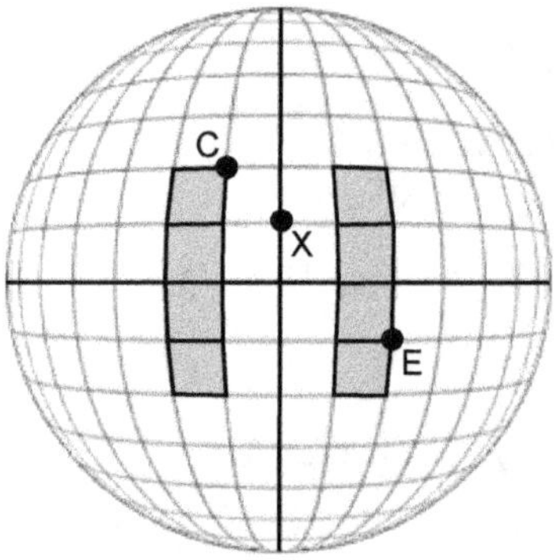

SBTP 10

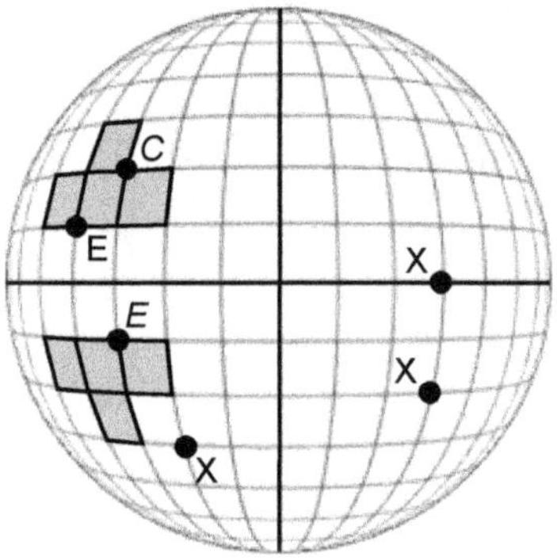

SBTP 11

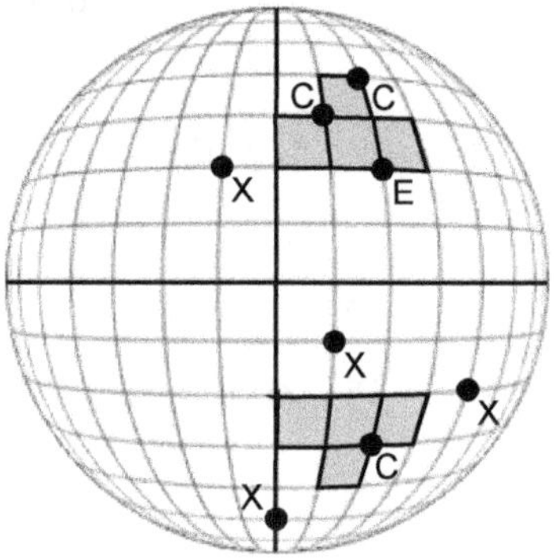

SBTP 12

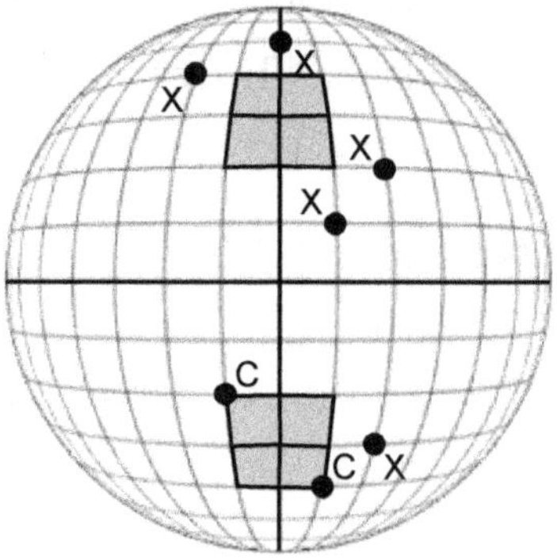

4.5

The approximate location of the *Almiranta* wreckage is (24° 50’ N, 80° 46’ W).

Answers Chapter 5

5.1

Exercises 1–8

1. *A*(0, 0, 0)	2. *B*(9, 0, 0)	3. *C*(9, 12, 0)	4. *D*(0, 12, 0)
5. *E*(0, 0, 4)	6. *F*(9, 0, 4)	7. *G*(9, 12, 4)	8. *H*(0, 12, 4)

Exercises 9–14

9. *P*(2, -5, 1)	10. *Q*(-8, -5, 1)	11. *R*(-8, 3, 1)	12. *T*(2, -5, 7)
13. *U*(-8, -5, 7)	14. *V*(-8, 3, 7)		

Exercises 15–20

15. *xz*-plane	16. *xy*-plane	17. *yz*-plane
18. *z*-axis	19. *x*-axis	20. *y*-axis

Exercises 21–23

21. (2, 2, 0); (2, 2, 2); (2, 1, 0); (2, 1, 2); (1, 2, 0); (1, 2, 2); (1, 1, 0); (1, 1, 2)

22. (-2, 1, 2); (-2, 1, 1); (-2, 2, 2); (-2, 2, 1); (-1, 1, 1); (-1, 1, 2); (-1, 2, 2); (-1, 2, 1)

23. (2, 1, 0); (2, 1, 1); (1, 1, 0); (1, 1, 1); (2, -2, 0); (2, -2, 1); (1, -2, 0); (1, -2, 1)

Exercises 24–26

24.

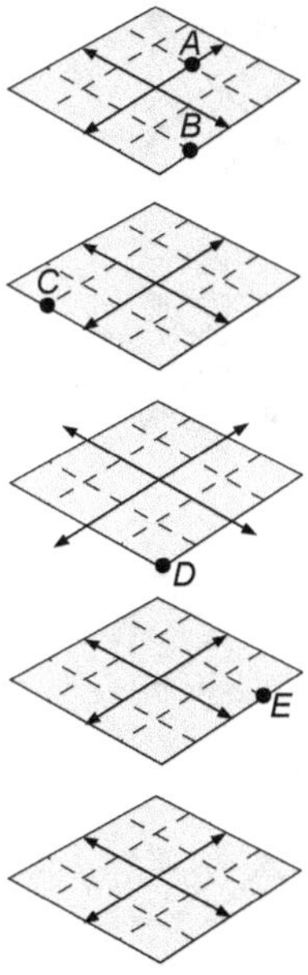

25.

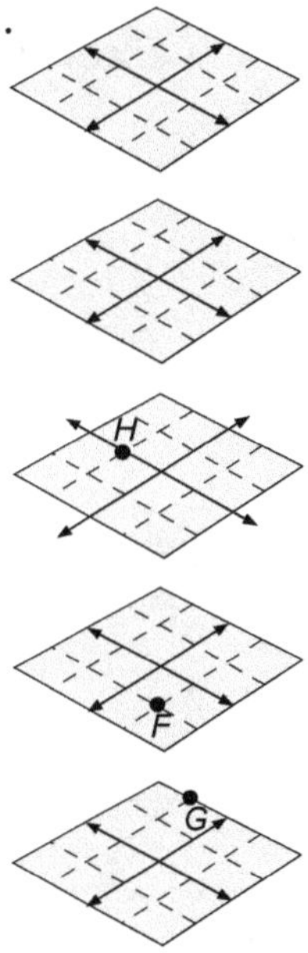

26.

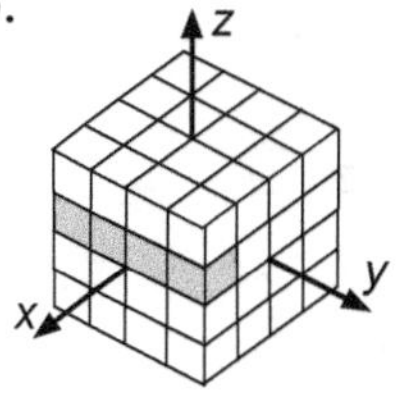

5.2

Answers for Exercises 1 and 2 are shown on Page 101.

Exercise 3

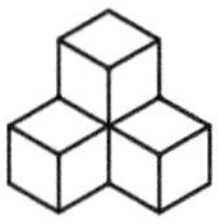

Exercise 4

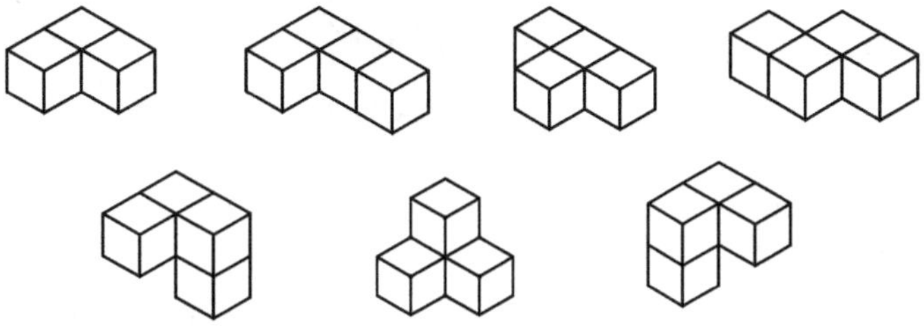

Exercise 5

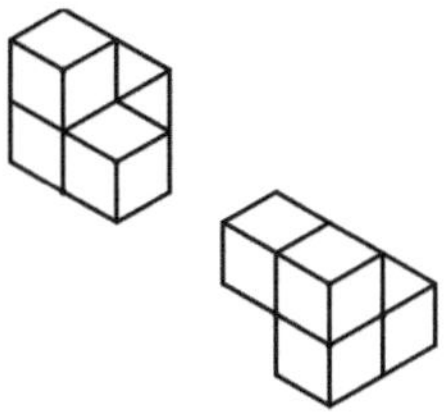

One end

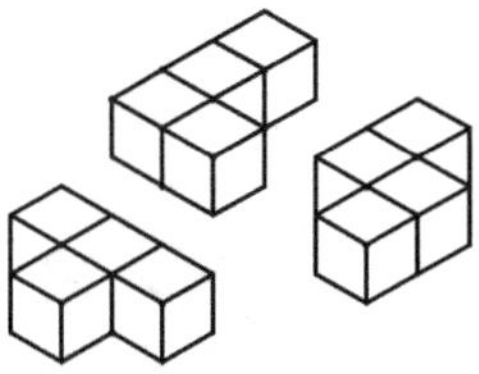

Flat middle

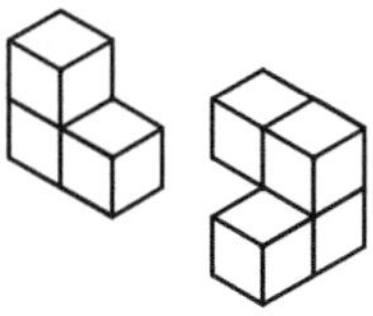

Other end

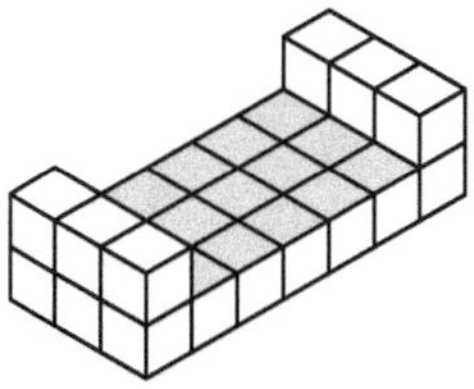

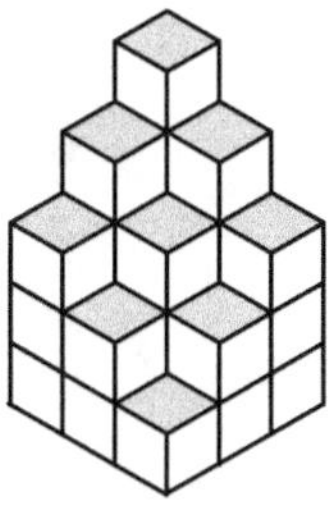

Assemble for bottom

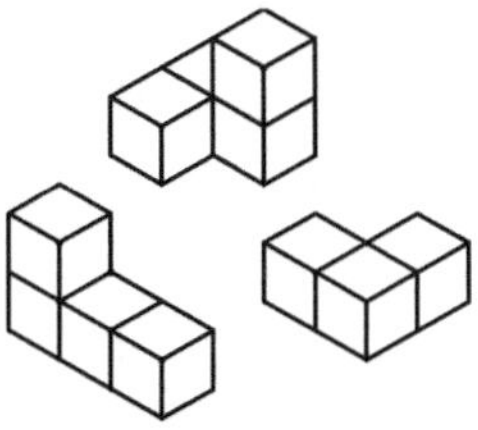

Add these three

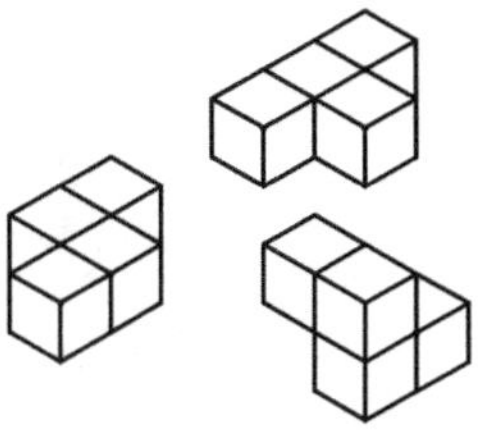

Finish with this

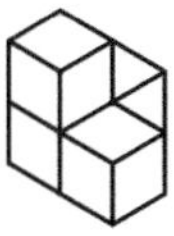

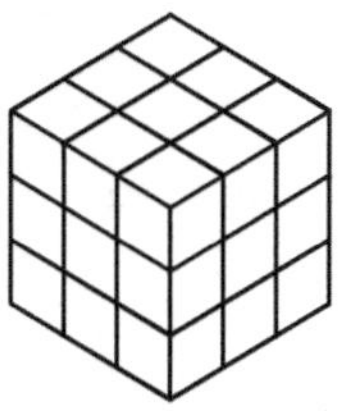

The cube can be assembled in the same way that you created the multiple staircase. The last piece is placed into the corner rather than on top.

5.3

Exercise 1

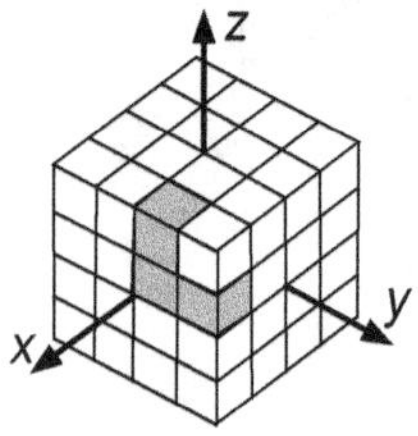

Exercise 2

Top Level
(z = 3)

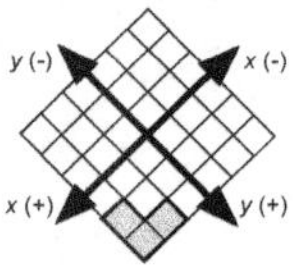

Level 2
(z = 2)

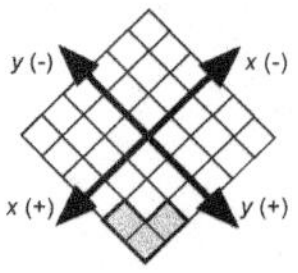

Level 1
(z = 1)

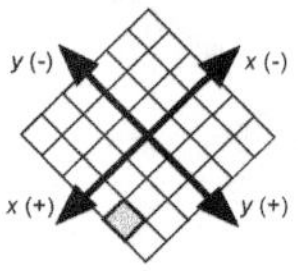

Middle Level
(z = 0)

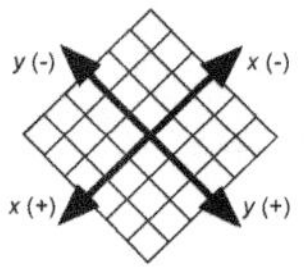

5.6

3-DBTP 1

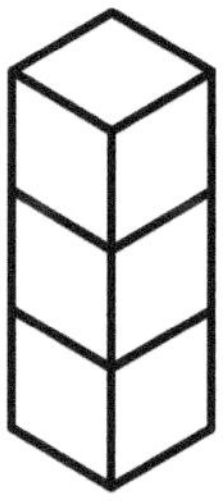

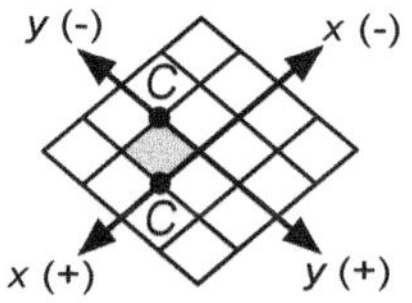

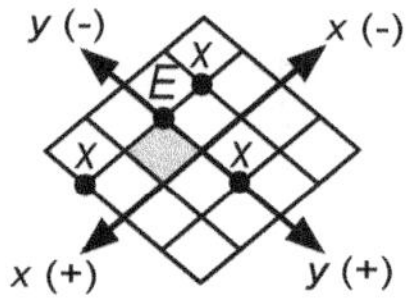

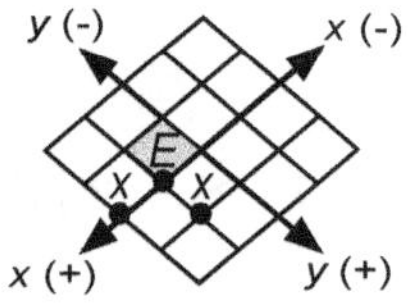

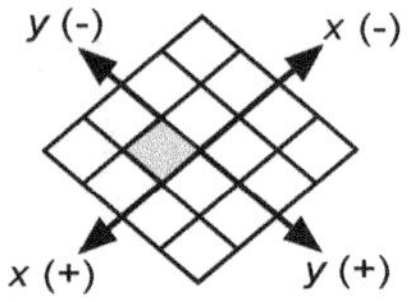

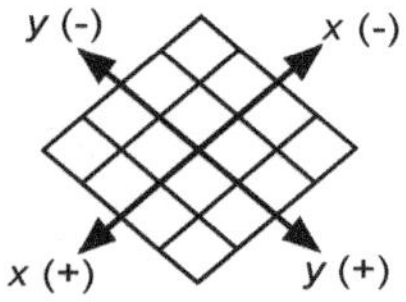

3-DBTP 2

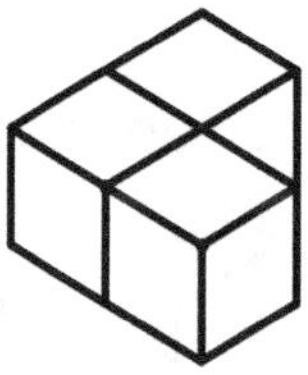

Top
z=2

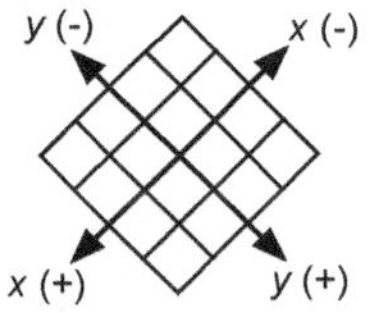

z=1

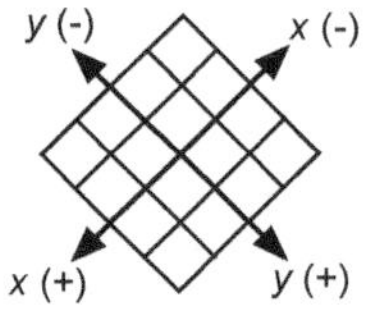

Middle
z=0

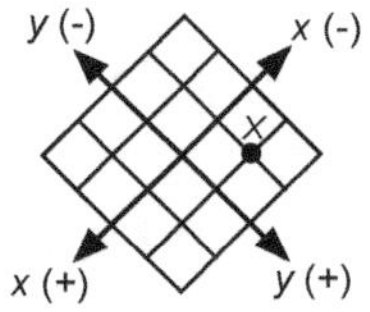

z= -1

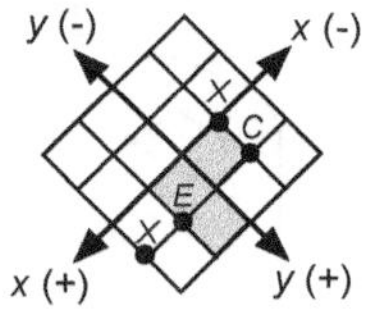

Bottom
z= -2

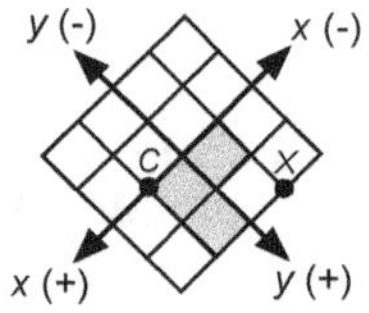

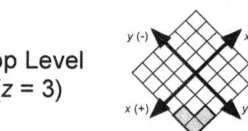

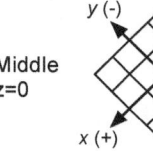

3-DBTP 3

Top
z=2

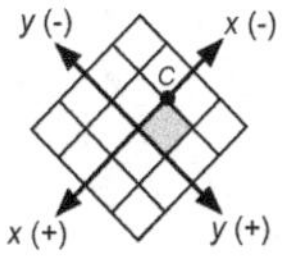

z=1

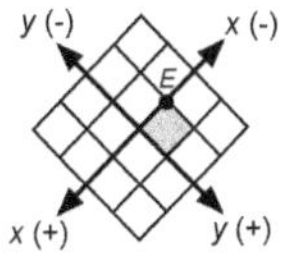

Middle
z=0

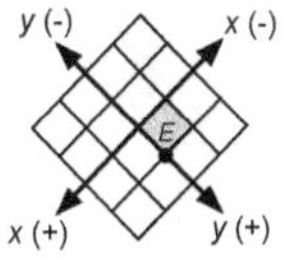

z= -1

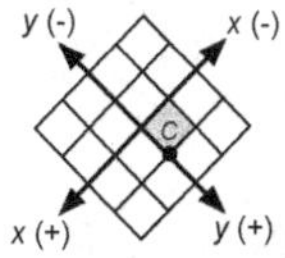

Bottom
z= -2

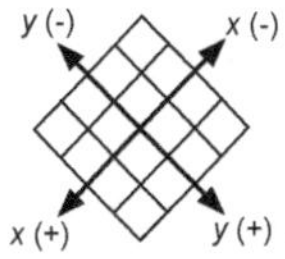

3-DBTP 4

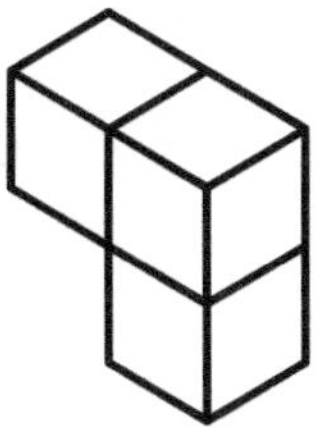

Top
z=2

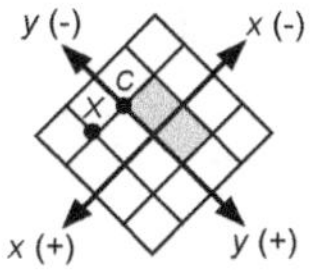

z=1

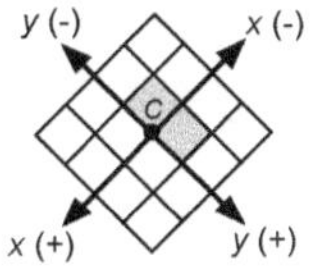

Middle
z=0

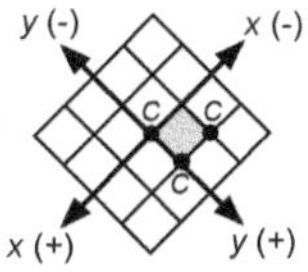

z= -1

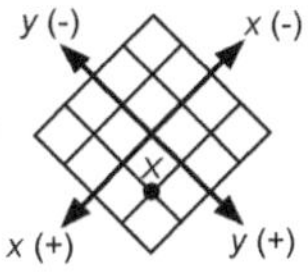

Bottom
z= -2

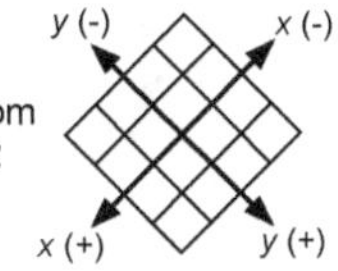

3-DBTP 5

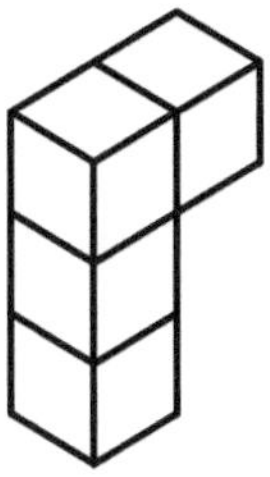

Top
z=2

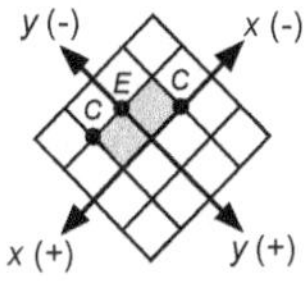

z=1

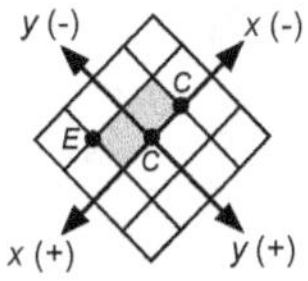

Middle
z=0

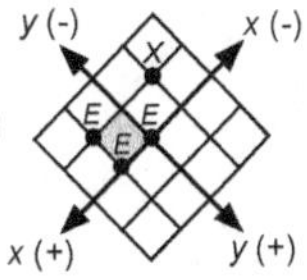

z= -1

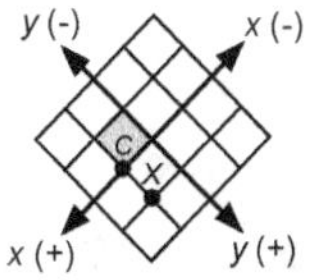

Bottom
z= -2

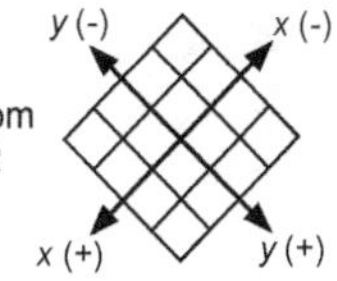

3-DBTP 6

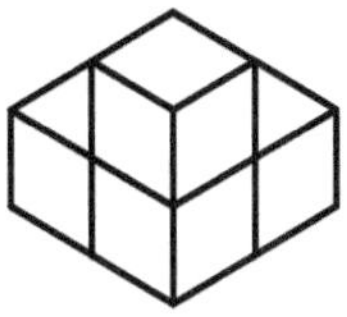

Top
z=2

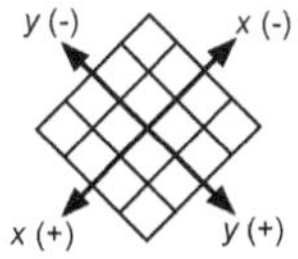

z=1

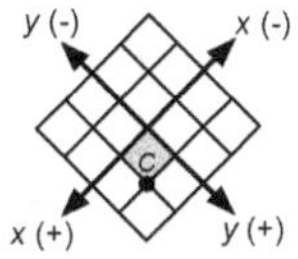

Middle
z=0

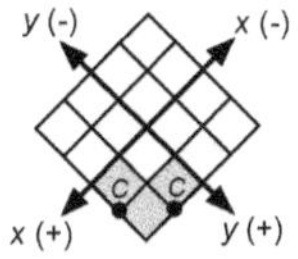

z= -1

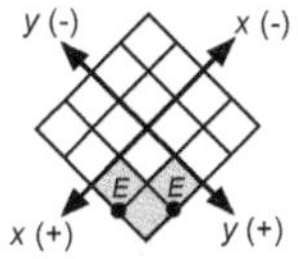

Bottom
z= -2

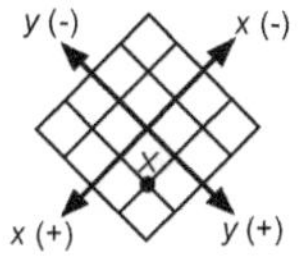

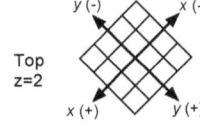

3-DBTP 7

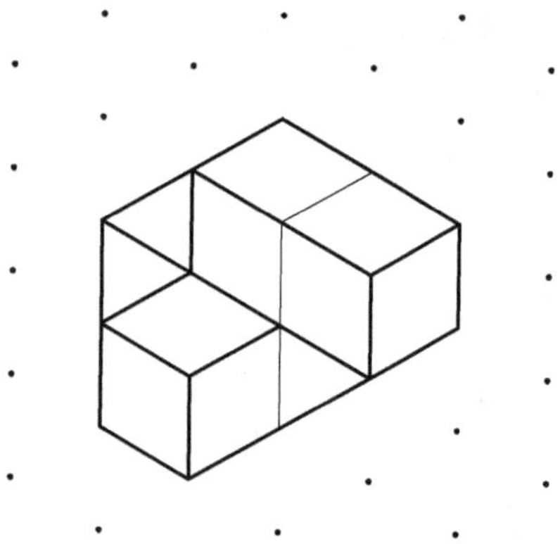

z = 3

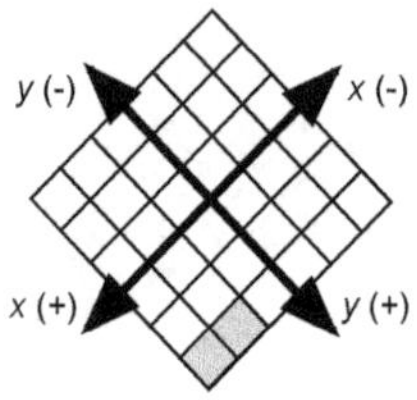

z = 2

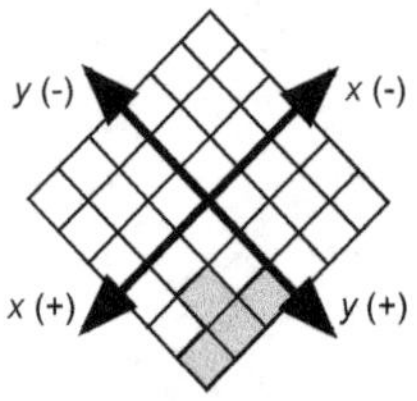

z = 1

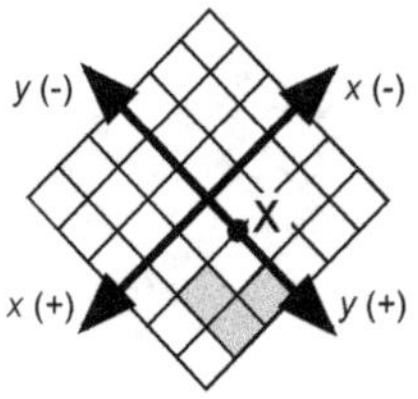

z = 0

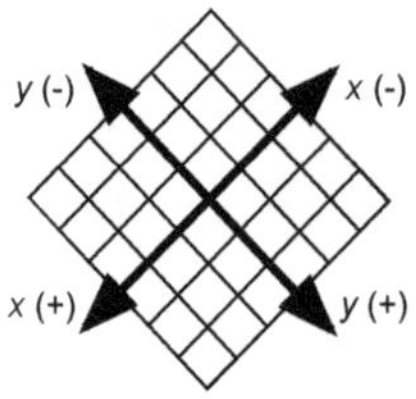

z = -1

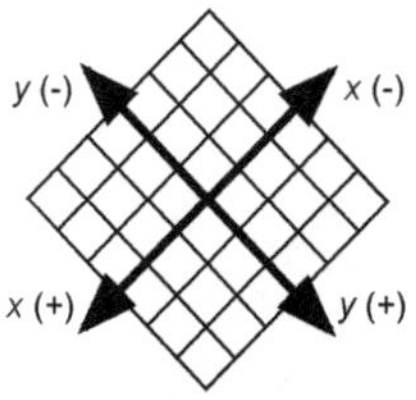

z = -2

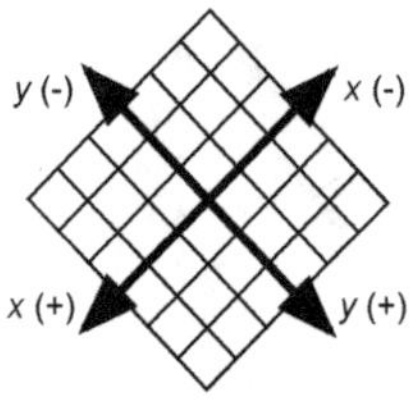

z = -3

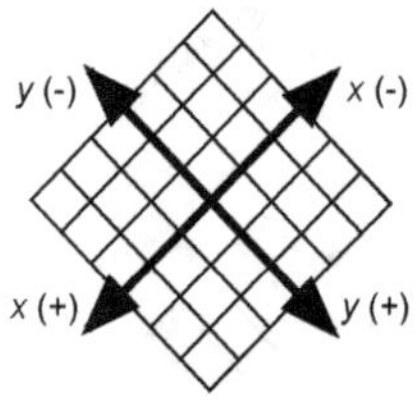

Answers Chapter 6

6.2

1. Freebooter Island

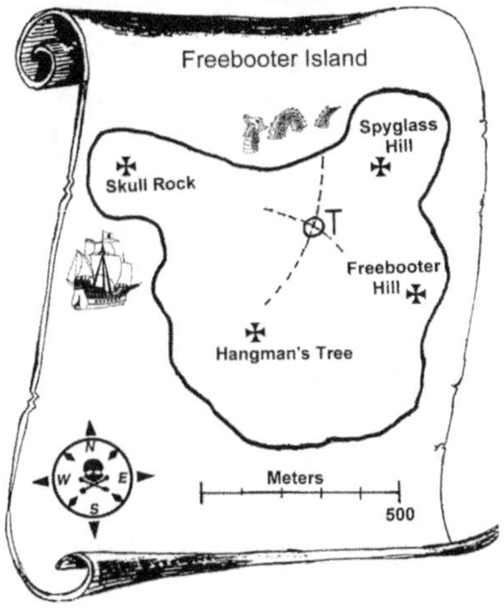

2. Turtle Island

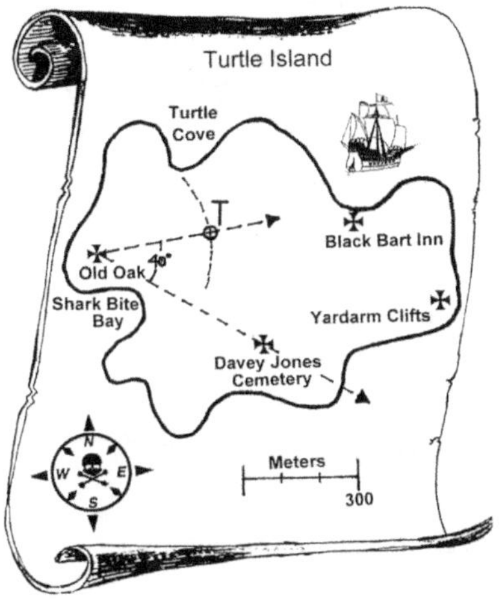

3. Calico Island

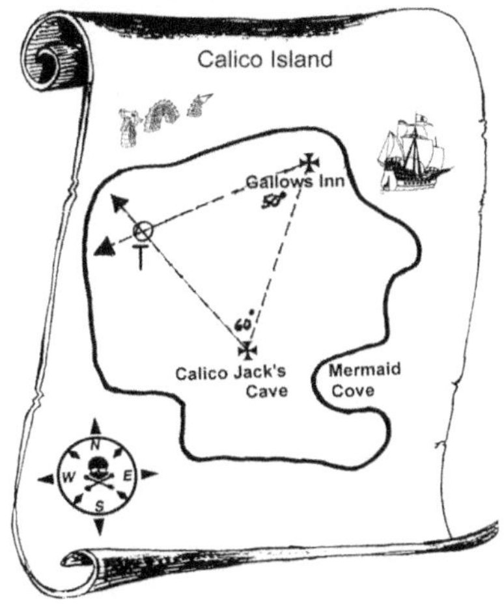

4. Swashbuckler's Island

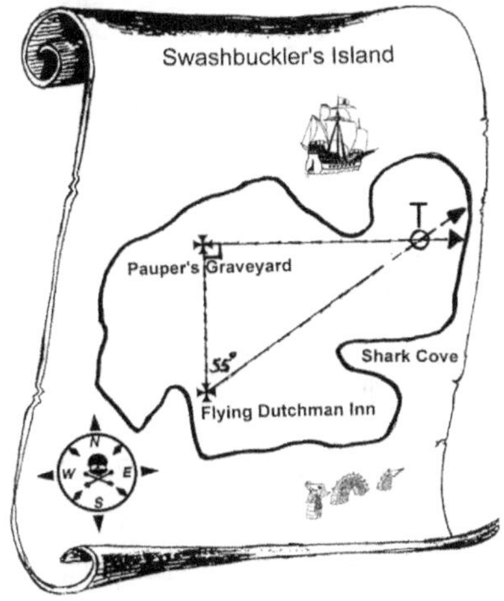

5. Isla Mauritia

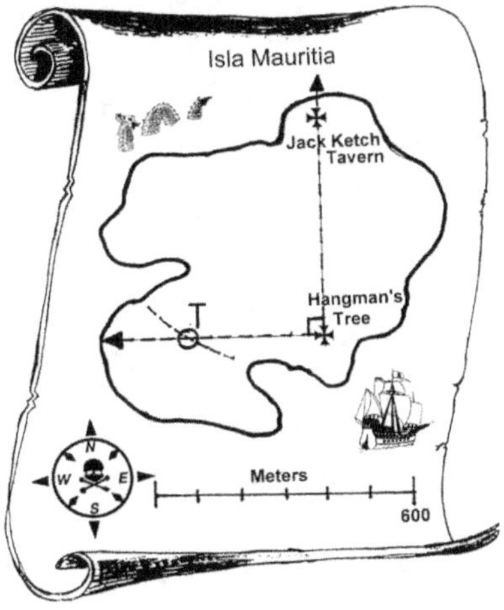

6. Barbossa Island

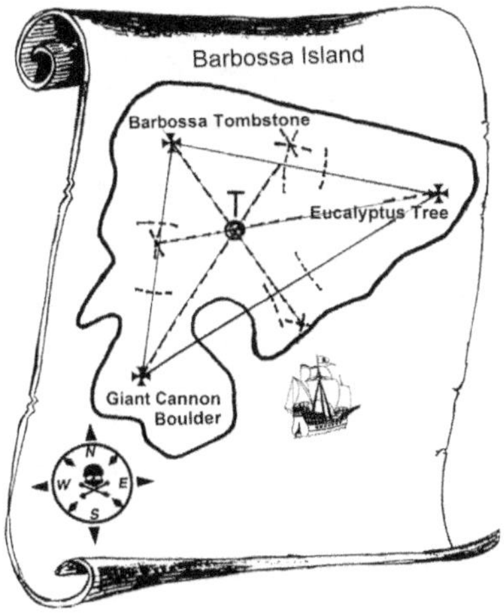

7. Crocodile Key

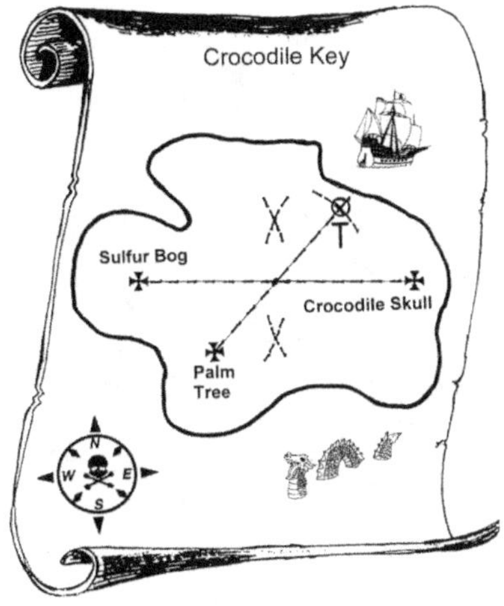

8. Isola Diavolo

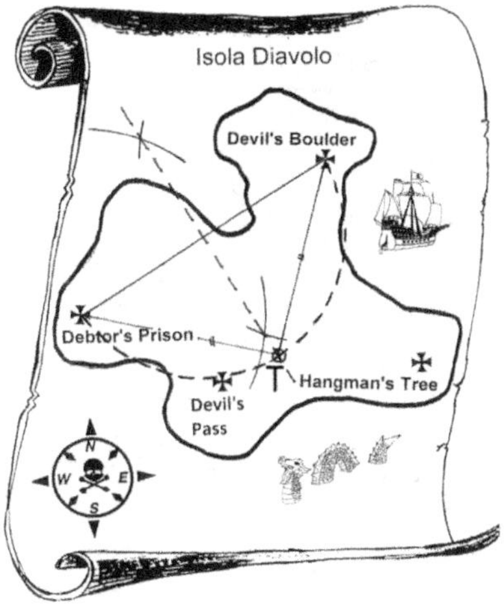

9. Torture Island

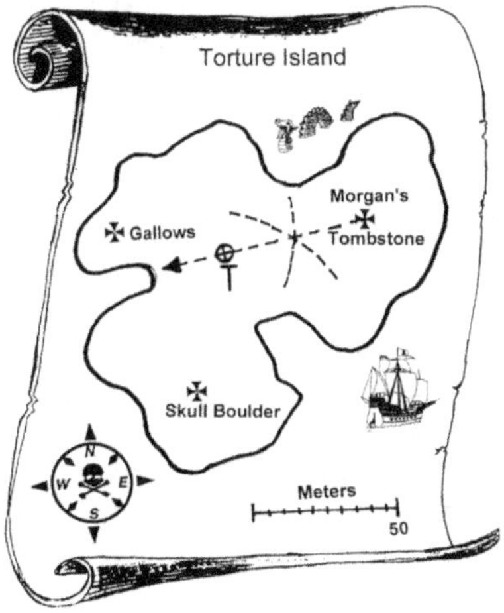

10. Isla Serpiente

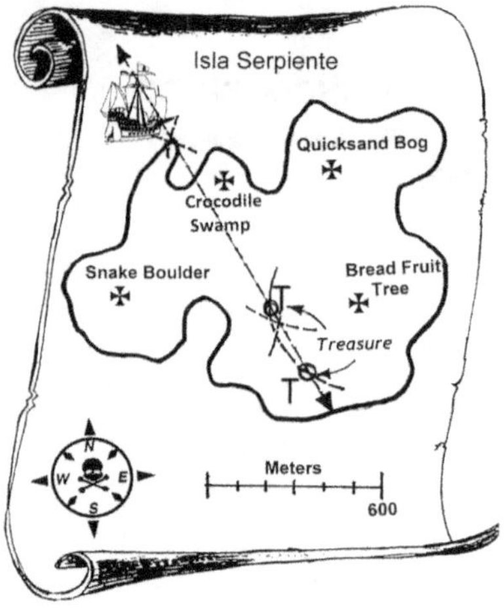

11. Isla Tortuga

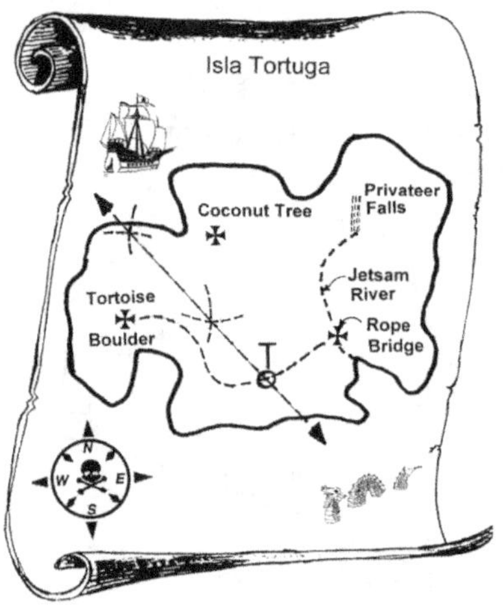

12. Spyglass Island

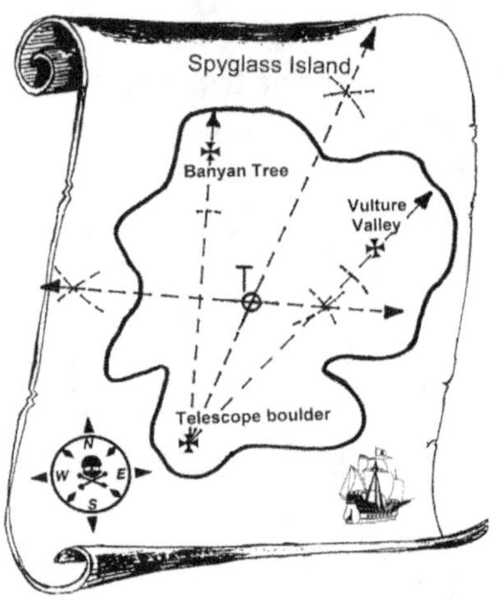

13. Mono Key

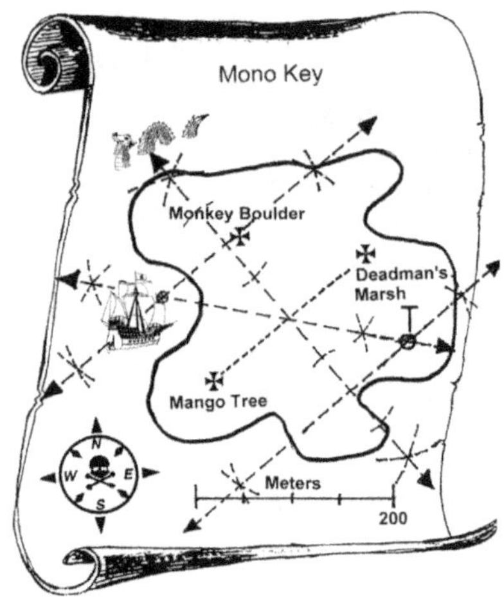

14. Isla Garuda

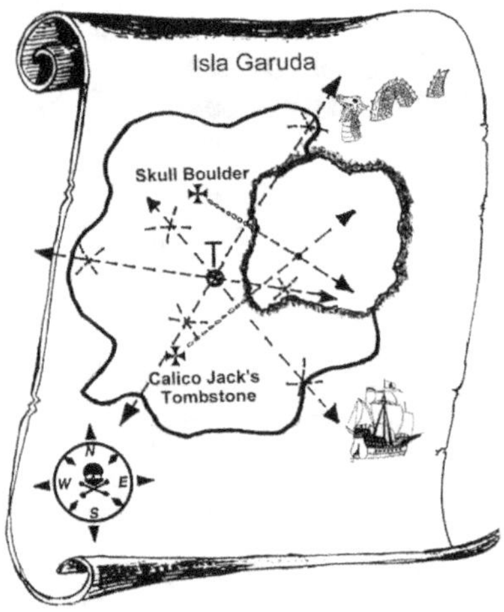

15. Long John Island

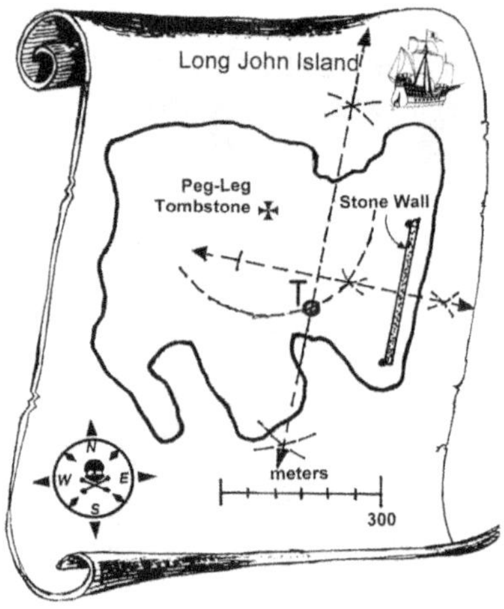

16. Parrot Island

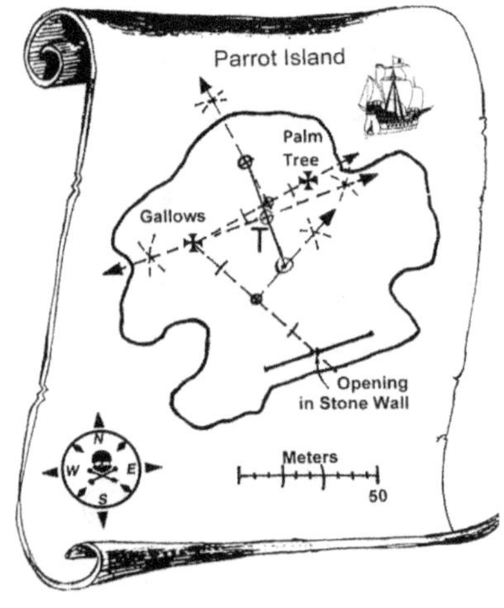

17. Cayman Key

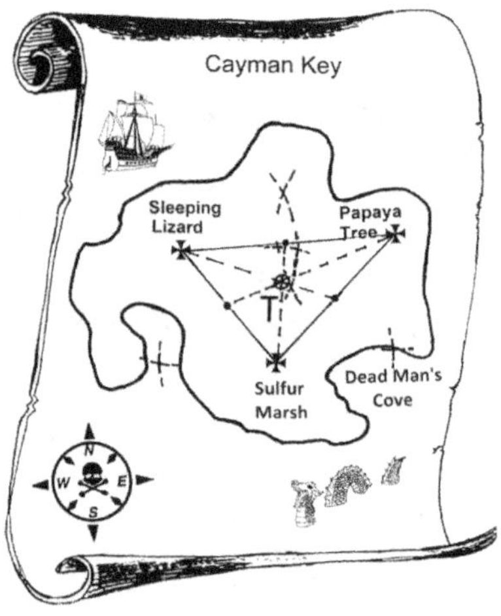

18. Skeleton Island

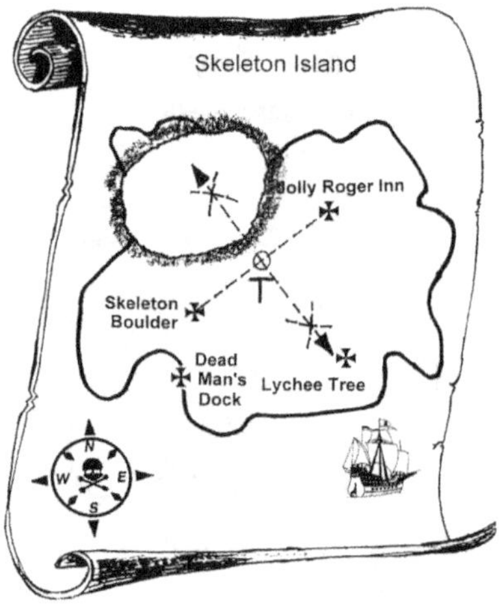

19. Buccaneer Island

There are a number of rectangles that can be formed with the given information: *ABGD*, *BDIJ*, *BFHD*, and *BCDE*. All four points must lie on the island since the Albatross Tavern and the treasure are on the island. Therefore *ABGD* is our rectangle. So our treasure is located at either point *A* or point *G* and the Albatross Tavern is located at the opposite point. Thus, unless we can find the remains of the Albatross Tavern on the island, we will have to dig at both locations to find the treasure.

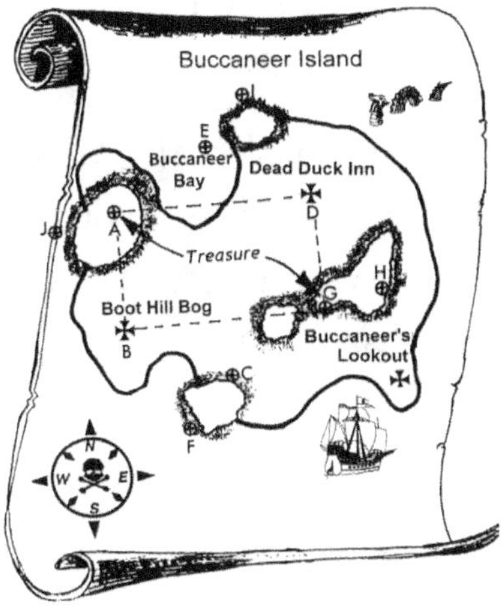

20. Grand Doubloon Island

Pick an arbitrary point to represent the gallows and follow the instructions to the treasure. Do it a second time. Pick another point and follow the instructions to the treasure. You should get the same location for the treasure! See below for an analytic derivation.

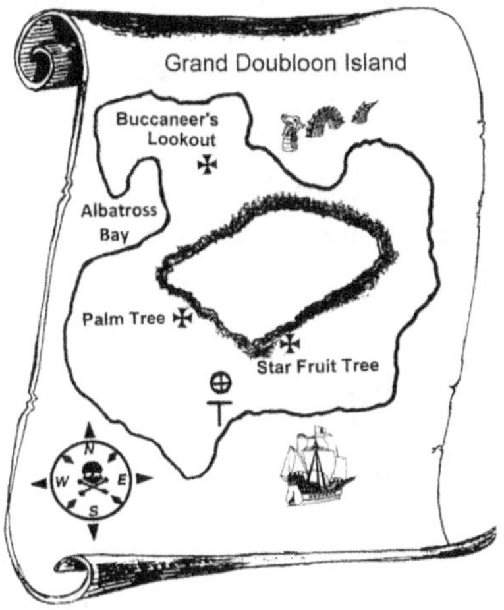

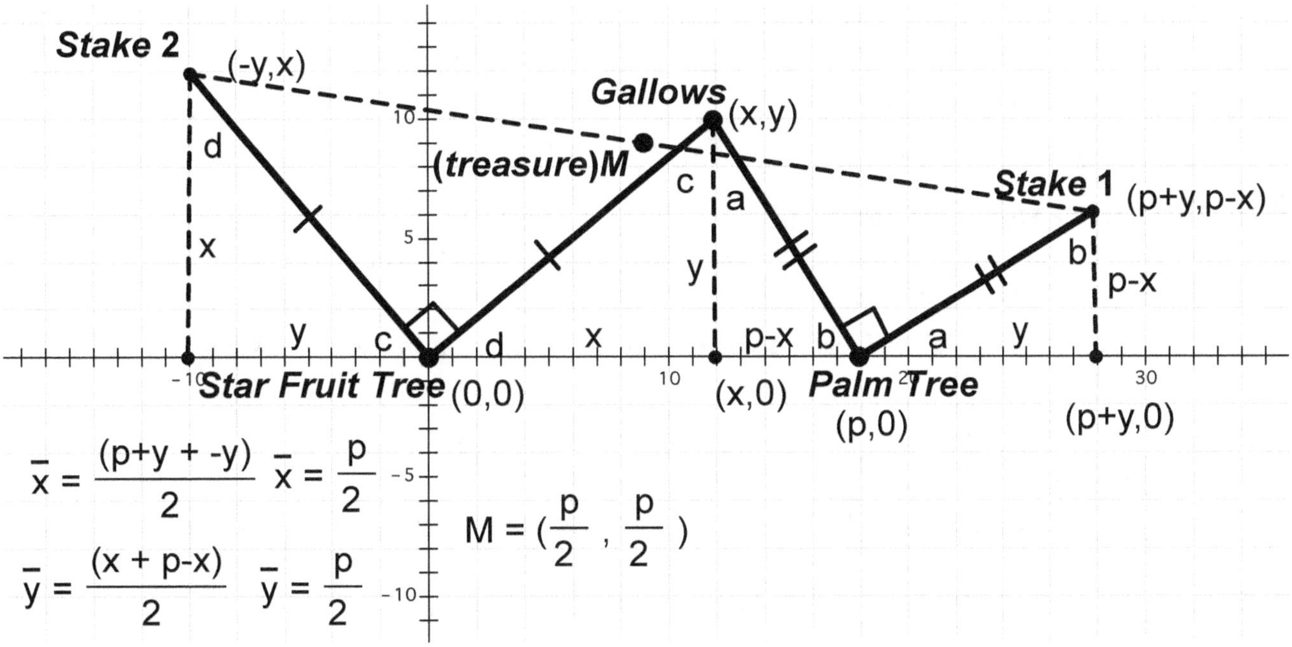

Answers Chapter 7

7.2

1. TDSUCTWSJV AK AF BSESAUS
2. The treasure is buried on Skull Island.
3. XEOI 7A TEGIW RSYXL XS0EVHW XLI SEO
4. Dig 2 meters down.
5. Gold is in the chest.
6. The treasure is with Davey Jones.
7. Doubloons here.
8. Dig 20 paces North.
9.

+	0	1	2	3	4
0	0	1	2	3	4
1	1	2	3	4	0
2	2	3	4	0	1
3	3	4	0	1	2
4	4	0	1	2	3

10. 2

11. 1

12. 25

13. Jack Sparrow hid the treasure.
14. STOJKB KOBJZVOB
15. Dig here for gold.
16. Davey Jones has the treasure.

D	W	I	T	H	T
E	L	V	E	C	R
I	I	W	R	A	E
R	S	W	S	P	A
U	N	I	A	T	S
B	S	I	E	R	U

7.4

1. Dig five meters south of the coconut tree and the treasure is yours.
2. Four feet below the gallows.
3. Treasure is buried with Captain Silvers.
4. Gold 5 meters south palm tree.

7.6 Island Notes Document

1. *Cayman Key translation*: Avast ye scallywag. Gold doubloons be yours should ye dig twenty paces north of the Mango Tree.
2. *Barbossa Island translation*: Treasure be yours matey if you dig midway between the Palm Tree and Crocodile Skull.
3. *Isla Sirena translation*: As ye steps off the ship at Dead Man's Cove walk forty paces fifty degrees east of north and my treasure awaits ye.
4. *Blackbeard Island translation*: If ye walk forty meters from Blackbeard's Tombstone towards Debtor's Prison ye shall dig for doubloons.
5. *Haunted Isle translation*: Drive a stake midway betwixt the Jolly Roger Inn and Skeleton

Boulder. From Dead Man's Dock walk twenty meters towards the stake and my treasure be yours.

6. *Skeleton Key translation*: Ahoy matey. The treasure be yours should you dig 15 meters from the Breadfruit Tree and 20 meters from Morgan's Grave.
7. *Doubloon Island translation*: At a distance of five meters from ye olde castle wall and twenty five meters from the cemetery gate, two possibilities there be. Dig not by Blackbeard's Tombstone but ah, the other there ye shall find me treasure mate.
8. *Skull Island translation*: Come lads tis treasure to be found. From Leaping Lizard Saloon walk straight as ye be across Jetsam River Bridge and continue straight for another fifty paces and dig.
9. *Privateer Island translation*: Rackam, Morgan, and Kidd. Ye shall find tombstones three. My treasure shall be buried equally from all three.
10. *Demon Island translation*: Pieces of Eight at Fortress Gate.
11. *Isla Tortuga translation*: The treasure is midway between the Gallows and Skull Rock.
12. *Isla Langosta translation*: As ye steps off the ship at Dead Man's Cove walk fifty paces 40 degrees east of north and my treasure awaits ye.
13. *Parrot Island translation*: Ye olde treasure be found 15 meters and 60 degrees west of south from Crows Nest Tavern.
14. *Silver's Island translation*: Long John's treasure is buried two hundred meters north from Calico Jack Cave.
15. *Crocodile Key translation*: The treasure is buried six meters from the Palm Tree and due north of the Gallows.
16. *Devil's Island translation*: From the Monolith at Mermaid Cove walk 40 meters at an angle of 35 degrees east of north and dig mates, dig.
17. *Isla Marsopa translation*: From Black Bart Inn walk towards Davy Jones Cemetery for twenty five steps, turn left and walk another five steps and the treasure be yours.
18. *Buccaneer Island translation*: Ye olde treasure be hidden fifty meters from the center of the Cold River Bridge and thirty meters from the Cemetery Wall.
19. *Monkey Island translation*: From the Hangman's Tree walk towards Skull Rock for 10 meters and there ye shall find doubloons aplenty.
20. *Crescent Key translation*: Twenty meters west of Jack Rackham Tombstone ye shall find treasure galore.
21. *Isla Mariposa translation*: Gold doubloons are to be found if ye walk from the Castle Gate 700 paces through the Twin Monoliths.
22. *Místico Island translation*: From the front steps of Jolly Roger Inn send one bucko walking in the direction of Skull Mountain for 100 meters and another bucko on a course towards Capricorn Point for 80 meters. The treasure location forms an equilateral triangle with the two buckos.
23. *Serpent Island translation*: Gold be yours if ye walk from Crocodile Skull Rock towards Gator Glen for a hundred meters turn right, walk sixty meters. Drive a stake. Dig midway betwixt your stake and the giant boulder atop Iguana Hill.
24. *Isla Tesoro translation*: Send one mate from Diablo Prison 80 paces towards Gangplank Saloon

and send a second mate from the Gallows 60 paces towards Hog's Head Tavern. Find the point midway between the two and treasure be ye reward.

25. *Isla de los Muerto translation*: From the Hangman's Tree walk 50 paces in the direction of Deadman's Dock. Turn and face north. Walk 40 paces, turn right, and walk another 30 paces east. Gold awaits your shovel.
26. *Shipwreck Island translation*: Place a matey at the midway point between the Monkey Pod tree and the Palm Tree. From the Hangman's Tree walk towards your matey counting your steps. If ye continue on the same distance ye shall find riches below.
27. *Emerald Island translation*: If ye knows yer geometry, treasure awaits ye. The treasure tis buried at the fourth point of a parallelogram formed by the Mango Tree, Coconut Tree, and Papaya Tree.
28. *Isla de Sangria translation*: Treasure chest of gold be found under a boulder in Cold River equally distant from the Orange Tree and the Lemon Tree.
29. *Isla de Oro translation*: From Hangman's Tree 50 meters and 45 degrees west of south for gold.
30. *Isla Plata translation*: Find the midpoint betwixt Jetty's Head Tavern and Devil's Spyglass. Find the midpoint betwixt the Monkey Pod tree and Quicksilver Mine. If ye follow me words, treasure be yours exactly betwixt the two midpoints.

7.6 Island Treasure Locations

1. Cayman Key

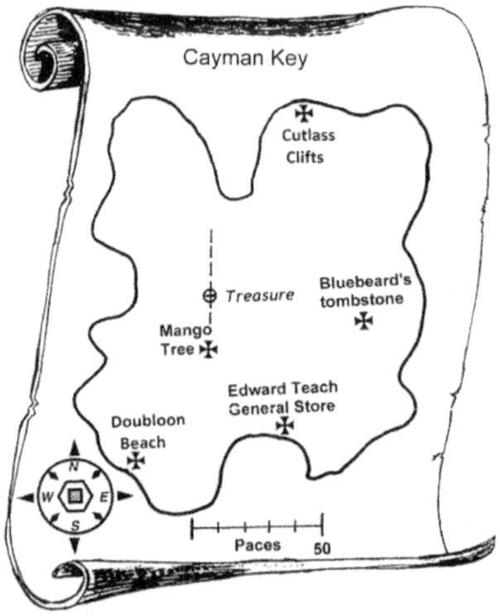

2. Barbossa Island

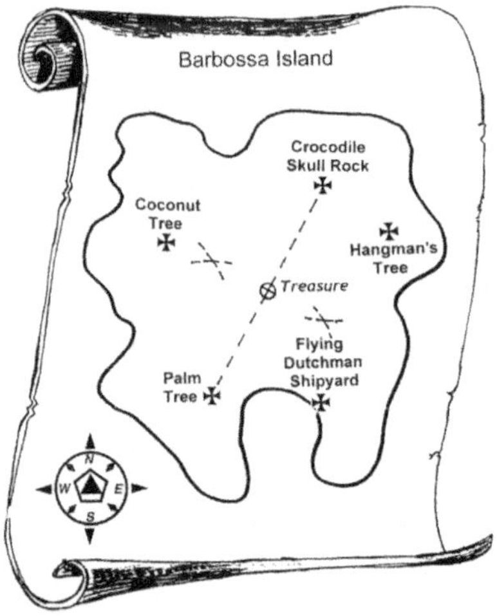

3. Isla Sirena

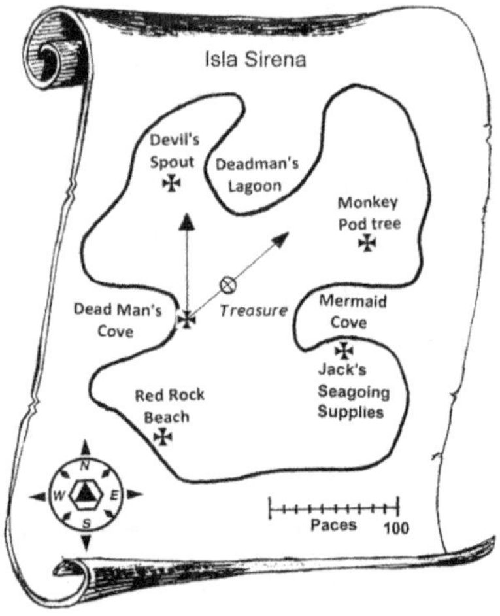

4. Blackbeard Island

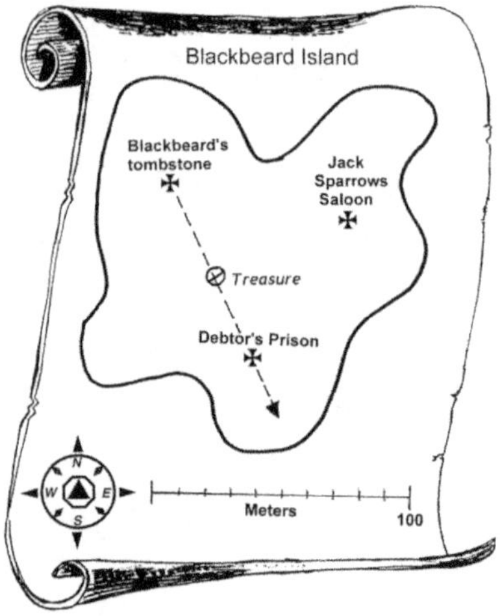

5. Haunted Isle

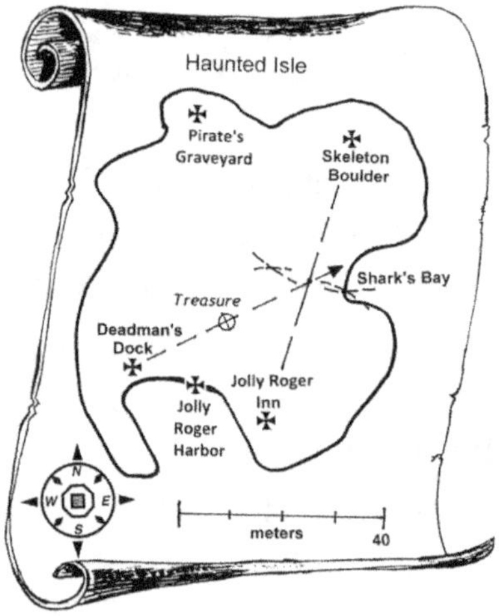

6. Skeleton Key

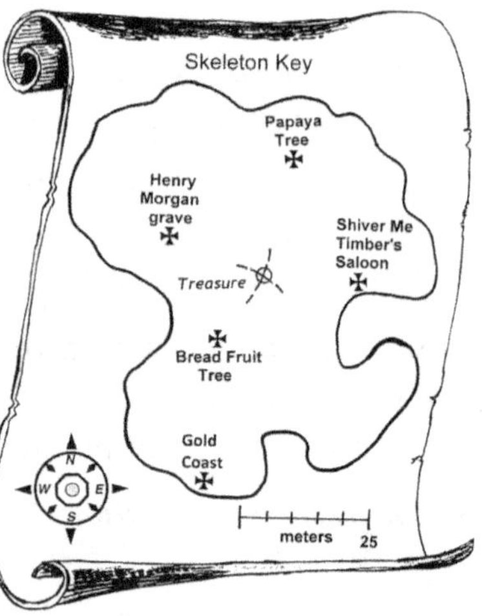

7. Doubloon Island

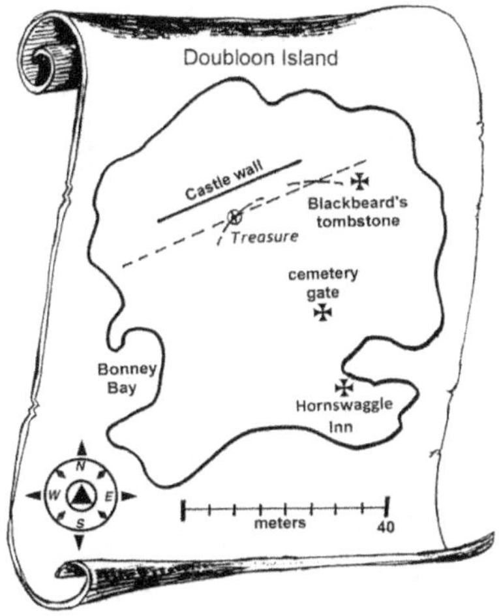

8. Skull Island

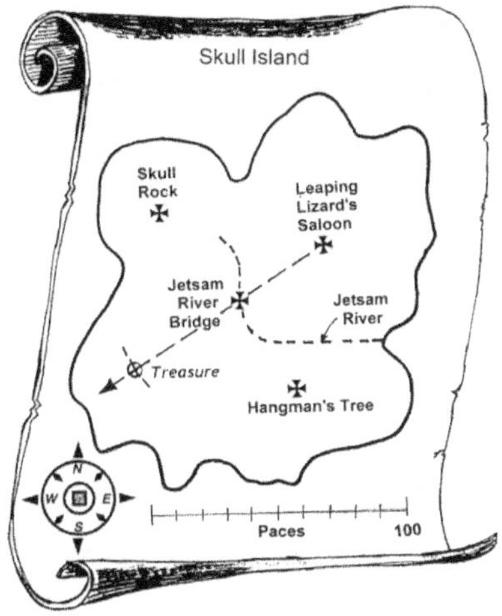

9. Privateer Island

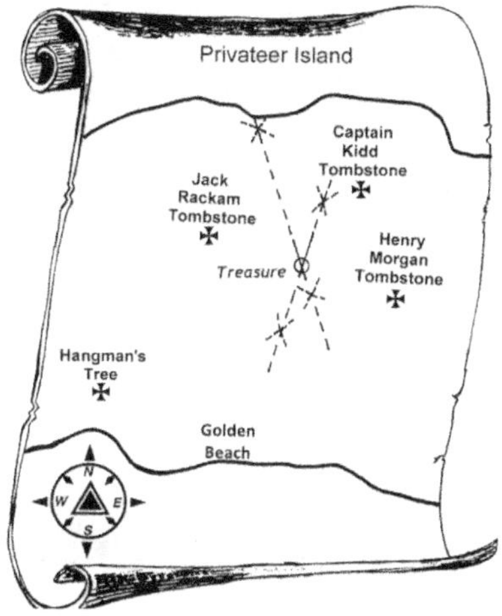

10. Demon Island

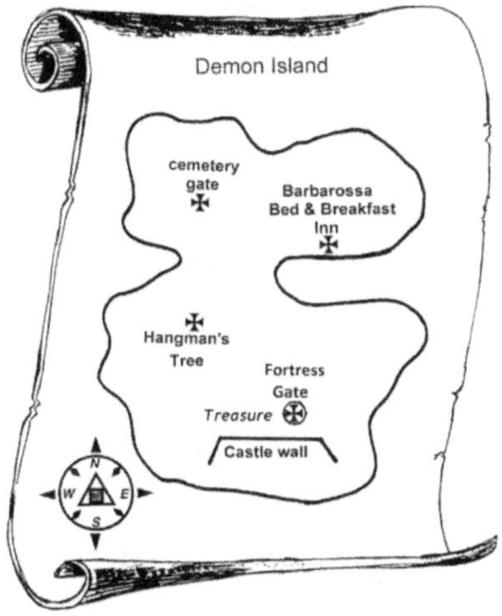

11. Isla Tortuga

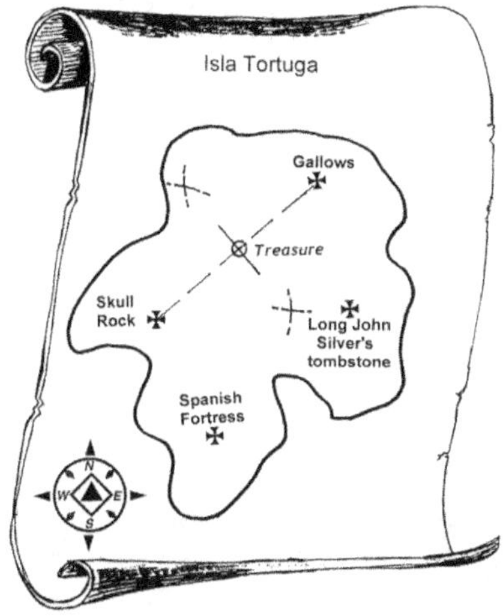

12. Isla Langosta

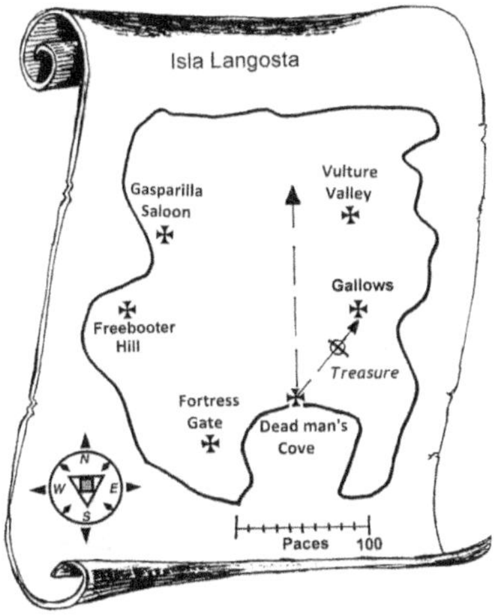

13. Parrot Island

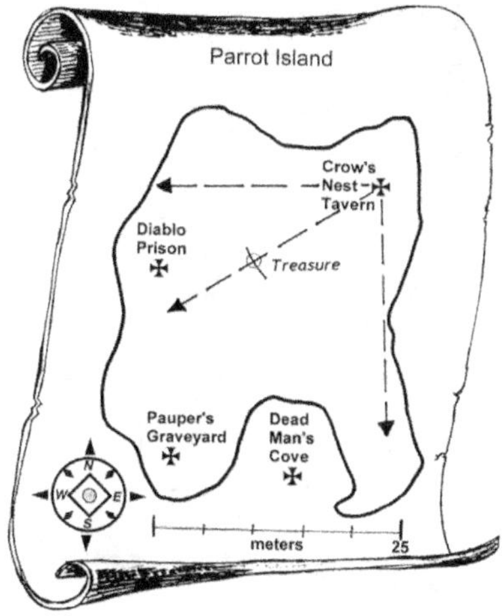

14. Silver's Island

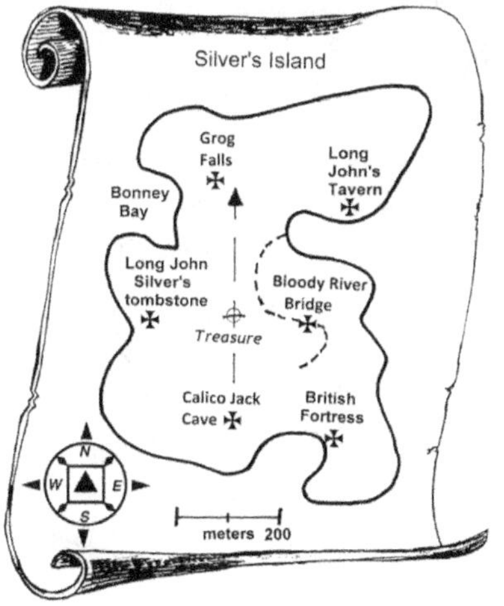

15. Crocodile Key

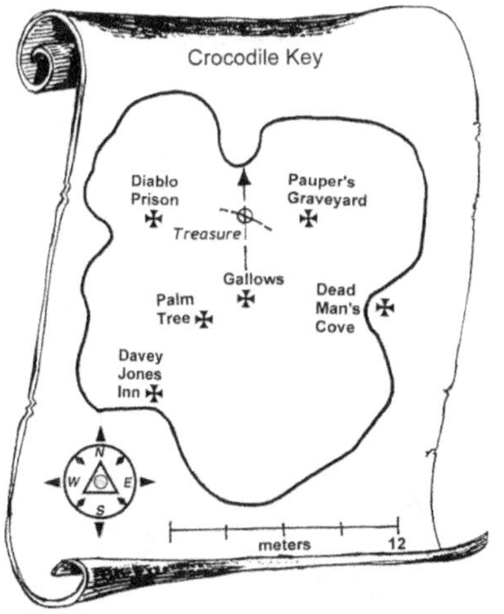

16. Devil's Island

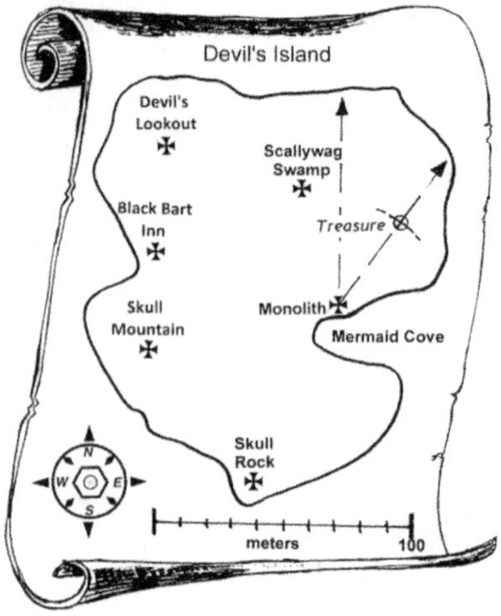

17. Isla Marsopa

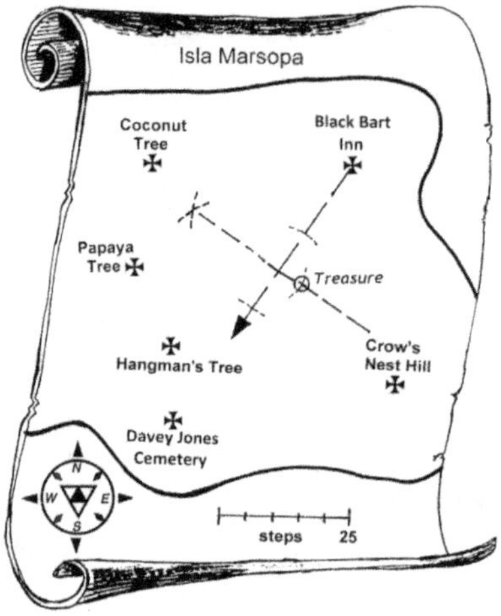

18. Buccaneer Island

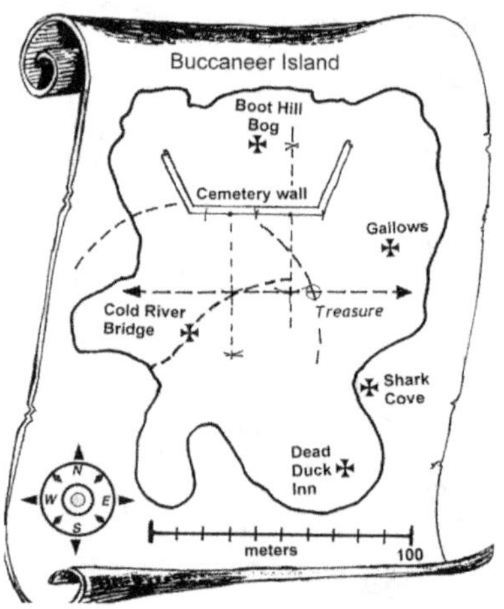

19. Monkey island

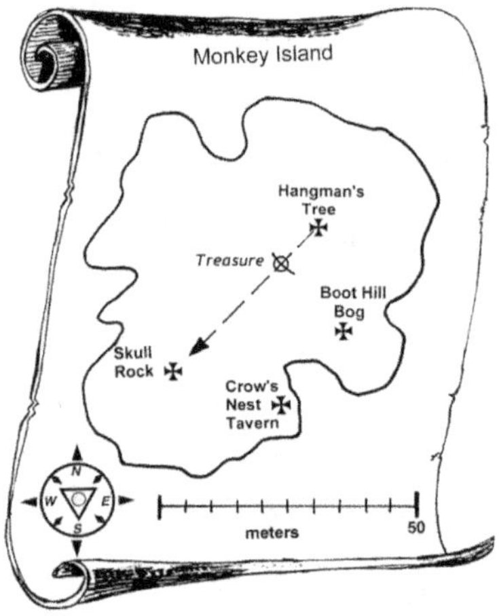

20. Crescent Key

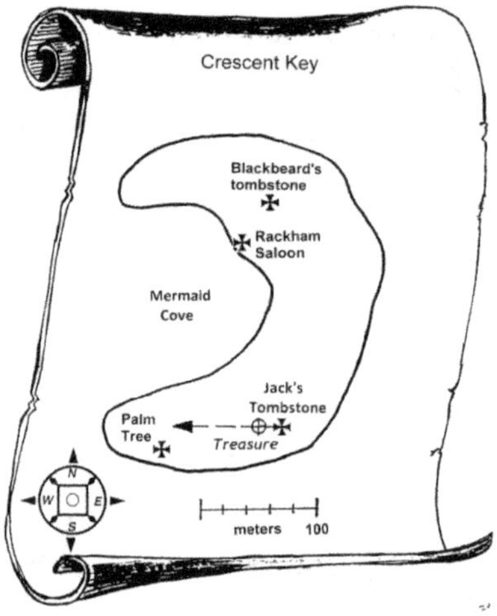

21. Isla Mariposa

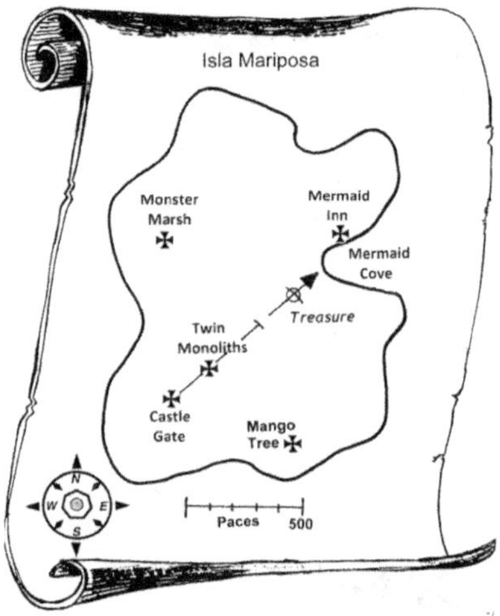

22. Mistico Island

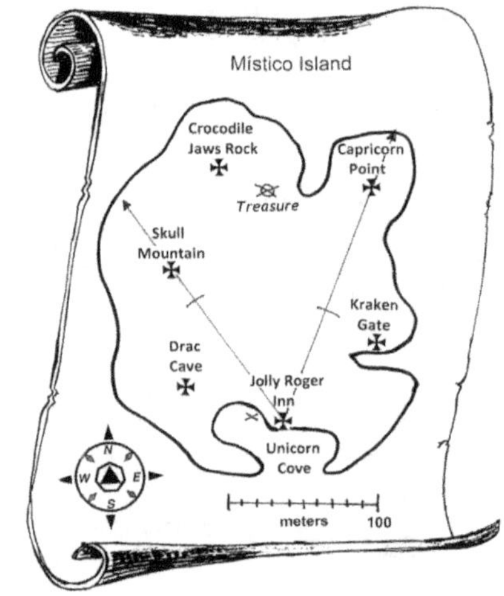

23. Serpent Island

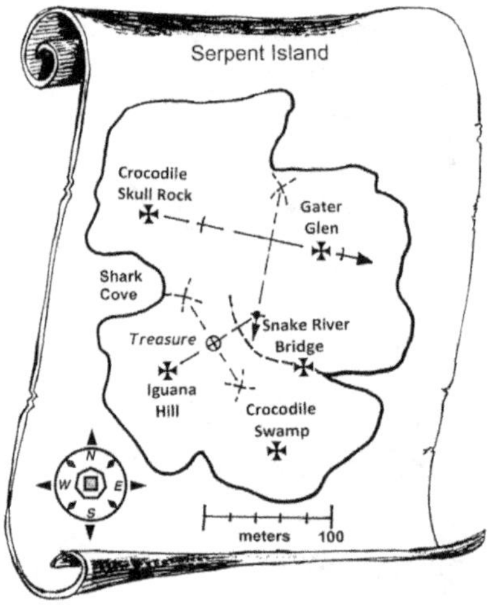

24. Isla Tesoro

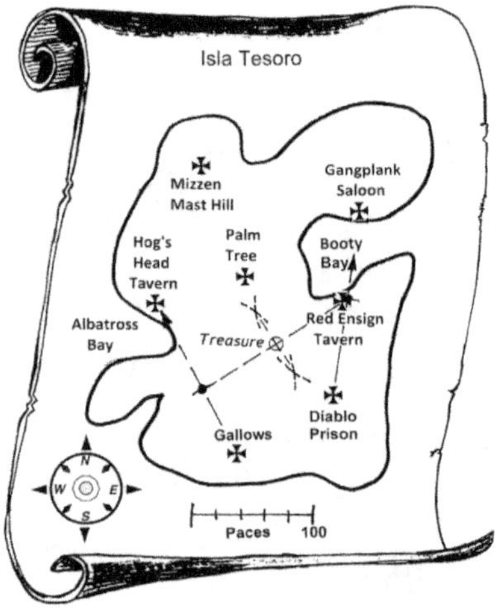

25. Isla de los Muerto

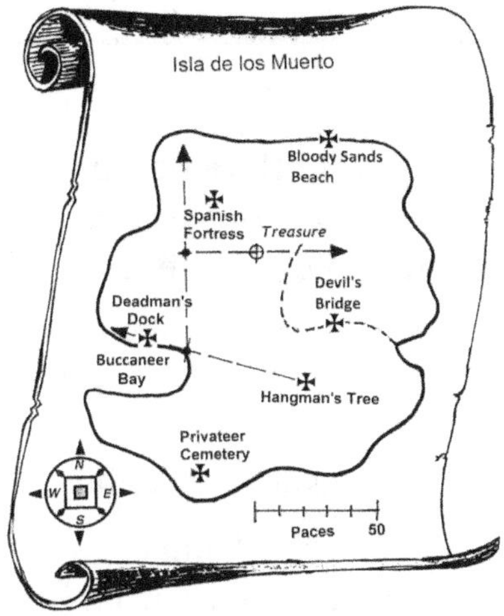

26. Shipwreck Island

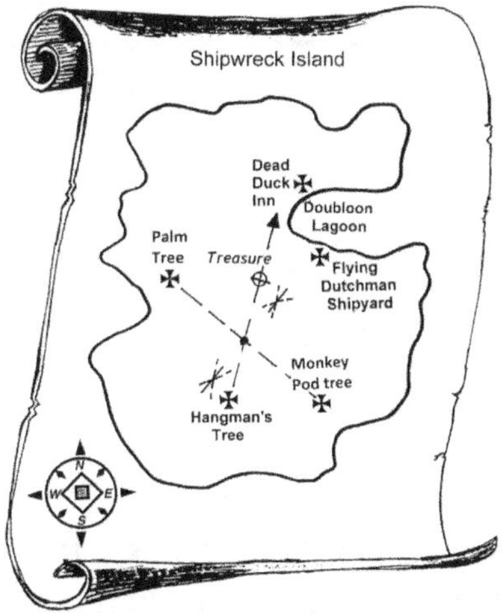

27. Emerald Island

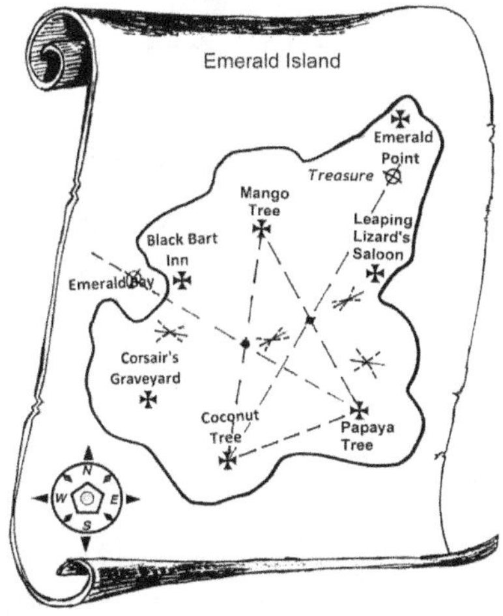

28. Isla de Sangria

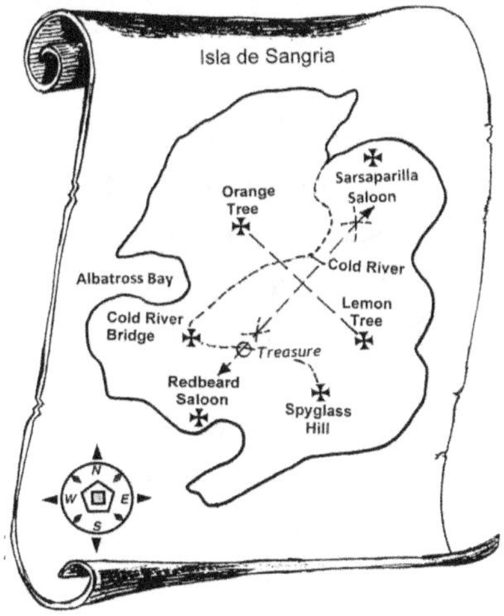

29. Isla de Oro

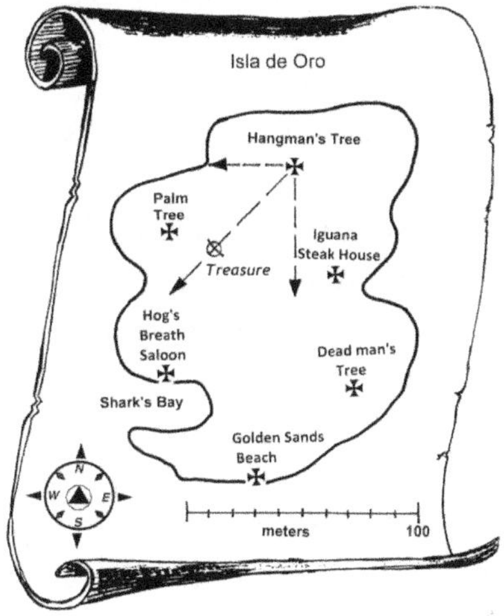

30. Isla Plata

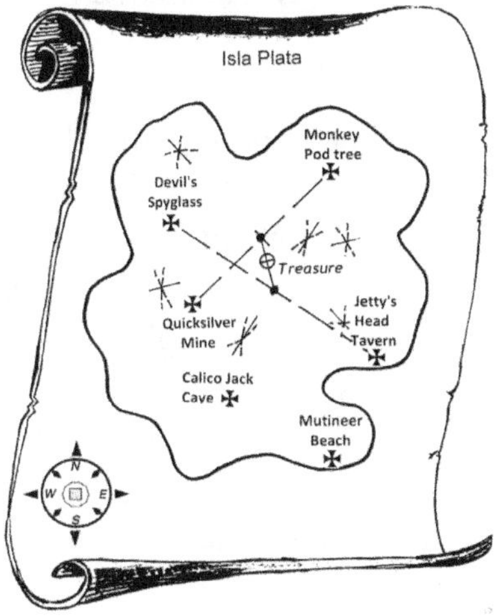

Footnotes

Chapter 1

1. *(1)* W. W. R. Ball and H. S. M. Coxeter, *Mathematical Recreations and Essays;* E. R. Berlekamp, J. H. Conway, and R. K. Guy, *Winning Ways for Your Mathematical Plays;* M. Gardner, *Mathematical Games;* J. S. Madachy, *Pentominoes: Some Solved and Unsolved Problems,* to name just a few.

2. *(16)* A **domino** is a rectangular tile with a line dividing its face into two squares containing spots, called pips. The most common set of dominoes contains all the possible combinations of zero (blank) to six spots. This set is known as a "double-six." The early American or European domino was made of ivory or hard, ebonized wood. Today the typical set is made of polystyrene plastic or bakelite.

The earliest mention of dominoes is from the Song Dynasty (960 –1279) China. The domino made its European appearance in Italy during the 18th century. The term "domino" comes from its resemblance to a costume worn during the annual *Carnevale di Venizia.* During the carnival, men and women wore hooded masquerade costumes, called domino, that were often made of black silk.

Chapter 2

3. *(24)* The classic game *Battleship* was played in mathematics classes long before it became a commercial product. Today, math teachers still use the classic version of *Battleship* to introduce the Cartesian coordinate system because it uses coordinates in the way they are used in mathematics, as the location of points (lattice points) on the rectangular grid. The Milton Bradley version of the game Battleship™, although enjoyable, may cause problems later for a student when they are introduced to the Cartesian coordinate system. The commercial version of Battleship™ uses a rectangular grid with numbers on the horizontal axis and letters on the vertical axis. The numbers represent the columns in the grid and the letters represent the rows in the grid. Squares, therefore, are located by pairing a number and a letter. The pair (C, 5) would represent a square region rather than a point. Thus if your goal is to teach the rectangular coordinate system, use the classic version, not the commercial game Battleship™.

4. *(26)* All 12 pentominoes are similar in shape to 12 letters of the alphabet. Thus we name them by their letter, such as the *I*-pentomino or the *L*-Pentomino. See below:

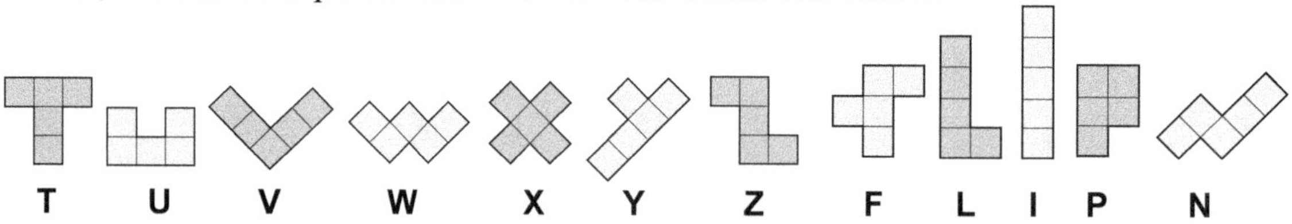

5. *(29)* Although the ancient Egyptians, Greeks, and Romans used coordinates for map making, it was Descartes who recognized the importance of establishing the correspondence of ordered pairs of numbers with points in a plane. With this correspondence, Descartes demonstrated that all of Euclidean geometry "held" in this coordinate system.

6. *(30)* A **square** is a quadrilateral with all its sides congruent and all its angles congruent. A **rectangle** is a quadrilateral with all its angles congruent (and thus they are right angles). A **rhombus** is a quadrilateral with all its sides congruent. A **parallelogram** is a quadrilateral with the opposite sides parallel. A **trapezoid** is a quadrilateral with exactly one pair of parallel sides. An **isosceles trapezoid** is a trapezoid with the non-parallel sides the same length. A **kite** is a quadrilateral with two distinct pairs of congruent consecutive sides.

Footnotes

Chapter 4

7. *(89)* **A Brief History of Time Zones**

For much of history, time was determined locally. Towns would set their clocks to 12 o'clock noon "solar time" when the sun reached its highest point each day. Due to rapid, long distance train travel developed in the late 19th century, the standardization of time became a necessity. In 1878, Sir Sanford Fleming proposed dividing the world into time zones. Since the Earth rotated once every 24 hours he proposed dividing it into 24 one-hour time zones. Since the circumference of the earth is 360° then every 15° of longitude would be one time zone ($24 \times 15° = 360°$). In 1884, the International Prime Meridian Conference was held in Washington D.C. The line of longitude through the Royal Observatory in Greenwich, England was designated the Prime Meridian or starting point for an east-west axis. Each of the 24 longitude lines became the centerlines of the 24 time zones. So 7.5° (7° 30') to the west and 7.5° (7° 30') to the east of the Prime Meridian is the time zone designated Greenwich Mean Time (GMT). The next time zone to the west would be called GMT+1. The next time zone to the east would be GMT-1. Most of Europe is in GMT-1. Because of physical and political issues, the boundaries for the time zones do not follow longitude lines exactly.

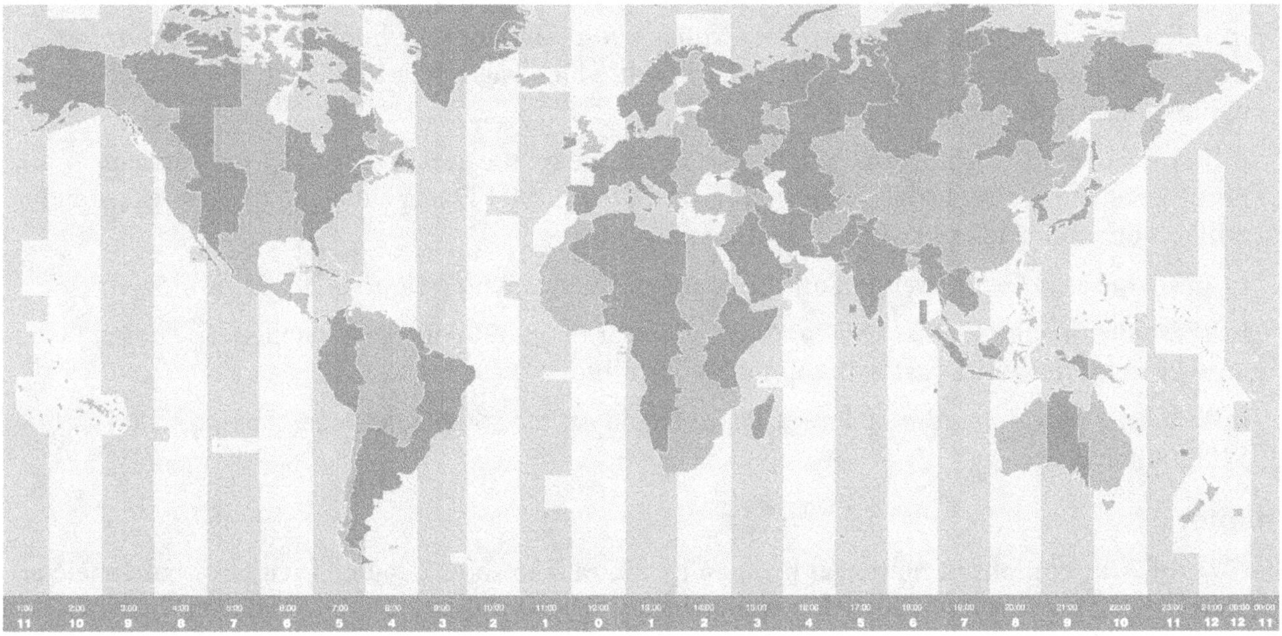

Try your hand at Exercises 1–3 using the map of GMT time zones shown above.

1. If it is 9 am in Greenwich, England, what time is it in New York City, USA (GMT-5)?
2. If it is 10 pm (GMT+10) in Sydney, Australia, what time is it in most of Europe (GMT+1)?
3. If it is Friday 10 pm in San Francisco, USA (GMT-8), what time is it in Sydney, Australia?

Answers: 1. 4 am 2. 1 pm 3. 4 pm, Saturday

8. *(95)* The *Mercedes* sank in the Battle of Cape St. Mary's, killing more than 200 sailors. The attack led Spain to declare war on Britain and enter the Napoleonic Wars.

9. *(95)* In 1555, the *Santa Maria Del Camino* was carrying 1.8 million pesos in gold and silver and an unspecified amount of gold, emeralds and pearls. It was caught in a hurricane and sunk near St. Lucie Inlet on the east coast of Florida.

- In 1563, *La Madalena* was sunk during a bad storm off the south Florida coast while carrying over 50 tons of silver in bullion plus 1,110 pounds of gold in small ingots and jewelry.

Footnotes

- In 1571, the *San Ignacio* and the *Santa Maria de la Limpia Concepcion*, carrying over 2.5 million pesos in treasure sunk off the northeast coast of Florida near St. Augustine.
- In 1589, a very large convoy of about 100 Spanish galleons sailed into a hurricane in the Bahaman Channel and sunk. One of the large treasure ships, *La Magdalena*, was carrying over 1.25 million pesos in treasure.
- In 1611, *Santa Ana Maria del Juncal* sank off Cabo de Apalachi. It was carrying several million pesos in silver bullion.
- In 1624, the Spanish galleon *El Espiritu Santo El Mayor* was sunk in a squall in the Bahaman Channel. It was carrying a cargo of 2.2 million pesos.
- In 1622, a fleet of 28 ships bound for Spain carrying silver, gold, emeralds, and pearls from the New World sailed head on into a hurricane along the Florida straits, west of the Florida Keys. Among the ships sunk was the *Atocha*, loaded with a cargo of 24 tons of silver, 180,000 pesos of silver coins, 582 copper ingots, and 125 gold bars and discs. Some of this treasure was found and salvaged by treasure-hunting pioneer Mel Fisher.
- In 1683, the Spanish galleon *Santissima Concepcion* sank during a hurricane. It was carrying over 1.8 million pesos in treasure, the majority of which was silver bullion, 1,500 pounds of gold bullion and worked gold.
- In 1715, a fleet of 12 ships was caught by a hurricane on the east coast of Florida between Fort Pierce and the Sebastian Inlet, sinking 11 of them. Mel Fisher salvaged these wrecks, and artifacts are still being recovered from them.
- In 1730, the ship *Genovase* sank off the coast of Jamaica with a cargo of $1.85 million.
- In 1880, the Spanish Galleon *Santa Rosa* sank near the mouth of the Suwannee River along the northern Florida Gulf Coast with a cargo of $5 million.
- In 1880, the *Maria Therese* sank near Padre Island off the south Texas coast taking with it $100,000 in cargo.

Chapter 5

10. *(97)* A **CT** or **computed tomography scan** uses x-rays to show detailed images of hard skeletal structures. A **PET** or **positron emission tomography scan** is a test that uses a radioactive material (a tracer) to look for abnormalities in the body. **MRI** or **magnetic resonance imaging** uses a large magnet and radio waves to look at soft tissue inside the body.

Chapter 7

11. *(136)* The **scytale** (rhymes with Italy) is a cylindrical tool used to encrypt and decrypt a transposition cipher. Ancient Greek military officers used this tool to communicate during battle. To send a message, the first officer would write a message on a strip of parchment wrapped around the cylinder. The parchment was then sent to the second officer who wrapped it around his identical cylinder to read the message.

Appendix 3

12. *(217)* As of February 2014, The Oriental Trading Company was selling a set of 12 inflatable Earth globes for under $14.00.

Illustration and Photo Credits

The author and publisher would like to thank the following for permission to reproduce their work. Any artwork not noted is in the public domain.

Introduction: Page iv – Pirates digging treasure illustration © iStockphoto/Verzh

Chapter 1: Page 1 – Photo of Solomon Golumb courtesy of Solomon Golumb

Chapter 2: Page 24 – Treasure chest illustration © iStockphoto/Elenita_1

Page 29 – Illustration of Descartes © iStockphoto/Graffisimo

Chapter 3: Page 61 – Image of radar screen © iStockphoto/enot-poloskun

Chapter 4: Page 85 – Photo of globe © iStockphoto/viafilms; illustration of Earth by Emily Reed

Page 87 – Photo of Taj Mahal © iStockphoto/adamkaz; Fallingwater,Dec08.jpg © Sturmvogel 66, http://commons.wikimedia.org/wiki/File:Fallingwater,Dec08.jpg / CC BY-SA 3.0*; photo of Doge's Palace © iStockphoto/matthewleesdixon; Kinkaku-ji Gold Pavilion close-up.jpg © Rdsmit4, http://commons.wikimedia.org/wiki/File:Kinkaku-ji_Gold_Pavilion_close-up.jpg / CC BY-SA 2.5*; photo of Alhambra © iStockphoto/THEPALMER; photo of Ankor Wat © iStockphoto/Veni; Sydney_Opera_House_-_Inside_1.jpg © Namiac, http://commons.wikimedia.org/wiki/File: Sydney_Opera_House_-_Inside_1.jpg / CC BY-SA 3.0; photo of Petronas Towers © iStockphoto/aleskramer

Page 88 – Image of Euclid © iStockphoto/ZU_09; images of Cardano and Archimedes © iStockphoto/HultonArchive; Omar Khayyam2.JPG © A. Venediktov, http://commons.wikimedia.org/wiki/File:Omar_Khayyam2.JPG / CC BY-SA 3.0; Srinivasa Ramanujan - OPC - 2.jpg © Konrad Jacobs, http://commons.wikimedia.org/wiki/File:Srinivasa_Ramanujan_-_OPC_-_2.jpg / CC BY-SA 2.0*

Page 89 – Normal_Mercator_map_85deg.jpg © Lars H. Rohwedder, http://commons.wikimedia.org/wiki/File:Normal_Mercator_map_85deg.jpg / CC BY-SA 3.0 / modified from original

Page 95 – Photo of Odyssey Explorer courtesy of Odyssey Marine Exploration, www.shipwreck.net; photo of Mel Fisher courtesy of Kim Fisher

Chapter 5: Page 97 – Photo of archaeological dig © iStockphoto/drduey; photo of diver © iStockphoto/GoodOlga; photo of physicians reading brain scan © iStockphoto/skynesher

Page 98 – Image of 3-D coordinate system by Emily Reed

Chapter 7: Page 135 – Image of Mary Queen of Scots © iStockphoto/traveler1116

Appendix 2: Page 207 – Photo of snowy cricket © Janice Stiefel

Appendix 3: Page 217 – Photo of Istvan Lenart courtesy of Istvan Lenart

Footnotes: Page 271 – Illustration of map showing time zones © iStockphoto/LdF

* Attribution-ShareAlike 3.0 Unported license – http://creativecommons.org/licenses/by-sa/3.0/deed
Attribution-ShareAlike 2.5 Generic – http://creativecommons.org/licenses/by-sa/2.5/deed
Attribution-ShareAlike 2.0 Generic – http://creativecommons.org/licenses/by-sa/2.0/deed

Books by Michael Serra

All the books listed below are available through our website **www.michaelserra.net**.

Discovering Geometry (various editions and ISBN)

Michael Serra's extensive classroom experience helped him shape a new approach to teaching geometry. The developmental focus of *Discovering Geometry* helps students review their comprehension of geometry and guides them in mastering the next level. You'll find many opportunities both to support students whose progress is slower and to challenge more advanced students. *Discovering Geometry* has proven effective in countless classrooms across the country. Published by Kendall Hunt (www.kendallhunt.com).

Patty Paper Geometry

ISBN 978-1-5595-3072-9

In *Patty Paper Geometry* students discover most of the properties in high school geometry by folding and tracing on patty paper. Constructions are performed more accurately and geometric discoveries are faster. Each of the 12 chapters includes spiraled exercise sets, providing constant review. Use *Patty Paper Geometry* as a supplement to your geometry program or even as a major course of study. Caution: *Patty Paper Geometry is addictive*!

Pirate Math Developing Mathematical Reasoning with Games and Puzzles

ISBN 978-0-9834-0991-5

Michael Serra combines the challenge of mathematics with the fun adventure of pirates and buried treasure. *Pirate Math* starts out with polyominoes and progresses to coordinate systems and geometry. Play the Buried Treasure game using a rectangle coordinate plane, a polar coordinate system, a spherical surface, and with three-dimensional areas. Ahoy matey, use the chapter on cryptography to help solve hidden messages to uncover the pirate booty.

Smart Moves Developing Mathematical Reasoning with Games and Puzzles

ISBN 978-0-9834-0990-8

Smart Moves has over 330 games and puzzles that focus on Sequential Reasoning. Sequential thinking is an important part of daily life from home building to writing computer code. The puzzles make excellent classroom openers, end-of-period thought provokers, or for students to work on outside the classroom. The Mathematical Connections highlights key math concepts such as vectors and graph theory. Using the puzzle tips in *Smart Moves* will engage students in solving problems, help them discover strategies, and encourage mathematical thinking.

What's Wrong With This Picture?

ISBN 978-1-5595-3584-7

Students love catching mistakes, especially in the classroom. In *What's Wrong with This Picture?* students are told in advance that at least one of the problems on each page is wrong. Watch students search for errors and in the process, learn critical thinking skills. There are 50 student activities, each with three to four geometry problems. The problems are usually visual but there are also word problems and proofs.

The Mathercise Series

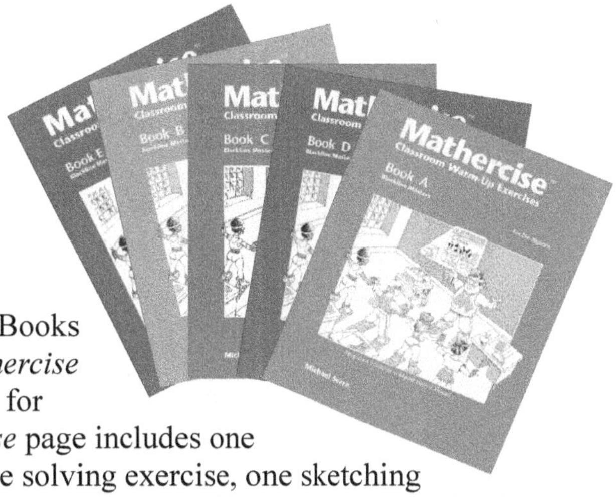

Mathercise Set (Books A through E)

ISBN 978-1-5595-3063-7

The *Mathercise Set* includes all five books, taking students from pre-algebra through pre-calculus.The sketching exercises involve spercentages, algebra, equations, averages, proportions, probability, and, in Books D and E, functions and analytic geometry. Each *Mathercise* book is a set of 50 black line masters, "class starters" for middle and high school math classes. Each *Mathercise* page includes one reasoning exercise (either inductive or deductive), one solving exercise, one sketching or graphing exercise, and space for a review exercise of your own design. Each 64-page book includes teaching tips, sample problems, answer keys, and reproducible answer sheets. *Mathercise* your students once or twice a week at the beginning of the class periods and you'll keep your students in shape and on track.

Mathercise A ISBN 978-1-5595-3059-0

Book A is for middle school and high school students not yet taking algebra. Some exercises involve solving equations in one-unknown, probability, averages, rate/time exercises.

Mathercise B ISBN 978-1-5595-3060-6

Book B is for students taking pre-algebra, algebra, or a first-year high school mathematics course. Exercises include sketching with two and three-dimensional drawing, with transformations.

Mathercise C ISBN 978-1-5595-3061-3

Book C is for students taking algebra, geometry, or a second-year high school mathematics course. Exercises include sketching with two and three-dimensional drawing, with transformations.

Mathercise D ISBN 978-1-5595-3062-0

Book D is for students who have taken a year of algebra and are taking geometry, advanced algebra, or a second or third-year high school mathematics course. Exercises include graphing quadratic, absolute value, and exponential functions.

Mathercise E ISBN 978-1-5595-3063-7

Book E is for students taking advanced algebra, pre-calculus, or a third or fourth-year high school mathematics course. Exercises include graphing functions, including sine and cosine functions.

www.ingramcontent.com/pod-product-compliance
Lightning Source LLC
Chambersburg PA
CBHW080727230426
43665CB00020B/2643
* 9 7 8 0 9 8 3 4 0 9 9 1 5 *